D1430568

Business
Ethics

Senior Contributing Authors
Stephen M. Byars, USC Marshall School Of Business
Kurt Stanberry, University Of Houston-Downtown

TABLE OF CONTENTS

Preface   1

1 Why Ethics Matter   7

   1.1 Being a Professional of Integrity   8
   1.2 Ethics and Profitability   13
   1.3 Multiple versus Single Ethical Standards   20

2 Ethics from Antiquity to the Present   27

   2.1 The Concept of Ethical Business in Ancient Athens   28
   2.2 Ethical Advice for Nobles and Civil Servants in Ancient China   35
   2.3 Comparing the Virtue Ethics of East and West   40
   2.4 Utilitarianism: The Greatest Good for the Greatest Number   44
   2.5 Deontology: Ethics as Duty   50
   2.6 A Theory of Justice   54

3 Defining and Prioritizing Stakeholders   67

   3.1 Adopting a Stakeholder Orientation   68
   3.2 Weighing Stakeholder Claims   72
   3.3 Ethical Decision-Making and Prioritizing Stakeholders   78
   3.4 Corporate Social Responsibility (CSR)   83

4 Three Special Stakeholders: Society, the Environment, and   93
   Government

   4.1 Corporate Law and Corporate Responsibility   94
   4.2 Sustainability: Business and the Environment   103
   4.3 Government and the Private Sector   117

5 The Impact of Culture and Time on Business Ethics   131

   5.1 The Relationship between Business Ethics and Culture   132
   5.2 Business Ethics over Time   139
   5.3 The Influence of Geography and Religion   144
   5.4 Are the Values Central to Business Ethics Universal?   149

6 What Employers Owe Employees   159

   6.1 The Workplace Environment and Working Conditions   160

6.2 What Constitutes a Fair Wage?   169
6.3 An Organized Workforce   177
6.4 Privacy in the Workplace   184

7 What Employees Owe Employers   195

7.1 Loyalty to the Company   196
7.2 Loyalty to the Brand and to Customers   203
7.3 Contributing to a Positive Work Atmosphere   207
7.4 Financial Integrity   212
7.5 Criticism of the Company and Whistleblowing   218

8 Recognizing and Respecting the Rights of All   231

8.1 Diversity and Inclusion in the Workforce   232
8.2 Accommodating Different Abilities and Faiths   239
8.3 Sexual Identification and Orientation   244
8.4 Income Inequalities   247
8.5 Animal Rights and the Implications for Business   252

9 Professions under the Microscope   265

9.1 Entrepreneurship and Start-Up Culture   266
9.2 The Influence of Advertising   271
9.3 The Insurance Industry   276
9.4 Ethical Issues in the Provision of Health Care   280

10 Changing Work Environments and Future Trends   295

10.1 More Telecommuting or Less?   296
10.2 Workplace Campuses   301
10.3 Alternatives to Traditional Patterns of Work   306
10.4 Robotics, Artificial Intelligence, and the Workplace of the Future   314

11 Epilogue: Why Ethics Still Matter   325

11.1 Business Ethics in an Evolving Environment   326
11.2 Committing to an Ethical View   329
11.3 Becoming an Ethical Professional   332
11.4 Making a Difference in the Business World   336

A The Lives of Ethical Philosophers   341

B   **Profiles in Business Ethics: Contemporary Thought Leaders**   347

C   **A Succinct Theory of Business Ethics**   357

  Index   365

Preface

Welcome to *Business Ethics*, an OpenStax resource. This textbook was written to increase student access to high-quality learning materials, maintaining highest standards of academic rigor at little to no cost.

About OpenStax

OpenStax is a nonprofit based at Rice University, and it's our mission to improve student access to education. Our first openly licensed college textbook was published in 2012, and our library has since scaled to over 25 books for college and AP® courses used by hundreds of thousands of students. OpenStax Tutor, our low-cost personalized learning tool, is being used in college courses throughout the country. Through our partnerships with philanthropic foundations and our alliance with other educational resource organizations, OpenStax is breaking down the most common barriers to learning and empowering students and instructors to succeed.

About OpenStax resources

Customization

Business Ethics is licensed under a Creative Commons Attribution 4.0 International (CC BY) license, which means that you can distribute, remix, and build upon the content, as long as you provide attribution to OpenStax and its content contributors.

Because our books are openly licensed, you are free to use the entire book or pick and choose the sections that are most relevant to the needs of your course. Feel free to remix the content by assigning your students certain chapters and sections in your syllabus, in the order that you prefer. You can even provide a direct link in your syllabus to the sections in the web view of your book.

Instructors also have the option of creating a customized version of their OpenStax book. The custom version can be made available to students in low-cost print or digital form through your campus bookstore. Visit the Instructor Resources section of your book page on OpenStax.org for information.

Art attribution in *Business Ethics*

In *Business Ethics*, most art contains attribution to its title, creator or rights holder, host platform, and license within the caption. Because the art is openly licensed, anyone may reuse the art as long as they provide the same attribution to its original source.

To maximize readability and content flow, some art does not include attribution in the text. If you reuse art from *Business Ethics* that does not have attribution provided, use the following attribution: Copyright Rice University, OpenStax, under CC BY 4.0 license.

Errata

All OpenStax textbooks undergo a rigorous review process. However, like any professional-grade textbook, errors sometimes occur. Since our books are web based, we can make updates periodically when deemed pedagogically necessary. If you have a correction to suggest, submit it through the link on your book page on openstax.org. Subject matter experts review all errata suggestions. OpenStax is committed to remaining transparent about all updates, so you will also find a list of past errata changes on your book page on openstax.org.

Format

You can access this textbook for free in web view or PDF through OpenStax.org, and for a low cost in print.

About *Business Ethics*

Business Ethics is designed to meet the scope and sequence requirements of the single-semester standardized business ethics course across all majors. This title includes innovative features designed to enhance student learning, including case studies, application scenarios, and links to video interviews with executives, all of which help instill in students a sense of ethical awareness and responsibility. The book provides an important opportunity for students to learn the core concepts of business ethics and understand how to apply those concepts to their professional lives.

Coverage and scope

Our *Business Ethics* textbook adheres to the scope and sequence requirements of introductory business ethics courses nationwide. We have endeavored to make the core theories and practical concepts of business ethics engaging, relevant, and accessible to students. The guiding themes of the textbook are to promote high ethical standards and to assist the integration of ethical thinking across the business school curriculum, with an end result of encouraging even greater ethical consciousness on the part of business practitioners beyond their graduation. We particularly emphasize the reality of today's global business community and observe that geography, culture, and time contribute to ethical concepts and constructs. With awareness of these issues in mind, the content of this textbook has been developed and arranged to emphasize the necessity—and difficulty—of ethical decision-making. The authors seek to help students recognize legal and moral issues, reason through the consequences of different courses of action, and promote social responsibility. The text emphasizes connections between topics such as ethical theories, legal responsibilities, the prioritization of stakeholders, and corporate social responsibility. The organization and pedagogical features were developed and vetted with feedback from business ethics instructors dedicated to the project.

Engaging feature boxes

Throughout *Business Ethics*, you will find features that engage students by taking selected topics a step further. Each feature box contains either a link to a deeper exploration of the topic at hand or critical thinking questions that may be geared toward class discussion, student projects, or written essays. Our features include:

- **Cases from the Real World**. This feature presents brief examples of real companies making ethical decisions in the midst of hectic competition. Each example includes follow-up critical thinking questions that encourage reflection on the case and how it relates to chapter concepts and themes.
- **What Would You Do?** This feature presents brief, fact-based scenarios in which students are challenged to put themselves into the shoes of ranking executives and balance a host of interests—some conflicting—as they make decisions for their businesses. Students provide an answer to a practical problem or ethical issue, as well as their reasoning.
- **Ethics across Time and Cultures**. This feature considers how geography, culture, and time influence the ethical values we have. Follow-up critical thinking questions allow for broader reflection on the chapter topics and encourage deeper integration of the chapter content.
- **Link to Learning.** This feature provides a very brief introduction to online resources and videos that are pertinent to students' exploration of the topic at hand. Link to Learning boxes allow students to connect easily to some of the most important thought leaders and concepts in the field of business ethics. The

purpose is to highlight the complexities of ethical decision-making.

Module materials that reinforce key concepts

- **Learning Objectives.** Every module begins with a set of clear and concise learning objectives. These objectives are designed to help the instructor decide what content to include or assign, and to guide students on what they can expect to learn. After completing the module and end-of-module exercises, students should be able to demonstrate mastery of the learning objectives.
- **Summaries.** Section summaries distill the information in each module for both students and instructors down to key, concise points addressed in the section.
- **Key Terms.** Key terms are bold and are followed by a definition in context. Definitions of key terms are also listed in the glossary, which appears at the end of the chapter.
- **Assessments.** Multiple-choice and short-answer review questions provide opportunities to recall and test the information students learn throughout each module.

Additional resources

Student and instructor resources

We've compiled additional resources for both students and instructors, including Getting Started Guides, a test bank, and comprehensive PowerPoint slides. Instructor resources require a verified instructor account, which you can apply for when you log in or create your account on OpenStax.org. Take advantage of these resources to supplement your OpenStax book.

Community Hubs

OpenStax partners with the Institute for the Study of Knowledge Management in Education (ISKME) to offer Community Hubs on OER Commons—a platform for instructors to share community-created resources that support OpenStax books, free of charge. Through our Community Hubs, instructors can upload their own materials or download resources to use in their courses, including additional ancillaries, teaching material, multimedia, and relevant course content. We encourage instructors to join the hubs for the subjects most relevant to their teaching and research, as an opportunity to both enrich their courses as well as to engage with other faculty.

To reach the Community Hubs, visit www.oercommons.org/hubs/OpenStax.

Technology partners

As allies in making high-quality learning materials accessible, our technology partners offer optional low-cost tools that are integrated with OpenStax books. To access the technology options for your text, visit your book page on OpenStax.org.

About the authors

Senior contributing authors

Stephen M. Byars, USC Marshall School of Business

Stephen Byars received his BA from Claremont McKenna College, his MA from the University of San Diego, and his PhD from the University of Southern California. He teaches business ethics and oral and written communication at the Marshall School of Business at USC to both graduate and undergraduate business majors. He has served as associate director of the USC Writing Program, temporary director of the Writing

Center within the Writing Program, and as director of the USC Marshall Consulting Program. His scholarly interests include business and professional ethics, the constructive mediation of disputes in the workplace, and those best practices that permit leaders to direct business in ways that engender community, social, and corporate good.

Kurt Stanberry, University of Houston-Downtown

Kurt Stanberry is a professor of legal studies in the College of Business at the University of Houston Downtown and has held the PLM Endowed Professorship since 2011. He is also a licensed attorney. He received his BA from Yale University, an MBA from the Graduate School of Business at Temple University, and a JD from the University of Houston College of Law.

Kurt teaches courses at the undergraduate and graduate level in business law, contracts, employment law, negotiations, ethics, and other related topics. He also conducts continuing education seminars in topics such as negotiations, leadership, diversity, and ethics for CPAs, CFPs, attorneys, and business executives, through organizations such as the AICPA, FEI, and TSCPA at the state and national levels. He has published numerous articles in scholarly journals, two textbooks, various practice manuals, and cases. Prior to joining the faculty at UHD, Kurt was a professor in the California State University System and was also a visiting professor in international programs in London, Bonn, Tokyo, and Seoul. He has been teaching and practicing law for over 30 years.

Contributing authors

Barbara Boerner, Brevard College

Robert Brancatelli, Fordham University

Wade Chumney, California State University, Northridge

Laura Dendinger, Wayne State College

Bill Nantz, Houston Community College

Mark Poepsel, Southern Illinois University Edwardsville

David Shapiro, Pennsylvania State University

Reviewers

Justin Bateh, Florida State College at Jacksonville

Ronald Berenbeim, New York University

Kenneth Bigel, Touro College

Cindy Briggs, Salt Lake Community College

Barbara Chappell, Walden University

Maureen Chisholm, Quincy College

Valerie Collins, Sheridan College

Dixon Cooper, Ouachita Baptist University

Anastasia Cortes, Virginia Polytechnic Institute

Sarah Esveldt, Carroll University

Rand Fandrich, New England College of Business

Charles Fenner, State University of New York Canton

Mehran Ferdowsian, Wilkes University

Betty Fitte, Tidewater Community College

Robert Freeborough, Berkeley College

Martha Helland, University of Sioux Falls

Amy Jordan, Loyola University Chicago

Stephanie Jue, University of Texas

Cheryl Keymer, North Arkansas College

Nai Lamb, University of Tennessee at Chattanooga

Jolene A. Lampton, Park University–Austin Campus

Barbara Limbach, Chadron State College

Marilyn Marousek, Barry University

Russ Meade, Husson University

Michael Pakaluk, Catholic University

Tatyana Pashnyak, Bainbridge State College

Roslyn Roberts, California State University, Sacramento

Amber Ruszkowski, Ivy Tech Community College

Richard Savior, State University of New York Empire State College

Lon Schiffbauer, Salt Lake Community College

Nathan Smith, Houston Community College

Anne Snell, Tulane University

Chris Suprenant, University of New Orleans

Glen Taylor, Paradise Valley Community College

Sonia Toson, Kennesaw State University

Joel Webb, Loyola University New Orleans

Andy Wible, Muskegon Community College

Jeffrey Yoder, Fairfield University

Figure 1.1 Each of us makes innumerable decisions every day. In a business context, these choices have consequences for ourselves and others whom we must take into account in our decision-making process. (credit: modification of "business paper office laptop" by "rawpixel"/Pixabay, CC0)

Chapter Outline

1.1 Being a Professional of Integrity
1.2 Ethics and Profitability
1.3 Multiple versus Single Ethical Standards

Introduction

Ethics consists of the standards of behavior to which we hold ourselves in our personal and professional lives. It establishes the levels of honesty, empathy, and trustworthiness and other virtues by which we hope to identify our personal behavior and our public reputation. In our personal lives, our ethics sets norms for the ways in which we interact with family and friends. In our professional lives, ethics guides our interactions with customers, clients, colleagues, employees, and shareholders affected by our business practices (Figure 1.1).

Should we care about ethics in our lives? In our practices in business and the professions? That is the central question we will examine in this chapter and throughout the book. Our goal is to understand why the answer is *yes*.

Whatever hopes you have for your future, you almost certainly want to be successful in whatever career you choose. But what does success mean to you, and how will you know you have achieved it? Will you measure it in terms of wealth, status, power, or recognition? Before blindly embarking on a quest to achieve these goals, which society considers important, stop and think about what a successful career means to you personally. Does it include a blameless reputation, colleagues whose good opinion you value, and the ability to think well of yourself? How might ethics guide your decision-making and contribute to your achievement of these goals?

1.1 | Being a Professional of Integrity

Learning Objectives

By the end of this section, you will be able to:

- Describe the role of ethics in a business environment
- Explain what it means to be a professional of integrity
- Distinguish between ethical and legal responsibilities
- Describe three approaches for examining the ethical nature of a decision

Whenever you think about the behavior you expect of yourself in your personal life and as a professional, you are engaging in a philosophical dialogue with yourself to establish the standards of behavior you choose to uphold, that is, your **ethics**. You may decide you should always tell the truth to family, friends, customers, clients, and shareholders, and if that is not possible, you should have very good reasons why you cannot. You may also choose never to defraud or mislead your business partners. You may decide, as well, that while you are pursuing profit in your business, you will not require that all the money on the table come your way. Instead, there might be some to go around to those who are important because they are affected one way or another by your business. These are your stakeholders.

Acting with Integrity

Clients, customers, suppliers, investors, retailers, employees, the media, the government, members of the surrounding community, competitors, and even the environment are **stakeholders** in a business; that is, they are individuals and entities affected by the business's decisions (Figure 1.2). Stakeholders typically value a leadership team that chooses the ethical way to accomplish the company's legitimate for-profit goals. For example, Patagonia expresses its commitment to environmentalism via its "1% for the Planet" program, which donates 1 percent of all sales to help save the planet. In part because of this program, Patagonia has become a market leader in outdoor gear.

Figure 1.2 Stakeholders are the individuals and entities affected by a business's decisions, including clients, customers, suppliers, investors, retailers, employees, the media, the government, members of the surrounding community, the environment, and even competitors. (attribution: Copyright Rice University, OpenStax, under CC BY 4.0 license)

Being successful at work may therefore consist of much more than simply earning money and promotions. It may also mean treating our employees, customers, and clients with honesty and respect. It may come from the sense of pride we feel about engaging in honest transactions, not just because the law demands it but because we demand it of ourselves. It may lie in knowing the profit we make does not come from shortchanging others. Thus, **business ethics** guides the conduct by which companies and their agents abide by the law and respect the rights of their stakeholders, particularly their customers, clients, employees, and the surrounding community and environment. Ethical business conduct permits us to sleep well at night.

LINK TO LEARNING

Are business ethics an oxymoron? Read "Why Ethics Matter" to understand (https://openstax.org/l/53oxymoron) just a few of the reasons to have values-driven management.

Nearly all systems of religious belief stress the building blocks of engaging others with respect, empathy, and honesty. These foundational beliefs, in turn, prepare us for the codes of ethical behavior that serve as ideal guides for business and the professions. Still, we need not subscribe to any religious faith to hold that ethical behavior in business is still necessary. Just by virtue of being human, we all share obligations to one another, and principal among these is the requirement that we treat others with fairness and dignity, including in our commercial transactions.

For this reason, we use the words *ethics* and *morals* interchangeably in this book, though some philosophers distinguish between them. We hold that "an ethical person" conveys the same sense as "a moral person," and we do not regard religious belief as a requirement for acting ethically in business and the professions. Because we are all humans and in the same world, we should extend the same behavior to all. It is the right way to behave, but it also burnishes our own professional reputation as business leaders of integrity.

Integrity—that is, unity between what we say and what we do—is a highly valued trait. But it is more than just consistency of character. Acting with **integrity** means we adhere strongly to a code of ethics, so it implies trustworthiness and incorruptibility. Being a professional of integrity means consistently striving to be the best person you can be in all your interactions with others. It means you practice what you preach, walk the talk, and do what you believe is right based upon reason. Integrity in business brings many advantages, not the least of which is that it is a critical factor in allowing business and society to function properly.

Successful corporate leaders and the companies they represent will take pride in their enterprise if they engage in business with honesty and fair play. To treat customers, clients, employees, and all those affected by a firm with dignity and respect *is* ethical. In addition, laudable business practices serve the long-term interests of corporations. Why? Because customers, clients, employees, and society at large will much more willingly patronize a business and work hard on its behalf if that business is perceived as caring about the community it serves. And what type of firm has long-term customers and employees? One whose track record gives evidence of honest business practice.

LINK TO LEARNING

In this interview, Mark Faris, a white-collar criminal convicted of fraud, claims that greed, arrogance, and ambition were motivating factors (https://openstax.org/l/53MarkFaris) in his actions. He also discusses the human ability to rationalize our behavior to justify it to ourselves. Note his proposed solutions: practicing ethical leadership and developing awareness at an individual level via corporate training.

Many people confuse legal and ethical compliance. They are, however, totally different and call for different standards of behavior. The concepts are not interchangeable in any sense of the word. The law is needed to establish and maintain a functioning society. Without it, our society would be in chaos. Compliance with these legal standards is strictly mandatory: If we violate these standards, we are subject to punishment as established by the law. Therefore, **compliance** in terms of business ethics generally refers to the extent to which a company conducts its business operations in accordance with applicable regulations, statutes, and laws. Yet this represents only a baseline minimum. Ethical observance builds on this baseline and reveals the principles of an individual business leader or a specific organization. Ethical acts are generally considered voluntary and personal—often based on our perception of or stand on right and wrong.

Some professions, such as medicine and the law, have traditional codes of ethics. The Hippocratic Oath, for example, is embraced by most professionals in health care today as an appropriate standard always owed to patients by physicians, nurses, and others in the field. This obligation traces its lineage to ancient Greece and the physician Hippocrates. Business is different in not having a mutually shared standard of ethics. This is changing, however, as evidenced by the array of codes of conduct and mission statements many companies have adopted over the past century. These have many points in common, and their shared content may eventually produce a code universally claimed by business practitioners. What central point might constitute such a code? Essentially, a commitment to treat with honesty and integrity customers, clients, employees, and others affiliated with a business.

The law is typically indebted to tradition and precedence, and compelling reasons are needed to support any change. Ethical reasoning often is more topical and reflects the changes in consciousness that individuals and society undergo. Often, ethical thought precedes and sets the stage for changes in the law.

Behaving ethically requires that we meet the mandatory standards of the law, but that is not enough. For example, an action may be legal that we personally consider unacceptable. Companies today need to be focused not only on complying with the letter of the law but also on going above and beyond that basic mandatory requirement to consider their stakeholders and do what is right.

LINK TO LEARNING

To see an example of a corporate ethical code (https://openstax.org/l/53J&Jcredo) or mission statement, visit Johnson & Johnson and read "Our Credo" written by former chair Robert Wood Johnson.

Forbes provides an annual list of companies recently deemed the most ethical (https://openstax.org/l/53EthicalBus) according to their standards and research.

Ends, Means, and Character in Business

How, then, should we behave? Philosophy and science help us answer this question. From philosophy, three different perspectives help us assess whether our decisions are ethical on the basis of reason. These perspectives are called **normative ethical theories** and focus on how people ought to behave; we discuss them in this chapter and in later chapters. In contrast, *descriptive ethical theories* are based on scientific evidence, primarily in the field of psychology, and describe how people tend to behave within a particular context; however, they are not the subject of this book.

The first normative approach is to examine the ends, or *consequences*, a decision produces in order to evaluate whether those ends are ethical. Variations on this approach include utilitarianism, teleology, and consequentialism. For example, **utilitarianism** suggests that an ethical action is one whose consequence achieves the greatest good for the greatest number of people. So if we want to make an ethical decision, we should ask ourselves who is helped and who is harmed by it. Focusing on consequences in this way generally does not require us to take into account the means of achieving that particular end, however. That fact leads us to the second normative theory about what constitutes ethical conduct.

The second approach does examine the *means,* or actions, we use to carry out a business decision. An example of this approach is **deontology**, which essentially suggests that it is the means that lend nobility to the ends. Deontology contends that each of us owes certain duties to others (*deon* is a Greek word for duty or obligation) and that certain universal rules apply to every situation and bind us to these duties. In this view, whether our actions are ethical depends only on whether we adhere to these rules. Thus, the means we use is the primary determinant of ethical conduct. The thinker most closely associated with deontology is the eighteenth-century German philosopher Immanuel Kant (Figure 1.3).

Kantianism (Deontology)

Immanuel Kant (1724–1804)

Human beings are creatures with *reason*.

Reason depends on respect for rules.

As creatures with reason, we are "duty bound" to follow logical ethical principles and avoid contradiction.

Figure 1.3   Immanuel Kant was an eighteenth-century philosopher, now associated with deontology, who spent nearly all his professional life teaching at the university in Königsberg (which today is Kaliningrad, the westernmost point in Russia). (credit right: modification of "Kant foto" by "Becker"/Wikimedia Commons, Public Domain)

The third normative approach, typically called **virtue theory**, focuses on the *character* of the decision-maker—a character that reflects the training we receive growing up. In this view, our ethical analysis of a decision is intimately connected with the person we choose to be. It is through the development of habits, the routine-actions in which we choose to engage, that we are able to create a character of integrity and make ethical decisions. Put differently, if a two-year-old is taught to take care of and return borrowed toys even though this runs contrary to every instinct they have, they may continue to perfect their ethical behavior so that at age forty, they can be counted on to safeguard the tens of millions of dollars investors have entrusted to their care in brokerages.

Virtue theory has its roots in the Greek philosophical tradition, whose followers sought to learn how to live a flourishing life through study, teaching, and practice. The cardinal virtues to be practiced were courage, self-control, justice, and wisdom. Socrates was often cited as a sage and a role model, whose conduct in life was held in high regard.

ETHICS ACROSS TIME AND CULTURES

Aristotle and the Concept of Phronesis, or Practical Wisdom

Phrónēsis (fro-NEE-sis) is a type of practical wisdom that enables us to act virtuously. In "The Big Idea: The Wise Leader," a *Harvard Business Review* article on leadership and ethical decision-making, Ikujiro Nonaka, a Japanese organizational theorist, and Hirotaka Takeuchi, a professor of Management Practice at Harvard Business School, discuss the gap between the theory and practice of ethics and which characteristics make a wise leader.[1] The authors conclude that "the use of explicit and tacit knowledge isn't enough; chief executive officers (CEOs) must also draw on a third, often forgotten kind of knowledge, called practical wisdom. Practical wisdom is tacit knowledge acquired from experience that enables people to make prudent judgments and take actions based on the actual situation, guided by values and morals."

The concept of practical wisdom dates back to Aristotle, who considered phronesis, which can also be defined as prudence, to be a key intellectual virtue. Phronesis enables people to make ethically sound judgments. According to the authors, phronetic leaders:

- practice moral discernment in every situation, making judgments for the common good that are guided by their individual values and ethics;
- quickly assess situations and envision the consequences of possible actions or responses;
- create a shared sense of purpose among executives and employees and inspire people to work together in pursuit of a common goal;
- engage as many people as possible in conversation and communicate using metaphors, stories, and other figurative language in a way that everyone can understand; and
- encourage practical wisdom in others and support the training of employees at all levels in its use.

In essence, the first question any company should ask itself is: "Do we have a moral purpose?" Having a moral purpose requires focusing on the common good, which precedes the accumulation of profit and results in economic and social benefits. If companies seek the common good, profits generally will follow.

Critical Thinking

In the article cited, the authors stress the importance of being well versed in the liberal arts, such as philosophy, history, literature, and in the fine arts to cultivate judgment. How do you think a strong background in the liberal arts would impart practical wisdom or help you make ethical decisions?

1.2 Ethics and Profitability

Learning Objectives

By the end of this section, you will be able to:

- Differentiate between short-term and long-term perspectives
- Differentiate between *stockholder* and *stakeholder*
- Discuss the relationship among ethical behavior, goodwill, and profit
- Explain the concept of corporate social responsibility

Few directives in business can override the core mission of maximizing shareholder wealth, and today that particularly means increasing quarterly profits. Such an intense focus on one variable over a short time (i.e., a **short-term perspective**) leads to a short-sighted view of what constitutes business success.

Measuring true profitability, however, requires taking a long-term perspective. We cannot accurately measure success within a quarter of a year; a longer time is often required for a product or service to find its market and gain traction against competitors, or for the effects of a new business policy to be felt. Satisfying consumers' demands, going green, being socially responsible, and acting above and beyond the basic requirements all take time and money. However, the extra cost and effort will result in profits in the long run. If we measure success from this longer perspective, we are more likely to understand the positive effect ethical behavior has on all who are associated with a business.

Profitability and Success: Thinking Long Term

Decades ago, some management theorists argued that a conscientious manager in a for-profit setting acts ethically by emphasizing solely the maximization of earnings. Today, most commentators contend that ethical business leadership is grounded in doing right by all stakeholders directly affected by a firm's operations, including, but not limited to, **stockholders**, or those who own shares of the company's stock. That is, business leaders do right when they give thought to what is best for *all* who have a stake in their companies. Not only that, firms actually reap greater material success when they take such an approach, especially over the long run.

Nobel Prize–winning economist Milton Friedman stated in a now-famous *New York Times Magazine* article in 1970 that the only "social responsibility of a business is to increase its profits."[2] This concept took hold in business and even in business school education. However, although it is certainly permissible and even desirable for a company to pursue profitability as a goal, managers must also have an understanding of the context within which their business operates and of how the wealth they create can add positive value to the world. The context within which they act is society, which permits and facilitates a firm's existence.

Thus, a company enters a **social contract** with society as whole, an implicit agreement among all members to cooperate for social benefits. Even as a company pursues the maximizing of stockholder profit, it must also acknowledge that all of society will be affected to some extent by its operations. In return for society's permission to incorporate and engage in business, a company owes a reciprocal obligation to do what is best for as many of society's members as possible, regardless of whether they are stockholders. Therefore, when applied specifically to a business, the social contract implies that a company gives back to the society that permits it to exist, benefiting the community at the same time it enriches itself.

LINK TO LEARNING

What happens when a bank decides to break the social contract? This press conference held by the National Whistleblowers Center (https://openstax.org/l/53Birken) describes the events surrounding the $104 million whistleblower reward given to former UBS employee Bradley Birkenfeld by the U.S. Internal Revenue Service. While employed at UBS, Switzerland's largest bank, Birkenfeld assisted in the company's illegal offshore tax business, and he later served forty months in prison for conspiracy. But he was also the original source of incriminating information that led to a Federal Bureau of Investigation examination of the bank and to the U.S. government's decision to impose a $780 million fine on UBS in 2009. In addition, Birkenfeld turned over to investigators the account information of more than 4,500 U.S. private clients of UBS.[3]

In addition to taking this more nuanced view of profits, managers must also use a different time frame for obtaining them. Wall Street's focus on periodic (i.e., quarterly and annual) earnings has led many managers to adopt a short-term perspective, which fails to take into account effects that require a longer time to develop. For example, charitable donations in the form of corporate assets or employees' volunteered time may not show a return on investment until a sustained effort has been maintained for years. A **long-term perspective** is a more balanced view of profit maximization that recognizes that the impacts of a business decision may not manifest for a longer time.

As an example, consider the business practices of Toyota when it first introduced its vehicles for sale in the

United States in 1957. For many years, Toyota was content to sell its cars at a slight loss because it was accomplishing two business purposes: It was establishing a long-term relationship of trust with those who eventually would become its loyal U.S. customers, and it was attempting to disabuse U.S. consumers of their belief that items made in Japan were cheap and unreliable. The company accomplished both goals by patiently playing its long game, a key aspect of its operational philosophy, "The Toyota Way," which includes a specific emphasis on long-term business goals, even at the expense of short-term profit.[4]

What contributes to a corporation's positive image over the long term? Many factors contribute, including a reputation for treating customers and employees fairly and for engaging in business honestly. Companies that act in this way may emerge from any industry or country. Examples include Fluor, the large U.S. engineering and design firm; illycaffè, the Italian food and beverage purveyor; Marriott, the giant U.S. hotelier; and Nokia, the Finnish telecommunications retailer. The upshot is that when consumers are looking for an industry leader to patronize and would-be employees are seeking a firm to join, companies committed to ethical business practices are often the first to come to mind.

Why should stakeholders care about a company acting above and beyond the ethical and legal standards set by society? Simply put, being ethical is simply good business. A business is profitable for many reasons, including expert management teams, focused and happy employees, and worthwhile products and services that meet consumer demand. One more and very important reason is that they maintain a company philosophy and mission to do good for others.

Year after year, the nation's most admired companies are also among those that had the highest profit margins. Going green, funding charities, and taking a personal interest in employee happiness levels adds to the bottom line! Consumers want to use companies that care for others and our environment. During the years 2008 and 2009, many unethical companies went bankrupt. However, those companies that avoided the "quick buck," risky and unethical investments, and other unethical business practices often flourished. If nothing else, consumer feedback on social media sites such as Yelp and Facebook can damage an unethical company's prospects.

CASES FROM THE REAL WORLD

Competition and the Markers of Business Success

Perhaps you are still thinking about how you would define success in your career. For our purposes here, let us say that success consists simply of achieving our goals. We each have the ability to choose the goals we hope to accomplish in business, of course, and, if we have chosen them with integrity, our goals and the actions we take to achieve them will be in keeping with our character.

Warren Buffet (Figure 1.4), whom many consider the most successful investor of all time, is an exemplar of business excellence as well as a good potential role model for professionals of integrity and the art of thinking long term. He had the following to say: "Ultimately, there's one investment that supersedes all others: Invest in yourself. Nobody can take away what you've got in yourself, and everybody has potential they haven't used yet. . . . You'll have a much more rewarding life not only in terms of how much money you make, but how much fun you have out of life; you'll make more friends the more interesting person you are, so go to it, invest in yourself."[5]

Figure 1.4   Warren Buffett, shown here with President Barack Obama in June 2010, is an investor and philanthropist who was born in 1930 in Omaha, Nebraska. Through his leadership of Berkshire Hathaway, he has become one of the most successful investors in the world and one of the wealthiest people in the United States, with an estimated total net worth of almost $80 billion. (credit: "President Barack Obama and Warren Buffett in the Oval Office" by Pete Souza/Wikimedia Commons, Public Domain)

The primary principle under which Buffett instructs managers to operate is: "Do nothing you would not be happy to have an unfriendly but intelligent reporter write about on the front page of a newspaper."[6] This is a very simple and practical guide to encouraging ethical business behavior on a personal level. Buffett offers another, equally wise, principle: "Lose money for the firm, even a lot of money, and I will be understanding; lose reputation for the firm, even a shred of reputation, and I will be ruthless."[7] As we saw in the example of Toyota, the importance of establishing and maintaining trust in the long term cannot be underestimated.

LINK TO LEARNING

For more on Warren Buffett's thoughts about being both an economic and ethical leader, watch this interview (https://openstax.org/l/53Buffet) that appeared on the PBS NewsHour on June 6, 2017.

Stockholders, Stakeholders, and Goodwill

Earlier in this chapter, we explained that stakeholders are all the individuals and groups affected by a business's decisions. Among these stakeholders are stockholders (or **shareholders**), individuals and institutions that own stock (or shares) in a corporation. Understanding the impact of a business decision on the stockholder and various other stakeholders is critical to the ethical conduct of business. Indeed, prioritizing the claims of various stakeholders in the company is one of the most challenging tasks business professionals face. Considering only stockholders can often result in unethical decisions; the impact on all stakeholders must be considered and rationally assessed.

Managers do sometimes focus predominantly on stockholders, especially those holding the largest number of shares, because these powerful individuals and groups can influence whether managers keep their jobs or are dismissed (e.g., when they are held accountable for the company's missing projected profit goals). And many believe the sole purpose of a business is, in fact, to maximize stockholders' short-term profits. However, considering only stockholders and short-term impacts on them is one of the most common errors business managers make. It is often in the long-term interests of a business *not* to accommodate stockowners alone but rather to take into account a broad array of stakeholders and the long-term and short-term consequences for a course of action.

Here is a simple strategy for considering all your stakeholders in practice. Divide your screen or page into three columns; in the first column, list all stakeholders in order of perceived priority (Figure 1.5). Some individuals and groups play more than one role. For instance, some employees may be stockholders, some members of the community may be suppliers, and the government may be a customer of the firm. In the second column, list what you think each stakeholder group's interests and goals are. For those that play more than one role, choose the interests most directly affected by your actions. In the third column, put the likely impact of your business decision on each stakeholder. This basic spreadsheet should help you identify all your stakeholders and evaluate your decision's impact on their interests. If you would like to add a human dimension to your analysis, try assigning some of your colleagues to the role of stakeholders and reexamine your analysis.

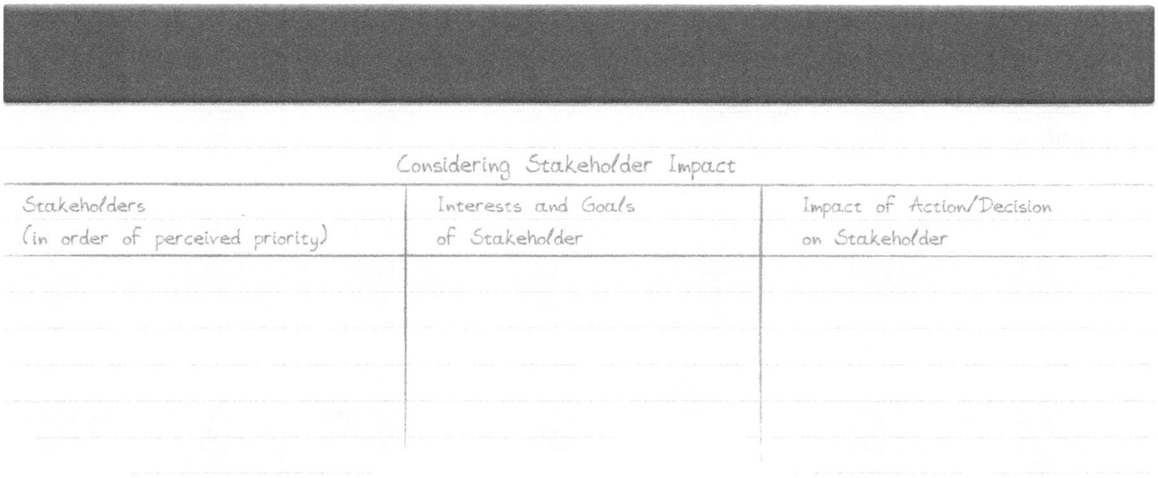

Considering Stakeholder Impact		
Stakeholders (in order of perceived priority)	Interests and Goals of Stakeholder	Impact of Action/Decision on Stakeholder

Figure 1.5   Imagine you are the CEO of a mid-sized firm—about five hundred employees—and your company is publicly traded. To understand what matters most to all your stakeholders, complete the preceding exercise to evaluate the impact of a particular action or decision. (attribution: Copyright Rice University, OpenStax, under CC BY 4.0 license)

The positive feeling stakeholders have for any particular company is called **goodwill**, which is an important component of almost any business entity, even though it is not directly attributable to the company's assets and liabilities. Among other intangible assets, goodwill might include the worth of a business's reputation, the value of its brand name, the intellectual capital and attitude of its workforce, and the loyalty of its established customer base. Even being socially responsible generates goodwill. The ethical behavior of managers will have a positive influence on the value of each of those components. Goodwill cannot be earned or created in a short time, but it can be the key to success and profitability.

A company's name, its corporate logo, and its trademark will necessarily increase in value as stakeholders view that company in a more favorable light. A good reputation is essential for success in the modern business world, and with information about the company and its actions readily available via mass media and the Internet (e.g., on public rating sites such as Yelp), management's values are always subject to scrutiny and open debate. These values affect the environment outside and inside the company. The **corporate culture**, for instance, consists of shared beliefs, values, and behaviors that create the internal or organizational context within which managers and employees interact. Practicing ethical behavior at all levels—from CEO to upper and middle management to general employees—helps cultivate an ethical corporate culture and ethical employee relations.

WHAT WOULD YOU DO?

Which Corporate Culture Do You Value?

Imagine that upon graduation you have the good fortune to be offered two job opportunities. The first is with a corporation known to cultivate a hard-nosed, no-nonsense business culture in which keeping long hours and working intensely are highly valued. At the end of each year, the company donates to numerous social and environmental causes. The second job opportunity is with a nonprofit recognized for a very different culture based on its compassionate approach to employee work-life balance. It also offers the chance to pursue your own professional interests or volunteerism during a portion of every work day. The first job offer pays 20 percent more per year.

Critical Thinking

- Which of these opportunities would you pursue and why?
- How important an attribute is salary, and at what point would a higher salary override for you the nonmonetary benefits of the lower-paid position?

Positive goodwill generated by ethical business practices, in turn, generates long-term business success. As recent studies have shown, the most ethical and enlightened companies in the United States consistently outperform their competitors.[8] Thus, viewed from the proper long-term perspective, conducting business ethically is a wise business decision that generates goodwill for the company among stakeholders, contributes to a positive corporate culture, and ultimately supports profitability.

You can test the validity of this claim yourself. When you choose a company with which to do business, what factors influence your choice? Let us say you are looking for a financial advisor for your investments and retirement planning, and you have found several candidates whose credentials, experience, and fees are approximately the same. Yet one of these firms stands above the others because it has a reputation, which you discover is well earned, for telling clients the truth and recommending investments that seemed centered on the clients' benefit and not on potential profit for the firm. Wouldn't this be the one you would trust with your investments?

Or suppose one group of financial advisors has a long track record of giving back to the community of which it is part. It donates to charitable organizations in local neighborhoods, and its members volunteer service hours toward worthy projects in town. Would this group not strike you as the one worthy of your investments? That it appears to be committed to building up the local community might be enough to persuade you to give it your business. This is exactly how a long-term investment in community goodwill can produce a long pipeline of potential clients and customers.

CASES FROM THE REAL WORLD

The Equifax Data Breach

In 2017, from mid-May to July, hackers gained unauthorized access to servers used by Equifax, a major credit reporting agency, and accessed the personal information of nearly one-half the U.S. population.[9] Equifax executives sold off nearly $2 million of company stock they owned after finding out about the hack in late July, weeks before it was publicly announced on September 7, 2017, in potential violation of insider trading rules. The company's shares fell nearly 14 percent after the announcement, but few expect Equifax managers to be held liable for their mistakes, face any regulatory discipline, or pay any penalties for profiting from their actions. To make amends to customers and clients in the aftermath of the hack, the company offered free credit monitoring and identity-theft protection. On September 15, 2017, the company's chief information officer and chief of security retired. On September 26, 2017, the CEO resigned, days before he was to testify before Congress about the breach. To date, numerous government investigations and hundreds of private lawsuits have been filed as a result of the hack.

Critical Thinking

- Which elements of this case might involve issues of legal compliance? Which elements illustrate acting legally but not ethically? What would acting ethically and with personal integrity in this situation look like?
- How do you think this breach will affect Equifax's position relative to those of its competitors? How might it affect the future success of the company?
- Was it sufficient for Equifax to offer online privacy protection to those whose personal information was hacked? What else might it have done?

A Brief Introduction to Corporate Social Responsibility

If you truly appreciate the positions of your various stakeholders, you will be well on your way to understanding the concept of **corporate social responsibility (CSR)**. CSR is the practice by which a business views itself within a broader context, as a member of society with certain implicit social obligations and environmental responsibilities. As previously stated, there is a distinct difference between legal compliance and ethical responsibility, and the law does not fully address all ethical dilemmas that businesses face. CSR ensures that a company is engaging in sound ethical practices and policies in accordance with the company's culture and mission, above and beyond any mandatory legal standards. A business that practices CSR cannot have maximizing shareholder wealth as its sole purpose, because this goal would necessarily infringe on the rights of other stakeholders in the broader society. For instance, a mining company that disregards its corporate social responsibility may infringe on the right of its local community to clean air and water if it pursues only profit. In contrast, CSR places all stakeholders within a proper contextual framework.

An additional perspective to take concerning CSR is that ethical business leaders opt to do *good* at the same time that they do *well*. This is a simplistic summation, but it speaks to how CSR plays out within any corporate setting. The idea is that a corporation is entitled to make money, but it should not only make money. It should also be a good civic neighbor and commit itself to the general prospering of society as a whole. It ought to make the communities of which it is part better at the same time it pursues legitimate profit goals. These ends are not mutually exclusive, and it is possible—indeed, praiseworthy—to strive for both. When a company approaches business in this fashion, it is engaging in a commitment to corporate social responsibility.

LINK TO LEARNING

U.S. entrepreneur Blake Mycoskie has created a unique business model (https://openstax.org/l/53TOMS) combining both for-profit and nonprofit philosophies in an innovative demonstration of corporate social responsibility. The company he founded, TOMS Shoes, donates one pair of shoes to a child in need for every pair sold. As of May 2018, the company has provided more than 75 million pairs of shoes to children in seventy countries.[10]

1.3 | Multiple versus Single Ethical Standards

Learning Objectives

By the end of this section, you will be able to:

* Analyze ethical norms and values as they relate to business standards
* Explain the doctrine of ethical relativism and why it is problematic
* Evaluate the claim that having a single ethical standard makes behaving consistently easier

Business people sometimes apply different ethical standards in different contexts, especially if they are working in a culture different from the one in which they were raised or with coworkers from other traditions. If we look outside ourselves for ethical guidance, relying on the context in which we find ourselves, we can grow confused about what is ethical business behavior. Stakeholders then observe that the messages we send via our conduct lack a consistent ethical core, which can harm our reputation and that of the business. To avoid falling back on **ethical relativism**, a philosophy according to which there is no right or wrong and what is ethical depends solely on the context, we must choose a coherent standard we can apply to all our interactions with others.

Some people who adopt multiple ethical standards may choose to exhibit the highest standards with their families, because these are the people they most revere. In a business setting, however, this same person may choose to be an unethical actor whose sole goal is the ruthless accumulation of wealth by any means. Because work and family are not the only two settings in which we live our lives, such a person may behave according to yet another standard to competitors in a sporting event, to strangers on the street, or to those in his or her religious community.

Although the ethical standard we adopt is always a choice, certain life experiences can have more profound effects on our choice than others. Among the most formative experiences are family upbringing and cultural traditions, broadly defined here to include religious and ethnic norms, the standard patterns of behavior within the context in which we live. Culture and family also influence each other because the family exists in and responds to its cultural context, as well as providing us with the bedrock for our deepest values. Regardless of this initial coding, however, we can choose the ethical standards we apply in the business context.

Why should we choose a single ethical code for all the contexts in which we live? The Greek philosophers and later proponents of the normative ethical theories we discussed earlier would say that if you apply your reason to determine how to behave, it makes rational sense to abide by a single ethical code for all interactions with all persons in all contexts. By doing so, you maximize your ethical behavior no matter who the other party is. Furthermore, you have an internally consistent behavior for all family, friends, customers, clients, and anyone else with whom you interact. Thus, we need not choose different values in different contexts, and when people see us in different situations, they are more likely to trust us because they see we uphold the same values regardless of the context.

Indeed, proponents of all the normative ethical theories would insist that the only rational choice is to have a single ethical standard. A deontologist would argue that you should adhere to particular duties in performing your actions, regardless of the parties with whom you interact. A utilitarian would say that any act you take should result in the greatest good for the greatest number. A virtue ethicist would state that you cannot be virtuous if you lack integrity in your behavior toward all.

Adopting a consistent ethical standard is both selfless and in the manager's self-interest. That is, would-be customers and clients are more likely to seek out a business that treats all with whom it interacts with honesty and fairness, believing that they themselves will be treated likewise by that firm. Similarly, business leaders who treat everyone in a trustworthy manner need never worry that they might not have impressed a potential customer, because they always engage in honorable commercial practices. A single standard of business behavior that emphasizes respect and good service appeals to all.

Normative ethics is about discovering right and delineating it from wrong; it is a way to develop the rules and norms we use to guide meaningful decision-making. The ethics in our single code are not relative to the time, person, or place. In this world, we all wear different hats as we go about our daily lives as employees, parents, leaders, students. Being a truly ethical person requires that no matter what hat we wear, we exhibit a single ethical code and that it includes, among others, such universal principles of behavior as honesty, integrity, loyalty, fairness, respect for law, and respect for others.

Yet another reason to adopt a universal ethical standard is the transparent character it nurtures in us. If a company's leadership insists that it stands for honest business transactions at every turn, it cannot prosecute those who defraud the company and look the other way when its own officers do the same. Stakeholders recognize such hypocrisy and rightly hold it against the business's leaders.

Business leaders are not limited to only one of the normative ethical theories we have described, however. Virtue theory, utilitarianism, and deontology all have advantages to recommend them. Still, what should not change is a corporate commitment to not make exceptions in its practices when those favor the company at the expense of customers, clients, or other stakeholders.

Moving from theory to daily life, we can also look at the way our reputation is established by the implicit and explicit messages we send to others. If we adopt ethical relativism, friends, family, and coworkers will notice that we use different standards for different contexts. This lack of consistency and integrity can alter their perception of us and likely damage our reputation.

WHAT WOULD YOU DO?

Taking Advantage of an Employee Discount

Suppose you work in retail sales for an international clothing company. A perk of the job is an employee discount of 25 percent on all merchandise you purchase for personal use. Your cousin, who is always looking for a bargain, approaches you in the store one day and implores you to give him your employee discount on a $100 purchase of clothes for himself.

Critical Thinking

- How would you handle this situation and why?
- Would it matter if the relative were someone closer to you, perhaps a brother or sister?
- If so, why?

🔑 Key Terms

business ethics the conduct by which companies and their agents abide by the law and respect the rights of their stakeholders, particularly their customers, clients, employees, and the surrounding community and environment

compliance the extent to which a company conducts its business operations in accordance with applicable regulation and statutes

corporate culture the shared beliefs, values, and behaviors that create the organizational context within which employees and managers interact

corporate social responsibility (CSR) the practice in which a business views itself within a broader context, as a member of society with certain implicit social obligations and responsibility for its own effects on environmental and social well-being

deontology a normative ethical theory suggesting that an ethical decision requires us to observe only the rights and duties we owe to others, and, in the context of business, act on the basis of a primary motive to do what is right by all stakeholders

ethical relativism a view that ethics depends entirely upon context

ethics the standards of behavior to which we hold ourselves in our personal and professional lives

goodwill the value of a business beyond its tangible assets, usually including its reputation, the value of its brand, the attitude of its workforce, and customer relations

integrity the adherence to a code of moral values implying trustworthiness and incorruptibility because there is unity between what we say and what we do

long-term perspective a broad view of profit maximization that recognizes the fact that the impact of a business decision may not manifest for a long time

normative ethical theories a group of philosophical theories that describe how people ought to behave on the basis of reason

shareholder an individual or institution that owns stock or shares in a corporation, by definition a type of stakeholder; also called stockholder

short-term perspective a focus on the goal of maximizing periodic (i.e., quarterly and annual) profits

social contract an implicit agreement among societal members to cooperate for social benefit; when applied specifically to a business, it suggests a company that responsibly gives back to the society that permits it to incorporate, benefiting the community at the same time that it enriches itself

stakeholders individuals and entities affected by a business's decisions, including customers, suppliers, investors, employees, the community, and the environment, among others

stockholder an individual or institution that owns stock or shares in a corporation, by definition a type of stakeholder; also called shareholder

utilitarianism a normative theory of ethics suggesting that an ethical act is the one whose consequences create the greatest good for the greatest number of people

virtue theory a normative theory that focuses on proper conduct guided by the training we received growing up

📖 Summary

1.1 Being a Professional of Integrity

Ethics sets the standards that govern our personal and professional behavior. To conduct business ethically, we must choose to be a professional of integrity. The first steps are to ask ourselves how we define success

and to understand that integrity calls on us to act in a way that is consistent with our words. There is a distinct difference between legal compliance and ethical responsibility, and the law does not fully address all ethical dilemmas that businesses face. Sound ethical practice meets the company's culture, mission, or policies above and beyond legal responsibilities. The three normative theories of ethical behavior allow us to apply reason to business decisions as we examine the result (utilitarianism), the means of achieving it (deontology), and whether our choice will help us develop a virtuous character (virtue ethics).

1.2 Ethics and Profitability

A long-term view of business success is critical for accurately measuring profitability. All the company's stakeholders benefit from managers' ethical conduct, which also increases a business's goodwill and, in turn, supports profitability. Customers and clients tend to trust a business that gives evidence of its commitment to a positive long-term impact. By exercising corporate social responsibility, or CSR, a business views itself within a broader context, as a member of society with certain implicit social obligations and responsibility for its own effects on environmental and social well-being.

1.3 Multiple versus Single Ethical Standards

The adoption of a single ethical code is the mark of a professional of integrity and is supported by the reasoned approach of each of the normative theories of business ethics. When we consistently maintain the same values regardless of the context, we are more likely to engender trust among those with whom we interact.

Assessment Questions

1. Which of these concepts relates to utilitarianism?
   A. consequences
   B. actions
   C. character
   D. duty

2. True or false? According to the Greek system of logic introduced by Socrates, normative ethical theories ultimately are grounded in reason.

3. Explain why ethical responsibilities go beyond legal compliance.

4. Describe the difference between normative and descriptive ethical theories.

5. Which of the following is not a stakeholder?
   A. the media
   B. corporate culture
   C. the environment
   D. customers

6. True or false? According to Milton Friedman, a company's social responsibility consists solely of bettering the welfare of society.

7. What is corporate social responsibility (CSR)?

8. Describe a practical way to prioritize the claims of stakeholders.

9. Describe how a company's ethical business practices affect its goodwill.

10. True or false? Family is generally a strong influence on our ethical standards.

11. Which normative ethical theory supports the idea of holding multiple ethical standards?

    A.   deontology

    B.   utilitarianism

    C.   virtue ethics

    D.   none of the above

12. Describe the benefits of having a single ethical standard.

 # Endnotes

1. Ikujiro Nonaka and Hirotaka Takeuchi, "The Big Idea: The Wise Leader," *Harvard Business Review*, May 2011. https://hbr.org/2011/05/the-big-idea-the-wise-leader.
2. Jia Lynn Yang, "Maximizing Shareholder Value: The Goal That Changed Corporate America," *Washington Post*, August 26, 2013. https://www.washingtonpost.com/business/economy/maximizing-shareholder-value-the-goal-that-changed-corporate-america/2013/08/26/26e9ca8e-ed74-11e2-9008-61e94a7ea20d_story.html?utm_term=.524082979f63.
3. David Kocieniewski, "Whistle-blower Awarded 104 Million by IRS," *New York Times*, September 11, 2012. http://www.nytimes.com/2012/09/12/business/whistle-blower-awarded-104-million-by-irs.html.
4. Jeffrey Liker, *The Toyota Way: Fourteen Management Principles from the World's Greatest Manufacturer* (New York: McGraw-Hill, 2005).
5. Zameena Mejia and Margaret Ward, "Warren Buffett Says This One Investment 'Supersedes All Others,'" *CNBC Make It*, October 4, 2017. https://www.cnbc.com/2017/10/04/warren-buffett-says-this-one-investment-supersedes-all-others.html.
6. Laurence A. Cunningham, "The Philosophy of Warren E. Buffett," *New York Times*, May 1, 2015. https://www.nytimes.com/2015/05/02/business/dealbook/the-philosophy-of-warren-e-buffett.html.
7. Laurence A. Cunningham, "The Philosophy of Warren E. Buffett," *New York Times*, May 1, 2015. https://www.nytimes.com/2015/05/02/business/dealbook/the-philosophy-of-warren-e-buffett.html.
8. Peter Georgescu, "Doing the Right Thing Is Just Profitable," *Forbes*, July 26, 2017. https://www.forbes.com/sites/petergeorgescu/2017/07/26/doing-the-right-thing-is-just-profitable/#360853967488.
9. Tyler Durden, "Massive Data Breach At Equifax: As Many As 143 Million Social Security Numbers Hacked," *Zero Hedge*, September 7, 2017. http://www.zerohedge.com/news/2017-09-07/massive-data-breach-equifax-many-143-million-social-security-numbers-hacked.
10. Arezou Naeini, Auditee Dutt, James Angus, Sarkis Mardirossian, and Sebastian Bonfanti, "A Shoe for a Shoe, and a Smile," *Business Today*, June 7, 2015. http://www.businesstoday.in/magazine/lbs-case-study/toms-shoes-shoes-for-free-cause-marketing-strategy-case-study/story/219444.html; TOMS.com, Giving shoes, https://www.toms.com/what-we-give-shoes.

2 Ethics from Antiquity to the Present

Figure 2.1 Their accuracy and practical use in the marketplace made scales, held aloft here by the figure of Justice in Bruges, Belgium, a common symbol in jurisprudence and law in the East and the West. Even today, the concept of counterbalancing different ideas and philosophies underlies many approaches to the law and ethics. (credit: modification of "Golden Lady Justice" by Emmanuel Huybrechts/Flickr, CC BY 2.0)

Chapter Outline

2.1 The Concept of Ethical Business in Ancient Athens
2.2 Ethical Advice for Nobles and Civil Servants in Ancient China
2.3 Comparing the Virtue Ethics of East and West
2.4 Utilitarianism: The Greatest Good for the Greatest Number
2.5 Deontology: Ethics as Duty
2.6 A Theory of Justice

Introduction

From the time of barter to the age of bitcoin, most people engaged in business transactions have sought trust. Without trust, which is a fundamental outcome of ethical behavior, not just business relationships but all relationships would collapse. To develop insight into our own concepts of ethics, this chapter looks at how ethical systems have developed over time, beginning with the distinction between ethics and the law.

Ethics are the standards of behavior to which we hold ourselves accountable in our personal and professional lives. Laws and regulations set the minimal standards by which society lives out those ethical norms. Because laws are minimal standards, it is not uncommon for an act to be legal but generally deemed unethical. The fact is that law and ethics are not always the same. Always, however, they are in dialogue, and each informs the other. The greatest challenge in business decision-making is moving beyond the letter of the law to create a culture of ethics (Figure 2.1).

Can you identify a moment in your life when it was hard to follow your conscience, or your personal morality conflicted with societal norms? What was the nature of the conflict, and how did you approach it?

2.1 | The Concept of Ethical Business in Ancient Athens

Learning Objectives

By the end of this section, you will be able to:

- Identify the role of ethics in ancient Athens
- Explain how Aristotelian virtue ethics affected business practices

It would be hard to overstate the influence of ancient Athens on Western civilization. Athenian achievements in the arts, literature, and government have molded Western consciousness. Perennial themes, such as the search for individual identity and each person's place in the world, appear in countless novels and Hollywood screenplays. The role of Athenian ethical theories in philosophy has been profound, and Athenian principles continue to be influential in contemporary philosophy. Ethics, as a form of applied philosophy, was a major focus among the leaders of ancient Athens, particularly teachers like Socrates, Plato, and Aristotle. They taught that ethics was not merely what someone did but who someone was. Ethics was a function of being and, as the guiding principle for dealings with others, it naturally applied as well to the sensitive areas of money and commerce.

Ancient Athens

Like a modern metropolis, the city-state (*polis*) of Athens in the fifth century BCE drew people from far afield who wanted a better life. For some, that life meant engaging in trade and commerce, thanks to the openness of the new democracy established under the lawgiver Cleisthenes in 508 BCE. Others were drawn to Athens' incredibly rich architecture, poetry, drama, religious practices, politics, and schools of philosophy. Youth traveled there hoping to study with such brilliant teachers as the mathematicians Archimedes and Pythagoras; dramatists like Sophocles and Euripides; historians Herodotus and Thucydides; Hippocrates, the father of medicine; and, of course, the renowned but enigmatic philosopher Socrates. More than being the equivalent of rock stars of their day, these thinkers, scholars, and artists challenged youth to pursue truth, no matter the cost to themselves or their personal ambitions. These leaders were interested not in fame or even in personal development but in the creation of an ideal society. This was the Golden Age of ancient Greece, whose achievements were so profound and enduring that they have formed the pillars of Western civilization for nearly two and a half millennia.

Philosophy, in particular, flourished during the Golden Age, with various schools of thought attempting to make sense of the natural and human worlds. The human world was thought to be grounded in the natural world but to transcend it in striking ways, the most obvious being humans use of reason and deliberation. Philosophers like Socrates, Plato, and Aristotle tackled fundamental questions of human existence with such insight that their ideas have remained relevant and universal even at the dawn of artificial intelligence. As British mathematician and philosopher Alfred North Whitehead (1861–1947) observed, "the safest general characterization of the European philosophical tradition is that it consists of a series of footnotes to Plato."[1]

Why are the insights of these Greek philosophers still relevant today? One reason is their development of the ancient concept of *virtue*. The person most closely associated with virtue in the West, and the development of what is now known as **virtue ethics**—that is, an ethical system based upon the exercise of certain virtues (loyalty, honor, courage) emphasizing the formation of character—is Plato's famous pupil Aristotle (384–322 BCE) (Figure 2.2).

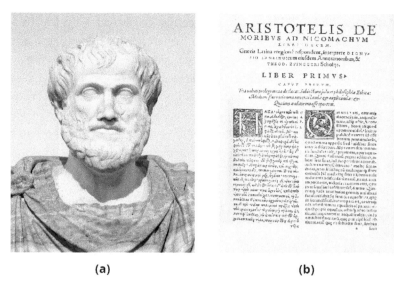

(a)   **(b)**

Figure 2.2   *Nicomachean Ethics*, by the ancient Greek philosopher Aristotle (a), is a rough collection of Aristotle's lecture notes to his students on how to live the virtuous life and achieve happiness; it is the oldest surviving treatment of ethics in the West. The collection was possibly named after Aristotle's son. This 1566 edition (b) was printed in both Greek and Latin. (credit a: modification of "Aristotle Altemps Inv8575" by "Jastrow"/Wikimedia Commons, Public Domain; credit b: modification of "Aristotelis De Moribus ad Nicomachum" by "Aavindraa"/Wikimedia Commons, Public Domain)

Aristotelian Virtue Ethics

For Aristotle, everything that exists has a purpose, or end, and has been designed to meet that end. For instance, the proper end of birds is to fly, that of fish to swim. Birds and fish have been designed with the appropriate means (feathers, fins) to achieve those ends. Teleology, from the Greek *telos* meaning goal or aim, is the study of ends and the means directed toward those ends. What is the *telos* of human beings? Aristotle believed it to be **eudaimonia**, or happiness. By this, he did not mean happiness in a superficial sense, such as having fun or being content. Rather, he equated happiness with human flourishing, which he believed could be attained through the exercise of the function that distinguishes humans from the natural world: reason.[2] For Aristotle, reason was supreme and best used to increase not wealth but character. "But what is happiness?" he asked. "If we consider what the function of man is, we find that happiness is a virtuous activity of the soul."[3]

However, because humans are endowed not only with reason but also with the capacity to act in an honorable and ethical manner, they may reject their end, either intentionally or by default. The great task of life, then, is to recognize and pursue happiness, no matter the constraints placed on the individual, the most dramatic of which are suffering and death. Birds and fish have little difficulty achieving their ends, and we can assume that much of this is due to their genetic coding. Because happiness might not be genetically encoded in human beings, they must learn how to be happy. How do they do that? According to Aristotle, *eudaimonia* is achieved by leading a virtuous life, which is attained over time. "Happiness is a kind of activity; and an activity clearly is developed and is not a piece of property already in one's possession."[4]

Aristotle identified two types of virtues, which the philosophical community of his day agreed were objective and not subjective. The two types were intellectual and moral. Intellectual virtues—including knowledge (*epistémē*), wisdom (*sophíā*), and, most importantly for Aristotle, prudence (**phrónēsis**), or practical wisdom—served as guides to behavior; that is, a person acted prudently based on the wisdom gained over time through the ongoing acquisition and testing of knowledge. To give an oversimplified but practical application of Aristotelian thinking, a hiring manager acts prudently when assessing a pool of candidates based on knowledge of their backgrounds and on insight gained after years of working in that role. The manager may even use intuitive reason regarding a candidate, which Aristotle believed was another way of arriving at truth. Understood in this way, the manager's intuition is an impression regarding character and someone's potential fit in an organization. Among the intellectual virtues, prudence played the major role because it helped individuals avoid excess and deficiency and arrive at the **golden mean** between the two. Prudence has been translated as "common sense" and "practical wisdom" and helps individuals make the right decision in the right way at the right time for the right reason. In Aristotle's view, only the truly prudent person could possess all the moral virtues.

The distinction Aristotle made is that the intellectual virtues are acquired purely through learning, whereas the moral virtues are acquired through practice and the development of habits. In contrast to the intellectual virtues, which focused on external acts, the moral virtues had to do with character. They included courage, self-control, liberality, magnificence, honor, patience, and amiability. Some of these virtues had different meanings in ancient Greece than they do today. "Liberal," for instance, referred not to a political or economic stance but rather to an aspect of personality. Someone would be considered liberal who was open and sharing of him- or herself and his or her talents without fear of rejection or expectation of reciprocity. The paragon of these virtues was the magnanimous individual, someone for whom fame and wealth held little attraction.[5] This person had self-knowledge; was not rash, quick to anger, or submissive to others; and acted with self-respect, control, and prudence. The magnanimous individual achieved happiness by leading a life characterized by reason and will. He or she remained in control of self and did not hand over his or her authority—or moral agency—to others, whether in judgment or in decision-making. "So, magnanimity seems to be a sort of crown of the virtues, because it enhances them and is never found apart from them. This makes it hard to be truly magnanimous, because it is impossible without all-round excellence," according to Aristotle.[6]

The relationship between the intellectual and the moral virtues was not as clear cut as it may appear, however, because Aristotle believed that action preceded character. In other words, the primary way to change character was through consistent, intentional behavior in the direction of virtue. Aristotle gave the example of courage. A person was not courageous first and then went about performing acts of courage. Rather, courage resulted from incremental change, small steps taken over time that molded the person's character. It relied on a recognition of justice, so that courage was directed toward the right end. The important task was developing the habit of leading the virtuous life. Anyone could do this; however, it was a discipline that had to be learned and practiced with dedication. We can see that this habit of virtue is especially relevant for business today, when the temptation to conform to an established organizational culture is overwhelming even when that culture may permit and even encourage questionable practices. Add the seductive power of money, and anyone's courage might be tested.

The most notable feature of virtue ethics is that it viewed the basic ethical unit—the fundamental agent of morality—as the individual, who lived out his or her worldview publicly. A life of virtue, therefore, took place in the economic and political spheres so that others might participate in and benefit from it. In Athenian society, it was important for business to be conducted competently and ethically. Even though Aristotle was suspicious of business, he acknowledged its importance in preserving and nurturing Athenian democracy. He also praised the creation of money to further the goal of justice, so that a shoemaker and a housebuilder, for instance, could trade their wares on an equal basis. Virtue in the marketplace was demonstrated through ethical behavior, according to Aristotle: "People do in fact seek their own good, and think that they are right to act in this way. It is from this belief that the notion has arisen that such people are prudent. Presumably, however, it is impossible to secure one's own good independently of domestic and political science."[7] This belief in the public nature of virtue was crucial for the flourishing of the city-state and also has implications for contemporary business, which must consider the individual, organization, industry, and society in its development and planning.

ETHICS ACROSS TIME AND CULTURES

Athenian Democracy

Just as time and place influence people's perception of ethics, so is their understanding of democracy also subjective.

You might be surprised to learn the Athenian version of democracy was significantly different from our own. For instance, although the word "democracy" comes from the Greek for people (*dêmos*) and power (*krátos*), only adult men who owned property could vote, and voting was direct; Athens was not a republic with elected representatives, like the United States. Resident aliens, or *metics*—those who change their home—were not eligible for citizenship and could not vote. They had limited rights and their status was second class, although this did not stop many of them from attaining wealth and fame. They were often among the best artisans, craftspeople, and merchants in the city-state. Metics were able to conduct business in the marketplace (*agora*) provided they paid special taxes yearly. One of the most famous was Aristotle, who was born outside Athens in northern Greece.

Women, even those who were citizens, were not allowed to vote and had limited rights when it came to property and inheritance. Their primary function in Athenian society was the care and management of the home. "The Athenian woman must be the perfect Penelope—a partner to the husband, a guard of the house, and one who practices the virtues defined by her husband. Physical beauty was not to be a goal, nor was it even a primary valued attribute. Total dedication to the welfare of husband, children, and household was the ultimate virtue"[8] (Figure 2.3).

Figure 2.3   Penelope and Odysseus in a scene from Homer's *Odyssey*, as depicted in 1802 by the German painter Johann Tischbein. For the ancient Greeks, Penelope represented all the virtues of a loving, dutiful partner. She remained faithful to her husband Odysseus despite his absence of some twenty years during and after the Trojan War. (credit: "Odysseus and Penelope" by H. R. Wacker and James Steakley/Wikimedia Commons, Public Domain)

Finally, not all transactions were as straightforward as selling Egyptian linen, dried fruit, or spices. Slave traders, too, brought their "wares" to market. Slavery was a customary part of many cultures throughout the ancient world, from Persia to Arabia and Africa and China. In Athens and its surrounding area, it is estimated that during the Golden Age (fifth century BCE) there were 21,000 citizens, 10,000 metics (non-native Athenians who still shared some of the benefits of citizenship), and 400,000 slaves.[9] Despite the Athenian emphasis on virtue and honor, there was little or no objection to owning slaves, because they formed an indispensable part of the economy, providing the labor for agriculture and food production.

Slavery persists even today. For instance, it is believed that nearly thirty million people worldwide are living and working as slaves, including three million in China and fourteen million in India.[10] Servitude also exists for migrant workers forced to live and work in inhuman conditions without recourse to legal help or even the basic necessities of life. Such conditions occur in industries as diverse as commercial fishing in Southeast Asia and construction in Qatar.[11]

Critical Thinking

- Consider how democracy has expanded since the Golden Age of Greece, eventually including universal suffrage and fundamental rights for everyone. Although we try not to judge cultures today as having right or wrong practices, we often judge earlier cultures and civilizations. How might you assess a practice like slavery in antiquity without imposing modern values on a civilization that existed more than two and a half millennia ago?
- Are there absolute truths and values that transcend time and space? If yes, where might these come from? If not, why not?

Honorable Behavior in Business

The common belief in ancient Greece that business and money were somehow tainted reflected Plato's concept that the physical world was an imperfect expression, or shadow, of the ideal. Everything in the physical world was somehow less than the ideal, and this included the products of human thought and labor. For example, a cow exists in the physical world as an imperfect and temporary expression of the ideal essence of a cow, what we might call "cowness." (This imperfection accounted for the many variations found in the earthly creature.) Business, as a human invention based on self-interest, also had no appreciable ideal or end. After all, what was the purpose of making money if not having more money? Any end beyond that was not evident. In other words, money existed simply to replicate itself and was fueled by avarice (the love of money) or greed (the love of material goods). "As for the life of the businessman, it does not give him much freedom of action. Besides, wealth is obviously not the good that we are seeking, because it serves only as a means; i.e., for getting something else," said Aristotle.[12]

Yet, business had an interesting effect that helped invigorate Athenian life and encouraged those engaged in it to be virtuous (or else risk their reputation). This effect was *association*. Business was based on the free and fair exchange of goods, which brought not only items of merchandise into association with each other but also buyers, sellers, and public officials. The way to ensure ethically sound association was through the exercise of prudence, especially in its demand that people act not rashly but deliberately. This deliberative aspect of prudence provided a way for buyers, sellers, and everyone engaged in a transaction to act honorably, which was of the utmost importance. Honor was not only a foundational virtue but the cultural environment in which the ancient world existed. One of the worst offenses anyone could commit, whether man, woman, free, or slave, was to act in a dishonorable way. Of course, although acting deliberately does not guarantee that one is acting honorably, for Athenians, acting in a calculated way was not an indication of dishonor. Dishonorable acts included any that disturbed the basic order (*dikē*) of life in which everyone had a role, including the gods.

Interestingly, the Aristotelian approach to business did not condemn money making or the accumulation of riches. What concerned Aristotle, particularly because of its harmful effects on the individual and the city-state, was greed. Aristotle considered greed an excess that tipped the scales of justice and led to scandal. Money might constitute the bait, but greed causes the person to reach out and grab as much as possible, falling into the trap of scandal. The Greeks considered the exercise of greed an irrational, and therefore ignoble, act. Only attention to honor and deliberative prudence could save someone from acting so foolishly.

Honor in ancient Greece was not just an individual characteristic but also a function of the group to which an individual belonged, and the person derived self-esteem from membership in that group. Civic virtue consisted of honorable living in community. Business scandals today often arise not from conflicts of interest but from conflicts of honor in which employees feel torn by their allegiance to a coworker, a supervisor, or the organization.[13] Although few people would use the term honor to describe contemporary workplace culture or corporate mission, nearly everyone understands the importance of reputation and its impact, positive or negative, on a business. Reputation is no accident. It is the product of a culture formed by individual and group effort. That effort is directed, intentional, and ongoing.

According to Aristotle, and later thinkers who expanded upon his work, such as thirteenth-century philosopher and theologian Thomas Aquinas, to act dishonorably casts disrepute on all concerned. Ends and means had to be aligned, particularly in business, which provided people's livelihoods and secured the economic health of the city-state. Acting honorably meant trying to be magnanimous in all transactions and rising above obsession with baser instincts. The honorable person was magnanimous, prudent, fair, and interested in self-advancement as long as it did not injure personal integrity or the body politic. The importance of prudence is evident because, said Aristotle, it is "concerned with human goods, i.e., things about which deliberation is possible; for we hold that it is the function of the prudent man to deliberate well; and nobody deliberates about things that cannot be otherwise, or that are not means toward an end, and that end is a practical good. And the man who is good at deliberation generally is the one who can aim, by the help of his calculation, at the best of the goods attainable."[14]

Aquinas further divided Aristotelian prudence into memory, reason, understanding, docility, shrewdness, foresight, circumspection, and caution.[15] To use these qualities in a constructive way, a business person had to direct them toward an appropriate end, which applies to business today just as it did in fourth-century Athens. A merchant could not make money in a random way but had to keep the needs of customers in mind and conduct business with fair prices and fees. This exercise of prudence was part of the cosmic order that ensured the right management of the home, the marketplace, and civilization itself. Similarly, committing fraud or deception to achieve an end, even if that end were good or just, was not considered an honorable act. Only when ends and means were aligned and worked in harmony were those engaged in the transaction considered virtuous. This virtue, in turn, would lead to the happiness Aristotle envisioned and toward which his entire system of virtue ethics aimed.

ETHICS ACROSS TIME AND CULTURES

Three Forms of Justice

Along with honor, justice—as depicted in the image at the beginning of this chapter—formed part of the cultural environment of Athenian society. Citizens often relied on litigation to settle disputes, particularly conflicts over business transactions, contracts, inheritance, and property. Justice existed in three forms, as it does today: legal, commutative, and distributive. In *legal justice*, the city-state was responsible for establishing fair laws for the welfare of its citizens. *Commutative justice* characterized relationships among individuals. Courts attempted to correct harms inflicted and return what had been unlawfully taken away from plaintiffs. *Distributive justice* governed the duty of the city-state to distribute benefits and burdens equitably among the people.

We can see these forms of justice at work today in very practical ways. For instance, within the framework of commutative justice, businesses are often held responsible ethically and financially for any harm caused by their products. And distributive justice is debated in such hotly contested issues as corporate and individual tax rates, universal health coverage, state and federal income assistance, subsidized housing, social security eligibility, college tuition aid (e.g., Pell grants), and similar programs designed to create a "safety net" for those least fortunate. Some safety net programs have been criticized for their excessive cost, inefficiency, and unfairness to those who pay into them while receiving no benefit or say in their administration.

Critical Thinking

- How is the ancient concept of distributive justice understood in today's political debate?
- What are the underlying values that inform each side of the debate (e.g., values like wealth maximization and corporate social responsibility)?
- Can these sides be reconciled and, if so, what must happen to bring them together? Does virtue have a role to play here; if so, how?

How, exactly, did honor and deliberative prudence prevent someone from acting foolishly in life and
unethically in business? And what does it look like to follow these virtues today?

2.2 Ethical Advice for Nobles and Civil Servants in Ancient China

Learning Objectives

By the end of this section, you will be able to:

- Identify the key features of Confucian virtue ethics
- Explain how Confucian virtue ethics can be applied to contemporary business

The teachings and writings of Confucius (551–479 BCE; also called Kung Fu Tzu or Master Kung) not only have
endured more than two and a half millennia but have influenced Chinese culture to such a degree that they
remain part of the national character. In classical Confucianism, the practice of virtue constitutes the essence
of governance. Differing from Aristotelian virtue (*arête*), Confucian virtue emphasizes relationships. Aristotle
shows how a self-determining person might live well in society. Confucius showed how a relationship-
determining person can live well with others. The reasons for this distinction will become clearer throughout
the section.

As an iconic figure, Confucius had an impact on politics, literature, civil administration, diplomacy, and religion
in China. Yet, by most accounts, he considered himself a failure, never having achieved the position and
security he sought during his lifetime. However, his story is a testament to the reward of a life lived with
integrity and simplicity.

Social Upheaval in Ancient China

More than a century and a half before Aristotle and on the other side of the globe, Confucius, a wandering
preacher from the principality of Lu in China, also struggled to answer life's questions, although in a practical
rather than a philosophical way. Confucius committed himself to healing the social divisions that were tearing
China apart under the declining Zhou Dynasty. Those divisions led to what historians call the "Period of the
Warring States," which persisted for two hundred years after Confucius's death. It was a time of constant
warfare and violence.[16] To counter the social disintegration he found everywhere, Confucius looked to the
past, or "the wisdom of the ancients." He called for a "return to *li*," which was the proper order of the universe
in which everyone had a role to play and there was harmony in the world.[17]

We might see this harmony in a contemporary business setting as a team of people bringing different talents
to bear on a specific project for the good (and profit) of the company. In this sense, *li* refers to doing those
tasks in collaboration with others to achieve the mission of the organization. For Confucius, *li* was expressed
through ritual acts. When the correct rituals were followed in the right way with the right intention for the
right end, all was well. Of course, corporate rituals also exist, and like all ritual acts, they reinforce cohesion

and identity within the group. Identifying them helps improve employee awareness, productivity, and, perhaps, happiness. One example of this would be new-employee orientation, which is intended to acclimate newcomers to the corporate culture, the company ethos, and the traditions associated with the way the firm does business. Finally, anticipating Aristotle's golden mean, *li* emphasized the middle ground between deficiency and excess. "Nothing in excess" was its guiding principle.[18]

Huston Smith, noted historian of world religions, has observed that the widespread adoption of Confucius's teachings within a generation of his death was not due to the originality of his ideas.[19] What made the humble scholar the greatest cultural force in China's history was chance. Confucius appeared on the scene at the right time, offering a fractured country an alternative to two extremes, neither of which was working. These were a realism that was tyrannical and relied on brute force to restrain the rivaling factions, and an idealistic approach called Mohism that was based on universal love and mutual aid. Confucius rejected the first as crude and the second as utopian.[20] Instead, he offered a practical but empathetic approach, a sort of tough love for the times.

LINK TO LEARNING

Read this article that gives a helpful historical background on Confucianism (https://openstax.org/l/53Confucianism) to learn more.

Confucian Virtue Ethics

Scholars believe that, like Aristotle, Confucius stressed the virtuous life in his ethical system, with the goal of creating a ***junzi***, or a person who was gracious, magnanimous, and cultured: in other words, a flourishing human being. A *junzi* exhibited refinement, self-control, and balance in all things, acting neither rashly nor timidly. Such a person was the opposite of a "small" individual, who spent his or her time embroiled in petty rivalries and for whom power was the ultimate measure of success.

The concept of *junzi* and the Aristotelian magnanimous individual have much in common, except that for Confucius, there was added urgency. To be a *junzi* was a matter not just of honor but of survival. It is no exaggeration to say that China's very existence depended upon the ability of individuals—nobles and peasants alike—to rise above the barbarity around them and embrace a way of life directed both outward toward social, political, and administrative reform and inward toward spiritual development. Confucius (Figure 2.4) believed that living the virtues he taught would achieve both these ends.

Figure 2.4   Confucius (Kung Fu-tzu or Master Kung), depicted here in front of the Confucius Temple in Beijing, lived during a turbulent period in China's history. He sought to end violence and chaos through a return to order, harmony, and reverence, especially within the family. (credit: "KongZi, Confucius Temple with Gold Roof, Main Statue" by "klarititemplateshop.com"/Flickr, CC BY 2.0)

The keystone of Confucius's deliberate tradition was the *dao* of humanity, or the Way, which established humanity as the answer to rampant lawlessness.[21] Confucius believed people were inherently good and that the way to stop inhuman behavior was to make them even better, or more human. He identified three means to do this, which we explore next: "whole-hearted sincerity and truthfulness," the "constant mean," and "expediency" (*quan*).[22] Specific virtues like moral character, righteousness, wisdom, courage, respect, filial piety, and simplicity formed part of these means. Someone who lived virtuously became more human, which resulted in a flourishing individual and an ordered world.

"Whole-hearted sincerity and truthfulness" meant more than sincerity, because even liars can be convincing. The sincerity Confucius had in mind was closer to loyalty, and the thing to which humans had to be loyal was truth. Confucius intended to counter the blind loyalty that had contributed to the eruption of anarchy throughout China. For instance, if a subject were called upon to offer advice, the subject had to be truthful, even though the ruler might not like the advice, which actually happened to Confucius, causing him to resign his post as minister of justice in Lu.[23] What a subject owed the ruler was not cloying deference but the truth, which would benefit everyone in the long run. The implications for ethical behavior in modern corporations may be obvious. Reporting unethical behavior as a whistleblower or even standing up for truth in a meeting is sometimes easier said than done, which is why living virtuously requires disciplined practice and the support of like-minded individuals.

The "constant mean" refers to balance between excess and deficiency in an existential and in a practical sense. We are to follow the middle path, avoiding extremes of thought and action through ritual acts. We cannot claim to lead a balanced life; we must show it by performing acts that maintain personal and collective order. The *Book of Li* catalogues many of these acts, which form a guide for proper living, indicating the correct way to maintain the five great relationships that support Chinese society: parent/child, husband/wife, elder/junior sibling, master/apprentice, and ruler/subject. Confucius and his peers believed that properly observing these key five relationships was essential for social good and would invoke divine favor on the people.

Note that three of these are relationships within the family. The family was the basic unit of society and Confucius's hope for reform, because it was the primary and most influential school of character, virtue, and conscience. Thus, the return to *li* takes on greater significance than a simple longing for an idyllic past. As Huston Smith noted, "that three of the Five Relationships pertain within the family is indicative of how important Confucius considered this institution to be. In this he was not inventing but continuing the Chinese assumption that the family is the basic unit of society. This assumption is graphically embedded in Chinese legend, which credits the hero who 'invented' the family with elevating the Chinese from the animal to human level."[24]

WHAT WOULD YOU DO?

Yijing

The five great relationships upon which Chinese civilization is built prescribed definite roles for the social classes and sexes. As in ancient Greece, women in ancient China were in charge of domestic duties and care of the family. They were neither expected nor believed able to assume duties outside the home and certainly not in the competitive world of business. Yet consider the fictional case of Yijing.

Yijing was the daughter of the merchant Bei Li, who sold farming tools and agricultural products in Cao, which bordered Lu. Bei Li's business was very successful and he took great pride in it. He had three sons who worked with him, but none had the head for business that his daughter Yijing had. Moreover, none of them wanted to take over the business after his death. When Yijing begged for a chance to run the business for her father, he agreed, but he insisted she disguise herself as a man when traveling and doing business in the family name. If people knew she was a woman, they would ridicule the family and take advantage of her. Although surprised by her father's request, Yijing agreed and eventually took over the business, making it extremely prosperous.

Critical Thinking

If you were Yijing, what would you have done?

For Confucius, the third approach to the Way of humanity was the doctrine of expediency. Where Buddhism and Taoism advocated compassion and Mohism advocated universal love, Confucianism defined righteousness as the virtue that would temper compassion and love so that people could live together not just peacefully but justly.[25] Righteousness included a practical approach to problem solving that helped politics, diplomacy, and civil administration to flourish. This expediency, or **quan**, is a noteworthy feature of Confucianism. Originally referring to a piece of metal used in balancing scales, *quan* is applied when weighing options in a moral dilemma and acts as a counterbalance to achieve fairness, enabling parties in a transaction to arrive at an equitable agreement. Ultimately, *quan* allows people and institutions to prioritize responsive action over ritual and serves as the way to align what people do with who they are, thus allowing them to become more human. For the businessperson, it might mean not fleeing the "tawdry" world of the marketplace but recognizing the humanity within it.

One example of the use of *quan* is the Broad Group, a Chinese manufacturer of central air conditioning products. The company produces clean energy systems and has developed an alternative to Freon. The new coolant has changed the way energy is delivered to such an extent that Zhang Yue, the company's chief executive officer, was awarded the Champions of the Earth prize by the United Nations in 2011 for his work in green energy.[26] Certainly, there is more opportunity for sustainable manufacturing and ethical business practices throughout China, and the state is attempting to promote such efforts.

A Confucian Business Model

The spirituality that emerges from *quan* as righteousness is not solely about the individual; it is about the act itself, that is, the transaction, whether that takes place in a market, shop, or loading dock. When righteousness is directed outward in this way, it becomes justice, compelling all parties in a transaction to act in good faith or risk upsetting the proper order of things. Justice in this sense allows for wealth creation, investment, and strategic planning as long as all fulfill their roles and act in the manner of a *junzi*. An overarching spirituality of business may even develop, arising from the people who collectively make up the company. This is a traditionally Confucian way of looking at corporate culture, as the reflection of a larger network of relationships.

The other two Confucian ways of humanity also relate to business, because wholeheartedness and sincerity can serve as models of risk assessment, requiring clearheaded thinking and action balanced with respect for markets, competitors, and stakeholders. The *dao* of humanity rejects the premise that greed reigns supreme by itself. Instead, its ethical counterpart is truth. Both qualities exist within business practices. In this ethical framework, loyalty to truth is not just a stock phrase but a commitment to value in all aspects of an enterprise, such as sales, finance, marketing, and the employment and hiring chain. An investment advisor might recommend the constant mean to clients so their money is in a diversified portfolio with a long-term strategy. The *dao* of humanity, wholeheartedness, sincerity, and the other virtues are treated in *The Analects* (Figure 2.5).

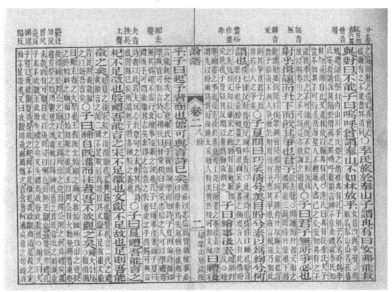

Figure 2.5 *The Analects of Confucius* is a collection of Confucius's teachings and sayings regarding the virtuous life and how to attain harmony. They were compiled by his followers and written with ink and brush on strips of bamboo. (credit: "Rongo Analects 02" by "Fukutaro"/Wikimedia Commons, Public Domain)

Some have criticized Confucianism for impeding progress in China in areas like education, the natural sciences, and business, because it has failed to adapt to the modern context. High-frequency trading, blockchain technology, artificial intelligence, and robotics do not work with cultural values thousands of years old, these critics say, so what we need is a new consciousness for a new era in human history. However, these criticisms miss the point. Confucius was interested in the same thing that concerned Aristotle—namely, the character of the person or persons making decisions rather than the decisions themselves. The importance of character has been proven repeatedly through business scandals like Enron, LIBOR, and the 2008 financial crisis, as well as the recent problems of Uber and Volkswagen, in which personal irresponsibility resulted in disaster. Indeed, business schools now offer seminars for executives integrating virtue ethics—both Aristotelian- and Confucian-inspired models—in leadership development.

LINK TO LEARNING

For a concise breakdown of the rise and collapse of Enron, see The Crime Network's episode on Enron (https://openstax.org/l/53Enron) in its *Corrupt Crimes* series.

The recent campaign of China's central government against unethical business practices has made a point of prosecuting executives for corruption in the form of bribery, kickbacks, and embezzlement, demonstrating that some Confucian thought has survived from ancient times. Jack Ma, cofounder of the giant Chinese ecommerce site Alibaba, has called this "clean communism," which might be another way of characterizing the form of state-sponsored capitalism that exists in China.[27] Of course, the former Communist regime did not embrace Confucian virtue. Mao Zedong was deeply suspicious of Confucius, holding him to be a relic of the Imperial Era and having little value for the new China he intended to create with the founding of the People's Republic of China in 1949.

LINK TO LEARNING

To what extent are children in China responsible for their parents' businesses? In this article, Kelly Zong, daughter of billionaire Zong Qinghua, explains how she believes modern-day China has "lost its soul" (https://openstax.org/l/53China) through selfish individualism and an obsession with wealth. If Kelly Zong is correct, would it be safe to say that China needs another return to ancient wisdom? Why or why not? Do you agree with her assessment of the current generation and individualism?

2.3 | Comparing the Virtue Ethics of East and West

Learning Objectives

By the end of this section, you will be able to:

- Compare the origins and goals of virtue ethics in the East and the West
- Describe how these systems each aimed to establish a social order for family and business
- Identify potential elements of a universally applied business ethic

Aristotle and Confucius each constructed an ethical system based on virtue, with Aristotle's ultimate aim being happiness and Confucius's being harmony. Each addressed a particular problem. For Aristotle, happiness consisted of the search for truth, which, in turn, required a centered, stable individual who could surmount misfortune or weak character. Confucius looked to settle the soul of the Chinese people by creating a system that reflected the heavenly order on Earth. Both systems rely on reasoned means to achieve reasoned ends.

East Meets West

Given the vastly different cultural and historical settings of ancient Greece and China, you may be surprised to find similarities between the Aristotelian and Confucian systems of virtue ethics. Yet not only are there similarities but the two systems share the theme of control. For Aristotle, control manifested itself through the deliberative process of *phrónēsis*, resulting in virtuous living, harmony, and happiness. This application of practical wisdom was related to self-restraint, or temperance. In Confucian virtue ethics, control was a function of self-regulation; primitive instincts were held at bay and the person gained the capacity and courage to act more humanely (Figure 2.6). This achievement of control benefited not only the individual but also the family and, by extension, the nation. Self-regulation was Confucius's way of establishing order.

CONTROL		
	Aristotle	Confucius
Characteristics	*phrónēsis* self-restraint temperance	self-regulation ability courage
Behavior	virtuous living harmony happiness	*junzi* *ru* (humanity)

Figure 2.6   The Aristotelian and Confucian systems of virtue ethics have in common the theme of control, as this comparison shows. (attribution: Copyright Rice University, OpenStax, under CC BY 4.0 license)

In a business context, control bears directly on **managerial ethics**, which is a way of relating to self, employees, and the organization that balances individual and collective responsibility, and in which management also includes planning, organizing, and leading to achieve organizational goals.[28] A self-controlled, disciplined manager is able to work through layers of bureaucracy and the complexities of human interaction to attain goals in a way that is responsible and profitable and that enhances the organization's mission and culture. These goals are achieved not at the expense of stakeholders but in a way that is fair for all. We might even say that righteousness leads to justice, which includes profit. We saw earlier that neither Aristotle nor Confucius disapproved of profit as long as it benefitted humanity in some way. Both men would have a very definite opinion about the optimization of shareholder wealth.

Despite these similarities between the two traditions, there are differences—the most notable being the locus of ethics. Aristotle placed this locus on individuals, who were called to fulfill their purpose honorably, accepting fate with dignity and aplomb. The basis of this acceptance was reason. For Confucius, reflecting the historical plight of China, the locus was the family, which he envisioned as putting an end to anarchy and setting the nation on its proper course by providing the basic pattern of relationships for personal and professional life. To be sure, family counted for Aristotle just as the individual counted for Confucius, but the emphasis in each system was different. Aristotle acknowledged that "a solitary man has a hard life, because it is not easy to keep up a continuous activity by oneself; but in company with others and in relation to others it is easier."[29]

Regardless of the source of ethical behavior, those engaged in business were required to act with accountability and responsibility. They were accountable to customers and suppliers when delivering commodities like figs, pottery, or olive oil. And they had to conduct themselves responsibly to maintain their personal and professional reputation. Thus, business was the perfect expression of ethics in both East and West, because it provided a forum within which virtues were tested in very real ways. Confucius urged each follower to be a great or humane person, or *ru*, not a small one.[30] This was so important that the school established after his death was known as the Ru School, and the principles it taught are called Ruism.[31]

Personal and Professional Roles

Another important characteristic of Eastern and Western systems of virtue ethics is the integration of personal and professional life. A person could not act one way at home and a completely different way in public, especially civic leaders, merchants, teachers, and rulers. The modern tendency to compartmentalize various aspects of ourselves to accommodate circumstances would have puzzled those living in ancient Greece or China. A retail manager who contributes generously to help protect endangered species but thinks nothing of working the sales staff to the point of burnout to achieve monthly goals has not successfully integrated the personal and the professional, for instance, and even poses obstacles to individual happiness and life in the community. Everyone desires efficiency in business, but compartmentalizing our personal and professional ideals can lead to "dispersed personal accountability" in an organization and the kind of financial meltdown that occurred, through greed and rule-breaking, in the housing and financial industries and led to the worldwide recession of 2008.[32]

What might the integration of personal and professional life look like, and how can we apply it within the relationships that are the foundation of business? To answer this question, consider the essence of the virtuous person that each ethical system strove to create. For Aristotle, the virtuous person saw the truth in every kind of situation. Once acknowledged and recognized, the truth could not be denied without compromising honor. Similarly, Confucius taught that "A gentleman will not, for the space of a meal, depart from humanity. In haste and flurry, he adheres to it; in fall and stumble, he adheres by it."[33]

Despite the emphasis these systems placed on character, however, character was not ultimately what defined the virtuous individual, family, city-state, or nation. Instead, it was the individual's transformation, through education, into a different kind of being who will act virtuously even if no one is watching. When the person concentrates on the means used to achieve an end, eventually the means become a way of life even more important than the end itself. It is not merely that the means must match the end, but that they come to define the virtuous person.

The integration of personal and professional lives has two effects: motive and awareness. Motive is the willingness to do the right thing because it is the right thing, even though there may be no perceived benefit. Arguably, it is here that the individual's true nature is revealed. The other effect, awareness, is the ability to see the ethical dimension in all events, choices, decisions, and actions. Many business scandals could be avoided if more people understood the value of human capital and the need to see the larger picture; to put it differently: responsibility over profitability. Or, as Confucius would say, it is the person who can broaden the Way, not the Way that broadens the person.[34]

Is There a Universal Ethics?

A fundamental question in the study of ethics is whether we can identify universal, objective moral truths that cut across cultures, geographic settings, and time. At the most foundational level, the answer might be yes. As Aristotle noted, ethics is not a science but an art.[35] Perhaps the best way to answer the question is to consider the methods used for moral decision-making. This strategy would be in line with Aristotelian and Confucian models if we assume that once they attain insight, most people will follow their conscience and act in reasonable, responsible ways. Methods of decision-making then could be adapted to any context or dilemma. But what constitutes a reasonable, responsible method, and who gets to choose it?

It is possible that standards of ethical conduct could be created to guide business affairs fairly and justly. Such standards already exist in most industries and professions. The Generally Accepted Accounting Principles (GAAP) give direction to those working in accounting and finance in the United States. The International Standards Organization offers guidelines and protocols for many industries. Together with governmental regulation, these might serve as the basis for ethical behavior, perhaps even globally. Of course, those fashioning guidelines would have to be sensitive to individual autonomy and national sovereignty, especially when it comes to international jurisdiction, privacy, and human rights. For example, the International Financial Reporting Standards serve as a kind of international GAAP to help companies report financial results in a common accounting language across national boundaries.

Despite our best efforts, someone who wishes to conduct business selfishly and unethically always will be drawn to do so unless given a compelling incentive not to. It is evident why Aristotle and Confucius stressed the importance of schooling. Perhaps what is needed now, building on these two ancient approaches, is business education focused on transformation rather than on conformity to guidelines. This proposal touches the core of both Aristotelian and Confucian teachings: training and education. Training and education help internalize in us more altruistic business practices. They also permit greater integration between our personal and professional understandings of the way we should treat friends, family, customers, and clients. No matter the context, we are then encouraged to treat others with honesty and respect, so that even someone certain to get away with the most outrageous corruption or money-laundering scheme would not do it. Why not? Because doing so would be a betrayal of the person's conscience and identity. A business education that is truly effective—one for the twenty-first century—would produce a graduate who could stand up and say no to that kind of self-betrayal.

WHAT WOULD YOU DO?

Scenario with Aristotle and Confucius

Imagine a scenario in which Aristotle and Confucius sit down to discuss Chiquita Brands International, a global produce conglomerate that paid "protection" money to right-wing and Marxist guerrilla groups in Colombia between 1997 and 2004 to ensure there would be no violence against its employees, banana plantations, and facilities. The payment violated the U.S. Foreign Corrupt Practices Act (1977), which prohibits bribes and kickbacks to foreign officials. Chiquita claimed it was the victim of extortion and had no choice. However, for its actions, it eventually paid $25 million in fines to the U.S. government. In 2007, a group of Colombians filed a lawsuit against the company under the Alien Tort Claims Act, alleging that, because of its illegal payments, Chiquita was "complicit in extrajudicial killings, torture, forced disappearances, and crimes against humanity" perpetrated against plantation workers by the guerilla "death squads."[36] The case went to the U.S. Supreme Court in 2015, but the Court declined to hear it.

Critical Thinking

- What do you suppose Confucius and Aristotle, teachers of virtue ethics, would say about the Colombians' case, and how would they go about assessing responsibility? What would they identify as the crime committed? Would they think the executives at Chiquita had acted prudently, cravenly, or deceitfully?
- What would you do if confronted with this case?

LINK TO LEARNING

The Business and Human Rights Resource Centre provides helpful, detailed information concerning ethics cases and the role of business in society, including more information about the Chiquita lawsuit (https://openstax.org/l/53Chiquita) and other interesting cases.

2.4 | Utilitarianism: The Greatest Good for the Greatest Number

Learning Objectives

By the end of this section, you will be able to:

- Identify the principle elements of Jeremy Bentham's utilitarianism
- Distinguish John Stuart Mill's modification of utilitarianism from Bentham's original formulation of it
- Evaluate the role of utilitarianism in contemporary business

Although the ultimate aim of Aristotelian virtue ethics was *eudaimonia*, later philosophers began to question this notion of happiness. If happiness consists of leading the good life, what is good? More importantly, who decides what is good? Jeremy Bentham (1748–1842), a progressive British philosopher and jurist of the Enlightenment period, advocated for the rights of women, freedom of expression, the abolition of slavery and of the death penalty, and the decriminalization of homosexuality. He believed that the concept of good could be reduced to one simple instinct: the search for pleasure and the avoidance of pain. All human behavior could be explained by reference to this basic instinct, which Bentham saw as the key to unlocking the workings of the human mind. He created an ethical system based on it, called utilitarianism. Bentham's protégé, John Stuart Mill (1806–1873), refined Bentham's system by expanding it to include human rights. In so doing, Mill reworked Bentham's utilitarianism in some significant ways. In this section we look at both systems.

Maximizing Utility

During Bentham's lifetime, revolutions occurred in the American colonies and in France, producing the Bill of Rights and the *Déclaration des Droits de l'Homme* (Declaration of the Rights of Man), both of which were based on liberty, equality, and self-determination. Karl Marx and Friedrich Engels published *The Communist Manifesto* in 1848. Revolutionary movements broke out that year in France, Italy, Austria, Poland, and elsewhere.[37] In addition, the Industrial Revolution transformed Great Britain and eventually the rest of Europe from an agrarian (farm-based) society into an industrial one, in which steam and coal increased manufacturing production dramatically, changing the nature of work, property ownership, and family. This period also included advances in chemistry, astronomy, navigation, human anatomy, and immunology, among other sciences.

Given this historical context, it is understandable that Bentham used reason and science to explain human behavior. His ethical system was an attempt to quantify happiness and the good so they would meet the conditions of the scientific method. Ethics had to be empirical, quantifiable, verifiable, and reproducible across time and space. Just as science was beginning to understand the workings of cause and effect in the body, so ethics would explain the causal relationships of the mind. Bentham rejected religious authority and wrote a rebuttal to the Declaration of Independence in which he railed against natural rights as "rhetorical nonsense, nonsense upon stilts."[38] Instead, the fundamental unit of human action for him was *utility*—solid, certain, and factual.

What is utility? Bentham's fundamental axiom, which underlies utilitarianism, was that all social morals and government legislation should aim for producing the greatest happiness for the greatest number of people. Utilitarianism, therefore, emphasizes the consequences or ultimate purpose of an act rather than the character of the actor, the actor's motivation, or the particular circumstances surrounding the act. It has these characteristics: (1) universality, because it applies to all acts of human behavior, even those that appear to be done from altruistic motives; (2) objectivity, meaning it operates beyond individual thought, desire, and perspective; (3) rationality, because it is not based in metaphysics or theology; and (4) quantifiability in its reliance on utility.[39]

ETHICS ACROSS TIME AND CULTURES

The "Auto-Icon"

In the spirit of utilitarianism, Jeremy Bentham made a seemingly bizarre request concerning the disposition of his body after his death. He generously donated half his estate to London University, a public university open to all and offering a secular curriculum, unusual for the times. (It later became University College London.) Bentham also stipulated that his body be preserved for medical instruction (Figure 2.7) and later placed on display in what he called an "auto-icon," or self-image. The university agreed, and Bentham's body has been on display ever since. Bentham wanted to show the importance of donating one's remains to medical science in what was also perhaps his last act of defiance against convention. Critics insist he was merely eccentric.

Figure 2.7   At his request, Jeremy Bentham's corpse was laid out for public dissection, as depicted here by H.H. Pickersgill in 1832. Today, his body is on display as an "auto-icon" at University College, London, a university he endowed with about half his estate. His preserved head is also kept at the college, separate from the rest of the body.) (credit: "Mortal Remains of Jeremy Bentham, 1832" by Weld Taylor and H. H. Pickersgill/Wikimedia Commons, CC BY 4.0)

Critical Thinking

- What do you think of Bentham's final request? Is it the act of an eccentric or of someone deeply committed to the truth and courageous enough to act on his beliefs?
- Do you believe it makes sense to continue to honor Bentham's request today? Why is it honored? Do requests have to make sense? Why or why not?

Bentham was interested in reducing utility to a single index so that units of it could be assigned a numerical and even monetary value, which could then be regulated by law. This **utility function** measures in "utils" the value of a good, service, or proposed action relative to the utilitarian principle of the greater good, that is, increasing happiness or decreasing pain. Bentham thus created a "hedonic calculus" to measure the utility of proposed actions according to the conditions of intensity, duration, certainty, and the probability that a certain consequence would result.[40] He intended utilitarianism to provide a reasoned basis for making judgments of value rather than relying on subjectivity, intuition, or opinion. The implications of such a system on law and public policy were profound and had a direct effect on his work with the British House of Commons, where he was commissioned by the Speaker to decide which bills would come up for debate and vote. Utilitarianism provided a way of determining the total amount of utility or value a proposal would produce relative to the harm or pain that might result for society.

Utilitarianism is a consequentialist theory. In **consequentialism**, actions are judged solely by their consequences, without regard to character, motivation, or any understanding of good and evil and separate from their capacity to create happiness and pleasure. Thus, in utilitarianism, it is the consequences of our actions that determine whether those actions are right or wrong. In this way, consequentialism differs from Aristotelian and Confucian virtue ethics, which can accommodate a range of outcomes as long as the character of the actor is ennobled by virtue. For Bentham, character had nothing to do with the utility of an action. Everyone sought pleasure and avoided pain regardless of personality or morality. In fact, too much reliance on character might obscure decision-making. Rather than making moral judgments, utilitarianism weighed acts based on their potential to produce the most good (pleasure) for the most people. It judged neither the good nor the people who benefitted. In Bentham's mind, no longer would humanity depend on inaccurate and outdated moral codes. For him, utilitarianism reflected the reality of human relationships and was enacted in the world through legislative action.

To illustrate the concept of consequentialism, consider the hypothetical story told by Harvard psychologist Fiery Cushman. When a man offends two volatile brothers with an insult, Jon wants to kill him; he shoots but misses. Matt, who intends only to scare the man but kills him by accident, will suffer a more severe penalty than his brother in most countries (including the United States). Applying utilitarian reasoning, can you say which brother bears greater guilt for his behavior? Are you satisfied with this assessment of responsibility? Why or why not?[41]

LINK TO LEARNING

A classic utilitarian dilemma considers an out-of-control streetcar and a switch operator's array of bad choices. Watch the video on the streetcar thought experiment (https://openstax.org/l/53streetcar) and consider these questions. How would you go about making the decision about what to do? Is there a right or wrong answer? What values and criteria would you use to make your decision about whom to save?

Synthesizing Rights and Utility

As you might expect, utilitarianism was not without its critics. Thomas Hodgskin (1787–1869) pointed out what he said was the "absurdity" of insisting that "the rights of man are derived from the legislator" and not nature.[42] In a similar vein, the poet Samuel Taylor Coleridge (1772–1834) accused Bentham of mixing up morality with law.[43] Others objected that utilitarianism placed human beings on the same level as animals and turned people into utility functions. There were also complaints that it was mechanistic, antireligious, and too impractical for most people to follow. John Stuart Mill sought to answer these objections on behalf of his mentor but then offered a synthesis of his own that brought natural rights together with utility, creating a new kind of utilitarianism, one that would eventually serve to underpin neoclassical economic principles.[44]

Mill's father, James, was a contemporary and associate of Bentham's who made sure his son was tutored in a rigorous curriculum. According to Mill, at an early age he learned enough Greek and Latin to read the historians Herodotus and Tacitus in their original languages.[45] His studies also included algebra, Euclidean geometry, economics, logic, and calculus.[46] His father wanted him to assume a leadership position in Bentham's political movement, known as the Philosophical Radicals.[47] Unfortunately, the intensity and duration of Mill's schooling—utilitarian conditions of education—were so extreme that he suffered a nervous breakdown at the age of twenty years. The experience left him dissatisfied with Bentham's philosophy of utility and social reform. As an alternative, Mill turned to Romanticism and poets like Coleridge and Johann Wolfgang Goethe (1749–1832).[48] What he ended up with, however, was not a rejection of utilitarianism but a synthesis of utility and human rights.

Why rights? No doubt, Mill's early life and formation had a great deal to do with his championing of individual freedom. He believed the effort to achieve utility was unjustified if it coerced people into doing things they did not want to do. Likewise, the appeal to science as the arbiter of truth would prove just as futile, he believed, if it did not temper facts with compassion. "Human nature is not a machine to be built after a model, and set to do exactly the work prescribed for it, but a tree, which requires to grow and develop itself on all sides, according to the tendency of the inward forces which make it a living thing," he wrote.[49] Mill was interested in humanizing Bentham's system by ensuring that everyone's rights were protected, particularly the minority's, not because rights were God given but because that was the most direct path to truth. Therefore, he introduced the **harm principle**, which states that the "only purpose for which power can be rightfully exercised over any member of a civilized community, against his will, is to prevent harm to others. His own good, either physical or moral, is not a sufficient warrant." [50]

To be sure, there are limitations to Mill's version of utilitarianism, just as there were with the original. For one, there has never been a satisfactory definition of "harm," and what one person finds harmful another may find beneficial. For Mill, harm was defined as the set back of one's interests. Thus, harm was defined relative to an individual's interests. But what role, if any, should society play in defining what is harmful or in determining who is harmed by someone's actions? For instance, is society culpable for not intervening in cases of suicide, euthanasia, and other self-destructive activities such as drug addiction? These issues have become part of the public debate in recent years and most likely will continue to be as such actions are considered in a larger social context. We may also define intervention and coercion differently depending on where we fall on the political spectrum.

Considering the social implications of an individual action highlights another limitation of utilitarianism, and one that perhaps makes more sense to us than it would to Bentham and Mill, namely, that it makes no provision for emotional or cognitive harm. If the harm is not measurable in physical terms, then it lacks significance. For example, if a reckless driver today irresponsibly exceeds the speed limit, crashes into a concrete abutment, and kills himself while totaling his vehicle (which he owns), utilitarianism would hold that in the absence of physical harm to others, no one suffers except the driver. We may not arrive at the same conclusion. Instead, we might hold that the driver's survivors and friends, along with society as a whole, have suffered a loss. Arguably, all of us are diminished by the recklessness of his act.

LINK TO LEARNING

Watch this video for a summary of utilitarian principles (https://openstax.org/l/53utilitarian) along with a literary example of a central problem of utility and an explanation of John Stuart Mill's utilitarianism.

The Role of Utilitarianism in Contemporary Business

Utilitarianism is used frequently when business leaders make critical decisions about things like expansion, store closings, hiring, and layoffs. They do not necessarily refer to a "utilitarian calculus," but whenever they take stock of what is to be gained and what might be lost in any significant decision (e.g., in a cost-benefit analysis), they make a utilitarian determination. At the same time, one might argue that a simple cost-benefits analysis is not a utilitarian calculus unless it includes consideration of all stakeholders and a full accounting of externalities, worker preferences, potentially coercive actions related to customers, or community and environmental effects.

As a practical way of measuring value, Bentham's system also plays a role in risk management. The utility function, or the potential for benefit or loss, can be translated into decision-making, risk assessment, and strategic planning. Together with data analytics, market evaluations, and financial projections, the utility function can provide managers with a tool for measuring the viability of prospective projects. It may even give them an opportunity to explore objections about the mechanistic and impractical nature of utilitarianism, especially from a customer perspective.

Utilitarianism could motivate individuals within the organization to take initiative, become more responsible, and act in ways that enhance the organization's reputation rather than tarnish it. Mill's *On Liberty* (Figure 2.8), a short treatment of political freedoms in tension with the power of the state, underscored the importance of expression and free speech, which Mill saw not as one right among many but as the foundational right, reflective of human nature, from which all others rights derive their meaning. And therein lay the greatest utility for society and business. For Mill, the path to utility led through truth, and the main way of arriving at truth was through a deliberative process that encouraged individual expression and the clash of ideas.

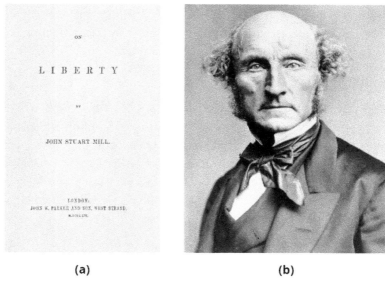

(a)   **(b)**

Figure 2.8 In *On Liberty* (1859) (a), John Stuart Mill (b) combined utility with human rights. He emphasized the importance of free speech for correcting error and creating value for the individual and society. (credit a: modification of "On Liberty (first edition title page via facsimile)" by "Yodin"/Wikimedia Commons, Public Domain; credit b: modification of "John Stuart Mill by London Stereoscopic Company, c1870" by "Scewing"/Wikimedia Commons, Public Domain)

As for Mill's harm principle, the first question in trying to arrive at a business decision might be, does this action harm others? If the answer is yes, we must make a utilitarian calculation to decide whether there is still a greater good for the greatest number. Then we must ask, who are the others we must consider? All stakeholders? Only shareholders? What does harm entail, and who decides whether a proposed action might be harmful? This was the reason science and debate were so important to Mill, because the determination could not be left to public opinion or intuition. That was how tyranny started. By introducing deliberation, Mill was able to balance utility with freedom, which was a necessary condition for utility.

Where Bentham looked to numerical formulas for determining value, relying on the objectivity of numbers, Mill sought value in reason and in the power of language to clarify where truth lies. The lesson for contemporary business, especially with the rise of big data, is that we need both numbers and reasoned principles. If we apply the Aristotelian and Confucian rule of the mean, we see that balance of responsibility and profitability makes the difference between sound business practices and poor ones.

2.5 Deontology: Ethics as Duty

Learning Objectives

By the end of this section, you will be able to:

- Explain Immanuel Kant's concept of duty and the categorical imperative
- Differentiate between utilitarianism and deontology
- Apply a model of Kantian business ethics

Unlike Bentham and Mill, Immanuel Kant (1724–1804) was not concerned with consequences of one's actions or the harm caused to one's individual interests. Instead, he focused on motives and the willingness of individuals to act for the good of others, even though that action might result in personal loss. Doing something for the right reason was much more important to Kant than any particular outcome.

Aroused From "Dogmatic Slumber"

In 1781, at the age of fifty-six years, Kant published *Critique of Pure Reason* (*Kritik der Reinen Vernunft*) in Königsberg, Prussia (Figure 2.9).[51] Almost immediately, it transformed him from an obscure professor of metaphysics and logic into a preeminent figure in the world of philosophy. In the 800-page tome, Kant criticized the way rationalism ("pure reason") had assumed the mantle of absolute truth, supplanting both religious faith and empirical science. Kant referred to the unquestioned acceptance of rationalism as *dogmatism*. Whether Christian or revolutionary, dogmatic thinking was to be avoided because it obscured the truths of science and religion through flawed logic.

(a)

(b)

Figure 2.9 First published in 1781, Immanuel Kant's *Critique of Pure Reason* provided a new system for understanding experience and reality. It defended religious faith against atheism and the scientific method against the skepticism of the Enlightenment. (credit a: modification of "Immanuel Kant (1724-1804)" by "Daube aus Böblingen"/Wikimedia Commons, Public Domain; credit b: modification of "Title page of 1781 edition of Immanuel Kant's Critique of Pure Reason" by "Tomisti"/Wikimedia Commons, Public Domain)

Kant credited the skepticism of empirical philosopher David Hume (1711–1776) with awakening him from "dogmatic slumber," although he disagreed with Hume, who claimed that the mind did not exist at all but was the result of mental associations derived from sensory experience.[52] For Kant, reality could be discerned not through reasoning or sensory experience alone but only by understanding the nature of the human mind. Kant argued that sensory experience did not create the mind but rather that the mind created experience through its internal structures. And within the mind's complex structures there also existed an inherent and unconditional duty to act ethically, which Kant called the "categorical imperative," first outlined in *Groundwork of the Metaphysic of Morals* (1785).[53]

In its initial form, Kant's described his concept of the **categorical imperative** as follows: "Act only according to that maxim whereby you can, at the same time, will that it should become a universal law."[54] Kant's categorical (or unconditional) imperative has practical applications for the study of ethics. The categorical imperative contains two major suppositions: (1) We must act on the basis of goodwill rather than purely on self-interested motives that benefit ourselves at the expense of others; (2) we must never treat others as means toward ends benefitting ourselves without consideration of them also as ends in themselves. Kant held that observing the categorical imperative as we consider what actions to take would directly lead to ethical actions on our part.

LINK TO LEARNING

Watch this video about the categorical imperative (https://openstax.org/l/53categorical) to learn more.

How do you see the imperative working in your own life? Within your family? In your personal and professional relationships? Does Kant's understanding of the relationship between art and beauty accord with your own?

In Kant's view, rationalism and empiricism prevented people from perceiving the truth about their own nature. What was that truth? What was sufficient to constitute it? Kant identified an a priori world of knowledge and understanding in which truth lay in the structures and categories of the mind that were beyond perception and reason. This was a radical concept for the times.

In the end, Kant's systematic analysis of knowing and understanding provided a much-needed counterweight to the logic of Enlightenment rationalism. The existence of the mental structures he proposed has even been confirmed today. For instance, the scientific consensus is that humans are born with cognitive structures designed specifically for language acquisition and development. Even more surprising, there may be similar cognitive structures for morality, conscience, and moral decision-making.[55] So, it is quite possible that conscience, if not happiness, may have a genetic component after all, although Kant himself did not believe the categories of the understanding or the a priori structures of the mind were biological.

LINK TO LEARNING

Read a good survey of Kant's critique of Enlightenment rationalism and of empiricism (https://openstax.org/l/53KantCritique) in this article.

Utilitarianism and Deontology

From a Kantian perspective, it is clear that adherence to duty is what builds the framework for ethical acts. This is in direct contradiction of Bentham's view of human nature as selfish and requiring an objective calculus for ethical action to result. Kant rejected the idea of such a calculus and believed, instead, that perceptions were organized into preexisting categories or structures of the mind. Compare his notion of an ordered and purposeful universe of laws with the similar *logos*, or logic, of the ancient Greeks. One of those laws included implementation of the categorical imperative to act ethically, in accordance with our conscience. However, even though that imperative ought to be followed without exception, not everyone does so. In Kant's moral teachings, individuals still had free will to accept or reject it.

There is a definite contrast between utilitarianism, even Mill's version, and Kant's system of ethics, known as deontology, in which duty, obligation, and good will are of the highest importance. (The word is derived from the Greek *deon*, meaning duty, and *logos* again, here meaning organization for the purpose of study.[56]) An ethical decision requires us to observe only the rights and duties we owe to others, and, in the context of business, act on the basis of a primary motive to do what is right by all stakeholders. Kant was not concerned with utility or outcome—his was not a system directed toward results. The question for him was not how to attain happiness but how to become worthy of it.

Rather like Aristotle and Confucius, Kant taught that the transcendent aspects of human nature, if followed, would lead us inevitably to treat people as ends rather than means. To be moral meant to renounce uninformed dogmatism and rationalism, abide by the categorical imperative, and embrace freedom, moral sense, and even divinity. This was not a lofty or unattainable goal in Kant's mind, because these virtues constituted part of the systematic structuring of the human mind. It could be accomplished by living truthfully or, as we say today, authentically. Such a feat transcended the logic of both rationalism and empiricism.

WHAT WOULD YOU DO?

Les Misérables

You may have seen the very popular Broadway show or movie *Les Misérables*, based on Victor Hugo's epic nineteenth-century French novel of the same name. The main character, Jean Valjean, steals a loaf of bread to feed his sister's starving family and is arrested and sent to prison. If we apply conventional reasoning and principles of law to his crime, Valjean genuinely is guilty as charged and we do not need to consider any extenuating circumstances. However, in a Kantian ethical framework, we would take into account Valjean's motives as well as his duty to treat his sister's family as ends in themselves who deserve to live. Valjean's fate demonstrates what might occur when there is a gap between the legal and the moral. Clearly, Valjean broke the law by stealing the bread. However, he acted morally by correcting a wrong and possibly saving human lives. According to Kantian ethics, Valjean may have been ethical in stealing bread for his family, particularly because the action was grounded in good will and provided benefit to others more than to himself.

Critical Thinking

- It has been said that in Kantian ethics, duty comes before beauty and morality before happiness. Can you think of other instances when it is appropriate to break one moral code to satisfy another, perhaps greater one? What are the deciding factors in each case?
- What would you do if you were Jean Valjean?

Kantian Business Ethics

Unlike utilitarianism, which forms the philosophical foundation for most cost-benefit analysis in business, Kantian ethics is not so easily applied. On one hand, it offers a unique opportunity for the development of individual morality through the categorical imperative to act ethically, which emphasizes humanity and autonomy.[57] This imperative addresses one major side of business ethics: the personal. Character and moral formation are crucial to creating an ethical culture. Indeed, business ethics is littered with cases of companies that have suffered damaging crises due to their leaders' lack of commitment to act on the basis of a good will and with regard for what benefits others. Recent examples include Uber, where a toxic work environment was allowed to prevail, and Volkswagen, which knowingly misrepresented the emissions level of its cars.[58] Such examples exist in government as well, as the recent Theranos and "Fat Leonard" scandals confirm.[59] The latter consisted of graft and corruption in the U.S. Navy's Pacific fleet and has been a continual source of embarrassment for an institution that prides itself on the honorable conduct of its officers. One person can make a difference, either positively or negatively.

On the other hand, Kant's categorical imperative is just that: categorical or unconditional. It calls for morally upright behavior regardless of external circumstance or the historical context of a proposed act or decision. Kant affirmed that "the moral law is an imperative, which commands categorically, because the law is unconditioned."[60] Unconditional ethics could be a challenge for a global organization dealing with suppliers, customers, and competitors in sometimes vastly different cultures. It raises a larger philosophical issue: namely, was Kant correct in believing that morality and mental categories are independent of experience? Or can they be culturally conditioned, and, if so, does that make them relative rather than absolute, as Kant believed them to be?

This question whether ethics is universal is distinctly Kantian, because Kant believed that not only must a moral agent act with others' interests in mind and have the right intentions, but also that the action be universally applicable. Think of how Kantian ethics might be applied not just on an individual level but throughout an organization, and then society. Kant would judge a corporate act to be ethical if it benefitted others at the same time it benefitted company leadership and stockholders, and if it did not place their interests above those of other stakeholders. If loyalty to a coworker conflicted with loyalty to a supervisor or the organization, for instance, then acts resulting from such loyalty might not meet the conditions of deontology. Either the supervisor or the company would be treated as a means rather than an end. Although the qualitative or humanizing element of Kantian ethics has broad appeal, it runs into limitations in an actual business setting. Whether the limitations have good or bad effects depends on the organization's culture and leadership. In general, however, most companies do not adhere to strict Kantian theories, because they look to the outcome of their decisions rather than focusing on motives or intentions.

CASES FROM THE REAL WORLD

Samsung

In the fall of 2016, Samsung Electronics experienced a massive public relations disaster when its Galaxy Note 7 smartphones started exploding due to faulty batteries and casings. Initially, the company denied there were any technical problems. Then, when it became obvious the exploding phones posed a safety and health threat (they were banned from airplanes), Samsung accused its suppliers of creating the problem. In reality, the rush to beat Apple's iPhone 7 release date was the most likely reason corners were cut in production. Samsung finally owned up to the problem, recalled more than two million phones worldwide, and replaced them with new, improved Galaxy Note 7s.

The company's response and its replacement of the phones went a long way toward defusing the disaster and even boosting the company's share price. Whether management knew it, its response was Kantian. Samsung focused on the end (i.e., customer safety and satisfaction) with the motive of doing the ethically responsible thing. Although some might argue the company could have done far more and much more quickly, perhaps it still acted in accordance with the categorical imperative. What do you think?

Critical Thinking

- How might the categorical imperative become a part of organizational culture? Could it ever work in business?
- Do you see the categorical imperative as applicable to your own interests and hope for a career?

2.6 | A Theory of Justice

Learning Objectives

By the end of this section, you will be able to:

- Evaluate John Rawls's answer to utilitarianism
- Analyze the problem of redistribution
- Apply justice theory in a business context

This chapter began with an image of Justice holding aloft scales as a symbol of equilibrium and fairness. It ends with an American political philosopher for whom the equal distribution of resources was a primary concern. John Rawls (1921–2002) wanted to change the debate that had prevailed throughout the 1960s and 1970s in the West about how to maximize wealth for everyone. He sought not to maximize wealth, which was a utilitarian goal, but to establish justice as the criterion by which goods and services were distributed among the populace. Justice, for Rawls, had to do with fairness—in fact, he frequently used the expression **justice as fairness**—and his concept of fairness was a political one that relied on the state to take care of the most disadvantaged. In his **justice theory**, offered as an alternative to the dominant utilitarianism of the times, the idea of fairness applied beyond the individual to include the community as well as analysis of social injustice with remedies to correct it.

Justice Theory

Rawls developed a theory of justice based on the Enlightenment ideas of thinkers like John Locke (1632–1704) and Jean-Jacques Rousseau (1712–1778), who advocated **social contract theory**. Social contract theory held that the natural state of human beings was freedom, but that human beings will rationally submit to some restrictions on their freedom to secure their mutual safety and benefit, not subjugation to a monarch, no matter how benign or well intentioned. This idea parallels that of Thomas Hobbes (1588–1679), who interpreted human nature to be selfish and brutish to the degree that, absent the strong hand of a ruler, chaos would result. So people willingly consent to transfer their autonomy to the control of a sovereign so their very lives and property will be secured. Rousseau rejected that view, as did Rawls, who expanded social contract theory to include justice as fairness. In *A Theory of Justice* (1971), Rawls introduced a universal system of fairness and a set of procedures for achieving it. He advocated a practical, empirically verifiable system of governance that would be political, social, and economic in its effects.

Rawls's justice theory contains three principles and five procedural steps for achieving fairness. The principles are (1) an "original position," (2) a "veil of ignorance," and (3) unanimity of acceptance of the original position.[61] By **original position**, Rawls meant something akin to Hobbes' understanding of the state of nature, a hypothetical situation in which rational people can arrive at a contractual agreement about how resources are to be distributed in accordance with the principles of justice as fairness. This agreement was intended to reflect not present reality but a desired state of affairs among people in the community. The **veil of ignorance** (Figure 2.10) is a condition in which people arrive at the original position imagining they have no identity regarding age, sex, ethnicity, education, income, physical attractiveness, or other characteristics. In this way, they reduce their bias and self-interest. Last, **unanimity of acceptance** is the requirement that all agree to the contract before it goes into effect. Rawls hoped this justice theory would provide a minimum guarantee of rights and liberties for everyone, because no one would know, until the veil was lifted, whether they were male, female, rich, poor, tall, short, intelligent, a minority, Roman Catholic, disabled, a veteran, and so on.

The five procedural steps, or "conjectures," are (1) entering into the contract, (2) agreeing unanimously to the contract, (3) including basic conditions in the contract such as freedom of speech, (4) maximizing the welfare of the most disadvantaged persons, and (5) ensuring the stability of the contract.[62] These steps create a system of justice that Rawls believed gave fairness its proper place above utility and the bottom line. The steps also supported his belief in people's instinctual drive for fairness and equitable treatment. Perhaps this is best seen in an educational setting, for example, the university. By matriculating, students enter into a contract that includes basic freedoms such as assembly and speech. Students at a disadvantage (e.g., those burdened with loans, jobs, or other financial constraints) are accommodated as well as possible. The contract between the university and students has proven to be stable over time, from generation to generation. This same procedure applies on a micro level to the experience in the classroom between an individual teacher and students. Over the past several decades—for better or worse—the course syllabus has assumed the role of a written contract expressing this relationship.

Rawls gave an example of what he called "pure procedural justice" in which a cake is shared among several people.[63] By what agreement shall the cake be divided? Rawls determined that the best way to divide the cake is to have the person slicing the cake take the last piece. This will ensure that everyone gets an equal amount. What is important is an independent standard to determine what is just and a procedure for implementing it.[64]

The Problem of Redistribution

Part of Rawls's critique of utilitarianism is that its utility calculus can lead to tyranny. If we define pleasure as that which is popular, the minority can suffer in terrible ways and the majority become mere numbers. This became clear in Mills's attempt to humanize Bentham's calculus. But Mills's harm principle had just as bad an effect, for the opposite reason. It did not require anyone to give up anything if it had to be done through coercion or force. To extend Rawls's cake example, if one person owned a bakery and another were starving, like Jean Valjean's sister in *Les Misérables*, utilitarianism would force the baker to give up what he had to satisfy the starving person without taking into account whether the baker had greater debts, a sick spouse requiring medical treatment, or a child with educational loans; in other words, the *context* of the situation matters, as opposed to just the consequences. However, Mill's utilitarianism, adhering to the harm principle, would leave the starving person to his or her own devices. At least he or she would have one slice of cake. This was the problem of distribution and redistribution that Rawls hoped to solve, not by calculating pleasure and pain, profit and loss, but by applying fairness as a normative value that would benefit individuals and society.[65]

The problem with this approach is that justice theory is a radical, egalitarian form of liberalism in which redistribution of material goods and services occurs without regard for historical context or the presumption many share that it inherently is wrong to take the property legally acquired by one and distribute it to another. Rawls has been criticized for promoting the same kind of coercion that can exist in utilitarianism but on the basis of justice rather than pleasure. Justice on a societal level would guarantee housing, education, medical treatment, food, and the basic necessities of life for everyone. Yet, as recent political campaigns have shown, the question of who will pay for these guaranteed goods and services through taxes is a contentious one. These are not merely fiscal and political issues; they are philosophical ones requiring us to answer questions of logic and, especially in the case of justice theory, fairness. And, naturally, we must ask, what is fair?

Rawls's principles and steps assume that the way in which the redistribution of goods and services occurs would be agreed upon by people in the community to avoid any fairness issues. But questions remain. For one, Rawls's justice, like the iconic depiction, is blind and cannot see the circumstances in which goods and services are distributed. Second, we may question whether a notion of fairness is really innate. Third, despite the claim that justice theory is not consequentialist (meaning outcomes are not the only thing that matters), there is a coercive aspect to Rawls's justice once the contract is in force, replacing utility with mandated fairness. Fourth, is this the kind of system in which people thrive and prosper, or, by focusing on the worst off, are initiative, innovation, and creativity dampened on the part of everyone else? Perhaps the most compelling critic of Rawls in this regard was his colleague at Harvard University, Robert Nozick (1938–2002), who wrote *A Theory of Entitlement* (1974) as a direct rebuttal of Rawlsian justice theory.[66] Nozick argued that the power of the state may never ethically be used to deprive someone of property he or she has legally obtained or inherited in order to distribute it to others who are in need of it.

Still, one of the advantages of justice theory over the other ethical systems presented in this chapter is its emphasis on method as opposed to content. The system runs on a methodology or process for arriving at truth through the underlying value of fairness. Again, in this sense it is similar to utilitarianism, but, by requiring unanimity, it avoids the extremes of Bentham's and Mill's versions. As a method in ethics, it can be applied in a variety of ways and in multiple disciplines, because it can be adapted to just about any value-laden content. Of course, this raises the question of content versus method in ethics, especially because ethics has been defined as a set of cultural norms based on agreed-upon values. Method may be most effective in determining what those underlying values are, rather than how they are implemented.

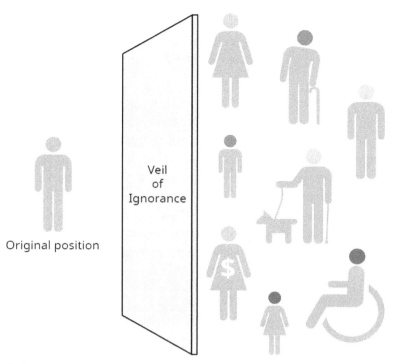

Figure 2.10   The "veil of ignorance" in Rawls's "original position." Those in the original position have no idea who they will be once the veil (wall) has been lifted. Rawls thought such ignorance would motivate people in the community to choose fairly. (attribution: Copyright Rice University, OpenStax, under CC BY 4.0 license)

LINK TO LEARNING

The "veil of ignorance" is a central concept in Rawls's justice theory. What is it? What does it attempt to accomplish? Watch this video on how "ignorance can improve decision-making" (https://openstax.org/l/53Rawls) to explore further.

Justice in Business

Although no ethical framework is perfect or fits a particular era completely, Rawls's justice theory has distinct advantages when applied to business in the twenty-first century. First, as businesses become interdependent and globalized, they must pay more attention to quality control, human resources, and leadership in diverse settings. What will give greater legitimacy to an organization in these areas than fairness? Fairness is a value that is cross-cultural, embraced by different social groups, and understood by nearly everyone. However, what is considered fair depends on a variety of factors, including underlying values and individual characteristics like personality. For instance, not everyone agrees on whether or how diversity ought to be achieved. Neither is there consensus about affirmative action or the redistribution of resources or income. What is fair to some may be supremely unfair to others. This presents an opportunity for engaged debate and participation among the members of Rawls's community.

Second, as we saw earlier, justice theory provides a method for attaining fairness, which could make it a practical and valuable part of training at all levels of a company. The fact that its content—justice and fairness—is more accessible to contemporary people than Confucian virtue ethics and more flexible than Kant's categorical imperative makes it an effective way of dealing with stakeholders and organizational culture.

Justice theory may also provide a seamless way of engaging in corporate social responsibility outwardly and employee development inwardly. Fairness as a corporate doctrine can be applied to all stakeholders and define a culture of trust and openness, with all the corresponding benefits, in marketing, advertising, board development, client relations, and so on. It is also an effective way of integrating business ethics into the organization so ethics is no longer seen as the responsibility solely of the compliance department or legal team. Site leaders and middle managers understand fairness; employees probably even more so, because they are more directly affected by the lack of it. Fairness, then, is as much part of the job as it is an ongoing process of an ethics system. It no doubt makes for a happier and more productive workforce. An organization dedicated to it can also play a greater role in civic life and the political process, which, in turn, helps everyone.

WHAT WOULD YOU DO?

John Rawls's Thought Experiment

John Rawls's original position represents a community in which you have no idea what kind of person you will end up being. In this sense, it is like life itself. After all, you have no idea what your future will be like. You could end up rich, poor, married, single, living in Manhattan or Peru. You might be a surgeon or fishing for sturgeon. Yet, there is one community you will most likely be a part of at some point: the aged. Given that you know this but are not sure of the details, which conditions would you agree to *now* so that senior citizens are provided for? Remember that you most likely will join them and experience the effects of what you decide now. You are living behind not a spatial veil of ignorance but a temporal one.

Critical Thinking

- What are you willing to give up so that seniors—whoever they might be—are afforded care and security in their later years?
- Should you have to pay into a system that provides medical coverage to other people less health conscious than you? Why or why not?

🔑 Key Terms

categorical imperative Kant's unconditional precept that we must "act only according to that maxim whereby you can, at the same time, will that it should become a universal law"; to act on the basis of good will rather than purely self-interested motives and never treat others as means toward an end without consideration of them as ends in themselves

consequentialism an ethical theory in which actions are judged solely by their consequences without regard to character, motivation, or absolute principles of good and evil and separate from their capacity to produce happiness and pleasure

eudaimonia the happiness or human flourishing that results from virtuous activity; it is more than contentment or satisfaction

golden mean in Aristotelian virtue ethics, the aim of ethical behavior, a value between excess and deficiency

harm principle the idea that the only purpose for which the power of the state can rightly be used is to prevent harm to others

junzi a person who is gracious, magnanimous, and cultured; a flourishing human being

justice as fairness Rawls's summary of the essence of his theory of justice

justice theory the idea of fairness applied beyond the individual to include the community as well as analysis of social injustice with remedies to correct it

li the proper order of the universe and the customs and rituals that support order and harmony on Earth

managerial ethics a way of relating to self, employees, and the organization that balances individual and collective responsibility

original position in Rawls's justice theory, a hypothetical situation in which rational people can arrive at a contractual agreement about how resources are to be distributed in accordance with the principles of justice as fairness

phrónēsis prudence or practical wisdom; the intellectual virtue Aristotle considered most important

quan expediency; a practical consideration of the relative rightness of options when considering a moral dilemma

social contract theory a theory that holds the natural state of human beings is freedom, but that human beings will rationally submit to some restrictions on their freedom to secure their mutual safety and benefit

unanimity of acceptance in Rawls's theory, the requirement that all agree to the contract before it goes into effect

utility function a measure, in "utils," of the value of a good, service, or proposed action relative to the utilitarian principle of the greater good, that is, increasing happiness or decreasing pain

veil of ignorance in Rawls's theory, a condition in which people arrive at the original position imagining they have no identity regarding age, sex, ethnicity, education, income, physical attractiveness, or other characteristics; in this way, they reduce their bias and self-interest

virtue ethics an ethical system based on the exercise of certain virtues (loyalty, honor, courage) emphasizing the formation of character

📄 Summary

2.1 The Concept of Ethical Business in Ancient Athens

The role of ethics in Athens during Greece's Golden Age (fifth century BCE) was substantial. Aristotle focused on the role of virtue in developing individual character and social stability. He believed a person's actions determined whether he or she was virtuous, and the point of the virtuous life was happiness, or *eudaimonia*.

Aristotle identified two types of virtues: intellectual and moral. Intellectual virtues were acquired through learning and served as guides to behavior by helping the individual discover truth. Moral virtues were acquired through habit and built character by helping someone pursue what is beneficial and avoid what is harmful in daily life. Aristotle considered *phrónēsis*, or prudence, the most important virtue, because of its practical application.

The thirteenth-century philosopher and theologian Thomas Aquinas agreed with Aristotle that to act dishonorably casts disrepute on all concerned. Ends and means had to be aligned, particularly in business, which provided people's livelihoods and secured the economic health of the city-state.

2.2 Ethical Advice for Nobles and Civil Servants in Ancient China

Confucius (551–479 BCE) attempted to revise ancient Chinese traditions and mores to counter the social chaos of his times. His system of virtue ethics emphasized relationships and, when followed faithfully, led to the *dao* of humanity, that is, true harmonious living. There were three ways to achieve *dao*: "whole-hearted sincerity and truthfulness," the "constant mean," and "expediency" (*quan*). Someone who lived virtuously became more humane, which resulted in a flourishing individual and an ordered nation.

In Confucian virtue ethics, business was viewed as a network of relationships dependent on trust and righteousness. Righteousness was a form of justice that compelled everyone to act in good faith. Considered in this way, justice allows for wealth creation, investment, and strategic planning as long as everyone fulfills his or her role and acts in accordance with the basic pattern of relationships Confucius identified.

2.3 Comparing the Virtue Ethics of East and West

Aristotle and Confucius each constructed an ethical system based on virtue, with Aristotle's anticipated result being happiness and Confucius's being harmony. For Aristotle, happiness consisted of the search for truth. Confucius looked to create a system that put an end to civil chaos. Although both systems relied on reason and control to achieve their ends, Aristotle placed the locus of ethical behavior on individuals, but he held that a moral upbringing and good political governance also contributed to the formation of moral character. Confucius saw this locus in the family, which provided the basic pattern of relationships for personal and professional life. Reason prevailed throughout, as in the cultivation of a more just and humane person.

In a business context, reason and control bear directly on management, leadership, and corporate culture. They constitute a way of cultivating individual virtue and corporate ethos such that the two go hand in hand. The environment or culture of an organization needs individuals of character who can follow their conscience and experience moral conversion. We might envision the emergence of universal values like reason and control that nurture both the individual and the organization.

2.4 Utilitarianism: The Greatest Good for the Greatest Number

Jeremy Bentham developed a quantifiable method for determining what was beneficial and what was detrimental. He called this method utilitarianism, because its basic unit, the "util," acted like a monetary unit. Bentham's protégé, John Stuart Mill, refined this system to include human rights. His "harm principle" is an outstanding element in his version of utilitarianism.

Utilitarianism in business can lead to a bottom-line mentality in which decisions are based on achieving the greatest good for the organization as it pertains to the greatest number of stakeholders, including shareholders and all others affected by the actions of the organization The outcome is the determining factor, not the intent of the actors or whether people are treated humanely.

2.5 Deontology: Ethics as Duty

Rejecting dogmatic thinking of all kinds, Kant believed people were not the sum total of reactions to stimuli but complex beings with innate structures of understanding and inborn moral sensitivity. In his view, everyone had a duty to obey a categorical imperative to do the just and moral thing, regardless of the consequences. The outcome of an act was not as important as the intent of the actor and whether the act treated others as ends or means. Here, Kant reflected Aristotelian virtue ethics in seeing people as ends in themselves and not as "living tools" or human resources.

This view does not typically govern most management decisions in business; arguably, utilitarianism is the efficient, go-to theory on which corporate leaders often rely. Yet a Kantian understanding of business ethics remains viable even today and sometimes displays itself in the most compassionate and humane actions that evolving commercial organizations take.

2.6 A Theory of Justice

Rawls developed a theory of justice based on social contract theory, holding that the natural state of human beings is freedom, not subjugation to a monarch, no matter how benign or well intentioned. Rawls's theory views human beings as inherently good and, echoing Kant, inclined toward moral rectitude and action. In his theory, Rawls included the "veil of ignorance," which ensures objectivity in our choices and the avoidance of bias. Criticism of Rawls's theory focuses primarily on the issue of distribution, because decisions made in ignorance can neither reward innovation and enterprise nor encourage risk.

Assessment Questions

1. Which of the following is not an intellectual virtue according to Aristotle?
   A.   the basic order of life
   B.   knowledge
   C.   wisdom
   D.   prudence

2. Deliberative prudence does all the following except _____.
   A.   align ends and means
   B.   encourage prodigality
   C.   avoid conflict
   D.   prevent rash behavior

3. True or false? According to Aristotle, happiness is a virtuous activity of the soul.

4. True or false? It is possible to act deliberately and shrewdly in a good way or toward a good end.

5. How might virtue ethics apply to contemporary business?

6. *Quan* means which of the following?
   A.   adherence to the past
   B.   philosophic tradition
   C.   practicality
   D.   insistence on protocol

7. *The Analects of Confucius* _____.
   A. are similar to Aristotle's *Nicomachean Ethics*
   B. represent an oral tradition
   C. reflect Buddhist ideals
   D. codify a system of virtue ethics

8. True or false? Confucian virtue ethics is similar to the Aristotelian version in that both are very practical.

9. True or false? According to Confucius, the hope for reform of Chinese society was a centralized planning system.

10. How can wholeheartedness and sincerity serve as models of risk assessment?

11. "Control" as used in this section does not refer to which of the following?
   A. reverence
   B. *phrónēsis*
   C. temperance
   D. Confucian self-regulation

12. Managerial ethics is related to which of the following?
   A. shareholder wealth
   B. righteousness
   C. bureaucracy
   D. honor

13. True or false? In both East and West, the means used to achieve a certain end are often more important than the end.

14. True or false? Individualism was the greatest value in Confucian ethics.

15. Utilitarianism is a system that _____.
   A. considers historical conditions
   B. approaches Aristotelian deliberation
   C. builds on natural law theory
   D. attempts to quantify the good

16. In *On Liberty*, John Stuart Mill _____.
   A. proposes a harm principle
   B. exalts libertarianism
   C. prescribes a consequentialist answer to ethical crises
   D. rejects rights

17. True or false? John Stuart Mill's emphasis on human rights distinguishes him from Jeremy Bentham.

18. How does utilitarianism affect contemporary business practice?

19. Does the value that John Stuart Mill placed on the deliberative process and individual expression as the main ways of arriving at truth have any relevance for political debate today?

20. Immanuel Kant objected to dogmatism in _____.
   A.   religion
   B.   science
   C.   both A and B
   D.   neither A nor B

21. True or false? Immanuel Kant contended that people often interpret reason subjectively.

22. True or false? A criticism of Immanuel Kant's categorical imperative is that its refusal ever to permit exceptions in acting ethically is impossible to observe in life.

23. What are the essential differences between John Stuart Mill's version of utilitarianism and Immanuel Kant's deontology?

24. How does Kantian ethics work in a business setting?

25. John Rawls's theory of justice is based on which of the following?
   A.   cognitive structures
   B.   moral duty
   C.   social contract theory
   D.   survival of the fittest

26. The "veil of ignorance" ensures which of the following?
   A.   mass delusion
   B.   objectivity
   C.   self-reliance
   D.   Enlightenment reason

27. True or false? John Rawls's theory of justice is mainly non-Utilitarian.

28. A distinguishing characteristic of justice theory is that it emphasizes method over content.

29. What challenges does Rawlsian justice theory present when it comes to the redistribution of goods and services in society?

Endnotes

1.   Alfred North Whitehead, *Process and Reality. An Essay in Cosmology. Gifford Lectures Delivered in the University of Edinburgh During the Session 1927–1928.* (Cambridge, UK: Cambridge University Press, 1929).
2.   Robert C. Solomon, "Business and the Humanities: An Aristotelian Approach to Business Ethics" in *Business as a Humanity*, eds. Thomas J. Donaldson, R. Edward Freeman. The Ruffin Series in Business Ethics, ed. R. Edward Freeman. (New York: Oxford University Press, 1994), 66-67.
3.   Aristotle, *The Nicomachean Ethics*, translated by J.A.K. Thomson. (New York: Penguin Books, 2004), 1097b.
4.   Aristotle, *The Nicomachean Ethics*, translated by J.A.K. Thomson. (New York: Penguin Books, 2004), 1169b.
5.   Aristotle, *The Nicomachean Ethics*, translated by J.A.K. Thomson. (New York: Penguin Books, 2004), 1124b–1125a.
6.   Aristotle, *The Nicomachean Ethics*, translated by J.A.K. Thomson. (New York: Penguin Books, 2004), 1123b.
7.   Aristotle, *The Nicomachean Ethics*, translated by J.A.K. Thomson. (New York: Penguin Books, 2004), 1142a.
8.   William O'Neal, "The Status of Women in Ancient Athens," *International Social Science Review* 68, no. 3 (1993): 118.
9.   Nigel Wilson, ed., s.v. "Demography" in *Encyclopedia of Ancient Greece.* (New York: Routledge, 2006), 213–216.
10. South Morning China Post, "2.9 Million Trapped in Modern-Day Slavery in China, 30 Million Worldwide," October 17, 2013; updated October 18, 2013. http://www.scmp.com/news/world/article/1333894/29-million-trapped-modern-day-slavery-china-30-million-worldwide.
11. Patrick Winn, "Slavery on Thai Fishing Boats Is Straight from the 18th Century," June 23, 2013. http://www.businessinsider.com/thailand-slavery-fishing-boats-2013-6; Amar Toor, "Soccer and Slavery: World Cup Dogged by Reports of Labor Abuse in Qatar," October 3, 2013. https://www.theverge.com/2013/10/3/4797842/qatar-faces-allegations-of-slave-migrant-labor-ahead-of-world-cup-2022.
12. Aristotle, *The Nicomachean Ethics*, translated by J.A.K. Thomson. (New York: Penguin Books, 2004), 1096a.
13. Solomon, "Business and the Humanities: An Aristotelian Approach to Business Ethics," 70.
14. Aristotle, *The Nicomachean Ethics*, translated by J.A.K. Thomson. (New York: Penguin Books, 2004), 1141b.
15. Marta Rocchi et al, "Margin Call: What if John Tuld Were Christian? Thomistic Practical Wisdom in Financial Decision-Making," Working

     Paper no. 01/17 (Pamplona: Universidad de Navarra, Facultad de Ciencias Económicas y Empresariales, 2017), 6. https://papers.ssrn.com/sol3/papers.cfm?abstract_id=2936288.

16. Huston Smith, ed., "Confucianism" in *The World's Religions*. (New York: HarperCollins, 1991), 160.

17. Daryl Koehn, "East Meets West: Toward a Universal Ethic of Virtue for Global Business," *Journal of Business Ethics* 116, no. 4 (2013): 712.

18. Huston Smith, ed., "Confucianism," in *The World's Religions*. (New York: HarperCollins, 1991), 175.

19. Huston Smith, ed., "Confucianism," in *The World's Religions*. (New York: HarperCollins, 1991), 158–159.

20. Huston Smith, ed., "Confucianism," in *The World's Religions*. (New York: HarperCollins, 1991), 166–167.

21. Chichung Huang, *The Analects of Confucius: A Literal Translation with Introduction and Notes*. (New York: Oxford University Press, 1997), 14.

22. Chichung Huang, *The Analects of Confucius: A Literal Translation with Introduction and Notes*. (New York: Oxford University Press, 1997), 23.

23. Chichung Huang, *The Analects of Confucius: A Literal Translation with Introduction and Notes*. (New York: Oxford University Press, 1997), 22 (16.1).

24. Huston Smith, ed., "Confucianism" in *The World's Religions*. (New York: HarperCollins, 1991), 176.

25. Chichung Huang, *The Analects of Confucius: A Literal Translation with Introduction and Notes*. (New York: Oxford University Press, 1997), 6.

26. UBS, "You May Be Surprised at Which Country Is Setting an Example for the Future of Sustainable Cities," January 8, 2018. https://mashable.com/2018/01/08/china-sustainable-cities/#qTP12grk4uqc.

27. Josh Horwitz, "Jack Ma Has Some Thoughts on China's 'Clean' Communism and the US's Divided Politics," November 30, 2017. https://qz.com/1142604/jack-ma-has-some-thoughts-on-chinas-clean-communism-and-the-uss-divided-politics/.

28. Peter R. Woods and David A. Lamond, "What Would Confucius Do?: Confucian Ethics and Self-Regulation in Management," *Journal of Business Ethics* 102, no. 4 (2011): 670.

29. Aristotle, *The Nicomachean Ethics*, translated by J.A.K. Thomson. (New York: Penguin Books, 2004), 1170a.

30. Chichung Huang, *The Analects of Confucius: A Literal Translation with Introduction and Notes*. (New York: Oxford University Press, 1997), 6.13.

31. Chichung Huang, *The Analects of Confucius: A Literal Translation with Introduction and Notes*. (New York: Oxford University Press, 1997), 34.

32. Robert Hinkley, *Time to Change Corporations: Closing the Citizenship Gap*. (New York: CreateSpace Independent Publishing Platform, 2011), 53.

33. Chichung Huang, *The Analects of Confucius: A Literal Translation with Introduction and Notes*. (New York: Oxford University Press, 1997), 4.5.

34. Chichung Huang, *The Analects of Confucius: A Literal Translation with Introduction and Notes*. (New York: Oxford University Press, 1997), 15.29.

35. Aristotle, *The Nicomachean Ethics*, translated by J.A.K. Thomson. (New York: Penguin Books, 2004), 1140b.

36. Business & Human Rights Resource Centre, "Chiquita Lawsuits (re Columbia)." https://business-humanrights.org/en/chiquita-lawsuits-re-colombia (accessed November 7, 2017).

37. R.J.W. Evans and Hartmut Pogge von Strandmann, "1848–1849: A European Revolution?" in *The Revolutions in Europe 1848–1849: From Reform to Reaction*, eds. R.J.W. Evans, Hartmut Pogge von Strandmann, (Oxford: Oxford University Press, 2000), 1–8.

38. David Armitage, *The Declaration of Independence: A Global History*. (Cambridge, MA: Harvard University Press, 2007), 80.

39. Michael Quinn, "Jeremy Bentham, 'The Psychology of Economic Man,' and Behavioural Economics," *Oeconomia* 6, no. 1 (2016): 3–32.

40. Jeremy Bentham, *An Introduction to the Principles of Morals and Legislation*. (London: Clarendon Press, 1823), 30.

41. Max H. Bazerman and Ann E. Tenbrunsel, "Ethical Breakdowns," *Harvard Business Review*, April 2011.

42. Thomas Hodgskin, *The Natural and Artificial Right of Property, Contrasted*. (London: R. Steil, 1832). http://oll.libertyfund.org/titles/hodgskin-the-natural-and-artificial-right-of-property-contrasted.

43. *Encyclopedia of Philosophy*, s.v. "Coleridge, Samuel Taylor (1772–1834)," (by Michael Moran). http://www.encyclopedia.com/humanities/encyclopedias-almanacs-transcripts-and-maps/coleridge-samuel-taylor-1772-1834 (accessed November 13, 2017).

44. Ian Shapiro, "Lecture 7 – The Neoclassical Synthesis of Rights and Utility." http://oyc.yale.edu/political-science/plsc-118/lecture-7 (accessed November 14, 2017).

45. John Stuart Mill, "*Autobiography*." I. http://www.gutenberg.org/cache/epub/10378/pg10378-images.html (accessed November 13, 2017).

46. John Stuart Mill, "*Autobiography*." I. http://www.gutenberg.org/cache/epub/10378/pg10378-images.html (accessed November 13, 2017).

47. *The Stanford Encyclopedia of Philosophy*, s.v. "John Stuart Mill. 1. Life," (by Christopher Macleod). https://plato.stanford.edu/entries/mill/ (accessed November 13, 2017).

48. *The Stanford Encyclopedia of Philosophy*, s.v. "John Stuart Mill. 1. Life," (by Christopher Macleod). https://plato.stanford.edu/entries/mill/ (accessed November 13, 2017).

49. John Stuart Mill, "*On Liberty*," p. 111. http://www.gutenberg.org/files/34901/34901-h/34901-h.htm (accessed November 14, 2017).

50. John Stuart Mill, "*On Liberty*," p. 18. http://www.gutenberg.org/files/34901/34901-h/34901-h.htm (accessed November 14, 2017).

51. Immanuel Kant, *Critique of Practical Reason*. http://www.gutenberg.org/cache/epub/5683/pg5683-images.html (accessed November 19, 2017).

52. David Hume, *A Treatise of Human Nature*, Section I. https://www.gutenberg.org/files/4705/4705-h/4705-h.htm#link2H_4_0042 (accessed November 18, 2017), I.

53. Immanuel Kant, *Critique of Practical Reason*, I. http://www.gutenberg.org/cache/epub/5683/pg5683-images.html (accessed November 19, 2017).

54. Immanuel Kant, *Grounding for the Metaphysics of Morals. On a Supposed Right to Lie Because of Philanthropic Concerns*, translated by James W. Ellington. (Indianapolis, IN: Hackett, 1993), 30.

55. Edward O. Wilson, "The Biological Basis of Morality," *The Atlantic*, April 1998; *Internet Encyclopedia of Philosophy*, s.v. "Morality and Cognitive Science" (by Regina A. Rini). https://www.iep.utm.edu/m-cog-sc/.

56. *Stanford Encyclopedia of Philosophy*, s.v. "Deontological Ethics" (by Larry Alexander and Michael Moore). https://plato.stanford.edu/entries/ethics-deontological/ (accessed November 19, 2017).

57. Immanuel Kant, *Critique of Practical Reason*, Preface. http://www.gutenberg.org/cache/epub/5683/pg5683-images.html (accessed November 19, 2017).

58. Biz Carson, "Cocaine and Groping—Bombshell Report on Uber's Work Environment Makes It Sound Awful and Full of Bros," *Business Insider*, February 22, 2017. http://www.businessinsider.com/another-negative-report-about-uber-work-environment-2017-2; Jack Ewing, "Engineering a Deception: What Led to Volkswagen's Diesel Scandal," *New York Times*, March 16, 2017. https://www.nytimes.com/interactive/2017/business/volkswagen-diesel-emissions-timeline.html.

59. Mark D. Faram, "2 Navy Officers Sentenced in 'Fat Leonard' Case," *Navy Times*, March 7, 2018. https://www.navytimes.com/news/your-navy/2018/03/07/o-6-and-o-5-sentenced-in-fat-leonard-case/ (accessed March 8, 2018); Sarah Ashley O'Brien, "Theranos Founder Elizabeth Holmes Charged With Massive Fraud," *CNN*, March 14, 2018. http://money.cnn.com/2018/03/14/technology/theranos-fraud-scandal/index.html.

60. Immanuel Kant, *Critique of Practical Reason*, VII. http://www.gutenberg.org/cache/epub/5683/pg5683-images.html (accessed November 19, 2017).

61. John Rawls, *A Theory of Justice*. (Cambridge, MA: Harvard University Press, 2009), 120, 136.

62. John Rawls, *A Theory of Justice.* (Cambridge, MA: Harvard University Press, 2009), 121, 464.
63. John Rawls, *A Theory of Justice.* (Cambridge, MA: Harvard University Press, 2009), 85.
64. John Rawls, *A Theory of Justice.* (Cambridge, MA: Harvard University Press, 2009), 85.
65. *Stanford Encyclopedia of Philosophy*, s.v. "John Rawls. 3.3 Reasonable Pluralism and the Public Political Culture" (by Leif Wenar). https://plato.stanford.edu/entries/rawls/ (accessed November 20, 2017).
66. *Stanford Encyclopedia of Philosophy*, s.v. "Robert Nozick's Political Philosophy" (by Eric Mack). https://plato.stanford.edu/entries/nozick-political/ (accessed March 9, 2018).

Figure 3.1 Starbucks, based in Seattle, Washington, is a company with more than 250,000 employees and locations across the globe. It directly affects countless stakeholders beyond its institutional investors and millions of customers, from coffee growers and milk producers, to urban and suburban communities and developers, to local, state, and national governments. (credit: modification of "StarbucksVaughanMills" by "Raysonho"/Wikimedia Commons, CC0)

Chapter Outline

3.1 Adopting a Stakeholder Orientation

3.2 Weighing Stakeholder Claims

3.3 Ethical Decision-Making and Prioritizing Stakeholders

3.4 Corporate Social Responsibility (CSR)

Introduction

In May 2018, in the wake of a global uproar after two black men in a Philadelphia Starbucks were arrested while awaiting a friend, Starbucks closed its approximately eight thousand U.S. stores to conduct racial bias training (Figure 3.1).[1] The company also officially changed its policy to allow people to visit its stores and restrooms without making a purchase, hoping to avoid more incidents like this one (sparked by a white employee calling 9-1-1 when the men did not buy anything). The two men who were arrested eventually settled with Starbucks for an undisclosed sum.

As one of the largest beverage retailers in the world, Starbucks directly affects countless stakeholders: food and drink distributors; coffee and tea growers; milk producers; urban and suburban communities; local, state, and national governments; more than 300,000 employees and 1,600 institutional investors; and millions of customers.[2] The company's decision to close its U.S. stores for half a day was financially costly, and the training session could never fully solve the problem of conscious or unconscious bias. But the firm believed it was the right thing to do. Why does it matter to its stakeholders what Starbucks does? What role do stakeholders play in a company's decisions about its ethical behavior, and why?

3.1 | Adopting a Stakeholder Orientation

Learning Objectives

By the end of this section, you will be able to:

- Identify key types of business-stakeholder relationships
- Explain why laws do not dictate every ethical responsibility a company may owe key stakeholders
- Discuss why stakeholders' welfare must be at the heart of ethical business decisions

Have you ever had a stake in a decision someone else was making? Depending on your relationship with that person and your level of interest in the decision, you may have tried to ensure that the choice made was in your best interests. Understanding your somewhat analogous role as a stakeholder in businesses large and small, local and global, will help you realize the value of prioritizing stakeholders in your own professional life and business decisions.

Stakeholder Relationships

Many individuals and groups inside and outside a business have an interest in the way it brings products or services to market to turn a profit. These stakeholders include customers, clients, employees, shareholders, communities, the environment, the government, and the media (traditional and social), among others. All stakeholders should be considered essential to a business, but not all have equal priority. Different groups of stakeholders carry different weights with decision makers in companies and assert varying levels of interest and influence. As we examine their roles, consider how an organization benefits by working with its stakeholders and how it may benefit from encouraging stakeholders to work together to promote their mutual interests.

What are the roles of an organization's many stakeholders? We begin with the internal stakeholders. The board of directors—in a company large enough to have one—is responsible for defining and evaluating the ongoing mission of a business after its founding. It broadly oversees decisions about the mission and direction of the business, the products or services offered, the markets in which the business will operate, and salary and benefits for the senior officers of the organization. The board also sets goals for income and profitability. Its most important function is to select and hire the chief executive officer (CEO) or president. The CEO is usually the only employee who reports directly to the board of directors, and he or she is charged with implementing the policies the board sets and consulting with them on significant issues pertaining to the company, such as a dramatic shift in products or services offered or discussions to acquire—or be acquired by—another firm.

In turn, the CEO hires executives to lead initiatives and carry out procedures in the various functional areas of the business, such as finance, sales and marketing, public relations, manufacturing, quality control, human resources (sometimes called human capital), accounting, and legal compliance. Employees in these areas are internal stakeholders in the success of both their division and the larger corporation. Some interact with the outside environment in which the business operates and serve as contact points for external stakeholders, such as media and government, as well.

In terms of external stakeholders for a business, customers certainly are an essential group. They need to be able to trust that products and services are backed by the integrity of the company. They also provide reviews, positive or negative, and referrals. Customers' perceptions of the business matter, too. Those who learn that a business is not treating employees fairly, for instance, may reconsider their loyalty or even boycott the business to try to influence change in the organization. Stakeholder relationships, good and bad, can have compound effects, particularly when social media can spread word of unethical behavior quickly and widely.

Key external stakeholders are usually those outside of the organization who most directly influence a business's bottom line and hold power over the business. Besides customers and clients, suppliers have a great deal of influence and command a great deal of attention from businesses of all sizes. Governments hold power through regulatory bodies, from federal agencies such as the Environmental Protection Agency to the local planning and zoning boards of the communities in which businesses exist. These latter groups often exercise influence over the physical spaces where businesses work and try to grow (Figure 3.2).

Figure 3.2 Maryland's former Lieutenant Governor, Anthony Brown, hosts a 2014 small-business stakeholder roundtable discussion. Governments consider local businesses to be stakeholders in economic decision-making. Small businesses have their own local and regional stakeholders, who are influenced by the products and services they offer and the decisions they make in building their businesses. (credit: modification of "Lt. Governor Host MBE_Small Business Stakeholders Roundtable Discussion" by "Maryland GovPics"/Flickr, CC BY 2.0)

Businesses are responsible to their stakeholders. Every purchase of a product or a service carries with it a sort of promise. Buyers promise that their money or credit is good, and businesses promise a level of quality that will deliver what is advertised. The relationship can quickly get more complex, though. Stakeholders also may demand that the businesses they patronize give back to the local community or protect the global environment while developing their products or providing services. Employees may demand a certain level of remuneration for their work. Governments demand that companies comply with laws, and buyers in business-to-business exchanges (B2B, in business jargon) demand not only high-quality products and services but on-time delivery and responsive maintenance and service should something go wrong. Meeting core obligations to stakeholders is primarily about delivering good products and services, but it is also about communicating and preparing for potential problems, whether from within the company or from external circumstances like a natural disaster.

Ethical Responsibilities Often Extend Beyond Legal Requirements

We have seen that stakeholders include the people and entities invested in and influential in the success of an organization. It is also true that stakeholders can have multiple, and simultaneous, roles. For example, an employee can also be a customer and a stockholder.

Any transaction between a stakeholder and a business organization may appear finite. For instance, after you purchase something from a store you leave and go home. But your relationship with the store probably continues. You might want to repurchase the item or ask a question about a warranty. The store may have collected future marketing data about you and your purchases through its customer loyalty program or your use of a credit card.

Samsung, based in South Korea, is a large, multinational corporation that makes a variety of products, including household appliances such as washers and dryers. When Samsung's washers developed a problem with the spin cycle in 2017, the company warned customers that the machines could become unbalanced and tip over, and that children should be kept away. The problem persisted, however, and Samsung's responsibility and legal exposure increased. The eventual fix was to offer all owners of the particular washer model a full refund even if the customer did not have a complaint, and to offer free pick up of the machine as well. The recall covered almost three million washers, which ranged in price from $450 to $1500. By choosing to spend billions to rectify the problem, Samsung limited its legal exposure to potential lawsuits, settlement of which would likely have far exceeded the refunds it paid. This example demonstrates the weight of the implicit social contract between a company and its stakeholders and the potential impact on the bottom line if that contract is broken.

When a product does not live up to its maker's claims for whatever reason, the manufacturer needs to correct the problem to retain or regain customers' trust. Without this trust, the interdependence between the company and its stakeholders can fail. By choosing to recognize and repay its customer stakeholders, Samsung acted at an **ethical maximum**, taking the strongest possible action to behave ethically in a given situation. An **ethical minimum**, or the least a company might do that complies with the law, would have been to offer the warning and nothing more. This may have been a defensible position in court, but the warning might not have reached all purchasers of the defective machine and many children could have been hurt.

Each case of a faulty product or poorly delivered service is different. If laws reach above a minimum standard, they can grow cumbersome and impede business growth. If businesses adhere only to laws and ethical minimums, however, they can develop poor reputations and people can be harmed. The ethically minimal course of action is not illegal or *necessarily* unethical, but the company choosing it will have failed to recognize the value of its customers.

CASES FROM THE REAL WORLD

Amazon Sets a Demanding Pace on the Job

In a visit to an Amazon distribution center, a group of business students and their professors met with the general manager.[3] After taking them on an extensive tour of the five-acre facility, the general manager commented on the slowness of the visitors' walking pace. He described the Amazon Pace, a fast, aggressive walk, and confirmed that the average employee walks eight or nine miles during a shift. These employees are called "pickers," and their task is to fill an order and deliver it to the processing and packing center as quickly as possible. The design of the center is a trade secret that results in a random distribution of products. Therefore, the picker has to cover a number of directions and distances while filling an order. Those who cannot keep up the pace are usually let go, just as would be those who steal.

Critical Thinking

- Does the requirement to walk an average of eight or nine miles at a fast pace every day strike you as a reasonable expectation for employees at Amazon, or any other workplace? Why or why not? Should a company that wants to impose this requirement tell job applicants beforehand?
- Is it ethical for customers to patronize a company that imposes this kind of requirement on its employees? And if not, what other choices do customers have and what can they do about it?
- The center's general manager may have been exaggerating about the Amazon Pace to impress upon his visitors how quickly and nimbly pickers fill customer orders for the company. If not, however, is such a pace sustainable without the risk of physiological and psychological stress?

The law only partly captures the ethical obligations firms owe their stakeholders. One way many companies go beyond the legally required minimum as employers is to offer lavish **amenities**—that is, resources made available to employees in addition to wages, salary, and other standard benefits. They include such offerings as on-site exercise rooms and other services, company discounts, complimentary or subsidized snacks or meals, and the opportunity to buy stock in the company at a discounted price. Astute business leaders see the increased costs of amenities as an investment in retaining employees as long-term stakeholders. Stakeholder loyalty within and outside the firm is essential in sustaining any business venture, no matter how small or large.

WHAT WOULD YOU DO?

The Social Responsibility of Business

There are two opposing views about how businesses, and large publicly held corporations in particular, should approach ethics and social responsibility. One view holds that businesses should behave ethically within the marketplace but concern themselves *only* with serving shareholders and other investors. This view places economic considerations above all others. The other view is that stakeholders are not the means to the end (profit) but are ends in and of themselves as human beings (see our earlier discussion of deontological ethics in Ethics from Antiquity to the Present). Thus, the **social responsibility of business** view is that being responsible to customers, employees, and a host of other stakeholders should be not only a corporate concern but central to a business's mission. In essence, this view places a premium on the careful consideration of stakeholders. Consider what approach you might take if you were the CEO of a multinational corporation.

Critical Thinking

- Would your business be driven primarily by a particular social mission or simply by economics?
- How do you think stakeholder relationships would influence your approach to business? Why?

LINK TO LEARNING

Read a detailed consideration of the social responsibility of business in the form of polite but fiercely oppositional correspondence between economist Milton Friedman and John Mackey, founder and CEO of Whole Foods (https://openstax.org/l/53WholeFoods) to learn more.

One challenge for any organization's managers is that not all stakeholders agree on where the company should strive to land when it chooses between ethical minimums and maximums. Take stockholders, for example. Logically, most stockholders are interested in maximizing the return on their investment in the firm, which earns profit for them in the form of dividends. Lynn Stout, late Professor of Law at Cornell Law School, described the role of shareholder in this way:

> "Shareholders as a class want companies to be able to treat their stakeholders well, because this encourages employee and customer loyalty . . . Yet individual shareholders can profit from pushing boards to exploit committed stakeholders—say, by threatening to outsource jobs unless employees agree to lower wages, or refusing to support products customers have come to rely on unless they buy expensive new products as well. In the long run, such corporate opportunism makes it difficult for companies to attract employee and customer loyalty in the first place." [4]

Essential to Stout's point is that shareholders do not necessarily behave as a class. Some will want to maximize their investment even at a cost to other stakeholders. Some may want to extend beyond the legal minimum and seek a long-term perspective on profit maximization, demanding better treatment of stakeholders to maximize future potential value and to do more good than harm.

In the long run, stakeholder welfare must be kept at the heart of each company's business operations for these significant, twin reasons: It is the right thing to do and it is good for business. Still, if managers need additional incentive to act on the basis of policies that benefit stakeholders, it is useful to recall that stakeholders who believe their interests have been ignored will readily make their displeasure known, both to company management and to the much wider community of social media.

3.2 Weighing Stakeholder Claims

Learning Objectives

By the end of this section, you will be able to:

- Explain why stakeholders' claims vary in importance
- Categorize stakeholders to better understand their claims

As we saw earlier in this chapter and in Why Ethics Matter, the law only partially captures the ethical obligations firms owe their stakeholders. A particular **stakeholder claim**, that is, any given stakeholder's interest in a business decision, may therefore challenge the ethical stance even of an organization that complies with the law. For example, some community members may oppose the opening of a "big box" chain store that threatens the livelihoods of small-business owners in the area, while shareholders, creditors, employees, and consumers within the nearby neighborhoods support it as an additional opportunity for profit and quality goods at competitive prices. Conflicts like this illustrate how complicated prioritizing stakeholder claims can be, particularly when there are ethical pros and cons on both sides. A big box store may offer a wider selection of goods at lower prices, for example, and create jobs for teens and part-time workers.

A related theme to recall is that even though all stakeholder claims are important for a company to acknowledge, not all claims are of equal importance. Most business leaders appreciate that a company's key stakeholders are essential to its efficient operation and growth, and that its overall mission, goals, and limited resources will force its managers to make choices by prioritizing stakeholders' needs. In this section, we look at ethical ways in which business managers can begin to make those decisions.

The Ethical Basis of Stakeholders' Claims

Stakeholder claims vary in their significance for a firm. According to Donaldson and Preston,[5] there are three theoretical approaches to considering stakeholder claims: a descriptive approach, an instrumental approach, and a normative approach. The **descriptive approach** sees the company as composed of various stakeholder groups, each with its own interests. These interests impinge on the company to a greater or lesser degree; thus, the main point of the descriptive approach is to develop the most accurate model and act on it in ways that weigh and balance these interests as fairly as possible. The **instrumental approach** connects stakeholder management and financial outcomes, proposing that appropriate management of stakeholder interests is important and useful because it contributes to a positive bottom line.

The **normative approach** considers stakeholders as ends in themselves rather than simply as means to achieve better financial results. According to Donaldson and Preston, in the normative approach "the interests of all stakeholders are of intrinsic value. That is, each group of stakeholders merits consideration for its own sake and not merely because of its ability to further the interests of some other group, such as the shareowners."[6] This approach is the one that most appropriately represents ethical stakeholder theory, according to Donaldson and Preston, and it places an objective consideration of all stakeholders' interests ahead of fiscal considerations alone.

We can also view these three approaches to stakeholders as occupying levels of increasing comprehensiveness. At the lowest level is the descriptive approach, which merely sets the stage for consideration of stakeholder claims and concerns. The instrumental aspect combines a consideration for profit along with other stakeholder concerns and attempts to balance these interests with particular attention to the way the company and its shareholders might be affected. The normative approach takes the most comprehensive view of the organization and its stakeholders, putting the focus squarely on stakeholders. Although Donaldson and Preston stress that the descriptive and instrumental approaches are integral to stakeholder theory, they contend that the fundamental basis of stakeholder theory is normative.[7]

Of course, these are theoretical approaches, and the extent to which any of them is implemented in a given company will vary. But unfortunately, the decision to disconnect from stakeholders is both real and expensive for a corporation. A 2005 survey of customers of 362 companies is demonstrative: "Only 8% of customers described their experience as 'superior.' However, 80% of the companies surveyed believe that the experience they have been providing is indeed superior."[8] Another study found significant links between levels of customer satisfaction and a firm's performance, including rates of retention, overall revenue, and stock price.[9] Enlightened companies spend time and resources testing their stakeholders' concerns and eliciting their feedback while there is time to incorporate it into management decisions.

This article discusses a recent video showing United Airlines removing ticketed, seated passengers from a plane to make room for four of its employees who needed to fly to another airport (https://openstax.org/l/53VideoUnited) igniting debate over company policies and how they are implemented. This related article about the United Airlines overbooking situation (https://openstax.org/l/53United) provides some more information.

Upon being asked to deplane and take a later flight, should a customer who has booked the fare for the earlier flight have the right to refuse? Which stakeholder(s) do you think United valued more in this incident? Why?

Airlines overbook to ensure that despite any no-shows or cancellations, any given flight will have as many occupied seats as possible, because an unoccupied seat represents lost revenue. In terms of valuing stakeholders, does this strategy make sense to you? Why or why not?

A classic example of negative consumer reaction is the response that met Ford Motor Company's 1958 introduction of the Edsel (Figure 3.3). Ford had done extensive research to create a luxury family sedan aimed at an upper-income segment of the market then dominated by Buick, Oldsmobile, and Chrysler. However, the market did not identify Ford products with high status, and the Edsel did not last three years in the marketplace. Ford failed to serve the investors, suppliers, and employees who depended on the company for their livelihoods. Of course, the corporation survived that failure, perhaps because it learned the lessons of stakeholder management the hard way.

Figure 3.3   This Edsel Pacer was manufactured in 1958, the first year of production of the ill-fated Ford model, which ceased production in November 1959. (credit: modification of "Edsel Pacer 2-door Hardtop 1958 front" by "Redsimon"/Wikimedia Commons, CC BY 2.5)

Entertainers too (as well as their clubs, venues, and studios) are sensitive to the views of their stakeholders—that is, fans and the consuming public as a whole. Scarlett Johansson recently signed on to play the role of Dante "Tex" Gill in a biographical film (or "biopic"). Gill had been identified as female at birth but spent much of his professional career self-identifying as male. When the casting was announced in July 2018, it provoked a controversy among transgender rights groups, and within a few days, Johansson announced she had withdrawn from the role.[10] "In light of recent ethical questions raised surrounding my casting as Dante Tex Gill, I have decided to respectfully withdraw my participation in the project. . . . While I would have loved the opportunity to bring Dante's story and transition to life, I understand why many feel he should be portrayed by a transgender person, and I am thankful that this casting debate, albeit controversial, has sparked a larger conversation about diversity and representation in film," she said.[11]

Defining Stakeholder Categories

To better understand stakeholder theory and, ultimately, manage stakeholder claims and expectations, it may be helpful to take a closer look at categories of stakeholders. One way to categorize stakeholders is by defining their impact. For example, regulatory stakeholders including stockholders, legislatures, government regulators, and boards of directors are **enabling stakeholders** because they permit the firm to function. **Normative stakeholders** such as competitors and peers influence the norms or informal rules of the industry; **functional stakeholders** are those who influence inputs, such as suppliers, employees, and unions, and those influencing outputs such as customers, distributors, and retailers. Finally, **diffused stakeholders** include other organizations such as nongovernmental organizations (NGOs), voters, and mass media organizations with less direct relationships but potential for meaningful impacts on firms (Figure 3.4).[12]

Figure 3.4   Grouping stakeholders into meaningful categories according to relationship types allows an organization to prioritize stakeholders' claims. (attribution: Copyright Rice University, OpenStax, under CC BY 4.0 license)

As the Figure 3.4 shows, enabling and functional stakeholders are those active in design, production, and marketing. They provide input for the products or services the organization distributes in the form of output. Companies should identify *all* the stakeholders shown in the figure and consider how they are linked to the firm. Although the diffused linkage stakeholders will vary according to place and time, the enabling, functional, and normative linkage stakeholders are constant, because they are integral to the operation of the firm. Stakeholders, in turn, can exert some control and authority by serving on the board of directors, by exercising their power as purchasers, by being elected to public office, or by joining employees' unions.

In many cases, if one stakeholder effects a change in the firm, other stakeholders will be affected. For example, if an NGO raises concerns about unequal pay of laborers on a rubber plantation that provides raw materials for gasket makers, the supplier may be forced to equalize pay, incurring additional expense. The supplier has taken the ethical action, but ultimately the cost is likely passed through the supply chain to the end user, the retail purchaser at the local car dealer. The supplier could also have absorbed the additional cost, diminishing the bottom line and reducing returns for stockholders, who may withdraw their investment from the company. Although this model of stakeholder relationships is complex, it is useful in understanding the impact of each individual group on the organization as a whole.

James E. Grunig, now professor emeritus at University of Maryland, and Todd Hunt, who together developed the organizational linkage model in Figure 3.4, looked at these relationships through the lens of four "publics" or cohorts: the nonpublic, the latent, the aware, and the active. These publics are distinguished by their degree of awareness of a problem and ability to do something about it. In the nonpublic cohort, no problem is recognized or exists. For the latent public, a problem is there but the public does not recognize it. The aware public recognizes that a problem exists. The active public is aware of the problem and organizes to respond to it. These categories help the organization design its message about a problem and decide how to communicate. Herein lies the ethical significance. If an organization is aware of a problem and the public is not, the organization has an opportunity to communicate and guide the public in recognizing and dealing with it, as the example of Johnson & Johnson's Tylenol product in the following box illustrates.

CASES FROM THE REAL WORLD

The Chicago Tylenol Murders

In the fall of 1982, Johnson & Johnson faced a public relations nightmare when customers in Cook County, Illinois, began dying—eventually, a total of seven people died—after taking over-the-counter, Tylenol-branded acetaminophen capsules. Analysis showed the presence of potassium cyanide, a fatal poison in no way connected with the production of the pill. Johnson & Johnson voluntarily removed all Tylenol products from the U.S. marketplace and offered to pay full retail price for any pills returned to the company. This represented about thirty million bottles of capsules worth more than $100 million. (Significantly, too, Johnson & Johnson decided on this wide-ranging action despite the fact that it and law enforcement realized the cyanide poisoning was limited to Cook County, Illinois.)

Because Tylenol was a flagship product bringing in significant revenue, this was an extreme action but one based on the company's ethics, rooted in its corporate credo. Investigation showed that someone had tinkered with the bottles and injected cyanide into the product in stores. Although no one was ever apprehended, the entire drug industry responded, following Johnson & Johnson's lead, by introducing tamper-proof containers that warned consumers not to use the product if the packaging appeared in any way compromised.

The strong ethical stance taken by Johnson & Johnson executives resulted in immediate action that reassured the public. When the company eventually returned Tylenol to the market, it introduced it first to clinics, hospitals, and physicians' offices, promoting medicine's professional trust in the product. The strategy was successful. Before the poisonings, Tylenol had 37 percent of the market of over-the-counter analgesics. That plunged to 7 percent in fall 1982 but was resurrected to 30 percent by fall 1983.

Critical Thinking

- In its corporate credo, Johnson & Johnson identifies multiple stakeholders: users of its products (output), employees (input), employees' families (diffused linkage), and the government (enabling linkage). Applying Grunig and Hunt's theory, do you believe Johnson & Johnson acted as an enlightened company that includes and communicates with a variety of publics?
- U.S. business leaders are often accused of acting on a short-term obsession with profitability at the expense of the long-term interests of their corporation. Which aspects of the Tylenol crisis demonstrate a short-term perspective? Which show the value of a longer-term perspective?

LINK TO LEARNING

With the adoption of its credo, Johnson & Johnson became one of the first corporations to create something like a mission statement. Read the Johnson & Johnson credo (https://openstax.org/l/53J&JCredo) to learn more.

On the other hand, a company might try to manage a problem by covering it up or denying it. For example, Volkswagen had data that showed its diesel engine's emissions exceeded U.S. pollution standards. Rather than redesign the engine, Volkswagen engineers installed a unit in each car to interpret the emissions as if they met Environmental Protection Agency standards. When the fraud was discovered, Volkswagen was required to buy back millions of cars. As of September 2017, the company had incurred fines and expenses in excess of $30 billion, and some employees had gone to jail. Such damage is bad enough, but loss of reputation and the trust of consumers and stockholders has hurt the company's value and share price.[13] Volkswagen's management of stakeholder relationships was poor and extremely expensive. Once-loyal stakeholders became part of an aware and active public—a group of people united by a common problem and organized for satisfaction, sometimes demanding compensation.[14]

A challenge for business leaders is to assign appropriate weights to stakeholder claims on their companies in an ethical manner. This task is even more difficult because a claim is not necessarily a formal process. "Essentially, stakeholders 'want something' from an organization. Some want . . . to influence what the organization does . . . and others are, or potentially could be, concerned with the way they are affected by the organization."[15]

If a stakeholder has its own identity or voice, or if members of a stakeholder group are many, the claim can be clear and direct, such as in the case of a union negotiating for better pay and benefits, or a community trying to lure a corporation to open operations there. Think of the enormous effort communities around the world make to try to get the Olympics or World Cup organizers to bring the competition to their locale. In spite of significant investment and debt, these communities see a real advantage to their local economy.

Many stakeholder claims are indirect, or "voiceless," due perhaps to their representing relatively few individuals relative to the size and power of the organization and the time required to evoke a response from a large, bureaucratic company. If you have ever had a problem with a cable television or satellite company, you can immediately understand this stakeholder relationship, because it is so difficult to find someone with enough authority to make a decision on behalf of the company. Some companies count on individuals' growing frustrated and giving up on the claim. An indirect stakeholder claim might also be one that affects future generations, such as concerns about air and water pollution. For example, University of Southern California law professor Christopher D. Stone introduced in 1972 what was then a radical concept for the law in the United States, that the environment itself is entitled to legal standing in the courts. If this were so, then the environment might also be eligible for certain protections under the law. Appearing at the dawn of increasing social awareness of ecologic concerns, Stone's influential law review article "Should Trees Have Standing?" gave many environmentalists a new legal philosophy to harness in defense of the natural world.[16]

LINK TO LEARNING

Try playing a game of stakeholder identification, mapping, and analysis, such as this one from the "Gamestorming" website (https://openstax.org/l/53Gamestorming) to learn more.

3.3 Ethical Decision-Making and Prioritizing Stakeholders

Learning Objectives

By the end of this section, you will be able to:

- Identify the factors that affect stakeholder prioritization
- Explain why priorities will vary based upon the interest and power of the stakeholder
- Describe how to prioritize stakeholder claims, particularly when they conflict

If we carry the idea of stakeholder to the extreme, every person is a stakeholder of every company. The first step in **stakeholder management**, the process of accurately assessing stakeholder claims so an organization can manage them effectively, is therefore to define and prioritize stakeholders significant to the firm. Then, it must consider their claims.

Given that there are numerous types of stakeholders, how do managers balance these claims? Ethically, no group should be treated better than another, and managers should respond to as many stakeholders as possible. However, time and resource limitations require organizations to prioritize claims as stakeholder needs rise and fall.

Stakeholder Prioritization

First, it may help to speak to the expectations that any stakeholders may have of a particular business or institution. It depends on particular stakeholders, of course, but we can safely say that all stakeholders expect a form of satisfaction from an organization. If these stakeholders are shareholders (stockowners), then they generally wish to see a high return on their purchase of company shares. If, on the other hand, they are employees, they typically hope for interesting tasks, a safe work environment, job security, and rewarding pay and benefits. If, yet again, the stakeholders are members of the community surrounding a business, they usually wish that the company not harm the physical environment or degrade the quality of life within it.

So the task confronting an organization's management begins with understanding these multiple and sometimes conflicting expectations and ethically deciding which stakeholders to focus on and in what sequence, if not all stakeholders cannot be addressed simultaneously, that is, **stakeholder prioritization**. It helps to actively gather information about all key stakeholders and their claims. First, managers must establish that an individual with a concern is a member of a stakeholder group. For example, a brand may attract hundreds or thousands of mentions on Twitter each day. Which ones should be taken seriously as representative of key stakeholders? Brand managers look for patterns of communication and for context when deciding whether to engage with customers in the open expanses of social media platforms.

LINK TO LEARNING

Read this article "Five Questions to Identify Key Stakeholders" (https://openstax.org/l/53FiveQuestions) in the *Harvard Business Review* to learn more about identifying your key stakeholders.

After establishing that a key stakeholder group is being represented, the manager should identify what the company needs from the stakeholder. This simply helps clarify the relationship. If nothing is needed immediately or for the foreseeable future, this does not mean the stakeholder group does not matter, but it can be a good indication that the stakeholder need not be prioritized at the moment.

Note that managers are often considering these questions in real time, usually with limited resources and power, and that circumstances can change in a matter of moments. In one sense, all representatives of a company are constantly practicing stakeholder prioritization. It need not be a formal process. At times, it is a question of which supplier should be praised or prodded or which customer has a larger order to fill or a special request that might be met. What matters is establishing that someone is a stakeholder, that the concern is currently important, and that the relationship matters for the growth of the business.

If the firm cannot survive without this particular stakeholder or replace him or her relatively easily, then such a person should have priority over other stakeholders who do not meet this criterion. Key suppliers, lucrative or steady customers, and influential regulators must all be attended to but not necessarily capitulated to. For example, a local state legislator representing the district where a business is located may be urging the legislature to raise business taxes to generate more revenue for the state. By him- or herself, the legislator may not have sufficient political clout to persuade the legislature to raise taxes. Yet wise business leaders will not ignore such a representative and will engage in dialogue with him or her. The legislator may eventually be able to win others over to the cause, so it behooves perceptive management to establish a working relationship with him or her.

Not every stakeholder can command constant attention, and no firm has unlimited time or resources, so in one sense, this prioritizing is simply the business of management. Combine the inherent priority of the stakeholder relationship with the level of **exigency**, that is, the level of urgency of a stakeholder claim, to arrive at a decision about where to begin focusing resources and efforts.

Stakeholder prioritization will also vary based on time and circumstance. For example, a large retailer facing aggressive new competitors must prioritize customer service and value. With Amazon acquiring Whole Foods and drastically cutting prices, the grocery chain's customer base may very well grow because prices could become more attractive while the perception of high quality may persist. Potential customers may no longer need to economize by shopping elsewhere.[17] Whole Foods' competitors, on the other hand, must now prioritize customer service, whereas before they could compete on price alone. Whole Foods can become a serious competitor to discount grocery stores like ALDI and Walmart.

Another way to prioritize stakeholder relationships is with a matrix of their power and interest. As Figure 3.5 shows, a stakeholder group can be weighted on the basis of its influence (or power) over and interest in its relationship to the firm. A stakeholder with a high level of both power and interest is a key stakeholder. If this type of stakeholder group encounters a problem, its priority rises.

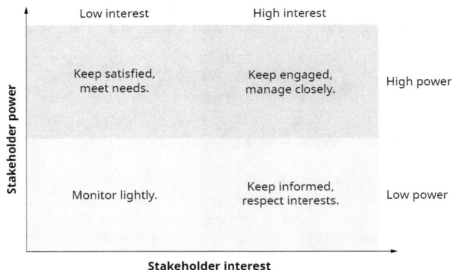

Figure 3.5 Stakeholder priority can be expressed as a relationship between the stakeholder group's influence or power and the interest the stakeholder takes in the relationship. (attribution: Copyright Rice University, OpenStax, under CC BY 4.0 license)

On the supplier side, a small farmer or seasonal supplier could fall in the low-power, low-interest category, particularly if that farmer were selling various retailers produce from his or her fields. However, if that same farmer could connect to a huge purveyor like Kroger, he or she could sell this giant customer its entire crop. This relationship places the farmer in the low-power, high-interest category, meaning he or she will most likely have to make price adjustments to make the sale.

The model's focus on power reveals a need for any company to carefully cultivate relationships with stakeholders. Not all stakeholders have equal influence with a firm. Still, no organization can blithely ignore any stakeholder without potentially debilitating economic consequences. For example, now that Amazon has acquired Whole Foods and increased the size of the customer stakeholder group, it must also find ways to personalize its communications with this group, because personal service has traditionally been more a hallmark of Whole Foods than of Amazon.

Successful business practice today hinges on the ethical acknowledgement of stakeholder claims. It is the right thing to do. Not only that, it also engenders satisfied stakeholders, whether they be customers, stockowners, employees, or the community in which a firm is located. Naturally, satisfied stakeholders lead to the financial well-being of a company.

Managing Stakeholder Expectations

Stakeholder management does not work if the firm's prioritizing decisions are based on flawed, inaccurate, or incomplete information. Some tools are available to help. MITRE is a nonprofit research and development consulting firm that helps governments and other large organizations with many stakeholders conduct stakeholder assessment. The MITRE *Guide to Stakeholder Assessment and Management* lays out a five-step system for stakeholder management.[18]

Overall, MITRE stresses that an organization must sustain trust with its stakeholders through communication efforts. To accomplish this, however, stakeholders must first be clearly identified and then periodically reidentified, because stakeholder cohorts change in size and significance over time. The concerns or claims of stakeholders are identified through data gathering and analysis. Sometimes a firm will conduct surveys or focus groups with customers, suppliers, or other stakeholders. Other times, product usage data will be available as a function of sales figures and marketing data. For software in web and mobile applications, for example, user data may be readily available to show how stakeholders are using the company's digital services or why they appear to be purchasing its products. Another source of stakeholder data is social media, where firms can monitor topics stakeholders of all types are talking about. What matters is gathering relevant and accurate data and ensuring that key stakeholders are providing it. In the next step, managers present the results of their research to the company's decision makers or make decisions themselves.[19] Finally, stakeholders should be informed that their concerns were taken into consideration and that the company will continue to heed them. In other words, the firm should convey to them that they are important.

LINK TO LEARNING

One methodology for prioritizing stakeholder claims is the Stakeholder Circle, developed by Dr. Linda Bourne. Visit the Stakeholder Management website detailing the five key actions an organization can take using this model (https://openstax.org/l/53StakeCircle) to learn more.

WHAT WOULD YOU DO?

Malaysia Airlines

Malaysia Airlines is owned by individual investors and the Malaysian government, which took over the company in 2014 after two mysterious jet crashes. The airline has lost money and struggled since that time, going through three CEOs. The current CEO, Peter Bellew, is experienced in tourism and travel and has been asked to cut costs and increase revenues. His strategy is to maximize the number of Malaysian Muslims (who make up more than 60 percent of the population) flying to Mecca for hajj, the annual holy pilgrimage and an obligation for all Muslims who are well enough to travel and can afford the trip. Bellew plans to provide charter flights to make the pilgrimage easier on travelers.[20]

Critical Thinking

- Describe the passenger stakeholder claims on Malaysia Airlines.
- Describe the government stakeholder claims on Malaysia Airlines.

- What would you advise Bellew to identify as a priority—the demand from pilgrims for easy travel at a reduced price or the demand from the government for profitable operations? Explain your answer.

Because every firm, no matter its mission, ultimately depends on the marketplace, its clients or customers are often high-priority stakeholders. Ethically, the company owes allegiance to customer stakeholders, but it also has an opportunity and perhaps a responsibility to shape their expectations in ways that encourage its growth and allow it to continue to provide for employees, suppliers, distributors, and shareholders.

We should note, too, that nonprofit organizations are beholden, for the most part, to the same rules that apply to for-profits for their sustainability. Nonprofits typically provide a service that is just as dependent on cash flow as is the service or product of a for-profit. A significant difference, of course, is that the client or customer for a nonprofit's service often is unable to pay for it. Therefore, the necessary cash must come from other sources, often in the form of donations or endowments. Hence, those who give to philanthropies constitute essential stakeholders for these nonprofits and must be acknowledged as such.

Wesley E. Lindahl, who studies and advises nonprofits, notes that philanthropies have an ethical obligation to safeguard the donations that come their way. He likens this to a stewardship, because the monies given to charities are gifts intended for others very much in need of them. So those who manage nonprofits have a special obligation to ensure that these donations are well spent and distributed appropriately.[21]

There are three major components to bringing about change in customer or donor expectations: (1) customer receptivity to a product or service offered by the company, (2) acknowledgement of the gap between customer receptivity and corporate action to reduce it, and (3) a system to bring about and maintain change in customer desires to bring it in line with precisely what the corporation can deliver. One example of firms altering customers' habits is the evolution of beverage containers. Most soft drinks and other beverages such as beer were once delivered in reusable glass bottles. Customers were motivated to return the bottles by the refund of a minimal cash deposit originally paid at the time of purchase. The bottles had to be thick and sturdy for reuse, which resulted in substantial transportation costs, due to their weight.

To reduce these costs of manufacturing and transportation, manufacturers first redesigned production to be local, and then, when technology allowed, introduced aluminum cans and pull tabs. Eventually, the cardboard carton that held bottles together was replaced by a plastic set of rings to hold aluminum cans together. Now, however, customers and other stakeholders object to the hazard these rings present to wildlife. Some firms have responded by redesigning their packaging yet again. This ongoing process of developing new packaging, listening to feedback, and redesigning the product over time ultimately changed stakeholder behavior and modernized the beverage industry. Stakeholders are essential parts of a cycle of mutual interest and involvement.

ETHICS ACROSS TIME AND CULTURES

Going King Sized in the United States and Crashing on the Couch in China

IKEA is a multinational corporation with a proven track record of listening to stakeholders in ways that improve relationships and the bottom line. The Swedish company has had success in the United States and, more recently, in China by adapting to local cultural norms. For example, in the United States, IKEA solicited the concerns of many of its approximately fifty thousand in-store customers and even visited some at home. The company learned, among other things, that U.S. customers assumed IKEA featured only European-size beds. In fact, IKEA has offered king-size beds for years; they simply were not on display. IKEA then began to focus on displaying furniture U.S. consumers were more familiar with and so grew its bedroom furniture sales in 2012 and 2013.[22]

As IKEA expands into China, it has welcomed a different trend—people taking naps on the furniture on display. "While snoozing is prohibited at IKEA stores elsewhere, the Swedish retailer has long permitted Chinese customers to doze off, rather than alienate shoppers accustomed to sleeping in public."[23] Adapting to local culture, as these examples demonstrate, is one way a company can respond to stakeholder wishes. The firm abandons some of its usual protocols in exchange for increasing consumer identification with its products.

IKEA appears to have learned what many companies with a global presence have concluded: Stakeholders, and particularly consumer-stakeholders, have different expectations in different geographic settings. Because a firm's ethical obligations include listening and responding to the needs of stakeholders, it behooves all international companies to appreciate the varying perspectives that geography and culture may produce among them.

Critical Thinking

- Does IKEA have a system to influence stakeholder behavior? If so, describe the system and explain who changes more under the system, IKEA or its consumers.
- Does IKEA's strategy reflect a normative approach to managing stakeholder claims? If so, how?

The ethical responsibility of a stakeholder is to make known his or her preferences to the companies he or she purchases from or relies on. Such communication can lead to an increased commitment on the part of corporations to improve. To the extent they do so, companies act more ethically in responding to the wishes and needs of their stakeholders.

3.4 | Corporate Social Responsibility (CSR)

Learning Objectives

By the end of this section, you will be able to:

- Define corporate social responsibility and the triple bottom line approach
- Compare the sincere application of CSR and its use as merely a public relations tool
- Explain why CSR ultimately benefits both companies and their stakeholders

Thus far, we have discussed stakeholders mostly as individuals and groups outside the organization. This section focuses on the business firm as a stakeholder in its environment and examines the concept of a corporation as a socially responsible entity conscious of the influences it has on society. That is, we look at the role companies, and large corporations in particular, play as active stakeholders in communities. Corporations, by their sheer size, affect their local, regional, national, and global communities. Creating a positive impact in these communities may mean providing jobs, strengthening economies, or driving innovation. Negative impacts may include doing damage to the environment, forcing the exit of smaller competitors, and offering poor customer service, to name a few. This section examines the concept of a corporation as a socially responsible entity conscious of the influences it has on society.

Corporate Social Responsibility Defined

In recent years, many organizations have embraced corporate social responsibility (CSR), a philosophy (introduced in Why Ethics Matter,) in which the company's expected actions include not only producing a reliable product, charging a fair price with fair profit margins, and paying a fair wage to employees, but also caring for the environment and acting on other social concerns. Many corporations work on prosocial endeavors and share that information with their customers and the communities where they do business. CSR, when conducted in good faith, is beneficial to corporations and their stakeholders. This is especially true for stakeholders that have typically been given low priority and little voice, such as the natural environment and community members who live near corporate sites and manufacturing facilities.

CSR in its ideal form focuses managers on demonstrating the social good of their new products and endeavors. It can be framed as a response to the backlash corporations face for a long track record of harming environments and communities in their efforts to be more efficient and profitable. Pushback is not new. Charles Dickens wrote about the effects of the coal economy on nineteenth-century England and shaped the way we think about the early industrial revolution. The twentieth-century writer Chinua Achebe, among many others, wrote about colonization and its transformative and often painful effect on African cultures. Rachel Carson first brought public attention to corporation's chemical poisoning of U.S. waterways in her 1962 book *Silent Spring*.

Betty Friedan's *The Feminine Mystique* (1963) critiqued the way twentieth-century industrialization boxed women into traditional roles and limited their agency. Kate Chopin's novel *The Awakening* (1899) and the nineteenth-century novels of Jane Austen had already outlined how limited options were for women despite massive social and economic shifts in the industrializing West. Stakeholder communities left out of or directly harmed by the economic revolution have demanded that they be able to influence corporate and governmental economic practices to benefit more directly from corporate growth as well as entrepreneurship opportunities. The trend to adopt CSR may represent an opportunity for greater engagement and involvement by groups mostly ignored until now by the wave of corporate economic growth reshaping the industrialized world.

CSR and the Environment

Corporations have responded to stakeholder concerns about the environment and sustainability. In 1999, Dow Jones began publishing an annual list of companies for which sustainability was important. Sustainability is the practice of preserving resources and operating in a way that is ecologically responsible in the long term.[24] The Dow Jones Sustainability Indices "serve as benchmarks for investors who integrate sustainability considerations into their portfolios."[25] There is a growing awareness that human actions can, and do, harm the environment. Destruction of the environment can ultimately lead to reduction of resources, declining business opportunities, and lowered quality of life. Enlightened business stakeholders realize that profit is only one positive effect of business operations. In addition to safeguarding the environment, other ethical contributions that stakeholders could lobby corporate management to make include establishing schools and health clinics in impoverished neighborhoods and endowing worthwhile philanthropies in the communities where companies have a presence.

Other stakeholders, such as state governments, NGOs, citizen groups, and political action committees in the

United States apply social and legal pressure on businesses to improve their environmental practices. For example, the state of California in 2015 enacted a set of laws, referred to as the California Transparency in Supply Chains Act, which requires firms to report on the working conditions of the employees of their suppliers. The law requires only disclosures, but the added transparency is a step toward holding U.S. and other multinational corporations responsible for what goes on before their products appear in shiny packages in stores. The legislators who wrote California's Supply Chains Act recognize that consumer stakeholders are likely to bring pressure to bear on companies found to use slave labor in their supply chains, so forcing disclosure can bring about change because corporations would rather adjust their relationships with supply-chain stakeholders than risk alienating massive numbers of customers.[26]

As instances of this type of pressure on corporations increase around the world, stakeholder groups become simultaneously less isolated and more powerful. Firms need customers. Customers need employment, and the state needs taxes just as firms need resources. All stakeholders exist in an interdependent network of relationships, and what is most needed is a sustainable system that enables all types of key stakeholders to establish and apply influence.

People, Planet, Profit: The Triple Bottom Line

How can corporations and their stakeholders measure some of the effects of CSR programs? The **triple bottom line (TBL)** offers a way. TBL is a measure described in 1994 by John Elkington, a British business consultant (Figure 3.6), and it forces us to reconsider the very concept of the "bottom line." Most businesses, and most consumers for that matter, think of the bottom line as a shorthand expression of their financial well-being. Are they making a profit, staying solvent, or falling into debt? That is the customary bottom line, but Elkington suggests that businesses need to consider not just one but rather three measures of their *true* bottom line: the economic and also the social and environmental results of their actions. The social and environmental impacts of doing business, called people and planet in the TBL, are the *externalities* of their operations that companies must take into account.

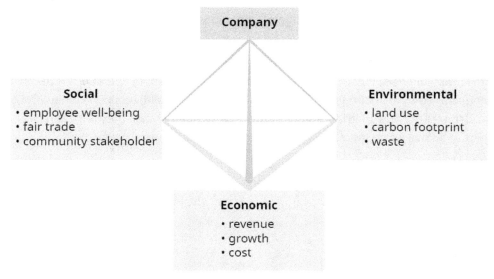

Figure 3.6   The three components of the triple bottom line are interrelated. (attribution: Copyright Rice University, OpenStax, under CC BY 4.0 license)

The TBL concept recognizes that external stakeholders consider it a corporation's responsibility to go beyond making money. If increasing wealth damages the environment or makes people sick, society demands that the corporation revise its methods or leave the community. Society, businesses, and governments have realized that all stakeholders have to work for the common good. When they are successful at acting in a socially responsible way, corporations will and should claim credit. In acting according to the TBL model and promoting such acts, many corporations have reinvested their efforts and their profits in ways that can ultimately lead to the development of a sustainable economic system.

CSR as Public Relations Tool

On the other hand, for some, CSR is nothing more than an opportunity for publicity as a firm tries to look good through various environmentally or socially friendly initiatives without making systemic changes that will have long-term positive effects. Carrying out superficial CSR efforts that merely cover up systemic ethics problems in this inauthentic way (especially as it applies to the environment), and acting simply for the sake of public relations is called **greenwashing**. To truly understand a company's approach toward the environment, we need to do more than blindly accept the words on its website or its advertising.

CASES FROM THE REAL WORLD

When an Image of Social Responsibility May Be Greenwashing

Ben and Jerry's Ice Cream started as a small ice cream stand in Vermont and based its products on pure, locally supplied dairy and agricultural products. The company grew quickly and is now a global brand owned by Unilever, an international consumer goods company co-headquartered in Rotterdam, The Netherlands, and London, United Kingdom.

According to its statement of values, Ben and Jerry's mission is threefold: "Our Product Mission drives us to make fantastic ice cream—for its own sake. Our Economic Mission asks us to manage our Company for sustainable financial growth. Our Social Mission compels us to use our Company in innovative ways to make the world a better place."

With its expansion, however, Ben and Jerry's had to get its milk—the main raw ingredient of ice cream—from larger suppliers, most of which use confined-animal feeding operations (CAFOs). CAFOs have been condemned by animal-rights activists as harmful to the well-being of the animals. Consumer activists also claim that CAFOs contribute significantly to pollution because they release heavy concentrations of animal waste into the ground, water sources, and air.

Critical Thinking

- Does the use of CAFOs compromise Ben and Jerry's mission? Why or why not?
- Has the growth of Ben and Jerry's contributed to any form of greenwashing by the parent company, Unilever? If so, how?

LINK TO LEARNING

Read Ben and Jerry's Statement of Mission (https://openstax.org/l/53BenJerry) **for more on the** company's values and mission.

Coca-Cola provides another example of practices some would identify as greenwashing. The company states the following on its website:

> "Engaging our diverse stakeholders in long-term dialogue provides important input that informs our decision making, and helps us continuously improve and make progress toward our 2020 sustainability goals . . . We are committed to ongoing stakeholder engagement as a core component of our business and sustainability strategies, our annual reporting process, and our activities around the world. As active members of the communities where we live and work, we want to strengthen the fabric of our communities so that we can prosper together." [27]

Let us take a close look at this statement. "Engaging stakeholders in long-term dialogue" appears to describe an ongoing and reciprocal relationship that helps improvement be continuous. Commitment to "stakeholder engagement as a core component of business and sustainability strategies" appears to focus the company on the requirement to conduct clear, honest, transparent reporting.

Currently 20 percent of the people on Earth consume a Coca-Cola product each day, meaning a very large portion of the global population belongs to the company's consumer stakeholder group. Depending on the process and location, it is estimated that it takes more than three liters of water to produce a liter of Coke. Each day, therefore, millions of liters of water are removed from the Earth to make Coke products, so the company's water footprint can endanger the water supplies of both employee and neighbor stakeholders. For example, in Chiapas, Mexico, the Coca-Cola bottling plant consumes more than one billion liters of water daily, but only about half the population has running water.[28] Mexico leads the world in per capita consumption of Coke products.

If consumers are aware only of Coca-Cola's advertising campaigns and corporate public relations writings online, they will miss the very real concerns about water security associated with it and other corporations producing beverages in similar fashion. Thus it requires interest on the part of stakeholders to continue to drive real CSR practices and to differentiate true CSR efforts from greenwashing.

The Ultimate Stakeholder Benefit

CSR used in good faith has the potential to reshape the orientation of multinational corporations to their stakeholders. By positioning themselves as stakeholders in a broader global community, conscientious corporations can be exemplary organizations. They can demonstrate interest and influence on a global scale and improve the way the manufacture of goods and delivery of services serve the local and global environment. They can return to communities as much as they extract and foster automatic financial reinvestment so that people willing and able to work for them can afford not only the necessities but a chance to pursue happiness.

In return, global corporations will have sustainable business models that look beyond short-term growth forecasts. They will have a method of operating and a framework for thinking about sustained growth with stakeholders and *as* stakeholders. Ethical stakeholder relationships systematically grow wealth and opportunity in dynamic fashion. Without them, the global consumer economy may fail. On an alternate and ethical path of prosperity, today's supplier is a consumer in the next generation and Earth is still inhabitable after many generations of dynamic change and continued global growth.

🔑 Key Terms

amenities resources made available to employees in addition to wages, salary, and other standard benefits

descriptive approach a theory that views the company as composed of various stakeholders, each with its own interests

diffused stakeholder a stakeholder with an interest in a company's decisions and whose impacts on a firm can be large even if the relationship is generally weaker than other types

enabling stakeholder a stakeholder who permits an organization to function within the economic and legal system

ethical maximum the strongest action a company can choose to behave ethically in a given situation

ethical minimum the least a company might do to claim it holds an ethically positive position

exigency the level of urgency of a stakeholder claim

functional stakeholder a stakeholder whose relationships influence or govern an organization's inputs and outputs

greenwashing carrying out superficial CSR efforts that merely cover up systemic ethics problems for the sake of public relations

instrumental approach a theory proposing that good management of stakeholders is important because it can help the bottom line

normative approach a theory that considers stakeholders as ends unto themselves rather than means to achieve a better bottom line

normative stakeholder a stakeholder in the organization's industry who influences its norms or informal rules

social responsibility of business the view that stakeholders are not the means to the end (profit) but are ends in and of themselves as human beings

stakeholder claim a particular stakeholder's interest in a business decision

stakeholder management the process of accurately assessing stakeholder claims so an organization can manage them effectively

stakeholder prioritization the process of deciding which stakeholders to focus on and in what sequence

triple bottom line (TBL) a measure that accounts for an organization's results in terms of its effects on people, planet, and profits

📄 Summary

3.1 Adopting a Stakeholder Orientation

An organization has duties and responsibilities with regard to each stakeholder; however, the implicit social contract between business and society means that meeting legal requirements might support only minimal ethical standards. Society on the whole and in the long run requires that business consider a broader range of duties in its relationships with key stakeholders.

3.2 Weighing Stakeholder Claims

There are three approaches to stakeholder theory: the descriptive approach, the instrumental approach, and the normative approach. The normative approach takes the most comprehensive view of the organization and its stakeholders and is the fundamental basis of stakeholder theory. Organizations can analyze stakeholder claims by classifying them on the basis of their intensity and impact on the firm, as well as on the basis of their relationship to the firm. Such classifications may include enabling stakeholders, normative stakeholders, functional stakeholders, and diffused stakeholders. Using the lens of the four "publics" (the nonpublic, the latent, the aware, and the active), we can also understand a stakeholder claim on the basis of the public's degree of awareness of a problem and ability to do something about it.

3.3 Ethical Decision-Making and Prioritizing Stakeholders

Business leaders prioritize those stakeholders who have immediate needs or high urgency or great significance to the organization, and the identity of these groups may shift over time. Stakeholders can also be prioritized on the basis of their relationship to the organization using a matrix of their power and interest. Steps in the MITRE stakeholder management process are to establish trust, identify stakeholders, gather and analyze appropriate data, present information to management, and let stakeholders know they matter. Because customers are often considered high-priority stakeholders, it can be essential for corporations and nonprofit organizations to manage any expectations that customers (or donors) may have.

3.4 Corporate Social Responsibility (CSR)

Most organizations must practice genuine corporate social responsibility to be successful in the modern marketplace. The triple bottom line places people and the planet on equal standing with profit in the mission of an organization. The genuine practice of CSR, unlike greenwashing, requires a commitment to an additional stakeholder, the planet, whose continued healthy existence is essential for any organization to operate.

Assessment Questions

1. Maintaining trust between stakeholders and organizations is _____.
   A.   the stakeholder's responsibility
   B.   an ethical minimum
   C.   an ethical maximum
   D.   a social contract

2. True or false? Companies are required to provide amenities to their employees to fulfill the social contract between management and employees as stakeholders.

3. Choose your favorite brand. List at least five of its key stakeholder groups.

4. A shareholder is a stakeholder who _____.
   A.   holds stock for investment
   B.   has a general interest in the fate of all publicly traded companies
   C.   focuses on the means by which firms get their products to market
   D.   always purchases the product or service of a particular company

5. A stakeholder claim _____.
   A.   is usually a complaint
   B.   is always financial
   C.   is any matter of concern for the corporation or company
   D.   is the same as a lawsuit

6. Explain how the normative approach to stakeholder theory informs the instrumental aspect and the descriptive approach.

7. What is the most important quadrant in the influence/interest matrix, and why?

8. In correct order, the stakeholder management steps adapted from the approach of the MITRE consulting firm are to _____.

    A. build trust, identify stakeholders, prioritize claims, visualize changes, and perform triage

    B. build trust, identify stakeholders, gather and analyze data, present results, make changes, and prepare a communication strategy

    C. build trust, identify stakeholders, gather and analyze data, present findings to management, and communicate key messages to stakeholders conveying the company's appreciation of them

    D. identify stakeholders, gather and analyze data, make changes, and present results

9. True or false? Stakeholder management practice ultimately is about valuing stakeholder contributions to a firm, no matter how significant, inspired, or influential that contribution might not be.

10. Name the three components of the triple bottom line.

11. What does the California Transparency in Supply Chains Act require of businesses that operate in California?

12. True or false? Corporate social responsibility is a voluntary action for companies.

13. The Dow Jones Sustainability Indices provides information for _____.

    A. investors who seek quick profit

    B. investors who seek long-term returns

    C. investors who value CSR in companies

    D. marketing promotions of each of its members

 Endnotes

1. "The Latest: Police Release Call from Starbucks Employee," Associated Press, April 17, 2018. https://apnews.com/7c0b3793ca244e128effc1019bde194c.
2. "Starbucks," *Fortune*. http://fortune.com/fortune500/starbucks/; "Starbucks Corporation Institutional Ownership," Nasdaq. https://www.nasdaq.com/symbol/sbux/institutional-holdings; "Starbucks Company Profile," Starbucks. https://www.starbucks.com/about-us/company-information/starbucks-company-profile (accessed June 18, 2018).
3. Michael Nunez, "New Horror Story Proves Working for Amazon Is More Soul-Crushing Than We Thought," Gizmodo, March 7, 2016. https://gizmodo.com/new-horror-story-proves-working-for-amazon-is-more-soul-1763323814.
4. Lynn A. Stout, "The Shareholder Value Myth," Paper 771 (Ithaca, NY: Cornell Law Faculty Publications 2013), 6. http://scholarship.law.cornell.edu/cgi/viewcontent.cgi?article=2311&context=facpub.
5. Thomas Donaldson and Lee E. Preston, "The Stakeholder Theory of the Corporation: Concepts, Evidence, and Implications," *The Academy of Management Review* 20, no. 1 (1995): 65–91.
6. Thomas Donaldson and Lee E. Preston, "The Stakeholder Theory of the Corporation: Concepts, Evidence, and Implications," *The Academy of Management Review* 20, no. 1 (1995): 65–91.
7. Thomas Donaldson and Lee E. Preston, "The Stakeholder Theory of the Corporation: Concepts, Evidence, and Implications," *The Academy of Management Review* 20, no. 1 (1995): 65–91.
8. Christopher Meyer and Andre Schwager, "Understanding Customer Experience," *Harvard Business Review*, February 2007. https://hbr.org/2007/02/understanding-customer-experience.
9. Paul Williams and Earl Naumann, "Customer Satisfaction and Business Performance: A Firm-Level Analysis," *Journal of Services Marketing* 25, no. 1 (2011): 20–32.
10. Mia Galuppo, "Scarlett Johansson Drops Out of 'Rub & Tug' Trans Film Following Backlash," *Hollywood Reporter*, July 13, 2018. https://www.hollywoodreporter.com/news/scarlett-johansson-drops-trans-film-rub-tug-backlash-1127003.
11. Aaron Hicklin, "Exclusive: Scarlett Johansson Withdraws from *Rub & Tug*," *Out*, July 13, 2018. https://www.out.com/out-exclusives/2018/7/13/exclusive-scarlett-johansson-withdraws-rub-tug.
12. Brad L. Rawlins, "Prioritizing Stakeholders for Public Relations," Institute for Public Relations, March 2006. https://www.instituteforpr.org/wp-content/uploads/2006_Stakeholders_1.pdf.
13. Charles Riley, "Volkswagen's Diesel Scandal Costs Hit $30 Billion," *CNN Money*, September 29, 2017. http://money.cnn.com/2017/09/29/investing/volkswagen-diesel-cost-30-billion/index.html.
14. Miles Brignall, "Volkswagen's US Compensation Deal Leaves British Drivers Fuming," *The Guardian*, October 29, 2016. https://www.theguardian.com/money/2016/oct/29/volkswagen-us-compensation-deal-british-drivers-fuming; Soraya Sarhaddi Nelson, "German Consumers Fight Automakers for Compensation in Emissions Scandal," All Things Considered, November 10, 2017. https://www.npr.org/2017/11/10/563378729/german-consumers-fight-automakers-for-compensation-in-emissions-scandal.
15. P1 Examining Team, "All About Stakeholders – Part 1," ACCA. http://www.accaglobal.com/us/en/student/exam-support-resources/professional-exams-study-resources/p1/technical-articles/stakeholders-part1.html (accessed August 5, 2018).
16. Christopher D. Stone, "Should Trees Have Standing? Toward Legal Rights for Natural Objects," *Southern California Law Review* 45, (1972): 450–501.

17. Nathaniel Meyersohn, "Why Kroger Is Making Its Own Clothes," *CNN Money*, November 3, 2017. http://money.cnn.com/2017/11/03/news/companies/kroger-clothes/index.html.
18. "Systems Engineering Guide. Stakeholder Assessment and Management," MITRE. https://www.mitre.org/publications/systems-engineering-guide/enterprise-engineering/transformation-planning-and-organizational-change/stakeholder--assessment-and-management (accessed May 1, 2018).
19. "Systems Engineering Guide. Stakeholder Assessment and Management," MITRE. https://www.mitre.org/publications/systems-engineering-guide/enterprise-engineering/transformation-planning-and-organizational-change/stakeholder--assessment-and-management (accessed May 1, 2018).
20. John Anthony, "Malaysia Airlines Prepares for Rebranding, CEO Mueller Says," *Stuff*, October 2, 2015. https:www.stuff.co.nz/business/industries/72625417/Malaysia-Auirlines-prepares-for-rebranding-CEO-Christoph-Mueller-says.
21. Wesley E. Lindahl, "The Fundraising Process," in *Understanding Nonprofit Organizations*, 2nd ed, eds. J. Steven Ott and Lisa A. Dicke (Philadelphia: Westview Press, 2012), 123.
22. Jenna Goudreau, "How IKEA Leveraged the Art of Listening to Global Dominance," *Forbes*, January 30, 2013. https://www.forbes.com/sites/jennagoudreau/2013/01/30/how-ikea-leveraged-the-art-of-listening-to-global-dominance/#6ab8eefc2b09.
23. Dan Levin, "Shh. It's Naptime at Ikea in China," *New York Times*, August 26, 2016. https://www.nytimes.com/2016/08/27/world/what-in-the-world/shh-its-naptime-at-ikea-in-china.html.
24. Victoria Knowles, "What's the Difference Between CSR and Sustainability?" *2degrees*, March 25, 2014. https://www.2degreesnetwork.com/groups/2degrees-community/resources/whats-difference-between-csr-and-sustainability/.
25. "Dow Jones Sustainability Indices," RobecoSAM. http://www.sustainability-indices.com/index-family-overview/djsi-family-overview/#tab-1 (accessed August 5, 2018); "Results Announced for 2017 Dow Jones Sustainability Indices Review," RobecoSAM, September 7, 2017. http://www.sustainability-indices.com/images/170907-djsi-review-2017-en-vdef.pdf.
26. Kamala Harris, "The California Transparency in Supply Chains Act. A Resource Guide," California Department of Justice, 2015. https://oag.ca.gov/sites/all/files/agweb/pdfs/sb657/resource-guide.pdf.
27. Coca-Cola Company, "2016 Sustainability Report: Stakeholder Engagement," August 18, 2017. http://www.coca-colacompany.com/stories/stakeholder-engagement#2.
28. Martha Pskowski, "Coca-Cola Sucks Wells Dry in Chiapas, Forcing Residents to Buy Water," *Salon*, September 16, 2017. https://www.salon.com/2017/09/16/coca-cola-sucks-wells-dry-in-chiapas-forcing-residents-to-buy-water_partner/.

4 | Three Special Stakeholders: Society, the Environment, and Government

Figure 4.1 The Japanese concept of *nemawashi* broadly means "laying the groundwork" or "building strong roots." In a business ethics context, *nemawashi* means building a strong foundation for an action or project by reaching out to all stakeholders and seeking their input, demonstrating how much the organization values their opinion as it builds support from the ground up. (attribution: Copyright Rice University, OpenStax, under CC BY 4.0 license)

Chapter Outline

4.1 Corporate Law and Corporate Responsibility

4.2 Sustainability: Business and the Environment

4.3 Government and the Private Sector

Introduction

Good business leaders know that a commitment to sustainability and corporate social responsibility (CSR) requires a strong foundation, one upon which a company can build and expand its commitment to every aspect of the organization.[1] Companies that truly intend to incorporate CSR into their long-term strategy start by soliciting input from a large and diverse group of stakeholders, followed by a transparent process of implementation, commitment, and enforcement. Corporate social responsibility is more than just another policy; it's a philosophy, capturing the essence of *nemawashi*, or "building strong roots" (Figure 4.1). CSR also demonstrates that a company is willing to commit the financial and human resources necessary to make it a reality, rather than just a talking point.

This chapter looks at sustainability and CSR from the perspective of a diverse constituency, including managers, employees, investors, government regulators, competitors, customers and clients, the community, and the environment. If you were a CEO, would you be willing to commit the time and money to incorporate CSR the right way in your company? Why might some businesses hesitate to use a *nemawashi*-style approach?

4.1 | Corporate Law and Corporate Responsibility

Learning Objectives

By the end of this section, you will be able to:

- Explain how investors and owners benefit from doing business as a corporate entity
- Define the concept of shareholder primacy
- Discuss the conflict between shareholder primacy and corporate social responsibility

Corporate law, which enables businesses to take advantage of a legal structure that separates liability from ownership and control, was introduced in most states in the nineteenth century. The separation of ownership and liability means that, unlike sole proprietors and members of partnerships, owners of modern business corporations enjoy the advantage of limited liability for the corporation's debts and other financial obligations, a concept at the heart of a U.S. economic system built on capitalism.

The Advantages of Corporate Status

The concept of **limited liability** means that the owners (shareholders or stockholders) of corporations, as well as directors and managers, are protected by laws stating that in most circumstances, their losses in case of business failure cannot exceed the amount they paid for their shares of ownership (Figure 4.2). The same protection applies to owners of some other business entities such as limited liability companies (LLCs). An LLC is similar to a corporation in that owners have limited liability; however, it is organized and managed more like a partnership. For purposes of granting owners the protection of limited liability, several types of entities are possible within each state, including a corporation, an LLC, a limited liability partnership, and a limited partnership.

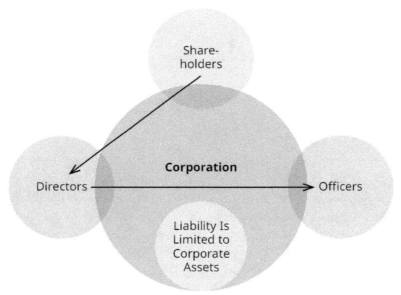

Figure 4.2   Corporate shareholders elect directors who appoint the company's officers—all of whom benefit from limited liability. (attribution: Copyright Rice University, OpenStax, under CC BY 4.0 license)

Without state incorporation laws, business owners would be subject to personal liability for business losses, which could create several disadvantages. Ownership would be riskier, so owners could have more difficulty selling their ownership interests. They could also be subject to a pro rata share of income taxes. These types of personal financial liability could limit the ability of businesses to raise capital by selling stock. Limited liability, by reducing the amount a shareholder can lose from investing in a corporation by buying its stock, increases the investment's attractiveness to potential new shareholders. Ultimately, corporate status increases both the potential number of willing investors and the amount of capital they are likely to invest. After all, would you be willing to invest your money in a business if you knew not only that you could lose the capital you invested, but also that you could be sued personally for any and all debts of the business?

Corporate status is conferred upon a business by state law (statute) when a state issues the business a charter of incorporation. The protective shield of corporate status enables businesses to socialize their losses in a way that traditional proprietorships and partnerships are not able to do. *Socializing* a loss is a means to amortize it or spread it out over society in general, so the owners do not absorb it individually. Amortization is similar to the idea behind insurance, in which many people bear a small share in a loss, rather than one or a few people bearing all of it. Therefore, it is accurate to say that society enables corporations to exist, both by passing laws that create them and by limiting the financial risk exposure of their owners. Since our society grants for-profit businesses the right to incorporate and make unlimited profits with limited liability, a reasonable person could conclude that corporations owe a debt to society in return. Corporations' **quid pro quo**—a Latin term meaning *this for that*—is acceptance of corporate social responsibility, to benefit the many stakeholders to whom corporations may owe a duty, including customers, the community, the environment, employees, media, and the government (Figure 4.3).

Figure 4.3   A corporation's typical stakeholders include (but are not limited to) its customers or clients, the community in which it operates, the natural environment, its employees, the media, and the government. (attribution: Copyright Rice University, OpenStax, under CC BY 4.0 license)

Balancing the Many Responsibilities of a Corporation

A longstanding ethical debate about corporate social responsibility asks whether, in fact, a corporation owes a duty to society or only to its shareholders. The line of important court cases shaping this issue spans almost a century and includes a series of landmark cases involving the Ford Motor Company, the Wrigley Company, and Hobby Lobby.

In *Dodge v. Ford Motor Company* (1919), the Michigan Supreme Court ruled in favor of **shareholder primacy**, saying that founder Henry Ford must operate the Ford Motor Company primarily in the profit-maximizing interests of its shareholders.[2] In the traditional corporate model, a corporation earns revenue and, after deducting expenses, distributes the profits to shareholders in the form of dividends. Ford had announced that his company would stop paying big dividends to shareholders and instead would use its profits to achieve several other goals, including improving product quality, expanding company facilities, and perhaps most surprisingly, lowering prices. Shareholders then sued Ford, asking the court to order Ford Motor Company to continue allocating the lion's share of profits to high dividend payments. (It is ironic that the named shareholders who sued Ford were the Dodge brothers, former Ford suppliers who had recently started their own car company.)

At the trial, Ford (Figure 4.4) testified that he believed his company was sufficiently profitable to consider its broader obligation and engage in activities to benefit the public, including its workers and customers. This was a unique position for the founder and primary owner of a large corporation to take in the early twentieth century. During the rise of capitalism in the United States, most owners sought only to maximize profits, because that was the primary basis of their ability to attract capital and to reinvest in the company. Most investors were interested in a healthy return on their investment, rather than any type of social good. Shareholders contended that the concern Ford expressed for his workers and customers was both improper and illegal. The court agreed, and Ford was forced to abandon his managerial goal of balancing profits and realizing broader social goals.[3]

(a)   (b)

Figure 4.4   In 1913, workers are shown laboring on a Ford assembly line (a) in Highland Park, Michigan. In *Dodge v. Ford Motor Company* (1919), the Michigan Supreme Court ruled that Henry Ford (b) must operate the Ford Motor Company primarily in the profit-maximizing interests of its shareholders rather than in the broader interests of his workers and customers. (credit a: modification of "Ford assembly line - 1913" by unknown/ Wikimedia Commons, Public Domain; credit b: modification of "Portrait of Henry Ford" by Hartsook/Wikimedia Commons, Public Domain)

Ironically, in the same case, the court upheld the validity of a doctrine known as the **business judgment rule**, a common-law principle stating that officers, directors, and managers of a corporation are not liable for losses incurred when the evidence demonstrates that decisions were reasonable and made in good faith, which gives corporate management latitude in deciding how to run the company.[4] Essentially, the business judgment rule holds that a court will not second-guess the decisions of a company's managers or directors.

The legality and appropriateness of social responsibility as a business policy have followed a long and winding road since 1919. In the 1950s and 1960s, for example, some state courts rejected the shareholder primacy doctrine, instead ruling that a broad interpretation of the business judgment rule allowed managers discretion when it came to allocating company assets, including using them for programs demonstrating social awareness.

In 1968, in a highly publicized case, the court ruled that the board of directors of the Wrigley Company, of baseball and chewing gum fame, had a significant amount of discretion in determining how to balance the interests of stakeholders.[5] The case of *Shlensky v. Wrigley* (1968) revolved around William Wrigley Jr.'s ownership of the Chicago Cubs. The baseball team had steadfastly refused to install the lights necessary for playing night games at Wrigley Field, even though every other stadium in major league baseball had lights. Instead, the Cubs had respected the local community's belief that night baseball games and their associated lights would negatively affect the surrounding neighborhood, creating more opportunities for crime. In the view of some investors, however, the Cubs' decision was depressing profits for shareholders. The shareholders brought a challenge against the Wrigley Company, but the Cubs' owners won the case.

The Wrigley case represented a shift from the idea that corporations should pursue only the maximization of shareholder value, as had been held in the Ford Motor Company case.[6] As a follow-up to this case, lights were finally installed at Wrigley Field in 1988, but only after the owner, William Wrigley III, had sold the team (in 1981) to the Tribune Company, a large media conglomerate that fought for six years to install lights. However, the case stands as precedent for the ability of management to balance various interests and profits when making decisions.

Dodge v. Ford (1919) and *Shlensky v. Wrigley* (1968) established the dynamic nature of the debate over the shareholder primacy doctrine and indicated a shift in both legal thought and precedent toward allowing management greater latitude in deciding how to best manage a corporation. A more recent decision, *Burwell v. Hobby Lobby* (2014), demonstrated what some may consider the double-edged sword of this latitude.[7] In a 5–4 decision in favor of Hobby Lobby, the Supreme Court ruled that some corporations (those that are closely held by a few shareholders) can object on ethical, moral, or religious grounds to the Affordable Care Act's rule that health insurance policies must cover various forms of contraception; such companies can elect not to offer such coverage.

The majority opinion in the case was written by Justice Samuel Alito, joined by Chief Justice John Roberts and Justices Antonin Scalia, Clarence Thomas, and Anthony Kennedy. In essence, the Court ruled that business owners could place their personal values first and follow their own agenda. The case received a great deal of publicity, some of it quite negative. Essentially, the Court held in this case that "corporate law does not require for-profit corporations to pursue profit at the expense of everything else,"[8] similar to the ruling in the Chicago Cubs/Wrigley Field case.

The decision was a victory for the family that owns Hobby Lobby and has been praised by some and criticized by others for expanding the rights of corporate owners. Some analysts believe it represents more than just an expansion of management prerogative and enlarges the right of corporations to be treated as a "person." The Hobby Lobby case can be interpreted to mean the people who control corporations (owners and/or management) may act on their own values in a way that might well be inconsistent with the interests of employees and other minority shareholders. In the majority decision, Alito wrote, "A corporation is simply a form of organization used by human beings to achieve desired ends. When rights, whether constitutional or statutory, are extended to corporations, the purpose is to protect the rights of these people."[9] Hobby Lobby is primarily owned by one family, and Alito's comments seem to suggest that another interpretation would limit the applicability of the case to only closely held corporations, in which the majority of the stock is owned by a small number of shareholders.

Some might think Henry Ford's attempt to forego profits in order to pay workers higher wages was a good choice but not find Hobby Lobby's preference for limiting female employees' health insurance benefits on religious grounds to be so. However, the law must be interpreted logically: If you give management the prerogative to put one social issue ahead of profits, should management not also be able to pursue any social issue of its choosing? An extension of the logic used in the Hobby Lobby case could lead to an expansion of the corporate rights of the personhood doctrine, for example, by allowing the individual right to privacy to become a shield against regulatory scrutiny by government agencies (although a corporation is not a natural person).

Another potential problem with giving management greater rights to pursue social agendas is protecting the interests of minority shareholders who disagree with the majority. Since corporation law is state law, the protections for minority shareholders vary widely, but owners of a small number of shares have little or no power to influence the choices the corporation makes. Some states allow cumulative voting for seats on the board of directors, which increases minority shareholder power. Others permit buyouts or dissolution statutes that apply to closely held corporations. However, in a traditional large corporation, none of these protections for minority interests are likely to apply. Of course, another option is for disgruntled shareholders to sell their shares.

The Two Sides of the Corporate Responsibility Debate

The issue of corporate social responsibility is the subject of high-level global discussion and debate among leaders in the public and private sectors, such as the World Economic Forum Annual Meeting in Davos, Switzerland. Numerous respected academic centers also hold forums on CSR, such as the Center on Democracy, Development, and the Rule of Law at Stanford University and the Harvard Law School Forum on Corporate Governance and Financial Regulation.

As we have seen, slow but steady acceptance of CSR as a legitimate business concept has led to the legal and ethical position that corporate directors and managers may exercise business judgment and discretion in running a corporation. This development has come about for multiple reasons: a) the fact that society allows LLCs to exist, b) the sheer magnitude of the economic power corporations possess, and c) the desire of corporations to act responsibly in order to avoid more extensive government regulation. Managers are usually accorded significant latitude as long as they can point to a rational interpretation of their actions as benefiting the corporation as a whole in the long term. The combination of economic and political power in the world's largest corporations necessitates that executives consider the interests of a broader set of stakeholders, rather than only stockholders. Indeed, social, environmental, and charitable programs often create shareholder value rather than take away from it. And honoring obligations to all stakeholders in a corporation—including those who own no stock shares—is the **moral minimum** a firm must undertake to satisfy the base threshold for acting ethically.

A recent study by researchers at Princeton and the University of Texas indicates that corporations benefit from following CSR policies in multiple ways.[10] These benefits are collectively called a "halo effect" and can add value to the business. As an example, consumers frequently take CSR spending as an indirect indicator that a company's products are of high quality, and often they are also more willing to buy these products as an indirect way of donating to a good cause.

However, some economists, such as Milton Friedman, Henry Hazlitt, Adam Smith, and others, have argued that CSR initiatives based on environmental or social justice instead *limit* shareholder wealth.[11] The Nobel Prize-winning economist Milton Friedman (1912–2006) believed shareholders should be able decide for themselves what social initiatives to donate to or to take part in, rather than having a business executive decide for them. He argued that both government regulation and corporate social initiatives allow an outside third party to make these choices for shareholders.

In Friedman's opinion, too much power assumed by corporate management in pursuing a social agenda might ultimately lead to a form of corporate autocracy. Supporters of the profit maximization principle believe it is a waste of corporate resources to reduce air pollution below the level required by law, to require vendors to participate in a sustainable supply chain initiative, or to pay lower-level employees a salary above the legally mandated minimum wage. Friedman asserted that "doing good deeds" is not the job of corporations; it is the right of those people who want to do them but should not be imposed on those who do not. His philosophy asserts that socially oriented initiatives are analogous to a form of outside regulation, resulting in higher costs to those corporations that follow socially responsible policies.

When Friedman was laying out this position in the 1970s, it reflected the prevailing opinion of a majority of U.S. shareholders and commentators on corporate law at that time. In the years since then, however, Friedman's perspective has fallen into disfavor. This does not invalidate his point of view, but it does demonstrate that public opinion about corporations is subject to change over time. The subjectivity or relativity with which we view companies along with their perceived rights and responsibilities is a major theme this text addresses.

Do corporate directors owe a specific fiduciary duty to shareholders? A **fiduciary duty** is a very high level of legal responsibility owed by those who manage someone else's money, which includes the duties of care and loyalty. Some examples of relationships that include a fiduciary duty are those between a trustee of an estate and its beneficiary, and between a fund manager and a client. According to the American Bar Association, the business judgment rule states "that as fiduciaries, corporate directors owe the corporation and its shareholders fiduciary duties of diligence and fidelity in performing their corporate duties. These fiduciary obligations include the duty of care and the duty of loyalty . . . the duty of care consists of an obligation to act on an informed basis; the duty of loyalty requires the board and its directors to maintain, in good faith, the corporation's and its shareholders' best interests over anyone else's interests."[12] So it would seem that the answer is yes, corporate directors do have a specific fiduciary duty to promote the best interests of the corporation. But what exactly does that duty entail? Does that specifically mean returning profits to shareholders in the form of dividends? As we have seen, these questions have frequently spilled over into the courts, in the form of shareholder lawsuits challenging the actions of directors and/or management.

LINK TO LEARNING

Fiduciary duty also includes a duty of communication, as you can read in the oft-cited Meinhard v. Salmon case (https://openstaxcollege.org/l/53MeinVSal) from 1928, where the New York Court of Appeals held that business partners may have a fiduciary duty to one another regarding business opportunities that arise during the course of the partnership.

UCLA law professor Steven Bainbridge wrote in the *New York Times*: "If directors were allowed to deviate from shareholder wealth maximization, they would inevitably turn to indeterminate balancing standards, which provide no accountability."[13] As support for his position, Bainbridge pointed to a 2010 case, *eBay Domestic Holdings Inc. v. Newmark*, in which a Delaware court ruled that corporate directors are bound by fiduciary duties and standards that include "acting to promote the value of the corporation for the benefit of its stockholders."[14]

However, Lynn Stout, a professor at Cornell University Law School, wrote a contrasting piece in the *New York Times* in which she said, "There is a common belief that corporate directors have a legal duty to maximize corporate profits and shareholder value—even if this means skirting ethical rules, damaging the environment or harming employees. But this belief is utterly false. Modern corporate law does not require for-profit corporations to pursue profit at the expense of everything else, and many do not."[15] Her opinion is based in part on the Hobby Lobby decision referenced above.

Thus, while ethicists may agree that corporations do indeed owe social responsibilities to society, legal experts still differ over this point. The fact that we have seen inconsistent decisions from the courts over the last century confirms the lack of legal consensus. Of course, both legal and ethical opinion are always in flux, so where the debate stands today in no way indicates where it will be in ten years. On this issue, public opinion, as well as that of politicians and even the courts, is like a pendulum swinging back and forth, usually between points of view that are center-right or center-left, rather than at the extremes. However, the pendulum is reset every so often, and the arc within which it swings may differ from era to era.

CASES FROM THE REAL WORLD

Unilever "Enhancing Livelihoods" through Project Shakti

According to management guru Peter Drucker, whose ideas significantly contributed to the foundations of thought about the workings of the modern business corporation, workers "need to know the organization's mission and to believe in it." How do organizations ensure this commitment? By satisfying workers' values.[16] A program undertaken by Unilever, the Dutch-British multinational company co-headquartered in Rotterdam and London, illustrates the kind of values-oriented corporate endeavor Drucker describes. Project Shakti is a Unilever CSR initiative in India that links corporate social responsibility and financial opportunities for local women.[17] It is considered a leading example of micro-entrepreneurship, and it expands the concept of sustainability to include not only environmental issues but also economic opportunity and financial networking in underdeveloped areas.

The goal, according to Unilever, is to give rural Shakti women the ability to earn money for themselves and their families as micro-entrepreneurs. Unilever's subsidiary in India, Hindustan Lever, has started training programs for thousands of women in small towns and villages across India to help them understand how to run their own small sole proprietorships as distributors of the company's products. With support from a team of rural sales managers, women who had been unable to support themselves are now becoming empowered by learning how a supply chain works, what products Hindustan Lever produces, and how to distribute them. The sales managers also act in a consulting capacity to help with business basics, money management, negotiations, and related skills that help the women run their businesses effectively.

The program was so successful that Unilever expanded it to include Shakti men, typically the sons, brothers, or husbands of the women already running businesses. The men, who are essentially like delivery drivers, sell Unilever products using bicycles for transportation, enabling them to cover a larger area than women cover on foot. The women spend most of their time running the business.

Project Shakti has enlisted more than 100,000 rural participants, which includes about 75,000 women. The project has changed their lives in ways that are profound, and not only because of the income earned. The women now have increased self-esteem based on a sense of empowerment, and they finally feel they have a place in Indian society. According to the Unilever Sustainable Living Plan, Project Shakti is one of the best and most sustainable ways the company can address women's social concerns. It allows Unilever to conduct business in a socially responsible manner, helping women to help themselves while extending the reach of its products.

Critical Thinking

- Do you believe Unilever sponsors the Shakti program to help women, to boost its own profits, or both? Explain your answer.
- If Unilever has mixed motives, does this discredit the company in your eyes? Should it?
- How is this program an example of both corporate and personal sustainability?
- Could this model program be duplicated elsewhere, in another area and with different products? Why or why not?

It is clear that many different stakeholders value corporate social responsibility, including some investors, shareholders, employees, customers, and suppliers. Indeed, some businesses look at CSR as providing a perfect long-term strategic opportunity to strengthen company fundamentals while contributing to society at the same time. Effective corporate leaders will get try to get investors on board with the idea of CSR, avoiding or minimizing the potential for any litigation related to maximization of profits. And innovative companies are finding ways to create value for both the business and society simultaneously.[18]

Data analysis indicates that following a policy of corporate social responsibility does not have to mean losing money; on the contrary, many corporations that use an ethical approach to doing business are actually quite profitable. Mutual funds, recognizing that investors care about sustainable investing, now offer socially responsible funds, and third-party ratings companies, such as Morningstar, rate the funds so potential investors can evaluate how well the companies in them are meeting environment, social, and governance challenges. An example of such a fund is the Calvert Fund, which describes itself as a "leader in responsible investing with a mission to deliver superior long-term performance to our clients and to enable them to achieve positive impact."[19]

LINK TO LEARNING

This website for Ellevest (https://openstaxcollege.org/l/53Ellevest) takes you to a digital investment platform run by women for women clients. The idea was launched in 2016 by Sallie Krawcheck, who had worked for large Wall Street firms and experienced first-hand the challenges of using an ethical approach to investing in traditional firms, especially for women.

The chart below analyzes mutual funds and their rate of return over several different time periods; included are examples of both general index funds and "socially responsible" or social index funds (Figure 4.5). If we compare the two general index funds at the top to the three funds at the bottom that invest in socially responsible companies, we see a competitive return on investment in the social funds. Social responsibility does not mean lower profitability.

Relative Profitability of Socially Responsible and Other Index Mutual Funds				
Index or Fund	Holdings (Number of Different Stocks Held in Fund)	Year-to-Date Return	2-Year Return	5-Year Return
S&P 500 Index	500	8.2%	7.4%	81.4%
NASDAQ Index	3,176	6.5%	12.5%	108%
Vanguard FTSE Social Index	407	7.7%	5.7%	96.7%
TIAA-CREF Social	793	12.1%	0.1%	66.8%
iShares Social	403	8.1%	6.5%	78.8%

General index fund   Social index fund

Source: Zacks, Abhijit Ghosh. "Top Ranked Socially Responsible Mutual Funds." Yahoo! Finance. April 30, 2014.

Figure 4.5 This chart demonstrates that social responsibility can be profitable. (attribution: Copyright Rice University, OpenStax, under CC BY 4.0 license)

LINK TO LEARNING

Being socially responsible does not necessarily mean being unprofitable. This video interview with George Pohle (https://openstaxcollege.org/l/53IBMGlobal) reveals how ensuring that CSR is at the core of a business's strategy can yield financial benefits. Pohle is the vice president and global leader of the Business Strategy Consulting Division at IBM Global Business Services.

4.2 Sustainability: Business and the Environment

Learning Objectives

By the end of this section, you will be able to:

- Explain the concept of earth jurisprudence
- Evaluate the claim that sustainability benefits both business and the environment
- Identify and describe initiatives that attempt to regulate pollution or encourage businesses to adopt clean energy sources

Public concern for the natural environment is a relatively new phenomenon, dating from the 1960s and Rachel Carson's seminal book *Silent Spring*, published in 1962. In 1992, Cormac Cullinan's *Wild Law* proposed "earth justice" or "earth jurisprudence," a concept underlying the law's ability to protect the environment and effectively regulate businesses that pollute. The preoccupation with business success through investment in corporations, in contrast, is a much older concept, dating back at least to the creation of the British East India Company in 1600, and the widespread emergence of the corporation in Europe in the 1700s. If you were a business owner, would you be willing to spend company resources on environmental issues, even if not required to do so by law? If so, would you be able to justify your actions to shareholders and investment analysts as smart business decisions?

Environmental Justice

If a business activity harms the environment, what rights does the environment have to fight back? Corporations, although a form of business entity, are actually considered persons in the eyes of the law. Formally, **corporate personhood**, a concept we touched on in the preceding section, is the legal doctrine holding that a corporation, separate and apart from the people who are its owners and managers, has some of the same legal rights and responsibilities enjoyed by natural persons (physical humans), based on an interpretation of the word "person" in the Fourteenth Amendment.[20]

The generally accepted constitutional basis for allowing corporations to assert that they have rights similar to those of a natural person is that they are organizations of people who should not be deprived of their rights simply because they act collectively. Thus, treating corporations as persons who have legal rights allows them to enter into contracts with other parties and to sue and be sued in a court of law, along with numerous other legal rights. Before and after the Supreme Court's ruling in *Citizens United v. Federal Election Commission* (2010), which upheld the First Amendment free-speech rights of corporations, there have been numerous challenges to the concept of corporate personhood; however, none have been successful. Thus, U.S. law considers corporations to be persons with rights protected under key constitutional amendments, regulations, and case law, as well as responsibilities under the law, just as human persons have.

A question that logically springs from judicial interpretations of corporate personhood is whether the environment should enjoy similar legal status. Should the environment be considered the legal equivalent of a person, able to sue a business that pollutes it? Should environmental advocates have been able to file a lawsuit against BP (formerly British Petroleum) on behalf of the entire Gulf of Mexico for harm created by the 2010 Deepwater Horizon oil spill (discussed in more detail in the government regulation section of this chapter), which, at five million barrels, was ten times larger than the famous Exxon Valdez spill and remains the largest and most widespread ocean oil spill in the history of the global petroleum industry? Furthermore, the Deepwater Horizon spill affected not only thousands of businesses and people, but also the entirety of the Gulf of Mexico, which will suffer harm for years to come. Should the Gulf of Mexico have legal standing to sue, just like a person?

While U.S. jurisprudence has not yet officially recognized the concept that Earth has legal rights, there are examples of progress. Ecuador is now the first country to officially recognize the concept.[21] The country rewrote its Constitution in 2008, and it includes a section entitled "Rights for Nature." It recognizes nature's right to exist, and people have the legal authority to enforce these rights on behalf of the ecosystem, which can itself be named as a litigant in a lawsuit.

Earth jurisprudence is an interpretation of law and governance based on the belief that society will be sustainable only if we recognize the legal rights of Earth as if it were a person. Advocates of earth jurisprudence assert that there is legal precedent for this position. As pointed out earlier in this chapter, it is not only natural persons who have legal rights, but also corporations, which are artificial entities. Our legal system also recognizes the rights of animals and has for several decades. According to earth jurisprudence advocates, officially recognizing the legal status of the environment is necessary to preserving a healthy planet for future generations, in particular because of the problem of "invisible pollution."

Businesses that pollute the environment often hide what they are doing in order to avoid getting caught and facing economic, legal, or social consequences. The only witness may be Earth itself, which experiences the harmful impact of their invisible actions. For example, as revealed in a recent report,[22] companies all over the world have for years been secretly burning toxic materials, such as carbon dioxide, at night. A company that needs to dump a toxic substance usually has three choices: dispose of it properly at a safe facility, recycle and reuse it, or secretly dump it. There is no doubt that dumping is the easiest and cheapest option for most businesses.

As another example, approximately twenty-five million people board cruise ships every year, and as a result, cruise ships dump one billion gallons (3.8 billion liters) of sewage into the oceans annually, usually at night so no one sees or smells it. Friends of the Earth, a nongovernmental organization (NGO) concerned with environmental issues, used data from the U.S. Environmental Protection Agency (EPA) to calculate this figure.[23] The sewage dumped into the sea is full of toxins, including heavy metals, pathogens, bacteria, viruses, and pharmaceutical drugs (Figure 4.6). When invisibly released near coasts, this untreated sewage can kill marine animals, contaminate seafood, and sicken swimmers, and no one registers the damage except the ocean itself. Many believe the environment should have the right not to be secretly polluted in the dead of night, and Earth should have rights at least equal to those of corporations.

Figure 4.6   A warning in Honolulu regarding the damage done by ocean dumping. (credit: "No Dumping - Drains to Ocean" by Daniel Ramirez/Wikimedia Commons, CC BY 2.0)

Cormac Cullinan, an environmental attorney, author, and leading proponent of earth jurisprudence, often collaborates with other environmental advocates such as Thomas Berry, an eco-theologian, scholar, and author. Cullinan, Berry, and others have written extensively about the important legal tenets of earth jurisprudence; however, it is not a legal doctrine officially adopted by the United States or any of its states to date. The concept of earth justice is tied indirectly to the economic theory of the "tragedy of the commons," a phrase derived from British economist William Forster Lloyd, who, in the mid-nineteenth century, used a hypothetical example of unregulated grazing on common land to explain the human tendency to act independently, putting self-interest first, without regard for the common good of all users. The theory was later popularized by ecologist and philosopher Garrett Hardin, who tied it directly to environmental issues. In other words, when it comes to natural resources, the **tragedy of the commons** holds that people generally use as much of a free resource as they want, without regard for the needs of others or for the long-term environmental effects. As a way of combating the tragedy of the commons, Cullinan and others have written about the concept of earth justice,[24] which includes the following tenets:

"The Earth and all living things that constitute it have fundamental rights, including the right to exist, to have a habitat or a place to be.

Humans must adapt their legal, political, economic, and social systems to be consistent with the fundamental laws or principles that govern how the universe functions.

Human acts, including acts by businesses that infringe on the fundamental rights of other living things violate fundamental principles and are therefore illegitimate and unlawful."[25]

LINK TO LEARNING

The concept of earth justice relies heavily on Garrett Hardin's discussion of the tragedy of the commons (https://www.openstax.org/l/53TragOfCom) in *Science* in 1968.[26] This classic analysis of the environmental dilemma describes how, from colonial times, Americans regarded the natural environment as something to be used for their own farming and business ends. Overuse, however, results in the inevitable depletion of resources that negatively affects the environment, so that it eventually loses all value.

Today, supporters of the environment assert that government has both a right and an obligation to ensure that businesses do not overuse any resource, and to mandate adequate environmental protection when doing so. In addition, some form of fee may be collected for using up a natural resource, such as severance taxes imposed on the removal of nonrenewable resources like oil and gas, or deposits required for possible cleanup costs after projects have been abandoned. As part of the growing acceptance of the concept of earth justice, several nonprofit educational organizations and NGOs have become active in both lobbying and environmental litigation. One such organization is the Center for Earth Jurisprudence (housed at the Barry School of Law in Orlando), a nonprofit group that conducts research in this area.

LINK TO LEARNING

The following video describing the Center for Earth Jurisprudence (https://www.openstax.org/l/53EarthJuris) discusses support for laws that legally protect the sustainability of life and health on Earth, focusing upon the springs and other waters of Florida.

Why Sustainability Is Good for Business

The notion that the environment should be treated as a person is relatively new. But given the prominence of the environmental movement worldwide, no well-managed business today should be conducted without an awareness of the tenuous balance between the health of the environment and corporate profits. It is quite simply good business practice for executives to be aware that their enterprise's long-term sustainability, and indeed its profitability, depend greatly on their safeguarding the natural environment. Ignoring this interrelationship between business and the environment not only elicits public condemnation and the attention of lawmakers who listen to their constituents, but it also risks destroying the viability of the companies themselves. Virtually all businesses depend on natural resources in one way or another.

Progressive corporate managers recognize the multifaceted nature of **sustainability**—a long-term approach to business activity, environmental responsibility, and societal impact. Sustainability affects not only the environment but also other stakeholders, including employees, the community, politics, law, science, and philosophy. A successful sustainability program thus requires the commitment of every part of the company. For example, engineers are designing manufacturing and production processes to meet the demands of companies dedicated to sustainability, and the idea of company-wide sustainability is now mainstream. Many of the largest companies in the world see sustainability as an important part of their future survivability.

The Global 100 and Sustainability's Strategic Worth

Corporate Knights is a Canadian research and publishing company that compiles an annual list called the Global 100, identifying the world's most sustainable companies.[27] The 2018 edition of the list, presented at the World Economic Forum in Davos, Switzerland, shows that an increasing number of major multinational companies take sustainability seriously, including many U.S. businesses. The highest-ranking U.S. company is technology giant Cisco, which ranks seventh on the Global 100 list.[28] Other U.S. companies in the top twenty-five include Autodesk, Merck, and McCormick & Co. The countries with the best representation on the list are primarily from North America and Western Europe: the United States (18), France (15), the United Kingdom (10), Germany (7), Brazil (5), Finland (5), and Sweden (5).

You may expect that companies dedicated to sustainability would be less profitable in the long run as they face additional costs. In fact, data from the Global 100's return on investment shows this is not the case. Let's examine the evidence. If an investor had put $250 in Global 100 companies in 2005, it would have been worth $580 in 2015, compared to $520 for the same amount invested in a typical index fund. The Global 100's cumulative return on high-sustainability firms is about 25 percent higher than a traditional investment.[29]

Cisco Systems, number seven on the global list, is a good example of how green procurement and sustainable sourcing have become a regular part of the supply chain. At Cisco, according to a top-level supply chain executive, "we take seriously the responsibility of delivering products in an ethical and environmentally responsible manner."[30] Cisco relies on its Supplier Code of Conduct to set standards for suppliers so they follow fair labor practices, ensure safe working conditions, and reduce their **carbon footprint**, the amount of carbon dioxide and other carbon compounds released by the consumption of fossil fuels, which can be measured quantitatively (see the link below). Cisco is in the process of embedding sustainability into supply chain management at all levels.

LINK TO LEARNING

Do you know what your carbon footprint is? This personal footprint calculator (https://www.openstax.org/l/53CarbonFoot) allows you to find out where you stand.

Another company dedicated to sustainability is Siemens, which was ranked number nine on the 2018 list. Siemens is a multinational industrial conglomerate headquartered in Germany, whose businesses range from power plants to electrical systems and equipment in the medical field and high-tech electronics. Siemens was rated the most energy-efficient firm in its sector, because it produced more dollars in revenue per kilowatt used than any other industrial corporation. This is a standard technique to judge efficiency and demonstrates that Siemens has a low carbon footprint for a company in the industries in which it operates. The commitment of Siemens to sustainability is further demonstrated by its decision to manufacture and sell more environmentally friendly infrastructure products such as green heating and air conditioning systems.

Cisco and Siemens show that businesses across the globe are starting to understand that for a supply chain to be sustainable, companies and their vendors must be partners in a clean and safe environment. Do businesses simply pay lip service to environmental issues while using all available natural resources to make as much money as they can in the present, or are they really committed to sustainability? There is abundant evidence that sustainability has become a policy adopted by businesses for financial reasons, not simply public relations.

McKinsey & Company is one of the world's largest management consulting firms and a leader in the use of data analytics, both qualitative and quantitative, to evaluate management decisions. McKinsey conducts periodic surveys of companies around the world on matters of importance to corporate leaders. In the 2010 survey, 76 percent of executives agreed that sustainability provides shareholders long-term value, and in the 2014 survey, entitled "Sustainability's Strategic Worth," the data indicated that many companies consider cost savings to be the number-one reason for adopting such policies. Cost cutting, improved operations, and efficiency were indicated as the primary reasons for adopting sustainability policies by over one-third of all companies (36%).[31]

Other major studies have demonstrated similar results. Grant Thornton is a leading global accounting and consulting firm. Its 2014 report on CSR showed that the top reason companies cite for moving towards more environmentally responsible business practices is financial savings. Grant Thornton conducted more than 2,500 interviews with clients and business executives in approximately thirty-five countries to discover why companies are making a commitment to sustainable practices. The study found that cost management was the key reason for sustainability (67%).[32]

A specific example is Dell Computers, headquartered outside Austin, Texas, and with operations all over the world. The "Dell Legacy of Good Plan" has set a goal to reduce greenhouse gas emissions from all facilities and operations by 50 percent by the year 2020, along with several other environmental goals. As part of this overall plan, Dell created the Connected Workplace, a flex-work program allowing alternative arrangements such as variable work hours to avoid rush hour, full- or part-time work at home flexibility, and job sharing. This sustainability initiative helps the company avoid about seven thousand metric tons of greenhouse gas emissions, and, directly related to the financial benefit of sustainability, it saves the company approximately $12 million per year.[33]

However, adopting sustainability policies may require a long-term outlook. A recent article in the *Harvard Business Review* discussed the issue of sustainability and how it can create real cost savings (Figure 4.7). "It's hard for companies to recognize that sustainable production can be less expensive. That's in part because they have to fundamentally change the way they think about lowering costs, taking a leap of faith . . . that initial investments made in more-costly materials and methods will lead to greater savings down the road. It may also require a willingness to buck conventional financial wisdom by focusing not on reducing the cost of each part but on increasing the efficiency of the system as a whole."[34]

Figure 4.7 Sustainability can create long-term cost savings for companies. (credit: work by Nattanan Kanchanaprat/Pixabay, CC0)

Sustainability Standards

The International Organization for Standardization, or ISO, is an independent NGO and the world's largest developer of voluntary international business standards. More than twenty thousand ISO standards now cover matters such as sustainability, manufactured products, technology, food, agriculture, and even healthcare. The adoption and use of these standards by companies is voluntary, but they are widely accepted, and following ISO certification guidelines results in the creation of products and services that are clean, safe, reliable, and made by workers who enjoy some degree of protection from workplace hazards.

In the environmental area, the ISO 14000 series of standards promotes effective environmental management systems in business organizations by providing cost-effective tools that make use of best practices for environmental management. These standards were developed in the 1990s and updated in 2015; they cover everything from the eco-design (ISO 14006) of factories and buildings to environmental labels (ISO 14020) to limits on the release of greenhouse gasses (ISO 14064). While their adoption is still voluntary, a growing number of countries allow only ISO 14000-certified companies to bid on public government contracts, and the same is true of some private-sector companies (Figure 4.8).

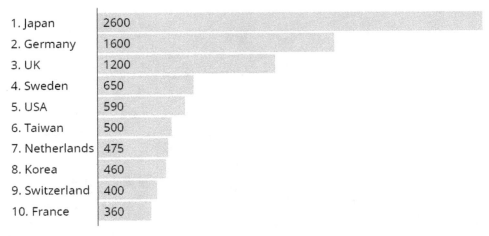

Figure 4.8   According to recent reports, close to fifteen thousand companies worldwide have chosen to be ISO 14000 certified, including Nissan, Ford, and IBM. (attribution: Copyright Rice University, OpenStax, under CC BY 4.0 license)

Another type of sustainability standard with which businesses may elect to comply is LEED certification. LEED stands for Leadership in Energy and Environmental Design, and it is a rating system devised by the U.S. Green Building Council to evaluate a structure's environmental performance. The most famous example is the Empire State Building in New York City, which was awarded LEED Gold status (for existing buildings). The LEED certification was the result of a multimillion-dollar rebuilding program to bring the building up to date, and the building is the tallest in the United States to receive it. There are dozens of other examples of large commercial buildings, such as the Wells Fargo Tower in Los Angeles, as well as thousands of smaller buildings and residential homes. LEED certification is the driver behind the ongoing market transformation towards sustainable design in all types of structures, including buildings, houses, and factories.

The High Cost of Inaction

According to estimates from the EPA, by the year 2050, Earth's population will be about ten billion people. Dramatic population growth has had a very significant and often negative human impact on the planet. Not only are there more people to feed, house, and care for, but new technologies allow businesses to harness natural resources in unprecedented amounts. NGOs and government agencies alike have taken notice. For years, the Department of State and the Department of Defense have considered climate change to be a potential threat to the long-term security of the United States. If unmanaged, climate change could pose a risk to both U.S. security and Department of Defense facilities and operations.[35] Other respected organizations are also alerting the public to the risks of ignoring climate change.

The Union of Concerned Scientists (UCS) has released a detailed report identifying approximately twenty serious risks that will be faced if the problem is not addressed in a substantial way. These risks include rising seas and increased coastal flooding, more intense and frequent heat waves, more destructive hurricanes, wildfires that last longer and produce more damage, and heavier precipitation in some areas and more severe droughts in other areas. In addition to extreme weather events, there would likely be widespread forest death in the Rocky Mountains and other mountain ranges, the destruction of coral reefs, and shifts in the ranges of plants and animals. Both military bases and national landmarks would be at risk, as would the electrical grid and food supply. The UCS, with a membership consisting of the world's most respected scientists, bases its projections on scientific research studies that have produced empirical evidence of climate change. Its official position is that "global warming is already having significant and very costly effects on communities, public health, and our environment."[36]

Environmental protection and climate change issues receive varying degrees of support at the national level, depending on the commitment different presidents make to them. During periods in which the administration in Washington demonstrates a lower priority for climate change issues, such as the Trump administration's announced intention to withdraw from the Paris Climate Accord, private companies may take the lead on actions to reduce global warming emissions.

For example, Microsoft founder Bill Gates recently announced the creation of a private initiative to invest $20 billion on climate-related research and development over the next five years. This is an example of government-funded early experimental research that a business may be able to turn into a commercially viable solution. If government steps back, private-sector companies concerned about long-term sustainability may have to take a leadership role.[37] Ultimately, it requires the cooperation of public and private efforts to address climate change; otherwise, the impacts will continue to intensify, growing more costly and more damaging."[38]

LINK TO LEARNING

This video produced by the National Oceanic and Atmospheric Administration (https://www.openstax.org/l/53NOAAvid) in conjunction with the State Department and an Oregon state agency shows the magnitude of ocean pollution. As of 2017, only two states (California and Hawaii) have banned plastic bags, according to the National Conference of State Legislatures.[39]

Sustainability often requires the public and private sectors to cooperate. Inaction contributes to disasters like the 2017 devastation of Houston by Hurricane Harvey and of Puerto Rico by Hurricane Maria. There is often tension between developers who want to build and cities that try to legislate for more green space. Green space not only offers a place for recreation and enjoyment of nature, but also provides essential natural drainage for rain and flood waters, reducing the likelihood that developed areas will end up underwater in a storm.

WHAT WOULD YOU DO?

Flooding in Houston: Is the Status Quo Sustainable?

A symbiotic relationship exists between development and flooding in urban areas such as Houston, Texas. Imagine you are a member of the urban planning commission for the city council of Houston, which recently suffered traumatic flood damage from several major storms, including Hurricanes Harvey and Ike, and Tropical Storm Allison, all of which occurred since 2001 and caused a total of approximately

$75 billion in damages.[40] The floods also caused dozens of deaths and changed the lives of millions who lived through them. Future storms may increase in severity, because climate change is warming ocean waters.

The mayor and the city council have asked the planning commission to propose specific solutions to the flooding problem. This solution must not rely exclusively on taxpayer funds and government programs, but rather must include actions by the private sector as well.

One of the most direct solutions is a seemingly simple tradeoff: The greater Houston area must reduce the percentage of land covered by concrete while increasing the percentage of land dedicated to green space, which acts like a sponge to absorb flood waters before they can do severe damage. The planning commission thinks the best way to accomplish this is to issue a municipal ordinance requiring corporate developers and builders to set aside as green space an amount of land at least equal to what will be covered by concrete, (neighborhoods, office buildings, parking lots, shopping centers). However, this will increase the cost of development, because it means more land will be required for each type of project, and as a result, developers will have higher land costs.

Critical Thinking

- As a member of the urban planning commission, you will have to convince the stakeholders that a proposal to require more green space is a workable solution. You must get everyone, including developers, investors, neighborhood homeowner associations, politicians, media, and local citizens, on board with the idea that the benefit of sustainable development is worth the price. What will you do?
- Is this a matter that should be regulated by the local, state, or federal government? Why?
- Who pays for flood damage after a hurricane? Are your answers to this question and the preceding one consistent?

U.S. government agencies, such as the National Aeronautics and Space Administration (NASA) and National Oceanic and Atmospheric Administration, have identified many challenges in which sustainability can make a positive contribution. These include climate change, decreasing supplies of clean water, loss of ecological systems, degradation of the oceans, air pollution, an increase in the use and disposal of toxic substances, and the plight of endangered species.[41] Progress toward solving these challenges depends in part on deciding who should help pay for the protection of global environmental resources; this is an issue of both environmental and distributive justice.

One way to address the issue of shared responsibility between corporations and society is the implementation of a "cap and trade" system. According to the Environmental Defense Fund, **cap and trade** is a viable approach to addressing climate change by curbing emissions that pollute the air: The "cap" is a limit on greenhouse gas emissions—if companies exceed their cap, they must pay penalties—whereas the "trade" allows companies to use the free market to buy and sell pollution allowances that permit them to emit a certain amount of pollution.

At present, there are more questions than answers, including how much of the responsibility lies with governments, how this responsibility can be allocated between developed and developing nations, how much of the cost should the private sector bear, and how should these divisions of cost and responsibility be enforced. Private companies must bear part of the cost, and the business sector recognizes they have some responsibility, but many disagree on whether that should be in the form of after-the-fact fines, or before-the-fact fees and deposits paid to the government. Regulations may very well have to be international in scope, or companies from one country may abuse the environment in another.

ETHICS ACROSS TIME AND CULTURES

Is It Ethical to Dump Toxic Waste in Countries That Allow It?

Should a multinational company take advantage of another country's lack of regulation or enforcement if it saves money to do so?

A *New York Times* news correspondent reporting from Nigeria found a collection of steel drums stacked behind a village's family living compound. In this mid-1990s case, ten thousand barrels of toxic waste had been dumped where children live, eat, and drink.[42] As safety and environmental hazard regulations in the United States and Europe have driven toxic waste disposal costs up to $3,000 per ton, toxic waste brokers are looking for the poorest nations with the weakest laws, often in West Africa, where the costs might be closer to $3 per ton. The companies in this incident were looking for cheap waste-dumping sites, and Nigeria agreed to take the toxic chemical waste without notifying local residents. Local people wearing shorts, t-shirts, and sandals unloaded barrels of polychlorinated biphenyls, placing them next to a residential area. Nigeria has often been near the top of the United Nations' list of most corrupt nations, with government leaders cutting deals to line their own pockets while exposing their citizens to environmental hazards.

A more recent example occurred in Côte d'Ivoire (Ivory Coast) in 2006, when residents discovered that hundreds of tons of "slops" (chemicals) from a foreign-owned ship had been dumped near Abidjan, the country's commercial capital. The ship was owned by a multinational energy company named Trafigura. According to a report from Amnesty International, more than 100,000 residents were sickened, leading to fifteen deaths. Trafigura had illegally dumped the toxic waste in Côte d'Ivoire after searching for a disposal site in several other countries.[43]

Critical Thinking

- Should a U.S. or European company take advantage of a country's weak approach to business and political ethics?
- Would your answer change if your decision saved your company $1 million?

Inaction on issues of sustainability can lead to long-term environmental consequences that may not be reversible (the death of ocean coral, the melting of polar ice caps, deforestation). Another hurdle is that it is sometimes difficult to convince companies and their investors that quarterly or annual profits are short-term and transitory, whereas environmental sustainability is long-term and permanent.

Environmental Economics and Policy

Some politicians and business leaders in the United States believe that the U.S. system of capitalism and free enterprise is the main reason for the nation's prosperity over the past two hundred years and the key to its future success. Free enterprise was very effective in facilitating the economic development of the United States, and many people benefited from it. But it is equally true that this could not have happened without the country's wealth of natural resources like oil, gas, timber, water, and many others. When we consider the environment and the role of sustainability, the question is not whether our system works well with an abundance of natural resources. Rather, we should ask how well it would work in a nation, indeed in a world, in which such resources were severely limited.

Does business, as the prime user of these resources, owe a debt to society? The *Harvard Business Review* recently conducted a debate on this topic on its opinion/editorial pages. Business owes the world everything and nothing, according to Andrew Winston, author and consultant on environmental and social challenges. "It's an important question," he wrote, "but one that implies business should do the socially responsible thing out of a sense of duty. This idea is a distraction. Sustainability in business is not about philanthropy, but about profitability, innovation, and growth. It's just plain good business."[44] On the other hand, Bart Victor, professor at Vanderbilt University's Owen Graduate School of Management, wrote, "Business is far more powerful and deeply influential than any competing ideological force, political force or environmental force . . . business now has to see itself and its responsibilities and obligations in a new way."[45]

Using deontological or duty-based reasoning, we might conclude that business does owe a debt to the environment. A basic moral imperative in a normative system of ethics is that someone who uses something must pay for it. In contrast, a more utilitarian philosophy might hold that corporations create jobs, make money for shareholders, pay taxes, and produce things that people want; thus, they have done their part and do not owe any other debt to the environment or society at large. However, utilitarianism is often regarded as a "here and now" philosophy, whereas deontology offers a longer-term approach, taking future generations into account and thus aligning more with sustainability.

Should businesses have to pay more in fees or taxes than ordinary citizens for public resources or infrastructure they use to make a profit? Consider the example of fracking: West Texas has seen a recent boom in oil and gas drilling due to this relatively new process. Fracking is short for hydraulic fracturing, which creates cracks in rocks beneath Earth's surface to loosen oil and gas trapped there, thus allowing it to flow more easily to the surface. Fracking has led to a greatly expanded effort to drill horizontally for oil and gas in the United States, especially in formations previously thought to be unprofitable, because there was no feasible way to get the fossil fuels to the surface. However, it comes with a significant downside.

Fracking requires very heavy equipment and an enormous amount of sand, chemicals, and water, most of which must be trucked in. Traffic around Texas's small towns has increased to ten times the normal amount, buckling the roads under the pressure of a never-ending stream of oil company trucks. The towns do not have the budget to repair them, and residents end up driving on dangerous roads full of potholes. The oil company trucks are using a public resource, the local road system, often built with a combination of state and local taxpayer funds. They are obviously responsible for more of the damage than local residents driving four-door sedans to work. Shouldn't the businesses have to pay a special levy to repair the roads? Many think it is unfair for small towns to have to burden their taxpayers, most of whom are not receiving any of the profits from oil and gas development, with the cost of road repair. An alternative might be to impose a Pigovian tax, which is a fee assessed against private businesses for engaging in a specific activity (proposed by British economist A. C. Pigou). If set at the proper level, the tax is intended as a deterrent to activities that impose a net cost—what economists call "negative externalities"—on third parties such as local residents.

This issue highlights one of many environmental debates sparked by the fracking process. Fracking also causes the overuse and pollution of fresh water, spills toxic chemicals into the ground water, and increases the potential for earthquakes due to the injection wells drilled for chemical disposal. Ultimately, as is often the case with issues stemming from natural resource extraction, local residents may receive a few short-term benefits from business activity related to drilling, but they end up suffering a disproportionate share of the long-term harm.

One method of dealing with the long-term harm caused by pollution is a **carbon tax**, that is, a "pay-to-pollute" system that charges a fee or tax to those who discharge carbon into the air. A carbon tax serves to motivate users of fossil fuels, which release harmful carbon dioxide into the atmosphere at no cost, to switch to cleaner energy sources or, failing that, to at least pay for the climate damage they cause, based on the amount of greenhouse gas emissions generated from burning fossil fuels. A proposal to implement a carbon tax system in the United States has been recommended by many organizations, including the conservative Climate Leadership Council (CLC).[46] Exxon Mobil, Shell, British Petroleum, and Total, along with other oil companies and a number of large corporations in other industries, recently announced their support for the plan to tax carbon emissions put forth by the CLC.[47]

LINK TO LEARNING

Visit the Carbon Tax Center (https://www.openstax.org/l/53CarbonTax) to learn about the carbon tax as a monetary disincentive.

Would this "pay-to-pollute" method actually work? Will companies agree to repay the debt they owe to the environment? Michael Gerrard, the director of the Sabin Center for Climate Change Law at Columbia University Law School, said, "If a sufficiently high carbon tax were imposed, it could accomplish a lot more for fighting climate change than liability lawsuits."[48] Initial estimates are that if the program were implemented, companies would pay more than $200 billion a year, or $2 trillion in the first decade, an amount deemed sufficient to motivate the expanded use of renewable sources of energy and reduce the use of nonrenewable fossil fuels.

Some environmental organizations, including the Nature Conservancy and the World Resources Institute, are also endorsing the plan, as are some legislators in Washington, DC. "The basic idea is simple," Senator Sheldon Whitehouse (D-RI) said. "You levy a price on a thing you don't want—carbon pollution—and you use the revenue to help with things you do want."[49] According to the senator, a U.S. carbon tax or a fee of $45 per metric ton would reduce U.S. carbon emissions by more than 40 percent in the first decade. This is an idea with global support, and it has already been tried. The World Bank has data indicating that forty countries, along with some major cities, have already enacted such programs, including all countries of the EU, as well as New Zealand and Japan.

CASES FROM THE REAL WORLD

Corporate and Personal Choices Regarding the Environment of the Future

The car manufacturer Tesla is developing new technologies to allow people to reduce their carbon footprint. In addition to a line of electric cars, the company makes other renewable energy products, such as roofing tiles that act as solar energy panels, and promotes longer-term projects such as the Hyperloop, a high-speed train project jointly designed by Tesla and SpaceX.

Of course, if businesses are to succeed in selling environmentally friendly products, they must have consumers willing to buy them. A homeowner has to be ready to spend 20 percent more than the cost of a traditional roof to install solar roofing tiles that reduce the consumption of electricity generated by fossil fuels (Figure 4.9).

Figure 4.9   Although solar panels can reduce your carbon footprint, the tiles are much more expensive than standard roofing tiles. (credit: "Typical Solar Installation" by Tim Fuller/Flickr, CC BY 2.0)

Another personal decision is whether to buy a $35,000 Tesla Model 3 electric car. While it reduces the driver's carbon footprint, it requires charging every 250 miles, making long-distance travel a challenge until a national system of charging stations is in place.

Tesla's founder, Elon Musk, is also the founder of SpaceX, an aerospace manufacturer that produces and launches the only space-capable rockets currently in existence in the United States. Thus, when NASA wants to launch a rocket, it must do so in partnership with SpaceX, a private company. It is often the case that private companies develop important advances in technology, with incentives from government such as tax credits, low-interest loans, or subsidies. This is the reality of capital-intensive, high-tech projects in a free-market economy, in which government spending may be limited for budgetary and political reasons. Not only is SpaceX making the rockets, but it is making them reusable, with long-term sustainability in mind.

Critical Thinking

- Should corporations and individual consumers bear joint responsibility for sustaining the environment? Why or why not?
- What obligation does each of us have to be aware of our own carbon footprint?
- If individual consumers have some obligation to support environmentally friendly technologies, should all consumers bear this responsibility equally? Or just those with the economic means to do so? How should society decide?

LINK TO LEARNING

Elon Musk, founder of the electric car manufacturer Tesla and other companies, recently spoke at a global conference held at the Panthéon-Sorbonne University in Paris. In this video, Musk explains the

effect of carbon dioxide emissions on climate change (https://www.openstax.org/l/53ElonTalk) **in clear
and simple terms.**

Government and the Private Sector

Learning Objectives

By the end of this section, you will be able to:

- Identify three public health issues that might warrant government regulation
- Explain what is meant by "revolving door" in a political context
- Compare constitutional arguments for and against government regulation of industry

Ideally, all levels of government—local, state, and federal—should work with each other and with private-sector businesses to accomplish a fair and rational balance between their respective roles in maintaining a just society. Rarely does one actor alone solve a problem; more often, it takes either a state-federal or a government-business partnership to make a significant impact on a social or economic challenge. Such partnerships are often quite effective, according to Deloitte, a global consulting and accounting firm.[50]

For example, the federal Clean Air Act of 1970 gives the EPA nationwide authority, but controlling air pollution, which does not recognize borders, also necessitates that state governments play a very significant role in enforcing environmental standards. In turn, about half the states also allow major cities to have their own air quality regulatory programs. "Think globally, act locally" seems to capture the essence of government regulation in air quality. For decades, California has had an air-quality program that not only attempts to comply with mandates in the federal program but also goes a step further to create state-specific rules, such as stricter auto emissions guidelines.

In another example, in May 2017, the Environment and Natural Resources Division of the U.S. Department of Justice, together with the EPA and the Texas Commission on Environmental Quality, announced a settlement with Vopak, a Houston energy company, related to air-quality violations by the company.[51] Both federal and state government agencies had filed actions against Vopak, stating that the company failed to comply with Clean Air Act requirements to properly manage equipment at its on-site wastewater treatment facility, resulting in excess emissions of a variety of hazardous air pollutants, as well as volatile organic compounds, in an area classified as not meeting ground-level ozone standards. Per the settlement terms, the company, at considerable cost, "will install state-of-the art pollution controls at the wastewater treatment system and use infrared cameras" to detect otherwise undetectable air pollution from its chemical storage tanks. Additionally, Vopak will pay a $2.5 million civil penalty.[52]

Sustainability and the Public Interest

For two centuries, businesses have profited from using and selling the nation's natural resources. The tradeoff in a free but regulated economic system such as that in the United States is to allow the continued extraction of natural resources but to require a commitment to protection of the environment in return. This bargain promotes long-term sustainability by balancing the interests of the environment, state and local governments, and users of natural resources. However, this public-private collaboration is not without controversy.

WHAT WOULD YOU DO?

The Keystone XL Pipeline

The case of the Keystone XL pipeline is an example of the emotional aspect of many environmental disputes, as our nation tries to come to grips with sustainability issues. Local and national opponents of the Keystone XL pipeline, which would carry crude oil from Canada to the Texas Gulf Coast, have protested for years to stop its construction (Figure 4.10). These efforts accelerated after President Trump approved the pipeline in March 2017, reversing President Obama's decision to reject it on environmental grounds. It appears that the pipeline is likely to be completed, pending legal action still unresolved in Nebraska.

Figure 4.10   Groups across the political spectrum have come together to protest the proposed Keystone pipeline route. (credit: modification of "Protest against the proposed KeystoneXL tar sands pipeline" by Fibonacci Blue/Flickr, CC BY 2.0)

To fight the pipeline, some opponents have used legal strategies such as court challenges in Nebraska, where regulators have not yet approved its route through the state. Other methods include tactics learned in the fight against the Dakota Access pipeline, in which protestors blocked equipment, occupied construction sites, and fought company employees and law enforcement officers. Protestors have vowed to use the same tactics against the Keystone XL. As Tom Goldtooth, executive director of the Indigenous Environmental Network, told reporters, "Our dedication to stop this pipeline isn't just for the future determination of our lives as human beings but also for the future of all generations of life, and that we stay true to the understandings of protecting mother earth to the fullest degree and do it in a prayerful way."[53]

Opponents of projects such as Keystone XL are not always divided along political party lines, geography, age, or other demographics. Bret Clanton is a rancher and a registered Republican who doesn't fit the standard profile of an environmentalist. The TransCanada Oil Company told him it planned to dig up three miles of his land to lay a section of the Keystone XL pipeline and bulldoze another two and half miles for an access road. "I've lived here all my life and this ground is pretty much as God, or whoever, made it, and I just want it to stay that way," Clanton said. He fought the pipeline from the beginning and lobbied the state government for several years, but he and the others may lose their legal challenges.[54]

Environmentalists now face a conundrum. Should they accept the pipeline and its potential for harm? Or should they advance to more aggressive tactics such as destroying property to forestall it and hope that a candidate friendlier to environmentalists is elected in 2020? Is nonlethal violence justified in the pursuit of environmental justice?

Critical Thinking

- How should society and governments react to aggressive environmental protest?
- How would you balance a protestor's First Amendment right of free speech, expression, and assembly with concern for public safety and protection of property?

When discussing the topic of sustainability as a function of responsible and sustainable business conduct, we consider not only environmental health but also public health. Polluting the environment is bad for public health, but so too are a wide variety of inherently dangerous products from alcohol to tobacco to guns to drugs. The World Health Organization estimates that alcohol is the cause of close to 7 percent of all deaths each year globally, or about 3.5 million people, and total global sales of alcohol are well over $1 trillion per year.[55] The question is whether society should allow businesses to market, sell, and profit from a product that causes so many deaths and creates a significant public health problem. The same question can be asked about tobacco, on which businesses make over half a trillion dollars annually and which the United States has struggled to regulate for years. Some businesses are acting on their own to rein in the sale or use of harmful products. In 2014, CVS, a drugstore and health care giant, chose to stop selling tobacco products, because such sales do not support its corporate mission.[56]

Few issues are the source of as much public debate as guns, but it is clear that gun violence in the United States is a major public health challenge. There are about 35,000 deaths per year in the United States due to firearms, and another 75,000 nonfatal firearm injuries. However, thousands of businesses profit from gun sales. Annual revenue in the gun and ammunition manufacturing industry is close to $14 billion, producing a profit of $1.5 billion, whereas the annual revenue of gun and ammunition stores is an additional $3 billion, resulting in a profit of $500 million.[57] Based on these facts, should the sale of guns remain relatively unregulated, or, in the interest of public health, should the government increase regulatory efforts in this area? On the corporate front, after the most recent fatal mass shooting at a high school in Parkland, Florida, several companies took action without waiting for the law to change. Dick's Sporting Goods announced it will no longer sell semi-automatic assault rifles, such as the AR-15, as has Kroger, which owns Fred Meyer stores. Walmart has announced it will no longer sell guns to anyone under twenty-one years of age.

Another pressing social issue is opioid abuse. In 2016, there were approximately sixty thousand deaths due to drug overdoses, almost double the number of gun deaths. Profits from the sale of these drugs are in the tens of billions of dollars, and the pharmaceutical industry spends $100 million lobbying Congress not to regulate it more stringently. Some local government entities are suing opioid drug manufacturers,[58] and, in the private sector, CVS recently announced it would now fill opioid prescriptions with supplies for only seven days. While opioids are legal and often legitimately prescribed for pain management, a large part of the problem is that they are also overprescribed.[59] Given these facts, should pharmaceutical corporations be allowed to profit from this product? What ethical or legal responsibilities do those in the medical community have for the problem?

Although sustainability discussions justifiably focus on the protection of human life and public health issues, a related ethical issue close to the hearts of many citizens is animal rights. Businesses have begun to take notice of public demands in this area, as evidenced by a 2017 *Fortune* article about the Yoox Net-a-Porter Group.[60]

Net-a-Porter is a large, online retailer (with $2 billion/year in sales) that markets top-line brands such as Prada, Gucci, and Michael Kors. After a survey of its customers showed that a significant majority want the company to forgo fur products, it decided to forbid the use of fur in its entire line. Other big-name brands such as Armani, Hugo Boss, North Face, Nautica, and Timberland have followed Net-a-Porter's lead and recently announced fur-free policies.

Related developments are taking place in the cosmetics and food industries. Many cosmetics companies have announced cruelty-free product testing policies for products ranging from makeup to hairspray. In the food industry, the U.S. Department of Agriculture recently reported that cage-free eggs account for approximately one-quarter of the wholesale shell egg market.[61] Why? Sales and profits are the answer, along with sustainability. According to research conducted by Walmart, over 75 percent of the retail giant's customers said they would be more likely to shop at a store that improves its policies related to animal welfare. Thus, not only Walmart but also supermarket chains such as Kroger have announced the gradual implementation of cage-free egg-buying policies, as have fast food giants such as McDonald's and Burger King.[62] Such changes are often prompted, if not driven, by the influence of informed consumer stakeholders who are demanding the products they want to buy.

The Revolving Door between Government Regulation and the Private Sector

While private companies may take the initiative in response to public demand, and intergovernmental cooperation can accomplish many good things, sometimes the solution is for a private-sector company or industry to work directly with the government, as we saw with the example of Space X. Given the pressure on federal, state, and local agencies to reduce their budgets, many have increasingly turned to public-private partnerships, or P3s, as a means to solve problems.

Sometimes, however, the relationship between business and government can become too close, as when executives from the private sector leave their jobs to work for government agencies, becoming the regulators rather than the regulated, and then return to industry in a kind of "revolving door" effect. For example, Goldman Sachs, one of the world's largest financial services firms, has seen many of its executives take senior leadership positions in the presidential administrations of both Democrats and Republicans, including the present secretary of the treasury, Steven Mnuchin. The same trend is occurring on a global level; Mario Draghi, the president of the European Central Bank, was previously a vice chair and managing director of Goldman Sachs International, and Mark Carney, the governor of the Bank of England, worked for Goldman Sachs as well. The large number of executives from one of the biggest investment banks in the world moving in and out of government service causes some critics to warn of the "fox guarding the hen house" approach to regulation. Is the relationship between government and the private sector sometimes too cozy? Does this revolving door in fact result in bad policy?

Of course, it would be incorrect to assume, because multiple executives of a firm landed in government positions, that the firm is automatically guilty of wrongdoing. Goldman Sachs has created several programs with ethical goals. The company encourages clients to consider environmental and sustainability issues, and it backs green bonds, which are used to fund projects that have positive environmental and/or climate benefits. In truth, our government would find it difficult to function without the expertise from the private sector supplementing that of the public sector in public service positions.

Research by the Federal Reserve Bank of Kansas City demonstrates how regulation and legislation in this area must strike a balance between encouraging and discouraging executives from the private sector to serve in high-level government positions. Our system of government service does not want to run the risk of undermining "the ability of regulatory agencies to seek and retain top level talent, but at the same time we do not want to impair the independence of government policy-makers."[63]

A quick look at some figures indicates the scope of the problem. A 2008 General Accounting Office survey of fifty large defense contractors revealed that almost ninety thousand people who had left the Department of Defense in the preceding eight years were afterwards employed by private-sector companies doing business with the government as contractors.[64] While legal restrictions exist to limit the revolving door effect, most relate only to direct government contracting. Private-sector companies seeking to acquire talent by hiring former employees of the federal government must be aware of the statutory and regulatory restrictions and their associated penalties.

One rule says former senior government employees may not make any communication with or appearance before their former agency, with the intent to influence the agency, for one year after leaving service. The ban is extended to two years for certain "very senior" officials.[65] Penalties for violations can include fines of up to $50,000 per violation and/or twice the amount of compensation received. On a company level, the penalty can be up to $500,000 per violation and/or twice the amount of the contract. Moreover, individuals who intentionally violate the law may be subject to criminal penalties, which can include up to five years in jail.

In 2009, shortly after he took office, President Obama issued an executive order requiring all executive agency appointees to take an ethics pledge as a prerequisite for accepting appointment. The pledge included a lobbying ban and restrictions on appointees and lobbyists entering and leaving the government. For instance, appointees entering the government had to agree not to participate in any matter both "directly and substantially" related to their former employer or clients for two years.[66] However, because these ethical restrictions were implemented by way of executive order, not federal statute, they may vary from president to president. Ethical questions have been raised about traditional conflict of interest concepts in the present administration, because people currently serving in it have retained ownership of private companies rather than selling them or placing them in blind trusts.

Of course, the relationship between government and business is an important one, and expertise in a field can be extremely valuable to both sides in a business-government partnership. However, this collaboration should be transparent and subject to public scrutiny, as noted by the Brookings Institution, one of the oldest nonprofit public policy think tanks. In a report entitled "Amateur Government: When Political Appointees Manage the Federal Bureaucracy," the Institution warns against the potential for conflicts of interest stemming from allowing too many industry executives to move into government service, set overtly pro-industry policies, and then go back to their higher-paying, private-sector jobs. The key is to seek a balance.[67]

Government Regulation and the Constitution

Over the past decade, many politicians have run for office on a platform of reducing government regulation. There are at least two closely related positions on reducing federal government regulation. The first is essentially a **states' rights** position that seeks to limit the powers of the federal government to those very specifically enumerated in the Constitution. It is based on principles embodied in the Tenth Amendment and on a narrow interpretation of the Commerce Clause. The Tenth Amendment reserves to the states any right not specifically delegated to the federal government. The **Commerce Clause** is the part of the Constitution that gives the federal government the right to regulate commerce between states.

The second, related view of government regulation holds that "less is better" at all levels, whether state or federal. Its followers simply seek to reduce the size of government and regulation at every level. Some might attribute this position to a libertarian or "small government" philosophy.

These two philosophies might be characterized as less government regulation vs. no government regulation, other than military defense. The preference for state regulation is often based on a belief in the business community that many states are softer on regulation that the federal government, or that states are closer to the problems businesses face and are more efficient at addressing them. However, there is little clear evidence that one branch of government is more efficient than another. The real challenge is weighing the benefits of regulation against the costs, and finding the right balance between over- and under-regulation. Weak regulation can allow a business to cut corners. For instance, auto emission regulations intended to go into effect by certain dates have been delayed multiple times during the 1980s and the early 2000s. The Obama administration announced plans to enforce tougher rules, but the current administration has said it plans to delay implementation. Auto emission regulations have become politically charged, constantly changing depending on the party in power, and some states have responded with their own legislation instead of waiting for the federal stalemate to end. Regulation that is consistently enforced in the effort to achieve the long-term goal, such as cleaner air, is preferable to a moving target.

A third position is that government is not necessarily a bad thing. Such a "federalist" philosophy might assert that centralized government provides an array of benefits for citizens. For example, in the *Federalist Papers*, Alexander Hamilton emphasized that a well-intentioned central government was not the enemy of liberty but rather the best means of securing the rights achieved through the passage of the Constitution. He and others also pointed out an advantage of federal over state government—a large republic such as the United States would actually benefit from a larger electorate and a larger pool of qualified leaders, and competing state and regional interests would be more balanced under federal regulation.

Acceptance of one or the other of these philosophies may lean an administration towards more or less regulation, as well as calibrating its response to aggressive lobbying by industries seeking to reduce regulation they view as burdensome. The results for the environment and/or public health can sometimes be disastrous.

CASES FROM THE REAL WORLD

BP Deepwater Horizon Oil Spill and Government Regulation

The company that owned and operated the Deepwater Horizon drilling rig, Transocean Ltd., contracted in 2010 with BP to drill a very deep water offshore oil well in the Gulf of Mexico, in a field called the Macondo. The drilling operation failed and ultimately led to an infamous environmental and human disaster called the Deepwater Horizon spill that has since been the subject of intense scrutiny and litigation.[68] Eleven workers were killed and seventeen were injured, and at least five million barrels of oil poured into the ocean in the largest such spill in history. The environmental harm was epic in scale (Figure 4.11). Five years later, tar balls still dotted the beach. Oil buried beneath the sand offshore still gets pushed toward the beach whenever the surf is rough. Offshore islands have disappeared because the mangrove roots were coated in oil, killing the trees. Once the mangrove root framework that holds the land together was destroyed, the islands were washed away within a few years. Louisiana was already losing land at a concerning pace, and more has been lost since the spill. Scientists confirm that the disaster has accelerated the pace of the loss.[69]

Figure 4.11 The 2010 Deepwater Horizon oil rig fire and resulting river of oil in the Gulf of Mexico. (credit left: modification of "Deepwater Horizon offshore drilling unit on fire" by the US Coast Guard/ Wikimedia Commons, Public Domain; credit right: modification of "Defense.gov photo essay 100506-N-6436W-023" by Michael B. Watkins/Wikimedia Commons, Public Domain)

Many question whether more regulation and a better relationship between regulators and the oil industry might have prevented the Deepwater Horizon disaster. Transocean, the rig owner/operator, did not install a relatively inexpensive safety device, an acoustically triggered shutoff valve, which most experts agree could have stopped the flow of oil from the well into the Gulf. Congress had not mandated such a device, largely as a result of oil industry lobbying, and since it wasn't required, BP and Transocean were free to act as they pleased.

Other nations with offshore drilling activities, such as Norway and Brazil, mandate that all oil rigs be equipped with backup acoustically triggered shutoff valves as a safety measure. Norway has a stellar reputation for safety related to its North Sea offshore drilling. Two-thirds of Statoil, its largest oil company, is owned by the government, and, as a result, the company does not lobby the government for weakened regulation. The same is true of Petrobras, the Brazilian oil company.[70] Partial government ownership makes public/private-sector cooperation more likely and is therefore likely to improve safety as well.

Critical Thinking

- Should the U.S. government pass a law requiring the use of the automatic shutoff valves on oil rigs in its waters?
- Should privately owned oil companies be allowed to lobby against safety regulations?
- Research whether public attitudes in the United States support stronger offshore drilling safety regulations. What do you think accounts for your findings?

Questions of regulation and political influence have become even more sensitive in recent years, following the decision in *Citizens United v. Federal Election Commission* (2010).[71] In **Citizens United**, the U.S. Supreme Court ruled 5–4 that laws preventing corporations from using general treasury funds for political advertising violated the First Amendment's guarantee of freedom of speech. In other words, the government may not prevent corporations from spending money to support or oppose candidates in elections. With this decision, the Court invalidated numerous campaign finance reform laws. Many commentators think the decision opened the floodgates for special-interest groups to spend without limit in U.S. elections.

LINK TO LEARNING

Visit the U.S. Supreme Court case website (https://openstaxcollege.org/l/53OyezCase) named Oyez. Read the *Citizens United* case, both the majority decision and the minority dissents. Judicial language can be a bit difficult to understand, so you may have to read it twice, but it's worth it, because of the importance of the case.

What does *Citizens United* mean for businesses? Business entities may now seek to persuade the voting public by spending an unlimited amount of money on political ads, whether through social media or traditional print and broadcast media. Businesses opposed to government regulation can spend without limit to help elect candidates whose position on reduced regulation is the same as theirs, thereby increasing the pressure on Congress to deregulate. Many think the profusion of money in U.S. politics is one cause of the partisan divide that often paralyzes the legislative branch and unduly influences the executive branch.

One of the sponsors of the corporate governance law known as the Sarbanes-Oxley Act (SOX), Senator Paul Sarbanes (D-MD), is among those who would like to see financial limits on business lobbying groups and political action committees, several of which are attempting to repeal current regulations such as SOX, which is tough on business fraud. **Sarbanes-Oxley**, passed in 2002 in response to several highly publicized corporate fraud cases that took down companies such as Enron and WorldCom, mandates reporting transparency in areas ranging from finance to accounting to supply chain activities. Essentially, it ensures that we now consider it both unethical *and* illegal to deceive shareholders, creditors, and the public at large.

Sarbanes-Oxley applies to publicly traded companies and is enforced by the Securities and Exchange Commission. It covers multiple topics such as the independence of corporate boards and outside certified public accounting firms that audit corporations. The law also makes the CEO and CFO personally responsible for errors in annual audits—thus making it harder to "cook the books." Finally, it prohibits company loans to executives and grants protection to whistleblowers.

Some critics thought compliance with SOX might be too costly. However, after more than a decade of enforcement, it is now clear to most that Sarbanes-Oxley was, and is, a necessary regulatory step. It has allowed for significant progress to be made in slowing down the kind of unethical conduct that led to the Enron fraud. Although SOX technically applies only to publicly traded companies, many private companies also adopt SOX-style internal controls and transparency, as do not-for-profits such as universities and hospitals.

Key Terms

business judgment rule the principle that officers, directors, and managers of a corporation are not liable for losses incurred when the evidence demonstrates that decisions were reasonable and made in good faith

cap and trade a system that limits greenhouse gas emissions by companies while allowing them to buy and sell pollution allowances

carbon footprint the amount of carbon dioxide and other carbon compounds released by the consumption of fossil fuels

carbon tax a pay-to-pollute system in which those who discharge carbon into the air pay a fee or tax

Citizens United a 2010 Supreme Court ruling in favor of unlimited spending by individuals and corporations on political campaigns

Commerce Clause an enumerated power listed in the Constitution giving the federal government the right to regulate commerce between states

corporate personhood the legal doctrine holding that a corporation, separate and apart from the people who are its owners and managers, has some of the same legal rights and responsibilities enjoyed by natural persons

fiduciary duty a very high level of legal responsibility owed by those who manage someone else's money, which includes the duties of care and loyalty

limited liability a business owner's protection against loss of personal assets, granted with corporate status

moral minimum the minimal actions or practices a business must undertake to satisfy the base threshold for acting ethically

quid pro quo the tradeoff someone makes in return for getting something of value; from the Latin meaning *this for that*

Sarbanes-Oxley legislation passed in 2002 that mandates reporting transparency by businesses in areas ranging from finance to accounting to supply chain activities

shareholder primacy a company's duty to maximize profits for stockholders

states' rights a view that states should have more governing authority than the federal government, based on the Tenth Amendment, which reserves to the states any right not specifically delegated to the federal government

sustainability a long-term approach to the interaction between business activity and societal impact on the environment and other stakeholders

tragedy of the commons an economy theory highlighting the human tendency to use as much of a free natural resource as wanted without regard for others' needs or for long-term environmental effects or issues

Summary

4.1 Corporate Law and Corporate Responsibility

While some argue that corporations have a primary duty to maximize profits for the benefit of shareholders, others assert that businesses have a duty to the society in which they operate, a duty that serves as the basis of the CSR philosophy. Many court cases have addressed the issue, but it has not been conclusively resolved.

Despite the ongoing ethical debate, being a good corporate citizen is a goal toward which most contemporary corporations strive. An effective CSR policy usually means that companies have to commit to both an internal

and external approach to ethics. Corporate social responsibility and good corporate governance are in reality just two sides of the very same coin. Social responsibility does not mean lower profitability.

4.2 Sustainability: Business and the Environment

Adopting sustainability as a strategy means protecting the environment. Society has an interest in the long-term survival, indeed the flourishing, of ecological habitats and natural resources, and we ask and expect companies to respect this societal goal in their business activities.

When analyzing what a business owes society in return for the freedom to extract our natural resources, we must balance development and preservation. It may be easy to say from afar that a business should cut back on how much it pollutes the air, but what happens when that means cutting back on fossil fuel use and transitioning to electric vehicles, a choice that affects everyone on a personal level?

4.3 Government and the Private Sector

One challenge in a free enterprise system is balancing the need for government regulation and private-sector corporate managers' need for independence in running their businesses. The Sarbanes-Oxley Act tries to strike this balance by mandating transparency in corporate governance. This debate also includes the question whether businesses operating in the private sector ought to do public good on their own, regardless of whether the government mandates it. For example, many companies make a commitment to keep the environment clean, and to do so by going above and beyond what the law requires.

Assessment Questions

1. True or false? Corporations that embrace CSR policies consistently produce a lower rate of return on investment for shareholders.

2. True or false? Milton Friedman's economic philosophy advocates increased government regulation to ensure that corporations are socially responsible.

3. Which of the following is *not* true?
   A.   Shareholder primacy is the clear legal precedent in the United States.
   B.   Maximizing shareholder profits is a legitimate goal of management.
   C.   Dividends are paid out of corporate profits.
   D.   Companies that pursue CSR policies can also be profitable.

4. Industries like to be in control of their own destiny and as a result prefer self-regulation to laws imposed by governments. Self-regulation is often _____.
   A.   based on external codes of conduct
   B.   enforced by the courts
   C.   in conflict with common law
   D.   less costly for firms than government regulation

5. Identify two benefits for a company following a policy of corporate social responsibility (CSR).

6. What is earth jurisprudence?

7. Which of the following best describes the tragedy of the commons?

    A. People are always willing to sacrifice for the good of society.

    B. People are likely to use all the natural resources they want without regard to others.

    C. The common good of the people is a popular corporate goal.

    D. Tragedies occur when there is too much government regulation.

8. ISOs are sustainability standards for businesses _____.

    A. promulgated by the state government

    B. promulgated by the federal government

    C. promulgated by the World Trade Organization

    D. none of the above

9. True or false? If environmental harm is discovered, the business entity causing it is frequently held liable by both the government and the victims of the harm in separate proceedings.

10. Which of the following is a potentially effective way to reduce global warming?

    A. build more coal-burning power plants

    B. build more diesel-burning cars

    C. implement a carbon tax

    D. implement tax-free gasoline

11. True or false? The law prohibits all executives from serving in senior government posts and then leaving to go back to work for the same company in the private sector.

12. True or false? Air pollution is regulated by three levels of government: local, state, and federal.

13. Which of the following is true?

    A. Very few business executives have ever left private jobs to go into government service.

    B. Most government regulatory agencies are funded by donations.

    C. Numerous executives have left Goldman Sachs to go to work for the government.

    D. Few people leave government service to go into the private sector.

14. Which of the following constitutional provisions gives regulatory power to the federal government?

    A. First Amendment

    B. Tenth Amendment

    C. Commerce Clause

    D. Supremacy Clause

15. The *Citizens United* case _____.

    A. upheld existing law limiting spending on behalf of political candidates

    B. overturned existing law

    C. sent the case back to the lower court to be re-tried

    D. created more restrictive limits on political spending

16. What Amendment was at the center of the *Citizens United* case? Explain.

Endnotes

1.   Patrick Moorhead, "Cisco's CSR Program under CEO Chuck Robbins Is Flourishing," *Forbes*, March 9, 2016. https://www.forbes.com/sites/patrickmoorhead/2016/03/09/ciscos-csr-program-under-ceo-chuck-robbins-is-flourishing/#46e003c2574e.

2.   Dodge v. Ford Motor Company, 204 Mich. 459, 170 N.W. 668 (Mich. 1919).

3.   Dodge v. Ford Motor Company, 204 Mich. 459, 170 N.W. 668 (Mich. 1919).

4. Dodge v. Ford Motor Company, 204 Mich. 459, 170 N.W. 668 (Mich. 1919).
5. Shlensky v. Wrigley, 237 N.E. 2d 776 (Ill. App. 1968).
6. Shlensky v. Wrigley, 237 N.E. 2d 776 (Ill. App. 1968).
7. Burwell v. Hobby Lobby, 573 U.S. _____ (2014).
8. Burwell v. Hobby Lobby, 573 U.S. _____ (2014).
9. Burwell v. Hobby Lobby, 573 U.S. _____ (2014).
10. "Corporate Social Responsibility: The Halo Effect," *The Economist*, June 25, 2015. https://www.economist.com/news/business/21656218-do-gooding-policies-help-firms-when-they-get-prosecuted-halo-effect.
11. Milton Friedman, *Capitalism and Freedom*. (Chicago: University of Chicago Press. 1963).
12. Lindsay Llewellyn, "Breaking Down the Business-Judgment Rule," *American Bar Association*, May 30, 2013. http://apps.americanbar.org/litigation/committees/commercial/articles/spring2013-0513-breaking-down-the-business-judgement-rule.html.
13. Stephen Bainbridge, "A Duty to Shareholder Value," Opinion Pages, *New York Times*, April 16, 2015. https://www.nytimes.com/roomfordebate/2015/04/16/what-are-corporations-obligations-to-shareholders/a-duty-to-shareholder-value.
14. Stephen Bainbridge, "A Duty to Shareholder Value," Opinion Pages, *New York Times*, April 16, 2015. https://www.nytimes.com/roomfordebate/2015/04/16/what-are-corporations-obligations-to-shareholders/a-duty-to-shareholder-value.
15. Lynn Stout, "Corporations Don't Have to Maximize Profits," Opinion Pages, *New York Times*, April 16, 2015. https://www.nytimes.com/roomfordebate/2015/04/16/what-are-corporations-obligations-to-shareholders/corporations-dont-have-to-maximize-profits.
16. Rick Wartzman, "What Peter Drucker Knew About 2020," *Harvard Business Review*, October 16, 2014. https://hbr.org/2014/10/what-peter-drucker-knew-about-2020.
17. Unilever. https://www.unilever.com/sustainable-living/values-and-values/.
18. Tracey Keys, et al., "Making the Most of Corporate Social Responsibility," *McKenzie Quarterly*, December 2009. https://www.mckinsey.com/global-themes/leadership/making-the-most-of-corporate-social-responsibility.
19. Calvert. https://www.calvert.com/.
20. H.J. Graham, *Everyman's Constitution*. (Madison: State Historical Society of Wisconsin, 1968). See also H.J. Graham, "The 'Conspiracy Theory' of the Fourteenth Amendment," *Yale Law Journal* 47, no. 3 (1938): 341–403. doi: 10.2307/791947.
21. "Ecuador Adopts Rights of Nature in Constitution," *The Rights of Nature*. https://therightsofnature.org/ecuador-rights/.
22. M. Triassi, et al., "Environmental Pollution from Illegal Waste Disposal and Health Effects," *Int J Environ Res Public Health* 12, no. 2 (2015): 1216–1236. doi: 10.3390/ijerph120201216.
23. Gwynn Guilford, *Quartz*, December 9, 2014. https://qz.com/308970/cruise-ships-dump-1-billion-tons-of-sewage-into-the-ocean-every-year/.
24. *State of the World 2010 Transforming Cultures from Consumerism to Sustainability*. Washington, DC: The Worldwatch Institute, 2010.
25. Rights of Nature, "Principles of Earth Jurisprudence." https://therightsofnature.org/principles-of-earth-jurisprudence/.
26. Garrett Hardin, "The Tragedy of the Commons," *Science* 162, no. 3859 (1968): 1243–1248. doi: 10.1126/science.162.3859.1243.
27. Jeff Kauflin, "The World's Most Sustainable Companies 2017," *Forbes*, January 17, 2017. https://www.forbes.com/sites/jeffkauflin/2017/01/17/the-worlds-most-sustainable-companies-2017/#2773f73a4e9d.
28. Corporate Knights, "2018 Global 100." http://www.corporateknights.com/reports/global-100/.
29. Jeff Kauflin, "The World's Most Sustainable Companies 2017," *Forbes*, January 17, 2017. https://www.forbes.com/sites/jeffkauflin/2017/01/17/the-worlds-most-sustainable-companies-2017/#2773f73a4e9d.
30. 3BLMedia, "2015 Cisco Corporate Social Responsibility Report: Supply Chain," 2015. http://3blmedia.com/News/2015-Cisco-Corporate-Social-Responsibility-Report-Supply-Chain.
31. McKinsey & Co., "Sustainability's Strategic Worth," 2016. http://csr-raadgivning.dk/wp-content/uploads/2016/02/Sustainabilitys-strategic-worth-McKinsey-Global-Survey-results-McKinsey-July-2014.pdf.
32. Paul Raleigh, "Corporate Social Responsibility: Beyond Financials," *Grant Thornton*, August 13, 2014. https://www.grantthornton.global/en/insights/articles/Corporate-social-responsibility/.
33. Jessica Lyons Hardcastle, "Dell's Flexible Work Programs Save $12M, Reduce GHGs," *Environmental Leader*, July 10, 2014. https://www.environmentalleader.com/2014/07/dells-flexible-work-programs-save-12m-reduce-ghgs/.
34. Knut Haanaes, "Making Sustainability Profitable," *Harvard Business Review*, March 2013. https://hbr.org/2013/03/making-sustainability-profitable.
35. Adam Wernick, "The U.S. Defense Department Takes Climate Change Seriously," Public Radio International, October 8, 2017. https://www.pri.org/stories/2017-10-08/us-defense-department-takes-climate-change-seriously.
36. Union of Concerned Scientists, "Global Warming Impacts." https://www.ucsusa.org/our-work/global-warming/science-and-impacts/global-warming-impacts#.WjQa11WnF0w.
37. Lucy P. Marcus, "Why Strong Ties between Business and Government Matter," *The Guardian*, January 4, 2016. https://www.theguardian.com/business/2016/jan/04/why-strong-ties-between-business-and-government-matter-r-and-d.
38. Union of Concerned Scientists, "Global Warming Impacts." https://www.ucsusa.org/our-work/global-warming/science-and-impacts/global-warming-impacts#.WjQa11WnF0w.
39. National Conference on State Legislatures, "State Plastic and Paper Bag Legislation," July 5, 2017. http://www.ncsl.org/research/environment-and-natural-resources/plastic-bag-legislation.aspx.
40. Elizabeth Chuck, "Hurricane Harvey: How Many Billions of Dollars in Damage Will Historic Storm Cost?" NBC News, August 30, 2017. https://www.nbcnews.com/storyline/hurricane-harvey/how-many-billions-damage-will-harvey-cost-s-anyone-s-n797521.
41. NASA, "Report on Climate Change," March 22, 2018. https://climate.nasa.gov/evidence/.
42. James Brooke, "Waste Dumpers Turning to West Africa," *New York Times*, July 17, 1998. http://www.nytimes.com/1988/07/17/world/waste-dumpers-turning-to-west-africa.html?pagewanted=all.
43. Financial Transparency Coalition, "Cross-border Dumping of Hazardous Waste," August 20, 2010. https://financialtransparency.org/hazardous-waste/.
44. Andrew Winston, "Business Owes the World Everything . . . and Nothing," *Harvard Business Review*, May 4, 2010. https://hbr.org/2010/05/business-owes-the-world-everyt.html.
45. Lew Harris, "Business Owes Significant Obligations to Society," *Newswise*, February 23, 2000. https://www.newswise.com/articles/business-owes-significant-obligations-to-society.
46. Climate Leadership Council, "The Four Pillars of Our Carbon Dividends Plan." https://www.clcouncil.org/our-plan/.
47. John Schwartz, "Exxon Mobil Lends Its Support to a Carbon Tax Proposal," *New York Times*, June 20, 2017. https://www.nytimes.com/2017/06/20/science/exxon-carbon-tax.html.
48. John Schwartz, "Exxon Mobil Lends Its Support to a Carbon Tax Proposal," *New York Times*, June 20, 2017. https://www.nytimes.com/2017/06/20/science/exxon-carbon-tax.html.
49. Katy Lederer, "Why Can't Republicans Support a Carbon Tax?" *The New Yorker*, November 9, 2015. https://www.newyorker.com/business/

currency/why-cant-republicans-support-a-carbon-tax.
50. Lauren Rosenbaum, "The growing complexity of social and economic challenges is driving new, innovative forms of collaboration between governments and businesses." *Deloitte*, March, 19, 2013. https://www2.deloitte.com/insights/us/en/focus/business-trends/2013/partnerships-for-the-future.html.
51. U.S. Department of Justice, "Under Agreement with United States and State of Texas, Vopak to Reduce Hazardous Air Pollution at Chemical Storage Facility," May 17, 2017. https://www.justice.gov/opa/pr/under-agreement-united-states-and-state-texas-vopak-reduce-hazardous-air-pollution-chemical.
52. U.S. Department of Justice, "State-Federal Cooperation in Environmental Enforcement," May 24, 2017. https://www.justice.gov/archives/opa/blog/state-federal-cooperation-environmental-enforcement.
53. Ben Wolfgang, "Environmentalists, Tribes Promise Dakota Access-style Camps, Protests to Stop Keystone XL Pipeline," *The Washington Times*, March 24, 2017. http://www.washingtontimes.com/news/2017/mar/24/keystone-xl-pipeline-environmentalists-tribes-prom/.
54. Oliver Laughland and Laurence Mathieu-Léger, "Keystone Pipeline Defiance Triggers Further Assault on Citizens' Rights," *The Guardian*, May 3, 2017. https://www.theguardian.com/us-news/2017/may/03/keystone-pipeline-protests-land-rights-south-dakota.
55. World Health Organization, "Global Status Report on Alcohol and Health," 2011. http://www.who.int/substance_abuse/publications/global_alcohol_report/msbgsruprofiles.pdf.
56. Larry Merlo, "Message from Larry Merlo, President and CEO," February 5, 2014. https://cvshealth.com/thought-leadership/message-from-larry-merlo-president-and-ceo.
57. Louis Jacobson, "Counting Up How Much the NRA Spends on Campaigns and Lobbying," *Politifact*, October 11, 2017. http://www.politifact.com/truth-o-meter/article/2017/oct/11/counting-up-how-much-nra-spends/.
58. Mattie Quinn, "The Opioid Files: Hundreds of States and Cities Are Suing Drug Companies," *Governing*, November 13, 2017. http://www.governing.com/topics/health-human-services/gov-opioid-lawsuits-companies-states-cities.html.
59. Owen Amos, "Why Opioids Are Such an American Problem?" *BBC News*, October 25, 2017. http://www.bbc.com/news/world-us-canada-41701718.
60. Matthew Prescott, "Why Animal Cruelty Is Bad Business," *Fortune*, June 23, 2017. http://fortune.com/2017/06/23/animal-cruelty-stop-human-society-welfare-businesses-companies/.
61. "Egg Markets Overview," USDA AMS Agricultural Analytics Division, July 20, 2018. https://www.ams.usda.gov/sites/default/files/media/Egg%20Markets%20Overview.pdf.
62. Matthew Prescott, "Why Animal Cruelty Is Bad Business," *Fortune*, June 23, 2017. http://fortune.com/2017/06/23/animal-cruelty-stop-human-society-welfare-businesses-companies/.
63. Janet Yellen, "Financial Stability a Decade after the Onset of the Crisis," *Symposium Federal Reserve Bank of Kansas City*, August 25, 2017. https://www.federalreserve.gov/newsevents/speech/yellen20170825a.htm.
64. Dave Nadler and Ryan P. McGovern, "Top Ten Things Every Government Contractor Should Know about Post-Government Employment and 'Revolving Door' Restrictions," Association of Corporate Counsel, September 2015. http://www.acc.com/_cs_upload/vl/membersonly/InfoPAK/584525_11.pdf.
65. Dave Nadler and Ryan P. McGovern, "Top Ten Things Every Government Contractor Should Know about Post-Government Employment and 'Revolving Door' Restrictions," Association of Corporate Counsel, June 18, 2013. http://www.acc.com/legalresources/publications/topten/tttegcskapeardr.cfm?bcsi-ac-a70e1c0dc9ec8868=2719437500000002IZDw7%2FkDT%2FHOA2foH2ESHqJFX%2FQEYQAAAgAAAD+gbAGEAwAAUgAAAHsnLwA.
66. Dave Nadler and Ryan P. McGovern, "Top Ten Things Every Government Contractor Should Know about Post-Government Employment and 'Revolving Door' Restrictions," Association of Corporate Counsel, June 18, 2013.
67. David M. Cohen, "Amateur Government: When Political Appointees Manage the Federal Bureaucracy," The Brookings Institution, 1996. https://www.brookings.edu/wp-content/uploads/2016/06/amateur.pdf.
68. EPA, "Deepwater Horizon – BP Gulf of Mexico Oil Spill." https://www.epa.gov/enforcement/deepwater-horizon-bp-gulf-mexico-oil-spill.
69. Debbie Elliott, "5 Years after BP Oil Spill, Effects Linger and Recovery Is Slow," NPR, April 20, 2015. https://www.npr.org/2015/04/20/400374744/5-years-after-bp-oil-spill-effects-linger-and-recovery-is-slow
70. Russell Gold, et al., "Leaking Oil Well Lacked Safeguard Device," *Wall Street Journal*, April 28, 2010. https://www.wsj.com/articles/SB10001424052748704423504575212031417936798.
71. Citizens United v. Federal Election Commission, 558 U.S. 310 (2010).

The Impact of Culture and Time on Business Ethics

Figure 5.1 Business ethics do not exist in a vacuum. They are a reflection of the underlying values of a society and the way society lives out those values over time. This experience is captured in language, culture, religious traditions, and modes of thinking, all of which have varied throughout history and influence the conduct of business in a range of ways. (credit: modification of "atlas close up dark dirty" by Aaditya Arora/Pexels, CC0)

Chapter Outline

5.1 The Relationship between Business Ethics and Culture

5.2 Business Ethics over Time

5.3 The Influence of Geography and Religion

5.4 Are the Values Central to Business Ethics Universal?

Introduction

Ethics is a construct of considerable significance to human beings. Some suggest ethics emerged to allow families and clans to cooperate in harsh environments. Others point to its use in governing trade and commerce, even simple bartering. Still others say ethical behavior is wired into the cognitive structures of the brain, explaining why we find codes of ethics and morality in texts as diverse as the Code of Hammurabi (a Babylonian code of law nearly four thousand years old), the Bible, the Napoleonic Code, and *The Analects of Confucius*, all of which outline ways for people to live together in society.

Whatever its origin, ethics has almost certainly existed throughout human time and varied with language, culture, history, and geography (Figure 5.1). Are there underlying values that transcend time and place, however? If so, do the protocols of business ethics embody these values? For instance, we see respect for others in Dubai, where tea accompanies negotiations; in Tokyo, where formal words and bows come first; and in Lima, where polite inquiries about the family precede business. Is respect, therefore, a universal value?

In short, to what degree is any code of business ethics conditioned by culture, time, and geography? Given that individuals are responsible only for their own behavior, is it possible for business ethics to be universal?

5.1 | The Relationship between Business Ethics and Culture

Learning Objectives

By the end of this section, you will be able to:

- Describe the processes of acculturation and enculturation
- Explain the interaction of business and culture from an ethical perspective
- Analyze how consumerism and the global marketplace might challenge the belief system of an organization

It has been said that English is the language of money and, for that reason, has become the language of business, finance, trade, communication, and travel. As such, English carries with it the values and assumptions of its native speakers around the world. But not all cultures share these assumptions, at least not implicitly. The sick leave or vacation policies of a British investment bank, for instance, may vary greatly from those of a shoe manufacturer in Laos. Because business and capitalism as conducted today have evolved primarily from European origins and profits are measured against Western standards like the U.S. dollar, the ethics that emerges from them is also beholden primarily (but not exclusively) to Western conceptions of behavior. The challenge for business leaders everywhere is to draw out the values of local cultures and integrate the best of those into their management models. The opportunities for doing so are enormous given the growing impact of China, India, Russia, and Brazil in global commerce. The cultures of these countries will affect the dominant business model, possibly even defining new ethical standards.

Business Encounters Culture

To understand the influence of culture on business ethics, it is essential to understand the concepts of enculturation and acculturation. In its most basic anthropological sense, **enculturation** refers to the process by which humans learn the rules, customs, skills, and values to participate in a society. In other words, no one is born with culture; all humans, regardless of their origin, have to learn what is considered appropriate behavior in their surrounding cultures. Whereas enculturation is the acquisition of any society's norms and values, **acculturation** refers specifically to the cultural transmission and socialization process that stems from cultural exchange. The effects of this blending of cultures appear in both the native (original) culture and the host (adopted) culture. Historically, acculturation has often been the result of military or political conquest. Today, it also comes about through economic development and the worldwide reach of the media.

One of the earliest real estate deals in the New World exemplifies the complexity that results when different cultures, experiences, and ethical codes come into contact. No deed of sale remains, so it is difficult to tell exactly what happened in May 1626 in what is now Manhattan, but historians agree that some kind of transaction took place between the Dutch West India Company, represented by Pieter Minuit, the newly appointed director-general of the New Netherland colony, and the Lenape, a Native American tribe (Figure 5.2). Which exact Lenape tribe is unknown; its members may have been simply passing through Manhattan and could have been the Canarsee, who lived in what is today southern Brooklyn.[1] Legend has it that the Dutch bought Manhattan island for $24 worth of beads and trinkets, but some historians believe the natives granted the Dutch only fishing and hunting rights and not outright ownership. Furthermore, the price, acknowledged as "sixty guilders" (about $1000 today), could actually represent the value of items such as · farming tools, muskets, gun powder, kettles, axes, knives, and clothing offered by the Dutch. Clearly, the reality was more nuanced than the legend.[2]

Figure 5.2 The 1626 purchase of Manhattan as depicted by Alfred Fredericks in *The Popular Science Monthly* of 1909. (credit: "The Purchase of Manhattan Island" by "Ineuw"/Wikimedia Commons, Public Domain)

The "purchase" of Manhattan is an excellent case study of an encounter between two vastly different cultures, worldviews, histories, and experiences of reality, all within a single geographic area. Although it is a misconception that the native peoples of what would become the United States did not own property or value individual possession, it is nevertheless true that their approach to property was more fluid than that of the Dutch and of later settlers like the English, who regarded property as a fixed commodity that could be owned and transferred to others. These differences, as well as enforced taxation, eventually led to war between the Dutch and several Native American tribes.[3] European colonization only exacerbated hostilities and misunderstandings, not merely about how to conduct business but also about how to live together in harmony.

LINK TO LEARNING

For more information, read this article about the Manhattan purchase and the encounter between European and Native American cultures (https://openstax.org/l/53Manhattan) and also this article about Peter Minuit (https://openstax.org/l/53PeterMinuit) and his involvement. What unexamined assumptions by both parties led to problems between them?

Two major conditions affect the relationship between business and culture. The first is that business is not culturally neutral. Today, it typically displays a mindset that is Western and primarily English-speaking and is reinforced by the enculturation process of Western nations, which tends to emphasize individualism and competition. In this tradition, business is defined as the exchange of goods and services in a dedicated market for the purpose of commerce and creating value for its owners and investors. Thus, business is not open ended but rather directed toward a specific goal and supported by beliefs about labor, ownership, property, and rights.

In the West, we typically think of these beliefs in Western terms. This worldview explains the misunderstanding between Minuit, who assumed he was buying Manhattan, and the tribal leaders, who may have had in mind nothing of the sort but instead believed they were granting some use rights. The point is that a particular understanding of and approach to business are already givens in any particular culture. Businesspeople who work across cultures in effect have entered the theater in the middle of the movie, and often they must perform the translation work of business to put their understanding and approach into local cultural idioms. One example of this is the fact that you might find *sambal* chili sauce in an Indonesian McDonald's in place of Heinz ketchup, but the restaurant, nevertheless, is a McDonald's.

The second condition that affects the relationship between business and culture is more complex because it reflects an evolving view of business in which the purpose is not solely generating wealth but also balancing profitability and responsibility to the public interest and the planet. In this view, which has developed as a result of political change and economic globalization, organizations comply with legal and economic regulations but then go beyond them to effect social change and sometimes even social justice.[4] The dominant manufacture-production-marketing-consumption model is changing to meet the demands of an increasing global population and finite resources. No longer can an organization maintain a purely bottom-line mentality; now it must consider ethics, and, therefore, social responsibility and sustainability, throughout its entire operation. As a result, local cultures are assuming a more aggressive role in defining their relationship with business prevalent in their regions.

Had this change taken place four centuries ago, that transaction in Manhattan might have gone a little differently. However, working across cultures can also create challenging ethical dilemmas, especially in regions where corruption is commonplace. A number of companies have experienced this problem, and globalization will likely only increase its incidence.

CASES FROM THE REAL WORLD

Petrobras

If you were to do a top-ten list of the world's greatest corruption scandals, the problems of Petrobras (*Petróleo Brasileiro*) in Brazil surely would make the list. The majority state-owned petroleum conglomerate was a party to a multibillion-dollar scandal in which company executives received bribes and kickbacks from contractors in exchange for lucrative construction and drilling contracts. The contractors paid Petrobras executives upward of five percent of the contract amount, which was funneled back into slush funds. The slush funds, in turn, paid for the election campaigns of certain members of the ruling political party, *Partido dos Trabalhadores*, or Workers Party, as well as for luxury items like race cars, jewelry, Rolex watches, yachts, wine, and art.[5]

The original investigation, known as Operation Car Wash (*Lava Jato*), began in 2014 at a gas station and car wash in Brasília, where money was being laundered. It has since expanded to include scrutiny of senators, government officials, and the former president of the republic, Luiz Inácio Lula da Silva. The probe also contributed to the impeachment and removal of Lula's successor, Dilma Rousseff. Lula and Rousseff are members of the Workers Party. The case is complex, revealing Chinese suppliers, Swiss bank accounts where money was hidden from Brazilian authorities, and wire transfers that went through New York City and caught the eye of the U.S. Department of Justice. In early 2017, the Brazilian Supreme Court justice in charge of the investigation and prosecution was mysteriously killed in a plane crash.

It is hard to imagine a more tragic example of systemic breakdown and individual vice. The loss of trust in government and the economy still affects ordinary Brazilians. Meanwhile, the investigation continues.

Critical Thinking

- Is there any aspect of the case where you think preventive measures could have been taken either by management or government? How would they have worked?
- Do you think this case represents an example of a culture with different business ethics than those practiced in the United States? Why or why not? How might corporations with international locations adjust for this type of issue?

LINK TO LEARNING

Read this article about the Petrobras case (https://openstax.org/l/53Petrobras) to learn more.

Balancing Beliefs

What about the ethical dimensions of a business in a developed country engaging in commerce in an environment where corruption might be more rampant than at home? How can an organization remain true to its mission and what it believes about itself while honoring local customs and ethical standards? The question is significant because it goes to the heart of the organization's values, its operations, and its internal culture. What must a business do to engage with local culture while still fulfilling its purpose, whether managers see that purpose as profitability, social responsibility, or a balance between the two?

Most business organizations hold three kinds of beliefs about themselves. The first identifies the purpose of business itself. In recent years, this purpose has come to be the creation not just of shareholder wealth but also of economic or personal value for workers, communities, and investors.[6] The second belief defines the organization's mission, which encapsulates its purpose. Most organizations maintain some form of mission statement. For instance, although IBM did away with its formal mission statement in 2003, its underlying beliefs about itself have remained intact since its founding in 1911. These are (1) dedication to client success, (2) innovation that matters (for IBM and the world), and (3) trust and personal responsibility in all relationships.[7] President and chief executive officer (CEO) Ginni Rometty stated the company "remain[s] dedicated to leading the world into a more prosperous and progressive future; to creating a world that is fairer, more diverse, more tolerant, more just."[8]

LINK TO LEARNING

Johnson & Johnson was one of the first companies to write a formal mission statement, and it is one that continues to earn praise. This statement has been embraced by several succeeding CEOs at the company, illustrating that a firm's mission statement can have a value that extends beyond its authors to serve many generations of managers and workers. Read Johnson & Johnson's mission statement (https://openstax.org/l/53Johnson) to learn more.

Finally, businesses also go through the process of enculturation; as a result, they have certain beliefs about themselves, drawn from the customs, language, history, religion, and ethics of the culture in which they are formed. One example of a company whose ethics and ethical practices are deeply embedded in its culture is Merck & Co., one of the world's largest pharmaceutical companies and known for its strong ethical values and leadership. As its founder George W. Merck (1894–1957) once stated, "We try to remember that medicine is for the patient. We try never to forget that medicine is for the people. It is not for the profits. The profits follow, and if we have remembered that, they have never failed to appear. The better we have remembered it, the larger they have been."[9] Culture is deeply rooted, but businesses may make their own interpretations of its accepted norms.

LINK TO LEARNING

Merck & Co. is justly lauded for its involvement in the fight to control the spread of river blindness in Africa. For more information, watch this World Bank video about Merck & Co.'s efforts to treat river blindness (https://openstax.org/l/53Merck&Co) and its partnership with international organizations and African governments.

Our beliefs are also challenged when a clash occurs between a legal framework and cultural norms, such as when a company feels compelled to engage in dubious and even illegal activities to generate business. For example, the German technology company Siemens has paid billions of dollars in fines and judgments for bribing government officials in several countries. Although some local officials may have expected to receive bribes to grant government contracts, Siemens was still bound by national and international regulations forbidding the practice, as well as by its own code of ethics. How can a company remain true to its mission and code of ethics in a highly competitive international environment (Figure 5.3)?

Figure 5.3 Ethical decision-making in a global context requires a broad perspective. Business leaders need to know themselves, their organization's mission, and the impact of their decisions on local communities. They also must be open to varying degrees of risk. (credit: "accomplishment action adventure atmosphere" by unknown/Pixabay, CC0)

Business performance is a reflection of what an organization believes about itself, as in the IBM and Merck examples.[10] Those beliefs, in turn, spring from what the individuals in the organization believe about it and themselves, based on their communities, families, personal biographies, religious beliefs, and educational backgrounds. Unless key leaders have a vision for the organization and themselves, and a path to achieving it, there can be no balance of beliefs about profitability and responsibility, or integration of business with culture. The Manhattan purchase was successful to the degree that Minuit and the tribal leaders were willing to engage in an exchange of mutual benefit. Yet this revealed a transaction between two very different commercial cultures. Did each group truly understand the other's perception of an exchange of goods and services? Furthermore, did the parties balance personal and collective beliefs for the greater good? Given the distinctions between these two cultures, would that even have been possible?

Consumerism and the Global Marketplace

To paraphrase the ancient Greek philosopher Heraclitus (c. 535–475 BCE), the one constant in life is change. Traditional norms and customs have changed as the world's population has grown more diverse and urbanized, and as the Internet has made news and other resources readily available. The growing emphasis on **consumerism**—a lifestyle characterized by the acquisition of goods and services—has meant that people have become defined as "consumers" as opposed to citizens or human beings. Unfortunately, this emphasis eventually leads to the problem of diminishing marginal utility, with the consumer having to buy an ever-increasing amount to reach the same level of satisfaction.

At the same time, markets have become more diverse and interconnected. For example, South Korean companies like LG and Samsung employ 52,000 workers in the United States,[11] and many U.S. companies now manufacture their products abroad. Such globalization of their domestic markets has allowed U.S. consumers to enjoy products from around the world, but it also presents ethical challenges. The individual consumer, for instance, may benefit from lower prices and a greater selection of goods, but only by supporting a company that might be engaged in unethical practices in its overseas supply or distribution chains. Producers' choices about wages, working conditions, environmental impact, child labor, taxation, and plant safety feature in the creation of each product brought to market. Becoming aware of these factors requires consumers to engage in an investigation of the business practices of those parties they will patronize and exercise a certain amount of cultural and ethical sensitivity.

CASES FROM THE REAL WORLD

Overseas Manufacturing

How can the purchase of a pair of sneakers be seen as an ethical act? Throughout the 1990s, the U.S. shoe and sportswear manufacturer Nike was widely criticized for subcontracting with factories in China and Southeast Asia that were little more than sweatshops with deplorable working conditions. After responding to the criticisms and demanding that its suppliers improve their workplaces, the company began to redeem itself in the eyes of many and has become a model of business ethics and sustainability. However, questions remain about the relationship between business and government.

For instance, should a company advocate for labor rights, a minimum wage, and unionization in developing countries where it has operations? What responsibility does it have for the welfare of a contractor's workers in a culture with differing customs? What right does any Western company have to insist that its foreign contractors observe in their factories the protocols required in the West? What, for example, is sacred about an eight-hour workday? When Nike demands that foreign manufacturers observe Western laws and customs about the workplace, arguably this is capitalist imperialism. Not only that, but Western firms will be charged more for concessions regarding factory conditions. Perhaps this is as it should be, but Western consumers must then be prepared to pay more for material goods than in the past.

Some argue that demanding that companies accept these responsibilities imposes cultural standards on another culture through economic pressure. Others insist there should be universal standards of humane employee treatment, and that they must be met regardless of where they come from or who imposes them. But should the market dictate such standards, or should the government?

The rise of artificial intelligence and robotics will complicate this challenge because, in time, they may make offshoring the manufacture and distribution of goods unnecessary. It may be cheaper and more efficient to bring these operations back to developed countries and use robotic systems instead. What would that mean for local cultures and their economies? In Nike's case, automation is already a concern, particularly as competition from its German rival, Adidas, heats up again.[12]

Critical Thinking

- What ethical responsibilities do individual consumers have when dealing with companies that rely on overseas labor?
- Should businesses adopt universal workplace standards about working conditions and employee protections? Why or why not?
- What would be required for consumers to have the necessary knowledge about a product and how it was made so that they could make an informed and ethical decision? The media? Commercial watchdog groups? Social-issues campaigns? Something else?

Read this report, "A Race to the Bottom: Trans-Pacific Partnership and Nike in Vietnam," to learn more (https://openstax.org/l/53Nike) **about this issue.**

In considering the ethical challenges presented by the outsourcing of production to lower costs and increase profits, let us return to the example of IBM. IBM has a responsibility to provide technology products of high quality at affordable prices in line with its beliefs about client success, innovation, and trust. If it achieved these ends in a fraudulent or otherwise illegal way, it would be acting irresponsibly and in violation of both U.S. and host country laws and as well as the company's own code of ethics. These constraints appear to leave little room for unethical behavior, yet in a globalized world of intense competition, the temptation to do anything possible to carve out an advantage can be overpowering. This choice between ends and means is reminiscent of the philosophers Aristotle and Kant, both of whom believed it impossible to achieve just ends through unjust means.

But what about consumer responsibility and the impact on the global community? Western consumers tend to perceive globalization as a phenomenon intended to benefit them specifically. In general, they have few compunctions about Western businesses offshoring their manufacturing operations as long as it ultimately benefits them as consumers. However, even in business, ethics is not about consumption but rather about human morality, a greater end. Considering an expansion of domestic markets, what feature of this process enables us to become more humane rather than simply pickier consumers or wasteful spenders? It is the opportunity to encounter other cultures and people, increasing our ethical awareness and sensitivity. Seen in this way, globalization affects the human condition. It raises no less a question than what kind of world we want to leave to our children and grandchildren.

5.2 | Business Ethics over Time

Learning Objectives

By the end of this section, you will be able to:

- Describe the ways ethical standards change over time
- Identify major shifts in technology and ethical thinking over the last five hundred years
- Explain the impact of government and self-imposed regulation on ethical standards and practices in the United States

Besides culture, the other major influence in the development of business ethics is the passage of time. Ethical standards do not remain fixed; they transform in response to evolving situations. Over time, people change, technology advances, and cultural mores (i.e., acquired culture and manners) shift. What was considered an appropriate or accepted business practice one hundred or even fifty years ago may not carry the same moral weight it once did. However, this does not mean ethics and moral behavior are relative. It simply acknowledges that attitudes change in relationship to historical events and that cultural perspective and the process of acculturation are not stagnant.

Shifts in Cultural and Ethical Standards

We find an example of changing cultural mores in the fashion industry, where drastic evolution can occur even over ten years, let alone a century. The changes can be more than simply stylistic ones. Clothing reflects people's view of themselves, their world, and their values. A woman in the first half of the twentieth century might be very proud to wear a fox stole with its head and feet intact (Figure 5.4). Today, many would consider that an ethical faux pas, even as the use of fur remains common in the industry despite active campaigns against it by organizations such as People for the Ethical Treatment of Animals. At the same time, cosmetics manufacturers increasingly pledge not to test their products on animals, reflecting changing awareness of animals' rights.

Figure 5.4   Philanthropist Anne Morgan, wife of banker and industrialist J.P. Morgan, wearing a fur stole circa 1915. (credit: "Anne Morgan, wearing fur stole, ca. 1915" by "Elisa.rolle"/Wikimedia Commons, Public Domain)

Bias is built into the human psyche and expressed through our social structures. For this reason, we should avoid making snap judgments about past eras based on today's standards. The challenge, of course, is to know which values are situational—that is, although many values and ethics are relative and subjective, others are objectively true, at least to most people. We can hardly argue in favor of slavery, for example, no matter in which culture or historical era it was practiced. Of course, although some values strike us as universal, the ways in which they are interpreted and applied vary over time, so that what was once acceptable no longer is, or the reverse.

ETHICS ACROSS TIME AND CULTURES

When Even Doctors Smoked

From the 1940s to the 1970s, cigarettes were as common as water bottles are today. Nearly everyone smoked, from judges in court to factory workers and pregnant women. Edward Bernays, the Austrian-American founder of the field of public relations, promoted smoking among women in a 1929 campaign in New York City in which he marketed Lucky Strike cigarettes as "torches of freedom" that would lead to equality between men and women. However, by the late 1960s, and in the wake of the release of the landmark Surgeon General's report on "Smoking and Health" on January 11, 1964, it had become clear that there was a direct link between cigarette smoking and lung cancer. Subsequent research has added heart and lung diseases, stroke, and diabetes. Smoking has decreased in Western countries but remains well established in the global East and South, where cigarette manufacturers actively promote the products in markets like Brazil, China, Russia, and Singapore, especially among young people.

Critical Thinking

Are such practices ethical? Why or why not?

LINK TO LEARNING

Explore these statistics on cigarette smoking in young adults from the CDC (https://openstax.org/l/53CDCsmoking) and these charts on the global state of smoking from the World Bank (https://openstax.org/l/53GlobalSmoking) for information about cigarette use in the United States and globally, including demographic breakdowns of smoking populations.

Thus, we acknowledge that different eras upheld different ethical standards, and that each of these standards has had an impact on our understanding of ethics today. But this realization raises some basic questions. First, what should we discard and what should we keep from the past? Second, on what basis should we make this decision? Third, is history cumulative, progressing onward and upward through time, or does it unfold in different and more complicated ways, sometimes circling back upon itself?

The major historical periods that have shaped business ethics are the age of mercantilism, the Industrial Revolution, the postindustrial era, the Information Age, and the age of economic globalization, to which the rise of the Internet contributed significantly. Each of these periods has had a different impact on ethics and what is considered acceptable business practice. Some economists believe there may even be a postglobalization phase arising from populist movements throughout the world that question the benefits of free trade and call for protective measures, like import barriers and export subsidies, to reassert national sovereignty.[13] In some ways, these protectionist reactions represent a return to the theories and policies that were popular in the age of mercantilism.

Unlike capitalism, which views wealth creation as the key to economic growth and prosperity, **mercantilism** relies on the theory that global wealth is static and, therefore, prosperity depends on extracting wealth or accumulating it from others. Under mercantilism, from the sixteenth to the eighteenth centuries, the exploration of newly opened markets and trade routes coincided with the impulse to colonize, producing an ethical code that valued acculturation by means of trade and often brute force. European powers extracted raw commodities like cotton, silk, diamonds, tea, and tobacco from their colonies in Africa, Asia, and South America and brought them home for production. Few questioned the practice, and the operation of business ethics consisted mainly of protecting owners' interests.

During the Industrial Revolution and the postindustrial era, in the nineteenth and early twentieth centuries, business focused on the pursuit of wealth, the expansion of overseas markets, and the accumulation of capital. The goal was to earn as high a profit as possible for shareholders, with little concern for outside stakeholders. Charles Dickens (1812–1870) famously exposed the conditions of factory work and the poverty of the working class in many of his novels, as did the American writer Upton Sinclair (1878–1968). Although these periods witnessed extraordinary developments in science, medicine, engineering, and technology, the state of business ethics was perhaps best described by critics like Ida Tarbell (1857–1944), who said of industrialist John D. Rockefeller (1839–1937) (Figure 5.5), "Would you ask for scruples in an electric dynamo?"[14]

(a)   (b)

Figure 5.5   Ida Tarbell (a) was a pioneer of investigative journalism and a leading "muckraker" of the Progressive Era. She is perhaps best known for her exposé of the business practices of John D. Rockefeller (b), founder of the Standard Oil Company. (credit a: modification of "TARBELL, IDA M." by Harris & Ewing/Library of Congress, Public Domain; credit b: modification of "John D. Rockefeller 1885" by "DIREKTOR"/Wikimedia Commons, Public Domain)

With the advent of the Information and Internet ages in the late twentieth and early twenty-first centuries, a code of professional conduct developed for the purpose of achieving goals through strategic planning.[15] In the past, ethical or normative rules were imposed from above to lead people toward right behavior, as the company defined it. Now, however, more emphasis is placed on each person at a firm embracing ethical standards and following those dictates to arrive at the appropriate behavior, whether at work or when off the clock.[16] The creation of human resources departments (increasingly now designated as human capital or human assets departments) is an outgrowth of this philosophy, because it reflects a view that humans have a unique value that ought not be reduced simply to the notion that they are instruments to be manipulated for the purposes of the organization. Millennia earlier, Aristotle referred to "living tools" in a similar but critical way.[17] Although one characteristic of the information age—access to information on an unprecedented scale—has transformed business and society (and some say made it more egalitarian), we must ask whether it also contributes to human flourishing, and to what extent business should concern itself with this goal.

A Matter of Time

What effect does time have on business ethics, and how is this effect achieved? If we accept that business today has two purposes—profitability and responsibility—we might assume that business ethics is in a much better position now than in the past to affect conduct across industries. However, much of the transformation of business over time has been the result of direct government *intervention*; one recent example is the Dodd–Frank Wall Street Reform and Consumer Protection Act that followed the financial crisis of 2008. Yet, despite such regulation and increased management vigilance in the form of ethics training, compliance reporting, whistleblower programs, and audits, it is tempting to conclude that business ethics is in worse shape than ever. The Information Age and the Internet may even have facilitated unethical behavior by making it easier to move large sums of money around undetected, by enabling the spread of misinformation on a global scale, and by exposing the public to the theft and misuse of vast stores of personal data gathered by companies as diverse as Equifax and Facebook.

However, since the mercantile era, there has been a gradual increase in awareness of the ethical dimension of business. As we saw in the preceding chapter, businesses and the U.S. government have debated and litigated the role of corporate social responsibility throughout the twentieth century, first validating the rule of shareholder primacy in *Dodge v. Ford Motor Company* (1919) and then moving away from a strict interpretation of it in *Shlensky v. Wrigley* (1968). In *Dodge v. Ford Motor Company* (1919), the Michigan Supreme Court famously ruled that Ford had to operate in the interests of its shareholders as opposed to its employees and managers, which meant prioritizing profit and return on investment. This court decision was made even though Henry Ford had said, "My ambition is to employ still more men, to spread the benefits of this industrial system to the greatest possible number, to help them build up their lives and their homes. To do this we are putting the greatest share of our profits back in the business."[18] By mid-century and the case of *Shlensky v. Wrigley* (1968), the courts had given boards of directors and management more latitude in determining how to balance the interests of stakeholders.[19] This position was confirmed in the more recent case of *Burwell v. Hobby Lobby* (2014), which held that corporate law does not require for-profit corporations to pursue profit at the expense of everything else.

Governmental regulation and legal interpretations have not been the only avenues of change over the past century. The growing influence of consumers has been another driving force in recent attempts by businesses to self-regulate and voluntarily comply with global ethical standards that ensure basic human rights and working conditions. The United Nations (UN) Global Compact is one of these standards. Its mission is to mobilize companies and stakeholders to create a world in which businesses align their strategies and operations with a set of core principles covering human rights, labor, the environment, and anticorruption practices. The Global Compact is a "voluntary initiative based on CEO commitments to implement universal sustainability principles and to undertake partnerships in support of UN goals."[20] Of course, as a voluntary initiative, the initiative does not bind corporations and countries to the principles outlined in it.

LINK TO LEARNING

Read the Ten Principles of the United Nations Global Compact (https://openstax.org/l/53UNcompact) urging corporations to develop a "principled approach to doing business." The principles cover human rights, labor, the environment, and corruption.

Whenever we look at the ways in which our perception of ethical business practice changes over time, we should note that such change is not necessarily good or bad but rather a function of human nature and of the ways in which our views are influenced by our environment, our culture, and the passage of time. Many of the examples discussed thus far illustrate a gradual increase in social awareness due to the actions of individual leaders and the historical era in which they found themselves. This does not mean that culture is irrelevant, but that human nature exists and ethical inclination is part of that nature. Historical conditions may allow this nature to be expressed more or less fully. We might measure ethical standards according to the degree they allow human compassion to direct business practice or, at least, make it easier for compassion to hold sway. We might then consider ethics not just a nicety but a constitutive part of business, because it is an inherent human trait. This is a perspective Kant and Rawls might have agreed with. Ethical thinking over time should be measured, deliberate, and open to examination.

5.3 | The Influence of Geography and Religion

Learning Objectives

By the end of this section, you will be able to:

- Describe the impact of geography on global relationships and business ethics
- Explain how religion informs ethical business practice around the world

Business ethics guides people to practice commerce professionally and honestly and in a way that permits as many as possible to flourish. However, as we have seen, the ethical standards by which business is conducted can vary depending on culture and time. Geography and regional cultural practices also play a significant role. As global markets become increasingly connected and interdependent, we navigate more of our valued relationships across international boundaries.

Business as Global Relationships

Global relationships teach us to be sensitive not just to other languages and customs but also to other people's worldviews. A company looking to move its production to another country may be interested in setting up supply, distribution, and value chains that support human rights, worker safety, and equity for women, while the local culture is excited about the economic benefits it will gain from the company's investment in employment and the local tax base and infrastructure. These goals need not be in conflict, but they must be integrated if the company is to reach an ethically sound agreement with the host country. Dialogue and openness are crucial to this process, just as they are in every other kind of relationship.

Geography affects a business's relationship with almost any type of stakeholder, from stockholders and employees to customers, the government, and the environment. Hence the growing importance of **localization**, the process of adapting a product for non-native environments and languages, especially other nations and cultures. Such adaption often starts with language translation but may include customizing content or products to the tastes and consumption habits of the local market; converting currencies, dates, and other measurements to regional standards; and addressing community regulations and legal requirements.

Research has shown that successful leaders and organizations with global responsibilities "need to understand and exceed the leadership expectations in the cultures they are interacting with."[21] In its study of leadership effectiveness and organizational behavior across cultures, the GLOBE leadership project of the Beedie School of Business at Simon Fraser University in Vancouver, Canada, found leader effectiveness is contextual and strongly connected to cultural and organizational values. The study also concluded that, although leaders learn to adapt to cultural expectations, they often have to exceed those expectations to be truly successful.[22] In other words, business has a role beyond merely reflecting the culture in which it operates.

One element of business culture you may not realize is based on local custom and culture is the notion of time. Unlike the notion of historical time discussed in the previous module, the concept of time in business—people's approach to punctuality, for example—varies widely in different cultures. To put it in economic terms, all cultures share the resource of time, but they measure and use that resource very differently. These differences might significantly affect the foundation of any business relationships you may want to establish around the world. For this and many other reasons, basic cultural literacy must be at the forefront of any ethical system that governs business behavior.

Consider, for example, that in the United States, we might speak of "a New York minute," "the nick of time," "the eleventh hour," and so on. Such expressions make sense in a culture where the enculturation process emphasizes competition and speed. But even among Western business cultures, conceptions of time can differ. For example, the Italian *subito* and the German *sofort* both refer to something happening "at once" or "straightaway," but with different expectations about when the action, in fact, will take place. And some cultures do not measure the passage of time at all.

Generally, the farther east and south we travel from the United States, the more time becomes relational rather than chronological. In Kenya, *tutaonana baadaye* means "see you later," although "later" could be any time, open to context and interpretation. The nomadic inhabitants of North Africa known as the Tuareg sit down to tea before discussing any business, and as a rule, the longer the time spent in preliminary conversation, the better. A Tuareg proverb has it that the first cup of tea is bitter like life, the second sweet like love, and the third gentle like death.[23] Compare this with the Western attitude that "time flies" and "time is money." Finally, Westerners doing business in some English-speaking African countries have learned that if they want something immediately, they have to say "now now" as "now" by itself does not convey the desired sense of immediacy.

Another aspect of international business relationships is the question of personal space. In Nigeria, for example, standing either too close or too far from someone to whom you are speaking might be seen as impolite. In some cultures, touch is important in establishing connection, whereas in others it may be frowned upon. As a general rule, "contact" cultures—where people stand closer together when interacting, touch more often, and have more frequent direct eye contact—are found in South America, the Middle East, and southern Europe, while "noncontact" cultures—where eye contact and touching are less frequent, and there is less physical proximity during interactions—are in northern Europe, the Far East, and the United States. So, the seemingly innocuous gesture of a handshake to cement a new business relationship might be viewed very differently depending on where it occurs and who is shaking hands.

All of this speaks to the awareness and cultural sensitivity that must be exhibited by an ethical manager doing business in a region different from his or her own. Certain mistakes, particularly accidental ones and those not motivated by malicious design, will likely be forgiven. Still, a global ethical demeanor requires that we be as conscious as possible as to what constitutes courtesy wherever we find ourselves conducting business.

WHAT WOULD YOU DO?

Tucked In, Tucked Out

Time and space are just two examples of cultural characteristics that you may take for granted but that are not universal. Business attire is another, as is humor, which is notoriously hard to translate across languages and cultures. And, of course, miscommunications can occur not just across regional boundaries and business cultures but even within them. For example, unless you are a barista at a hipster coffee bar, it may not be a good idea to wear piercings, tattoos, or colorfully dyed hair to work. Employers have the right to establish a dress code and expect employees to abide by it.

In the movie *The Intern*, Robert De Niro's senior character wears conservative blue and gray suits to his job at an e-commerce fashion startup, whereas the younger men dress very casually. At one point in the film, De Niro's character asks, "Doesn't anybody tuck in their shirt?" Leaving your shirt untucked has become more acceptable in recent years, and the black t-shirt and jeans favored in Silicon Valley are now quite fashionable in some business environments.

Many today would disagree with the old adage that "clothes make the man," yet studies show that well-dressed employees are held in higher esteem and may earn more, on average, than those who dress down. The age of uncomfortable dresses and starched white shirts may be over, but cultural standards, along with underlying values that prioritize, say, innovation over uniformity, change over time and even within the same company.

Critical Thinking

- How do you think clothing choices affect the relationships we form at work or in other business situations?
- What is your opinion about workplace dress codes, and how far should employers go in setting dress and other behavior standards? Why are these standards important (or not) from an ethical perspective?
- How do you think clothing might affect an international company's approach to business ethics?

LINK TO LEARNING

The Italian Jesuit priest Matteo Ricci (1552–1610) learned Mandarin, adopted Chinese dress, translated Confucian texts into Latin, and was welcomed into the Chinese emperor's court as a scholar. His message was religious, not commercial, but his respectful attitude allowed him to be accepted and trusted by the emperor and administrators. Learn more about Ricci's approach and the relationship between Western and Ming Chinese views of ethics (https://openstax.org/l/53Ricci) on this webpage.

Religion and Ethics

A major factor in the difference that geography and culture make in our ethical standards is the influence of religious practice. For example, just as the current debate over the redistribution of goods and services has Christian roots, so the Industrial Revolution in England and northern Europe looked to Protestant Christianity in particular for the values of frugality, hard work, industriousness, and simplicity. Until the seventeenth century, religion and ethics were nearly inseparable. Many believed that people could not be persuaded to do the right thing without the threat of eternal damnation. The Enlightenment's attempt to peel religion away from ethics was short-lived, with even Kant acknowledging the need to base morality on something beyond the rationalism of his time.

Religions are neither uniform nor monolithic, of course, nor are they unchanging over time. The core of Christianity, for instance, does not change, but its emphasis in any given period does. Moreover, the state or crown often worked side by side with the church in the past, choosing certain teachings over others to promote its own interests. This cooperation was evident during the era of mercantilism when the issue of personhood, or the privilege of having the freedom and capacity to make decisions and act morally, was hotly debated in the context of slavery, a practice that had been going on for centuries in the Christian West and the Islamic East. Although the church officially opposed slavery, the conquest of new lands was justified theologically as bringing salvation and civilization to populations considered savage and unsophisticated. Christianity was thought to save them from their pagan ways just as Islam and the message of the prophet saved unbelievers in the East. Behavioral norms for the clergy were founded and supported by the divine right of kings and the authority of religious tradition (Figure 5.6). Commerce and trade followed these norms.

Figure 5.6   Just as concepts of time and space vary from culture to culture, so do the influence of religious tradition and authority on ethics and what is considered appropriate behavior, whether individual or corporate. The Taj Mahal is not the Palace of Versailles. (credit left: modification of "Taj Mahal" by Suraj rajiv/ Wikimedia Commons, CC BY 4.0; credit right: modification of "Cour de Marbre du Château de Versailles October 5, 2011" by Kimberly Vardeman/Wikimedia Commons, CC BY 2.0)

By the time of the Industrial Revolution and postindustrial eras, Protestantism and its values of frugality, hard work, and simplicity (the "Protestant ethic") had helped create a culture of individualism and entrepreneurship in the West, particularly in Great Britain and the United States. In fact, the Protestant work ethic, religion, and a commitment to hard work all are intertwined in the business history of both these countries. One example of this singular association is John D. Rockefeller, who, in the late nineteenth and early twentieth centuries, commanded the attention given today to Bill Gates and Warren Buffet as emblems of free enterprise.

No one was more convinced of the link between religious faith and success in business than Rockefeller, who clung to his Baptist faith from his early years until his death in 1937. The richest person of his age, Rockefeller earned his fortune as the founder and major shareholder of Standard Oil but always regarded his billions as a public trust rather than his personal prize. "As his fortune grew big enough to beggar the imagination, [Rockefeller] retained his mystic faith that God had given him money for mankind's benefit . . . or else why had He lavished such bounty on him?"[24] Despite criticism, even from family members, Rockefeller donated enormous sums to many causes, especially medical research (in the form of Rockefeller University) and higher education. He financed the founding of the University of Chicago as an institution that would train students to pursue their professional and business interests under the guidance of Christian faith.

Still, as Ida Tarbell pointed out in her work, Rockefeller's business ethics were not above reproach. In making his fortune, he pursued markedly Darwinian practices revealing a conviction in survival of the fittest. Later in life, and as his philanthropic motivation increased, his endowment of several charitable causes more fully reflected his belief as to how God wished him to dispose of a sizable portion of his wealth.

LINK TO LEARNING

Watch this episode of "American Experience" on John D. Rockefeller, Sr. from the Public Broadcasting System (https://openstax.org/l/53Rockefeller) **to learn more about him.**

Of course, Rockefeller's concept of stewardship—an attitude toward money and capital that stresses care and responsibility rather than pure utility—can be found across cultures and religions in various forms, and there are many similarities among the Judaic, Islamic, and Christian views of money and its use toward a greater end. All three of these religions teach that no harm should be done to others, nor should people be treated as means toward a material end like wealth. Yet what role does a religious concept of stewardship play in the ethics of the twenty-first century? The Enlightenment attempted to separate religion and ethics but could not. Are the two concepts inextricably linked? Might the business leaders of today succeed where the Enlightenment failed?

Although religious practices and cultural assumptions remain strongly in place, fewer people in the West today profess a religion than in the past.[25] Does this development affect the way you approach business relationships and conduct negotiations? Might we see a universal, secular code of ethics developing in place of religion? If so, how would it accommodate the differences across time, regions, and cultures discussed in this chapter? The Universal Declaration of Human Rights, adopted by the United Nations General Assembly in December 1948, contains a list of basic human rights such as the right to life, liberty, due process, religion, education, marriage, and property. Business ethics will have to balance all these factors when adopting standards of conduct and local practices.

WHAT WOULD YOU DO?

Ramadan

Jillian Armstrong leads an external audit team reviewing the financial statements of Islamabad Investment Bank in Islamabad, Pakistan. It is Ramadan, and the employees on her team are Muslims who fast each day for a month. Jillian has never fasted and believes the practice can be harmful over prolonged periods, especially in the heat of summer. She proposes several times that team members keep up their strength by drinking water or tea, but her suggestions are met with awkward silence. She has decided to leave well enough alone as long as everyone does their work, but now she faces a dilemma. What should she do for lunch? Should she eat in her office, out of sight of the team and bank employees? Have lunch in one of the local restaurants that cater to Westerners? Or perhaps fast with her team and eat at sundown?

Critical Thinking

- What do you think would be the effect of Jillian's accepting the local custom but continuing her own personal preference at mealtimes?
- Can two ways of life exist side by side at work? Why or why not?

5.4 | Are the Values Central to Business Ethics Universal?

Learning Objectives

By the end of this section, you will be able to:

- Explain the difference between relative and absolute ethical values
- Discuss the degree to which compliance is linked with organizational responsibility and personal values
- Identify the criteria for a system of normative business ethics
- Evaluate the humanistic business model

One of the perennial themes in business ethics—indeed, in ethics in general—is the difference between relative and absolute values. Is it possible to identify a set of universal values that is consistent across cultures and time? We might begin with always honoring the terms of a contract, consistently treating customers and partners with honesty, and never cheating. Where could we go from there? No matter our culture, geography, or time, could we identify some basic normative behaviors to govern business conduct in general?

Absolute Values versus Relative Values

To put this question another way, is there a set of **universal values** that all can endorse? Are there "human values" that apply everywhere despite differences in time, place, and culture (Figure 5.7)? If not, and if ethical standards are relative, are they worth having? Again, the UN Universal Declaration of Human Rights is a useful starting point for the way business can conduct itself. Let us look at how it is possible to align business with human rights in such a way that both profitability and responsibility are honored across the globe.

Figure 5.7 The pursuit of happiness is as near a universal human trait as we can find. It is not a coincidence that it appears in the American Declaration of Independence (1776), which was written by Thomas Jefferson and inspired by the British Enlightenment philosopher John Locke. However, the nature of human happiness is subjective. For example, everyone must eat to survive, but not everyone would agree that eating chocolate-raspberry cake brings happiness. (credit: "Happiness Is a Piece of Cake Close Up Photography" by Antonio Quagliata/Pexels, CC0)

According to the Union Internationale des Avocats, an international, nongovernmental association of legal professionals, corruption "corrodes the democratic principles of accountability, equality, and transparency. It poses an extremely high cost to the citizenry, it saps the credibility of government and it places companies under an unbearable economic burden."[26] The UN Convention Against Corruption has called corruption "an insidious plague" that exists everywhere and "hurts the poor disproportionately by diverting funds intended for development, undermining a Government's ability to provide basic services, feeding inequality and injustice and discouraging foreign aid and investment."[27] Corruption appears to exist everywhere, so it would seem to require a persistent and consistent answer everywhere. Can business ethics provide one?

Business ethics exists on three levels: the individual, the organizational, and the societal. At the organizational and societal levels, laws, regulations, and oversight can go a long way toward curtailing illegal activity. Business ethics motivates managers to (1) meet legal and industry governing and reporting requirements and (2) shape corporate culture so that corrupt practices such as bribery, embezzlement, and fraud have no place in the organization. In the ideal case, the organization's culture never allows the latter, because scandals not only damage reputations but they make companies and countries much less attractive to investors. Corruption is expensive: According to the World Economic Forum, no less than $2 trillion is lost each year worldwide as a result of corruption, a staggering waste not just of resources but of credibility for business in general.[28]

At the individual level, when corruption takes place, it is a matter of conscience. Corruption can be defeated only by individuals acting in accordance with their conscience and being supported by systems and corporate culture that encourage such action. Transparency, whistleblower programs, ethics training, and modeling of appropriate behavior by upper management can create the conditions for employees to act ethically, but conscience is a personal phenomenon. So, although the work of national, regional, and international organizations can limit corruption through enforcement and the prosecution of cases (as was the case with the revelation of the so-called Panama Papers), corruption will not be reduced in any significant way unless efforts have been made to form individual conscience and teach practical ways to act on it.

LINK TO LEARNING

Read the article "Perspective: Panama Papers and 'responsible' journalism" on the Panama Papers and how journalists might hold the corporate world to account in cases of fraud and corruption (https://openstax.org/l/53PanamaPapers) for a detailed explanation.

Although ethical practice has been directly influenced by religion, as noted, ethics is not religion and religious belief is not a prerequisite for a commitment to business ethics. For example, although what constitutes ethical behavior in Islamic society is strongly linked to religious values, secular philosophers can endorse a highly developed commitment to commercial ethics, too. Furthermore, most religions have high ethical standards but do not address many of the problems faced in business. And although a good system of law incorporates ethical standards, the law can and sometimes does deviate from what is ethical. Finally, in the same vein, ethics is not science. The social and natural sciences provide data to make better ethical choices, but science cannot tell people what they ought to do (nor should it).

Absolute values do exist. Abstaining from cheating customers, defrauding clients, lying, and murder are fairly objective ethical values; the reason for making any exceptions must be carefully laid out. Ethical systems, whether utilitarian, rights based, or based on natural law and virtue ethics, are attempts to translate absolute values like these into workable solutions for people. From these systems has emerged a basic set of ethical norms for the business world.

Business Ethics and Compliance

A hallmark of any profession is the existence of ethical guidelines, often based on values like honesty, integrity, and objectivity. Organizational responsibility is fairly straightforward: Comply with applicable local, state, national, and international regulations. Compliance can be an immense task for industries like aerospace, pharmaceuticals, banking, and food production, due to the large number of employees involved, the certification of them that sometimes is necessary, and the requisite record keeping. Still, legal requirements are usually clear, as are the ways an organization can exceed them (as do, for example, companies such as Whole Foods, Zappos, and Starbucks). Personal responsibility is a different matter. It is either less clear what to do or harder to do it because of constant pressure to increase the organization's profitability and the perception that "everybody else is doing it."[29]

In the United States, companies spend more than $70 billion annually on ethics training; worldwide, the figure is more than double that.[30] Unfortunately, in the United States, much of this money is spent on merely meeting the minimum requirements of compliance, so that if there is ever a problem with the Department of Justice or the Securities and Exchange Commission, the organization is insulated from criticism or liability because its employees have engaged in the recommended training. Federal Sentencing Guidelines for felonies and serious misdemeanors now carry mandatory prison time for individual executives who are convicted. These guidelines also are designed to help organizations with compliance and reporting, and they introduce seven steps toward that end: (1) create a Code of Ethics, (2) introduce high-level oversight, (3) place ethical people in positions of authority, (4) communicate ethics standards, (5) facilitate employee reporting of misconduct, (6) react and respond to instances of misconduct, and (7) take preventive steps.

Many organizations focus on the letter of the law so that they can claim "good faith" in their effort to create an ethical environment. However, middle managers and employees often complain their ethics training consists of passing a computerized sexual harassment or fraud program once a year but that nothing is done to address issues in a substantive way or to change the culture of the organization, even those that have experienced problems.[31] The focus still seems to be on organizational responsibility and compliance as opposed to individual responsibility and the formation of ethical conscience. We might argue that it is not the business of business to form people in their conscience, but the result of not doing so has become expensive for everyone concerned.[32]

The damage done to an organization's or government's reputation due to scandal can be enormous and long lasting. The 2017 conviction for bribery and embezzlement of Lee Jae-yong, heir to the Samsung electronics empire, was part of a widespread corruption scandal that brought down the president of South Korea. Bribery was also at the heart of the FIFA (Fédération Internationale de Football Association) corruption scandal, in which soccer officials, marketing executives, and broadcasters were accused of racketeering, wire fraud, and money laundering by the U.S. Department of Justice in 2015. The Volkswagen emissions scandal also began in 2015, when the Environmental Protection Agency cited the German automaker for violating the Clean Air Act by cheating on emissions tests. To date, the fallout has cost the company nearly $30 billion in fines.

As the LIBOR (London Interbank Offered Rate) scandal, in which banks were manipulating rates to profit from trades, showed, ethical breakdowns often occur because systems fail or people make bad decisions, and sometimes both. In the case of LIBOR, the United Kingdom's Serious Fraud Office determined there were inadequate systems of oversight in the setting of rates and that individual executives encouraged rate fixing, which led to the conviction of several traders, at least one of whom still maintains his innocence.[33] The result was a staggering $6 billion cumulative fine for the banks involved (i.e., Barclay's, J.P. Morgan Chase, Citicorp, Royal Bank of Scotland, and Deutsche Bank).[34]

LINK TO LEARNING

Read this article on the LIBOR scandal and the consequences (https://openstax.org/l/53LIBOR) for an in-depth overview.

If there is anything to be learned from these scandals, it is that organizations will succumb to ethics crises if they do not pay attention to their organizational culture and foster their employees' growth as moral beings. This is even more important in industries like banking that are more susceptible to unethical behavior because of the great sums of money that change hands. Compliance is important, but business managers must attempt to go above and beyond to clearly model and enforce the highest standards of ethical behavior.

Normative Business Ethics

Normative business ethics should address systemic issues such as oversight and transparency as well as the character of individuals who make up the organization. Human flourishing may not be the immediate concern of business, but managers and employees have a significant impact on business performance. Giving employees common-sense advice and training in practical ways to counter unethical behavior, as well as ethical role models at the top of the organization, can be more effective than prevention. There are programs that do this, such as "Giving Voice to Values" at the Darden School of Business at the University of Virginia.[35] These programs are effective for their ability to help individuals act on their principles. As effective as they may be, however, they beg the larger question not of how someone can act on what their conscience tells them but how to determine what their conscience is telling them in the first place.

One model of ethical behavior, sometimes called the **humanistic business model**, may provide the answer for businesses that wish to achieve the dual goal of human flourishing and responsible profits. In this model, organizations focus on employees as a vital part of the operation and support them in their professional training, health care, education, family responsibilities, and even spiritual concerns. Leaders create positive relationships with stakeholders, including their employees, to cultivate investor goodwill and because they believe in the underlying values of trust and authenticity. The influence of positive psychology is evident, and there is much to commend in this kinder approach to the job of management that makes an effort to establish "sustainable human welfare."[36] However, happy employees are one thing; the human flourishing identified by Aristotle and John Stuart Mill is quite another. What, then, is missing from humanistic business?

The problem is that if anything flourishes in this model, it is often the business rather than the employees. After all, free enterprise has the interests of the enterprise at heart. But employees are human beings first, which means any attempt to improve their welfare must begin by thinking of them as human beings rather than as employees. How can businesses do this?

One alternative is to put the humanities into business. Businesses currently rely heavily on data analytics, algorithms, and statistical analyses to drive decision-making. The use of these tools is often backed by social science research in consumer behavior, behavioral finance, and cognitive studies. But looking to the humanities to understand business is an opportunity to engage business in subjects and ideas that have a tremendous, if often overlooked, impact on people. After all, literature that has stood the test of time can provide tremendous insight into human behavior, and Homer or Shakespeare may be more relevant to contemporary executive leadership than a business seminar on how to motivate employees.

In fact, we could argue that anything that makes an impact on people should legitimately be within the scope of business. Richard DeGeorge (1933–) of the University of Kansas describes what adding the humanities to business education entails:

> "Students do not need psychosociological jargon in their business interactions. They do need to understand people and their motives, to know how to read and judge character, and to have the ability to imagine themselves in another's shoes, be they those of a competitor, a boss, or a subordinate. For those dedicated to the case method, novels, short stories, and plays offer an inexhaustible storehouse of riches, more detailed, subtle, and complete than most cases written up for courses."[37]

In DeGeorge's humanities model, business ethics would not prepare students to *do* certain things, for which they likely will be trained by their employers, but to *be* certain persons. DeGeorge suggests that "a course in the philosophy of business would enable students to think about the foundations of business—its values, ends, purpose, and justification . . . philosophy could add a critical element to business education, an element that would keep business education always alive and prevent it from becoming an accepted, orthodox ideology."[38]

Finally, if normative business ethics is to recognize and, ultimately, be based on the individual, it must address another human trait: bias. Intellectual, emotional, and social biases affect all decision-making, including those of an ethical nature. Some bias is good, as in having a favorable disposition toward those who work hard in intellectually honest ways. Bias also rewards those who support and nurture the best elements of a culture, whether corporate, social, or political. But it becomes dangerous when people use it to blind themselves to the reality around them, reinforce hardened positions even in the face of contradictory evidence, and shirk their responsibility as moral beings.

An example of bias occurs when employees engage in unethical activity because it has been sanctioned by higher-ups. They abdicate personal responsibility by assigning blame elsewhere. However, no amount of rationalization of the fear of job loss, financial pressure, desire to please a supervisor, and the rest, can justify such behavior, because it diminishes **moral agency**, the self-awareness, freedom, and ability to make choices based on our perception of right and wrong. And such agency needs to be at the heart of business ethics. After all, we cannot make a commitment to serve customers, develop leaders, and improve life for all stakeholders unless there is freedom and moral agency, the necessary ingredients in establishing an attitude of concern, that is, respect for oneself and for others, including all appropriate stakeholders.

ETHICS ACROSS TIME AND CULTURES

"What's Love Got to Do with It?"

Philosopher and historian Martin Buber (1878–1965) taught that love is not a feeling but a responsibility of one person for another. Feelings may come and go, but the solidarity that people have with each other and the care they take with one another define them as human beings (Figure 5.8). Thus, love, as responsibility, depends on relationships based on good faith and concern. Business, too, is about relationships. Without a relationship of trust, there can be no exchange of goods or services upon which economies are built.

Many people question the place of love in a business setting. When seen from Buber's perspective, however, love is not an idyllic feeling but a driving force for justice and care. This does not deny the need for profit and financial success. It simply emphasizes the other side of the twofold purpose of business (profit and responsibility). In fact, John Mackey, the founder of Whole Foods, has said that love has been the basis of his success in business, which translates into care and concern for customers beyond profit and for workers beyond productivity (Figure 5.8).[39]

Figure 5.8   If there is anything that transcends time, place, and culture, it is love. The search for a universally applied set of ethics always comes back to it. But what does love look like in a business setting? (credit: "Love Is All You Need Signage" by Jacqueline Smith/Pexels, CC0)

Recall the statement by IBM quoted earlier in the chapter: "[IBM] remain[s] dedicated to leading the world into a more prosperous and progressive future; to creating a world that is fairer, more diverse, more tolerant, more just."[40]

Critical Thinking

- Can Martin Buber's notion of love play a role in business? What would that look like?
- What responsibilities do companies have regarding justice and care? Should business ethics be grounded only on more concrete tenets? Why or why not?

🔑 Key Terms

acculturation the cultural transmission and socialization process that stems from cultural exchange

consumerism a lifestyle characterized by the acquisition of goods and services

enculturation the process by which humans learn the rules, customs, skills, and values to participate in a society

humanistic business model a business model for balancing profitability and responsibility fairly, especially with regard to stakeholders

localization the process of adapting a product for non-native environments and languages, especially in other nations and cultures

mercantilism the economic theory that global wealth is static and prosperity comes from the accumulation of wealth through extraction of resources or trade

moral agency the self-awareness, freedom, and ability to make choices based on one's perception of right and wrong

universal values ethical principles that apply everywhere despite differences in time, geography, and culture

🗐 Summary

5.1 The Relationship between Business Ethics and Culture

Culture has a tremendous influence on ethics and its application in a business setting. In fact, we can argue that culture and ethics cannot be separated, because ethical norms have been established over time by and make sense to people who share the same background, language, and customs. For its part, business operates within at least two cultures: its organizational culture and the wider culture in which it was founded. When a business attempts to establish itself in a new environment, a third culture comes into play. With increasingly diverse domestic and global markets and the spread of consumerism, companies must consider the ethical implications of outsourcing production and resist the temptation to look the other way when their values are challenged by the reality of overseas supply or distribution chains.

5.2 Business Ethics over Time

As a function of culture, ethics is not static but changes in each new era. Technology is a driving force in ethical shifts, as we can see in tracing changes from the age of mercantilism to the Industrial Revolution to the postindustrial era and the Information Age. Some of the most successful recent efforts to advance ethical practices have come from influences outside industry, including government regulation and consumer pressure.

5.3 The Influence of Geography and Religion

Business is primarily about relationships—with employees, business partners, and customers and clients. Ethical standards and practices governing these relationships depend on the environment they exist in, an environment that, in turn, depends on additional factors such as geography and religion. Religion's role in business is less certain today; we are perhaps more likely to see a universal, secular code of ethics develop than to see religion serve as common ground for different cultures to come together.

5.4 Are the Values Central to Business Ethics Universal?

Any system of business ethics must consider the processes of enculturation and acculturation as well as the fact that ethical standards may shift depending on geography or time, even if certain underlying ethical values (e.g., prohibitions against lying, fraud, or murder) may remain constant. It is usually in a business's best interest to promote human flourishing within the organization, providing comprehensive training along a humanistic business model, which applies the social sciences to ensure profitability and responsibility in an organization as well as happy, productive employees.

▣ Assessment Questions

1. The fact that a McDonald's in Indonesia might provide *sambal* chili sauce to its customers rather than ketchup is as an example of _____.
   A. acculturation
   B. consumerism
   C. enculturation
   D. globalization

2. What is the major difference between enculturation and acculturation?

3. How might consumerism be at odds with the growing concern for business ethics?

4. True or False? Globalization is evidence that business is culturally neutral.

5. Protecting owners' interests was a common feature of _____.
   A. the Industrial Revolution
   B. the Information Age
   C. the Dodd-Frank Act
   D. muckraking

6. True or false? All ethical standards are relative and should be treated as such.

7. True or false? The United Nations Global Compact is a set of standards that is binding worldwide.

8. What did the decision in *Shlensky v. Wrigley* (1968) establish in ethical terms? How does it compare to the decision in *Dodge v. Ford Motor Company* (1919)?

9. Values of Protestant Christianity were often used to justify _____.
   A. mercantilism
   B. Standard Oil's overseas investments
   C. business success during the Industrial Revolution
   D. secular humanism

10. True or false? Religion continues to be a forceful influence on ethical systems.

11. Define localization and name at least three items that might be included as part of a localization effort.

12. How would you reconcile cultural differences between so-called contact and noncontact cultures in the context of business negotiations?

13. Businesses today are concerned with balancing profitability with responsibility. Therefore, they should _____.

    A. pay attention to culture

    B. go beyond compliance

    C. hire moral people

    D. hire outside consultants to monitor their supply chain.

14. What are the levels upon which business ethics exists?

    A. compliance and governance

    B. federal, state, and local

    C. normative and descriptive

    D. individual, organizational, and societal

15. Why is conscience the locus or center of ethical behavior in business?

16. Describe the challenge of identifying a universal set of ethics.

17. How does humanities in ethics differ from a humanistic business model?

 # Endnotes

1. Janos Marton, "Today in NYC History: How the Dutch Actually Bought Manhattan (The Long Version)," Untapped Cities. https://untappedcities.com/2015/05/06/today-in-nyc-history-how-the-dutch-actually-bought-manhattan-the-long-version/ (accessed December 5, 2017).
2. Nathanial Benchley, "The 24$ Swindle," *American Heritage*. http://www.americanheritage.com/content/24-swindle (accessed December 5, 2017).
3. Ojibwa, "The Governor Krieft War," Native American Netroots. http://nativeamericannetroots.net/diary/968 (accessed December 7, 2017).
4. David Gelles and Claire Cain Miller, "Business Schools Now Teaching #MeToo, N.F.L. Protests and Trump," *New York Times*, December 25, 2017. https://www.nytimes.com/2017/12/25/business/mba-business-school-ethics.html.
5. Jonathan Watts, "The Long Read Operation Car Wash: Is This the Biggest Corruption Scandal in History?" *The Guardian*, June 1, 2017. https://www.theguardian.com/world/2017/jun/01/brazil-operation-car-wash-is-this-the-biggest-corruption-scandal-in-history.
6. David Gautschi, "The Liberal Arts: What Business Needs Now" (speech, Orono, Maine, May 4, 2016), Phi Beta Kappa induction, University of Maine.
7. Ovidijus Jurevicius, "Mission Statement of IBM," Strategic Management Insight. https://www.strategicmanagementinsight.com/mission-statements/ibm-mission-statement.html (accessed December 15, 2017).
8. IBM homepage. https://www.ibm.com/ibm/us/en/ (accessed December 15, 2017).
9. George W. Merck, "Medicine Is for the Patient, Not for the Profits" (speech, Richmond, Virginia, December 1, 1950), Medical College of Virginia at Richmond. https://www.merck.com/about/our-people/gw-merck-doc.pdf.
10. Michael Avari and Robert Brancatelli, "Integrating Virtue into the Jesuit Business School Curriculum," *Journal of Jesuit Business Education* 5, no. 1 (2014): 71–87.
11. Nancy McLernon, "Protectionism Is a Negative-Sum Game," *Wall Street Journal*, December 11, 2017.
12. Jennifer Bissell-Linsk, "Nike's Focus on Robotics Threatens Asia's Low-Cost Workforce," *Financial Times*, October 22, 2017. https://www.ft.com/content/585866fc-a841-11e7-ab55-27219df83c97 (accessed December 26, 2017).
13. "Concept and Stages of World's Economy Development," JBEM. http://www.jbem.lt/concept-stages-worlds-economy-development/ (accessed January 1, 2018).
14. Ron Chernow, *Titan: The Life of John D. Rockefeller, Sr.* (New York: Random House, 1998), 534.
15. Alasdair MacIntyre, *After Virtue*, 3rd ed. (South Bend: University of Notre Dame Press, 2007), 86.
16. Alasdair MacIntyre, *After Virtue*, 3rd ed. (South Bend: University of Notre Dame Press, 2007), 74–75.
17. Aristotle, *Nicomachean Ethics*, translated by J.A.K. Thomson. (New York: Penguin Books, 2004), 1161b: "the slave is a living tool in the same way that a tool is an inanimate slave."
18. Dodge v. Ford Motor Company, Illinois College of Law. https://law.illinois.edu/wp-content/uploads/2018/06/Aviram-July-27.pdf, pp. 10–14 (accessed January 9, 2018).
19. Shlensky v. Wrigley, 237 NE 2d 776 (Ill. App. 1968).
20. United Nations Global Compact, "Our Mission." https://www.unglobalcompact.org/what-is-gc/mission (accessed February 9, 2018).
21. Global Leadership & Organizational Behavior Effectiveness (GLOBE), "GLOBE CEO Study 2014," GLOBE. http://globeproject.com/study_2014 (accessed May 1, 2018).
22. Global Leadership & Organizational Behavior Effectiveness (GLOBE), "Overview," GLOBE. http://globeproject.com/studies.
23. Fabrizio Gatti, *Bilal: Viaggiare, Lavorare, Morire da Clandestini*. (Milano: Bibliotecca Universale Rizzoli), 51–53.
24. Ron Chernow, *Titan: The Life of John D. Rockefeller*. (New York: Random House, 1998), 467.
25. "Religious Landscape Study," Pew Research Center. http://www.pewforum.org/religious-landscape-study/ (accessed January 15, 2018).
26. João Miguel Barros, "15 Observations on the Phenomenon of Corruption: An Engaged Perspective from Macau," Union Internationale des Avocats.
27. United Nations Office on Drugs and Crime, "Foreword" in "United Nations Convention against Corruption," unodc.org. http://www.unodc.org/documents/treaties/UNCAC/Publications/Convention/08-50026_E.pdf (accessed January 15, 2018).

28. Stéphanie Thomson, "We Waste $2 Trillion a Year on Corruption. Here Are Four Better Ways to Spend That Money," Weforum.org. https://www.weforum.org/agenda/2017/01/we-waste-2-trillion-a-year-on-corruption-here-are-four-better-ways-to-spend-that-money/ (accessed January 11, 2018).

29. Tom Fox, "White Collar Criminals and Their Flagrant Rationalizations," fcpablog.com. http://www.fcpablog.com/blog/2017/9/29/tom-fox-white-collar-criminals-and-their-flagrant-rationaliz.html (accessed January 16, 2018).

30. Josh Bersin, "Spending on Corporate Training Soars: Employee Capabilities Now a Priority," forbes.com. https://www.forbes.com/sites/joshbersin/2014/02/04/the-recovery-arrives-corporate-training-spend-skyrockets/#4b6b313c5a73 (accessed January 16, 2018).

31. L.V. Anderson, "Ethics Trainings Are Even Dumber Than You Think," slate.com. http://www.slate.com/articles/business/the_ladder/2016/05/ethics_compliance_training_is_a_waste_of_time_here_s_why_you_have_to_do.html (accessed January 17, 2018).

32. Max H. Bazerman and Ann E. Tenbrunsel, "Ethical Breakdowns," *Harvard Business Review*, April 2011. https://hbr.org/2011/04/ethical-breakdowns; Kristen Dooley, "The LIBOR Scandal," *Review of Banking and Financial Law*, 32 no. 1 (2012): 2–12.

33. James McBride, "Understanding the LIBOR Scandal," Council on Foreign Relations. https://www.cfr.org/backgrounder/understanding-libor-scandal (accessed January 17, 2018).

34. ABC News. "Barclays, UBS Among Six Top Banks Fined Nearly $US6bn for Rigging Foreign Exchange, Libor Rates." http://www.abc.net.au/news/2015-05-21/us-britain-fine-top-banks-nearly-6-bn-for-forex-libor-abuses/6485510 (accessed March 17, 2018).

35. Institute for Business in Society, "Giving Voice to Values," University of Virginia Darden School of Business. http://www.darden.virginia.edu/ibis/initiatives/giving-voice-to-values/ (accessed January 13, 2018).

36. Humanistic Management Center, "The Three Stepped Approach to Humanistic Management," Humanistic Management Center. http://www.humanisticmanagement.org/cgi-bin/adframe/about_humanistic_management/the_three_stepped_approach_to_humanistic_management/index.html (accessed January 13, 2018).

37. Richard T. De George, "Business as a Humanity: A Contradiction in Terms?" in *Business As a Humanity*, eds. Thomas J. Donaldson, R. Edward Freeman, The Ruffin Series in Business Ethics, ed. R. Edward Freeman. (New York: Oxford University Press, 1994), 16.

38. Richard T. De George, "Business as a Humanity: A Contradiction in Terms?" in *Business As a Humanity*, eds. Thomas J. Donaldson, R. Edward Freeman, The Ruffin Series in Business Ethics, ed. R. Edward Freeman. (New York: Oxford University Press, 1994), 17.

39. John Mackey, "Rethinking the Social Responsibility of Business," wholefoodsmarket.com, September 28, 2005. http://www.wholefoodsmarket.com/blog/john-mackeys-blog/rethinking-social-responsibility-of-%C2%A0business (accessed March 17, 2018).

40. IBM homepage. https://www.ibm.com/ibm/us/en/ (accessed January 13, 2018).

Figure 6.1 Fifty years ago, corporate and regulatory boardrooms were almost exclusively male and white, as this meeting of the Federal Open Market Committee, an executive committee of the Federal Reserve banking system, demonstrates. How much has this changed today? (credit: modification of "FOMC meeting, 1970s" by Harris & Ewing/Wikimedia Commons, Public Domain)

Chapter Outline

6.1 The Workplace Environment and Working Conditions

6.2 What Constitutes a Fair Wage?

6.3 An Organized Workforce

6.4 Privacy in the Workplace

Introduction

The 2020 Gender Diversity Index shows that many *Fortune* 1000 boards of directors still lack diversity.[1] Women and minorities continue to be underrepresented at the chief executive officer (CEO) level too.[2] Does this sameness merely look bad, or are there ethical and business reasons why top U.S. management should be more diverse (Figure 6.1)?

A demographic disconnect between leadership and workforce influences working conditions in many ways. For example, if more women held leadership roles, would workplace sexual harassment have come to light before the #MeToo movement? Would more companies offer paid family leave? If minorities were better represented at the executive level, would corporate lobbyists advocate differently for immigration and health care policies? When 70 percent of boardroom seats are occupied by white men,[3] who make up only 30 percent of the population, many people's views, ideas, and opinions will go unheard in decisions that affect their lives and livelihoods. We have seen progress, but much remains to be accomplished. Does management have an ethical duty to try to diversify top leadership? Whatever individual responses we might offer to each of these questions, a significant theme in this chapter is that ethical behavior in the workplace is most effectively instituted when it is modeled by senior leadership.

6.1 | The Workplace Environment and Working Conditions

Learning Objectives

By the end of this section, you will be able to:

- Identify specific ethical duties managers owe employees
- Describe the provisions of the Occupational Safety and Health Act
- Identify Equal Employment Opportunity Commission protections, including those against sexual harassment at work
- Describe how employees' expectations of work have changed

All employees want and deserve a workplace that is physically and emotionally safe, where they can focus on their job responsibilities and obtain some fulfillment, rather than worrying about dangerous conditions, harassment, or discrimination. Workers also expect fair pay and respect for their privacy. This section will explore the ethical and legal duties of employers to provide a workplace in which employees want to work.

Ethical Decision-Making and Leadership in the Workplace

A contemporary corporation always owes an ethical, and in some cases legal, duty to employees to be a responsible employer. In a business context, the definition of this responsibility includes providing a safe workplace, compensating workers fairly, and treating them with a sense of dignity and equality while respecting at least a minimum of their privacy. Managers should be ethical leaders who serve as role models and mentors for all employees. A manager's job, perhaps the most important one, is to give people a reason to come back to work tomorrow.

Good managers model ethical behavior. If a corporation expects its employees to act ethically, that behavior must start at the top, where managers hold themselves to a high standard of conduct and can rightly say, "Follow my lead, do as I do." At a minimum, leaders model ethical behavior by not violating the law or company policy. One who says, "Get this deal done, I don't care what it takes," may very well be sending a message that unethical tactics and violating the spirit, if not the letter, of the law are acceptable. A manager who abuses company property by taking home office supplies or using the company's computers for personal business but then disciplines any employee who does the same is not modeling ethical behavior. Likewise, a manager who consistently leaves early but expects all other employees to stay until the last minute is not demonstrating fairness.

Another responsibility business owes the workforce is transparency. This duty begins during the hiring process, when the company communicates to potential employees exactly what is expected of them. Once hired, employees should receive training on the company rules and expectations. Management should explain how an employee's work contributes to the achievement of company-wide goals. In other words, a company owes it to its employees to keep them in the loop about significant matters that affect them and their job, whether good or bad, formal or informal. A more complete understanding of all relevant information usually results in a better working relationship.

That said, some occasions do arise when full transparency may not be warranted. If a company is in the midst of confidential negotiations to acquire, or be acquired by, another firm, this information must be kept secret until a deal has been completed (or abandoned). Regulatory statutes and criminal law may require this. Similarly, any internal personnel performance issues or employee criminal investigations should normally be kept confidential within the ranks of management.

Transparency can be especially important to workers in circumstances that involve major changes, such as layoffs, reductions in the workforce, plant closings, and other consequential events. These kinds of events typically have a psychological and financial impact on the entire workforce. However, some businesses fail to show leadership at the most crucial times. A leader who is honest and open with the employees should be able to say, "This is a very difficult decision, but one that I made and will stand behind and accept responsibility for it." To workers, euphemisms such as "right sizing" to describe layoffs and job loss only sounds like corporate doublespeak designed to help managers justify, and thereby feel better (and minimize guilt), about their (or the company's) decisions. An ethical company will give workers advance notice, a severance package, and assistance with the employment search, without being forced to do so by law. Proactive rather than reactive behavior is the ethical and just thing to do.

Historically, however, a significant number of companies and managers failed to demonstrate ethical leadership in downsizing, eventually leading Congress to take action. The Worker Adjustment and Retraining Notification (WARN) Act of 1989 has now been in effect for almost three decades, protecting workers and their families (as well as their communities) by mandating that employers provide sixty days' advance notice of mass layoffs and plant closings (Figure 6.2). This law was enacted precisely because companies were not behaving ethically.

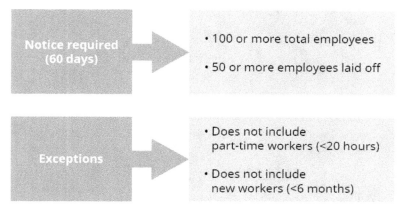

Figure 6.2 The WARN law mandates advance notice of mass layoffs to workers so that they can adequately prepare for such an event. (attribution: Copyright Rice University, OpenStax, under CC BY 4.0 license)

A report by the Cornell University Institute of Labor Relations indicated that, prior to passage of WARN, only 20 percent of displaced workers received written advance notice, and those who did received very short notice, usually a few days. Only 7 percent had two months' notice of their impending displacement.[4] Employers typically preferred to get as many days of work as possible from their workforces before a mass layoff or closing, figuring that workers might reduce productivity or look for other jobs sooner if the company were transparent and open about its situation. In other words, when companies put their own interests and needs ahead of the workforce, we can hardly call that ethical leadership.

Other management actions covered by WARN include outsourcing, automation, and artificial intelligence in the workplace. Arguably, a company has an ethical duty to notify workers who might be adversely affected even if the WARN law does not apply, demonstrating that the appropriate ethical standard for management often exceeds the minimum requirements of the law. Put another way, the law sometimes is often slow to keep up with ethical reflection on best management practices.

Workplace Safety under the Occupational Safety and Health Act

The primary federal law ensuring physical safety on the job is the Occupational Safety and Health Act (**OSHA**), which was passed in 1970.[5] The goal of the law is to ensure that employers provide a workplace environment free of risk to employees' safety and health, such as mechanical or electrical dangers, toxic chemicals, severe heat or cold, unsanitary conditions, and dangerous equipment. OSHA also refers to the Occupational Safety and Health Administration, which operates as a division of the Department of Labor and oversees enforcement of the law. This act created the National Institute for Occupational Safety and Health (NIOSH), which serves as the research institute for OSHA and enunciates appropriate standards for safety and health on the job.

Employer obligations under OSHA include the duty to provide a safe workplace free of serious hazards, to identify and eliminate health and safety hazards (Figure 6.3), to inform employees of hazards present on the job and institute training protocols sufficient to address them, to extend to employees protective gear and appropriate safeguards at no cost to them, and to publicly post and maintain records of worker injuries and OSHA citations.

Figure 6.3   Harry McShane, who celebrated his sixteenth birthday a month or so before this photo was taken by social reformer and photographer Lewis Wickes Hine, lost his left arm as a result of a workplace injury in May 1908 in Cincinnati, Ohio. McShane had already been working in the factory for more than two years. Before federal safety regulations (such as OSHA and FLSA), catastrophic injuries on the job were common, as was the presence of children in the workforce. McShane received no compensation for his injuries. (credit: modification of "Lewis Wickes Hines - Harry McShane 1908" by "Fordmadoxfraud"/Wikimedia Commons, Public Domain)

OSHA and related regulations give employees several important rights, including the right to make a confidential complaint with OSHA that might result in an inspection of the workplace, to obtain information about the hazards of the workplace and ways to avoid harm, to obtain and review documentation of work-related illnesses and injuries at the job site, to obtain copies of tests done to measure workplace hazards, and protection against any employer sanctions as a consequence of complaining to OSHA about workplace conditions or hazards.[6] A worker who believes his or her OSHA rights are being violated can make an anonymous report. OSHA will then establish whether there are reasonable grounds for believing a violation exists. If so, OSHA will conduct an inspection of the workplace and report any findings to the employer and employee, or their representatives, including any steps needed to correct safety and health issues.

OSHA has the authority to levy significant fines against companies that commit serious violations. The largest imposed to date were against BP, the oil company responsible for the largest oil spill in U.S. history, discussed in the feature box on BP Deepwater Horizon Oil Spill and Government Regulation. OSHA took into account that seventeen workers died on BP's rig, Deepwater Horizon, as a result of the initial explosion and fire in April 2010. Consequently, rig-worker safety was upgraded by statute. Total OSHA penalties issued to BP from 2005 to 2009 exceed $102 million.[7]

Other large fines issued over the last thirty years include $2.8 million against Union Carbide for violations related to an explosion and fire at its plant in Seadrift, Texas, in March 1991; $8.2 million levied against Samsung Guam in the wake of numerous worksite accidents at Guam's International Airport in 1995; and $8.7 million against Imperial Sugar in connection with an explosion at the company's plant in Port Wentworth, Georgia, in February 2008.[8] More recently, OSHA fined the producers of *The Walking Dead* $12,675 (the maximum allowable for a single citation) in the wake of the death of a stuntman working on an episode of the television show in Georgia in July 2017.[9] These fines demonstrate that the agency is serious about trying to protect the environment and workers. However, for some, the question remains whether it is more profitable for a business to gamble on cutting corners on safety and pay the fine if caught than to spend the money ahead of time to make workplaces completely safe. OSHA fines do not really tell the whole story of the penalties for workplace safety issues. There can also be significant civil liability exposure and public relations damage, as well as worker compensation payments and adverse media coverage, making an unsafe workplace a very expensive risk on multiple levels.

LINK TO LEARNING

Read this OSHA Fact Sheet about fines and penalties (https://openstax.org/l/53OSHA) **to learn more.**

A Workplace Free of Harassment

Employers have an ethical and a legal duty to provide a workplace free of harassment of all types. This includes harassment based on sex, race, religion, national origin, and any other protected status, including disability. Employees should not be expected to work in an atmosphere where they feel harassed, prejudiced against, or disadvantaged. The two complaints most frequently filed with the Equal Employment Opportunity Commission (**EEOC**), which strives to eliminate racial, gender, and religious discrimination in the workplace, are sexual harassment and racial harassment. Together, these categories made up two-thirds of all cases filed during 2017. More than thirty thousand complaints of sexual, gender, racial, or creedal harassment are filed each year, illustrating the frequency of the problem.[10]

The EEOC enforces Title VII of the Civil Rights Act (CRA) of 1964, which prohibits workplace discrimination including **sexual harassment**.[11] (As discussed elsewhere in the text, the CRA also protects employees from discrimination based on race, gender, religion, and national origin.) According to EEOC guidelines, it is unlawful to sexually harass a person because of that person's sex, either through explicit offers in exchange for sexual favors (known as quid pro quo) or through actions at a broader more systemic level that create a "hostile working environment." Sexual harassment includes unwelcome touching, requests for sexual favors, any other verbal or physical harassment of a sexual nature, offensive remarks based on a person's sex, and off-color jokes. The harasser can be the victim's supervisor (which creates company liability the first time it happens) or a peer coworker (which usually creates liability after the second time it happens, assuming the company had notice of the first occurrence). It can even be someone who is not an employee, such as a client or customer, and the law applies to men and women. Thus, the victim and the harasser both can be either a woman or a man, and offenses include both opposite-sex and same-sex harassment.

Although the law does not prohibit mild teasing, offhand comments, or isolated incidents that are not serious, harassment does become illegal when, according to the law, it is so frequent "that it creates a hostile or offensive work environment or when it is so severe that it results in an adverse employment decision (such as the victim being fired or demoted)."[12] It is management's responsibility to prevent harassment through education, training, and enforcement of a policy against it, and failure to do so will result in legal liability for the company.

Two relatively recent examples of workplace environments that descended into the worst excesses of sexist and other inappropriate behavior occurred at American Apparel and Uber. In both cases, principal leaders were mostly men who engaged in ruthless, no-holds-barred management practices that benefitted only those subordinates who most resembled the leaders themselves. Such environments may thrive for a while, but the long-term consequences can include criminal violations that produce hefty fines and imprisonment, bankruptcy, and radical upheaval in corporate management. At American Apparel and at Uber, these events resulted in the dismissal of each company's CEO, Dov Charney (who also was the founder of the company) and Travis Kalanick (who was one of the corporation's founders), respectively.[13]

In 2017 and 2018, a renewed focus on sexual harassment in the workplace and other inappropriate sexual behaviors brought a stream of accusations against high-profile men in politics, entertainment, sports, and business. They included entertainment industry mogul Harvey Weinstein; Pixar's John Lasseter; on-air personalities Matt Lauer and Charlie Rose; politicians such as Roy Moore, John Conyers, and Al Franken; and Uber's Kalanick, to name just a few (Figure 6.4).

(a)   (b)

Figure 6.4 Major figures in the news and entertainment industries, as well as Silicon Valley, have been accused of sexual harassment and often terminated or forced into retirement. Examples include Matt Lauer of NBC (a) and Travis Kalanick at Uber (b). (credit a: modification of "Hires 090402-N-0696M-018b" by Chad J. McNeeley/Wikimedia Commons, Public Domain; credit b: modification of "GES Opening Plenary on June 23, 2016" by GES Photo/Flickr, Public Domain)

The workplace harassment problem has continued for many decades despite the EEOC's enforcement efforts; it remains to be seen whether new public scrutiny will prompt a permanent change in the workplace. The Ford Motor Company serves as a relevant example. Decades after Ford tried to address sexual harassment at two Chicago-area assembly plants, the abuse at the plants evidently continues. According to legal action filed with the EEOC in the early 1990s, conditions for women working at some Ford auto assembly plants were hostile. Female employees alleged they were groped, that men pressed against them and simulated sex acts, and that men even masturbated in front of them. They further asserted that men would routinely make crude comments about the figures of female coworkers, and graffiti depictions of penises were everywhere—carved into tables, spray painted onto floors, and scribbled on walls. Managers and floor supervisors were accused of giving women better assignments in return for sex and punishing those who refused.[14]

In the 1990s, lawsuits and an EEOC action led to a $22 million settlement in which Ford admitted to widespread misconduct and committed to crack down on the offenders. However, it seems Ford still did not learn its lesson, or, after almost three decades, the memory dimmed and they slipped right back into old habits. In August 2017, the EEOC reached a new $10 million settlement with Ford for sexual and racial harassment at the two Chicago plants. Though Ford did not admit any wrongdoing in the recent settlement, it appears that neither millions of dollars in earlier damages nor promises by management led to any serious change. The *New York Times* interviewed some of the women at Ford,[15] and Sharon Dunn, who was a party of the first case and is now again a party of the second, said, "For all the good that was supposed to come out of what happened to us, it seems like Ford did nothing. If I had that choice today, I wouldn't say a damn word."

A Satisfied Workforce

Although the workplace should be free of harassment and intimidation of every sort, and management should provide a setting where all employees are treated with dignity and respect, ideally, employers should go much further.

Most people spend at least one-third and possibly as much as one-half of their waking hours at work. Management, therefore, should make work a place where people can thrive, that fosters an atmosphere in which they can be engaged and productive. Workers are happier when they like where they work and when they do not have to worry about childcare, health insurance, or being able to leave early on occasion to attend a child's school play, for example. For our grandparents' generation, a good job was dependably steady, and employees tended to stay with the same employer for years. There were not many extras other than a secure job, health insurance, and a pension plan. However, today's workers expect these traditional benefits and more. They may even be willing to set aside some salary demands in exchange for an environment featuring perquisites (or "perks"; nonmonetary benefits) such as a park-like campus, an on-the-premises gym or recreational center, flextime schedules, on-site day care and dry cleaning, a gourmet coffee house or café, and more time off. This section will explore how savvy managers establish a harmonious, compassionate workplace while still setting expectations of top performance.

Happy employees are more productive and more focused, which enhances their performance and leads to better customer treatment, fewer sick days, fewer on-the-job accidents, and less stress and burnout. They are more focused on their work, more creative, and better team players, and they are more likely to help others and demonstrate more leadership qualities. How, then, does an employer go about the process of making workers happy? Research has identified several pitfalls that managers should avoid if they want to have a good working relationship with their direct reports and, indeed, all their employees.[16] One is making employees feel like they are *just* employees. To be happy at work, employees, instead, need to feel like they know each other, have friends at work, are valued, and belong. Another pitfall is remaining aloof or above your employees. Taking an authentic interest in who they are as people really does matter. When surveys ask employees, "Do you feel like your boss cares about you?," too frequently the answer is no. One way to show caring and interest is to recognize when employees are making progress; another might be to take a personal interest in their lives and families. Asking employees to share their ideas and implementing these ideas whenever possible is another form of acknowledgement and recognition. Pause and highlight important milestones people achieve, and ensure that they feel their contributions are noticed by saying thank you.

Good advice to new managers includes making work fun. Allow people to joke around as appropriate so that when mistakes occur they can find humor in the situation and move forward without fixating simply on the downside. Celebrate accomplishments. Camaraderie and the right touch of humor can build a stronger workplace culture. Encourage exercise and sleep rather than long work hours, because those two factors improve employees' health, focus, attention, creativity, energy, and mood. In the long run, expecting or encouraging people to regularly work long hours because leaving on time looks bad is counterproductive to the goals of a firm. Accept that employees need to disengage sometimes. People who feel they are always working because their management team expects they must remain in touch via e-mail or mobile phone can become tremendously stressed. To combat this, companies should not expect their workers to be available around the clock, and workers should not feel compelled to be so available. Rather, employers should allow employees to completely disengage regularly so they can focus on their friends and families and tend to their own personal priorities. By way of international comparison, according to a recent article in *Fortune*, Germany and France have actually gone as far as banning work-related e-mails from employers on the weekends, which is a step in the right direction, even if only because disconnecting from work is now mandated by law.[17]

Employers must decide exactly how to spend the resources they have allocated to labor, and it can be challenging to make the right decision about what to provide workers (Figure 6.5). Should managers ask employees what they want? Benchmark the competition? Follow the founder's or the board's recommendations? How does a company make lifestyle benefits fair and act ethically when there is backlash against family-friendly policies from people who do not have their own families? Unlike the purchase of raw materials, utilities, and other budgetary items, which is driven primarily by cost and may present only a few choices, management's offering of employee benefits can present dozens of options, with costs ranging from minimal to very high. Work-at-home programs may actually cost the company very little, for example, whereas health insurance benefits may cost significantly more. In many other industrialized countries, the government provides (i.e., subsidizes) benefits such as health insurance and retirement plans, so a company does not have to weigh the pros and cons (i.e., do a cost-benefit analysis) of what to offer in this area. In the United States, employee benefits become part of a cost-benefit analysis, especially for small and mid-sized companies. Even larger companies today are debating what benefits to offer.

Figure 6.5 Workplace or clubhouse? Some companies offer playful perks in an effort to attract the best employees and increase worker satisfaction. (credit: work by Jason Putsche Photography/Spark Baltimore, CC BY 4.0)

Management has to decide not only how much money to spend on benefits and perks but precisely what to spend the money on. Another decision is what benefit choices management should allow each employee to make, and which choices to make for the workforce as a whole. The best managers communicate regularly with their workforce; as a result, they are more likely to know (and be able inform top management about) the types of perks most desired and most likely to attract and keep good workers. Figure 6.6 shows that men and women do not always want the same benefits, which presents a challenge for management. For instance, many women place about twice as much value as many men do on day care (23%–11%) and on paid family leave (24%–14%). Also valued more highly generally by women than by men are better health insurance, work-from-home options, and flexible hours, whereas more men value an on-site gym and free coffee more than women typically do.

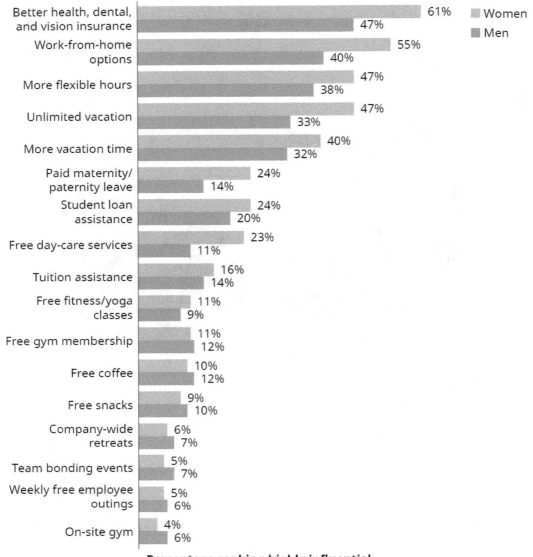

How Men and Women Rank Benefit Importance as a Tradeoff to Earnings

Percentage ranking highly influential

Source: Jones, Kerry. "The Most Desirable Employee Benefits." *Harvard Business Review*. Feb 15, 2017.
(Some data from FRACTL. "The Cost of Employee Happiness." http://www.frac.tl/employee-benefits-study/)

Figure 6.6   As this chart shows, men and women view the importance of various benefits differently, even if their top-ranked benefits are the same (i.e., better insurance, work-from-home options, and more flexible hours). (attribution: Copyright Rice University, OpenStax, under CC BY 4.0 license)

Age and generation also play a role in the types of perks that employees value. Workers aged eighteen to thirty-five rank career advancement opportunities (32%) and work-life balance (33%) as most important to them at work. However, 42 percent of workers older than thirty-five say work-life balance is the most important feature. This is likely because Generation X (born in the years 1965–1980) place a high value on opportunities for work-life balance, although, like Baby Boomers (born in the years 1946–1964), they also value salary and a solid retirement plan. On the other hand, Millennials (born in the years 1981–1997) appreciate flexibility: having a choice of benefits, paid time off, the ability to telecommute, flexible hours, and opportunities for professional development.[18]

The menu of benefits and perks thus depends on several variables, such as what the company can afford, whether employees value perks over the more direct benefit of higher pay, what the competition offers, what the industry norm is, and the company's geographic location. For example, Google is constantly searching for ways to improve the health, well-being, and morale of its "Googlers." The company is famous for offering unusual perks, like bicycles and electric cars to get staff around its sprawling California campus. Additional benefits are generous paid parental leave for new parents, on-site childcare centers at one location, paid leaves of absence to pursue further education with tuition covered, and on-site physicians, nurses, and health care. Other perks are gaming centers, organic gardens, eco-friendly furnishings, a pets-at-work policy, meditation and mindfulness training, and travel insurance and emergency assistance on personal and work-related travel. On the death of a Google employee, his or her spouse or domestic partner is compensated with a check for 50 percent of the employee's salary each year for a decade. In addition, all a deceased employee's stock options vest immediately for the surviving spouse or domestic partner. Furthermore, a deceased employee's children receive $1000 per month until they reach the age of nineteen, or until the age of twenty-three if they are full-time students.[19]

LINK TO LEARNING

Of course, Google is not the only company that offers good perks. Another is the software giant SAS. Glassdoor has an article describing some interesting benefits offered by other companies (https://openstax.org/l/53perks) in 2017. Do a quick comparison of a few of these companies. Do the perks influence your choice? Would you be willing to work for any of them?

In addition to offering benefits and perks, managers can foster a healthy workplace by applying good "people skills" as well. Managers who are respectful, open, transparent, and approachable can achieve two goals simultaneously: a workforce that is happier and also one that is more productive. Good management requires constant awareness that each team member is also an individual working to meet both personal and company goals. Effective managers act on this by regularly meeting with employees to recognize strengths, identify constructive ways to improve on weaknesses, and help workers realize collective and individual goals. Ethical businesses and good managers also invest in efforts like performance management and employee training and development. These commitments call for giving employees frequent and honest feedback about what they do well and where they need improvement, thereby enabling them to develop the skills they need, not only to succeed in the current job but to move on to the next level. Fostering teamwork by treating people fairly and acknowledging their strengths is also an important responsibility of management. Ethical managers, therefore, demonstrate most, if not all, of the following qualities: cultural awareness, positive attitude, warmth and empathy, authenticity, emotional intelligence, patience, competence, accountability, respectful, and honesty.

6.2 What Constitutes a Fair Wage?

Learning Objectives

By the end of this section, you will be able to:

- Explain why compensation is a controversial issue in the United States
- Discuss statistics about the gender pay gap
- Identify possible ways to achieve equal pay for equal work
- Discuss the ethics of some innovative compensation methods

The Center for Financial Services Innovation (CFSI) is a nonprofit, nonpartisan organization funded by many of the largest American companies to research issues affecting workers and their employers. Findings of CFSI studies indicate that employee financial stress permeates the workplaces of virtually all industries and professions. This stress eats away at morale and affects business profits. A recent CFSI report details data showing that "85% of Americans are anxious about their personal financial situation, and admit that their anxiety interferes with work. Furthermore, this financial stress leads to productivity losses and increased absenteeism, healthcare claims, turnover and costs affecting workers who cannot afford to retire."[20] The report also indicates that employees with high financial anxiety are twice as likely to take unnecessary sick time, which is can be expensive for an employer.

The CFSI report makes clear that ensuring workers are paid a fair wage is not only an ethical practice; it is also an effective way to achieve employees' highest and most productive level of performance, which is what every manager wants. In the process, it also makes workers more loyal to the company and less likely to jump ship at the first sign of a slightly better wage somewhere else.

The concept of a fair wage has a greater significance than simply one worker's pay or one company's policy. It is an economic concept critical to the nation as a whole in an economic system like capitalism, in which individuals pay for most of what they need in life rather than receiving government benefits funded by taxes. The ethical issues for the business community and for society at large are to identify democratic systems that can effectively eradicate the financial suffering of the poorest citizens and to generate sufficient wages to support the economic sustainability of all workers in the United States. Put another way, has the real income of average American workers declined so much over the past few decades that it now threatens the productivity of the largest economy in the world?

Economic Data as an Indicator of Fair Wages

The Pew Research Center indicates that over the thirty-five years between 1980 and 2014, the inflation-adjusted hourly wages of most middle-income American workers were nearly stagnant, rising just 6 percent, or an average of less than 0.2 percent, per year.[21] (The Pew Research Center defines middle-class adults as those living in households with disposable incomes ranging from 65 percent to 200 percent of the national median, which is approximately $60,000.) The data collected by the Economic Policy Institute, a nonprofit, nonpartisan think tank, show the same stagnant trend.[22] Contrast this picture with the wages of high-income workers, which rose 41 percent over the same years. Many economists, political leaders, and even business leaders admit that increasing wage and wealth disparities are not a sustainable pattern if the U.S. economy is to succeed in the long term.[23] Wage growth for all workers must be fair, which, in most cases, means higher wages for low- and middle-income workers. Figure 6.7 presents evidence of the growth of the income gap in the United Sates since the start of the great recession in 2007.

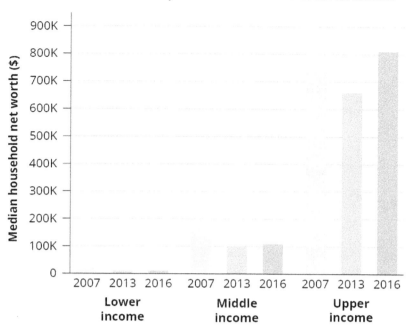

Source: Kochhar, Rakesh, and Anthony Cilluffo. "How Wealth Inequality Has Changed in the U.S. since the Great Recession, by Race, Ethnicity and Income." Pew Research Center. Nov 1, 2017.

Figure 6.7 Stagnant income has been the reality for lower- and middle-income American adults, with income in 2016 actually lower than it was 10 years before. This has not been the case for upper-income adults. (attribution: Copyright Rice University, OpenStax, under CC BY 4.0 license)

No reasonable person, regardless of profession or political party, would dispute that employees are entitled to a fair or just wage. Rather, it is in the *calculation* of a fair wage that the debate begins. Economists, sociologists, psychologists, and politicians all have opinions about this, as have most workers. Some of the factors that feature in calculations are federal and state minimum-wage standards, the cost of living, and the rate of inflation. Should a fair wage include enough money to raise a family, too, if the wage earner is the sole or principal support of a family?

Figure 6.8 shows the growth, or lack of growth, in the buying power of a minimum-wage earner since 1940. Compare the twenty-year period of 1949 through 1968 with the fifty-year period from 1968 through 2017. The difference has created a sobering reality for many workers. In the nearly six decades since 1960, the inflation-adjusted real minimum wage actually declined by 23 percent. That means minimum-wage workers did not even break even; the value of their wages declined over fifty years, meaning they have effectively worked half a century with no raise. In the following chart, *nominal wage* represents the actual amount of money a worker earns per hour; *real wage* represents the nominal wage adjusted for inflation. We consider real wages because nominal wages do not take into account changes in prices and, therefore, do not measure workers' actual purchasing power.

Figure 6.8   The graph contrasts the U.S. *nominal wage* (dollar amount) and the *real wage* (dollar amount's purchasing power) over the last seventy-five years, indicating a steady decline in purchasing power experienced by most workers. (attribution: Copyright Rice University, OpenStax, under CC BY 4.0 license)

One positive development for minimum-wage workers is that state governments have taken the lead in what was once viewed primarily as a federal issue. Today, most states have a higher minimum hourly wage than the federal minimum of $7.25. States with the highest minimum hourly wages are Washington ($11.50), California and Massachusetts ($11.00), Arizona and Vermont ($10.50), New York and Colorado ($10.40), and Connecticut ($10.00). Some cities have even higher minimum hourly wages than under state law; for example, San Francisco and Seattle are at $15.00. As of the end of 2017, twenty-nine states had higher minimum hourly wages than the federal rate, according to Bankrate.com (Figure 6.9).

Minimum Wage by State, 2017

$7.25 – $7.99
$8.00 – $8.74
$8.75 – $9.49
$9.50 – $10.24
$10.25 – $11.50

Source: Lerner, Michele. "Find the Minimum Wage in Your State." Bankrate. January 23, 2017.
(Data from the National Conference of State Legislatures, the U.S. Department of Labor, and state websites.)

Figure 6.9 As of 2017, there is a patchwork quilt of state-level minimum wage laws. (attribution: Copyright Rice University, OpenStax, under CC BY 4.0 license)

Unfair Wages: The Gender Pay Gap

Even after all possible qualifiers have been added, it remains true that women earn less than men. Managers sometimes offer multiple excuses to justify pay inequities between women and men, such as, "Women take time off for having babies" or "Women have less experience," but these usually do not explain away the differences. The data show that a woman with the same education, experience, and skills, doing the same job as a man, is still likely to earn less, at all levels from bottom to top. According to a study by the Institute for Women's Policy Research, even women in top positions such as CEO, vice president, and general counsel often earn only about 80 percent of what men with the same job titles earn.[24] Data from the EEOC over the five years from 2011 through 2015 for salaries of senior-level officials and managers (defined by the EEOC as those who set broad policy and are responsible for overseeing execution of those policies) show women in these roles earned an average of about $600,000 per year, compared with their male counterparts, who earned more than $800,000 per year.[25] That $200,000 difference amounts to a wage gap of about 35 percent each year.

The same is true in mid-level jobs as well. In a long-term study of compensation in the energy industry, researchers looked at the job of a land professional—who negotiates with property owners to lease land on which the oil companies then drill wells—and found evidence of women consistently getting paid less than men for doing the same job. Median salaries were compared for male and female land professionals with similar experience (one to five years) and educational background (bachelor's degree), and men earned $7000 more per year than their female counterparts.[26]

Doesn't the law require men and women to be paid the same? The answer is yes and no. Compensation discrimination has been illegal for more than fifty years under a U.S. law called the Equal Pay Act, passed in 1963. But the problem persists. Women earned about 60 percent of what men earned in 1960, and that value had risen to only 80 percent by 2016. Given these historic rates, women are not projected to reach pay equity until at least 2059, with projections based on recent trends predicting dates as late as 2119.[27] These are aggregate data; thus, they include women and men with the same job, or similar jobs, or jobs considered to fall in the same general category, but the data do not compare the salary of a secretary to that of a CEO, which would be an unrealistic comparison.

Equal pay under the law means equal pay for the "same" job, but not for the "equivalent" job. Those companies wishing to avoid strict compliance with the law may use several devices to justify unequal pay, including using slightly different job titles, slightly different lists of job duties, and other techniques that lead to different pay for different employees doing essentially the same job. Women have taken employers to court for decades, only to find their lawsuits unsuccessful because proving individual compensation discrimination is very difficult, especially given that multiple factors can come into play in compensation decisions. Sometimes class-action lawsuits have been more successful, but even then plaintiffs often lose.

Can anything be done to achieve equal pay? One step would be to pass a new law strengthening the rules on equal pay, but two recent attempts to pass the Paycheck Fairness Act (S.84, H.R.377) and the Fair Pay Act (S.168, H.R.438) narrowly failed.[28] These or similar bills, if ever enacted into law, would significantly reduce wage discrimination against those who work in similar job categories by establishing equal pay for "equivalent" work, rather than the current law which uses the term "same" job. The idea of pay equivalency is closely related to **comparable worth**, a concept that has been put into action on a limited basis over the years, but never on a large scale. Comparable worth holds that workers should be paid on the basis of the worth of their job to the organization. Equivalent work and comparable worth can be important next steps in the path to equal pay, but they are challenging to implement because they require rethinking the entire basis for pay decisions.

LINK TO LEARNING

Though the federal government has not yet passed the Paycheck Fairness Act, some states have taken action on their own. The website for the National Conference of State Legislatures' section on state equal pay laws (https://openstax.org/l/53PayLaws) provides a chart listing states that go beyond the current federal law to mandate equal pay for comparable or equivalent work. Look up your state in the chart. How does it compare with others in this regard?

If a woman's starting salary for the first job of her career is less than that of a man, the initial difference, even if small, tends to cause a systemic, career-long problem in terms of pay equity. Researchers at Temple University and George Mason University found that if a new hire gets $5000 more than another worker hired at the same time, the difference is significantly magnified over time. Assuming an average annual pay increase of 5 percent, an employee starting with a $55,000 salary will earn at least $600,000 more over a forty-year career than an employee who starts an equivalent job with a $50,000 salary. This significantly affects many personal decisions, including retirement, because, all other things equal, a lower-paid woman will have to work three years longer than a man to earn the same amount of money over the course of her career.[29]

ETHICS ACROSS TIME AND CULTURES

European Approaches to the Gender Pay Gap

The policies of other nations can offer some insight into how to address pay inequality. Iceland, for example, has consistently been at the top of the world rankings for workplace gender equality in the World Economic Forum survey.[30] A new Icelandic law went into effect on January 1, 2018, that makes it illegal to pay men more than women, gauged not by specific job category, but rather in all jobs collectively at any employer with twenty-five or more employees, a concept known as an aggregate salary data approach.[31] The burden of proof is on employers to show that men and women are paid equally or they face a fine. The ultimate goal is to eliminate all pay inequities in Iceland by the year 2022. The United Kingdom has taken a first step toward addressing this issue by mandating pay transparency, which requires employers with 250 workers or more to publish details on the gaps in average pay between their male and female employees.[32]

Policies not directly linked to salary can help as well. German children have a legal right to a place in kindergarten from the age of three years, which has allowed one-third of mothers who could not otherwise afford nursery school or kindergarten to join the workforce.[33] In the United Kingdom, the government offers up to thirty hours weekly of free care for three- and four-year-old children to help mothers get back in the workforce. Laws such as these allow women, who are often the primary caregivers in a household, to experience fewer interruptions in their careers, a factor often blamed for the wage gap in the United States.

The World Economic Forum reports that about 65 percent of all Organization for Economic Cooperation and Development (OECD) countries have introduced new policies on pay equality, including requiring many employers to publish calculations every year showing the gender pay gap.[34] Steps such as the collection and reporting of aggregate salary data, or some form of early education or subsidized childcare, are positive steps toward eventually achieving the goal of wage equality.

Critical Thinking

- Which of these policies do you think would be the most likely to be implemented in the United States and why?
- How would each of the normative theories of ethical behavior (virtue ethics, utilitarianism, deontology, and justice theory) view this issue and these proposed solutions?

Part of the reason that initial pay disparity is heightened over a career is that when a worker changes jobs, the new employer usually asks what the employee was making in his or her last job and uses that as a baseline for pay in the new job. To combat the problem of history-based pay, which often hurts women, eight states (and numerous municipalities) in the United States now ban employers from asking job applicants to name their last salary.[35] Although this restriction will not solve the entire problem, it could have a positive effect if it spreads nationally. In a survey by the executive search firm Korn Ferry, forty-six of one hundred companies said they usually comply with the legal requirements in force in the strictest of the locations in which they operate, meaning workers in states without this law might not be asked about their salary history during new-job negotiations either.[36]

Experiments in Compensation

Whether we are discussing fair wages, minimum wages, or equal wages, the essence of the debate often boils down to ethics. What should people get paid, who should determine that, and should managers and upper management do only what is required by law or go above and beyond if that means doing what they think is right? Organizational pay structures are set by a variety of methods, including internal policies, the advice of outside compensation consultants, and external data, such as market salaries.

An innovative compensation decision in Seattle may provide some insight. In 2011, a young man earning $35,000 a year told his boss at Gravity, a credit-card payments business, that his earnings were not sufficient for a decent life in expensive Seattle. The boss, Dan Price, who cofounded the company in 2004, was somewhat surprised as he had always taken pride in treating employees well. Nevertheless, he decided his employee was right. For the next three years, Gravity gave every employee a 20 percent annual raise. Still, profit continued to outgrow wages. So Price announced that over the *next* three years, Gravity would phase in a minimum salary of $70,000 for all employees. He reduced his own salary from $1 million to $70,000, to demonstrate the point and help fund it. The following week, five thousand people applied for jobs at Gravity, including a Yahoo executive who took a pay cut to transfer to a company she considered fun and meaningful to work for.

Price's decision started a national debate: How much should people be paid? Since 2000, U.S. productivity has increased 22 percent, yet inflation-adjusted median wages have increased only 2 percent. That means a larger share of capitalism's rewards are going to shareholders and top executives (who already earn an average of three hundred times more than typical workers, up from seventy times more just a decade ago), and a smaller share is going to workers. If Gravity profits while sharing the benefits of capitalism more broadly, Price's actions will be seen as demonstrating that underpaying the workforce hurts employers. If it fails, it may look like proof that companies should not overpay.

Price recognized that low starting salaries were antithetical to his values and felt that struggling employees would not be motivated to maintain the high quality that made his company successful with that compensation. He calls the $70,000 minimum wage an ethical and moral imperative rather than a business strategy, and, though it will cost Gravity about $2 million per year, he has ruled out price increases and layoffs. More than half the initial cost was offset by his own pay cut, the rest by profit. Revenue continues to grow at Gravity, along with the customer base and the workforce. Currently, the firm has a retention rate of 91 percent.[37] Yet Price says managers' scorecards should measure purpose, impact, and service, as much as profit.

Michael Wheeler, a professor at Harvard Business School who teaches a course called "Negotiation and The Moral Leader," recently discussed the aftermath of Dan Price's decision at Gravity. He interviewed other entrepreneurs about their plans for creative compensation to help develop a happy and motivated workforce, and it appears that some other companies are taking notice of how successful Gravity has been since Price made the decision to pay his workers more.[38] One of these entrepreneurs was Megan Driscoll, the CEO of Pharmalogics Recruiting, who, after hearing Dan Price speak to a group of executives, was inspired to raise the starting base pay of her employees by 33 percent. When Driscoll put her plan to work, her business had forty-six employees and $6.7 million in revenue. A year later, staff and revenues had jumped to seventy-two and $15 million, respectively. Driscoll points to data showing her people are working harder and smarter after the pay raise than before. There has been a 32 percent increase in clients, and the client retention rate doubled to 80 percent.[39]

Stephan Aarstol, CEO of Tower Paddleboards, wanted to give his workers a raise, but his company did not have the cash. Instead, Aarstol boldly cut the work day to five hours from the ten hours most employees had been working. Essentially that doubled their pay, and as a result, he says, employee focus and engagement have skyrocketed, as have company profits.[40]

Managers must carefully balance the short term, such as quarterly profits, versus long-term sustainability as a successful company. This requires recognizing the value of work that each person contributes and devising a fair, and sometimes creative, compensation plan.

6.3 An Organized Workforce

Learning Objectives

By the end of this section, you will be able to:

- Discuss trends in U.S. labor union membership
- Define codetermination
- Compare labor union membership in the United States with that in other nations
- Explain the relationship between labor productivity gains and the pay ratio in the United States

The issue of worker representation in the United States is a century-old debate, with economic, ethical, and political aspects. Are unions good for workers, good for companies, good for the nation? There is no single correct response. Your answer depends upon your perspective—whether you are a worker, a manager, an executive, a shareholder, or an economist. How might an ethical leader address the issue of the gap between labor's productivity gains and their relatively stagnant wages as compared with that of management?

Organized Labor

Americans' longstanding belief in individualism makes some managers wonder why employees would want or need to be represented by a labor union. The answer is, for the same reasons a CEO wants to be represented by an attorney when negotiating an employment contract, or that an entertainer wants to be represented by an agent. Unions act as the agent/lawyer/negotiator for employees during **collective bargaining**, a negotiation process aimed at getting management's agreement to a fair employment contract for members of the union. Everyone wants to be successful in any important negotiation, and people often turn to professionals to help them in such a situation.

However, in the United States, as elsewhere around the globe, the concept of worker organization has been about more than simply good representation. Unionization and worker rights have often been at the core of debates related to class economics, political power, and ethical values. There are legitimate points on each side of the union debate (Table 6.1).

Pros and Cons of Unions

Pros of Unions	Cons of Unions
Unions negotiate increased pay and benefits for workers.	Unions can make it harder to fast-track promotions for high-performing workers and/or get rid of low-performing ones.

Table 6.1

Pros and Cons of Unions

Pros of Unions	Cons of Unions
Unions create a formal dispute resolution process for workers.	Workers are required to pay union dues/fees that some might rather not pay.
Unions act as an organized lobbying group for worker rights.	Unions sometimes lead to a closed culture that makes it harder to diversify the workforce.
Collective bargaining agreements often set norms for employment for an entire industry—benefiting all workers, including those who are not at a union company.	Collective bargaining contracts can drive up costs for employers and lead to an adversarial relationship between management and workers.

Table 6.1

The value of unions is a topic that produces significant disagreement. Historically, unions have attained many improvements for workers in terms of wages and benefits, standardized employment practices, labor protections (e.g., child labor laws), workplace environment, and on-the-job safety. Nevertheless, sometimes unions have acted in their own interests to sustain their own existence, without primary concern for the workers they represent.

The history of the worker movement (summarized in the video in the following Link to Learning) reveals that in the first half of the twentieth century, wages were abysmally low, few workplace safety laws existed, and exploitive working conditions allowed businesses to use child labor. Unions stepped in and played an important role in leveling the playing field by representing the interests of the workers. Union membership grew to a relatively high level (33% of wage and salary workers) in the 1950s, and unions became a force in politics. However, their dominance was relatively short-lived, not least because in the 1960s, the federal government started to enact employment laws that codified many of the worker protections unions had championed. In the 1980s and 1990s, the U.S. economy gradually evolved from manufacturing, where unions were strong, to services, where unions were not as prevalent. The service sector is more difficult to organize, due to a variety of factors such as the historical absence of unions in the sector, workers' widely differing work functions and schedules, challenging organizational status, and white-collar bias against unions.

LINK TO LEARNING

This three-minute video entitled "The Rise and Fall of U.S. Labor Unions" (https://openstax.org/l/53LaborUnions) summarizes the history of the union movement. It is based on information from University of California Santa Cruz Professor William Domhoff and the University of Houston Bauer College of Business.

These developments, along with the appearance of state right-to-work laws, have led to a decline in unions and their membership. **Right-to-work laws** give workers the option of not joining the union, even at companies where the majority has voted to be represented by a union, resulting in lower membership. Right-to-work laws attempt to counter the concept of a union shop or **closed shop**, which requires that all new hires automatically be enrolled in the labor union appropriate to their job function and that union dues automatically be deducted from their pay.

Some question the fairness of right-to-work laws, because they allow those who do not join the union to get the same pay and benefits as those who do join and who pay unions dues for their representation. On the other hand, right-to-work laws provide workers the right of choice; those who do not want to join a union are not forced to do so. Those who do not choose to join may end up having a strained relationship with union workers, however, when a union-mandated strike occurs. Some non-union members, and even union members, elect to cross the picket line and continue to work. Traditionally, these "scabs," as they are derisively labeled by unions, have faced both overt and subtle retaliation at the hands of their coworkers, who prioritize loyalty to the union.

Twenty-eight states have right-to-work laws (Figure 6.10). Notice that many right-to-work states, such as Michigan, Missouri, Indiana, Wisconsin, Kentucky, Tennessee, Alabama, and Mississippi, are among the top ten states where automobiles are manufactured and unions once were strong.

States with Right-to-Work Laws

Source: National Conference of State Legislatures. "Right-to-Work Resources." http://www.ncsl.org/research/labor-and-employment/right-to-work-laws-and-bills.aspx.

Figure 6.10 Right-to-work states have typically been clustered in the South and Southeast, where unions have been traditionally less prevalent. (attribution: Copyright Rice University, OpenStax, under CC BY 4.0 license)

According to the U.S. Bureau of Labor Statistics, total union membership in the United States dropped to 20 percent of the workforce in 1980; by 2016, it was down to about half that (Figure 6.11).[41] Public sector (government) workers have a relatively high union membership rate of 35 percent, more than five times that of private-sector workers, which is at an all-time low of 6.5 percent. White-collar workers in education and training, as well as first responders such as police and firefighters now have some of the highest unionization rates, also 35 percent. Among states, New York continues to have the highest union membership rate at 23 percent, whereas South Carolina has the lowest, at slightly more than 1 percent.

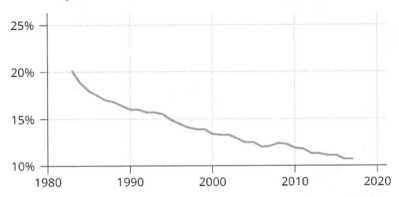

Percentage of U.S. Workers Who Are Union Members, 1983–2017

Sources: Miller, Kevin. American Association of University Women. "The Simple Truth about the Gender Pay Gap." Spring 2018. Bureau of Labor Statistics. "Union Affiliation Data from the Current Population Survey." May 16, 2018.

Figure 6.11 Union membership in the United States has steadily declined since 1980. (attribution: Copyright Rice University, OpenStax, under CC BY 4.0 license)

Codetermination is a workplace concept that goes beyond unionization to embrace shared governance, in which management and workers cooperate in decision-making and workers have the right to participate on the board of directors of their company. Board-level representation by employees is widespread in European Union countries. Most codetermination laws apply to companies over a certain size. For example, in Germany, they apply to companies with more than five hundred employees.[42] The labor union movement never has been quite as strong in the United States as in Europe—the trade-union movement began in Europe and remains more vibrant there even today—and codetermination is thus not common in U.S. companies (Table 6.2).

Unionization as Percentage of Workforce in Eight Industrialized Nations

Country	Workforce in Unions, %
Australia	25
Canada	30
France	9
Germany	26
Italy	35
Japan	22

Table 6.2 Labor union membership remains much higher in Europe and other Group of Seven (G7) countries than in the United States. Only France has a lower percentage of union membership.[43]

Unionization as Percentage of Workforce in Eight Industrialized Nations

Country	Workforce in Unions, %
Sweden	82
United Kingdom	29
United States	12

Table 6.2 Labor union membership remains much higher in Europe and other Group of Seven (G7) countries than in the United States. Only France has a lower percentage of union membership.[43]

Codetermination has worked relatively well in some countries. For example, in Germany, workers, managers, and the public at large support the system, and it has often resulted in workers who are more engaged and have a real voice in their workplaces. Management and labor have cooperated, which, in turn, has led to higher productivity, fewer strikes, better pay, and safer working conditions for employees, which is a classic win-win for both sides.

Pay and Productivity in the United States

Some managers, politicians, and even members of the general public believe unions are a big part of the reason that U.S. companies have difficulty competing in the global economy. The conservative think tank Heritage Foundation conducted a study that concluded unions may be responsible, in part, for a slower work process and reduced productivity.[44] However, multiple other studies indicate that U.S. productivity is up.[45]

Productivity in the United States increased 74 percent in the period 1973 to 2016, according to the OECD. In global productivity rankings, most studies indicate the United States ranks quite high, among the top five or six countries in the world and number two on the list compiled by the OECD (Table 6.3).

Productivity in 2015 by Country (Sample of Eight Industrialized Nations)

Country	Productivity (output/hours worked)
Australia	102.20
Canada	109.45
Germany	105.90
Japan	103.90
Mexico	105.10
South Korea	97.60

Table 6.3 This table compares 2015 productivity among several industrialized nations. U.S. productivity ranks high on the list.[46]

Productivity in 2015 by Country (Sample of Eight Industrialized Nations)

Country	Productivity (output/hours worked)
United Kingdom	100.80
United States	108.87

Table 6.3 This table compares 2015 productivity among several industrialized nations. U.S. productivity ranks high on the list.[46]

During the same period as the productivity gains discussed in the preceding paragraph, 1973 to 2016, wages for U.S. workers increased only 12 percent. In other words, productivity has grown six times more than pay. Taken together, these facts mean that American workers, union members or not, should not shoulder the blame for competitive challenges faced by U.S. companies. Instead, they are a relative bargain for most companies. Figure 6.12 compares productivity and pay and demonstrates the growing disparity between the two, based on data collected by the Economic Policy Institute.

Employee Productivity and Compensation, 1950–2010

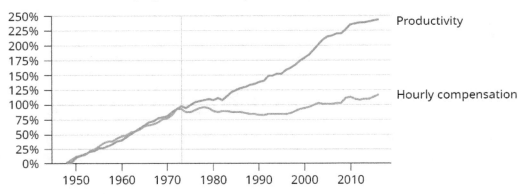

Source: Economic Policy Institute. "The Productivity-Pay Gap." Oct 2017. Based on analysis of data from BLS Labor Productivity and Costs program, Bureau of Labor Statistics Current Employment Statistics public data series and Employer Costs for Employee Compensation, and Bureau of Economic Analysis National Income and Product Accounts (Tables 2.3.4, 6.2, 6.3, 6.9, 6.10, and 6.11).

Figure 6.12   In the last four decades, wages in the United States have not kept up with productivity. According to the Economic Policy Institute, from 1948 to 1973, hourly compensation rose 91 percent, which closely follows productivity gains of 97 percent. However, from 1973 to 2013, hourly compensation rose only 9 percent, whereas productivity rose 74 percent in the same period. (attribution: Copyright Rice University, OpenStax, under CC BY 4.0 license)

Is Management Compensation Fair?

We gain yet another perspective on labor by looking at management compensation relative to that of employees. Between 1978 and 2014, inflation-adjusted CEO pay increased by almost 1,000 percent in the United States, while worker pay rose 11 percent.[47] A popular way to compare the fairness of a company's compensation system with that in other countries is the widely reported **pay ratio**, which measures how many times greater CEO pay is than the wages for the average employee.

The average multiplier effect in the United States is in the range of three hundred. This means that CEO pay is, on average, three hundred times as high as the pay of the average worker in the same company. In the United

Kingdom, the multiplier is twenty-two; in France, it is fifteen; and in Germany, it is twelve.[48] The 1965 U.S. ratio was only twenty to one, which raises the question, why and how did CEO pay rise so dramatically high in the United States compared with the rest of the world? Are CEOs in the United States that much better than CEOs in Germany or Japan? Do American companies perform that much better? Is this ratio fair to investors and employees? A large part of executive compensation is in the form of stock options, which frequently are included in the calculation of an executive's salary and benefits, rather than direct salary. However, this, in turn, raises the question of whether all or a portion of the general workforce should also share in some form of stock options.

LINK TO LEARNING

Some corporate boards claim executive pay is performance based; others claim it is a retention strategy to prevent CEOs from going to another company for more money. This video shows former CEO Steven Clifford discussing CEO pay (https://openstax.org/l/53CEOPay) and claiming that U.S. executives often dramatically, and in many cases unjustifiably, boost their own pay to astronomical levels, leaving shareholders and workers wondering why. He also discusses how it can be stopped.

Everyone wants to be paid fairly for their work. Whether CEO or administrative assistant, engineer or assembly-line worker, we naturally look out for our own best interest. Thus, management compensation is a topic that often causes resentment among the rank and file, especially when organized workers go on strike. From the employee viewpoint, the question is why management often wants to hold the line when it comes to everyone's wages but their own.

CASES FROM THE REAL WORLD

Verizon Strike

More than forty thousand Verizon workers went on strike in 2016 (Figure 6.13). The strike was eventually settled, with workers getting a raise, but bitter feelings and distrust remained on both sides. Workers thought management salaries were too high; management thought workers were seeking excessive raises. To continue basic phone services for its customers during the strike, Verizon called on thousands of non-union employees to perform the strikers' work. Non-union staff had to cross picket lines formed by fellow employees to go to work each day during the strike. Enmity toward these picket-line crossers was exceptionally high among some union members.

Figure 6.13   Union workers from the Communications Workers of America and the International Brotherhood of Electrical Workers are shown walking a Verizon picket line. They are protesting Verizon's decision to not provide pay raises. (credit: modification of "Verizon on Strike" by Marco Verch/Flickr, CC BY 2.0)

Critical Thinking

- How does management reintroduce civility to the workplace to keep peace between different factions?
- How could Verizon please union workers after the strike without firing the picket-line crossers, some of whom were Verizon union employees who consciously chose to cross the picket line?

6.4 | Privacy in the Workplace

Learning Objectives

By the end of this section, you will be able to:

- Explain what constitutes a reasonable right to privacy on the job
- Identify management's responsibilities when monitoring employee behavior at work

Employers are justifiably concerned about threats to and in the workplace, such as theft of property, breaches of data security, identity theft, viewing of pornography, inappropriate and/or offensive behavior, violence, drug use, and others. They seek to minimize these risks, and that often requires monitoring employees at work. Employers might also be concerned about the productivity loss resulting from employees using office technology for personal matters while on the job. At the same time, however, organizations must balance the valid business interests of the company with employees' reasonable expectations of privacy.

Magnifying ethical and legal questions in the area of privacy is the availability of new technology that lets employers track all employee Internet, e-mail, social media, and telephone use. What kind and extent of monitoring do you believe should be allowed? What basic rights to privacy ought a person have at work? Does your view align more closely with the employer's or the employee's?

Legal and Ethical Aspects of Electronic Monitoring

Monitored workstations, cameras, microphones, and other electronic monitoring devices permit employers to oversee virtually every aspect of employees' at-work behavior (Figure 6.14). Technology also allows employers to monitor every aspect of computer use by employees, such as downloads of software and documents, Internet use, images displayed, time a computer has been idle, number of keystrokes per hour, words typed, and the content of e-mails. According to a survey by the American Management Association, 48 percent of employers used a form of video monitoring in the workplace, and 67 percent monitored employee Internet use. In 30 percent of the organizations responding to the survey, this electronic monitoring had ultimately led to an employee's termination. [49]

Figure 6.14   Electronic monitoring often captures data from cameras, computers, and listening devices. This information can then be used against employees accused of violating company policy, raising privacy concerns. (credit left: modification of "Surveillance video cameras, Gdynia" by Paweł Zdziarski/Wikimedia Commons, CC 2.5; credit right: credit: modification of "Keylogger-screen-capture-example" by "FlippyFlink"/Wikimedia Commons, Public Domain)

The laws and regulations governing electronic monitoring are somewhat indirect and inconsistent. Very few specific federal statutes directly regulate private employers when it comes to broad workplace privacy issues. However, monitoring is subject to various state rules under both statutory and common law, and sometimes federal and state constitutional provisions as well. The two primary areas of the law related to workplace monitoring are a federal statute called the Electronic Communications Privacy Act of 1986 (ECPA) and various state common law protections against invasion of privacy.[50]

Although the ECPA may appear to prohibit an employer from monitoring its employees' oral, wire, and electronic communications, it contains two big exceptions that weaken its protection of employees' rights. One is the **business purpose exception**. This allows employers—on the basis of legitimate business purposes—to monitor electronic and oral communications, and employers generally assert a legitimate business purpose to be present. The other widely used exception is the **consent exception**, which allows employers to monitor employee communications provided employees have given their consent. According to the Society for Human Resource Management, the ECPA definition of electronic communication applies to the electronic transmission of communications but not to their electronic storage. Therefore, courts have distinguished between monitoring electronic communications such as e-mail during transmission and viewing e-mails in storage. Viewing emails during transmission is broadly allowed, whereas viewing stored e-mail is considered similar to searching an employee's private papers and thus is not routinely allowed under the ECPA unless certain circumstances apply (e.g., the e-mails are stored in the employer's computer systems).[51]

In general, it is legal for a company to monitor the use of its own property, including but not limited to computers, laptops, and cell phones. According to the ECPA, an employer-provided computer system is the property of the employer, and when the employer provides employees with a laptop they can take home, it likely violates no laws when it monitors everything employees do with that computer, whether business-related or personal. The same is true of an employer-provided cell phone or tablet, and always true when an employer gives employees notice of a written policy regarding electronic monitoring of equipment supplied by the company. Generally, the same is *not* true of equipment owned by the employee, such as a personal cell phone.

However, an important distinction is based on the issue of consent. The consent provision in the ECPA is not limited to business communications only; therefore, a company might be able to assert the right to monitor personal electronic communications if it can show employee consent (although this is very likely to worry employees, as discussed in the next section). Another consideration is whose e-mail server is being used. The ECPA and some state laws generally make it illegal for employers to intercept private e-mail by using an employee's personal log-on/user ID/password information.

Although the ECPA and National Labor Relations Act are both federal laws, individual states are free to pass laws that impose greater limitations, and several states have done so. Some require employers to provide employees advance written notice that specifies the types or methods of monitoring to which they will be subjected. Examples of state laws creating some degree of protection for workers include laws in California and Pennsylvania that require consent of both parties before any conversation can be monitored or recorded.

Employees can bring common law privacy claims to challenge employer monitoring. (Common laws are those based on prior court decisions rather than on legislatively enacted statutes.) To prevail on a common law claim of invasion of privacy, which is a tort, the employee must demonstrate a right to privacy with respect to the information being monitored. Several state constitutions, such as those in Louisiana, Florida, South Carolina, and California, expressly provide citizens a right to privacy, which may protect employees with respect to monitoring of their personal electronic information and personal communication in the workplace.

One additional regulatory consideration applicable to electronic monitoring is whether the company's workforce is unionized. The National Labor Relations Board, the federal labor law agency, has ruled that the video surveillance of any portion of the workplace is a condition of employment subject to collective bargaining and must be agreed to by the union before implementation, so employees have notice. If a workplace is not unionized (the majority are not), then this federal regulation requiring notice does not apply, and as stated previously in this chapter, if there is any protection at all, it would have to be given by state regulation (which is rare in the private [nongovernmental] sector).

What Constitutes a Reasonable Monitoring Policy?

Many employees generally are not be familiar with the specific details of the law. They may feel offended by monitoring, especially of their own equipment. Companies must also consider the effect on workplace morale if everyone feels spied upon, and the risk that some high-performing employees may decide to look elsewhere for career opportunities. Employers should develop a clear, specific, and reasonable monitoring policy. The policy should limit monitoring to that which is directly work related. For example, if a company is concerned about productivity and the goal of monitoring is to keep tabs on employee performance, then neither keystroke logging nor screenshot recording is necessary; software designed to show idle time or personal Internet use would be more helpful in identifying wasted time, which is the ultimate goal.

Employers should always remember their business goals when monitoring employees. It is not only a matter of treating employees ethically; it also makes good business sense to ensure that monitoring pertains only to business matters and does not unnecessarily intrude into the privacy of employees. Perhaps most importantly, in the interest of fairness, the monitoring policy must be communicated to the employees. When, if ever, is it acceptable to monitor without notice to the employee and without his or her knowledge?

LINK TO LEARNING

This notice by the State of Connecticut (https://openstax.org/l/53notice) mandates that all employers inform employees of the kinds of electronic monitoring of their activities and communications that may be undertaken at work, and the responsibilities of an employer. Read the notice and decide whether you think it is a reasonable policy. Would it make sense to the average worker? Do you think it is unfair to either party?

The Connecticut policy in the preceding Link to Learning applies to all employers (i.e., in state and in private sector workplaces). However, many states have policies that apply only to employees who work for the government. State employees hold a special status that conveys certain state constitutional rights with regard to due process, reasonable searches, and related legal doctrines. The same is true for federal government employees and the U.S. Constitution, which means the government has a duty of fairness in employee surveillance. It does not mean, however, that the government cannot monitor its employees at all, as demonstrated by an incident involving a California police officer. In a unanimous decision in *Ontario v. Quon*,[52] the U.S. Supreme Court in 2010 ruled in favor of a police chief in Ontario, California, who read nearly five hundred text messages sent by one of his sergeants on a police-issued pager. Many of the text messages were personal and some were sexually explicit. Only a few dozen were work related. The justices agreed that constitutional limits on unreasonable searches by public employers (under the Fourth Amendment) were minimal given a work-related purpose.

This decision creates precedent for more than 25 million employees of federal, state, and local governments and limits their expectation of privacy when using employer-issued tools. "Because the search [by the police chief] was motivated by a legitimate work-related purpose and because it was not excessive in scope, the search was reasonable," said Justice Anthony M. Kennedy.

In the private sector, where employees are not working for the government and the constitutional prohibition on unreasonable searches and seizures has very little applicability, if any, employers have even more latitude in terms of employee monitoring than in a government setting. The *Ontario v. Quon* case in all likelihood would never even make it to court if the employer were a private-sector company, because the issue of whether getting the text message was a reasonable search and seizure under the Fourth Amendment does not apply in a nongovernment employment setting. The Constitution acts to limit government intrusions but does not generally restrict private companies in this type of situation. However, ethical considerations may encourage private-sector employers to treat their workers respectfully, even if not required by law.

WHAT WOULD YOU DO?

Security versus Privacy

You manage a large, high-end jewelry store with an international clientele. Your workforce of 150 is demographically diverse, and your employees are trustworthy as a rule. However, you have experienced some unexplained loss of inventory and suspect a couple of employees are stealing valuable pieces, removing them from backroom storage safes and handing them off to another person somewhere in the store who leaves with them or to a third person pretending to be a customer. To prevent this, your assistant managers are urging you to place discreet cameras in the restrooms and break rooms, where these exchanges are likely occurring. Some managers might be concerned about using cameras at all due to privacy issues; others might want to use them without notifying employees or putting up signs because they do not want to tip off the suspects or deal with the negative reaction of the workforce (although that brings up invasion of privacy issues). You are weighing the pros of catching the thieves against the possible loss of other employees' trust.

Critical Thinking

- What issues must you confront as you decide whether you will take the recommendation of your assistant managers?
- What, ultimately, will you do? Explain your decision.

Drug Testing in the Workplace

Key issues that arise about a drug testing or monitoring program begin with whether an employer wants or needs to do it. Is it required by law for a particular job, under state or local regulations? Is it for pre-employment clearance? Does the employer need employees' permission? Does a failed test require mandatory termination? With the exception of employers in industries regulated by the federal government, such as airlines, trucking companies, rail lines, and national security-related firms, federal law is not controlling on the issue of drug testing in the workplace; it is largely a state issue. At the federal level, the Department of Transportation does mandate drug testing for workers such as airline crews and railway conductors and has a specific procedure that must be followed. However, for the most part, drug testing is not mandatory and depends on whether the employer wants to do it. Multiple states do regulate drug testing, but to varying degrees, and there is no common standard to be followed.

Testing of job applicants is the most common form of drug testing. State laws typically allow it, but the employer must follow state rules, if they exist, about providing notice and following standard procedures intended to prevent inaccurate samples. Testing current employees is much less common, primarily due to cost; however, companies that do use drug testing include some in the pharmaceutical and financial services industries. Some states put legal constraints on drug testing of private-sector employees. For example, in a few states. the job must include the possibility of property damage or injury to others, or the employer must believe the employee is using drugs.

Challenging a drug test is difficult because tests are considered highly accurate. An applicant or employee can refuse to take the test, but that often means not being hired or losing the job, assuming the worker is an employee at will. The concept of **employment at will** affirms that either the employee or the employer may dissolve an employment arrangement at will (i.e., without cause and at any time unless an employment contract is in effect that stipulates differently). Most workers are considered employees at will because neither the employer nor employee is obligated to the other; the worker can quit or be fired at any time for any reason because there is no contractual obligation. In some states, the employee risks not only job loss but also the denial of unemployment benefits if fired for refusing to take a drug test. Thus, the key concept that makes drug testing possible is employment at will, which covers approximately 85 percent of the employees in the private sector (unionized workers and top executives have contracts and thus are not at will, nor are government employees who have due process rights). The only legal limitation is that, in some states, the drug testing procedure must be fair, accurate, and designed to minimize errors and false-positive results.

The drug testing process, however, raises some difficult privacy issues. Employers want and are allowed to protect against specimen tampering by taking such steps as requiring subjects to wear a hospital gown. Some employers use test monitors who check the temperature of the urine and/or listen as a urine sample is collected. According to the Cornell University Law School Legal Information Institute, some state courts (e.g., Georgia, Louisiana, Hawaii) have found it an unreasonable invasion of privacy for the monitor to watch an employee in the restroom; however, in other states (e.g., Texas, Nevada), this is allowed.[53]

Case examples abound of challenges based on privacy concerns. In an article in the *Harvard Journal of Law and Technology*, University of Houston Law School professor Mark Rothstein, who is director of the Health Law and Policy Institute, summarized examples of legal challenges.[54] In one case, the court ruled that an employer engaged in unlawful retaliation as defined by the Mine Safety and Health Act. The employer dismissed two employees who were required to urinate in the presence of others but found themselves unable to do so. In a different case, $125,000 in tort damages was awarded to a worker for invasion of privacy and negligent infliction of emotional distress as a consequence of his being forced to submit a urine sample as he was being directly observed.

🔑 Key Terms

business purpose exception an exception to the Electronic Communications Privacy Act of 1986 that permits
employers to monitor all oral and electronic communications, assuming they can show a legitimate
business purpose for doing so

closed shop a union environment that requires new hires to be automatically enrolled in the labor union and
union dues to be automatically deducted from their pay

codetermination a concept popular in Europe that gives workers the right to participate on the board of
directors of their company

collective bargaining union negotiations with an employer on behalf of employees

comparable worth the idea that pay should be based upon a job holder's worth to the organization rather
than on salary history

consent exception an exception to the Electronic Communications Privacy Act of 1986 that allows employers
to monitor employee communications provided employees have given their consent

EEOC the Equal Employment Opportunity Commission, created by the U.S. Civil Rights Act of 1964 and which
attempts to eliminate discrimination in the workplace based on race, gender, or creed

employment at will a legal philosophy that holds that either the employee or the employer may dissolve the
employment arrangement at will (i.e., without cause and at any time unless an employment contract is in
effect that stipulates differently)

OSHA the Occupational Safety and Health Act, which governs workplace safety, and the Occupational Safety
and Health Administration, which administers the act at the federal level

pay ratio the number of times greater the average executive's salary is than the average worker's

right-to-work law a state law that says a worker cannot be forced to join a union

sexual harassment unwelcome touching, requests for sexual favors, and other verbal or physical
harassment of a sexual nature from a supervisor, coworker, client, or customer

📖 Summary

6.1 The Workplace Environment and Working Conditions

A company and its managers need to provide a workplace at which employees want to work, free of safety
hazards and all types of harassment. Perks and benefits also make the company an attractive place to work.
Yet another factor is managers who make employees feel valued and respected. A company can use all these
tools to attract and retain top talent, helping to reach the goals of having a well-run company with a satisfied
workforce. Philosophers Aristotle and Immanuel Kant said taking ethical action is the right thing to do. The
decision to create an environment in which employees want to come to work each day is, in large part, an
ethical choice, because it creates a healthy environment for all to encounter. However, the bonus comes when
a satisfied workforce fosters increased quality and productivity, which leads to appreciative customers or
clients and increased profitability. There is a financial payoff in that a well-treated workforce is also a
productive one.

6.2 What Constitutes a Fair Wage?

The concept of paying people fairly can become complicated. It includes trying to allocate and compensate
workers in the most effective manner for the company, but it takes judgement, wisdom, and a moral
imperative to do it fairly. Managers must balance issues of compensation equity, employee morale,
motivation, and profits—all of which may have legal, ethical, and business elements. The issue of a fair wage is

particularly salient for those earning the minimum wage, which, in real terms, has declined by 23 percent since 1960, and for women, who continue to experience a significant pay gap as compared with their male counterparts.

6.3 An Organized Workforce

Employees seek fair treatment in the workplace and sometimes gain a negotiating advantage with management by choosing to be represented by a labor union. Union membership in the United States has fallen in recent years as federal and state law have expanded to include worker protections unions fought for, and as the nation has shifted from a manufacturing to a service economy. Public-sector employee groups such as teachers, professors, first responders, and nurses are unionized in some cities and states. U.S. workers have contributed to a long rise in productivity over the last forty years but have not generally shared in wage gains.

6.4 Privacy in the Workplace

Monitoring of employees, whether electronically or through drug testing, is a complex area of workforce management. Numerous state and federal legal restrictions apply, and employers must decide not only what they are legally allowed to do but also what they should do ethically, keeping in mind the individual privacy concerns of their employees.

Assessment Questions

1. How often should managers in a workplace anticipate an inspection from the Occupational Safety and Health Administration?

    A. every day

    B. once a month

    C. upon request or complaint

    D. never

2. True or false? Sexual harassment is unethical but not illegal.

3. What are examples of benefits or perks that women usually value more than men?

4. What can a company do to try to reduce sexual harassment?

5. According to data presented in the chapter, about how much do women earn in comparison with men doing the same job?

    A. a lot less (about 40%–50%)

    B. somewhat less (about 70%–80%)

    C. almost the same (95%)

    D. about the same (100%)

6. True or false? Minimum wages are established by federal law only.

7. True or false? Minimum wages have at least kept pace with the cost of living, because of the automatic cost-of-living adjustment clause in the law.

8. Why have some states raised minimum wages above the federal minimum?

9. What are some of the reasons that have contributed to women making less than men in similar jobs?

10. In the United States, CEO pay is on average _____ times as high as the pay of the average worker in the same company.

    A. 30

    B. 50

    C. 100

    D. 300

11. True or false: U.S. union membership today is at the lowest level since the 1950s.

12. True or false: The right to work without joining a union is controlled by federal law.

13. Why is union membership at an all-time low?

14. How does executive pay in the United States compare to that in other countries?

15. True or false? Advance permission from employees is required before they can be electronically monitored under federal law.

16. True or false? Workplace drug testing is completely prohibited in some states.

17. Why would a company want to monitor Internet use at work?

18. What are the two major exceptions to the Electronic Communications Privacy Act that weaken its protections of employee privacy rights?

19. Should drug testing of employees be allowed?

Endnotes

1. 2020 Women on Boards, "2020 Gender Diversity Index Key Findings," 2016. https://www.2020wob.com/companies/2020-gender-diversity-index (accessed January 5, 2018).

2. Valentina Zarya, "The Percentage of Female CEOs in the Fortune 500 Drops to 4%," *Fortune*, June 6, 2016. http://fortune.com/2016/06/06/women-ceos-fortune-500-2016/.

3. Elizabeth Olsen, "Study Finds Only Modest Gains by Women and Minorities on Fortune 500 Boards," *New York Times*, February 5, 2017. https://www.nytimes.com/2017/02/05/business/dealbook/fortune-500-board-directors-diversity.html.

4. R.G. Ehrenberg and G.H. Jacubson, "Why WARN? The Impact of Recent Plant-Closing and Layoff Prenotification Legislation in the United States [electronic version]" in *Employment Security and Labor Market Behavior*, ed. C. Buechtemann. (Ithaca, NY: Cornell University Press, 1993: 200–214).

5. Occupational Safety and Health Act, 29 U.S.C. §651 et seq. (1970)

6. Occupational Safety and Health Act, 29 U.S.C. §651 et seq. (1970)

7. Occupational Safety & Health Administration, "Top Enforcement Cases Based on Total Issued Penalty," U.S. Department of Labor. https://www.osha.gov/dep/enforcement/top_cases.html (accessed January 5, 2018).

8. Occupational Safety & Health Administration, "Top Enforcement Cases Based on Total Issued Penalty," U.S. Department of Labor. https://www.osha.gov/dep/enforcement/top_cases.html (accessed January 5, 2018).

9. Occupational Safety & Health Administration, "Top Enforcement Cases Based on Total Issued Penalty," U.S. Department of Labor. https://www.osha.gov/dep/enforcement/top_cases.html (accessed January 5, 2018).

10. U.S. Equal Employment Opportunity Commission, "Statistics." https://www.eeoc.gov/eeoc/statistics/ (accessed April 22, 2018).

11. Civil Rights Act, § 7, 42 U.S.C. § 2000e et seq. (1964).

12. U.S. Equal Employment Opportunity Commission, "Sexual harassment." https://www1.eeoc.gov//laws/types/sexual_harassment.cfm?renderforprint=1 (accessed July 11, 2018).

13. Jeffrey Dastin, "American Apparel Names New CEO, Officially Ousts Founder," *Reuters*, December 16, 2014. https://www.reuters.com/article/us-american-apparel-managementchanges-idUSKBN0JU2J220141216; Julie Carrie Wong, "Uber CEO Travis Kalanick Resigns Following Months of Chaos," *The Guardian*, June 21, 2017. https://www.theguardian.com/technology/2017/jun/20/uber-ceo-travis-kalanick-resigns.

14. Susan Chira and Catrin Einhorn, "How Tough Is It to Change a Culture of Harassment? Ask Women at Ford," *New York Times*, December 19, 2017. https://www.nytimes.com/interactive/2017/12/19/us/ford-chicago-sexual-harassment.html.

15. Susan Chira and Catrin Einhorn, How Tough Is It to Change a Culture of Harassment? Ask Women at Ford," *New York Times*, December 19, 2017. https://www.nytimes.com/interactive/2017/12/19/us/ford-chicago-sexual-harassment.html.

16. Barry Moltz, "Seven Secrets to Keeping Your Employees Happy," *American Express Small Business*, August 24, 2017. https://www.americanexpress.com/us/small-business/openforum/articles/7-secrets-to-keeping-your-employees-happy/.

17. David Z. Morris, "New French Law Bars Work Email After Hours," *Fortune*, January 1, 2017. http://fortune.com/2017/01/01/french-right-to-disconnect-law/.

18. Stephen Miller, "Millennials in the Dark About Their Benefits," SHRM.org, October 25, 2016. https://www.shrm.org/resourcesandtools/hr-topics/benefits/pages/millennials-benefits.

19. Investopedia, "Top Ten Reasons to Work at Google," *Investopedia*. https://www.investopedia.com/articles/investing/060315/top-10-reasons-work-google.asp.
20. Sohrab Kohli and Rob Levy, "Employee Financial Health: How Companies Can Invest in Workplace Wellness," Center for Financial Service Information, May 30, 2017. http://cfsinnovation.org/research/employee-financial-health/.
21. Drew Desilver, "For Most Workers, Real Wages Have Barely Budged for Decades," Pew Research Center, October 9, 2014. http://www.pewresearch.org/fact-tank/2014/10/09/for-most-workers-real-wages-have-barely-budged-for-decades/.
22. Lawrence Mishel, Elise Gould, and Josh Bivens, "Wage Stagnation in Nine Charts," Economic Policy Institute, January 6, 2015. http://www.epi.org/publication/charting-wage-stagnation/.
23. Lawrence Mishel, Elise Gould, and Josh Bivens, "Wage Stagnation in Nine Charts," Economic Policy Institute, January 6, 2015. http://www.epi.org/publication/charting-wage-stagnation/.
24. Ariane Hegewisch and Angela Edwards, "The Gender Wage Gap: 2011," Institute for Women's Policy Research, September 2012. https://iwpr.org/publications/the-gender-wage-gap-2011/ (accessed July 12, 2018).
25. The Republic, "The Gender Wage Gap in 6 Charts," azcentral.com, April 6, 2017. https://www.azcentral.com/story/money/business/economy/2017/04/06/gender-wage-gap-6-charts/100122100/.
26. Kurt Stanberry and Forrest Aven, "Unequal pay for equal work. Why women still lag behind after the 50th anniversary of the U.S. Equal Pay Act," *Compensation and Benefits Review Journal*, 45, no. 4, (2013): 193–199.
27. Kevin Miller, "The Simple Truth about the Gender Pay Gap," American Association of University Women. https://www.aauw.org/research/the-simple-truth-about-the-gender-pay-gap/ (accessed April 23, 2018).
28. Kurt Stanberry and Forrest Aven, "Unequal pay for equal work. Why women still lag behind after the 50th anniversary of the U.S. Equal Pay Act," *Compensation and Benefits Review Journal*, 45, no. 4 (2013): 193–199.
29. George Mason University, "Study Reveals the Secrets to Negotiating a Higher Salary," October 20, 2010. https://eagle.gmu.edu/newsroom/843/.
30. Laura Lyons Cole, "Iceland's New Law Aimed at Eliminating the gender pay gap places the Country in Stark Contrast to the United States," *Business Insider*, January 4, 2018. http://www.businessinsider.com/iceland-gender-pay-gap-law-2018-1.
31. Laura Lyons Cole, "Iceland's New Law Aimed at Eliminating the Gender Pay Gap Places the Country in Stark Contrast to the United States," *Business Insider*, January 4, 2018. http://www.businessinsider.com/iceland-gender-pay-gap-law-2018-1.
32. Liz Alderman, "Britain Aims to Close Gender Pay Gap with Transparency and Shame," *New York Times*, April 4, 2018. https://www.nytimes.com/2018/04/04/business/britain-gender-pay-gap.html.
33. "The Gender Pay Gap," *The Economist*, October 7, 2017. https://www.economist.com/news/international/21729993-women-still-earn-lot-less-men-despite-decades-equal-pay-laws-why-gender.
34. Lauren Lyons Cole, "Iceland's New Law Aimed at Eliminating the Gender Pay Gap Places the Country in Stark Contrast to the US," *Business Insider*, January 4, 2018. http://uk.businessinsider.com/iceland-gender-pay-gap-law-2018-1?IR=T&r=US
35. Jena McGregor, "Will Bans on Asking about Salary History Work?" *Houston Chronicle*, November 19, 2017. http://digital.olivesoftware.com/Olive/ODN/HoustonChronicle/shared/ShowArticle.aspx?doc=HHC%2F2017%2F11%2F19&entity=Ar04514&sk=921F5F6D&mode=text.
36. "Korn Ferry Executive Survey: New Laws Forbidding Questions on Salary History Likely Changes the Game for Most Employers," Korn Ferry, November 14, 2017. https://www.kornferry.com/press/korn-ferry-executive-survey-new-laws-forbidding-questions-on-salary-history-likely-changes-the-game-for-most-employers/ (accessed January 25, 2018).
37. Peter Georgescu, "What Are We Waiting For?" *Forbes*, January 24, 2018. https://www.forbes.com/sites/petergeorgescu/2018/01/24/what-are-we-waiting-for/#6d32c7c556e3.
38. Michael Wheeler,"3 years Ago, This Boss Set a $70,000 Minimum Wage for his Employees—and the Move Is Still Paying Off," CNBC, August 29, 2017. https://www.cnbc.com/2017/08/29/this-boss-set-a-70000-minimum-wage-for-his-employees-3-years-ago.html.
39. Michael Wheeler, "3 years Ago, This Boss Set a $70,000 Minimum Wage for his Employees—and the Move Is Still Paying Off," CNBC, August 29, 2017. https://www.cnbc.com/2017/08/29/this-boss-set-a-70000-minimum-wage-for-his-employees-3-years-ago.html.
40. Deep Patel, "Can This Shark Tank Company Take on an Industry Working a Five-Hour Day?" *Huffington Post*, June 3, 2016. https://www.huffingtonpost.com/deep-patel/can-this-shark-tank-compa_b_10243974.html.
41. U.S. Bureau of Labor Statistics, "Union Members Summary." https://www.bls.gov/news.release/union2.nr0.htm (accessed January 5, 2018).
42. Ewan McGaughey, "The Codetermination Bargains: The History of German Corporate and Labor Law," *Columbia Journal of European Law*, 23, no. 1 (2016); LSE Legal Studies Working Paper No. 10/2015. https://papers.ssrn.com/sol3/papers.cfm?abstract_id=2579932.
43. "Trade Union Membership Compared," Nationmaster. http://www.nationmaster.com/country-info/stats/Labor/Trade-union-membership#country (accessed July 12, 2018).
44. Michael Haberman, Why Unions Are Bad For Companies, Employees and Customers," Omega, June 25, 2009. http://omegahrsolutions.com/2009/06/why-unions-are-bad-for-companies-employees-and-customers.html.
45. "The Productivity–Pay Gap," Economic Policy Institute. https://www.epi.org/productivity-pay-gap/ (accessed April 22, 2018).
46. David Johnson, "These are the Most Productive Countries in the World," *Time*, January 4, 2017.
47. Paul Hodgson, "Top CEOs Make More Than 300 Times the Average Worker," *Fortune*, June 22, 2015. http://fortune.com/2015/06/22/ceo-vs-worker-pay/.
48. Steve McDonnell, "CEO Compensation in the US vs. the World," *Houston Chronicle*. http://work.chron.com/ceo-compensation-vs-world-15509.html (accessed January 15, 2018).
49. "Managing Workplace Monitoring and Surveillance," SHRM.org, February 18, 2016. https://www.shrm.org/resourcesandtools/tools-and-samples/toolkits/pages/workplaceprivacy.aspx (accessed January 15, 2018).
50. Electronic Communications Privacy Act, 18 U.S.C. §2511 et seq. (1986).
51. Another Evil HR Director, "Privacy in the Workplace," HRInConfidence, June 13, 2013. http://www.hrinconfidence.com/2013_06_01_archive.html
52. *Ontario v. Quon*, 560 U.S. 746 (2010).
53. Legal Information Institute, "Expectation of Privacy," Cornell Law School. https://www.law.cornell.edu/wex/expectation_of_privacy (accessed April 22, 2018).
54. Mark Rothstein, "Workplace Drug Testing: A Case Study in the Misapplication of Technology," *Harvard Journal of Law and Technology* 5, Fall (1991): 65–93.

What Employees Owe Employers

Figure 7.1 What responsibilities do employees have to coworkers and to the company, as well as to themselves, when they are on the job? (credit, clockwise from top left): modification of "Call Centre 2006" by "AaronY"/Wikimedia Commons, CC BY 2.0; credit: modification of "los bolleros" by Agustín Ruiz/Flickr, CC BY 2.0; credit: modification of "Training" by Cory Zanker/Flickr, CC BY 4.0; credit: modification of "Afghan women at a textile factory in Kabul" by Andrea Salazar/Wikimedia Commons, Public Domain; credit: modification of "GenoPheno" by Cory Zanker/Flickr, CC BY 4.0; credit: modification of "Group" by Cory Zanker/Flickr, CC BY 4.0; credit: modification of "doin' work" by Nick Allen/Flickr, CC BY 2.0)

Chapter Outline

7.1 Loyalty to the Company

7.2 Loyalty to the Brand and to Customers

7.3 Contributing to a Positive Work Atmosphere

7.4 Financial Integrity

7.5 Criticism of the Company and Whistleblowing

Introduction

What Employers Owe Employees discussed the duties, obligations, and responsibilities managers and companies owe their employees. This chapter looks at the other side of that relationship to weigh the ethical dimensions of being a worthy employee and responsible coworker (Figure 7.1).

Coworkers may express their opinions differently, for instance, agreeing or disagreeing, perhaps in very animated ways. Although we and our peers at work may not see eye to eye on every issue, we work best when we understand the need to get along and to show a degree of loyalty to our employer and each other, as well as to ourselves, our values, and our own best interests. Balancing these factors requires a concerted effort.

What would you do, for example, if one of your coworkers were being bullied or harassed by another employee or a manager? Suppose a former colleague tried to recruit you to her new firm. What is the ethical action for you to take? How would you react if you learned your company's managers were behaving unethically or breaking the law? Who could you tell, and what could you expect as a result? What is the right response if a client or customer behaves badly toward you as an employee representing your firm? How do you provide good customer service and support the company brand in the face of difficult working conditions?

7.1 Loyalty to the Company

Learning Objectives

By the end of this section, you will be able to:

- Define employees' responsibilities to the company for which they work
- Describe a non-compete agreement
- Explain how confidentiality applies to trade secrets, intellectual property, and customer data

The relationship between employee and employer is changing, especially our understanding of commitment and loyalty. An ethical employee owes the company a good day's work and his or her best effort, whether the work is stimulating or dull. A duty of loyalty and our best effort are our primary obligations as employees, but what they mean can change. A manager who expects a twentieth-century concept of loyalty in the twenty-first century may be surprised when workers express a sense of entitlement, ask for a raise after six months, or leave for a new job after twelve months. This chapter will explore a wide range of issues from the perspective of what and how employees contribute to the overall success of a business enterprise.

A Duty of Loyalty

Hard work and our best effort likely make sense as obligations we owe an employer. However, loyalty is more abstract and less easily defined. Most workers do not have employment contracts, so there may not be a specific agreement between the two parties detailing their mutual responsibilities. Instead, the common law (case law) of agency in each state is often the source of the rules governing an employment relationship. The usual depiction of duty in common law is the **duty of loyalty**, which, in all fifty states, requires that an employee refrain from acting in a manner contrary to the employer's interest. This duty creates some basic rules employees must follow on the job and provides employers with enforceable rights against employees who violate them.

In general terms, the duty of loyalty means an employee is obligated to render "loyal and faithful" service to the employer, to act with "good faith," and not to compete with but rather to advance the employer's interests.[1] The employee must not act in a way that benefits him- or herself (or any other third party), especially when doing so would create a conflict of interest with the employer.[2] The common law of most states holds as a general rule that, without asking for and receiving the employer's consent, an employee cannot hold a second job if it would compete or conflict with the first job. Thus, although the precise boundaries of this aspect of the duty of loyalty are unclear, an employee who works in the graphic design department of a large advertising agency in all likelihood cannot moonlight on the weekend for a friend's small web design business. However, employers often grant permission for employees to work in positions that do not compete or interfere with their principal jobs. The graphic designer might work for a friend's catering business, for example, or perhaps as a wedding photographer or editor of a blog for a public interest community group.

Moonlighting has become such a common phenomenon that the website Glassdoor now has a section reserved for such jobs. The Glassdoor website has a number of postings for different moonlighting opportunities (https://openstax.org/l/53moonlighting) to explore.

What *is* clear is that it is wrong for employees to make work decisions primarily for their own personal gain, rather than doing what is in the employer's best interest. An employee might have the authority to decide which other companies the employer will do business with, for example, such as service vendors that maintain the copiers or clean the offices. What if the employee owned stock in one of those companies or had a relative who worked there? That gives him or her an incentive to encourage doing business with that particular company, whether it would be best for the employer or not.

The degree to which the duty of loyalty exists is usually related to the degree of responsibility or trust an employer places in an employee. More trust equals a stronger duty. For example, when an employee has very extensive authority or access to confidential information, the duty can rise to its highest level, called a fiduciary duty, which is discussed in an earlier chapter.

Differing Concepts of Loyalty

There is no generally agreed-upon definition of an employee's duty of loyalty to his or her employer. One indicator that our understanding of the term is changing is that millennials are three times more likely than older generations to change jobs, according to a *Forbes* Human Resources Council survey (Figure 7.2).[3] About nine in ten millennials (91 percent) say they do not expect to stay with their current job longer than three years, compared with older workers who often anticipated spending ten years or even an entire career with one employer, relying on an implicit social contract between employer and employee that rewarded lifetime employment.

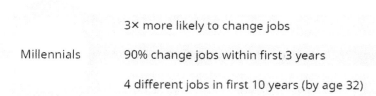

Source: Murdock, P. "The New Reality of Employee Loyalty." *Forbes*. Dec 12, 2017.

Figure 7.2 The data on millennials and job mobility indicate that millennials are more likely to "job hop" than their predecessors. (attribution: Copyright Rice University, OpenStax, under CC BY 4.0 license)

The Loyalty Research Center, a consulting firm, defines loyal employees as "being committed to the success of the organization. They believe that working for this organization is their best option . . . and loyal employees do not actively search for alternative employment and are not responsive to offers."[4] Likewise, Wharton School, University of Pennsylvania, professor Matthew Bidwell says there are two halves to the term: "One piece is having the employer's best interests at heart. The other piece is remaining with the same employer rather than moving on." Bidwell goes on to acknowledge, "There is less a sense that your organization is going to look after you in the way that it used to, which would lead [us] to expect a reduction in loyalty."[5]

Why are employees less likely to feel a duty of loyalty to their companies? One reason is that loyalty is a two-way street, a feeling developed through the enactment of mutual obligations and responsibilities. However, most employers do not want to be obligated to their workers in a legal sense; they usually require that almost all workers are employees "at will," that is, without any long-term employment contract. Neither state nor federal law mandates an employment contract, so when a company says an employee is employed at will, it is sending a message that management is not making a long-term commitment to the employee. Employees may naturally feel less loyalty to an organization from which they believe they can be let go at any time and for any legal reason (which is essentially what at-will employment means). Of course, at-will employment also means the employee can also quit at any time. However, freedom to move is a benefit only if the employee has mobility and a skill set he or she can sell to the highest bidder. Otherwise, for most workers, at-will employment usually works to the employer's advantage, not the employee's.

Another reason the concept of loyalty to an organization seems to be changing at all levels is the important role money plays in career decisions. When they see chief executive officers (CEOs) and other managers leaving to work for the highest bidder, subordinates quickly conclude that they, too, ought to look out for themselves, just as their bosses do, rather than trying to build up seniority with the company. Switching jobs can often be a way for employees to improve their salaries. Consider professional sports. For decades professional athletes were tied to one team and could not sell their services to the highest bidder, meaning that their salaries were effectively capped. Finally, after several court decisions (including the Curt Flood reserve clause case involving the St. Louis Cardinals and Major League Baseball),[6] players achieved some degree of freedom and can now switch employers frequently in an effort to maximize their earning potential.

The same evolution occurred in the entertainment industry. In the early years of the movie business, actors were tied to studios by contracts that prevented them from making movies for any other studio, effectively limiting their earning power. Then the entertainment industry changed as actors gained the freedom to sell their services to the highest bidder, becoming much more highly compensated in the process. Employees in any industry, not just sports and entertainment, benefit from being able to change jobs if their salary at their current job stagnates or falls below the market rate.

Another economic phenomenon affecting loyalty in the private sector was the switch from defined-benefit to defined-contribution retirement plans. In the former, often called a pension, employee benefits are usually sponsored (paid) fully by the employer and calculated using a formula based on length of employment, salary history, and other factors. The employer administers the plan and manages the investment risk, promising the employee a set payout upon retirement. In the defined-contribution plan, however, the employee invests a certain percentage of his or her salary in a retirement fund, often a 401(k) or 403(b) plan, where it is sometimes matched (partially or wholly) by the employer. (These savings plans with their seemingly strange designations are part of the U.S. Internal Revenue Code, and the letter/number combinations indicate subsections of the Code. 401(k) Plans typically are featured in for-profit employment settings and 403(b) plans in nonprofit environments.) Defined-benefit plans reward longevity in the firm, whereas defined-contribution plans reward high earnings over seniority. Thus, with the growth of defined-contribution plans, some reasons for staying with the same employer over time are no longer applicable.

According to PayScale's Compensation Best Practices Report, the two leading motivators people give for leaving their job are first, higher pay, and second, personal reasons (e.g., family, health, marriage, spousal relocation).[7] Of course, beyond money, workers seek meaning in their work, and it is largely true that money alone does not motivate employees to higher performance. However, it is a mistake for managers to think money is not a central factor influencing employees' job satisfaction. Money matters because if employees are not making enough money to meet their financial obligations or goals, they will likely be looking to for a higher-paying job. And, of course, increasing salary or other benefits can be a way of demonstrating both the company's loyalty to its employees and the role it believes employees' best interests play in its mission—navigating the aforementioned two-way street. For some employees, simply being acknowledged and thanked for their service and good work can go a long way toward sparking their loyalty; for others, more concrete rewards may be necessary.

Finally, many people work for themselves as freelance or contract workers in the new "gig" economy. They may take assignments from one or more companies at a time and are not employees in the traditional sense of the word. Therefore, it seems more reasonable that they would approach work in the same way a certified public accountant or attorney would—as completing a professional job for a client, after which they move on the next client, always keeping their independent status. We would not expect gig workers to demonstrate employer loyalty when they are not employees.

WHAT WOULD YOU DO?

The Ties That Bind

If building employee loyalty is a challenge for managers and they see their workers leaving for better opportunities, what can they do to change the situation? Some companies focus on team-building activities, company picnics, rock-climbing walls, or zip lines, but do these actually make workers decide to stay with their company for less salary? The answer is usually no. The reality is that salary plays an important role in an employee's decision to move to a new job. Therefore, retention bonuses are a popular and perhaps more successful technique for instilling loyalty. The company provides a payment to an employee contingent on his or her committing to remain at the company for a specific period.

According to a Glassdoor study,[8] when changing jobs, employees earn an average increase of more than 5 percent in salary alone, not including benefits. Thus, the offer of a salary increase and/or a retention or performance bonus can help turn many would-be former employees into newly loyal ones. The same study found that a 10 percent increase in pay upped the odds that an employee would stay at the company. According to Dr. Andrew Chamberlain, chief economist of Glassdoor, "While it is important to provide upward career paths for workers, a simple job title promotion may not be enough. Maintaining competitive pay is an important part of reducing turnover."[9]

Of course, a retention bonus may not be enough to keep someone at a job he or she hates, but it might help someone who likes the job to decide to stay. The Society for Human Resource Management believes retention plans should be part of an overall pay strategy, not merely giveaways for tenure.[10] Imagine that your colleague is considering leaving your firm for another company: Your manager has offered him a retention bonus to stay and your colleague is seeking your advice about what to do. What would you advise?

Critical Thinking

- What questions would you ask your colleague to better determine the advice you should give him or her?
- Consider your summer jobs, part-time employment, work-study hours on campus, and internships. What meant more to you—the salary you made or the extent to which you were treated as a real

contributor and not just a line on a payroll ledger? Or a combination of both?
- What lessons do you now draw about reciprocal loyalty between companies and their workers?

Confidentiality

In the competitive world of business, many employees encounter information in their day-to-day work that their employers reasonably expect they will keep confidential. Proprietary (private) information, the details of patents and copyrights, employee records and salary histories, and customer-related data are valued company assets that must remain in-house, not in the hands of competitors, trade publications, or the news media. Employers are well within their rights to expect employees to honor their **duty of confidentiality** and maintain the secrecy of such proprietary material. Sometimes the duty of confidentiality originates specifically from an employment contract, if there is one, and if not, the duty still exists in most situations under the common law of agency.

Most companies do not consider U.S. common law on confidentiality sufficient protection, so they often adopt employment agreements or contracts with employees that set forth the conditions of confidentiality. (Note that such contracts define a one-way obligation, from the employee to the employer, so they do not protect the at-will employee from being terminated without cause.) Typically, an employment agreement will list a variety of requirements. For example, although in most situations the law would already hold that the employer owns copyrightable works created by employees within the scope of their employment (known as *works for hire*), a contract usually also contains a specific clause stating that the company owns any and all such works and assigning ownership of them to the company. The agreement will also contain a patent assignment provision, stating that all inventions created within the scope of employment are owned by or assigned to the company.

LINK TO LEARNING

If one day you might be a freelancer, gig worker, or contractor, watch this video showing how a nondisclosure agreement can help you protect your ideas (https://openstax.org/l/53NDA) to learn more.

Employers also want to protect their **trade secrets**, that is, information that has economic value because it is not generally known to the public and is kept secret by reasonable means. Trade secrets might include technical or design information, advertising and marketing plans, and research and development data that would be useful to competitors. Often **nondisclosure agreements** are used to protect against the theft of all such information, most of which is normally protected only by the company's requirement of secrecy, not by federal intellectual property law. Federal law generally protects registered trademarks (commercial identifications such as words, designs, logos, slogans, symbols, and *trade dress*, which is product appearance or packaging) and grants creators copyrights (to protect original literary and artistic expressions such as books, paintings, music, records, plays, movies, and software) and patents (to protect new and useful inventions and configurations of useful articles) (Figure 7.3).

Figure 7.3 Registered trademarks and content covered by patents and copyrights are protected by law, but trade secrets have no official status and so do not enjoy the same level of federal protection. Thus, companies generally protect trade secrets internally, usually with employment agreements or contracts. (attribution: Copyright Rice University, OpenStax, under CC BY 4.0 license)

U.S. companies have long used **non-compete agreements** as a way to provide another layer of confidentiality, ensuring that employees with access to sensitive information will not compete with the company during or for some period after their employment there. The stated purpose of such agreements is to protect the company's **intellectual property**, which is the manifestation of original ideas protected by legal means such as patent, copyright, or trademark. To be enforceable, non-compete agreements are usually limited by time and distance (i.e., they are in effect for a certain number of months or years and within a certain radius of the employer's operations). However, some companies have begun requiring these agreements even from mid- and lower-level workers in an attempt to prevent them from changing jobs, including those who have no access to any confidential intellectual property. About 20 percent of the U.S. private-sector workforce, and about one in six people in jobs earning less than $40,000 a year, are now covered by non-compete agreements.[11] The increased use of such agreements has left many employees feeling trapped by their limited mobility.

LINK TO LEARNING

A template for a typical non-compete agreement (https://openstax.org/l/53noncompete) can be found at PandaDoc.

An ethical question arises regarding whether this practice is in the best interests of society and its workers, and some states are responding. California enacted a law in 2017 saying that most non-compete agreements are void, holding that although an employee may owe the employer a responsibility not to compete while employed, that duty ceases upon termination of employment.[12] In other words, an employee does not "belong" to a company forever. In California, therefore, a non-compete arrangement that limits employment after leaving the employer is now unenforceable. Does this law reflect the approach that most states will now take? A California company may still legally prohibit its employees from moonlighting during the term of their employment, particularly for a competitor.

CASES FROM THE REAL WORLD

Non-Compete Agreements

After an investigation by then–New York attorney general Eric Schneiderman, fast-food franchisor Jimmy John's announced in 2016 that it would not enforce non-compete agreements signed by low-wage employees that prohibited them from working at other sandwich shops, and it agreed to stop using the agreements in the future. Jimmy John's non-compete agreement had prohibited all workers, regardless of position, from working during their employment and for two years after at any other business that sold "submarine, hero-type, deli-style, pita, and/or wrapped or rolled sandwiches" in a geographic area within two miles of any Jimmy John's shop anywhere in the United States.[13]

Schneiderman said of the agreements, "They limit mobility and opportunity for vulnerable workers and bully them into staying with the threat of being sued." Illinois Attorney General Lisa Madigan had also initiated action, filing a lawsuit that asked the court to strike down such clauses. "Preventing employees from seeking employment with a competitor is unfair to Illinois workers and bad for Illinois businesses," Madigan said. "By locking low-wage workers into their jobs and prohibiting them from seeking better paying jobs elsewhere, the companies have no reason to increase their wages or benefits."[14]

Jimmy John's has more than 2,500 franchises in forty-six states, so its agreement meant it would be difficult for a former worker to get a job in a sandwich shop in almost any big city in the United States.

Critical Thinking

- Other than being punitive, what purpose do non-compete agreements serve when low-level employees are required to sign them?
- Suppose an executive chef or vice president of marketing or operations at Jimmy John's or any large sandwich franchise leaves the firm with knowledge of trade secrets and competitive strategies. Should he or she be compelled to wait a negotiated period of time before working for a competitor? Why or why not?
- What is fair to all parties when high-level managers possess unique, sensitive information about their former employer?

Employers may also insert a **nonsolicitation clause**, which protects a business from an employee who leaves for another job and then attempts to lure customers or former colleagues into following. Though these clauses have limitations, they can be effective tools to protect an employer's interest in retaining its employees and customers. However, they are particularly difficult for employees to comply with in relatively closed markets. Sample language for all the clauses we have discussed is found in Figure 7.4.

Non-Compete Clause
The Employee agrees that for a period of one year after the Employee no longer works for the Company, the Employee will not engage in the same or similar activities as were performed for the Company in any business within a 100-mile radius of the Company.

Nonsolicitation of Customers/Employees Clause
The Employee agrees that for a period of two years after the Employee no longer works for the Company, the Employee will not solicit customer, clients, and/or employees of the Company.

Confidentiality/ Non-Disclosure Clause
Employee agrees that during employment with the Company and following the termination of such employment for an unlimited term, the Employee shall not misappropriate, divulge, disclose, or make use of any confidential information, intellectual property, or trade secrets.

Figure 7.4 Common clauses found in employment contracts include those restricting competition and solicitation upon termination of the contract, as well as requiring confidentiality during and after employment. (attribution: Copyright Rice University, OpenStax, under CC BY 4.0 license)

A final clause an employee might be required to sign is a nondisparagement clause, which prohibits defaming or deliberately running down the reputation of the former employer.

7.2 Loyalty to the Brand and to Customers

Learning Objectives

By the end of this section, you will be able to:

- Describe how employees help build and sustain a brand
- Discuss how employees' customer service can help or hurt a business

A good employment relationship is beneficial to both management and employees. When a company's products or services are legitimate and safe and its employment policies are fair and compassionate, managers should be able to rely on their employees' dedication to those products or services and to their customers. Although no employee should be called upon to lie or cover up a misstep on the part of the firm, every employee should be willing to make a sincere commitment to an ethical employer.

Respecting the Brand

Every company puts time, effort, and money into developing a **brand**, that is, a product or service marketed by a particular company under a particular name. As Apple, Coca-Cola, Amazon, BMW, McDonald's, and creators of other coveted brands know, **branding**—creating, differentiating, and maintaining a brand's image or reputation—is an important way to build company value, sell products and services, and expand corporate goodwill. In the sense discussed here, the term "brand" encompasses an image, reputation, logo, tagline, or specific color scheme that is trademarked, meaning the company owns it and must give permission to others who would legally use it (such as Tiffany's unique shade of blue).

Companies want and expect employees to help in their branding endeavors. For example, according to the head of training at American Express, the company's brand is its product, and its mantra has always been, "Happy employees make happy customers."[15] American Express places significant emphasis on employee satisfaction because it is convinced this strategy helps protect and advance its brand. One company that uses positive employee involvement in branding is the technology conglomerate Cisco, which started a branding program on social media that reaches out to employees (Figure 7.5). Employees are encouraged to be creative in their brand-boosting posts in the program. The benefit is that prospective job candidates get a peek into Cisco life, and current employees feel the company trusts and values their ideas.[16]

Figure 7.5   These Cisco employees, part of a newly formed Virtual Customer Success team in India, help promote the brand and perhaps promote change as well. Women have been underrepresented in STEM careers (science, technology, engineering, math), and this group takes pride in the fact that they are part of a gender-balanced team. This photo was submitted as part of the annual #WeAreCisco #LoveWhereYouWork contest, with the hashtag #womenintech and the photo caption "Sorry, we're busy making a difference." (credit: modification of work by Shojana Ravi/Cisco, CC BY 4.0, used with the permission of https://thenetwork.cisco.com)

LINK TO LEARNING

Watch this video explaining the concept of brand loyalty (https://openstax.org/l/53BrandLoyal) to learn more.

However, protecting the brand can be a special challenge today, thanks to the ease with which customers and even employees can post negative information about the brand on the Internet and social media. Consider these examples in the fast-food industry. A photo posted on Taco Bell's Facebook page showed an employee licking a row of tacos. A Domino's Pizza employee can be seen in a YouTube video spitting on food, putting cheese into his nose and then putting that cheese into a sandwich, and rubbing a sponge used for dishwashing on his groin area.[17] On Twitter, a Burger King employee in Japan posted a photo of himself lying on hamburger buns while on duty.

The companies all responded swiftly. A Taco Bell spokesperson said the food was not served to customers and the employee in the photo was fired. The two Domino's employees behind the videos were fired and faced felony charges and a civil lawsuit; Domino's said the tainted food was never delivered. According to a Burger King news release, the buns in the photo were waste material because of an ordering mistake and were promptly discarded after the photo was taken; the employee in the photo was fired.

These examples demonstrate how much damage disloyal or disgruntled employees can create, especially on social media. All three companies experienced financial and goodwill losses after the incidents and struggled to restore public trust in their products. The immediate and long-term costs of such incidents are the reason companies invest in developing brand loyalty among their employees.

According to a *Harvard Business Review* interview with Colin Mitchell, global vice president, McDonald's Brand, McDonald's, good branding requires that a business think of marketing not just to its customers but also to its employees, because they are the "very people who can make the brand come alive for your customers".[18] The process of getting employees to believe in the product, to commit to the idea that the company is selling something worth buying, and even to think about buying it, is called **internal marketing**. Of course, some employees may not want to be the equivalent of a company spokesperson. Is it reasonable to expect an employee to be a kind of roving ambassador for the company, even when off the clock and interacting with friends and neighbors? Suppose employers offer employees substantial discounts on their products or services. Is this an equitable way to sustain reciprocal loyalty between managers and workers? Why or why not?

Internal marketing is an important part of the solution to the problem of employees who act as if they do not care about the company. It helps employees make a personal connection to the products and services the business sells, without which they might be more likely to undermine the company's expectations, as in the three fast-food examples cited in this section. In those cases, it is clear the employees did not believe in the brand and felt hostile toward the company. The most common problem is usually not as extreme. More often it is a lack of effort or "slacking" on the job. Employees are more likely to develop some degree of brand loyalty when they share a common sense of purpose and identity with the company.

LINK TO LEARNING

The Working Advantage website offers corporate discounts (https://openstax.org/l/53discount) to check out. Companies sometimes offer employees significant discounts to encourage them to buy, and support, their products.

Obligations to Customers

As the public's first point of contact with a company, employees are obliged to assist the firm in forming a positive relationship with customers. How well or poorly they do so contributes a great deal to customers' impression of the company. And customers' perceptions affect not only the company but all the employees who depend on its success for their livelihood. Thus, the ethical obligations of an employee also extend to interactions with customers, whom they should treat with respect. Employers can encourage positive behavior toward customers by empowering employees to use their best judgment when working with them.

LINK TO LEARNING

Watch this video giving a light-hearted take on bad customer service (https://openstax.org/l/53BadService) to learn more.

It may take only one bad customer interaction with a less-than-engaged or committed employee to sour brand loyalty, no matter how hard a company has worked to build it. In the same way, just one good experience can build up good will.

CASES FROM THE REAL WORLD

Redefining Customers

Sometimes engaged employees go above and beyond in the interest of customer service, even if they have no "customers" to speak of. Kathy Fryman is one such employee. Fryman was a custodian for three decades at a one hundred-year-old school in the Augusta (KY) Independent School District. She was not just taking care of the school building, she was also taking care of the people inside.[19]

Fryman fixed doors that would not close, phones that would not ring, and alarms that did not sound when they should. She kept track of keys and swept up dirty floors before Parents' Night. That was all part of the job of custodian, but she did much more.

Fryman would often ask the nurse how an ill student was doing. She would check with a teacher about a kid who was going through tough times at home. If a teacher mentioned needing something, the next day it would show up on his or her desk. A student who needed something for class would suddenly find it in his or her backpack. Speaking of Fryman, district superintendent Lisa McCrane said, "She just has a unique way of making others feel nurtured, comforted, and cared for." According to Fryman, "I need to be doing something for somebody."

Fryman's customers were not there to buy a product on which she would make a commission. Her customers were students and teachers, parents and taxpayers. Yet she provided the kind of service that all employers would be proud of, the kind that makes a difference to people every day.

Critical Thinking

- Is there a way for a manager to find, develop, and encourage the next Fryman, or is the desire to "do something good for somebody" an inherent trait in some employees that is missing in others?
- What is the appropriate means to reward a worker with Fryman's level of commitment? Her salary was fixed by school district pay schedules. Should she have been given an extra stipend for service above and beyond the expected? Additional time off with pay? Some other reward?
- Employees who display Fryman's zeal often do so for their own internal rewards. Others may simply want to be recognized and appreciated for their effort. If you were the superintendent in her district, how would you recognize Fryman? Could she, for example, be invited to speak to new hires about opportunities to render exceptional service?

Employees who treat customers well are assets to the company and deserve to be treated as such. Sometimes, however, customers are rude or disrespectful, creating a challenge for an employee who wants to do a good job. This problem is best addressed by management and the employee working together. In the Pizza Hut case that follows, an employee was placed in a bad situation by customers.

CASES FROM THE REAL WORLD

Is the Customer Always Right?

At an independently owned Pizza Hut franchise in Oklahoma,[20] two regular customers made sexually offensive remarks to a female employee named Lockard, who then told her boss she did not like waiting on them. One evening, these customers again entered the restaurant, and her boss instructed Lockard to wait on them. She did, but this time the customers became physically abusive. Although it is the employee's duty to provide good customer service, that does not mean accepting harassment.

Lockard sued her employer, the owner of the franchise, for failing to take her complaints seriously and for making her continue to suffer sexual harassment and assault by customers. The jury ruled in her favor, awarding her $360,000, and an appeals court upheld the judgment.

Critical Thinking

- Clearly, no employee should expect to be physically assaulted, but how far should an employee be expected to go in the name of customer service? Is taking verbal taunts expected? Why or why not?
- Just as every employee should treat customers and clients with respect, so every employer is ethically—and often legally—obligated to safeguard employees on the job. This includes establishing a workplace atmosphere that is safe and secure for workers. If you were the owner of this Pizza Hut franchise, what protections might you put in place for your employees?

7.3 Contributing to a Positive Work Atmosphere

Learning Objectives

By the end of this section, you will be able to:

- Explain employees' responsibility to treat their peers with respect
- Describe employees' duty to follow company policy and the code of conduct
- Discuss types of workplace violence

You may spend more time with your coworkers than you spend with anyone else, including your family and friends. Thus, your ability to get along with work colleagues can have a significant impact on your life, as well as your attitude toward your job and your employer. All sorts of personalities populate our workplaces, but regardless of their working style, preferences, or quirks, employees owe one another courtesy and respect. That does not mean always agreeing with them, because evaluating a diversity of perspectives on business problems and opportunities is often essential for finding solutions. At the same time, however, we are responsible for limiting our arguments to principles, not personalities. This is what we owe to one another as human beings, as well as to the firm, so worksite arguments do not inflict lasting harm on the people who work there or on the company itself.

Getting Along with Coworkers

An employee who gets along with coworkers can help the company perform better. What can employees do to help create a more harmonious workplace with a positive atmosphere?

One thing you can do is to keep an open mind. You may be wondering as you start a new job whether you will get along with your colleagues as well as you did at your old job. Or, if you did not get along with the people there and were looking for a change, you might fear things will be the same at the new job. Do not make any prejudgments. Get to know a bit about your new coworkers. Accept, or extend, lunch invitations, join weekend activities and office social events, and perhaps join those office traditions that bind long-serving employees and newcomers together in a collaborative spirit.

Another thing you can do it to remember to be kind. Everyone has a bad day every now and then, and if you spot a coworker having one, performing a random act of kindness may make that person's day better. You do not need to be extravagant. Offer to stay late to help the person meet a tight deadline, or bring coffee or a healthy snack to someone working on particularly difficult tasks. Remember the adage, "It's nice to be important, but it's more important to be nice."

For any relationship to succeed, including the relationship between coworkers, the parties must respect each other—and show it. Avoid doing things that might offend others. For example, do not take credit for someone else's work. Do not be narrow minded; when someone brings up a topic such as politics or religion, be willing to listen and tolerate differing points of view.

A related directive is to avoid sexual jokes, stories, anecdotes, and innuendos. You might think it is okay to talk about anything and everything at work, but it is not. Others may not find the topic funny and feel offended, and you may make yourself vulnerable to action by management if such behavior is reported. Your coworkers might be a captive audience, but you should never place them in an awkward position.

Make an effort to get along with everyone, even difficult people. You did not choose your coworkers, and some may be hard to get along with. But professionalism requires that we attempt to establish the best working relationships we can on the job, no matter the opinions we might have about our colleagues. Normally, we might like some of them very much, be neutral about some others, and genuinely dislike still others. Yet our responsibility in the workplace is to respect and act at least civilly toward all of them. We likely will feel better about ourselves as professionals and also live up to our commitments to our companies.

Finally, do no use social media to gossip. Gossiping at work can cause problems anywhere, perhaps especially on social media, so resist the urge to vent online about your coworkers. It makes you appear petty, small, and untrustworthy, and colleagues may stop communicating with you. You may also run afoul of your employer's social media policy and risk disciplinary action or dismissal.

Understanding Personalities

Understanding the various personalities at work can be a complex task, but it is a vital one for developing a sense of collegiality. One technique that may be helpful is to develop your own emotional intelligence, which is the capacity to recognize other people's emotions and also to know and manage your own. One aspect of using emotional intelligence is showing empathy, the willingness to step into someone else's shoes.

LINK TO LEARNING

Do you think you know yourself? Take this free online personality test (https://openstax.org/l/53personality) from IDR Labs; it may tell you something you did not know that you can use to your benefit at work.

All of us have different **workplace personalities**, which express the way we think and act on the job. There are many such personalities, and none is superior or inferior to another, but they are a way in which we exhibit our uniqueness on the job (Figure 7.6). Some of us lead with our brains and emphasize logic and reason. Others lead with our hearts, always emphasizing mercy over justice in our relationships with others.

Figure 7.6   Which type of personality are you? (credit: Jackson Ceszyk/Flickr, CC BY 4.0)

Employees can also have very different **work styles**, the way in which we are most comfortable accomplishing our tasks at work. Some of us gravitate toward independence and jobs or tasks we can accomplish alone. Others prefer team or project work, bringing us into touch with different personalities. Still others seek a mix of these environments. Some prioritize getting the job done as efficiently as possible, whereas others value the journey of working on the project with others and the shared experiences it brings. There is no right or wrong style, but it benefits any worker to know his or her preferences and something about the work personalities of colleagues. When in the office, the point for any of us individually is to appreciate what motivates our greatest success and happiness on the job.

WHAT WOULD YOU DO?

Personality Test

Imagine you are a department director with twenty-five employees reporting directly to you. Two of them are experts in their fields: You like and respect them individually, as do the others in your department, but they simply cannot get along with each other and so never work together.

How do you resolve this personality clash? You cannot simply insist that the two colleagues cooperate, because personalities do not change. Still, you have to do your best to establish an atmosphere in which they can least collaborate civilly. Even though managers have no power to change human nature or the personality conflicts that inevitably occur, part of their responsibility is to establish a harmonious working environment, and others will judge you on the harmony you cultivate in your department.

Critical Thinking

Working relationships are extremely important to an employee's job satisfaction. What options would you use to foster a cooperative working relationship in your department?

Reducing Workplace Violence

As recent incidents have shown—for example, the April 2018 shooting at YouTube headquarters in San Bruno, California[21]—workplace violence is a reality, and all employees play a role in helping make work a safe, as well as harmonious place. Employees, in fact, have a legal and ethical duty not to be violent at work, and managers have a duty to prevent or stop violence. The National Institute for Occupational Safety and Health reports that violence at work usually fits into one of four categories: traditional criminal intent, violence by one worker against another, violence stemming from a personal relationship, and violence by a customer.[22]

In violence based on traditional criminal intent, the perpetrator has no legitimate relationship to the business or its employees, and often the violence is part of a crime such as robbery or shoplifting. Violence between coworkers occurs when a current or former employee attacks another employee in the workplace. Worker-on-worker deaths account for approximately 15 percent of all workplace homicides. All companies are at risk for this type of violence, and contributing factors include failure to conduct a criminal background check as part of the hiring process.

When the violence arises from problems in a personal relationship, the perpetrator often has a direct relationship not with the business but with the victim, who is an employee. This category of violence accounts for slightly less than 10 percent of all workplace homicides. Women are at higher risk of being victims of this type of violence than men. In the fourth scenario, the violent person has a legitimate relationship with the business, perhaps as a customer or patient, and becomes violent while on the premises. A large portion of customer incidents occur in the nightclub, restaurant, and health care industries. In 2014, about one-fifth of all workplace homicides resulted from this type of violence.[23]

Codes of Conduct

Companies have a right to insist that their employees, including managers, engage in ethical decision-making. To help achieve this goal, most businesses provide a written code of ethics or code of conduct for all employees to follow. These cover a wide variety of topics, from workplace romance and sexual harassment to hiring and termination policies, client and customer entertainment, bribery and gifts, personal trading of company shares in any way that hints of acting on insider knowledge of the company's fortunes, outside employment, and dozens of others. A typical code of conduct, regardless of the company or the industry, will also contain a variety of standard clauses, often blending legal compliance and ethical considerations (Table 7.1).

Sample Code of Conduct

Compliance with all laws	Employees must comply with all laws, including bribery, fraud, securities, environmental, safety, and employment laws.
Corruption and fraud	Employees must not accept certain types of gifts and hospitality from clients, vendors, or partners. Bribery is prohibited in all circumstances.
Conflict of interest	Employees must disclose and/or avoid any personal, financial, or other interests that might influence their ability to perform their job duties.
Company property	Employees must treat the company's property with respect and care, not misuse it, and protect company facilities and other material property.
Cybersecurity and digital devices policy	Employees must not use company computer equipment to transfer illegal, offensive, or pirated material, or to visit potentially dangerous websites that might compromise the safety of the company network or servers; employees must respect their duty of confidentiality in all Internet interactions.
Social media policy	Employees may [or may not] access personal social media accounts at work but are expected to act responsibly, follow company policies, and maintain productivity.
Sexual harassment	Employees must not engage in unwelcome or unwanted sexual advances, requests for sexual favors, and other verbal or physical conduct of a sexual nature. Behaviors such as conditioning promotions, awards, training, or other job benefits upon acceptance of unwelcome actions of a sexual nature are always wrong.[24]
Workplace respect	Employees must show respect for their colleagues at every level. Neither inappropriate nor illegal behavior will be tolerated.

Table 7.1

LINK TO LEARNING

Exxon Mobil's Code of Conduct is typical of that of most large companies. Read Exxon Mobil's code of conduct (https://openstax.org/l/53Exxon) on their website, and note that it demands ethical conduct at every level of the organization. Exxon expects its leadership team to model appropriate behavior for all employees. Decide whether, if you were an Exxon employee, you would find the code understandable and clear regarding what is allowed and what is not. Still thinking as an employee, identify the section of the code you think is most important for you, and explain why.

Two areas that deserve special mention are cybersecurity and harassment. Recent news stories have highlighted the hacking of electronic tools such as computers and databases, and employees and managers can indirectly contribute to such data breaches through unauthorized web surfing, sloppy e-mail usage, and other careless actions. Large companies such as Equifax, LinkedIn, Sony, Facebook, and JP Morgan Chase have suffered the theft of customer information, leading to loss of consumer confidence; sometimes large fines have been levied on companies. Employees play a part in preventing such breaches by strictly following company guidelines about data privacy and confidentiality, the use and storage of passwords, and other safeguards that limit access to only authorized users.

LINK TO LEARNING

For more on recent data breaches, watch a couple of videos. Watch this video about how J.P. Morgan Chase's $13 billion fine was the largest in history (https://openstax.org/l/53JPMorgan) from *CBS Evening News*. Also watch this video about how the Sony PlayStation was hacked and data was stolen from 77 million users (https://openstax.org/l/53PlayStation) from *CBS Early*.

We are also witnessing an increased level of public awareness about harassment in the workplace, particularly because of the #MeToo movement that followed revelations in 2017 and 2018 of years of sexual predation by powerful men in Hollywood and Washington, DC, as well as across workplaces of all kinds, including in sports and the arts. A victim of sexual harassment can be a man or a woman, and/or the same sex as the harasser. The harasser can be a supervisor, coworker, other employee, officer/director, intern, consultant, or nonemployee. Whatever the situation, harassing and threatening behavior is wrong (and sometimes criminal) and should always be reported.

7.4 | Financial Integrity

Learning Objectives

By the end of this section, you will be able to:

- Describe an employee's responsibilities to the employer in financial matters
- Define insider trading
- Discuss bribery and its legal and ethical consequences

Employees may face ethical dilemmas in the area of finance, especially in situations such as bribery and insider trading in securities. Such dubious "profit opportunities" can offer the chance of realizing thousands or millions of dollars, creating serious temptation for an employee. However, insider trading and bribery are serious violations of the law that can result in incarceration and large fines.

Insider Trading

The buying or selling of stocks, bonds, or other investments based on nonpublic information that is likely to affect the price of the security being traded is called **insider trading**. For example, someone who is privy to information that a company is about to be taken over, which will cause its stock price to rise when the information becomes public, may buy the stock before it goes up in order to sell it later for an enhanced profit. Likewise, someone with inside information about a coming drop in share price may sell all his or her holdings at the current price before the information is announced, avoiding the loss other shareholders will suffer when the price falls. Although insider trading can be difficult to prove, it is essentially cheating. It is illegal, unethical, and unfair, and it often injures other investors, as well as undermining public confidence in the stock market.

Insider trading laws are somewhat complex. They have developed through federal court interpretations of Section 10(b)5 of the Securities Exchange Act of 1934, as well as through actions by the U.S. Securities and Exchange Commission (SEC). The laws identify several kinds of violations. These include trading by an insider (generally someone who performs work for the company) who possesses significant confidential information relevant to the valuation of the company's stock, and trading by someone outside of the company who is given this sort of information by an insider or who obtains it inappropriately. Even being the messenger (the one communicating material nonpublic information to others on behalf of someone else) can be a legal violation.

The concept of an "insider" is broad and includes officers, directors, and employees of a company issuing securities. A person can even constitute what is called a "temporary insider" if he or she temporarily assumes a unique confidential relationship with a firm and, in doing so, acquires confidential information centered on the firm's financial and operational affairs. Temporary insiders can be investment bankers, brokers, attorneys, accountants, or other professionals typically thought of as outsiders, such as newspaper and television reporters.

A famous case of insider trading, *Securities and Exchange Commission v. Texas Gulf Sulphur Co.* (1968), began with the discovery of the Kidd Mine and implicated the employees of Texas mining company.[25] When first notified of the discovery of a large and very valuable copper deposit, mine employees bought stock in the company while keeping the information secret. When the information was released to the public, the price of the stock went up and the employees sold their stock, making a significant amount of money. The SEC and the Department of Justice prosecuted the employees for insider trading and won a conviction; the employees had to give back all the money they had made on their trades. Insider trading cases are often highly publicized, especially when charges are brought against high-profile figures.

ETHICS ACROSS TIME AND CULTURES

Insider Trading and Fiduciary Duty

One of the most famous cases of insider trading implicated Michael Milken, Dennis Levine, and Martin Siegel, all executives of Drexel Burnham Lambert (DBL), and the company itself.[26] Ivan Boesky, also accused, was an arbitrageur, an outside investor who bet on corporate takeovers and appeared to be able to uncannily anticipate takeover targets, buy their stock ahead of time, and earn huge profits. Everyone wondered how; the answer was that he cheated. Boesky went to the source—the major investment banks—to get insider information. He paid Levine and Siegel to give him pretakeover details, an illegal action, and he profited enormously from nearly every major deal in the merger-crazy 1980s, including huge deals involving oil companies such as Texaco, Getty, Gulf, and Chevron.

The SEC started to become suspicious after receiving a tip that someone was leaking information. Investigators discovered Levine's secret Swiss bank account, with all the money Boesky had paid him. Levine then gave up Boesky in a plea deal; the SEC started watching Boesky and subsequently caught Siegel and Milken.

The penalties were the most severe ever given at the time. Milken, the biggest catch of all, agreed to pay $200 million in government fines, $400 million to investors who had been hurt by his actions, and $500 million to DBL clients—for a grand total of $1.1 billion. He was sentenced to ten years in prison and banned for life from any involvement in the securities industry. Boesky received a prison sentence of 3.5 years, was fined $100 million, and was permanently barred from working with securities. Levine agreed to pay $11.5 million and $2 million more in back taxes; he too was given a lifetime ban and was sentenced to two years in prison.

Milken and Levine violated their financial duties to their employer and the company's clients. Not only does insider trading create a public relations nightmare, it also subjects the company to legal liability. DBL ended up being held liable in civil lawsuits due to the actions of its employees, and it was also charged with violations of the Racketeer Influenced and Corrupt Organizations (RICO) Act) and ultimately failed, going bankrupt in 1990.

(As a note of interest regarding the aftermath of all of this for Milken, he has tried to redeem his image since his incarceration. He resolutely advises others to avoid his criminal acts and has endowed some worthy causes in Los Angeles.)

Critical Thinking

- Employers in financial services must have stringent codes of professional behavior for their employees to observe. Even given such a code, how should employees honor their fiduciary duty to safeguard the firm's assets and treat clients equitably? What mechanisms would you suggest for keeping employees in banking, equities trading, and financial advising within the limits of the law and ethical behavior?
- This case dominated the headlines in the 1980s and the accused in this case were all severely fined and received prison sentences. How do you think this case might be treated today?
- Should employees in these industries be encouraged or even required to receive ethical certification from the state or from professional associations? Why or why not?

Bribery and the Foreign Corrupt Practices Act

Another temptation that may present itself to employees is the offer of a bribe. A **bribe** is a payment in some material form (cash or noncash) for an act that runs counter to the legal or ethical culture of the work environment. Bribery constitutes a violation of the law in all fifty U.S. states, as well as of a federal law that prohibits bribery in international transactions, the Foreign Corrupt Practices Act. Bribery generally injures not only individuals but also competitors, the government, and the free-market system as a whole. Of course, often the bribe is somewhat less obvious than an envelope full of money. It is important, therefore, to understand what constitutes a bribe.

Numerous factors help establish the ethics (and legality) of gift giving and receiving: the value of the gift, its purpose, the circumstances under which it is given, the position of the person receiving it, company policy, and the law. Assuming an employee has decision-making authority, the company wants and has the right to expect him or her to make choices in *its* best interest, not the employee's own self-interest. For example, assume an employee has the authority to buy a copy machine for the company. The employer wants to get the best copy machine for the best price, taking into account quality, service, warranties, and other factors. But what if the employee accepts a valuable gift card from a vendor who sells a copy machine with higher operating and maintenance charges, and then places the order with that vendor. This is clearly not in the best interests of the employer. It constitutes a failure on the part of the employee to follow ethical and legal rules, and, in all likelihood, company policy as well. If a company wants its employees always to do the right thing, it must have policies and procedures that ensure the employees know what the rules are and the consequences for breaking them.

A gift may be only a well-intentioned token of appreciation, but the potential for violating company rules (and the law) is still present. A well-written and effectively communicated gift policy provides guidance to company employees about what is and is not appropriate to accept from a customer or vendor and when. This policy should clearly state whether employees are allowed to accept gifts on or outside the work premises and who may give or accept them. If gifts are allowed, the gift policy should define the acceptable value and type, and the circumstances under which an employee may accept a gift.

When in doubt about whether the size or value of a gift renders it impossible for an employee to accept it, workers should be advised to check with the appropriate officer or department within their company. Be it an "ethics hotline" or simply the human resources department, wise firms provide an easy protocol for employees to follow in determining what falls within and without the protocols for accepting gifts.

As an example of a gift policy, consider the federal government's strict rules.[27] A federal employee may not give or solicit a contribution for a gift to an official superior and may not accept a gift from an employee receiving less pay if that employee is a subordinate. On annual occasions when gifts are traditionally given, such as birthdays and holidays, an employee may give a superior a gift valued at less than $10. An employee may not solicit or accept a gift given because of his or her official position, or from a prohibited source, including anyone who has or seeks official action or business with the agency. In special circumstances such as holidays, and unless the frequency of the gifts would appear to be improper, an employee generally may accept gifts of less than $20. Gifts of entertainment, such as expensive restaurant meals, are also restricted. Finally, gifts must be reported when their total value from one source exceeds $390 in a calendar year. Some companies in the private sector follow similar rules.

Bribery presents a particular ethical challenge for employees in the international business arenas. Although every company wants to land lucrative contracts around the world, most expect their employees to follow both the law and company policy when attempting to consummate such deals. The U.S. law prohibiting bribery in international business dealings is the **Foreign Corrupt Practices Act** (FCPA), which is an amendment to the Securities and Exchange Act of 1934, one of the most important laws promoting transparency in corporate governance. The FCPA dates to 1977 and was amended in 1988 and 1998. Its main purpose is to make it illegal for companies and their managers to influence or bribe foreign officials with monetary payments or rewards of any kind in an attempt to get or keep business opportunities outside the United States. The FCPA is enforced through the joint efforts of the SEC and the Department of Justice.[28] It applies to any act by U.S. businesses, their representatives, foreign corporations whose stock is traded in U.S. markets, and all U.S. citizens, nationals, or residents acting in furtherance of a foreign corrupt practice, whether they are physically present in the United States or not (this is called the nationality principle). Antibribery law is a serious issue for companies with overseas business and cross-border sales. Any companies or individuals convicted of these activities may pay significant fines, and individuals can face prison time.

The FCPA prohibits an agent of any company incorporated in the United States from extending a bribe to a foreign government official to achieve a business advantage in that country, but it does not specifically prohibit the extension of a bribe to a private officer of a nongovernmental company in a foreign country. The definition of a foreign government official can be expansive; it includes not only those working directly for the government but also company officials if the company is owned or operated by the government. An exception is made for "facilitating or grease payments," small amounts of money paid to low-level government workers in an effort to speed routine tasks like processing paperwork or turning on electricity, but not to influence the granting of a contract.

Illegal payments need not be cash; they can include anything of value such as gifts and trips. For example, BHP Billiton, a U.S. energy company, and GlaxoSmithKline, a U.K. pharmaceutical company, were each fined $25 million for buying foreign officials tickets to the 2008 Olympic Games in Beijing, China.[29] Fines for violations like these can be large and can include civil penalties as well as forfeited profits. For example, Telia, a Swedish telecommunications provider whose shares are traded on Nasdaq, recently agreed to pay nearly a billion dollars ($965 million) in a settlement to resolve FCPA violations that consisted of using bribery to win business in Uzbekistan.[30]

LINK TO LEARNING

The SEC website provides an interactive list of the SEC's FCPA enforcement actions by calendar year and company name (https://openstax.org/l/53FCPA) for more information. Click on *Telia* to read more details on the case cited in the preceding paragraph. Do you think the penalty was too harsh, or not harsh enough? Why?

The potential effect of laws such as the FCPA that impose ethical duties on employees and the companies they work for is often debated. Although some believe the FCPA disadvantages U.S. firms competing in foreign markets, others say it is the backbone of an ethical free enterprise system. The argument against strong enforcement of the FCPA has some merit according to managers in the field, and there is a general sense that illegal or unethical conduct is sometimes necessary for success. An attorney for energy-related company Cinergy summed up the feelings of many executives: "Shame on the Justice Department's myopic view and inability to understand the realities of the world."[31] Some nations consider business bribery to be culturally acceptable and turn a blind eye to such activities.

The argument in favor of FCPA enforcement has its supporters as well, who assert that the law not only covers the activities of U.S. companies but also levels the playing field because of its broad jurisdiction over foreign enterprises and their officials. The fact is that since the United States passed the FCPA, other nations have followed suit. The 1997 Organization for Economic Cooperation and Development (OECD) Anti-Bribery Convention has been instrumental in getting its signatories (the United Kingdom and most European Union nations) to enact stricter antibribery laws. The United Kingdom adopted the Bribery Act in 2010, Canada adopted the Corruption of Foreign Officials Act of 1999, and European Union nations have done the same. There is also the OECD Convention on Combating Bribery of Foreign Public Officials in International Business Transactions, which has forty-three signatories, including all thirty-five OECD countries and eight other countries.

Companies and employees engaging in transactions in foreign markets face an increased level of regulatory scrutiny and are well served if they put ethics policies in place and enforce them. Companies must train employees at all levels to follow compliance guidelines and rules, rather than engaging in illegal conduct such as "under the table" and "off the books" payments (Figure 7.7).

Figure 7.7 "Under the table" and "off the books" are terms applied to payments that are really bribes. (credit: modification of "Graft for Everyone!" by Chris Potter/Flickr, CC BY 2.0)

Ethical Leadership

Of course, bribery is just one of many ethical dilemmas an employee might face in the workplace. Not all such dilemmas are governed by the clear-cut rules generally laid out for illegal acts such as bribery. Employees may find themselves being asked to do something that is legal but not considered ethical. For example, an employee might receive confidential proprietary knowledge about another firm that would give his or her firm an unfair competitive advantage. Should the employee act on this information?

WHAT WOULD YOU DO?

Should You Act on Information If You Have Doubts?

Assume you are a partner in a successful computer consulting firm bidding for a contract with a large insurance company. Your chief rival is a firm that has usually offered services and prices similar to yours. However, from a new employee who used to work for that firm, you learn that it is unveiling a new competitive price structure and accelerated delivery dates, which will undercut the terms you had been prepared to offer the insurance company. Assume you have verified that the new employee is not in violation of any non-compete or nondisclosure agreement and therefore the information was not given to you illegally.

Critical Thinking

Would you change prices and delivery dates to beat your rival? Or would you inform both your rival and potential customer of what you have learned? Why?

Most companies say they want all employees to obey the law and make ethical decisions. But employees typically should not be expected to make ethical decisions based just on gut instinct; they need guidance, training, and leadership to help them navigate the maze of grey areas that present themselves daily in business. This guidance can be provided by the company through standard setting and the development of ethical codes of conduct and policies. Senior managers modeling ethical behavior and so leading by direct example also provide significant direction.

7.5 | Criticism of the Company and Whistleblowing

Learning Objectives

By the end of this section, you will be able to:

- Outline the rules and laws that govern employees' criticism of the employer
- Identify situations in which an employee becomes a whistleblower

This chapter has explained the many responsibilities employees owe their employers. But workers are not robots. They have minds of their own and the freedom to criticize their bosses and firms, even if managers and companies do not always welcome such criticism. What kind of criticism is fair and ethical, what is legal, and how should a whistleblowing employee be treated?

Limiting Pay Secrecy

For decades, most U.S. companies enforced **pay secrecy**, a policy that prohibits employees from disclosing or discussing salaries among themselves. The reason was obvious: Companies did not want to be scrutinized for their salary decisions. They knew that if workers were aware of what each was paid, they would question the inequities that pay secrecy kept hidden from them.

Recently, the situation has begun to change. Ten states have enacted new laws banning employers from imposing pay secrecy rules: California, Colorado, Illinois, Louisiana, Maine, Michigan, Minnesota, New Hampshire, New Jersey, and Vermont.[32] The real game changer came in 2012, when multiple decisions by the National Labor Relations Board (NLRB) and various federal courts made it clear that most pay secrecy policies are unenforceable and violate federal labor law (National Labor Relations Act, 29 U.S.C. § 157-158).[33] Generally speaking, labor law lends employees the right to engage in collective activities, including that of discussing with each other the specifics of their individual employment arrangements, which includes how much they are paid. Moreover, the applicable sections of the 1935 National Labor Relations Act (NLRA) apply to union and non-union employees, so there is no exception made for companies whose employees are non-unionized, meaning the law protects all workers. In 2014, President Barack Obama issued an executive order banning companies that engaged in federal contracting from prohibiting such salary discussions.[34]

Opening up the discussion of pay acknowledges the growing desire of employees to be well informed and to have the freedom to question or criticize their company. If employees cannot talk about something at work because they think it will make their boss angry, where do they go instead? Social media can be a likely answer. Protections generally extend to salary discussions on Facebook or Twitter or Instagram; Section 7 of the NRLA protects two or more employees who act together or discuss improving their terms and conditions of employment in person or online, just as it does in other settings.

Speaking Out on Social Media

Does the First Amendment protect employees at work who criticize their boss or their company? Generally, no. That answer may surprise those who believe that the First Amendment protects all speech. It does not. The Bill of Rights was created to protect citizens from an overreaching government, not from their employer. The First Amendment reads as follows:

> "Congress shall make no law respecting an establishment of religion, or prohibiting the free exercise thereof; or abridging the freedom of speech, or of the press; or the right of the people peaceably to assemble, and to petition the Government for a redress of grievances."

The key words are "Congress shall make no law," meaning the content of speech is something the government and politicians cannot control with laws or policies. However, this right of free speech is generally not applicable to the private sector workplace and does not cover criticism of your employer.

Does that mean an employee can be fired for criticizing the company or boss? Yes, under most circumstances. Therefore, if someone posts a message on social media that says, "My boss is a jerk" or "My company is a terrible place to work," the likelihood is that the person can be fired without any recourse, assuming he or she is an employee at will (see the discussion of at-will employment earlier in this chapter). Unless the act of firing constitutes a violation under federal law, such as Title VII of the Civil Rights Act of 1964, the speech is not protected speech, and thus the speaker (the employee) is not protected.

At some point, all of us may get angry with our companies or supervisors, but we still have a duty to keep our disputes in-house and not make public any situations we are attempting to resolve internally. Employers typically are prohibited from discussing human resource matters relating to any specific employees. Employees, too, should keep complaints confidential unless and until crimes are charged or civil suits are filed.

CASES FROM THE REAL WORLD

Adrian Duane and IXL Learning

Adrian Duane had worked for IXL, a Silicon Valley educational technology company,[35] for about a year when he got into a dispute with his supervisor over Duane's ability to work flexible hours after he returned from medical leave following transgender surgery.

Duane posted a critical comment on Glassdoor.com after he said his supervisor refused to accommodate a scheduling request. Duane's critique said, in part: "If you're not a family-oriented white or Asian straight or mainstream gay person with 1.7 kids who really likes softball—then you're likely to find yourself on the outside. . . . Most management do not know what the word 'discrimination' means, nor do they seem to think it matters."[36]

According to court documents, Paul Mishkin, IXL's CEO, confronted Duane with a printout of the Glassdoor review during a meeting about his complaints, at which time IXL terminated Duane. IXL claimed the derogatory post showed "poor judgment and ethical values." Security had already cleared out Duane's desk and boxed his personal effects, and he was escorted from the premises. According to IXL, the company had granted Duane's requests for time off or modified work schedules and welcomes all individuals equally regardless of gender identity.

The NLRB heard Duane's case. Judge Gerald M. Etchingham said he did not believe the post was part of a concerted or group action among Duane's fellow employees at the company, and therefore it was not protected under the NLRA, because it was not an attempt to improve collective terms and conditions of employment. Furthermore, Etchingham said Duane's post was more like "a tantrum" and "childish ridicule" of his employer rather than speech protected under Section 7 of the NLRA. In other words, this was not an attempt to stimulate discussion but rather an anonymous one-way (and one-time) post. "Here, Duane's posting on Glassdoor.com was not a social media posting like Facebook or Twitter. Instead, Glassdoor.com is a website used by respondent and prospective employees as a recruiting tool to recruit prospective employees."[37]

The NLRB decision is an interesting step in the development of the law as the NLRB tries to apply the NLRA's protections to employee use of social media. Duane has a pending Equal Employment Opportunity Commission lawsuit alleging employment discrimination under Title VII of the Civil Rights Act of 1964.

Critical Thinking

- What ethical and legal obligations do employees have to refrain from badmouthing their employers in a fit of pique, especially on the firm's own website?
- Should management allow employees to criticize the company without fear of retaliation? Could management benefit from allowing such criticism? Why or why not?

The rules related to social media are evolving, but applicable laws do not generally distinguish between sites or locations in which someone might criticize an employer, so criticism of the boss remains largely unprotected speech. As discussed earlier, employees can go online and post information about wages, hours, and working conditions, and that speech is protected by federal statute. So, although some general complaints against employers are not protected under the First Amendment, they may be protected under the NLRA (because arguably they may be related to terms and conditions of employment). However, most courts agree that statements personally critical of the boss or the company on a basis other than wages and working conditions are not protected. Obviously, there is no protection when employees post false or misleading information on social media in an attempt to harm the company's reputation or that of management.

Whistleblowing: Risks and Rewards

The act of **whistleblowing**—going to an official government agency and disclosing an employer's violation of the law—is different from everyday criticism. In fact, whistleblowing is largely viewed as a public service because it helps society reduce bad workplace behavior. Being a whistleblower is not easy, however, and someone inclined to act as one should expect many hurdles. If a whistleblower's identity becomes known, his or her revelations may amount to career suicide. Even if they keep their job, whistleblowers often are not promoted, and they may face resentment not only from management but also from rank-and-file workers who fear the loss of their own jobs. Whistleblowers may also be blacklisted, making it difficult for them to get a job at a different firm, and all as a result of doing what is ethical.

Blowing the whistle on your employer is thus a big decision with significant ramifications. However, most employees do not want to cover up unethical or illegal conduct, nor should they. When should employees decide to blow the whistle on their boss or company? Ethicists say it should be done with an appropriate motive—to get the company to comply with the law or to protect potential victims—and not to get revenge on a boss at whom you are angry. Of course, even if an employee has a personal revenge motive, if the company actively is breaking the law, it is still important that the wrongdoing be reported. In any case, knowing when and how to blow the whistle is a challenge for an employee wanting to do the right thing.

The employee should usually try internal reporting channels first, to disclose the problem to management before going public. Sometimes workers mistakenly identify something as wrongdoing that was not wrongdoing after all. Internal reporting gives management a chance to start an investigation and attempt to rectify the situation. The employee who goes to the government should also have some kind of hard evidence that wrongful actions have occurred; the violation should be serious, and blowing the whistle should have some likelihood of stopping the wrongful act.

Under many federal laws, an employer cannot retaliate by firing, demoting, or taking any other adverse action against workers who report injuries, concerns, or other protected activity. One of the first laws with a specific whistleblower protection provision was the Occupational Safety and Health Act of 1970. Since passage of that law, Congress has expanded whistleblower authority to protect workers who report violations of more than twenty different federal laws across various topics. (There is no all-purpose whistleblower protection; it must be granted by individual statutes.)

A sample of the specific laws under which whistleblowing employees are protected can be found in the environmental area, where it is in the public interest for employees to report violations of the law to the authorities, which, in turn, helps the average citizen concerned about clean air and water. The Clean Air Act protects any employee reporting air emission violations from area, stationary, and mobile sources from any retaliation for such reporting. The Water Pollution Control Act similarly protects from retaliation any employee who reports alleged violations relating to discharge of pollutants into water.

Without the help of employees who are "on the ground" and see the violations occur, it could be difficult for government regulators to always find the source of pollution. Even when whistleblowers are not acting completely altruistically, their revelations may still be true and worthy of being brought to the public's attention. Thus, in such situations, the responsible employee becomes a steward of the public interest, and we all should want whistleblowers to come forward. Yet not all whistleblowers are white knights, and not all their firms are evil dragons worthy of being slain.

LINK TO LEARNING

Go to this U.S. Department of Labor website that lists all the laws under which whistleblowers have protection (https://openstax.org/l/53whistleblower) to learn more.

Blowing the whistle may bring the employee more than just intrinsic ethical rewards; it may also result in cash. The most lucrative law under which employees can blow the whistle is the False Claims Act (FCA), 31 U.S.C. §§ 3729–3733. This legislation was enacted in 1863, during the American Civil War, because Congress was worried that suppliers of goods to the Union Army might cheat the government. The FCA has been amended many times since then, and today it serves as a leading example of a statutory law that remains important after more than 150 years. The FCA provides that any person who knowingly submits false claims to the government must pay a civil penalty for each false claim, plus triple the amount of the government's damages. The amount of this basic civil penalty is regularly adjusted by the cost of living, and the current penalty range is from $5500 to $11,000.

More importantly for our discussion, the **qui tam provision** of the law allows private persons (called relators) to file lawsuits for violations of the FCA on behalf of the government and to receive part of any penalty imposed. The person bringing the action is a type of a whistleblower, but one who initiates legal action on his or her own rather than simply reporting it to a government agency. If the government believes it is a worthwhile case and intervenes in the lawsuit, then the relator (whistleblower) is entitled to receive between 15 and 25 percent of the amount the government recovers. If the government thinks winning is a long shot and declines to intervene in the lawsuit, the relator's share increases to 25 to 30 percent.

A few whistleblowers have become rich (and famous, thanks to an ABC News story), with awards ranging in the neighborhood of $100 million.[38] In 2012, a single whistleblower, Bradley Birkenfeld, a former UBS employee, was awarded $104 million by the Internal Revenue Service (IRS), making him the most highly rewarded whistleblower in history. Birkenfeld also spent time in prison for participating in the tax fraud he reported. In 2009, ten former Pfizer employees were awarded $102 million for exposing an illegal promotion of prescription medications. John Kopchinski, the original whistleblower and one of the ten, received $50 million. In another case involving the health care company HCA, two employees who blew the whistle on Medicare fraud ended up receiving a combined total of $100 million.

It is not just the size of the reward that should get your attention but also the amount of money these employees saved taxpayers and/or shareholders. They turned in companies that were cheating the Centers for Medicare and Medicaid Services (affecting taxpayers), the IRS (affecting government revenues), and private health insurance (affecting premiums). The public saved far more than the reward paid to the whistleblowers.

Incredibly high rewards such as the aforementioned are somewhat unusual, but according to National Whistleblower Center director Stephen Kohn, "Birkenfeld's and Eckard's rewards act like advertisements for the U.S. government's whistleblower programs, which make hundreds of rewards every year."[39] The FCA is one of four laws under which whistleblowers can receive a reward; the others are administered by the IRS, the SEC, and the Commodity Futures Trading Commission. Most whistleblowers do not get paid until the lawsuit and all appeals have concluded and the full amount of any monetary penalty has been paid to the government. Many complex cases of business fraud can go on for several years before a verdict is rendered and appealed (or a settlement is reached). An employee whose identity has been disclosed and who has been unofficially blacklisted may not see any reward money for several years.

CASES FROM THE REAL WORLD

Sherron Watkins and Enron

Enron is one of the most infamous examples of corporate fraud in U.S. history. The scandal that destroyed the company resulted in approximately $60 billion in lost shareholder value. Sherron Watkins, an officer of the company, discovered the fraud and first went to her boss and mentor, founder and chairperson Ken Lay, to report the suspected accounting and financial irregularities. She was ignored more than once and eventually went to the press with her story. Because she did not go directly to the SEC, Watkins received no whistleblower protection. (The Sarbanes-Oxley Act was not passed until after the Enron scandal. In fact, it was Watkins's circumstance and Enron's misdeeds that helped convince Congress to pass the law.[40])

Now a respected national speaker on the topic of ethics and employees' responsibility, Watkins talks about how an employee should handle such situations. "When you're faced with something that really matters, if you're silent, you're starting on the wrong path . . . go against the crowd if need be," she said in a speech to the National Character and Leadership Symposium, (a seminar to instill leadership and moral qualities in young men and women).

Watkins talks openly about the risk of being an honest employee, something employees should consider when evaluating what they owe their company, the public, and themselves. "I will never have a job in corporate America again. The minute you speak truth to power and you're not heard, your career is never the same again."

Enron's corporate leaders dealt with the looming crisis by a combination of blaming others and leaving their employees to fend for themselves. According to Watkins, "Within two weeks of me finding this fraud, [Enron president] Jeff Skilling quit. We did feel like we were on a battleship, and things were not going well, and the captain had just taken a helicopter home. The fall of 2001 was just the bleakest time in my life, because everything I thought was secure was no longer secure."

Critical Thinking

- Did Watkins owe an ethical duty to Enron, to its shareholders, or to the investing public to go public with her suspicions? Explain your answer.
- How big a price is it fair to ask a whistleblowing employee to pay?

LINK TO LEARNING

Visit the National Whistleblower Center website (https://openstax.org/l/53NWC) and learn more about some of the individuals discussed in this chapter who became whistleblowers.

Watch this video about one of the most famous whistleblowers, Sherron Watkins, former vice president of Enron (https://openstax.org/l/53Watkins) to learn more.

Sometimes employees, including managers, face an ethical dilemma that they seek to address from within rather than becoming a whistleblower. The risk is that they may be ignored or that their speaking up will be held against them. However, companies should want and expect employees to step forward and report wrongdoing to their superiors, and they should support that decision, not punish it. Sallie Krawcheck, a financial industry executive, was not a whistleblower in either the classical or the legal sense. She went to her boss with her discovery of wrongdoing at work, which means she had no legal protection under whistleblower statutes. Read her story in the following box.

CASES FROM THE REAL WORLD

Sallie Krawcheck and Merrill Lynch

Shortly after Sallie Krawcheck took over as chief of Merrill Lynch's wealth management division at Bank of America, she discovered that a mutual fund called the Stable Value Fund, a financial product Merrill had sold to customers as an investment for their 401k plans, was not as stable as its name implied. The team at Merrill had made a mistake by managing the fund in a way that assumed a higher risk than was acceptable to its investors, and the fund ended up losing much of its value. Unfortunately, because it was supposed to be a low-risk fund, the people who had invested in it, and who would suffer most from Merrill's mistakes, were earners of relatively modest incomes, including Walmart employees, who made up the largest group.

According to Krawcheck, she had two options. Option one was to say tough luck to the Stable Value Fund's investors, including the Walmart employees, explaining that all investments carry some degree of risk. Option two was to bail out the investors by pouring money into the fund to increase its value. Krawcheck had already been burned once by trying to be ethical. She had been head of CitiGroup's wealth management division (Smith Barney); in that capacity, she had made a decision to reimburse clients for some of their losses she felt were due to company mistakes. Rather than supporting her decision, however, CitiGroup terminated her, in large part for making the ethical decision rather than the profitable one. Now she was in the same predicament with a new company. Should Krawcheck risk her job again by choosing the ethical act, or should she make a purely financial decision and tell the 401k investors they would have to take the loss?

Krawcheck began talking to people inside and outside the company to see what they thought. Most told her to just keep her head down and do nothing. One "industry titan" told her there was nothing to be done, that everyone knows stable-value funds are not really stable. Unconvinced, Krawcheck took the problem to Bank of America's CEO. He agreed to back her up and put company money into the depleted stable-value funds to prop them up.

Krawcheck opted to be honest and ethical by helping the small investors and felt good about it. "I thought, ethical business was good business," she says. "It came down to my sense of purpose as well as my sense of my industry's purpose; it wasn't about some abstract ethical theorem . . . the answer wasn't that I got into the business simply to make a lot of money. It was because it was a business that I knew could have a positive impact on clients' lives."[41]

But the story does not really have a happy ending. Krawcheck writes that she thought at the time she had done the right thing *and* still had her job, a win/win outcome of a very tough ethical dilemma. However, speaking out did come at a cost. Krawcheck lost some important and powerful allies within the company, and although she did not lose her job at that time, she writes "the political damage was done; when that CEO retired, the clock began ticking down on my time at Bank of America, and before long I was 'reorganized out' of that role."[42]

Critical Thinking

- Could you do what Sallie Krawcheck did and risk being fired a second time? Why or why not?
- Krawcheck went on to start her own firm, Ellevest, specializing in investments for female clients. Why do you think she chose this route rather than moving to another large Wall Street firm?

WHAT WOULD YOU DO?

Underestimating and Overcharging

Suppose you are a supervising engineer at a small defense contractor of about one hundred employees. Your firm had barely been breaking even, but the recent award of a federal contract has dramatically turned the situation around. Midway through the new project, though, you realize that the principal partners in your firm have been overcharging the Department of Defense for services provided and components purchased. (You discovered this accidentally, and it would be difficult for anyone else to find it out.) You take this information to one of the principals, whom you know well and respect. He tells you apologetically that the overcharges became necessary when the firm seriously underestimated total project costs in its bid on the contract. If the overcharges do not continue, the firm will again be perilously close to bankruptcy.

You know the firm has long struggled to remain financially viable. Furthermore, you have great confidence in the quality of the work your team is providing the government. Finally, you feel a special kinship with nearly all the employees and particularly with the founding partners, so you are loath to take your evidence to the government.

Critical Thinking

What are you going to do? Will you swallow your discomfort because making the overcharges public may very well put your job and those of one hundred friends and colleagues at risk? Would the overall quality of the firm's work on the contract persuade you it is worth what it is charging? Or would you decide that fraud is never permissible, even if its disclosure comes at the cost of the survivability of the firm and the friendships you have within it? Explain your reasoning.

🔑 Key Terms

brand a type of product or service marketed by a particular company under a particular name

branding the process of creating, differentiating, and maintaining a particular image and/or reputation for a company, product, or service

bribe a payment in some form (cash or noncash) for an act that runs counter to the legal and ethical culture of the work environment

duty of confidentiality a common-law rule giving an employee responsibility to protect the secrecy of the employer's proprietary information, such as trade secrets, material covered by patents and copyrights, employee records and salary information, and customer data

duty of loyalty a common-law rule that requires an employee to refrain from acting in a manner contrary to the employer's interest

Foreign Corrupt Practices Act an amendment to the Securities and Exchange Act of 1934; its main purpose is to make it illegal for companies and their managers to influence or bribe foreign officials with monetary payments or rewards of any kind in an attempt to get or keep business opportunities outside the United States

insider trading the buying or selling of stocks, bonds, or other investments based on nonpublic information that is likely to favorably affect the price of the security being traded

intellectual property the manifestation of original ideas, protected by legal means such as patent, copyright, or trademark

internal marketing the process of getting employees to believe in the company's product and even to buy it

non-compete agreement a contract clause ensuring that employees will not compete with the company during or after employment there

nondisclosure agreement an agreement to prevent the theft of trade secrets, most of which are protected only by a duty of secrecy and not by federal intellectual property law

nonsolicitation clause an agreement that protects a business from an employee who leaves for another job and then attempts to lure customers or former colleagues away

pay secrecy a policy of some companies to prevent employees from discussing their salary with other workers

qui tam provision the section of the False Claims Act of 1863 that allows private persons to file lawsuits for violations of the act on behalf of the government as well as for themselves and so receive part of any penalty imposed

trade secret a company's technical or design information, advertising and marketing plans, and research and development data that would be useful to competitors

whistleblowing the act of reporting an employer to a governmental entity for violating the law

work style the way and order in which we are most comfortable accomplishing our tasks at work

workplace personality the manner in which we think and act on the job

📄 Summary

7.1 Loyalty to the Company

Although employees' and employers' concepts of loyalty have changed, it is reasonable to expect workers to have a basic sense of responsibility to their company and willingness to protect a variety of important assets such as intellectual property and trade secrets. Current employees should not compete with their employer in a way that would violate conflict-of-interest rules, and former employees should not solicit previous customers or employees upon leaving employment.

7.2 Loyalty to the Brand and to Customers

Employees have a duty to be loyal to the brand and treat customers well. Internal marketing is one process by which a company instills employee commitment to the brand and builds loyalty in its workforce. This loyalty should be a two-way street, however. If the company wants its employees to treat customers with respect, it must treat them with respect as well.

7.3 Contributing to a Positive Work Atmosphere

Ethical employees accept their role in creating a workplace that is respectful, safe, and welcoming by getting along with coworkers and doing what is best for the company. They also comply with corporate codes of conduct, which cover a wide range of behaviors, from financial dealings and bribery to sexual harassment. In addition, they are alert to any situation in the workplace that could escalate into violence. In short, the employee has a duty to be a responsible person in the job.

7.4 Financial Integrity

Legal and cultural differences may allow bribes in other countries, but bribery and insider trading (which allows someone with private information about securities to profit from that knowledge at the public's expense) are illegal in the United States, as well as unethical. A clear gift policy should be in place to help employees understand when it is acceptable to accept a gift from another employee or an outsider (such as a vendor), and to distinguish gifts from bribes.

7.5 Criticism of the Company and Whistleblowing

Employees should understand that there are limits to what can be posted about their employer online, just as there are limits to what they can say in the workplace, and that the First Amendment generally does not protect such speech. Whistleblowers are protected, and sometimes rewarded, for their willingness to come forward, but they can still face a hostile environment in some situations. Employees should not use whistleblowing as an attempt to get back at a boss or employer they do not like; rather, they should use it as a means to stop serious wrongdoing.

⧠ Assessment Questions

1. The common law concept that requires an employee to render loyal and faithful service to the employer is _____.

    A. the duty of confidentiality
    B. a non-compete agreement
    C. the duty of loyalty
    D. trade secret protection

2. An employee who works in the graphic design department of a large advertising agency most likely cannot moonlight after business hours for a friend's _____.

    A. bakery business
    B. web design business
    C. construction business
    D. landscaping design business

3. True or false? All fifty states require that an employee refrain from acting in a manner contrary to the employer's interest.

4. Based on a non-compete agreement, what should the employee avoid creating with the employer?

5. What duty requires an employee to maintain the secrecy of proprietary material, such as trade secrets, intellectual property, and customer data?

6. Which of the following is especially important for developing and maintaining employee loyalty to the brand?

    A. empowerment

    B. engagement

    C. commitment

    D. dedication

7. Efforts to get employees to believe in the product, to commit to the idea that the company is selling something worth buying, and even to think about buying it are part of _____.

    A. brand loyalty

    B. internal marketing

    C. employee engagement

    D. company identity

8. True or false? Employees are more likely to develop some degree of brand loyalty when they have a common sense of purpose and identity with the company.

9. Why should employees care about the way they treat customers?

10. A patient becomes violent on hospital premises after being turned down for the clinical trial of a new drug therapy. This scenario fits which of the following workplace violence categories?

    A. traditional criminal intent

    B. violence by one worker against another

    C. violence stemming from a personal relationship

    D. violence by a customer

11. Understanding the various personalities at work can be a complex task, but it is an important one for developing which of the following?

    A. collegiality

    B. emotional intelligence

    C. empathy

    D. personality harmony

12. True or false? Emotional intelligence is a willingness to step into someone else's shoes.

13. Regardless of their working style, preferences, or quirks, what do employees owe one another?

14. What are the four categories of violence at work, according to the National Institute for Occupational Safety and Health (NIOSH)?

15. The buying or selling of stocks, bonds, or other investments based on nonpublic information that is likely to favorably affect the price of the security being traded is which of the following?

    A. insider trading

    B. bribery

    C. illegal transaction

    D. manipulation

16. A payment in some form (cash or noncash) for an act that runs counter to the legal or ethical culture of the work environment is called _____.

    A. insider trading

    B. bribery

    C. illegal transaction

    D. manipulation

17. True or false? Because legal and cultural differences allow bribes in some other countries, U.S. firms and their employees are permitted to pay them.

18. Bribery generally injures individuals and which other entities?

19. List the factors that help establish the ethics (and legality) of gift giving and receiving.

20. Going to an official government agency and disclosing an employer's violation of the law is _____.

    A. insider trading

    B. whistleblowing

    C. free speech expression

    D. tattle telling

21. True or false? Most U.S. companies prohibit employees from disclosing or discussing salaries among themselves.

22. True or false? The First Amendment does not protect employees at work who criticize their boss or their company.

23. What kind of information can employees post online under the protection of federal statute?

24. What is typically not an appropriate motive for reporting the employer to authorities, unless the company is breaking the law?

25. What should the employees usually try first before going public with an accusation that their company may be breaking the law?

Endnotes

1. Schmidt v. Blue Lily Farms LLC, No. A08-1398. (Minn. Ct. App. July 21, 2009).

2. Restatement (Second) of Agency, § 394 (1958).

3. Peter Murdock, "The New Reality of Employee Loyalty," *Forbes*, December 12, 2017. https://www.forbes.com/sites/forbeshumanresourcescouncil/2017/12/28/the-new-reality-of-employee-loyalty/#f652ce34cf35.

4. "Declining Employee Loyalty: A Casualty of the New Workplace," Wharton School of Business, University of Pennsylvania, May 9, 2012. http://knowledge.wharton.upenn.edu/article/declining-employee-loyalty-a-casualty-of-the-new-workplace/.

5. "Declining Employee Loyalty: A Casualty of the New Workplace," Wharton School of Business, University of Pennsylvania, May 9, 2012. http://knowledge.wharton.upenn.edu/article/declining-employee-loyalty-a-casualty-of-the-new-workplace/.

6. Flood v. Kuhn, 407 U.S. 258 (1972).

7. Crystal Spraggins, "Yes, People Really Do Quit Jobs for More Money," PayScale, May 2015. https://www.payscale.com/compensation-today/2015/05/yes-people-really-do-quit-jobs-for-more-money.

8. "Why Employees Quit, According to New Glassdoor Economic Research," Glassdoor, February 2, 2017. https://www.glassdoor.com/press/employees-quit-glassdoor-economic-research/.

9.   "Why Employees Quit, According to New Glassdoor Economic Research," Glassdoor, February 2, 2017. https://www.glassdoor.com/press/
     employees-quit-glassdoor-economic-research/.
10. Rob Rogers, "Retention Compensation Plans—Please Stay! A Successful Retention Pay Strategy Isn't Merely a Giveaway for Tenure,"
     Society for Human Resource Management, February 26, 2015. https://www.shrm.org/resourcesandtools/hr-topics/compensation/pages/
     retention-compensation-plans.aspx.
11. Office of Economic Policy, U.S. Dept. of the Treasury, "Non-Compete Contracts: Economic Effects and Policy Implications," March 2016.
     https://www.treasury.gov/resource-center/economic-policy/Documents/UST%20Non-competes%20Report.pdf.
12. "New California Noncompete Law," The NonCompete Center. http://californianoncompete.com/ (accessed February 19, 2018).
13. Reuters, "Jimmy John's Will Stop Making Low-Wage Employees Sign Non-Compete Agreements," Fortune, June 22, 2016.
     http://fortune.com/2016/06/22/jimmy-johns-non-compete-agreements/.
14. Office of the Attorney General, State of Illinois, "Madigan Sues Jimmy John's for Imposing Unlawful Non-Compete Agreements on
     Sandwich Makers and Delivery Drivers," June 8, 2016. http://www.illinoisattorneygeneral.gov/pressroom/2016_06/20160608.html.
15. Marilyn Nagel, "How Are Your Employees Affecting Your Brand?" Huffington Post, September 23, 2013. https://www.huffingtonpost.com/
     marilyn-nagel/employee-engagement_b_3956204.html.
16. Jill Larsen, "Cisco's Employer Brand Puts Employees First," Cisco, December 12, 2016. https://newsroom.cisco.com/feature-
     content?type=webcontent&articleId=1809254.
17. "Taco Bell Worker Appears to Be Licking a Bunch of Taco Shells in This Facebook Picture," Huffington Post, June 3, 2013.
     https://www.huffingtonpost.com/2013/06/03/taco-bell-worker-licking_n_3377709.html; "Domino's Workers Disgusting YouTube Video:
     Spitting, Nose-Picking and Worse," Huffington Post, April 14, 2009. https://www.huffingtonpost.com/2009/04/14/dominos-workers-
     disgustin_n_186908.html.
18. Colin Mitchell, "Selling the Brand Inside," Harvard Business Review, January 2002. https://hbr.org/2002/01/selling-the-brand-inside.
19. Brenna Kelly, "Augusta Schools Custodian Kathy Fryman Takes Care of Building and the People Inside; Gets Fred Award," Northern
     Kentucky Tribune, September 23, 2017. http://www.nkytribune.com/2017/09/augusta-schools-custodian-kathy-fryman-takes-care-of-
     building-and-the-people-inside-gets-fred-award/.
20. LOCKARD, Plaintiff-Appellee, v. PIZZA HUT, INC., a corporation, doing business as Pizza Hut; A & M Food Services, Inc., a corporation, doing
     business as Pizza Hut, Defendants-Appellants. US Ct. App. Tenth Circuit (1998).
21. Robin Lindsay and Barbara Marcolini, "YouTube Shooting: Woman Wounds 3 Before Killing Herself, Police Say," New York Times, April 3,
     2018. https://www.nytimes.com/2018/04/03/us/youtube-shooting.html.
22. "4 Types of Workplace Violence: What's Your Greatest Risk?" Safety.BLR.com, December 23, 2015. https://safety.blr.com/workplace-safety-
     news/emergency-planning-and-response/violence-in-workplace/4-Types-of-Workplace-Violence-Whats-Your-Greatest-/.
23. Bureau of Labor Statistics, "Table A-6. Fatal Occupational Injuries Resulting from Transportation Incidents and Homicides, United States,
     2014." https://www.bls.gov/iif/oshwc/cfoi/cftb0291.pdf (accessed July 14, 2018).
24. Some phrasing borrowed from U.S. government standards: U.S. Department of State, "Sexual Harassment Policy." https://www.state.gov/
     s/ocr/c14800.htm (accessed March 1, 2018).
25. SEC v. Texas Gulf Sulphur Co., 401 F. 2d 833 (2d Cir. 1968).
26. Andrew Beattie, "Top 4 Most Scandalous Insider Trading Debacles," Investopedia, August 22, 2017. https://www.investopedia.com/
     articles/stocks/09/insider-trading.asp#ixzz56LjMgfhQ.
27. For information on rules on gifts in the federal government, see: Code of Federal Regulations, 5 CFR 2635 201–205 and 301–304, 81 FR
     48687 (August 2016).
28. Foreign Corrupt Practices Act, 15 U.S.C. § 78dd-1, et seq. (1977).
29. "SEC Enforcement Actions: FCPA Cases," U.S. Securities and Exchange Commission. https://www.sec.gov/spotlight/fcpa/fcpa-cases.shtml
     (accessed April 23, 2018).
30. "SEC Enforcement Actions: FCPA Cases," U.S. Securities and Exchange Commission. https://www.sec.gov/spotlight/fcpa/fcpa-cases.shtml
     (accessed April 23, 2018).
31. Stan Abrams, "The 'FCPA Is Bad for Business' Argument and the Reality of China FDI," Business Insider, August 3, 2012.
     http://www.businessinsider.com/the-fcpa-is-bad-for-business-argument-and-the-reality-of-china-fdi-2012-8.
32. Women's Bureau, "Pay Secrecy Fact Sheet," U.S. Department of Labor, Women's Bureau, August 2014. https://www.dol.gov/wb/media/
     pay_secrecy.pdf.
33. Kurt Stanberry and Forrest Aven, "Employer Restrictions on Salary Discussions among Employees: The Changing Landscape," World at
     Work Journal 23, no. 1 (2014).
34. Labor Law News Blog, "Can Employees Discuss Pay and Salaries?" GovDocs, April 23, 2014. https://www.govdocs.com/can-employees-
     discuss-pay-salaries/.
35. Erin Mulvaney, "An Employee Spoke Out on Glassdoor. Now the EEOC Is Suing His Company," BenefitsPRO, August 6, 2017.
     http://www.benefitspro.com/2017/06/08/an-employee-spoke-out-on-glassdoor-now-the-eeoc-is?page_all=1&slreturn=1517773094.
36. Erin Mulvaney, "An Employee Spoke Out on Glassdoor. Now the EEOC Is Suing His Company," BenefitsPRO, August 6, 2017.
     http://www.benefitspro.com/2017/06/08/an-employee-spoke-out-on-glassdoor-now-the-eeoc-is?page_all=1&slreturn=1517773094.
37. Erin Mulvaney, "An Employee Spoke Out on Glassdoor. Now the EEOC Is Suing His Company," BenefitsPRO, August 6, 2017.
     http://www.benefitspro.com/2017/06/08/an-employee-spoke-out-on-glassdoor-now-the-eeoc-is?page_all=1&slreturn=1517773094.
38. Alan Farnham, "7 Richest Snitches: Time to Rat Out Your Boss?" ABC News, September 17, 2012. http://abcnews.go.com/Business/biggest-
     whistleblower-rewards/story?id=17222028.
39. Alan Farnham, "7 Richest Snitches: Time to Rat Out Your Boss?" ABC News, September 17, 2012. http://abcnews.go.com/Business/biggest-
     whistleblower-rewards/story?id=17222028.
40. Shaheen Pasha, "Enron's Whistle Blower Details Sinking Ship," CNN Money, March 16, 2006. http://money.cnn.com/2006/03/15/news/
     newsmakers/enron/.
41. Sallie Krawcheck, "When to Risk Your Career for Ethical Reasons," Fast Company, January 1, 2017. https://www.fastcompany.com/3067239/
     when-to-risk-your-career-for-ethical-reasons.
42. Sallie Krawcheck, "When to Risk Your Career for Ethical Reasons," Fast Company, January 1, 2017. https://www.fastcompany.com/3067239/
     when-to-risk-your-career-for-ethical-reasons.

8

Recognizing and Respecting the Rights of All

Figure 8.1 The globalization of the economy highlights one of the advantages of a diverse workforce that can interact effectively with customers all over the world. (credit outside, clockwise from top left: modification of "GenoPheno" by Cory Zanker/Flickr, CC BY 4.0; credit: modification of "Look at that!" by Gabriel Rocha/Flickr, CC BY 2.0; credit: modification of "Eyes" by "Dboybaker"/Flickr, CC BY 2.0; credit: modification of "doin' work" by Nick Allen/Flickr, CC BY 2.0; credit: modification of "Man Young Face" by "gentlebeatz"/Pixabay, CC 0; credit: modification of "Training" by Cory Zanker/Flickr, CC BY 4.0; credit: modification of "los bolleros" by Agustín Ruiz/Flickr, CC BY 2.0; credit: modification of "Pithorgarh to Dharchulha on Nepal Border in Uttarakhand India (158)" by "rajkumar1220"/Flickr, CC BY 2.0; credit: modification of "mother and child" by Peter Shanks/Flickr, CC BY 2.0; credit: modification of "Afghan women at a textile factory in Kabul" by Andrea Salazar/Wikimedia Commons, Public Domain; credit: modification of "Open kitchen" by Dennis Wong/Flickr, CC BY 2.0; credit middle left: modification of "Begging for the photographer" by Pedro Ribeiro Simões/Flickr, CC BY 2.0; credit middle right: modification of "Calling it a day" by Staffan Scherz/Flickr, CC BY 2.0)

Chapter Outline

8.1 Diversity and Inclusion in the Workforce

8.2 Accommodating Different Abilities and Faiths

8.3 Sexual Identification and Orientation

8.4 Income Inequalities

8.5 Animal Rights and the Implications for Business

Introduction

Effective business managers in the twenty-first century need to be aware of a broad array of ethical choices they can make that affect their employees, their customers, and society as a whole. What these decisions have in common is the need for managers to recognize and respect the rights of all.

Actively supporting human diversity at work, for instance, benefits the business organization as well as society on a broader level (Figure 8.1). Thus, ethical managers recognize and accommodate the special needs of some employees, show respect for workers' different faiths, appreciate and accept their differing sexual orientations and identification, and ensure pay equity for all. Ethical managers are also tuned in to public sentiment, such as calls by stakeholders to respect the rights of animals, and they monitor trends in these social attitudes, especially on social media.

How would you, as a manager, ensure a workplace that values inclusion and diversity? How would you respond to employees who resisted such a workplace? How would you approach broader social concerns such as income inequality or animal rights? This chapter introduces the potential impacts on business of some of the most pressing social themes of our time, and it discusses ways managers can respect the rights of all *and* improve business results by choosing an ethical path.

8.1 | Diversity and Inclusion in the Workforce

Learning Objectives

By the end of this section, you will be able to:

- Explain the benefits of employee diversity in the workplace
- Discuss the challenges presented by workplace diversity

Diversity is not simply a box to be checked; rather, it is an approach to business that unites ethical management and high performance. Business leaders in the global economy recognize the benefits of a diverse workforce and see it as an organizational strength, not as a mere slogan or a form of regulatory compliance with the law. They recognize that diversity can enhance performance and drive innovation; conversely, adhering to the traditional business practices of the past can cost them talented employees and loyal customers.

A study by global management consulting firm McKinsey & Company indicates that businesses with gender and ethnic diversity outperform others. According to Mike Dillon, chief diversity and inclusion officer for PwC in San Francisco, "attracting, retaining and developing a diverse group of professionals stirs innovation and drives growth."[1] Living this goal means not only recruiting, hiring, and training talent from a wide demographic spectrum but also including all employees in every aspect of the organization.

Workplace Diversity

The twenty-first century workplace features much greater diversity than was common even a couple of generations ago. Individuals who might once have faced employment challenges because of religious beliefs, ability differences, or sexual orientation now regularly join their peers in interview pools and on the job. Each may bring a new outlook and different information to the table; employees can no longer take for granted that their coworkers think the same way they do. This pushes them to question their own assumptions, expand their understanding, and appreciate alternate viewpoints. The result is more creative ideas, approaches, and solutions. Thus, diversity may also enhance corporate decision-making.

Communicating with those who differ from us may require us to make an extra effort and even change our viewpoint, but it leads to better collaboration and more favorable outcomes overall, according to David Rock, director of the Neuro-Leadership Institute in New York City, who says diverse coworkers "challenge their own and others' thinking."[2] According to the Society for Human Resource Management (SHRM), organizational diversity now includes more than just racial, gender, and religious differences. It also encompasses different thinking styles and personality types, as well as other factors such as physical and cognitive abilities and sexual orientation, all of which influence the way people perceive the world. "Finding the right mix of individuals to work on teams, and creating the conditions in which they can excel, are key business goals for today's leaders, given that collaboration has become a paradigm of the twenty-first century workplace," according to an SHRM article.[3]

Attracting workers who are not all alike is an important first step in the process of achieving greater diversity. However, managers cannot stop there. Their goals must also encompass **inclusion**, or the engagement of all employees in the corporate culture. "The far bigger challenge is how people interact with each other once they're on the job," says Howard J. Ross, founder and chief learning officer at Cook Ross, a consulting firm specializing in diversity. "Diversity is being invited to the party; inclusion is being asked to dance. Diversity is about the ingredients, the mix of people and perspectives. Inclusion is about the container—the place that allows employees to feel they belong, to feel both accepted and different."[4]

Workplace diversity is not a new policy idea; its origins date back to at least the passage of the Civil Rights Act of 1964 (CRA) or before. Census figures show that women made up less than 29 percent of the civilian workforce when Congress passed Title VII of the CRA prohibiting workplace discrimination. After passage of the law, gender diversity in the workplace expanded significantly. According to the U.S. Bureau of Labor Statistics (BLS), the percentage of women in the labor force increased from 48 percent in 1977 to a peak of 60 percent in 1999. Over the last five years, the percentage has held relatively steady at 57 percent. Over the past forty years, the total number of women in the labor force has risen from 41 million in 1977 to 71 million in 2017.[5] The BLS projects that the number of women in the U.S. labor force will reach 92 million in 2050 (an increase that far outstrips population growth).

The statistical data show a similar trend for African American, Asian American, and Hispanic workers (Figure 8.2). Just before passage of the CRA in 1964, the percentages of minorities in the official on-the-books workforce were relatively small compared with their representation in the total population. In 1966, Asians accounted for just 0.5 percent of private-sector employment, with Hispanics at 2.5 percent and African Americans at 8.2 percent.[6] However, Hispanic employment numbers have significantly increased since the CRA became law; they are expected to more than double from 15 percent in 2010 to 30 percent of the labor force in 2050. Similarly, Asian Americans are projected to increase their share from 5 to 8 percent between 2010 and 2050.

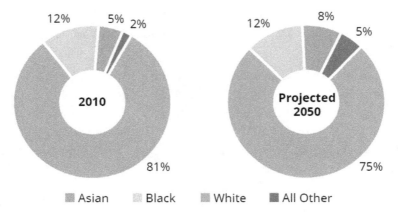

Workforce Makeup by Race, 2010 to 2050

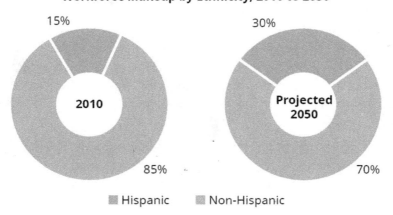

Workforce Makeup by Ethnicity, 2010 to 2050

Source: Toossi, Mitra. "Projections of the Labor Force to 2050: A Visual Essay." *Monthly Labor Review.* Oct. 2012. Data from U.S. Bureau of Labor Statistics.

Figure 8.2   There is a distinct contrast in workforce demographics between 2010 and projected numbers for 2050. (credit: attribution: Copyright Rice University, OpenStax, under CC BY 4.0 license)

Much more progress remains to be made, however. For example, many people think of the technology sector as the workplace of open-minded millennials. Yet Google, as one example of a large and successful company, revealed in its latest diversity statistics that its progress toward a more inclusive workforce may be steady but it is very slow. Men still account for the great majority of employees at the corporation; only about 30 percent are women, and women fill fewer than 20 percent of Google's technical roles (Figure 8.3). The company has shown a similar lack of gender diversity in leadership roles, where women hold fewer than 25 percent of positions. Despite modest progress, an ocean-sized gap remains to be narrowed. When it comes to ethnicity, approximately 56 percent of Google employees are white. About 35 percent are Asian, 3.5 percent are Latino, and 2.4 percent are black, and of the company's management and leadership roles, 68 percent are held by whites.[7]

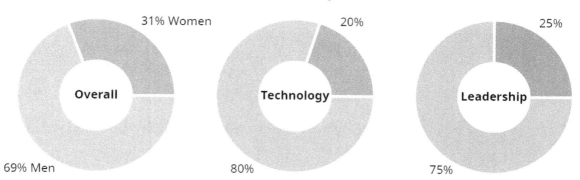

Source: Donnelly, Grace. "Google's 2017 Diversity Report Shows Progress Hiring Women, Little Changes for Minority Workers." *Fortune.* June 29, 2017.

Figure 8.3   Google is emblematic of the technology sector, and this graphic shows just how far from equality and diversity the industry remains. (credit: attribution: Copyright Rice University, OpenStax, under CC BY 4.0 license)

Google is not alone in coming up short on diversity. Recruiting and hiring a diverse workforce has been a challenge for most major technology companies, including Facebook, Apple, and Yahoo (now owned by Verizon); all have reported gender and ethnic shortfalls in their workforces.

The Equal Employment Opportunity Commission (EEOC) has made available 2014 data comparing the participation of women and minorities in the high-technology sector with their participation in U.S. private-sector employment overall, and the results show the technology sector still lags.[8] Compared with all private-sector industries, the high-technology industry employs a larger share of whites (68.5%), Asian Americans (14%), and men (64%), and a smaller share of African Americans (7.4%), Latinos (8%), and women (36%). Whites also represent a much higher share of those in the executive category (83.3%), whereas other groups hold a significantly lower share, including African Americans (2%), Latinos (3.1%), and Asian Americans (10.6%). In addition, and perhaps not surprisingly, 80 percent of executives are men and only 20 percent are women. This compares negatively with all other private-sector industries, in which 70 percent of executives are men and 30 percent women.

Technology companies are generally not trying to hide the problem. Many have been publicly releasing diversity statistics since 2014, and they have been vocal about their intentions to close diversity gaps. More than thirty technology companies, including Intel, Spotify, Lyft, Airbnb, and Pinterest, each signed a written pledge to increase workforce diversity and inclusion, and Google pledged to spend more than $100 million to address diversity issues.[9]

Diversity and inclusion are positive steps for business organizations, and despite their sometimes slow pace, the majority are moving in the right direction. Diversity strengthens the company's internal relationships with employees and improves employee morale, as well as its external relationships with customer groups. Communication, a core value of most successful businesses, becomes more effective with a diverse workforce. Performance improves for multiple reasons, not the least of which is that acknowledging diversity and respecting differences is the ethical thing to do.[10]

Adding Value through Diversity

Diversity need not be a financial drag on a company, measured as a cost of compliance with no return on the investment. A recent McKinsey & Company study concluded that companies that adopt diversity policies do well financially, realizing what is sometimes called a **diversity dividend**. The study results demonstrated a statistically significant relationship of better financial performance from companies with a more diverse leadership team, as indicated in Figure 8.4. Companies in the top 25 percent in terms of gender diversity were 15 percent more likely to post financial returns above their industry median in the United States. Likewise, companies in the top 25 percent of racial and/or ethnic diversity were 35 percent more likely to show returns exceeding their respective industry median.[11]

Likelihood of Financial Performance above Industry Median by Company Diversity Quartile

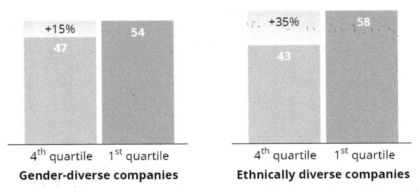

Source: Hunt, Vivian, Dennis Layton, and Sara Prince. McKinsey & Company. "Why Diversity Matters." Feb 2, 2015.

Figure 8.4   Companies with gender and ethnic diversity generally outperform those without it. (credit: attribution: Copyright Rice University, OpenStax, under CC BY 4.0 license)

These results demonstrate a positive correlation between diversity and performance, rebutting any claim that affirmative action and other such programs are social engineering that constitutes a financial drag on earnings. In fact, the results reveal a negative correlation between performance and lack of diversity, with companies in the bottom 25 percent for gender and ethnicity or race proving to be statistically less likely to achieve above-average financial returns than the average companies. Non-diverse companies were not leaders in performance indicators. Positive correlations do not equal causation, of course, and greater gender and ethnic diversity do not automatically translate into profit. Rather, as this chapter shows, they enhance creativity and decision-making, employee satisfaction, an ethical work environment, and customer goodwill, all of which, in turn, improve operations and boost performance.

Diversity is not a concept that matters only for the rank-and-file workforce; it makes a difference at all levels of an organization. The McKinsey & Company study, which examined twenty thousand firms in ninety countries, also found that companies in the top 25 percent for executive and/or board diversity had returns on equity more than 50 percent higher than those companies that ranked in the lowest 25 percent. Companies with a higher percentage of female executives tended to be more profitable.[12]

LINK TO LEARNING

Read the working paper "Is Gender Diversity Profitable? Evidence from a Global Survey," from the Peterson Institute for International Economics (https://openstax.org/l/53Peterson) for a closer look at the profitability of gender diversity.

Achieving equal representation in employment based on demographic data is the ethical thing to do because it represents the essential American ideal of equal opportunity for all. It is a basic assumption of an egalitarian society that all have the same chance without being hindered by immutable characteristics. However, there are also directly relevant business reasons to do it. More diverse companies perform better, as we saw earlier in this chapter, but why? The reasons are intriguing and complex. Among them are that diversity improves a company's chances of attracting top talent and that considering all points of view may lead to better decision-making. Diversity also improves customer experience and employee satisfaction.

To achieve improved results, companies need to expand their definition of diversity beyond race and gender. For example, differences in age, experience, and country of residence may result in a more refined global mind-set and cultural fluency, which can help companies succeed in international business. A salesperson may know the language of customers or potential customers from a specific region or country, for example, or a customer service representative may understand the norms of another culture. Diverse product-development teams can grasp what a group of customers may want that is not currently being offered.

Resorting to the same approaches repeatedly is not likely to result in breakthrough solutions. Diversity, however, provides usefully divergent perspectives on the business challenges companies face. New ideas help solve old problems—another way diversity makes a positive contribution to the bottom line.

The Challenges of a Diverse Workforce

Diversity is not always an instant success; it can sometimes introduce workplace tensions and lead to significant challenges for a business to address. Some employees simply are slow to come around to a greater appreciation of the value of diversity because they may never have considered this perspective before. Others may be prejudiced and consequently attempt to undermine the success of diversity initiatives in general. In 2017, for example, a senior software engineer's memo criticizing Google's diversity initiatives was leaked, creating significant protests on social media and adverse publicity in national news outlets.[13] The memo asserted "biological causes" and "men's higher drive for status" to account for women's unequal representation in Google's technology departments and leadership.

Google's response was quick. The engineer was fired, and statements were released emphasizing the company's commitment to diversity.[14] Although Google was applauded for its quick response, however, some argued that an employee should be free to express personal opinions without punishment (despite the fact that there is no right of free speech while at work in the private sector).

In the latest development, the fired engineer and a coworker filed a class-action lawsuit against Google on behalf of three specific groups of employees who claim they have been discriminated against by Google: whites, conservatives, and men.[15] This is not just the standard "reverse discrimination" lawsuit; it goes to the heart of the culture of diversity and one of its greatest challenges for management—the backlash against change.

In February 2018, the National Labor Relations Board ruled that Google's termination of the engineer did not violate federal labor law[16] and that Google had discharged the employee only for inappropriate but unprotected conduct or speech that demeaned women and had no relationship to any terms of employment. Although this ruling settles the administrative labor law aspect of the case, it has no effect on the private wrongful termination lawsuit filed by the engineer, which is still proceeding.

Yet other employees are resistant to change in whatever form it takes. As inclusion initiatives and considerations of diversity become more prominent in employment practices, wise leaders should be prepared to fully explain the advantages to the company of greater diversity in the workforce as well as making the appropriate accommodations to support it. Accommodations can take various forms. For example, if you hire more women, should you change the way you run meetings so everyone has a chance to be heard? Have you recognized that women returning to work after childrearing may bring improved skills such as time management or the ability to work well under pressure? If you are hiring more people of different faiths, should you set aside a prayer room? Should you give out tickets to football games as incentives? Or build team spirit with trips to a local bar? Your managers may need to accept that these initiatives may not suit everyone. Adherents of some faiths may abstain from alcohol, and some people prefer cultural events to sports. Many might welcome a menu of perquisites ("perks") from which to choose, and these will not necessarily be the ones that were valued in the past. Mentoring new and diverse peers can help erase bias and overcome preconceptions about others. However, all levels of a company must be engaged in achieving diversity, and all must work together to overcome resistance.

LINK TO LEARNING

Read this article for strategies on overcoming gendered meeting dynamics in the workplace (https://openstax.org/l/53meetings) from the *Harvard Business Review*.

CASES FROM THE REAL WORLD

Companies with Diverse Workforces

Texas Health Resources, a Dallas-area healthcare and hospital company, ranked No. 1 among *Fortune's* Best Workplaces for Diversity and No. 2 for Best Workplaces for African Americans.[17] Texas Health employs a diverse workforce that is about 75 percent female and 40 percent minority. The company goes above and beyond by offering English classes for Hispanic workers and hosting several dozen social and professional events each year to support networking and connections among peers with different backgrounds. It also offers same-sex partner benefits; approximately 3 percent of its workforce identifies as LGBTQ (lesbian, gay, bisexual, transgender, queer or questioning).

Another company receiving recognition is Marriott International, ranked No. 6 among Best Workplaces for Diversity and No. 7 among Best Workplaces for African Americans and for Latinos. African American, Latino, and other ethnic minorities account for about 65 percent of Marriott's 100,000 employees, and 15 percent of its executives are minorities. Marriott's president and CEO, Arne Sorenson, is recognized as an advocate for LGBTQ equality in the workplace, published an open letter on LinkedIn expressing his support for diversity and entreating then president-elect Donald Trump to use his position to advocate for inclusiveness. "Everyone, no matter their sexual orientation or identity, gender, race, religion disability or ethnicity should have an equal opportunity to get a job, start a business or be served by a business," Sorenson wrote. "Use your leadership to minimize divisiveness around these areas by letting people live their lives and by ensuring that they are treated equally in the public square."[18]

Critical Thinking

Is it possible that Texas Health and Marriott rank highly for diversity because the hospitality and healthcare industries tend to hire more women and minorities in general? Why or why not?

8.2 Accommodating Different Abilities and Faiths

Learning Objectives

By the end of this section, you will be able to:

- Identify workplace accommodations often provided for persons with differing abilities
- Describe workplace accommodations made for religious reasons

The traditional definition of diversity is broad, encompassing not only race, ethnicity, and gender but also religious beliefs, national origin, and cognitive and physical abilities as well as sexual preference or orientation. This section examines two of these categories, religion and ability, looking at how an ethical manager handles them as part of an overall diversity policy. In both cases, the concept of **reasonable accommodation** means an employer must try to allow for differences among the workforce.

Protections for People with Disabilities

In the United States, the Americans with Disabilities Act (ADA), passed in 1990, stipulates that a person has a disability if he or she has a physical or mental impairment that reduces participation in "a major life activity," such as work. An employer may not discriminate in offering employment to an individual who is diagnosed as having such a disability. Furthermore, if employment is offered, the employer is obliged to make reasonable accommodations to enable him or her to carry out normal job tasks. Making reasonable accommodations may include altering the physical workplace so it is readily accessible, restructuring a job, providing or modifying equipment or devices, or offering part-time or modified work schedules. Other accommodations could include providing readers, interpreters, or other necessary forms of assistance such as an assistive animal (Figure 8.5). The ADA also prohibits discriminating against individuals with disabilities in providing access to government services, public accommodations, transportation, telecommunications, and other essential services.[19]

Figure 8.5   A person with a service dog can usually perform all the essential function of the job, with some assistance. (credit: "DSC_004" by Aberdeen Proving Ground/Flickr, CC BY 2.0)

Access and accommodation for employees with physical or mental disabilities are good for business because they expand the potential pool of good workers. It is also ethical to have compassion for those who want to work and be contributing members of society. This principle holds for customers as well as employees. Recognizing the need for protection in this area, the federal government has enacted several laws to provide it. The Disability Rights Division of the U.S. Department of Justice lists ten different federal laws protecting people with disabilities, including not only the ADA but also laws such as the Rehabilitation Act, the Air Carrier Access Act, and the Architectural Barriers Act.

LINK TO LEARNING

The EEOC is the primary federal agency responsible for enforcing the ADA (as well as Title VII of the Civil Rights Act of 1964, mentioned earlier in the chapter). It hears complaints, tries to settle cases through administrative action, and, if cases cannot be settled, works with the Department of Justice to file lawsuits against violators. Visit the EEOC website (https://openstax.org/l/53EEOC) to learn more.

A key part of complying with the law is understanding and applying the concept of *reasonableness*: "An employer is required to provide a reasonable accommodation to a qualified applicant or employee with a disability unless the employer can show that the accommodation would be an **undue hardship**—that is, that it would require significant difficulty or expense."[20]

The law does not require an employee to refer to the ADA or to "disability" or "reasonable accommodation" when requesting some type of assistance. Managers need to be able to recognize the variety of ways in which a request for an accommodation is communicated. For example, an employee might not specifically say, "I need a reasonable accommodation for my disability" but rather, "I'm having a hard time getting to work on time because of the medical treatments I'm undergoing." This example demonstrates a challenge employers may face under the ADA in properly identifying requests for accommodation.

CASES FROM THE REAL WORLD

The ADA and Verizon Attendance Policy

Managers are usually sticklers about attendance, but Verizon recently learned an expensive lesson about its mandatory attendance policies from a 2011 class action lawsuit by employees and the EEOC. The suit asserted that Verizon denied reasonable accommodations to several hundred employees, disciplining or firing them for missing too many days of work and refusing to make exceptions for those whose absences were caused by their disabilities. According to the EEOC, Verizon violated the ADA because its no-fault attendance policy was an inflexible and "unreasonable" one-size-fits-all rule.

The EEOC required Verizon to pay $20 million to settle the suit, the largest single disability discrimination settlement in the agency's history. The settlement also forced Verizon to change its attendance policy to include reasonable accommodations for persons with disabilities. A third requirement was that Verizon provide regular training on ADA requirements to all mangers responsible for administering attendance policies.

Critical Thinking

- What are some specific rules that would fit within a fair and reasonable attendance policy?
- How would you decide whether an employee was taking advantage of an absenteeism policy?

Managing Religious Diversity in the Workplace

Title VII of the CRA, which governs nondiscrimination, applies the same rules to the religious beliefs (or nonbeliefs) of employees and job applicants as it does to race, gender, and other categories. The essence of the law mandates four tenets that all employers should follow: nondiscrimination, nonharassment, nonretaliation, and reasonable accommodation.

Regulations require that an employee notify the employer of a bona fide religious belief for which he or she wants protection, but the employee need not expressly request a specific accommodation. The employer must consider all possible accommodations that do not require violating the individual's beliefs and/or practices, such as allowing time off (Figure 8.6). However, the accommodation need not pose undue hardship on the firm, in terms of either scheduling or financial sacrifice. The employer must present proof of hardship if it decides it cannot offer an accommodation.

Figure 8.6   This calendar shows the significant number of holidays and observances an employer must consider with regard to time-off policies, including holidays of the three major religions, secular days, and other traditional days off. It may be a challenge to give everyone all preferred days off. (credit: modification of "2019 Calendar" by "Firkin"/openclipart, Public Domain)

Some cases of accommodation are based on cultural heritage rather than religion.

WHAT WOULD YOU DO?

Can Everyone's Wishes Be Accommodated?

You are a manager in a large Texas-based oil and gas company planning an annual summer company picnic and barbecue on the weekend of June 19. The oil industry has a long tradition of outdoor barbecues, and this one is a big morale-building event. However, June 19 is "Juneteenth," the day on which news of the Emancipation Proclamation reached slaves in Texas in 1865. Several African American employees always attend the barbecue event and are looking forward to it, but they also want to celebrate Emancipation Day, rich in history and culture and accompanied by its own official event. The picnic date cannot be easily rescheduled because of all the catering arrangements that had to be made.

Critical Thinking

- Is there a way to permit some employees to celebrate both occasions without inconveniencing

> others who will be attending only one?
> - What would you do as the manager, keeping in mind that you do not want to offend anyone?

Reasonable accommodation may require more than just a couple of hours off to go to weekly worship or to celebrate a holiday. It may extend to dress and uniform requirements, grooming rules, work rules and responsibilities, religious expression and displays, prayer or meditation rooms, and dietary issues.

LINK TO LEARNING

The Sikh faith dates to roughly the fourteenth century in India. Its practitioners have made their way to many Western nations, including the United Kingdom, Canada, Italy, and the United States. Sikhs in the West have experienced discrimination due to the distinctive turbans adult males wear, which are sometimes mistaken for Islamic apparel. Men are also required to wear a dagger called a *kirpan*. California law permits religious observers to wear a sheathed dagger openly, but not hidden away. Watch this video showing a San Joaquin County Sheriff's sergeant explaining the accommodation given to Sikhs to wear a kirpan in public (https://openstax.org/l/53kirpan) to learn more. How comfortable are you with permitting daggers to be carried openly in the workplace?

The law also protects those who do not have traditional beliefs. In *Welsh v. United States* (1970), the Supreme Court ruled that any belief occupying "a place parallel to that filled by the God of those admittedly qualifying for the exception" is covered by the law.[21] A nontheistic value system consisting of personal, moral, or ethical beliefs that is sincerely held with the strength of traditional religious views is deserving of protection. Protected individuals need not have a religion; indeed, if atheist or agnostic, they may have no religion at all.

Religion has become a hot-button issue for some political groups in the United States. Religious tolerance is the official national policy enshrined in the Constitution, but it has come under attack by some who want to label the United States an exclusively Christian nation.

CASES FROM THE REAL WORLD

The Abercrombie & Fitch Religious Discrimination Case

The U.S. Supreme Court, in a 2015 case involving Abercrombie & Fitch, ruled that that "an employer may not refuse to hire an applicant for work if the employer was motivated by avoiding the need to accommodate a religious practice," and that doing so violates the prohibition against religious discrimination contained in the CRA of 1964, Title VII. According to the EEOC general counsel David Lopez, "This case is about defending the American principles of religious freedom and tolerance. This decision is a victory for our increasingly diverse society."[22]

The case arose when, as part of her Muslim faith, a teenage girl named Samantha Elauf wore a hijab (headscarf) to a job interview with Abercrombie & Fitch. Elauf was denied a job because she did not conform to the company's "Look Policy," which Abercrombie claimed banned head coverings. Elauf filed a complaint with the EEOC alleging religious discrimination, and the EEOC, in turn, filed suit against Abercrombie & Fitch, alleging it refused to hire Elauf because of her religious beliefs and failed to accommodate her by making an exception to its "Look Policy."

"I was a teenager who loved fashion and was eager to work for Abercrombie & Fitch," said Elauf. "Observance of my faith should not have prevented me from getting a job. I am glad that I stood up for my rights, and happy that the EEOC was there for me and took my complaint to the courts. I am grateful to the Supreme Court for the decision and hope that other people realize that this type of discrimination is wrong and the EEOC is there to help."[23]

Critical Thinking

- Does a retail clothing store have an interest in employee appearance that it can justify in terms of customer sales?
- Does it matter to you what a sales associate looks like when you shop for clothes? Why or why not?

8.3 | Sexual Identification and Orientation

Learning Objectives

By the end of this section, you will be able to:

- Explain how sexual identification and orientation are protected by law
- Discuss the ethical issues raised in the workplace by differences in sexual identification and orientation

As society expands its understanding and appreciation of sexual orientation and identity, companies and managers must adopt a more inclusive perspective that keeps pace with evolving norms. Successful managers are those who willing to create a more welcoming work environment for all employees, given the wide array of sexual orientations and identities evident today.

Legal Protections

Workplace discrimination in this area means treating someone differently solely because of his or her sexual identification or sexual orientation, which can include, but is not limited to, identification as gay or lesbian (homosexual), bisexual, transsexual, or straight (heterosexual). Discrimination may also be based on an individual's association with someone of a different sexual orientation. Forms that such discrimination may take in the workplace include denial of opportunities, termination, and sexual assault, as well as the use of offensive terms, stereotyping, and other harassment.

Although the U.S. Supreme Court ruled in *United States v. Windsor* (2013) that Section 3 of the 1996 Defense of Marriage Act (which had restricted the federal interpretations of "marriage" and "spouse" to opposite-sex unions) was unconstitutional, and guaranteed same-sex couples the right to marry in *Obergefell v. Hodges* (2015),[24] marital status has little or no direct applicability to the circumstances of someone's employment. In terms of legal protections at work, the LGBTQ community is at a disadvantage because Title VII of the CRA does not address sexual orientation and federal law does not prohibit discrimination based on this characteristic. As of January 2018, twenty states prohibit sexual orientation discrimination in private and public workplaces and five more states prohibit sexual orientation discrimination only in public workplaces, not private (Figure 8.7).[25]

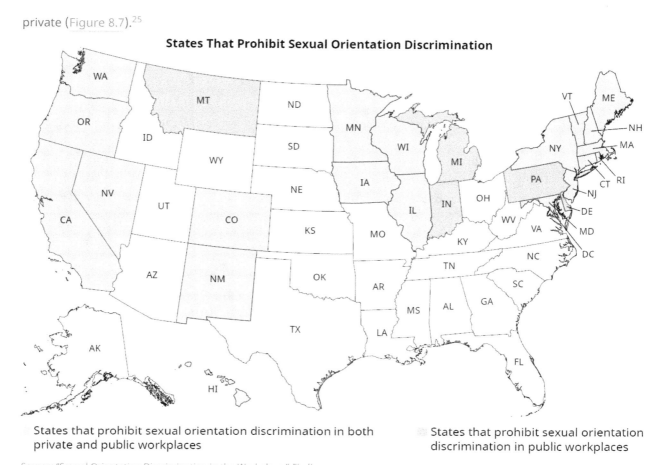

States That Prohibit Sexual Orientation Discrimination

States that prohibit sexual orientation discrimination in both private and public workplaces

States that prohibit sexual orientation discrimination in public workplaces

Source: "Sexual Orientation Discrimination in the Workplace." *FindLaw*.
http://employment.findlaw.com/employment-discrimination/sexual-orientation-discrimination-in-the-workplace.html.

Figure 8.7   State law in the United States varies in terms of protections and guarantees extended to LGBTQ employees of private companies. The geographic locations granting protection are clustered around the states that tend to vote for the Democratic party in national elections, with very little protection in the Great Plains or South. (attribution: Copyright Rice University, OpenStax, under CC BY 4.0 license)

In those states that do not have applicable state laws, employees risk adverse employment action simply for their LGBTQ status or for being married to a same-sex partner. Although legislation to address these circumstances has been introduced in Congress in previous sessions, none of the bills has yet passed. For example, a proposed law named the Equality Act is a federal LGBTQ nondiscrimination bill that would provide protections for LGBTQ individuals in employment, housing, credit, and education. But unless and until it passes, it remains up to the business community to provide protections consistent with those provided under federal law for other employees or applicants.

Ethical Considerations

In the absence of a specific law, LGBTQ issues present a unique opportunity for ethical leadership. Many companies choose to do the ethically and socially responsible thing and treat all workers equally, for example, by extending the same benefits to same-sex partners that they extend to heterosexual spouses. Ethical leaders are also willing to listen and be considerate when dealing with employees who may still be coming to an understanding of their sexual identification.

Financial and performance-related considerations come into play as well. Denver Investments recently analyzed the stock performance of companies before and after their adoption of LGBTQ-inclusive workplace policies.[26] The number of companies outperforming their peers in various industries increased after companies adopted LGBTQ-inclusive workplace policies. Once again, being ethical does not mean losing money or performing poorly.

In fact, states that have passed legislation considered anti-LGBTQ by the wider U.S. community, such as the Religious Freedom Restoration Act in Indiana or North Carolina's H.B. 2, the infamous "bathroom bill" that would require transgender individuals to use the restroom corresponding with their birth certificate, have experienced significant economic pushback. These states have seen statewide and targeted boycotts by consumers, major corporations, national organizations such as the National Collegiate Athletic Association, and even other cities and states.[27] In 2016, in response to H.B. 2, nearly seventy large U.S. companies, including American Airlines, Apple, DuPont, General Electric, IBM, Morgan Stanley, and Wal-Mart, signed an amicus ("friend of the court") brief in opposition to the unpopular North Carolina bill.[28] Indiana's Religious Freedom Restoration Act evoked a similar backlash in 2015 and public criticism from U.S. businesses.

To assess LGBTQ equality policies at a corporate level, the Human Rights Campaign foundation publishes an annual Corporate Equality Index (CEI) of approximately one thousand large U.S. companies and scores each on a scale of 0 to 100 on the basis of how LGBTW-friendly its benefits and employment policies are (Figure 8.8). More than six hundred companies recently earned a perfect score in the 2018 CEI, including such household names as AT&T, Boeing, Coca-Cola, Gap Inc., General Motors, Johnson & Johnson, Kellogg, United Parcel Service, and Xerox.[29]

States with the Most Corporate Equality Index (CEI) Companies

Percentage of Companies Scoring 100

Maryland	67
Massachusetts	65
Nevada	57
Minnesota	55
New York	53
Washington	53
Illinois	51
California	49
Connecticut	43
Kentucky	43

Source: Brant, Bobbi. "Best States to be Gay in Corporate America." Expert Market. (Based on data from Human Rights Foundation CEI 2015 and Human Rights Foundation SEI 2014.)

Figure 8.8   The Human Rights Campaign Foundation publishes an annual Corporate Equality Index to assess the LGBTQ equality policies of major U.S. corporations. A perfect score on the index is 100. These are the ten states with the highest percentages of "100 score" companies as of 2014–2015. (attribution: Copyright Rice University, OpenStax, under CC BY 4.0 license)

LINK TO LEARNING

Read the Human Rights Campaign's 2018 report (https://openstax.org/l/53HRC) for more on the Human Rights Campaign's CEI and its criteria.

Another organization tracking LGBTQ equality and inclusion in the workplace is the National LGBT Chamber of Commerce, which issues third-party certification for businesses that are majority-owned by LGBT individuals. There are currently more than one thousand LGBT-certified business enterprises across the country, although California, New York, Texas, Florida, and Georgia account for approximately 50 percent of them. Although these are all top-ranked states for new business startups in general, they are also home to multiple Fortune 500 companies whose diversity programs encourage LGBT-certified businesses to become part of their supply chains. Examples of large LGBT-friendly companies with headquarters in these states are American Airlines, JPMorgan Chase, SunTrust Bank, and Pacific Gas & Electric.

8.4 Income Inequalities

Learning Objectives

By the end of this section, you will be able to:

- Explain why income inequality is a problem for the United States and the world
- Analyze the effects of income inequality on the middle class
- Describe possible solutions to the problem of income inequality

The gap in earnings between the United States' affluent upper class and the rest of the country continues to grow every year. The imbalance in the distribution of income among the participants of an economy, or **income inequality**, is an enormous challenge for U.S. businesses and for society. The middle class, often called the engine of growth and prosperity, is shrinking, and new ethical, cultural, and economic problems are following from that change. Some identify income inequality as an ethical problem, some as an economic problem. Perhaps it is both. This section will address income inequality and the way it affects U.S. businesses and consumers.

The Middle Class in the United States

Data collected by economic researchers at the University of California show that income disparities have become more pronounced over the past thirty-five years, with the top 10 percent of income earners averaging ten times as much income as the bottom 90 percent, and the top 1 percent making more than forty times what the bottom 90 percent does.[30] The percentage of total U.S. income earned by the top 1 percent increased from 8 percent to 22 percent during this period. Figure 8.9 indicates the disparity as of 2015.

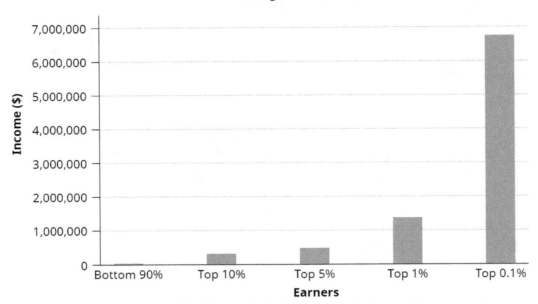

Source: Saez, Emmanuel. "Income and Wealth Inequality: Evidence and Policy Implications." *Contemporary Economic Policy* 35, no. 1 (Jan 2017): 7–25.

Figure 8.9   The 2015 data show the significant income disparity existing in the United States today—a gap that has increased significantly since 1980. (attribution: Copyright Rice University, OpenStax, under CC BY 4.0 license)

The U.S. economy was built largely on the premise of an expanding and prosperous middle class to which everyone had a chance of belonging. This ideal set the United States apart from other countries, in its own eyes and those of the world. In the years after World War II, the GI Bill and returning prosperity provided veterans with money for education, home mortgages, and even small businesses, all of which helped the economy grow. For the first time, many people could afford homes of their own, and residential home construction reached record rates. Families bought cars and opened credit card accounts. The culture of the middle class with picket fences, backyard barbecues, and black-and-white televisions had arrived. Television shows such as *Leave it to Beaver* and *Father Knows Best* reflected the "good life" desired by many in this newly emerging group. By the mid-1960s, middle-class wage earners were fast becoming the engine of the world's largest economy.

The middle class is not a homogenous group, however. For example, split fairly evenly between Democratic and Republican parties, the middle class helped elect Republican George W. Bush in 2004 and Democrat Barack Obama in 2008 and 2012. And, of course, a suburban house with a white picket fence represents a consumption economy, which is not everyone's idea of utopia, nor should it be. More importantly, not everyone had equal access to this ideal. But one thing almost everyone agrees on is that a *shrinking* middle class is not good for the economy. Data from the International Monetary Fund indicate the U.S. middle class is going in the wrong direction.[31] Only one-quarter of 1 percent of all U.S. households have moved up from the middle- to the upper-income bracket since 2000, while twelve times that many have slid to the lower-income bracket. That is a complete reversal from the period between 1970 and 2000, when middle-income households were more likely to move up than down. According to *Business Insider*, the U.S. middle class is "hollowing out, and it's hurting U.S. economic growth."[32]

Not only has the total wealth of middle-income families remained flat (Figure 8.10) but the overall percentage of middle-income households in the United States has shrunk from almost 60 percent in 1970 to only 47 percent in 2014, a very significant drop. Because consumers of comfortable means are a huge driver of the U.S. economy, with their household consumption of goods and services like food, energy, and education making up more than two-thirds of the nation's gross domestic product (GDP), the downward trend is an economic challenge for corporate America and the government. Business must be part of the solution. But exactly what can U.S. companies do to help address income inequality?

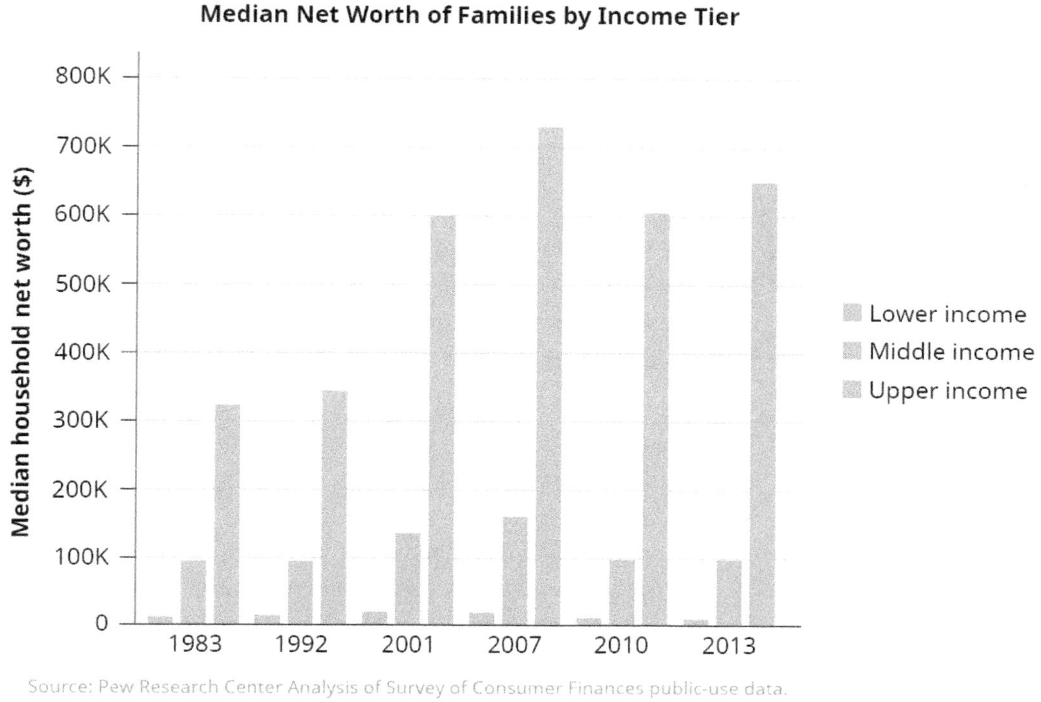
Median Net Worth of Families by Income Tier
Median household net worth ($)
800K
700K
600K
500K
400K
300K
200K
100K
0
1983
1992
2001
2007
2010
2013
Lower income
Middle income
Upper income
Source: Pew Research Center Analysis of Survey of Consumer Finances public-use data.

Figure 8.10 Lower- and middle-class wealth has remained stagnant or shrunk for the past thirty-five years while upper-class wealth has doubled. (attribution: Copyright Rice University, OpenStax, under CC BY 4.0 license)

Addressing Income Inequality

Robert Reich was U.S. Secretary of Labor from 1993 to 1997 and served in the administrations of three presidents (Gerald Ford, Jimmy Carter, and Bill Clinton). He is one of the nation's leading experts on the labor market and the economy and is currently the chancellor's professor of Public Policy at University of California, Berkeley, and a senior fellow at the Blum Center for Developing Economies. Reich recently told this story: "I was visited in my office by the chairman of one of the country's biggest high-tech firms. He wanted to talk about the causes and consequences of widening inequality and the shrinking middle class, and what to do about it." Reich asked the chairman why he was concerned. "Because the American middle class is the core of our customer base. If they can't afford our products in the years ahead, we're in deep trouble."[33]

Reich is hearing a similar concern from a growing number of business leaders, who see an economy that is leaving out too many people. Business leaders know the U.S. economy cannot grow when wages are declining, nor can their businesses succeed over the long term without a growing or at least a stable middle class. Other business leaders, such as Lloyd Blankfein, CEO of Goldman Sachs, have also said that income inequality is a negative development. Reich quoted Blankfein: "It is destabilizing the nation and is responsible for the divisions in the country . . . too much of the GDP over the last generation has gone to too few of the people."[34]

Some business leaders, such as Bill Gross, chair of the world's largest bond-trading firm, suggest raising the federal minimum wage, currently $7.25 per hour for all employers doing any type of business in interstate commerce (e.g., sending or receiving mail out of state) or for any company with more than $500,000 in sales. Many business leaders and economists agree that a higher minimum wage would help address at least part of the problem of income inequality; industrialized economies function best when income inequality is minimal, according to Gross and others who advocate for policies that bring the power of workers and corporations back into balance.[35] A hike in the minimum wage affects middle-class workers in two ways. First, it is a direct help to those who are part of a two-earner family at the lower end of the middle class, giving them more income to spend on necessities. Second, many higher-paid workers earn a wage that is tied to the minimum wage. Their salaries would increase as well.

Without congressional action to raise the minimum wage, states have taken the lead, along with businesses that are voluntarily raising their own minimum wage. Twenty-nine states have minimum wages that exceed the federal rate of $7.25 per hour. Costco, T.J. Maxx, Marshalls, Ikea, Starbucks, Gap, In-and-Out Burger, Whole Foods, Ben & Jerry's, Shake Shack, and McDonalds have also raised minimum wages in the past two years. Target recently announced a rise in its minimum wage to eleven dollars per hour, and banks, including Wells Fargo, PNC Financial Services, and Fifth Third Bank, announced a fifteen-dollar minimum wage.[36]

LINK TO LEARNING

Go to the National Conference of State Legislatures website for information about various laws in each state (https://openstax.org/l/53MinimumWage) and to look up the minimum wage law in your state.

The American Sustainable Business Council, in conjunction with Business for a Fair Wage, surveyed more than five hundred small businesses, and the results were surprising. A clear majority (58%–66%, depending on region) supported raising the minimum wage to at least ten dollars per hour.[37] Business owners were not simply being ethical; most understand that their business would benefit from an increase in consumers' purchasing power, and that this, in turn, would help the general economy. Frank Knapp, CEO of the South Carolina Small Business Chamber of Commerce representing five thousand business owners, said a higher minimum wage "will put more money in the hands of 300,000 South Carolinians who make less than ten dollars per hour and they will spend it here in our local economies. This minimum wage increase will also benefit another 150,000 employees who will have their wages adjusted. The resulting net $500 million increase in state GDP will be good for small businesses and good for the economy of South Carolina."[38]

In addition to paying a higher wage, businesses can help workers move to, or stay in, the middle class in other ways. For decades, some companies have hired many full-time workers as independent contractors because it saves them money on a variety of employee benefits they do not have to offer as a result. However, that practice shifts the burden to the workers, who now have to pay the full cost of their health insurance, workers' compensation, unemployment benefits, time off, and payroll taxes. A recent Department of Labor study indicates that employer costs for employee compensation averaged $35.64 per hour worked in September 2017; wages and salaries averaged $24.33 per hour worked and accounted for 68 percent of these costs, whereas benefit costs averaged $11.31 and accounted for the remaining 32 percent.[39] That means if employees on the payroll were paid as independent contractors, their pay would effectively be about one-third less, assuming they purchased benefits on their own. The 30 percent difference companies save by hiring independent contractors is often the margin between being in the middle class and falling below it.

ETHICS ACROSS TIME AND CULTURES

Falling Out of the Middle Class

Imagine a child living in a house with no power for lights, heat, or cooking, embarrassed to invite friends over to play or study, and not understanding what happened to a once-normal life. This is a story many middle-class families in the United States think could happen only to someone else, never to them. However, an HBO documentary entitled *American Winter* suggests the opposite is true; many seemingly solid middle-class families can slip all too easily into the lower class, into poverty, in houses that are dark with empty refrigerators.

The film, set in Portland, Oregon, tells the story of an economic tragedy. Families that were once financially stable are now barely keeping their heads above water. A needed job was outsourced or given to an independent contractor, or a raise failed to come even as necessities kept getting more expensive. The families had to try to pay for healthcare or make a mortgage payment when their bank account was overdrawn. Once-proud middle-class workers talk about the shame of having to ask friends for help or turn to public assistance as a last resort. The fall of the U.S. middle class is more than a line on an economic chart; it is a cold reality for many families who never saw it coming.

Critical Thinking

- Does a company have an ethical duty to find a balance between remaining profitable and paying all workers a decent living wage? Why or why not? Who decides what constitutes a fair wage?
- How would you explain to a board of directors your decision to pay entry-level workers a higher wage than required by law?

Yet sympathy for raising the minimum wage at either the federal or state level to sustain the middle class or reduce poverty in general has not been unanimous. Indeed, some economists have questioned whether a positive correlation exists between greater wages and a lowering of the poverty rate. Representative of such thought is the work of David Neumark, an economist at the University of California, Irvine, and William L. Wascher, a long-time economic researcher on the staff of the Board of Governors of the Federal Reserve System. They argue that, however well-meaning such efforts might be, simply raising the minimum wage can be counterproductive to driving down poverty. Rather, they maintain, the right calculus for achieving this goal is much more complex. As they put it, "we are hard-pressed to imagine a compelling argument for a higher minimum wage when it neither helps low-income families nor reduces poverty." Instead, the federal and state governments should consider a series of steps, such as the Earned Income Tax Credit, that would be more effective in mitigating poverty.[40]

Pay Equity as a Corollary of Income Equality

The issue of income inequality is of particular significance as it relates to women. According to the World Economic Forum (WEF), gender inequality is strongly associated with income inequality.[41] The WEF studied the association between the two phenomena in 140 countries over the past twenty years and discovered they are linked virtually everywhere, not only in developing nations. The issue of pay discrimination is addressed elsewhere in this textbook; however, the issue merits mention here as a part of the bigger picture of equality in the workplace. Adding to the disparity in income between men and women is the reality that many women are single mothers with dependent children and sometimes grandchildren. Hence, any reduction in their earning power has direct implications for their dependents, too, constituting injustice to multiple generations.

According to multiple studies, including those by the American Association of University Women and the Pew Research Center, on average, women are paid approximately 80 percent of what men are paid.[42] Laws that attempt to address this issue have not eradicated the problem. A recent trend is to take legislative action at the state rather than the federal level. A New Jersey law, for example, was named the Diane B. Allen Equal Pay Act to honor a retired state senator who experienced pay discrimination.[43] It will be the strongest such law in the country, allowing victims of discrimination to seek redress for up to six years of underpayment, and monetary damages for a prevailing plaintiff will be tripled.

The most significant part of the law, however, is a seemingly small change in wording that will have a big impact. Rather than requiring "equal pay for equal work," as does the federal law and most state laws aimed at the gender wage gap, the Diane B. Allen Equal Pay Act will require "equal pay for substantially similar work." This means that if a New Jersey woman has a different title than her male colleague but performs the same kinds of tasks and has the same level of responsibility, she must be paid the same. The new law recognizes that slight differences in job titles are sometimes used to justify pay differences but in reality are often arbitrary.

Minnesota recently passed a similar law, but it applies only to state government employees, not private-sector workers. It mandates that women be paid the same for comparable jobs and analyzes the work performed on the basis of how much knowledge, problem solving, and responsibility is required, and on working conditions rather than merely on job titles.

Ethical business managers will see this trend as an effort to address an ethical issue that has existed for well over a century and will follow the lead of states such as New Jersey and Minnesota. A company can help solve this problem by changing the way it uses job titles and creating a compensation system built on the ideas behind these two laws, which focus on job characteristics and not titles.

8.5 | Animal Rights and the Implications for Business

Learning Objectives

By the end of this section, you will be able to:

- Explain rising concerns about corporate treatment of animals
- Explain the concept of agribusiness ethics
- Describe the financial implications of animal ethics for business

Ethical questions about our treatment of animals arise in several different industries, such as agriculture, medicine, and cosmetics. This section addresses these questions because they form part of the larger picture of the way society treats all living things—including nonhuman animals as well as the environment. All states in the United States have some form of laws to protect animals; some violations carry criminal penalties and some carry civil penalties. Consumer groups and the media have also applied pressure to the business community to consider animal ethics seriously, and businesses have discovered money to be made in the booming business of pets. Of course, as always, we should acknowledge that culture and geography influence our understanding of ethical issues at a personal and a business level.

A Brief History of the Animal Rights Movement

Rhode Island, along with Boulder, Colorado, and Berkeley, California, led the way in enacting legislation recognizing individuals as guardians, not owners, of their animals, thus giving animals legal status beyond being just items of property. Many U.S. colleges now teach courses on animal rights law, there is strong support for granting fundamental legal rights to animals, and some attorneys, scientists, and ethicists dedicate their careers to animal rights.

The animal movement started in the late nineteenth century when the American Society for the Prevention of Cruelty to Animals (ASPCA) was formed, along with the American Humane Association. The American Welfare Institute and the Humane Society of the United States (HSUS) were established in the 1950s. The first federal animal protection law, the Humane Slaughter Act, was passed in the 1950s to avoid unnecessary suffering to farm animals (ten billion of which are killed every year). The most important U.S. law forbidding cruelty to animals in laboratory settings was enacted in 1966; the Animal Welfare Act requires basic humane conditions to be maintained for animals in testing facilities. Finally, in the 1970s and 1980s, the modern animal rights social movement emerged. It has led to an increased awareness of animal ethics by consumers and businesses.

However, despite significant progress, research using animals for product testing continues to be controversial in the United States, particularly because improved technology has offered humane and effective alternatives. The use of animals in biomedical research has drawn slightly less negative reaction than in consumer product testing, because of the more critical nature of the research. Though animal welfare laws have ameliorated some of the pain of animals used in biomedical research, ethical concerns remain, and veterinarians and physicians are demanding change, as are animal rights groups and policy and ethics experts. Increased integration of ethics in business conduct is operating alongside the desire to recognize **animal rights**, the entitlement of nonhuman animals to ethical treatment.

The Ethics of What We Eat

Concern for the welfare of animals beyond pets brings us to the agribusiness industry. This is where groups such as the ASPCA and HSUS have been particularly active. Agribusiness is a huge industry that provides us with the food we eat, including plant-based and animal-based foodstuffs. The industry has changed significantly over the past century, evolving from one consisting primarily of family and/or small businesses to a much larger one dominated mostly by large corporations. Aspects of this business with relevant and interrelated ethical questions range from ecology, animal rights, and economics to food safety and long-term sustainability (Figure 8.11). To achieve a high level of sustainability in the world's food supply chain, all stakeholders—the political sector, the business sector, the finance sector, the academic sector, and the consumer—must work in concert to achieve an optimal result, and a cost-benefit analysis of ethics in the food industry should include a recognition of all their concerns.

Figure 8.11   Each of the ethical considerations relating to agribusiness is interdependent with the others. For example, safe food production is a responsible use of natural resources, and consumers want to make informed choices based on responsible animal husbandry. (attribution: Copyright Rice University, OpenStax, under CC BY 4.0 license)

Experts predict that for us to meet the food needs of the world's population, we will need to double food production over the next fifty years. Given this, a high priority in the agribusiness industry ought to be to meet this demand for food at a reasonable price with products that are not a threat to human health and safety, animal health, or the limited resources in Earth's environment. However, to do so requires attention to factors such as soil and surface water conservation and protection of natural land and water areas. Furthermore, the treatment of animals by everyone in the livestock chain (e.g., livestock farmers, dealers, fish farmers, animal transporters, slaughterhouses) must be appropriate for a society with high legal and ethical standards.

The food chain can be truly sustainable only when it safeguards the social welfare and living environment of the people working in it. This means eliminating corruption, human rights violations (including forced labor and child labor), and poor working conditions. We must also encourage and empower consumers to make informed choices, which includes enforcing labeling regulations and the posting of relevant and accurate dietary information.

Finally, an analysis of the food supply chain must also include an awareness of people's food needs and preferences. For example, the fact that growing numbers of consumers are adopting vegetarian, vegan, gluten-free, or non–genetically modified organism diets is now apparent at responsive restaurants, grocery stores, and employer-provided cafés. For many, the ethical treatment of animals remains a philosophic issue; however, some rules about what foods are morally acceptable and how they are prepared for consumption (e.g., halal or kosher) are also grounded in faith, so animal rights have religious implications, too.

All in all, consumers' growing ethical sensitivity about what we eat could ultimately transform agribusiness. More acreage might be assigned to growing fruits and vegetables relative to those given over to livestock grazing, for instance. Or revelations about slaughterhouse processes may reduce our acceptance of the ways in which meat is processed for consumption. The economic consequences for agribusiness of such changes are difficult to underestimate.

LINK TO LEARNING

Peter Singer is an Australian-born philosopher who has teaching appointments at Princeton University and Monash University in Australia. His book *Animal Liberation*, originally published in 1975 but revised many times since, serves as a sort of bible for the animal rights movement. Yet Singer is highly controversial because he argues that some humans have fewer cognitive skills than some animals. Therefore, if we determine what we eat on the basis of sentience (the ability to think and/or feel pain), then many animals we eat should be off limits. Watch Singer's talk, "The Ethics of What We Eat," which was recorded at Williams College in December 2009 (https://openstax.org/l/53PeterSinger) as an introduction to Singer's philosophy.

The Use of Animals in Medical and Cosmetic Research

Viewpoints about animals used in medical research are changing in very significant ways and have resulted in a variety of initiatives seeking alternatives to animal testing. As an example, in conjunction with professionals from human and veterinary medicine and the law, the Yale University Hastings Program in Ethics and Health Policy, a bioethics research institute, is seeking alternatives to animal testing that focus on animal welfare.

Animals such as monkeys and dogs are used in medical research ranging from the study of Parkinson disease to toxicity testing and studies of drug interactions and allergies. There is no question that medical research is a valuable and important practice. The question is whether the use of animals is a necessary or even best practice for producing the most reliable results. Alternatives include the use of patient-drug databases, virtual drug trials, computer models and simulations, and noninvasive imaging techniques such as magnetic resonance imaging and computed tomography scans.[44] Other techniques, such as microdosing, use humans not as test animals but as a means to improve the accuracy and reliability of test results. In vitro methods based on human cell and tissue cultures, stem cells, and genetic testing methods are also increasingly available.

As for consumer product testing, which produces the loudest outcry, the Federal Food, Drug, and Cosmetic Act does not require that animal tests be conducted to demonstrate the safety of cosmetics. Rather, companies test formulations on animals in an attempt to protect themselves from liability if a consumer is harmed by a product. However, a significant amount of new research shows that consumer products such as cosmetics can be accurately tested for safety without the abuse of animals. Some companies may resist altering their methods of conducting research, but a growing number are now realizing that their customers are demanding a change.

Regulating the Use of Animals in Research and Testing

Like virtually every other industrialized nation, the United States permits medical experimentation on animals, with few limitations (assuming sufficient scientific justification). The goal of any laws that exist is not to ban such tests but rather to limit unnecessary animal suffering by establishing standards for the humane treatment and housing of animals in laboratories.

As explained by Stephen Latham, the director of the Interdisciplinary Center for Bioethics at Yale,[45] possible legal and regulatory approaches to animal testing vary on a continuum from strong government regulation and monitoring of all experimentation at one end, to a self-regulated approach that depends on the ethics of the researchers at the other end. The United Kingdom has the most significant regulatory scheme, whereas Japan uses the self-regulation approach. The U.S. approach is somewhere in the middle, the result of a gradual blending of the two approaches.

A movement has begun to win legal recognition of chimpanzees as the near-equivalent of humans, therefore, as "persons" with legal rights. This is analogous to the effort called environmental justice, an attempt to do the same for the environment (discussed in the section on Environmental Justice in Three Special Stakeholders: Society, the Environment, and Government). A nonprofit organization in Florida, the Nonhuman Rights Project, is an animal advocacy group that has hired attorneys to present a theory in court that two chimpanzees (Tommy and Kiko) have the legal standing and right to be freed from cages to live in an outdoor sanctuary (Figure 8.12). In this case, the attorneys have been trying for years to get courts to grant the chimps habeas corpus (Latin for "you shall have the body"), a right people have under the U.S. Constitution when held against their will. To date, this effort has been unsuccessful.[46] The courts have extended certain constitutional rights to corporations, such as the First Amendment right to free speech (in the 2010 *Citizens United* case). Therefore, some reason, a logical extension of that concept would hold that animals and the environment have rights as well.

Figure 8.12 This is Tommy the Chimpanzee's "home," a stretch of the word by any definition. The question in the court case brought on behalf of Tommy and Kiko, another chimpanzee, is whether animals should have the right of habeas corpus to be freed from involuntary confinement. (credit: From the film Unlocking The Cage. Directed by Chris Hegedus and D A Pennebaker. Copyrighted © 2015 Pennebaker Hegedus Films, Inc. All Rights Reserved. Used with permission.)

In cosmetic testing, the United States has relatively few laws protecting animals, whereas about forty other nations have taken more direct action. In 2013, the European Union banned animal testing for cosmetics and the marketing and sale of cosmetics tested on animals. Norway and Switzerland passed similar laws. Outside Europe, a variety of other nations, including Guatemala, India, Israel, New Zealand, South Korea, Taiwan, and Turkey, have also passed laws to ban or limit cosmetic animal testing. U.S. cosmetic companies will not be able to sell their products in any of these countries unless they change their practices. The Humane Cosmetics Act has been introduced but not yet passed by Congress. If enacted, it would end cosmetics testing on animals in the United States and ban the import of animal-tested cosmetics.[47] However, in the current antiregulatory environment, passage seems unlikely.

CASES FROM THE REAL WORLD

Beagles Freedom Project

Beagles are popular pets because—like most dogs—they are people pleasers, plus they are obedient and easy to care for (Figure 8.13). These same qualities make them the primary breed for animal testing: ninety-six percent of all dogs used in testing are beagles, leading animal-rights groups like the Beagle Freedom Project to make rescuing them a priority.[48] Even animal activists have to compromise to make progress, however, as the director of Beagle Freedom explains: "We have a policy position against animal testing. We don't like it philosophically, scientifically, even personally. . . . But that doesn't mean we can't find common ground, a common-sense solution, to bridge two sides of a very controversial and polarizing debate, which is animal testing, and find this area in the middle where we can get together to help animals."[49]

Figure 8.13   Through local events such as this one in Redondo Beach, California, the Beagle Freedom Project aims to raise awareness of the conditions prevalent for many dogs used in laboratory experimentation. (credit: modification of "JennyOetzell_46150" by "TEDxRB"/Flickr, CC BY 2.0)

Dogs used as subjects in laboratory experiments live in stacked metal cages with only fluorescent light, never walk on grass, and associate humans with pain. In toxicology testing, they are exposed to toxins at increasing levels to determine at what point they become ill. Before a beagle can be rescued, the laboratory has to agree to release it, which can be a challenge. If the laboratory is willing, the Beagle Freedom Project still has to negotiate, which usually means paying for all costs, including veterinary care and transportation, and absolving the laboratory of all liability, and then find the dog a home.

Alternatives to testing on beagles include three-dimensional human-skin-equivalent systems and a variety of advanced computer-based models for measuring skin irritation, for instance. According to the New England Anti-Vivisection Society, nonanimal tests are often more cost-effective, practical, and expedient; some produce results in a significantly shorter time.[50]

Critical Thinking

Why have U.S. cosmetics companies continued to use beagles for testing when there are more humane alternatives at lower costs?

According to the Humane Society of the United States, a more realistic alternative approach is to develop nonanimal tests that could provide more human safety data, including information about cancer and birth defects related to new products. Consumer pressure can also influence change. If consumer purchases demonstrate a preference for cruelty-free cosmetics and support ending cosmetics animal testing, businesses will get the message. Almost one hundred companies have already ceased testing cosmetics on animals, including The Body Shop, Burt's Bees, E.L.F. Cosmetics, Lush, and Tom's of Maine. Lists of such firms are maintained by People for the Ethical Treatment of Animals and similar organizations.[51]

LINK TO LEARNING

Cruelty Free International is an organization working to end animal experiments worldwide. It provides information about products that are not tested on animals in an effort to help consumers become more aware of the issues. Take a look at the Cruelty Free International website (https://openstax.org/l/53CrueltyFree) to learn more.

Companies will be wise to adapt to the increasing level of public awareness and consumer expectations, not least because U.S. culture now incorporates pets in almost every aspect of life. Dogs, cats, and other animals function as therapy pets for patients and those experiencing stress; an Uber-style dog service will bring dogs to work or school for a few minutes of companionship. Pets visit hospitals and act as service animals, appearing in restaurants, campuses, and workplaces where they would have been prohibited as recently as ten years ago. According to the American Pet Products Association (APPA), a trade group, two-thirds of U.S. households own a pet, and pet industry sales have tripled in the past fifteen years.[52] The APPA estimates U.S. spending on pets will reach almost $70 billion a year by 2018.

"People are fascinated by pets. We act and spend on them as if they were our children," says New York University sociology professor Colin Jerolmack, who studies animals in society.[53] As people increasingly want to include pets in all aspects of life, new and different industries have emerged and will continue to do so, such as tourism centered on the presence of pets and retail opportunities such as health insurance for animals, upscale stores, and new products specifically tailored for pets. With interest in pets at an all-time high, businesses cannot ignore the trend, either in terms of revenue to be earned or in terms of the ethical treatment of their fellow animals in laboratories.

 Key Terms

animal rights the entitlement of nonhuman animals to ethical treatment

diversity dividend the financial benefit of improved performance resulting from a diverse workforce

inclusion the engagement of all employees in the corporate culture

income inequality the unequal distribution of income among the participants of an economy

reasonable accommodation a change or adjustment to a job or other aspect of the work environment that permits an employee with a disability or other need to perform that job

undue hardship a difficulty or expense to the firm significant enough that reasonable accommodation may not be required

Summary

8.1 Diversity and Inclusion in the Workforce

A diverse workforce yields many positive outcomes for a company. Access to a deep pool of talent, positive customer experiences, and strong performance are all documented positives. Diversity may also bring some initial challenges, and some employees can be reluctant to see its advantages, but committed managers can deal with these obstacles effectively and make diversity a success through inclusion.

8.2 Accommodating Different Abilities and Faiths

To accommodate religious beliefs, the absence of formal religious faith, or disabilities, businesses should make every reasonable accommodation they can to allow workers to contribute to the company. This may require scheduling flexibility, the use of special devices, or simply an understanding manager.

8.3 Sexual Identification and Orientation

Although about half the states prohibit sexual orientation discrimination in private and public workplaces and a few do so in public workplaces only, federal law does not. Successful companies will not only follow the applicable law but also develop ethical policies to send a clear message that they are interested in job skills and abilities, not sexual orientation or personal life choices.

8.4 Income Inequalities

Income inequality has grown sharply while the U.S. middle class, though vital to economic growth, has continued to shrink. Currently, the federal minimum wage is $7.25 per hour, and many states simply follow the federal lead in establishing their own minimums. Though some economists dispute the existence of a simple, direct link between a shrinking middle class and governmental failure to raise the minimum wage at a sufficiently rapid pace, no one denies that businesses themselves could take the lead here by paying a higher minimum wage. Companies also can commit to hire workers as employees rather than as independent contractors and pay the cost of their benefits, and to pay women the same as men for similar work.

8.5 Animal Rights and the Implications for Business

Mainstream businesses from pharmaceutical and medical companies to grocers and restaurants must all consider the growing public awareness of the ethical treatment of nonhuman animals. This evolving concern has particular consequences for agribusiness in terms of what creatures we consider appropriate to cultivate and eat. Cosmetic companies are increasingly subject to legislative mandates in the global marketplace and to consumer pressure at home to adopt ethical policies with regard to animal testing. An aware consuming public can continue to force improvements in our treatment of animals.

⬚ Assessment Questions

1. Diversity and inclusion at all levels of a private-sector company is _____.
  A.   mandated by federal law
  B.   the approach preferred by many companies
  C.   required by state law in thirty states
  D.   contrary to the company's fiduciary duty to stockholders

2. Google _____.
  A.   has the most diverse workforce of any major U.S. company
  B.   uses a strict quota system in its hiring practices
  C.   is similar to other technology companies, most of which lag on diversity
  D.   promotes women at higher rates than men

3. True or false? Diversity programs may fail due to resistance from employees within a company.

4. Studies have been conducted on the financial performance of companies with high levels of diversity. Briefly discuss the results of such studies.

5. Since the passage of federal laws such as the Civil Rights Act of 1964, the percentage of women in leadership positions has improved but not reached parity with that of men. Briefly discuss the percentage of women in leadership positions in different industries and what might be some of the benefits of improving the representation of women.

6. The primary law prohibiting religious discrimination in the private sector workplace is _____.
  A.   the First Amendment of the Constitution
  B.   state law
  C.   Title VII of the Civil Rights Act
  D.   the Declaration of Independence

7. If an ADA accommodation is significantly expensive, _____.
  A.   the courts may rule that it is not reasonable
  B.   the courts may rule that it must be provided anyway
  C.   the EEOC guidelines do not apply
  D.   the federal government must subsidize the expense

8. True or false? There are no similarities between legal protections in the workplace for religion and disability.

9. The primary law prohibiting discrimination against disabled workers is the ADA. What is its main requirement?

10. Religious apparel and/or appearance are protected under Title VII's umbrella of religious nondiscrimination. Give an example.

11. Are individual states allowed to have laws protecting LGBTQ applicant or employee rights?

    A.   Yes, but it is not really necessary because federal law already protects them.

    B.   No, because it would violate federal law, which prohibits it.

    C.   Yes, some states extend this protection because there is no law at the federal level.

    D.   No, because the Supreme Court ruling in *Obergefell v. Hodges* now protects these rights.

12. True or false? Title VII of the Civil Rights Act prohibits discrimination based on sexual orientation.

13. Federal law does not currently protect LGBTQ applicants from discrimination in hiring. Are there any applicable state laws that do so?

14. Though federal law does not mandate it, do some companies nevertheless allow LGBTQ employees to extend insurance coverage to partners?

15. As of 2018, the current federal minimum wage is _____.

    A. $7.25 per hour

    B. $10 per hour

    C. $12.50 per hour

    D. $15 per hour

16. The middle class in the United States _____.

    A.   has steadily increased every year since World War II

    B.   has steadily declined every year since 1990

    C.   shows a significant decline since 2000

    D.   has grown since the recession of 2008

17. True or false? The percentage of income earned by the top 1 percent of households in the United States has more than doubled since the early 1980s.

18. Hiring a worker as an independent contractor saves an employer about 30 percent of the cost of an employee in benefits. Identify one or two of these benefits.

19. Do some states have laws mandating a higher wage than the federal minimum?

20. Laws protecting animal rights in cosmetic testing are _____.

    A.   more advanced in the United States than in the European Union

    B.   more advanced in the European Union than in the United States

    C.   more advanced in Asia than in the United States

    D.   more advanced in Asia than in the European Union

21. Alternatives to animal testing for cancer drugs _____.

    A.   do not exist

    B.   exist but are prohibitively expensive

    C.   exist and are not any more expensive than animal testing

    D.   exist and are far cheaper than animal testing

22. True or false? Cosmetics manufacturing is an area where testing with synthetic human skin is an acceptable substitute for animal testing.

23. True or false? There are not yet viable alternatives to animal testing in medical research.

24. Generally, Europe has more restrictions on animal testing than does the United States. How does this affect U.S. companies?

Endnotes

1. Novid Parsi, "Workplace Diversity and Inclusion Gets Innovative," Society for Human Resource Management, January 16, 2017.
    https://www.shrm.org/hr-today/news/hr-magazine/0217/pages/disrupting-diversity-in-the-workplace.aspx.
2. Novid Parsi, "Workplace Diversity and Inclusion Gets Innovative," Society for Human Resource Management, January 16, 2017.
    https://www.shrm.org/hr-today/news/hr-magazine/0217/pages/disrupting-diversity-in-the-workplace.aspx.
3. Novid Parsi, "Workplace Diversity and Inclusion Gets Innovative," Society for Human Resource Management, January 16, 2017.
    https://www.shrm.org/hr-today/news/hr-magazine/0217/pages/disrupting-diversity-in-the-workplace.aspx.
4. Novid Parsi, "Workplace Diversity and Inclusion Gets Innovative," Society for Human Resource Management, January 16, 2017.
    https://www.shrm.org/hr-today/news/hr-magazine/0217/pages/disrupting-diversity-in-the-workplace.aspx.
5. "Labor Force Statistics from the Current Population Survey. Household Data Annual Averages. 2. Employment Status of the Civilian
    Noninstitutional Population 16 Years and Over by Sex, 1977 to date," U.S. Bureau of Labor Statistics. https://www.bls.gov/cps/
    cpsaat02.htm (accessed July 22, 2018).
6. "Indicators (2013)," U.S. Equal Employment Opportunity Commission. https://www.eeoc.gov/eeoc/statistics/employment/jobpat-eeo1/
    2013_indicators.cfm (accessed January 10, 2018).
7. Google, https://diversity.google/annual-report/# (accessed July 10, 2018).
8. "Diversity in High Tech," U.S. EEOC. https://www.eeoc.gov/eeoc/statistics/reports/hightech/ (accessed January 12, 2018).
9. Lisa Eadicicco, "Google's Diversity Efforts Still Have a Long Way to Go," *Time*, July 1, 2016. http://time.com/4391031/google-diversity-
    statistics-2016/.
10. Pubali Neogy, "Diversity in Workplace Can Be a Game Changer," *Yahoo India Finance*, June 18, 2018. Neogy states that greater diversity in
    the workplace fosters "creativity and innovation," "opens global opportunities" for the firm, "fosters adaptability and better working
    culture," and generally "improves companies' bottom lines." https://in.finance.yahoo.com/news/diversity-workplace-can-game-changer-
    heres-183319670.html.
11. Vivian Hunt, Dennis Layton, and Sara Prince, "Why Diversity Matters," McKinsey & Company, January 2015. https://www.mckinsey.com/
    business-functions/organization/our-insights/why-diversity-matters.
12. Marcus Noland, Tyler Moran, and Barbara Kotschwar, "Is Gender Diversity Profitable? Evidence from a Global Survey," Working Paper
    16-3, Peterson Institute for International Economics, February 2016. https://piie.com/publications/working-papers/gender-diversity-
    profitable-evidence-global-survey.
13. Daisuke Wakabayashi, "Contentious Memo Strikes Nerve inside Google and Out," *New York Times*, August 8, 2017.
    https://www.nytimes.com/2017/08/08/technology/google-engineer-fired-gender-memo.html.
14. Bill Chappell and Laura Sydell, "Google Reportedly Fires Employee Who Slammed Diversity Efforts," *National Public Radio*, August 7, 2017.
    https://www.npr.org/sections/thetwo-way/2017/08/07/542020041/google-grapples-with-fallout-after-employee-slams-diversity-efforts.
15. Sara Ashley O'Brien, "Engineers Sue Google for Allegedly Discriminating against White Men and Conservatives," *CNN/Money*, January 8,
    2018. http://money.cnn.com/2018/01/08/technology/james-damore-google-lawsuit/index.html.
16. Daisuke Wakabayashi, "Google Legally Fired Diversity Memo Author, Labor Agency Says," *New York Times*, February 16, 2018.
    https://www.nytimes.com/2018/02/16/business/google-memo-firing.html.
17. Michael Bush and Kim Peters, "How the Best Companies Do Diversity Right," *Fortune*, December 5, 2016. http://fortune.com/2016/12/05/
    diversity-inclusion-workplaces/.
18. Michael Bush and Kim Peters, "How the Best Companies Do Diversity Right," *Fortune*, December 5, 2016. http://fortune.com/2016/12/05/
    diversity-inclusion-workplaces/.
19. "Titles I and V of the Americans with Disabilities Act of 1990 (ADA)," US Equal Employment Opportunity Commission. Approved July 26,
    1990. https:www.eeoc.gov/laws/statutes/ada.cfm.
20. Americans with Disabilities Act of 1990. Pub. L. 101-336.104 Stat. 328. (July 26, 1990).
21. Welsh v. United States, 398 U.S. 333, 90 S. Ct. 1792, 26 L. Ed. 2d 308; 29 CFR § 1605.1 (1970).
22. Equal Employment Opportunity Commission, "Supreme Court Rules in Favor of EEOC in Abercrombie Religious Discrimination Case," U.S.
    Equal Employment Opportunity Commission, June 1, 2015. https://www.eeoc.gov/eeoc/newsroom/release/6-1-15.cfm.
23. Equal Employment Opportunity Commission, "Supreme Court Rules in Favor of EEOC in Abercrombie Religious Discrimination Case," U.S.
    Equal Employment Opportunity Commission, June 1, 2015. https://www.eeoc.gov/eeoc/newsroom/release/6-1-15.cfm.
24. United States v. Windsor, 570, U.S. 744 (2013); Obergefell v. Hodges, 576 U.S. ___ (2015).
25. "Sexual Orientation Discrimination in the Workplace," *FindLaw*. http://employment.findlaw.com/employment-discrimination/sexual-
    orientation-discrimination-in-the-workplace.html (accessed January 16, 2018).
26. John N. Roberts and Cristian A. Landa, "Return on Equality™, the Real ROE: The Shareholder Case for LGBT Workplace Equality," *Denver
    Investments*, June 2015.
27. Jon Schuppe, "Corporate Boycotts Become Key Weapon in Gay Rights Fight," *NBC News*, March 26, 2016. https://www.nbcnews.com/news/
    us-news/corporate-boycotts-become-key-weapon-gay-rights-fight-n545721.
28. United States of America v. State of North Carolina et al., Amicus Curiae Brief by 68 Companies Opposed to H.B. 2 and in Support of
    Plaintiff's Motion for Preliminary Injunction, Case No. 1:16-cv-00425 (TDSJEP), July 8, 2016. http://ftpcontent4.worldnow.com/wbtv/pdf/
    Legal-brief-filed-by-68-businesses-opposing-HB2.pdf.
29. Gretel Kauffman, "Record Number of Corporations Earn Perfect Score for LGBTQ-Friendly Policies," *Christian Science Monitor*, December 6,
    2016. https://www.csmonitor.com/Business/2016/1206/Record-number-of-corporations-earn-perfect-score-for-LGBT-friendly-policies.
30. Emmanuel Saez, "Income and Wealth Inequality: Evidence and Policy Implications," *Contemporary Economic Policy*, 35, no. 1 (2017): 7–25.
31. Rachel Butt, "America's Shrinking Middle Class Is Killing the Economy," *Business Insider*, June 28, 2016. http://www.businessinsider.com/
    americas-shrinking-middle-class-hurts-economy-2016-6.
32. Rachel Butt, "America's Shrinking Middle Class Is Killing the Economy," *Business Insider*, June 28, 2016. http://www.businessinsider.com/
    americas-shrinking-middle-class-hurts-economy-2016-6.
33. Robert Reich, "Business leaders Worry about Shrinking Middle Class," *SF Gate*, June 27, 2014. http://www.sfgate.com/opinion/reich/article/
    Business-leaders-worry-about-shrinking-middle-5585515.php.
34. Robert Reich, "Business Leaders Worry about Shrinking Middle Class," *SF Gate*, June 27, 2014. http://www.sfgate.com/opinion/reich/
    article/Business-leaders-worry-about-shrinking-middle-5585515.php.
35. Robert Reich, "Business Leaders Worry about Shrinking Middle Class," *SF Gate*, June 27, 2014. http://www.sfgate.com/opinion/reich/
    article/Business-leaders-worry-about-shrinking-middle-5585515.php.
36. Jed Graham, "American's Paychecks Just Got a Lot Fatter, New Tax Data Show," *Investor's Business Daily*, January 4, 2018.
    https://www.investors.com/news/economy/americans-paychecks-just-got-a-lot-fatter-new-tax-data-show/.
37. Ross Eisenbray, "Businesses Agree—It's Time to Raise the Minimum Wage," Economic Policy Institute, October 20, 2014.

http://www.epi.org/blog/businesses-agree-time-raise-minimum-wage/.

38. Ross Eisenbray, "Businesses Agree—It's Time to Raise the Minimum Wage," Economic Policy Institute, October 20, 2014. http://www.epi.org/blog/businesses-agree-time-raise-minimum-wage/.

39. U.S. Bureau of Labor Statistics, "Employer Costs for Employee Compensation – September 2017," U.S. Department of Labor, June 8, 2017. https://www.bls.gov/news.release/pdf/ecec.pdf.

40. David Neumark and William L. Wascher, *Minimum Wages*. (Cambridge, MA: The MIT Press, 2008), 290. See particularly their conclusion, pp. 285–295.

41. Sonali Jain-Chandra, "Why Gender and Income Inequality Are Linked," World Economic Forum, October 27, 2015. https://www.weforum.org/agenda/2015/10/why-gender-and-income-inequality-are-linked/.

42. Kevin Miller, "The Simple Truth about the Gender Pay Gap," American Association of University Women. https://www.aauw.org/research/the-simple-truth-about-the-gender-pay-gap/ (accessed July 22, 2018).

43. Bryce Covert, "New Jersey's Equal Pay Law Is the New Gold Standard," *Huffington Post*, April 4, 2018. https://www.huffingtonpost.com/entry/opinion-covert-equal-pay-day-new-jersey_us_5acbc59be4b0337ad1ead22d.

44. "Animals in Science/Alternatives," NEAVS. https://www.neavs.org/alternatives/in-testing

45. Stephen Latham, "U.S. Law and Animal Experimentation: A Critical Primer," The Hastings Center, 2012. http://animalresearch.thehastingscenter.org/report/u-s-law-and-animal-experimentation-a-critical-primer/.

46. Lauren Choplin, "Habeas Corpus Experts Offer Support for Chimpanzee Rights Cases," Nonhuman Rights Project, March 8, 2018. https://www.nonhumanrights.org/blog/habeas-corpus-experts/.

47. "Fact Sheet: Cosmetic Testing," The Humane Society of the United States. http://www.humanesociety.org/issues/cosmetic_testing/qa/questions_answers.html?refer

48. "The Mission," Rescue and Freedom Project. http://bfp.org/about-bfp/ (accessed January 5, 2018).

49. Wendy Newell, "The Beagle Freedom Project Gives Retired Lab Dogs Forever Homes," *Dogster*, January 16, 2015. https://www.dogster.com/lifestyle/beagle-freedom-project-lab-animal-testing.

50. "Animals in Science/Alternatives," New England Anti-Vivisection Society, 2018. https://www.neavs.org/alternatives/in-testing (accessed January 9, 2018).

51. People for the Ethical Treatment of Animals, searchable database. https://features.peta.org/cruelty-free-company-search/index.aspx (accessed June 1, 2018).

52. "Pet Industry Market Size & Ownership Statistics," American Pet Products Association, 2017. http://www.americanpetproducts.org/press_industrytrends.asp (accessed January 9, 2018).

53. Jenna Goudreau, "The Pet Culture," *Forbes*, October 15, 2009. https://www.forbes.com/2009/10/15/pets-dogs-cats-forbes-woman-time-children.

Professions under the Microscope

Figure 9.1 What are the ethical challenges in entrepreneurship? In social media and advertising? In insurance and health care? This chapter examines these industries through an ethical lens. (credit: modification of "Health Care Medicine Healthy" by "ar130405"/Pixabay, CC0)

Chapter Outline

9.1 Entrepreneurship and Start-Up Culture
9.2 The Influence of Advertising
9.3 The Insurance Industry
9.4 Ethical Issues in the Provision of Health Care

Introduction

As consumers, employees, and community members, we see everywhere the extent to which business can contribute to either social well-being or harm. Some career paths invite special scrutiny because of their influential role in society and the extent to which they serve as magnets for business students. Friends and critics of these professions have studied the unique ethical issues they raise and individuals who pursue careers in these fields should give careful consideration to these findings to decide if the benefits outweigh the potential downsides.

Entrepreneurship, for instance, offers the opportunity to construct your own business in the hope of profit, but at some personal and financial cost. Are the potential gains being overplayed when, in fact, most entrepreneurial businesses fail? Advertising is the driver of sales, but are its claims honest and its delivery platforms, including social media, acting in good faith? Do they exert undue or biased influence on the gullible and the young? Insurance is necessary, but what is the proper and ethical role of property insurers, for example, in the face of increasingly dangerous natural disasters? Health care in the United States is extraordinarily expensive, especially compared with that in other industrialized nations, and access is too often limited to those with means. Should quality health care be a right for all rather than a privilege for the few?

Entrepreneurship and Start-Up Culture

Learning Objectives

By the end of this section, you will be able to:

- Identify ethical challenges relating to entrepreneurial start-ups
- Describe positive and negative effects of growth in a start-up
- Discuss the role of the founder in instilling an ethical culture

An **entrepreneur** is a business leader willing to risk starting a new company and offering a product or service he or she hopes will be sustainable and permit the firm to prosper. The entrepreneur may have to find the money required for this venture and typically draws on business experience gained by working for others first. Entrepreneurship often requires hard work, but the potential for economic payoff and career satisfaction appeals to many.

The Risks of Entrepreneurship

Although the risk of failure associated with starting a business is real and even high, we hear much in the media about success stories and little about those entrepreneurs who crash and burn. Perhaps the allure of entrepreneurship inevitably outshines any mention of the downside. Still, start-ups impose a higher than normal degree of risk, and we turn to the evidence for this now.

What is the specific nature of entrepreneurial risk? Different studies yield different results, but business consultant Patrick Henry reported that "75 percent of venture-backed startups fail." Henry added that "this statistic is based on a Harvard Business School study by Shikhar Ghosh. In a study by Statistical Brain, 'Startup Business Failure Rate by Industry,' the failure rate of all U.S. companies after five years was over 50 percent, and over 70 percent after ten years."[1]

This figure might be enough to chill the enthusiasm of any would-be entrepreneur who believes an exciting or novel concept is enough to support a successful company with a minimal amount of time and effort and a great deal of other people's money. Still, the ranks of start-ups expand prodigiously each month in the United States.

Even start-ups that beat the odds financially need to be watchful for a different sort of pitfall, an ethical failure that can be nourished by the very strengths that allow a company to get off the ground. That pitfall is the hubris or excessive pride that may characterize some entrepreneurs, particularly after they have had some initial success. Uber, an application-based, ride-hailing service, was founded in San Francisco by Travis Kalanick and Garrett Camp in 2009. If ever an idea matched the success potential of smartphones, it was this one. Offering a cheaper and more convenient service than hailing a cab on city streets, Uber was valued at $70 billion in 2017 and operated, with varying degrees of success, in seventy countries at that point. However, the corporate culture, especially at headquarters, left many observers aghast in early 2017 after an Uber engineer, Susan Fowler, blogged about her experiences there. Other employees substantiated much of her account, revealing an atmosphere rife with misogyny, homophobia, and sexual harassment.

This culture was permitted—even fostered—by Kalanick, who reigned unchecked for several years over what the *New York Times* labeled an "aggressive, unrestrained workplace culture."[2] Muted grumblings from quarters within the company never received much attention outside the firm, allowing Kalanick to become a high-flying role model for would-be entrepreneurs who wished to emulate his success. A reckoning finally arrived when Uber's board of directors asked him to resign his position as chief executive officer in June 2017.

Yet the workplace culture that prevailed during his years at the company was not unique to Uber. Many firms have experienced it. Holding destructive egos in check is an ethical challenge at many successful businesses, particularly at hard-riding start-ups. Founders and their start-up teams need to be aware of how deeply their attitudes toward others; their visible treatment of employees, customers, and clients; and their display of fairness will come to shape the company they are building. It is not enough for the founders to hypothesize, "we'll get around to establishing the right protocols after we're solvent." Nor is it adequate to insist that standards of courteous business practice will naturally emerge on their own. An initial culture either of ethics or its absence will set a tone from the first day of business. If the founders believe these niceties are not required of them owing to their genius or confidence, such arrogance will displace ethics as a best practice. To believe otherwise is self-deception.

Why Successful Start-Ups Change as They Grow

A legendary example of a start-up that still inspires many today is the Hewlett-Packard Corporation (HP). Its origins lie in the efforts of Bill Hewlett and David Packard, two Stanford University classmates in the 1930s. Much like members of a garage band, they started their company in a real garage, and the firm has outgrown its humble beginnings many times over (Figure 9.2).

Figure 9.2   Hewlett-Packard has restored the original garage in Palo Alto, California, in which its two cofounders, Bill Hewlett and David Packard, former Stanford University classmates, began work in 1938 on the electrical switches and sound oscillators that became their new company's first products. (credit: "HP Garage in Silicon Valley" by "MGA73bot2"/Wikimedia Commons, CC BY 2.0)

Start-ups are exciting. Many of their founders, like the late Steve Jobs of Apple, attain near-rock star status, and the companies *can* generate enormous profit. They allow many to do what they have always wanted to do and be their own bosses. Yet we often overlook the fact that even some of the most successful entrepreneurs experience many failures before they succeed, and long hours of hard work are typically required even for these failures. Smart entrepreneurs learn from their failures, but each lesson can be painful, frustrating, and time consuming.

A unique personality is required to weather the stresses and strains of a start-up, and it is a personality that tolerates much personal deprivation as it pursues the perceived highest goal of all, success for the firm, no matter what personal or collective costs might be entailed. The culture of entrepreneurialism allows for many business leaders and their staffs to be deprived of a portion of their humanity along the way to success. Thus, a preeminent ethical consideration is whether the result justifies this cost. At the very least, determined entrepreneurs must be advised of these possible sacrifices. They constitute the collateral damage of entrepreneurial dreams that any ambitious start-up founder should contemplate. Will one emerge at the end of the process as the sort of person one most wishes to be?

Even if a start-up becomes what its founders wish it to be—astronomically successful—inevitably it will change as it grows, acquires new locations, and hires more employees. These changes may eventually produce an organization with added layers—essentially, a hardened bureaucracy that slows down and complicates the management process. The company may no longer make essential decisions with the speed and nimbleness that once were possible. In short, success for a start-up is often accompanied by the risk of becoming, over time, exactly the traditional business structure its founders once rejected. So the founders of an entrepreneurial shop, and their successors, must guard against change that radically alters the original spirit of innovation and the free and rapid flow of information, even as the company grows. No business leader seeks bureaucracy, but it typically accompanies growth within any organization.

Particular problems that arise out of bureaucratization are additional layers of management, more codified procedures, and internal obstructions that surface as a business attempts to capitalize on its initial success. As more employees are added to the mix, the original team's sense of common purpose can become diluted.

Max Weber (1864–1920), the German academic, economist, and sociologist, appreciated the consequences of bureaucracy years ago. In *Wirtschaft und Gesellschaft* [*Economy and Society*], published posthumously in 1925, he pointed out, "in the private economy, [bureaucracy emerges] only in the most advanced institutions of capitalism."[3] Weber cemented the link between bureaucracy and capitalism further: "The development of the *money economy* [emphasis is Weber's] . . . is a presupposition of bureaucracy. Today it not only prevails but is predominant."[4]

Because start-ups constitute an "advanced" feature of capitalism, and because bureaucracy presupposes a "money economy," Weber prophesied that agile start-ups would be ripe for bureaucratization as they grow and age. Finally, he included this acknowledgement of the permanence of bureaucracy: "Once it is firmly established, bureaucracy is among those social structures which are the hardest to destroy."[5]

More recently, Michael A. Lutzker confirmed Weber's testimony on the inevitability of bureaucracy: "The administrative function has of course been a pervasive element of all societies, ancient, medieval, and modern, but Weber was among the first to recognize the distinctive character of bureaucracy in the modern era."[6]

Simply put, the very same success that permits a start-up to flourish often produces bureaucratic structures that chip away at the free-flowing camaraderie that allowed a handful of founders to act instantly and with one mind. As the staff expands, employees' ranks become more defined, titles and hierarchies appear, and individual achievements become harder to spot. This is what changes within a successful start-up, and it moves the company away from the more congenial atmosphere that characterized it at its outset. An original small partnership often becomes a corporate behemoth, and it takes on many of the attributes of those cubicle workplaces that frequently inspired its founders to strike out on their own in the first place.

All the better, then, if ethical practices that permit coworkers to bond as colleagues with a sense of commitment to each other and to their customers or clients emerge through a company's trial-and-error experience at the outset. Only if the founders and initial staff emphasize treating all stakeholders with honesty, courtesy, and respect will the new firm stand a chance of indelibly cementing ethics into its operating matrix.

Entrepreneurial Culture

A fairly common characteristic of successful start-ups is charismatic, driven founders with take-no-prisoner competitive mentalities, as was illustrated earlier in this chapter in the example of Kalanick and the leadership values at Uber. After all, it takes a thick skin and powerful ego to get through the inevitable disappointments that confront a start-up leader. Often, however, even when these self-assured personalities evade the most egregious behavior of a Kalanick, they still remain very difficult for others to abide. Many companies discover that a different leadership ethos is necessary as they grow. Could entrepreneurs still succeed if they also embraced a humanistic leadership style at the outset, or would this invariably undermine the already low initial odds of success? It is a difficult problem with which many firms wrestle. Dedicated employees may be put off by demanding leaders who are harsh, giving little back to loyal workers even after achieving success. New employees may decide the working climate is less congenial than they anticipated and simply leave. This turnstile effect of workers voting on management with their feet constitutes an ethical judgment of repugnant leadership at the top.

LINK TO LEARNING

Although no single set of traits identifies the ideal start-up leader, a demanding, driven nature is a fairly common characteristic. Consider these brief profiles of entrepreneurs: first, a profile on Walt Disney (https://openstax.org/l/53WaltDisney) and then a profile on Steve Jobs (https://openstax.org/l/53SteveJobs) as well as this video showing a contrasting view from Kerrie Laird (https://openstax.org/l/53KerrieLaird) at Vodafone.

After watching the videos, consider this thought experiment: Suppose the cult of the charismatic—but dogmatic—entrepreneurial leader such as Walt Disney or Steve Jobs were replaced with one steeped in a commitment to employee empowerment that Kerrie Laird claims for Vodafone? Could this change the culture at start-ups? If it could, do you believe that change would be for the better or worse?

These observations identify what may be unique to **entrepreneurial culture**. This is a combination of personality and management style often identified with those business leaders who strike out on their own, bring a start-up to life, and shape its initial business practices and culture on the job. If the enterprise is successful, the principles and philosophy of the founder become enshrined in the lore of the company, so that long after his or her departure, succeeding leaders find themselves beholden to the management philosophy exemplified from the early days of the firm.[7] As *you* seek the right leadership style to implement on the job, begin by asking precisely what kind of leader you would prefer to work for if you were not the boss. The answer you provide may very well be the best model to follow as you develop your own leadership personality, whether it is at a start-up or a more established company.

The first employees of a start-up realize what is at stake as the company tiptoes into new entrepreneurial waters. The founder may be the boss, but those associated with him or her sense a collaborative spirit that directly joins them to the founder as well as each other. There can be a genuine fraternity among those who have been with the firm since day 1 or shortly thereafter. Founding members of an entrepreneurial business are also often willing to undergo the strains and rigors attached to a start-up in return for an ownership stake in the company that allows them to profit handsomely from its later growth and success.

Newer staff, however, may not share this mindset. They may simply be seeking a secure position with a growing business rather than a chance to get in on the ground floor of a risky start-up. They will not necessarily have the tolerance for the demanding hours, chaos, and abrasive personalities that can characterize the early days of an enterprise. Can entrepreneurial founders shape a company's culture so it can accommodate talented employees who are looking for a corporate culture that supports some work–life balance?

Consider also the ethical practices of an entrepreneur and the ethical expectations of employees. Suppose that one of the distinguishing features woven into the fabric of the start-up is the respect extended to customers or clients. An entrepreneur typically promises always to hold customers in the highest regard, never lie to them, and serve them well. Furthermore, suppose this entrepreneur successfully instills this same ethos among all employees from the outset. Respect for customers is intended to become a distinguishing feature of the business; even if it causes monetary loss to the company, this entrepreneur will not cheat a client or misrepresent the company's services. Finally, presume that this ethos is embedded into the culture of the company while it is still in start-up mode.

Now, and literally against the odds, suppose the company becomes successful. This may signal the hardest time of all for the entrepreneur. Growth often accompanies success, and growth means, among other things, more employees. Not all these new hires will be as committed to the same degree of responsibility for customers. They will not necessarily set out to cheat clients, but they might lack the founder's enthusiasm for the most honorable treatment of customers. How can an entrepreneur ensure that the initial commitment carries over to the second generation of leadership? He or she cannot simply order it to happen—human nature usually does not respond so easily. So entrepreneurs must do their best to ensure that their version of customer service, one that prioritizes respect for clients, is passed along to new employees. It may be ingrained in the longest-serving employees, but it must be nurtured to the point where it has the same significance for the newest hires. This is where leadership mettle is tested to the severest degree.

CASES FROM THE REAL WORLD

Growing Up with a Start-Up

In the summer of 1970, a college senior named Paul Orfalea opened a store near the University of California, Santa Barbara, campus. He called it "Kinko's" after his own nickname and, with his partners, he sold college school supplies and around-the-clock copying services for students. After twenty-five years, Kinko's had grown to 1,200 stores and 23,000 employees, and Orfalea privately and lucratively sold it to FedEx.

Over the many years that Orfalea ran his start-up, his business became amazingly profitable but also imposed enormous stress on him and his founding partners and coworkers. As he put it, "I don't hide the fact that I have a problem with anger."[8] Since selling the company, Orfalea has spent many years mending relationships with those who worked most closely with him while he was building it.

What contributed to the tensions Orfalea felt while managing this burgeoning enterprise? Long hours, of course, but also the need he felt to sustain his initial success, to make each year more profitable than the last. Entrepreneurs often believe they are only as successful as their last quarter's profit and are driven to exceed it. Orfalea also felt that he alone was equipped to call others to account and veto what he felt were bad business ideas. Anger became a chief enemy he battled.

"In my mid- to late-forties," he said, "I struggled increasingly to manage my own emotional nature. Sometimes I felt I'd created a monster. The monster wasn't Kinko's, it was me."[9] Orfalea acknowledged the anger and resentment that he often felt toward other longtime staff at the company, which overpowered the respect that he knew he owed them. Consequently, he directed comments and actions at his colleagues that he has spent many subsequent years attempting to redress. All in all, he has labored diligently to repair friendships that he admits were frayed by his behavior alone.

After reflection, Orfalea now offers these recommendations to prospective entrepreneurs: Do not give way to your anger in the midst of the frustrating turns business inevitably takes. Do not take that anger home with you, either. Finally, try to be the person you most genuinely are, both at work and at home. It took Orfalea time to learn these lessons, but they are worthwhile for any would-be entrepreneur to ponder.[10]

Critical Thinking

- What price would you be willing to pay to pursue an entrepreneurial career? What price would you demand from your partners in the business? How long could you let work monopolize your life?
- In your opinion, was Orfalea right to manage Kinko's the way he did as it grew? Were the worries, anxieties, and bad moods he experienced inevitable? How would you avoid these?

9.2 The Influence of Advertising

Learning Objectives

By the end of this section, you will be able to:

- Discuss how social media has altered the advertising landscape
- Explain the influence of advertising on consumers
- Analyze the potential for subliminal advertising

The **advertising** industry revolves around creating commercial messages urging the purchase of new or improved products or services in a variety of media: print, online, digital, television, radio, and outdoor. Because as consumers we need and want to be informed, this feature of advertising is to the good. Yet some advertising is intended to lead to the purchase of goods and services we do not need. Some ads may make claims containing only the thinnest slice of truth or exaggerate and distort what the goods and services can actually deliver. All these tactics raise serious ethical concerns that we will consider here.

The Rise of Social Media

Relevant to any discussion of the influence and ethics of advertising is the emergence and dominance of social media, which now serve as the format within which many people most often encounter ads. Kelly Jensen, a digital-marketing consultant, observed that we inhabit a "Digital Era" in which "the internet is arguably the single most influential factor of our culture—transforming the way we view communication, relationships, and even ourselves. Social media platforms have evolved to symbolize the status of both individuals and businesses alike. . . Today, using social media to create brand awareness, drive revenue, engage current customers, and attract new ones isn't optional anymore. Now it is an absolute 'must.'"[11]

These are bold claims—as are the claims of some advertising—but Jensen argues convincingly that social media platforms reach many consumers, especially younger ones, who simply cannot be captured by conventional advertising schemes. For those who derive most of the significant information that shapes their lives solely through electronic sources, nothing other than social media–based appeals stands much chance of influencing their purchasing decisions.

This upending of conventional modes of advertising has begun to change the content of ads dramatically. It certainly presents a new stage on which people as young as their teens increasingly rely for help in choosing what to buy. Many marketers have come to appreciate that if they are not spreading the word about their products and services via an electronic source, many millennials will ignore it.[12]

Undeniably, a digital environment for advertising, selling, and delivering products and services functions as a two-edged sword for business. It provides lightning-quick access to potential customers, but it also opens pathways for sensitive corporate and consumer data to be hacked on an alarming scale. It offers astute companies nearly unlimited capacity to brand themselves positively in the minds of purchasers, but it simultaneously offers a platform for disgruntled stakeholders to assail companies for both legitimate and self-serving reasons.

Paul A. Argenti, who has taught business communication for many years at the Tuck School of Business at Dartmouth University, has studied this dilemma. As he put it, "mobile apps have created a new playground for cyber-thieves."[13] And consumer advocates and purchasers alike "now use technology to rally together and fuel or escalate a crisis—posing additional challenges for the corporation" in the crosshairs of criticism. Finally, "the proliferation of online blogs and social networking sites has greatly increased the visibility and reach of all current events, not excluding large corporate"[14] bungling.

Regardless of the delivery platform, however, any threat that the advertising of unnecessary or harmful products may pose to our autonomy as consumers is complicated by the fact that sometimes we willingly choose to buy goods or services we may not necessarily require. Sometimes we even buy things that have been proven to be harmful to us, such as cigarettes and sugary drinks. Yet we may *desire* these products even if we do not *need* them. If we have the disposable income to make these discretionary purchases, why should we not do so, and why should advertisers not advise us of their availability?

Does Advertising Drive Us to Unnecessary Purchases?

By definition, advertising aims to persuade consumers to buy goods and services, many of which are nonessential. Although consumers have long been encouraged to heed the warning caveat emptor (let the buyer beware), it is a valid question whether advertisers have any ethical obligation to rein in the oft-exaggerated claims of their marketing pitches. Most consumers emphatically would agree that they do.

The award-winning Harvard University economist John Kenneth Galbraith directly addressed this issue in *The Affluent Society*, first published in 1958. In what he depicted as the "the dependence effect," Galbraith bemoaned the power of corporations to harness wide-ranging advertising strategies, marketing efforts, and sales pitches to influence consumer purchasing decisions.[15] He asked whether it is possible for a sophisticated advertising campaign to create a demand for a product whose benefits are frivolous at best. If so, is there anything inherently wrong with that? Or are informed consumers themselves responsible for resisting tempting—though misleading—advertising claims and exercising their own best judgment about whether to buy a product that might be successful, not because it deserves to be but simply because of the marketing hype behind it? These questions remain fundamental to the manager's task of creating ethical advertising campaigns in which truthful content is prioritized over inducing wasteful consumption.

Psychological appeals form the basis of the most successful ads. Going beyond the standard ad pitch about the product's advantages, **psychological appeals** try to reach our self-esteem and persuade us that we will feel better about ourselves if we use certain products. If advertising frames the purchase of a popular toy as the act of a loving parent rather than an extravagance, for instance, consumers may buy it not because their child needs it but because it makes them feel good about what generous parents they are. This is how psychological appeals become successful, and when they do work, this often constitutes a victory for the power of psychological persuasion at the expense of ethical truthfulness.

Purchases are also affected by our notion of what constitutes a necessity versus a luxury, and that perception often differs across generations. Older consumers today can probably remember when a cell phone was considered a luxury, for instance, rather than a necessity for every schoolchild. On the other hand, many younger consumers consider the purchase of a landline unnecessary, whereas some older people still use a conventional phone as their main or even preferred means of communication. The cars and suburban homes that were once considered essential purchases for every young family are slowly becoming luxuries, replaced, for many millennials, by travel. Generational differences like these are carefully studied by advertisers who are anxious to make use of psychological appeals in their campaigns.

A consumer craze based on little more than novelty—or, at least, not on necessity or luxury in the conventional sense—is the Pet Rock, a recurring phenomenon that began in 1977. Pet Rocks have been purchased by the millions over the years, despite being nothing more than rocks. During the 2017 holiday shopping season, they retailed at $19.95.[16] Is this a harmless fad, or a rip-off of gullible consumers who are persuaded it can satisfy a real need? In the annals of marketing, the Pet Rock craze denotes one of the most successful campaigns—still unfolding today, though in subdued fashion—in support of so dubious a product.

As long as marketers refrain from breaking the law or engaging in outright lies, are they still acting ethically in undertaking influential advertising campaigns that may drive gullible consumers to purchase products with minimal usefulness? Is this simply the free market in operation? In other words, are manufacturers just supplying a product, promoting it, and then seeing whether customers respond positively to it? Or are savvy marketing campaigns exerting too much influence on consumers ill prepared to resist them? Many people have long asked exactly these questions, and we still have arrived at no clear consensus as to how to answer them. Yet it remains an obligation of each new generation of marketers to reflect on these points and, at the very least, establish their convictions about them.

A second ethical question is how we should expect reasonable people to respond to an avalanche of marketing schemes deliberately intended to separate them from their hard-earned cash. Are consumers obligated to sift through all the messages and ultimately make purchasing decisions in their own best interest? For example, does a perceived "deal" on an unhealthy food option justify the purchase (Figure 9.3)? These questions have no consensus answers, but they underlie any discussion of the point at which sophisticated advertising runs headlong into people's obligation to take responsibility for the wisdom of their purchases.

Figure 9.3 When an unwise purchase is made appealing, where does the consumer's responsibility for decision-making lie? Furthermore, if the purchase is spurred by children who are responding to advertising specifically directed at them, is consumer responsibility diminished? (credit: "Big Burgers - Asia (5490379696)" by Kinoko kokonotsu/Wikimedia Commons, CC BY 2.0)

No one would argue that children are particularly susceptible to the ads commercial television rains over them regularly. Generally, young children have not developed sufficient judgment to know what advertised products are good for them and which ones have little or no benefit or perhaps can even harm. Research has even shown that very young children have difficulty separating what is real on television from what is not. This is especially so as it pertains to advertising for junk food. Savvy marketers take advantage of the fact that young children (those younger than age seven or eight years) view advertising in the same manner they do information from trustworthy adults—that is, as very credible—and so marketers hone pitches for junk food directly to these children.[17]

What restrictions could we reasonably impose on those who gear their ads toward children? We could argue that they should take special care that ads targeting children make absolutely no exaggerated claims, because children are less capable of seeing through the usual puffery that most of us ignore. Children are more literal, and once they gain the ability to understand messages directed toward them, especially when voiced by adult authority figures, they typically accept these as truthful statements.

When adults make poor consumer choices, who is responsible? Is it ourselves? Is it our society and culture, which permit the barrage of marketing to influence us in ways we often come to regret? Is it the persuasive power of marketers, which we should rein in through law? Do adults have the right to some assistance from marketers as they attempt to carry out their responsibility to protect children from manipulative ads? We have no easy answers to these questions, though they have taken on special urgency as technology has expanded the range of advertising even to our smartphones.

Is Subliminal Advertising Real?

It may be possible for marketing to be unfairly persuasive in ways that overwhelm the better judgment of consumers. Whether it is the consumers' responsibility to resist or marketers' to tone down their appeals, or both, will continue to be debated. Yet the question of where responsibility lies when consumers are steered to make choices certainly has ethical ramifications.

Some psychologists and educational specialists claim that the very old and the very young are particularly ill prepared to exercise good judgment in the face of **subliminal advertising**, that is, embedded words or images that allegedly reach us only beneath the level of our consciousness. Other experts, however, disagree and insist that subliminal advertising is an urban myth that no current technology could create or sustain.

A U.S. journalist, Vance Packard, published *The Hidden Persuaders* in 1957, contending that subliminal messaging had already been introduced into some U.S. cinemas to sell more refreshments at the theaters' snack bars. Alarms sounded at the prospect, but it turned out that any data on which Packard was relying came from James Vicary, a U.S. market researcher who insisted he had engineered the feat in a cinema in New Jersey. No other substantiation was provided, and Vicary's claim was eventually dismissed as self-promotion, which he seemed to concede in an interview five years later. Although the immediate threat of subliminal advertising receded, some people remain concerned that such persuasion might indeed be possible, especially with the advent of better technologies, like virtual reality, to implement it.[18]

A 2015 study at the University of South Carolina found that thirsty test subjects placed in the role of shoppers in a simulated grocery store could be subliminally influenced in their choice of beverages *if* they were primed by images of various beverage brands within fifteen minutes of acknowledging being thirsty. After that window of time passed, however, any impact of subliminal messaging receded.[19]

So the scientific evidence establishing any real phenomenon of subliminal advertising is inconclusive. Put another way, the evidence to this point does not definitively demonstrate the existence of a current technology making subliminal marketing pitches possible. Given this, it cannot be clearly determined whether such a technology, if it did exist, would be effective. Another question is whether virtual reality and augmented reality might eventually make subliminal advertising viable. Real subliminal persuasion might render children, the elderly, and those with developmental disabilities more vulnerable to falling prey. Could even the most skeptical viewer resist a message so powerfully enhanced that the product can be sampled without leaving home? Would you be in favor of federal government regulation to prevent such ads? What sort of ethical imperatives would you be willing to request of or impose on sophisticated marketers?

LINK TO LEARNING

Is subliminal messaging real? Watch this video where BBC Earth Lab investigates a bit whimsically what truth might lie in the claim that subliminal advertising is real (https://openstax.org/l/53subliminal) **to learn more.**

Advertising plays a useful role in informing consumers of new or modified products and services in the marketplace, and wise purchasers will pay attention to it but with a discerning eye. Even the exaggerated claims that often accompany ads can serve a purpose as long as we do not unquestioningly accept every pitch as true.

9.3 | The Insurance Industry

Learning Objectives

By the end of this section, you will be able to:

- Discuss whether the underlying business model of the insurance industry is an ethical one
- Identify the reasons why the government offers certain kinds of insurance
- Discuss the ethical issues in insurers' decisions whether to offer disaster insurance
- Explain the concept of redlining

Although the concept of insurance dates back to antiquity, the insurance industry as a profession came of age in the seventeenth century, when maritime trade in valuable commodities like coffee, tea, cocoa, sugar, and silk became an immense industry, but one fraught with uncertainty. Merchants sought a means to limit their financial losses in the event their cargoes were lost at sea.

In England, merchants and shippers gathered together in associations, or syndicates, to distribute the risk of loss as evenly as possible. For a fee, individual merchants and ships' owners in these syndicates could buy insurance, essentially the right to be financially compensated by the syndicate's fund for their loss if their shipments or vessels sank. The first such association of traders and shippers began at Samuel Lloyd's coffee house, on Tower Street near the River Thames, in 1688. This was the origin of the huge insurance market now known as Lloyd's of London,[20] and from these early forms of group insurance sprang the profession as it exists today.

From the seventeenth century to the present, the profession has faced a fundamental ethical quandary: An insurance company makes money when purchaser fees, called **premiums**, are numerous and **claims**, requests for monetary compensation for covered losses, are few. But the reality is that accidents occur, whether they take the form of shipping losses, vehicular collisions, or home or business fires. So insurance carriers set customer premiums at a high enough rate to compensate themselves with a baseline profit when claims for compensation arise. The ethical question then is what constitutes a *reasonable* profit. The way the industry defines "reasonable" is directly reflected in the premiums it sets, which also take into account actuarial and statistical calculations of the historic frequency of the occurrence of various claims.

How Insurance Works

The irony of insurance coverage of any sort is that we buy it hoping never to use it. Still, business and consumers alike appreciate that a catastrophic loss can be financially devastating and so they seek to protect against it. Insurance coverage does not prevent illness, accidents, or other unforeseen events from occurring, but it does offer a means to recover, at least partially, from the monetary costs associated with them.

Insurance policies constitute a form of contract between insurers and the insured. To reduce their losses in those situations in which they must pay on a claim, insurers do their best to attach high premiums to the coverage and identify exclusions and limits on it. They worry about being forced to pay out on frivolous and exaggerated claims, while policyholders fear that on the rare occasions when they will have to file a claim, their reimbursement will be minuscule and/or their future premiums will rise. From the perspective of the consumer, the guarantee of a fair payout on a claim is the only inducement to pay insurance premiums in the first place.

WHAT WOULD YOU DO?

Valuing Your Inventory versus Valuing Your Employees

Assume you are the owner of a small apparel manufacturer with approximately fifty employees. Your business is located in a blighted area of town where the jobs you provide are important, but the insurance costs of doing business there are significant, too. Recently, fire and theft coverage has escalated in cost, but it is essential to protect your premises and inventory, and local ordinances require that you purchase it. You have customarily provided health coverage for your employees and their families, which many of them would not be able to afford if they had to bear the cost themselves. You would like to continue providing this coverage—though, due to your small employee base, you are not legally obligated to do so—but these costs have risen too. Finally, you would prefer to stay in this location, because you feel an obligation to your workers, most of whom live nearby, and because you feel welcomed by the community itself, which includes some longtime customers. Still, you may be forced to choose between paying for your employee health care costs and moving to a different area of town where fire and theft coverage would not cost as much.

Critical Thinking

- How will you make the decision within an ethical framework?
- What will you, your business, and your employees gain and lose based on what you decide?
- What, if anything, do you and your business owe the community of which you have been a part for so long?

Insurance protections are, in fact, limited. In August 2017, Hurricane Harvey dumped fifty-two inches of rain on Houston, Texas, accompanied by fierce winds. Tens of thousands of homes, stores, factories, and other industrial sites suffered severe damage and flooding. Although normal homeowners' and business owners' insurance provides for loss due to hurricane winds, it does not cover loss due to flooding. As *The Economist* observed in the immediate aftermath of the hurricane, "whereas wind damage is covered under most standard insurance policies in America, flood insurance is a government-run add-on that far from all homeowners buy. As a result, of over $30 billion in property losses in Texas, only 40 percent may be insured."[21]

Not only do few homeowners buy flood insurance; few private insurers offer it. After all, most insurance carriers are for-profit, and companies would make little money insuring everyone against flood damage in flood-prone areas. It would be a losing proposition for any carrier to undertake, because insurance companies enjoy their highest returns when claims are few and payouts small. But the federal government is not a commercial broker and does not intend to make a profit from extending any sort of insurance coverage. For that reason, the National Flood Insurance Act of 1968 established a way to dispense flood coverage through a federal agency. Today that supervising agency is the Federal Emergency Management Authority (FEMA), in partnership with the Department of Homeland Security (Figure 9.4). As of August 2017, just before Harvey struck, some five million households had taken out FEMA-sponsored flood coverage.[22]

Figure 9.4   The National Flood Insurance Program in the United States is part of the Federal Emergency Management Agency (FEMA). (credit: modification of "National Flood Insurance Program 50th Anniversary Logo – white background" by FEMA/fema.gov, Public Domain)

LINK TO LEARNING

Consumers' criticisms of the insurance industry are not limited to the United States; they pose an international issue for the profession. Read this *Sydney Morning Herald* article that explores the causes of controversy that haunt insurance carriers in Australia (https://openstax.org/l/53insurance) to learn more. Principally, they center on the lengths to which insurers might go to disallow a claim and so dispose of their obligation to pay out on it, at least according to some consumer watchdogs.

The California Earthquake Authority serves a similar function at the state level by managing privately funded insurance against earthquakes in California. The private brokers in the program make no profit from offering this coverage, but they do earn the right to offer (and profit from) other insurance in California.

The Ethical Dilemma of Insuring against Natural Disasters

We do not know with certainty what effect climate change will have on the incidence or severity of natural disasters (i.e., accidents that do not appear to have any direct human cause). We do know, however, that these events can be ruinously expensive, for the carriers that insure against them and for those who suffer them and must put their lives back together afterward.

Business writer Don Jergler said, for example, that "climate change has created a 'wildfire crisis in California,' which in turn is 'causing a fire insurance predicament.'" California insurance commissioner Dave Jones warned in December 2017, after a particularly disastrous fire season in California, that "insurers may start to back off writing insurance in some areas [of the state]," and this would pose a crisis for homeowners who consequently lost insurance protection against losses caused by wildfires.[23]

In Canada, too, "environmental risks linked to climate change are becoming important issues for insurers who need to consider their response to related risks and climate related losses whether arising from weather related events such as flood and storms or liability risks from third party claims."[24]

When insurance carriers must pay claimholders more often on claims arising from natural disasters, they lose money at a rate that could make them less willing to underwrite similar policies in the future. This unwillingness, in turn, would deny coverage against these disasters to an increasing number of individuals and companies. The high cost of disaster claims and subsequent shrinking of policy offerings are losses first experienced by the insurance industry, but they have rapid and dire consequences for policyholders.

Again, we come to the ethical conundrum as to what we might fairly expect from insurance carriers and from clients who seek to indemnify themselves against natural disasters. In regions where certain kinds of disasters are more likely to occur, is it reasonable to dictate that carriers still must provide coverage? If so, should we consider extending public subsidies to the carriers to protect them against catastrophic payouts? Should premiums be assigned on the basis of the incidence patterns and severity of risk associated with particular disasters in certain regions? With these questions, we return to the ethical consideration of what constitutes a reasonable profit for carriers and what premium policy holders ought to be charged for sufficient coverage.

The United States does not have the strong tradition of private/public ownership of industries, such as petroleum extraction or air travel that some other nations do.[25] Essentially, private/public ownership is an arrangement in which private (industry) and public (government) monies are combined to more safely bear an industry's risk and also share in its profit. It is often a successful partnership. When we consider the scale of loss that can result from natural disasters, and the extent of the public's need for protection from such loss, insurance may be a U.S. industry in which private/public ownership of some policies would be appropriate. The National Flood Insurance Program and the California Earthquake Authority are rare examples of public agencies managing insurance coverage that private insurers have declined to provide because the potential for profit is too low. Whether partnerships like this can and should be expanded, and whether they can be funded from federal and state budgets, are ethical questions for federal and state governments and policyholders alike.

CASES FROM THE REAL WORLD

What Does the Future Hold for the Insurance Industry?

Many insurance carriers enjoy a robust business. As an example, UnitedHealth Group Incorporated, headquartered in Minnesota, had about $185 million in sales in 2017 and employed approximately 230,000 people. Still, as an industry report from the business research company Hoovers established, insurers of all stripes, health or auto or property or anything else, face two major hurdles. First, they "are increasingly subject to a large number of regulations and reporting requirements by states. Consequently, some insurers have withdrawn from states that impose burdensome requirements." Second, large-scale "claims have become more common, creating problematic concentrations of risk for individual insurers. . . . And some risks can be large enough to drive insurers out of business or cause them to curtail services offered, increase rates, or leave states where risk is highest."[26] Thus, profits can be high within the industry, but so can payouts in the aftermath of major catastrophes. The report goes on to say that "floods, hurricanes, and tornadoes" produce the riskiest economic circumstances for the industry. Consequently, states in which these weather events are more common—Alabama, Florida, and North Carolina—have seen some carriers cease business operations within them.[27]

Critical Thinking

- In selecting coverage and setting prices, how does an insurance company choose the ethical

balance between making a reasonable profit and risking catastrophic losses of its own?
- Should the law require that carriers offer property insurance in states where harsh natural disasters occur? Or should federal and state monies be used to subsidize insurance companies' resources in these circumstances? In each case, why or why not?

Redlining: Discrimination in Insurance

A specific ethical challenge within the insurance profession is the tendency to engage in **redlining**. Redlining is the practice of assigning or denying coverage for certain policies, such as auto, homeowners, or business insurance, on the basis of the geographic neighborhoods where applicants for such coverage live, particularly inner-city neighborhoods. A variation on the practice is to charge considerably higher prices for the same coverage in different neighborhoods. Redlining assumes that the propensity for accidents, burglaries, fires, and other catastrophes is higher in some areas than others, so claims and costs will be higher for the insurance carrier.

At first glance, this practice appears to make economic sense from the perspective of both the insurer and the insured. Looking beneath the surface, however, reveals that redlined neighborhoods are often areas where racial and ethnic minorities live. No insurance carrier ever admits to engaging in discriminatory redlining (the term refers to an older practice by which insurance companies marked certain neighborhoods in red on print copies of coverage maps). Nearly every state in the United States forbids the practice. Yet a comprehensive 2017 study by *Consumer Reports* and ProPublica, a nonprofit research organization, indicated the phenomenon may remain very much a reality. This study focused on rates for auto insurance and found that for "decades, auto insurers have been observed to charge higher average premiums to drivers living in predominantly minority urban neighborhoods than to drivers with similar safety records living in majority white neighborhoods. Insurers have long defended their pricing by saying that the risk of accidents is greater in those neighborhoods, even for motorists who have never had one."[28]

The authors of the report compared auto insurance premiums and claims paid in four states (California, Illinois, Missouri, and Texas) and found similar results whether the carrier was Allstate, Geico, Liberty Mutual, or another. They contended "that many of the disparities in auto insurance prices between minority and white neighborhoods are wider than differences in risk can explain."[29] This is significant because laws do typically permit premium rates to be set according to the incidence of claims filed within certain neighborhoods. Yet laws never allow rates to be based solely or predominantly on the race or ethnicity of the residents in different neighborhoods. This is the essence of prohibited redlining. Professionals in the industry do well to steer clear of this practice or even the appearance of it, and that is the overriding theme of this study.

Drawing back, the ethical challenge for any responsible carrier is to ensure that the race, ethnicity, or creed of any policyholder plays absolutely no role in the premiums assigned him or her. There is no defensible reason to base a carrier's decision to extend or deny insurance coverage or assign the premium amount for it on these factors.

9.4 | Ethical Issues in the Provision of Health Care

Learning Objectives

By the end of this section, you will be able to:

- Identify ethical problems related to the availability and cost of health care in the United States and elsewhere
- Discuss recent developments in insuring or otherwise providing for health care in the United States

Private health care in the United States has historically been of high quality and readily available, but only for those who could afford it. This model for rationing health services is rare in the developed world and stands in dramatic contrast to the provision of health care in other industrialized economies. Those who provide health care and administer the health care system find that balancing the quality of, access to, and cost of medical care is an ethical dilemma in which they must continually engage.[30]

Multipayer Health Care in the United States

Typically in the United States, medical services have been dispensed through a **multipayer health care system**, in which the patient and others, such as an employer and a private health insurance company, all contribute to pay for the patient's care. Germany, France, and Japan also have multipayer systems. In a **single-payer health care system** such as those in the United Kingdom and Canada, national tax revenues pay the largest portion of citizens' medical care, and the government is the sole payer compensating those who provide that care. Contributions provided by employers and employees provide the rest. Both single- and multipayer systems help reduce costs for patients, employers, and insurers; both, especially single-payer, are also heavily dependent on taxes apportioned across employers and the country's population. In a single-payer system, however, because payment for health care is coordinated and dispensed by the government, almost no one lacks access to medical services, including visitors and nonpermanent residents.

Many reasons exist for the predominance of the multipayer system in the United States. Chief among these is the U.S. tradition that doctors' services and hospital care are privatized and run for profit. The United States has no federal health care apparatus that organizes physicians, clinics, and medical centers under a single government umbrella. Along with the profit motive, the fact that providers are compensated at a higher average rate than their peers abroad ensures that health care is more expensive in the United States than in most other nations.

The United States also has more health care professionals per citizen than most other countries, and more medical centers and clinics (Figure 9.5). One positive result is that the wait for most elective medical procedures is often shorter than in other countries, and travel time to a nearby medical facility is often less. Still, paying for health care remains one of the most controversial topics in the United States, and many question what it is that Americans gain from the current system to balance the cost. As an exhaustive study from The Commonwealth Fund asserted, "the United States spends far more on health care than other high-income countries, with spending levels that rose continuously over the past three decades. . . . Yet the U.S. population has poorer health than other countries."[31]

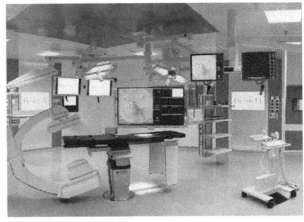

(a)   (b)

Figure 9.5   The Indiana University Health University Hospital (a) is an example of a contemporary medical center affiliated with a university medical school, in this case on the Indiana University–Purdue University Indianapolis campus. This is indicative of a common partnership through which hospitalization and medical-school education are made available in the United States. This type of affiliation also exists abroad, as evidenced by this state-of-the-art operating facility (b) at the Gemelli University Hospital in Rome, Italy. (credit a: modification of "Indiana University Hospital - IUPUI - DSC00508" by "Daderot"/Wikimedia Commons, Public Domain; credit b: modification of "Hybrid operating room for cardiovascular surgery at Gemelli Hospital in Rome" by "Pfree2014"/Wikimedia Commons, CC0)

Besides its inefficiencies, the state of U.S. health care raises challenging ethical issues for professionals in the field and for patients as well. What happens if many poorer people cannot afford health care? Should doctors treat them anyway? Who is qualified to receive subsidized (insured) health care? In the absence of universal health care, which is generally ensured elsewhere by a single-payer system that entitles everyone to receive care at very low cost, can the United States truly boast of being the richest nation on Earth? Put another way, when the least materially advantaged in a country do not have access to quality health care, what is the worth such a nation patently is assigning to those human beings residing within it?

Supporters of the status quo for health care in the United States may point to state-of-the-art facilities as evidence of its success. Yet other nations, such as Australia, the United Kingdom, and the Netherlands, have equal levels of medical technologies available for patients and are given much more favorable marks for universal health insurance and accessibility by The Commonwealth Fund.

The High Cost of Prescription Drugs

Discussions of health care accessibility have become politically charged, so for now it is enough to observe that not only is medical care enormously expensive in the United States but so are prescription drugs. According to William B. Schultz, an attorney writing in the *Washington Post* in 2017, "in the past 35 years, the only significant victory in the battle to control drug prices has been the enactment of legislation that established the generic drug program at the FDA [Federal Drug Administration]." Otherwise, he stated, "prescription drug prices account for 17 percent of the nation's health-care costs, up from 7 percent in the 1990s," and "prescription drug spending accounts for nearly 20 percent of total program spending for Medicare, the largest of the governmental health-care programs."[32] (Schultz is not entirely impartial; he is a partner in a law firm that represents generic drug providers, among other clients.)

LINK TO LEARNING

The *New York Times* asked its readers to relay their experiences as purchasers of prescribed medicines that they thought carried much too high a price tag. This article on some of the reader responses to drug prices (https://openstax.org/l/53DrugPrices) was reported by two journalists at the paper, Katie Thomas and Charles Ornstein.

The only way to recoup the enormous cost of developing new drugs, says the pharmaceutical industry, is to pass it along to consumers. Critics, on the other hand, assert that the much of the expense incurred within the industry results from the high cost of marketing new drugs. Wherever the truth lies in this debate, it remains that exorbitant prices for much-needed medicines dramatically reduce their social value when only a few individuals can actually afford to obtain them. What does it say of our priorities if we have the technology to create life-saving medicines but allow astronomic prices effectively to deny them to many patients who require them?

Paying for Health Care and Wellness

Within the multipayer system, many U.S. workers have traditionally looked to their employers or their unions to subsidize the cost of care and thereby make it available for them and their families. Many reasons explain why this is so. In contrast to the European and Canadian perspective, for example, in which both the state and employers are presumed to have an interest in and responsibility for underwriting the cost of health care, the traditional U.S. approach is that workers and their employers should be responsible for securing this coverage. This belief reflects an unease on the part of some about assigning services to the government, because this implies the need for a larger governing entity as well as additional taxes to sustain it. The sentiment also reflects a conviction on the part of some that self-reliance is always to be preferred when securing the necessities of life.

John E. Murray, a professor of economics at the University of Toledo, offered a related explanation. He cited the existence of industrial sickness funds in the United States, which arose in the late nineteenth and early twentieth centuries. These were monies "organized by workers through their employer or union [that] provided the rudiments of health insurance, principally consisting of paid sick leave, to a large minority of the industrial workforce of the late nineteenth and early twentieth centuries."[33] Murray stated that these funds declined in popularity not because they were ineptly administered or rendered bankrupt by World War I or the Great Depression but rather because they gave way to even more effective instruments in the form of group insurance policies offered by employers or labor unions.

So the U.S. worker's experience differed from that of European labor in that much significant health care coverage was provided under the auspices of unions and employers rather than the state. Murray noted another source of relief for workers who experienced illness or injury that prevented them from working for any period of time, and that was charity.[34] Specific versions of charity were offered by religious organizations, including Christian churches and Jewish synagogues. Often, these religious bodies banded together to provide monetary benefits for sick or injured members of their own faith who might otherwise have been denied health coverage due to prejudice.[35] The U.S. social experience featured more ethnic and cultural diversity, especially in the nineteenth and early twentieth centuries, than was present in many European nations, and a downside is the racial, ethnic, and religious prejudice it inspired.

A final distinction Murray pointed to is the past opposition of the American Medical Association to any sort of state-sponsored insurance. Early supporters of industrial sickness funds, including some physicians, anticipated that most doctors would support these funds as pathways ultimately directed to state-provided coverage. Instead, in 1920, "the American Medical Association voted officially to state its opposition to government health insurance. A sociologist concluded that from this time to the 1960s, physicians were the loudest opponents of government insurance."[36] By default, then, many U.S. workers came to rely more on their employers or unions than on any other source for coverage. However, this explanation does not answer the larger ethical question of who *should* provide health insurance to residents and citizens, a question that continues to roil politics and society in the nation even today.

More recently, large corporations have moved from providing one-size-fits-all insurance plans to compiling a menu of offerings to accommodate the different needs of their employees. Workers with dependent children may opt for maximum health care coverage for their children. Employees without dependents or a partner may elect a plan without this coverage and thereby pay lower premiums (the initial cost for coverage). Yet others might minimize their health-insurance coverage and convert some of the employer costs that are freed up into added pension or retirement plan value. Employers and workers have become creative in tailoring benefit plans that best suit the needs of employees (Figure 9.6). Some standard features of such plans are the **copayment**, a set fee per service paid by the patient and typically negotiated between the insurance carrier and the employer; the annual **deductible**, a preset minimum cost for health care for which the patient is responsible each year before the carrier will assume subsequent costs; and percent totals for certain medical or dental procedures that patients must pay before the carrier picks up the remainder.

Figure 9.6   Anthem Inc. (formerly WellPoint, Inc.), headquartered in Indianapolis, Indiana, is one of the largest health care vendors in the nation, with more than fifty thousand employees and nearly $2.5 billion in net revenue in fiscal year 2016. (credit: modification of "Company headquarters on Monument Circle in Indianapolis" by Serge Melki/Wikimedia Commons, CC BY 2.0)

Despite the intricacies of this customization, employers have found the group coverage policies they offer to be expensive for them too, more so with each passing year. Full health care coverage is becoming rarer as a standard employment benefit, and it is often available only to those who work full time. California, for example, stipulates that most workers need not be provided with employer health care coverage unless they work at least twenty hours a week.

Rising costs for both employers and employees have combined to leave fewer employees with health care benefits at any given time. Employees with limited or no coverage for themselves and their dependents often cope by cutting back on the medical attention they seek, even when doing so places their health at risk.

Whenever workers must skip medical services due to cost considerations, this places both them and their employers in an ethical quandary, because both typically want workers to be in good health. Furthermore, when employees must deny their dependents appropriate health care, this dilemma is all the more intensified.

To try to reduce the costs to themselves of employee health care insurance coverage, some companies have instituted **wellness programs** to try to ensure that their workforces are as healthy as possible. Some popular wellness program offerings are measures to help smokers quit, workout rooms on work premises or subsidized gym memberships, and revamped vending and cafeteria offerings that provide a range of healthier choices. Some companies even offer employees bonuses or other rewards for quitting smoking or achieving specific fitness goals such as weight loss or miles walked per week. Such employer efforts appear benign at first glance, because these measures truly can produce better health on the part of workers. Still, ethical questions arise as to who the true beneficiaries of such policies are. Is it the employees themselves or the companies for which they work? Furthermore, if such measures were to become compulsory rather than optional, would it still reflect managerial benevolence toward employees? We discuss this in the following paragraphs.

Wellness programs were inspired by *safety programs* first created by U.S. manufacturers in the 1960s. These companies included Chrysler, DuPont, and Steelcase. Safety programs were intended to reduce workplace accidents resulting in injuries and deaths. Over the years, such programs slowly but steadily grew in scope to encompass the general health of employees on the job. As these policies have expanded, they also have fostered some skepticism and resistance: "Wellness programs have attracted their share of criticism. Some critics argue workplace programs cross the line into employees' personal lives."[37] Ann Mirabito, a marketing professor at the Hankamer School of Business at Baylor University agrees there is potential for abuse: "It comes back to the corporate leader. . . . The best companies respect employees' dignity and offer programs that help employees achieve their personal goals."[38]

Employees who exercise, eat healthily, maintain their ideal weight, abstain from smoking, and limit their alcoholic consumption have a much better chance of remaining well than do their peers who undertake none of these activities. The participating employees benefit, of course, and so do their employers, because the health insurance they provide grows cheaper as their workers draw on it less. As Michael Hiltzik, a consumer affairs columnist for the *Los Angeles Times,* noted, "Smoking-cessation, weight-loss and disease-screening programs give workers the impression that their employers really care about their health. Ostensibly they save money too, since a healthy workforce is cheaper to cover and less prone to absenteeism."[39]

Certainly, employers are also serving their own interests by trying to reduce the cost of insuring their workers. But are there any actual disadvantages for employees of such wellness programs that employers might unethically exploit? Hiltzik suggested one: "The dark downside is that 'voluntary' wellness programs also give employers a window into their workers' health profiles that is otherwise an illegal invasion of their privacy."[41] Thus the health histories of workers become more transparent to their bosses, and, Hiltzik and others worry, this previously confidential information could allow managers to act with bias (in employee evaluation and promotion decisions, for instance) under cover of concern about employees' health.

The potential for intrusion into employee privacy through wellness programs is alarming; further, the chance for personal health data to become public as a consequence of enrolling in such programs is concerning. Additionally, what about wellness rules that extend to workers' behavior off the job? Is it ethical for a company to assert the right to restrict the actions of its employees when they are not on the clock? Some, such as researchers Richard J. Herzog, Katie Counts McClain, and Kymberleigh R. Rigard, argue that workers surrender a degree of privacy simply by going onto payroll: "When employees enter the workplace, they forfeit external privacy. For example, BMI [body mass index] can be visually calculated, smokers can be observed, and food intake monitored." They acknowledge, however, that "protecting privacy and enhancing productivity can provide a delicate balance."[40]

LINK TO LEARNING

As noted in previous chapters, we can find out a great deal about the ethical intentions of a company by studying its mission statement, although even the noblest statement is irrelevant if the firm fails to live up to it. Here is Anthem, Inc.'s very simple and direct mission statement (https://openstax.org/l/ 53AnthemMission) as an example from a health care insurer. What impression does this statement leave with you? Would you add or delete anything to it? Why or why not?

The Affordable Care Act

Health care reform on a major scale emerged in the United States with the passage of the Patient Protection and Affordable Care Act, more commonly known as the **Affordable Care Act (ACA)**, in March 2010, during the Obama Administration. The ACA (so-called Obamacare) represents a controversial plan that strikes its opponents as socialist. For its supporters, however, it is the first effective and comprehensive plan to extend affordable health care to the widest segment of the U.S. population. Furthermore, like most new federal policies, it has undergone tweaks and revision each year since becoming law. The ACA is funded by a combination of payments by enrollees and supplemental federal monies earmarked for this task.

The ACA mandates a certain level of preventive care, a choice of physicians and health care facilities, coverage at no extra cost for individuals with preexisting health conditions, protection against the cancellation of coverage solely on the basis of becoming ill, and mental health and substance abuse treatment, all of which must be met by carriers that participate in the plan. The ACA also permits its holders to select from a number of marketplace plans as opposed to the limited number of plans typically offered by any given employer.[42] All in all, it is a far-reaching and complex plan whose full implications for employers and their employees have yet to be appreciated. Preliminary results seem to indicate that employer-provided coverage on a comprehensive scale remains a cheaper alternative for those workers eligible to receive it.[43] Given the general efficiency of group insurance policies provided by U.S. employers, an ethical issue for all managers is whether these policies offer the best care for the greatest number of employees and so should be the responsibility of management to offer whenever it is possible to do so. Current law requires all companies employing fifty or more workers to make insurance available to that part of their workforce that qualifies for such coverage (e.g., by virtue of hours worked). Is it right, however, to leave the employees of smaller firms to their own devices in securing health care? Even if the law does not require it, we hold that an ethical obligation resides with small businesses to do everything in their power to provide this coverage for their employees.

Evidence of the intense debate the act has engendered is the Trump administration's attempts, beginning in January 2017, to repeal the ACA entirely, or at least to dilute significantly many of its provisions. Nearly immediately upon his inauguration, President Trump signed Executive Order 13765 in anticipation of ending the ACA. Also that same month, the American Health Care Act was introduced in the House of Representatives, again with an eye to eliminating or seriously weakening the existing act. Much political debate within both the House and Senate ensued in 2017, with proponents of the ACA seeking to ensure its survival and opponents attempting (but, as of this writing, failing) to repeal it.

The ACA represents the first far-reaching health care coverage to take effect since 1965, after many stalled or otherwise frustrated attempts. Since the passage that year of the Medicare and Medicaid Act, which provided health coverage to retired, elderly, and indigent citizens, many presidential administrations, Democrat and Republican alike, have worked to enlarge health care coverage for different segments of the national population. In addition to expanding eligibility for benefits, the Medicare and Medicaid Act had direct implications for business proprietors and their employees. For one, the act set up new automatic earnings deductions and tax schedules for workers and employers, and employers were made responsible for administering these plans, which help fund the programs' benefits.

The future of the ACA appears to depend on whether a Democrat or Republican sits in the White House and which party controls the Senate and the House in the U.S. Congress. Although legislation does hinge on the political sentiments of the president and the majority party in Congress, what is ethical does not lend itself to a majority vote. So regardless of whether the ACA survives, is revised, or is replaced entirely by new health care legislation, the provision of health care will likely continue to pose ethical implications for U.S. business and the workers who are employed by it.

The ethical debate over universal health care coverage is larger even than business and its employees, of course, but it still carries immense consequences for management and labor irrespective of how the ACA or other legislation fares in the halls of government and the courts. An ethical dilemma for employers is the extent to which they should make health coverage available to their workers at affordable rates, particularly if federal and state government plans provide little or no coverage for residents and the costs of employer-provided coverage continues to climb.

State-Level Experiments with Single-Payer Health Care Plans

Against the backdrop of federal attempts to institute national health care over the past several decades, some individual states in the United States have used their own resources to advance this issue by proposing mandated health care coverage for their citizens. For example, in April 2006, Massachusetts passed An Act Providing Access to Affordable, Quality, Accountable Heath Care, the first significant effort at the state level to ensure near-universal health care coverage.

The Massachusetts act created a state agency, the Commonwealth Health Insurance Connector Authority, to administer the extension of health care coverage to Massachusetts residents. In many ways, it served as the most significant precursor of and guide for the federal ACA, which would follow approximately four years later. By many accounts, the Massachusetts legislation has achieved its purposes with few negative consequences. As Brian C. Mooney, reporting in the *Boston Globe*, put it about five years after the act's passage: "A detailed *Globe* examination [of the implementation of the act] makes it clear that while there have been some stumbles—and some elements of the effort merit a grade of 'incomplete'—the overhaul, after five years, worked as well as or better than expected."[44]

The proposed Healthy California Act (SB 562) is another example. SB 562 passed in the California State Senate in June 2017. However, the Speaker of the Assembly, the lower house of the legislature, blocked a hearing of the bill at that time, and a hearing is necessary for the bill to advance to ratification. A new effort was initiated in February 2018 to permit the bill finally to be considered by the lower house. (Two differences between the California bill and the Massachusetts Act include the number of state residents who would be affected. Massachusetts has a population of about seven million compared to California's nearly forty million. A second distinction is that SB 562 is constitutes a single-payer plan, whereas the Massachusetts Act does not.)

Single-payer health care plans essentially concentrate both the administration of and payment for health care within one entity, such as a state agency. California's effort is a very simple plan on its face but complex in its implementation. Here is how Michael Hiltzik summarized the intent of California Senate Bill 562: "The program would take over responsibility for almost all medical spending in the state, including federal programs such as Medicare and Medicaid, employer-sponsored health plans, and Affordable Care Act plans. It would relieve employers, their workers and buyers in the individual market of premiums, deductibles and copays, paying the costs out of a state fund."[45] The bill would create a large, special program apparatus tentatively entitled Healthy California. It is contentious on many fronts, particularly in that it would create the largest single-payer health insurance plan sponsored by a U.S. state and the scope of the plan would necessitate a huge bureaucracy to administer it as well an infusion of state monies to sustain it. Furthermore, it would extend health care coverage to all residents of the state, including undocumented immigrants.

A specific hurdle to passage of Healthy California is that it would cost anywhere from $370 billion to $400 billion and would require federal waivers so California could assume the administration of Medicare and Medicaid in the state as well as the federal funds currently allotted to it. All these conditions would be enormously difficult and time consuming to meet, even if the federal government were sympathetic to California's attempts to do so. In 2018, that was decidedly not the case.

Is free or inexpensive access to health care a basic human right? If so, which elements within society bear the principal responsibility for providing it: government, business, workers, all these, or other agencies or individuals? This is a foundational ethical question that would invoke different responses on the part of nearly everyone you may ask.

ETHICS ACROSS TIME AND CULTURES

Free Universal Health Care

Except for the United States, the largest advanced economies in the world all provide a heavily subsidized **universal health care system**, that is, a publicly funded system that provides primary health services to all, usually at a nominal fee only and with no exclusions based on income or wealth. Although these systems are not perfect, their continued existence seems assured, regardless of the cultural or political framework of the various countries. A logical question is why the United States would be an outlier on this issue, and whether that might change in the future.

Some answers, as noted in the text, lie in the United States' historical reliance on a mostly private system, with approximately 83 percent of health care expenses provided by the private sector through insurers and employers (in contrast, this percentage in the United Kingdom is 17). A solution that has gained traction in recent years is conversion to a single-payer system. How might this work? One article estimates that the cost of instituting a national, single-payer health care insurance program in the United States would be $32 trillion over ten years. If this estimate is accurate, would it be an exorbitant price tag for such a program, or would it be money well spent in terms of making good health care available to all citizens?[46]

Critical Thinking

- Do you find it appropriate that health care costs be provided by a mix of private versus public sources?
- What advantages might single-payer health care offer over employer-provided coverage, care

provided under the ACA, or privately purchased health insurance?

As a nation, the United States has usually preferred a system predicated on private health care providers and insurers to pay for it. This arrangement has worked best in instituting high-quality care with minimal delays even for elective medical procedures. It has systematically failed, however, in establishing any sort of universal dispensation that is affordable for many citizens.

In the early twenty-first century, the United States is moving ever so slowly and with plenty of hiccups toward some degree of national or state management of health care. Precisely where these efforts will take us may not be clear for the next several years. The political, economic, and ethical dimensions of public management of our health care drive considerable controversy and very little agreement.

🔑 Key Terms

advertising commercial messages urging the purchase of new or improved products or services that reach us in every medium: print, online, digital, television, radio, and outdoor

Affordable Care Act (ACA) the Patient Protection and Affordable Care Act of 2010, often known as the Affordable Care Act or simply "Obamacare," a comprehensive federal health care management system

claim a request to an insurance carrier for monetary compensation for a loss sustained by a customer

copayment a partial charge for covered care negotiated by the provider and the employer and paid by the employee

deductible the annual portion of health care costs the patient must assume before full insurance coverage applies

entrepreneur a business leader willing to take on the risk of starting a new company and offering a product or service in the hope of a profit

entrepreneurial culture the combination of personality and management style with which entrepreneurs shape the initial business practices and ethical environment of their firm

multipayer health care system a means of providing health care in which the patient and others such as an employer and a private health insurance company all pay for the patient's care

premiums the fees customers pay for different forms of coverage

psychological appeal advertising intended to bolster consumers' self-esteem if certain products or services are purchased

redlining a discriminatory (and usually illegal) insurance practice of denying certain coverages in specific neighborhoods or selling them there at a higher price

single-payer health care system a means of providing health care in which state or national tax revenues would pay for citizens' medical care, with the government being the sole payer

subliminal advertising appeals including words and images that reach us at a level below our consciousness

universal health care system a means of providing health care to all, funded through taxes and overseen by the central or federal government

wellness programs employer initiatives that stress healthy eating, exercise, weight management, smoking cessation, and other efforts, to sustain employees' health and reduce health care costs

📄 Summary

9.1 Entrepreneurship and Start-Up Culture

The atmosphere surrounding entrepreneurs and their start-ups can provide a dizzying rush. The opportunities to create a company, be your own boss, make a dramatic impact on business, establish an entrepreneurial culture that will be adopted by others, and possibly become rich in the process certainly all appeal to our human nature. Still, the entrepreneurial lifestyle is challenging, and the success rate for start-ups is exceptionally low. Interpersonal conflicts are prevalent in start-up environments, and entrepreneurs who seek to stay true to their vision and ethical values face a difficult road. At many points, start-up founders have to choose how they most wish to be remembered: for the sake of their business success alone or also for the ethical fashion in which they attained that success and the humane culture they have embedded in their new firm. Sometimes these are mutually exclusive goals, but the most ethical entrepreneurs do their best to ensure that both objectives mesh for themselves and their firms. This lies at the heart of any definition of ethical leadership.

9.2 The Influence of Advertising

The Internet and social media present new canvasses for marketing that possess great power and for which rules and ethical norms are being developed. Psychological appeals and subliminal messaging present their own ethical issues. Discerning consumers currently must rely on their own sensibility to ferret out factual claims for advertised products and bear the burden of shielding those under their charge from the worst manipulative effects of marketing.

9.3 The Insurance Industry

Business owners and individuals are willing to pay insurance premiums in the hope that they will never have to be file a claim for reimbursement on their policy. Because the insurance industry profits only when claims are few and small, there may be a bigger role for government to play in managing disaster insurance through a private/public partnership, such as FEMA currently does to provide flood insurance and the California Earthquake Authority does where potentially disastrous earthquakes may occur. Ethical issues such whether to expand the use of public tax revenues to subsidize these partnerships need to be resolved.

9.4 Ethical Issues in the Provision of Health Care

The United States, unlike countries in Europe, has little tradition of merging the efforts of the state or federal government with that of private employers in the provision of health care. Although the quality of U.S. health care has rarely been challenged, its limited accessibility has posed ethical quandaries for business because many employees necessarily look to their employers for this benefit. The 2010 Affordable Care Act is an ambitious effort to meet the need for health care for all. Individual states have considered, and sometimes enacted, programs of their own to supply universal health care.

Assessment Questions

1. What characteristic is common to most entrepreneurs?
   A.   an advanced degree
   B.   deep management experience
   C.   a driven, highly competitive nature
   D.   a large network of business contacts

2. True or false? Entrepreneurs are usually motivated by the teamwork spirit.

3. Corporate culture comes from _____.
   A.   the commitment of the company's employees
   B.   the founder's idea of what the work environment should be like
   C.   government regulations about labor relations
   D.   the nature of the company's product or service

4. One danger a growing start-up can face is _____.
   A.   encroaching bureaucracy
   B.   lack of good employees
   C.   legal issues
   D.   venture capitalists

5. True or false? The phrase caveat emptor means the seller is principally responsible for purchase decisions, not the buyer.

6. True or false? Children are discerning viewers of television advertising.

7. Psychological appeals succeed when they _____.
    A. make consumers feel better about themselves
    B. let consumers compare themselves to their peers
    C. show consumers how to save money
    D. introduce new products

8. True or false? Even rational adults often fail to cast a suspicious eye to sophisticated ad pitches and end up making frivolous purchases.

9. Should insurance coverage be mandatory for in some U.S. areas, such as hurricane coverage in the Southeast, tornado coverage in the Midwest, earthquake coverage on the Pacific Coast? Why or why not? Should government subsidies help underwrite the cost of this coverage? Why or why not?

10. How prevalent has redlining been in the United States?

11. Premium rates for insurance coverage are based on statistical calculations of the historical rate of incidence of certain kinds of accidents, disasters, and theft, among other calamities against which we insure ourselves. Is this the most equitable way to assign these rates? Why or why not?

12. True or false? Business insurance is a relatively recent offering.

13. True or false? Insurance coverage offers a benefit we hope never to claim.

14. True or false? Employer-sponsored wellness programs have no downsides for employees.

15. True or false? Most European countries have multipayer health care systems like the United States.

16. In the European tradition, the main responsibility for supplying workers with health care lies with which of these groups?
    A. the government and labor unions
    B. labor unions
    C. nonprofit agencies and private companies
    D. individual workers

17. A job setting in which an employee gym and a snack bar featuring healthy foods and beverages were perks would benefit which of these groups?
    A. the owners/managers
    B. the customers or clients of the firm
    C. the employees
    D. all the above

18. Could an ethical case be made for managers dictating that employees adopt or avoid certain lifestyle practices (e.g., legally consuming cannabis) even when they are off the job? What would that argument be? What ethical counterarguments could be made?

 # Endnotes

1.   Patrick Henry, "Why Some Startups Succeed (and Why Most Fail)," *Entrepreneur*, February 18, 2017. https://www.entrepreneur.com/article/

288769.

2. Mike Isaac, "Inside Uber's Aggressive, Unrestrained Workplace Culture," *New York Times*, February 22, 2017. https://www.nytimes.com/2017/02/22/technology/uber-workplace-culture.html; David Swan, "Uber Boss Details New Direction," *The Australian,*" November 17, 2017. In the latter, Dara Khosrowshahi, Kalanick's replacement as CEO at Uber, outlines his attempts to move the company well beyond its poisonous atmosphere, observing that Uber "must adapt to become a great company where every person feels respected and challenged, can contribute in his or her own, and grow as an individual and as a professional."

3. H.H. Gerth and C. Wright Mills, eds., translators, *From Max Weber: Essays in Sociology* (New York: Oxford University Press, 1946), 196.

4. H.H. Gerth and C. Wright Mills, eds., translators, *From Max Weber: Essays in Sociology* (New York: Oxford University Press, 1946), 204.

5. H.H. Gerth and C. Wright Mills, eds., translators, *From Max Weber: Essays in Sociology* (New York: Oxford University Press, 1946), 228.

6. Michael A. Lutzker, "Max Weber and the Analysis of Modern Bureaucratic Organization: Notes Toward a Theory of Appraisal," *American Archivist*, 45, no. 2 (1982): 121.

7. The author worked for many years in the 1980s in human resources at the Walt Disney Company at its corporate site in Burbank, California. A popular training course offered in-house to employees new to professional or managerial roles was "Disney Way," in which the leadership culture of the company was traced back to its founding in 1926 and how that culture had remained greatly intact over the intervening years.

8. Paul Orfalea and Ann Marsh, *Copy This!* (New York: Workman Publishing Company, Inc., 2005), 99.

9. Paul Orfalea and Ann Marsh, *Copy This!* (New York: Workman Publishing Company, Inc., 2005), 105.

10. Paul Orfalea and Ann Marsh, *Copy This!* (New York: Workman Publishing Company, Inc., 2005), 99–115.

11. Kelly Jensen, "The Power a Social Media Policy Plugs into Your Brand," *QSRweb.com*, May 21, 2018. https://www.qsrweb.com/blogs/the-power-a-social-media-policy-plugs-into-your-brand/.

12. The Millennial Generation is defined by different metrics, depending on who the assessor is. For many, though, this generation consists of those who are currently (in 2018) 18 to 35 years of age. See "Global Marketing Analytics Market Analysis, Growth, Trends & Forecast 2018-2023, with an Expected CAGR of 13.17% - ResearchAndMarkets.com," *BusinessWire*. May 18, 2018. https://www.businesswire.com/news/home/20180518005174/en/Global-Marketing-Analytics-Market-Analysis-Growth-Trends.

13. Paul A. Argenti, *Corporate Communication*, 7th ed. (New York: McGraw Hill Education, 2016), 261.

14. Paul A. Argenti, *Corporate Communication*, 7th ed. (New York: McGraw Hill Education, 2016), 265.

15. John Kenneth Galbraith, *The Affluent Society*, 3rd ed. (New York: Houghton Mifflin Press, 1976), 103.

16. Pet Rock. http://www.petrock.com (accessed December 27, 2017).

17. See "Impact of Food Advertising on Children" in *Slogan*, January 31, 2018. The article states, "children less than eight are viewed by many child development researchers as vulnerable to misleading advertising. The intense marketing of high fat, high sugar foods to this age group is termed as exploitative because children do not understand that commercials are designed to sell products and they do not possess the cognitive ability to comprehend or evaluate the advertising." This applies regardless of the medium. https://global.factiva.com/ha/default.aspx#./!?&_suid=15282312820860079699790523521 72.

18. David Aaronovitch, "Subliminal Advertising: Unmasking the Myth or Menace in Hidden Messages," *The Times*, January 19, 2015. https://www.thetimes.co.uk/article/subliminal-advertising-unmasking-the-myth-or-menace-in-hidden-messages-xm3wnn0fnvx.

19. "Marketing Research; Researchers from University of South Carolina Report Recent Findings in Marketing Research (Drink Coca-Cola, Eat Popcorn, and Choose Powerade: Testing the Limits of Subliminal Persuasion)," *Marketing Weekly News,* December 18, 2015.

20. Robert D. Hogue, "Marine Insurance," *International Insurance Monitor*, 52, no. 4 (1999): 25–26; Shawn Moynihan and Caterina Pontoriero, "Inside Lloyd's: Demystifying the Inner Workings of the World's Most Famous Insurance Market," *National Underwriter Property & Casual*, October 6, 2016. Insurance "underwriters"—the name which remains in use today—were those agents who signed their names beneath the language of the contract.

21. "Hurricane Harvey Has Exposed the Inadequacy of Flood Insurance," *The Economist*, September 9, 2017. https://www.economist.com/finance-and-economics/2017/09/09/hurricane-harvey-has-exposed-the-inadequacy-of-flood-insurance.

22. "National Flood Insurance Program," Department of Homeland Security. https://www.fema.gov/national-flood-insurance-program (accessed August 8, 2018).

23. Don Jergler, "Climate Change and the 'Fire Insurance Predicament,'" *Insurance Journal*, February 8, 2018. Jergler quotes comments columnist Thomas Elias made in late January 2018 in the *San Diego Tribune*.

24. "What's on the Horizon for the Insurance Industry?" *Mondaq Business Briefing*, August 10, 2017. https://www.highbeam.com/doc/1G1-500231558.html.

25. As examples of this arrangement, consider Petrobras, the Brazilian oil giant that was founded in 1953 and has always featured some mix of government and private ownership. Currently, government direct and indirect ownership constitutes about 65 percent, with private investment making up the remaining 35 percent. Another instance is Malaysia Airlines, founded in the late-1940s, and for most of that time, it also has been held by some combination of government and private ownership.

26. "Insurance Carriers," Dun & Bradstreet. http://crmwebdev.mykonicaminolta.com/industryinfo/industryinfo.html?id=1901 (accessed August 7, 2018).

27. "Insurance Carriers," Dun & Bradstreet. http://crmwebdev.mykonicaminolta.com/industryinfo/industryinfo.html?id=1901 (accessed August 7, 2018).

28. Julia Angwin, et al., "Minority Neighborhoods Pay Higher Car Insurance Premiums Than White Areas with the Same Risk," *ProPublica Investigative Reporting*, April 5, 2017.

29. Julia Angwin, et al., "Minority Neighborhoods Pay Higher Car Insurance Premiums Than White Areas with the Same Risk," *ProPublica Investigative Reporting*, April 5, 2017.

30. "U.S. Can Learn from Other Nations' Health Care Systems," Harvard T.H. Chan School of Public Health. https://www.hsph.harvard.edu/news/hsph-in-the-news/health-care-system-aca (accessed August 8, 2018).

31. Eric C. Schneider, et al., "Mirror, Mirror 2017: International Comparison Reflects Flaws and Opportunities for Better U.S. Health Care," *The Commonwealth Fund*. July 2017. https://interactives.commonwealthfund.org/2017/july/mirror-mirror/

32. William B. Schultz, "Maryland's Price-Gouging Law Targets the Wrong Prescription Drugs," *Washington Post*, August 4, 2017.

33. John E. Murray, *Origins of American Health Insurance: A History of Industrial Sickness Funds* (New Haven: Yale University Press, 2007), xi.

34. John E. Murray, *Origins of American Health Insurance: A History of Industrial Sickness Funds* (New Haven: Yale University Press, 2007), 3.

35. A specific organization that serves as an example of this is the Knights of Columbus, chartered in New Haven, Connecticut, in 1882 as a "fraternal benefit society" of Roman Catholic workers (principally Irish and Italian Americans) who found themselves unable to qualify for other forms of coverage, because of their ethnic identities. In this earlier era, typically featuring only fathers as breadwinners, the Knights were formed most importantly to provide income for families whose husbands and fathers had experienced illness or injury or death on the job and so were unable to provide for their families. See the society's website, http://www.kofc.org/ (accessed August 8, 2018).

36. John E. Murray, *Origins of American Health Insurance: A History of Industrial Sickness Funds* (New Haven: Yale University Press, 2007), 17, 30–31.

37. Julie Carlson, "The Evolution of Workplace Wellness Programs," *Baylor Business Review* (Fall 2014): 21.

38. Julie Carlson, "The Evolution of Workplace Wellness Programs," *Baylor Business Review* (Fall 2014): 23.

39. Michael Hiltzik, "The Dark Side of 'Voluntary' Worker Wellness Programs," *Los Angeles Times*, December 27, 2017.

40. Richard J. Herzog, Katie Counts McClain, and Kymberleigh R. Rigard, "Governmentality, Biopolitical Control, and a Value Pluralist Perspective of Wellness Programs: Creating Utopian Employees," *Administrative Theory & Praxis* 38 (2016): 37–51. To appreciate the researchers' full embrace of wellness programs, note their assertion in the article's conclusion: "The creation of utopian employees, as discussed in this article, is better achieved by considering value pluralism when embracing the healthism paradigm and avoiding workplace dystopias." None of us wishes to work in a "dystopian" workplace, but are we ready to become "utopian employees"?

41. Michael Hiltzik, "The Dark Side of 'Voluntary' Worker Wellness Programs," *Los Angeles Times*, December 27, 2017.

42. "Patient Protection and Affordable Care Act," Healthcare.gov. https://www.healthcare.gov/glossary/patient-protection-and-affordable-care-act/ (accessed August 8, 2018).

43. Kris B. Mamula, "Affordable Care Act Rates in Pa. Will Rise, but Lower Than Expected," *Pittsburgh Post-Gazette*, June 6, 2018. Mamula's article is about insurer requests for an increase in their rates for coverage under the ACA in 2019 and the actual increase in these same rates for 2018 in three states: New York, Pennsylvania, and Washington. The prediction was that rates would increase approximately 5 percent in Pennsylvania for 2019 (as opposed to nearly 31 percent in 2018), more than 20 percent in New York, and nearly 20 percent in Washington. Mamula also observed that the rate of Pennsylvanians without any form of health insurance fell to a record low rate of 5.6 percent in 2018.

44. Brian C. Mooney, "'RomneyCare'—A Revolution That Basically Worked," *Boston Globe*, June 26, 2011; Massachusetts Health Connector. http://www.mahealthconnector.org.

45. Michael Hiltzik, "Complexities of Single-Payer Care," *Los Angeles Times*, February 11, 2018.

46. Kim Soffen, "Single-Payer Would Drastically Change Health Care in America. Here's How It Works," *Washington Post*, October 17, 2017.

Ethical managers will understand new business models and the new economies being driven by technological advances and the rise of robotics and artificial intelligence in the workplace. (credit: modification of "hand robot human divine spark" by "geralt"/Pixabay, CC0)

Chapter Outline

10.1 More Telecommuting or Less?

10.2 Workplace Campuses

10.3 Alternatives to Traditional Patterns of Work

10.4 Robotics, Artificial Intelligence, and the Workplace of the Future

Introduction

Beginning in the eighteenth century, in much of the Western world, the Industrial Revolution transformed the nature of work as industry displaced agriculture as the main driver of the economy and machines took over manual labor. Continuing technological changes have further altered the way people work and even the time and place where they do so. Growing numbers of people now spend some of their time working at home. Are they more productive without the distractions of the office or less productive without constant monitoring by managers? Some major companies like Apple, Amazon, Facebook, and Microsoft have constructed elaborate workplace campuses, offering unprecedented levels of amenities and even employee housing. Do these campuses facilitate the balancing of work and life, or do they blur the distinction and tie workers to their jobs instead?

Job sharing and flexible work schedules have emerged as alternatives to traditional patterns of work. These practices permit some workers to more easily fulfill work and life responsibilities. But does job sharing reflect employers' efforts to respond to workers' preferences or is it a move to reduce costs?

How will you prepare employees for the impact of robots at work (Figure 10.1) or manage the outsourcing of tasks to contractors in the gig economy? These challenges to traditional employment settings carry ethical implications for all stakeholders, including employers, employees, suppliers, customers, and clients.

10.1 | More Telecommuting or Less?

Learning Objectives

By the end of this section, you will be able to:

- Identify the benefits of permitting employees to work from home
- Explain the drawbacks of telecommuting for the business and for employees
- Discuss the ethical dilemmas related to telecommuting and some of the solutions

What if your business wanted to expand its local operations from six employees to ten but did not have the office space to add more workers? Today's businesses have a toolkit of technical solutions to set up working relationships with employees far and wide through voice, computer, video connections, and offsite work-sharing spaces. Coworkers can share files on a remote network server or on the cloud, and managers can use nontraditional methods to monitor activity and performance. Companies like General Assembly, WeWork, and Workbar are leasing access to communal spaces equipped for the business needs of remote workers. Telecommuting is therefore easier to implement than ever. But what exactly are the benefits and drawbacks of telecommuting, and what ethical issues does it raise?

Telecommuting and Its Advantages

The term **telecommuting** emerged in the 1970s to describe the practice of working at a specific location, whether the employee's home or an alternate office, to reduce commuting time to a centrally located office space or store. "Telework" was greatly facilitated by new telecommunications technology, including the Internet, e-mail, and mobile phones. Today, telecommuting means any mode of working at a remote location (home or other space) by virtue of an electronic connection and/or telephone and encompasses a variety of employment types, from gig assignments to part-time contract work to traditional full-time employment.

The most recent Census data reveal that almost four million U.S. employees skip the commute for at least part of each week, and according to a 2012 poll, worldwide, one in five workers telecommutes frequently, with approximately 10 percent working from home every day.[1] Figure 10.2 depicts the growth in telecommuting in the United States, China, India, France, Germany, and the United Kingdom. Clearly, employers are embracing telecommuting as a tool for flexibility, on a scale from occasional use to full-time implementation.[2]

Percentage of Employers Offering Telework Options

Source: Hess, Ken. "Death of the Office and Rise of the Telecommuter." Consumerization: BYOD. ZD Net. June 2, 2014. (Some data from Intuit.)

Figure 10.2   As more employers provide the opportunity for telework, fewer people are commuting to a corporate office every day. (attribution: Copyright Rice University, OpenStax, under CC BY 4.0 license)

Employees can connect to networked company computers from home and use work-enhancing tools on their laptops, tablets, and smartphones to make real-time connections by voice, text, or video with inexpensive or free applications (or "apps") like FaceTime and Skype. Other software solutions, like GoToMeeting or WebEx, make setting up and even recording a synchronous meeting with sound and video possible for even the smallest companies at fairly low cost. The communication and productivity tools that facilitate telecommuting can only grow in number and sophistication. Virtual reality tools like Microsoft's Mixed Reality allow a worker in one location to communicate with the holograph of another person in real time. For example, this technology could enable a job interview with a remote candidate. Of course, the use of technology brings with it the need to ensure information security and protection against hacking, including guaranteeing the authenticity of the persons engaging via this technology.

Employers allow employees to telecommute for a variety of reasons. First, it is a powerful recruiting tool for people who want to balance their work and personal lives. It allows employees to work a more flexible schedule to care for children or older relatives while maintaining a career and earning income.[3] Individuals with ability challenges also prefer the flexibility that telecommuting affords them.[4]

Telecommuting also reduces the hours that employees spend traveling to and from the job and can help keep cars off the road. Fewer workers commuting equals less crowding on public transportation.[5] Fewer cars mean less air pollution as well. The average U.S. employee (who commutes 30 miles and 60 minutes per day) will save more than $1000 on gas per year by telecommuting (along with associated costs of parking and vehicle upkeep and insurance).[6] Remote workers can continue to do their jobs despite weather conditions that impede travel. They are not exposed to sick coworkers' germs and may take fewer sick days (which sometimes translates to fewer sick days company-wide). Remote employees are also seldom late for work or early to leave when their workday starts at home.

More broadly, there is a good deal of evidence suggesting that telecommuting has beneficial effects on worker productivity. For example, a call-center study reported in the *Harvard Business Review* found that telecommuting employees made 13.5 percent more calls, resigned their positions at only half the usual rate, and had much higher job satisfaction compared with employees who did not telecommute.[7] The Colorado Department of Transportation, in a study of telecommuting productivity for a branch that issued permits, found 48 percent faster turnaround times for issuing permits and 5 percent more calls for telecommuters.[8] Furthermore, studies of JD Edwards teleworkers found them to be 20 to 25 percent more productive than their office colleagues; American Express employees who worked from home were 43 percent more productive than workers in the office.[9] With none of the distractions of a traditional office setting, like water-cooler gossip and long lunches, and with the happier attitude, workers tend to enjoy when they have control over their work lives. Telecommuting facilitates increased efficiency and productivity and also typically results in higher retention of workers, thereby reducing recruiting and training costs for firms.

Studies have shown that a person who commutes for an hour a day experiences added stress, anxiety, social isolation, and possibly depression.[10] Perhaps that is why companies that implement telecommuting experience less absenteeism overall.[11] It may also be easier to collaborate when not sharing a limited amount of space (such as in a cubicle forest), and people may be more willing to share resources with one another when the total number of workers present at the facility is reduced. Another point is that there may be less chatting and gossip among remote workers who are not in daily contact with each other or their colleagues.

Employers may be attracted to telecommuting for other reasons. Having remote employees can reduce office-space costs.[12] In fact, a company can consider expanding even when there is no available real estate or capital to enlarge or improve the physical facilities. Companies that hire remote employees can also widen their pool of potential applicants.[13] They can choose recruits with better job skills than the local population could provide and expand their sales and marketing territory by hiring employees based in a new area.

Finally, there are many external environmental benefits of telecommuting. We have seen that a business that reduces total office space also reduces its impact on the environment.[14] Remote workers would increase their individual consumption of utilities while working at home, but chances are that their home's energy consumption partially continues during the time spent at a traditional job as well (Figure 10.3).

Employee Benefits
• Saves time
• Reduces spending on gas
• Decreases stress
• Improves work-life balance

Other Benefits
• Reduces greenhouse emissions
• Decreases dependence on oil imports
• Aligns with future trending (Bring Your Own Device, Software as a Service)

Employer Benefits
• Reduces spending on real estate, utilities, overhead
• Increases employee productivity

Figure 10.3   Telecommuting is becoming more common around the world. The phenomenon stands to benefit remote workers and also their employers. (credit photograph: Cory Zanker/Flickr, CC BY 4.0; figure attribution: Copyright Rice University, OpenStax, under CC BY 4.0 license)

The Drawbacks of Telecommuting

In 2013, Yahoo's then–chief executive officer (CEO), Marissa Mayer, ended the company's work-at-home policy, contending that the change would boost communication and collaboration by bringing people back to the office to work with their colleagues face to face.[15] IBM, Aetna, and Bank of America followed her lead, citing a greater need for collaborative communication to compete with smaller firms.[16] A backlash in the media followed this announcement, because working at home is popular among Yahoo employees. Yahoo has since shown greater flexibility in allowing some employees to once again work at home.[17] But recent research does reveal that employees collaborate more creatively when they meet to discuss projects face to face. This finding has important implications for firms dependent on research and development for their future growth. In fact, Steve Jobs designed the Pixar facility to increase the likelihood of conversations that would promote idea generation.[18]

Corporate culture is not easy to convey over distance. The remote worker might have developed certain working habits at a different company with a different corporate culture (sometimes in another country). It can be challenging to help employees adapt to the culture of a new company when they work remotely.[19]

It is also more difficult for employers to monitor some kinds of work-related progress when an employee is working remotely. The likelihood of miscommunication increases when everything must be transmitted electronically or virtually.[20] A manager cannot "manage by walking around" when the worker is remote. There are no incidental opportunities to witness a worker interacting with a client or customer.[21] Workers may also be more hesitant to ask for direction on a project. Some managers worry that employees will slack off if there is no one there to watch them.[22]

The remote worker may have qualms about privacy when his or her personal life inevitably intersects with the workday (as when a family member walks into the room or the dog barks during a conference call).[23] Children may be confused when it seems like their parent is home but is not available for meals or play or homework help. It may be difficult for remote workers to maintain a work-life balance when their home becomes their office (especially if their hours are flexible). Workers may have to set aside living space for a home office and spend money to buy computing equipment, a desk, and other supplies.

Furthermore, it is difficult for an on-site technology team to provide technical assistance or secure data at the level the company may require when people are working at home. Moreover, when the definition of the workplace begins to blur, who is responsible for injuries that occur on the job at home? The employer is unable to exercise the same control over safety measures that holds in a traditional workplace.[24]

There may also be productivity concerns. Some remote workers will rise to the challenge of motivating themselves to work diligently. In fact, studies have shown that some remote workers are more productive than their traditional counterparts.[25] But it is not easy to sort potential employees into workers and procrastinators without some period of trial and error, which may be costly.

Not all fields are equally suited to telecommuting. Some jobs require consistent in-person contact with clients or customers, such as counseling, physical therapy, and medicine.[26] Some industries need the highest computer security, such as banking and finance. Other work settings, such as law enforcement, have increased needs for building security that would make working remotely an unsafe alternative for employees.[27]

The biggest drawback of telecommuting for the individual employee is the bias that studies reveal in employer attitudes. Most managers, after all, attained their status in a traditional job. When some employees telecommute and others do not, those who are in the physical presence of the employer every day can more easily make an impression (good or bad) simply by interacting with their manager. There is also some indication that employees who opt for a nontraditional work arrangement may be penalized if they are perceived as lazy or less dedicated than those who maintain traditional work hours. Employers might have a stronger recollection of the work produced by the employee they see regularly than they do of the work a remote employee is submitting online. Therefore, promotions and important projects may go to employees who are more visible. The remote employee might eventually be left without equal footing in the push for increased pay and status.

The Ethical Challenges of Telecommuting

Ethical employers must juggle the potential ethical challenges of managing remote employees, including developing trust in remote workers, encouraging trust among project team members when some are working remotely, keeping equity in mind when reviewing the performance of remote and in-office staff, and deciding which employees get to work remotely. Supervisors also must guard against abuse of the remote-work opportunity, maintain the security of the remote employee's work-related data, foster a level of collaboration that is vital to product development, and protect the remote worker's safety.[28] How can managers meet these challenges?

Although it is easy to consider allowing telecommuting for those who simply ask, managers should instead categorize jobs (not people) by their suitability for remote work. Best Buy recently announced it would modify its work-from-home policy for employees in its corporate office, changing it from a perquisite (or "perk") of employment to one granted by management on a case-by-case basis and mindful of the circumstances of individual workers.[29]

Managers should also carefully set up a framework of policies to govern at-home work and ensure fairness. For example, there could be a standard for how much time each person should spend in the office. The Massachusetts Institute of Technology created a remote pilot project in its Executive Education Program.[30] Employees were encouraged to work remotely two or three days each week and to be present in the office each Wednesday. After six months of the pilot program, 100 percent of the employees recommended its continuation.

LINK TO LEARNING

Watch this video tracing some of the history of workplaces and speculating about innovations in the future, many of which relate to telecommuting (https://openstax.org/l/53telecommute) to lean more. Keep a list of the telecommuting-specific innovations and identify any ethical concerns related to them.

Managers should set clear expectations for remote workers, such as maintaining professionalism while working and accomplishing a certain volume of work or number of tasks by a certain time. Those who meet these goals should be rewarded. In the interests of fairness and equity, neither expectations nor rewards should differ from those established for in-house workers.

The ethical employer communicates trust in his or her employees when implementing telecommuting. That trust is based on respect for the employee's motivation and the recognition that the employee has needs that are important in establishing work-life balance.[31] Perhaps the employer's vote of confidence in the employee's ability to work well remotely is the reason that productivity tends to increase in successful telecommuting programs. [32] The Figure 10.4 caption lists some of the best practices of successful telecommuting programs.

Figure 10.4   Telecommuting is more likely to succeed when remote employees are provided with the right technology, are empowered by inclusion in the corporate culture, and interact with colleagues in a manner that clearly expresses their expectations, values, and trust. (credit: modification of "daily bw: hanging out with my coworkers" by Mike McCune/Flickr, CC BY 2.0)

It would be unethical to place workers without assistance in a new situation in which they can easily fail. Telecommuting workers must be trained in time-management skills so they can maintain their productivity in an environment that may have more or different distractions than a traditional workplace and may make different demands on their time. Training should also strengthen communication skills, such as responding to messages promptly, that help ensure success in a remote setting. To help guard against the risk that telecommuting employees will be unfairly considered "out of sight, out of mind," the ethical company will adopt written expectations about timely communication in both directions. For instance, it should ensure that managers' lines of communication are as open to their remote employees as they are to those who can drop by their desk or office to chat.

Finally, many firms with successful telecommuting programs create a social network among employees. They sponsor online social occasions to help employees bond even though they are not in the same place. Workers can then find a way to have some virtual fun, despite the distance that might separate them.[33]

10.2 | Workplace Campuses

Learning Objectives

By the end of this section, you will be able to:

- Compare the workplaces of yesterday, today, and the future
- Describe the benefits and potential drawbacks of workplace campuses
- Identify ethical challenges in the development of workplace campuses

The physical workplace is changing. Most companies still inhabit traditional office spaces in which managers and employees each have an allotted space, whether an office, a cubicle, or just a desk. However, a growing number are redesigning their spaces with fewer separate offices, substituting flexible or shareable work stations built around communal space.[34] The idea is that such "open plan" environments allow for more collaboration and brainstorming because employees are no longer walled off from one another. Shared, multipurpose spaces open to all allow people to gather informally throughout the day. In effect, then, these changes are aimed to augment productivity.

In another trend, companies like Apple, Microsoft, Facebook, Amazon, and Alphabet (which owns Google) are developing expansive campus-like facilities that offer generous on-site amenities like recreation centers, fine dining, parks, walking and biking paths, climbing walls, free snacks, child-care facilities, basketball courts, haircuts and massages, and laundry, dry-cleaning, and car wash operations, in airy spaces often powered by renewable energy sources (Figure 10.5).[35] Facebook and Alphabet/Google have plans for building mega-corporate campuses that also include housing. Facebook plans to reserve 15 percent of its housing units for low-income neighbors, but, in both cases, it is anticipated that most residents of these campuses will be employees.[36] Presumably, workers who do not have to commute to and from work every day will be happier and more productive.

Figure 10.5   This herb garden at the Googleplex, Google's headquarters, is an outdoor area where workers can sit and contemplate nature. The garden is part of a farm-to-table program to teach Googlers about how their food is grown. (credit: "Googleplex" by Pamela Carls/Flickr, CC BY 2.0)

New workplace arrangements like these effectively serve as fringe benefits for employees that presumably offer the flexibility and work-life balance promised by corporate recruiters. Yet, looking from a different angle, we might consider the motivations behind these complexes to be less than altruistic, because such campuses encourage workers to stay in the office far longer than they might otherwise. Is this the case? Furthermore, if so, do they result in the same or higher levels of productivity? What ethical challenges do they present for the employer and the employee?

Workplace Campuses and Historical Precedents

Traditional workspaces are designed to allow each person to get the maximum amount of work completed each day, spending most of the time alone in a fairly utilitarian environment with minimal distractions. The size and location of the offices indicate status (corner offices are prized), and lunchrooms or cafeterias and water coolers provide the only place for brief social encounters.

State-of-the-art workplaces today, however, incorporate technology and encourage collaboration. Ergonomic furniture is available for comfort, and laptops and tablets allow workers to move around the facility as desktop computers could not. In fact, workers in the new flexible workplace spend less than 50 percent of their time at a desk.[37] Moreover, as we discussed in the previous section, many enjoy the flexibility of telecommuting as needed. Furthermore, in open-plan spaces, all work positions locations are alike; status is not signaled by location or size.

LINK TO LEARNING

Watch this promotional video for one technology company whose employees work in a campus-like setting (https://openstax.org/l/53CompanyCampus) to learn about some of the benefits.

As early as the 1960s, large companies like Bell Labs built suburban compounds for their corporate headquarters, but they were a far cry from the campus settings of Apple and Google today. Bell Labs' design, for example, was a series of laboratories and office buildings grouped together, with a functional cafeteria.

Workplace campuses are also modeled on university campuses that provide a relatively complete work and living environment for students. As noted, Facebook and Google are building apartments near their corporate campuses. Facebook's new project, named Willow Village, is near Menlo Park, California, and will include some fifteen hundred units. Employees who lease an apartment there will be eligible for a company bonus.[38] The future workplace campuses and mega-corporate campuses with housing bear a superficial resemblance to nineteenth- and early twentieth-century "company towns," which existed around the world.

In a company town, the stores, entertainment venues, and housing were all owned by the same company, which also employed everyone in a local factory or mine.[39] The remote locations of factories sometimes made it necessary for such employers to provide workers with housing and a means to acquire the necessities of life, but those who lived and worked in the company town paid for all purchases from their wages, which, of course, went straight back to the employer. The owners and builders of company towns, like George Pullman or Henry Ford, were often idealists who envisioned creating a social utopia.[40] But the towns and their owners could also be paternalistic and self-serving. Indeed, company towns created what is called a monopsony in the labor market, where there is only a single buyer, and the economic analysis of monopsony shows that with the lack of competition for labor, wages of workers are suppressed. That is, "a monopsonist in the labor market can leverage its market power. Because it is the only firm hiring, it can pay its workers less."[41]

Company towns began to disappear when cars became affordable and employees could drive to work. However, all that driving lengthened some workdays and disrupted the balance people enjoyed between working hours and personal time. Like telecommuting, corporate villages are one approach to cut down drive time. However, critics of Facebook's Willow Village are calling the property "Zucktown" and wondering whether the development will further blur the work-life balance for employees of Mark Zuckerberg's social media company.

CASES FROM THE REAL WORLD

Acuity's Workplace Campus

Employees at Acuity, an insurance provider in Sheboygan, Wisconsin, enjoy amenities beyond the imagining of the average U.S. worker. The company offers flexible workdays, on-site leadership training, tuition reimbursement for continuing education, and company scholarships. Its $130 million campus also provides an on-site fitness center complete with a climbing wall, a garden, and a cafeteria serving nutritious meals. Employees are offered the services of an on-site massage therapist, and there are on-site banking and dry-cleaning services.

The campus was designed to be a showpiece at the entrance to the town of Sheboygan. In fact, it features a working Ferris wheel and a theater-in-the-round that seats two thousand, which the company makes available for community events and town hall meetings.

Critical Thinking

- What do you think about a company that would build a multimillion-dollar workplace campus that also serves as a center for community events?
- What does the investment communicate about the company's core values and stakeholder focus?
- Should company facilities be only for employees?

The Pursuit of Work-Life Balance

Twenty-five percent of U.S. employees in multiple industries were recently surveyed and reported feeling "super stressed" as they juggled work and home responsibilities.[42] Daily stress from trying to maintain work-life balance can produce health effects like reduced immunity and inadequate sleep. Stressed workers are also less productive in the workplace.

Efforts to offer employees an ever-widening array of amenities appear to be an effort by employers to create work-life balance and make their companies more desirable as places of employment. The idea is that life is simpler if food is readily available and free at work, if a doctor's office or hair salon is just down the hall, and if home is right on campus.

Some research shows that millennials believe integrating work and leisure in some combination fosters work-life balance.[43] They may see less need to have clear boundaries between their work world and their home life as technology pushes them to be connected in so many ways that once did not exist but now seem inescapable (e.g., an employee of a global firm that conducts business around the clock may never be truly separated from the office due to connectivity provided by mobile devices).

Have employers then crossed a line with these perks? Have they created an expectation that the employee who works on a corporate campus where all needed services are provided will, in turn, be accessible for long hours of work on a regular basis? Are the amenities really velvet handcuffs that tie employees to work? Living right next to work clearly will reduce commuting time, and via this path, it may promote work-life balance. But the expectation that long hours should be routine just because they are possible will hamper, rather than facilitate, the quest for work-life balance. Furthermore, to the extent that mega-corporate campuses do tie workers to their jobs, reduced worker mobility means that labor markets will be less able to adjust to changing conditions.

The Ethical Challenges of Workplace Campuses

It is hard to imagine that anyone could find fault with a job that came with all the amenities of a campus-like environment. However, the all-encompassing aspect of these workplaces means a manager's job description greatly expands to include small-city management functions. As the April 2018 shooting of employees at YouTube's headquarters suggests, corporate campuses may have a greater need for security, with duties that dovetail those of the city police. Growth of the compound will challenge managers to comply with city planning and zoning regulations. How should these villages within a city contribute to the municipal services they need for the population they draw? Should the city be able to require a greater tax contribution from mega-corporate campus developers that equals the load they add to the city's fiscal responsibilities?

A New Slice of the Apple?

In 2011, Steve Jobs, founder of Apple, appeared before the Cupertino City Council to present his proposal for a new Apple headquarters on the outskirts of the city. The project, which was approved, is known as the "Ring." It encompasses 2.8 million square feet and cost some $5 billion to construct. Jobs planned the innovative facility to inspire engineers and programmers charged with creating new Apple devices and tools (Figure 10.6). Its shape is meant to allow them to collaborate while maintaining a connection to nature. Jobs (who died in 2011) also hoped the building would enable Apple to better safeguard its secrets, because it is large enough to house so many employees and data systems in one secure location. The building is sustainable due to solar panels that provide all its energy needs, and the campus includes nine thousand drought-resistant trees planted to withstand a changing climate. Parking is limited by design to encourage employees to use public transportation and share rides.[44]

Figure 10.6 This likeness of the Apple Ring provides a sense of the scale of the building, which boasts a four-story cafeteria. (attribution: Copyright Rice University, OpenStax, under CC BY 4.0 license)

Critics, however, say the Ring's outer-city location and inward-looking shape, giving many in it a view of only the other side of the building, discourage employees from being a part of Cupertino's life.[45] Others argue that remodeling an existing building in the heart of the city would have done more for Cupertino's local economy. Ninety percent of Ring workers are not local; they commute to their jobs, and so they might not have made an impact on the city even if Apple had made a different decision. Shareholders also objected to the facility because of its cost, which may have reduced Apple's ability to issue more corporate dividends.[46] However, Jobs' approach to the Apple campus is unquestionably part of a growing trend to create company compounds.

Critical Thinking

- Should a company build in the inner city to integrate its workforce with the community and reduce the traffic consequences of adding its workforce to the local population?

- Is it better for a company to support local restaurants or build its own restaurant facilities?
- Is it ethical for a company to spend so much on building a corporate facility instead of increasing shareholder dividends?
- Should there be zoning laws regarding corporate campuses?

10.3 Alternatives to Traditional Patterns of Work

Learning Objectives

By the end of this section, you will be able to:

- Explain the benefits, drawbacks, and ethical issues of job sharing and flextime
- Describe the business models that have emerged in the new millennium
- Discuss the ethical challenges businesses face in the gig economy

New ideas about the way we work and for how long, as well as the business models we use, are challenging many traditional business strategies. Job sharing and flexible hours (or flextime), the access or sharing economy, and the rise of gig workers all force us to evaluate how they affect management, employees, and customers alike. Although new business models provide increased autonomy and flexibility, they have also led to the rise of what some call the new *precariat*.[47] The precariat, for "precarious proletariat," is a new social class of people whose work offers little predictability or security. The existence of such a class raises ethical dilemmas for business managers, who may be tempted to substitute gig workers, to whom benefits like health insurance are ordinarily not provided, for regular employees entitled to costly benefits.[48]

Job Sharing and Flextime

In **job sharing**, two or more employees perform the work of a full-time position, each taking part of the total workload for the job. For example, one job-sharing employee might work three eight-hour shifts a week and the other would take two such shifts at the same job. In some ways, job sharing is simply another name for part-time work. The two people need not work equal numbers of hours, but they perform a single job, doing the same tasks and shouldering the same responsibilities. Unlike nurses, who work shifts but each has their own job, job sharers work one job between them.

Most people in the United States seek a full-time job of thirty-five hours a week or more, usually because they want the income and benefits (such as health insurance) that often come with such a job. But some are willing to forego full-time work because they need or want to care for children or an elderly or ailing family member, pursue their education, run a business on the side, or volunteer. Allowing two people to share a job is an option that can lead to enhanced work-life balance for both individuals. A job-sharing parent can work weekends only, for example, saving on daycare costs during the week.

Many job sharers report less stress and an increased ability to produce high-quality work. Studies have shown that many accomplish more in a shorter workweek due to higher morale.[49] Typically there is less absenteeism when the team can plan around the appointments and vacations of each individual.[50] Job sharing may also reduce the absenteeism of employees with children by providing increased flexibility to cover family emergencies or obligations. There is even a synergistic effect when two people bring their insights to problems that one person would usually face alone.[51]

Employers find that hiring two individuals to fill one job also opens the door to recruiting new talent. Job sharing might allow an employer to retain a knowledgeable associate who is ready to cut back work hours. Furthermore, an employee who is leaving or retiring can share the job for a time to train a replacement.

Many job sharers apply for jobs as a team. Those who have successfully shared a job advocate for setting clear performance expectations and progress checkpoints. Two employees might share an e-mail account and brief each other daily on their work.[52] Specific examples include translators of legal documents at an international law firm—one translator takes the morning shift; the other, the afternoon. Or technical writers at an engineering firm—one might work Monday through Wednesday noon; the other, Wednesday afternoon through Friday. This scenario works when common documents are being written or translated. If the job sharers are equally competent, work can be passed off to one another at specific intervals.

Other aspects of job sharing actually benefit employers, but not necessarily employees. Replacing a full-time position with two or more part-time employees may allow an employer to avoid paying for the benefits to which a full-time employee would be entitled, such as health insurance mandated by the Affordable Care Act, and sometimes optional benefits as well. The number of involuntary part-time workers varies over the course of the business cycle: In 2009, as a consequence of the Great Recession, U.S. Department of Labor statistics put the number of involuntary part-time workers at more than nine million; in mid-2018, that number was just below five million.[53]

There are some purely business drawbacks to job sharing. First, the practice does not work in all fields. Second, some work can suffer because of the extra time, and sometimes expense, necessary for coordination between job-sharing partners, especially if neither is formally in charge.[54] Job-sharing arrangements also presuppose that the two people are going to work together collaboratively, but competitive instincts could lead one partner to withhold information or even sabotage the project. Another drawback is the "two Mondays effect"—the potential productivity loss due to the time it takes each partner to get up to speed on the first day back.[55] Finally, some managers do not want the added responsibility of managing two people instead of one.

LINK TO LEARNING

Job sharing has many advantages for employees and employers alike. Watch this video about some of the benefits of job sharing (https://openstax.org/l/53JobShare) to learn more.

The ethical question raised by job sharing boils down to whether the employer is hiring job sharers to improve productivity and meet employee preferences, or hiring part-time workers to improve profitability at the employees' expense. The ethical employer hires employees to best serve the needs of the customer and the company while respecting the needs of each employee. The first step in ethically managing a job-sharing partnership is to pick the right job to share. Data-entry jobs and those that require less supervision and coordination between partners are more easily managed. Then, with both employees present, the manager should spend some time creating a shared written agreement about procedures to follow and responsibilities to accept.[56] Follow-up is important to be sure job sharers are working cooperatively and meeting their goals.

WHAT WOULD YOU DO?

Staffing Trade-offs

You are a department head in a mid-sized clothing manufacturing firm in a time of high unemployment. Your manager is always worrying about the bottom line and cash flow. She has asked you, as marketing employees retire or leave, to split a number of their positions into part-time jobs that do not require the company to offer benefits like health insurance. Your boss says many job applicants want this kind of employment. You are not so sure. You are reluctant to replace jobs offering good benefits with jobs that offer none, and you are seeking powerful arguments with which to persuade your boss to abandon the plan.

Critical Thinking

- What points support the job-sharing plan? How would it benefit the company? The employees?
- What negative effects might it have on the company and the employees?
- Is job sharing better for some positions in a department than for others?
- Do you have any concerns about potential employment discrimination if this plan is implemented? If so, what would they be?
- Is creating job-sharing positions the right thing for the company/customers/employees to do in this situation?

The practice of offering flexible hours, or **flextime**, lets employees choose their own start and finish time each day, arriving and leaving earlier or later than the normal 9-to-5 workday. Parents benefit particularly because they are better able to schedule their work around their children's lives. Women are the predominant users of this family-friendly work policy.[57]

Flextime was a starting place for creative new approaches to work. Teams now trade shifts to accommodate members' needs for time off. Some companies allow a compressed work week that caters to the efficient employee who can get a week's work done in less than forty hours. In some professions, such as accounting, employees might be allowed a reduced schedule during the off season.[58]

All these variations allow employers to recruit a more diverse workforce. No longer is it necessary that someone be free of weekday responsibilities to have full-time work and gainful employment. Flextime also benefits clients and customers because companies can extend their hours of operation when workers are willing to cover flexible shifts.[59]

Ethical employers base the decision to allow flextime on a clear and well-written policy that relies on objective job-related criteria. Without an objective policy, employees could claim discrimination if all were not eligible.[60] Employers should also be aware of the law; in some states, daily work hours are set by law, and allowing some employees to work more than eight hours a day might require payment of overtime.

Some studies have found a troubling bias against employees who request a later start to the workday.[61] Managers may incorrectly regard people who prioritize an early start as more desirable employees and attribute a request for a late start to lack of motivation. Managers need greater supervisory skills to ensure flextime workers are using their time productively and to effectively manage teams in which some are working flexible hours and others are not.

The Access Economy and Online Platforms

The **access economy** is essentially a resource circulation system in which consumers participate on both sides of a transaction, as both providers and obtainers of resources (the transaction is usually facilitated by a third party acting as a go-between). The model, sometimes called peer-to-peer (or P2P), is particularly popular when the asset is expensive to obtain and is not fully consumed by the user (such as a house or condo). In the traditional capitalist economic model, goods are bought and sold by businesses and individuals, but in the access or sharing economy, goods and services are traded on the basis of access rather than ownership.

In this business model, owners make money from underused assets. The global online hospitality marketplace is an example. Airbnb says consumer-hosts in San Francisco who rent out their homes do so for an average of about sixty nights a year, making almost $10,000 from such rentals. Car owners using the service RelayRides make an average of $250 a month from allowing others to use their cars. This helps consumers supplement their incomes or even finance the purchase of the assets they share. Many of the original sharing-economy businesses are now household names, including Airbnb, Uber, and Lyft; thousands more are part of the P2P decentralized markets.

Most sharing or collaborative economy business models use the Internet to facilitate transactions, so it might be more accurate to refer to them as part of the *online platform economy*. However, whereas some facilitate the renting of assets, such as real estate (think Airbnb), others are essentially selling labor (think Task Rabbit), and some bridge the two categories by offering a combination (think Lyft) (see Figure 10.7). The new business models all have something in common, however: a decentralized and democratized marketplace featuring broad-scale participation, with consumers serving multiple roles.

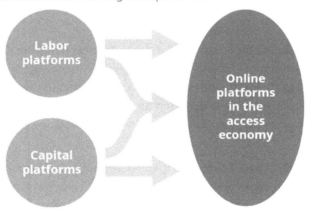

Figure 10.7   Online platforms have enabled a variety of access-economy models, including those driven by labor or capital and some by both. Examples include Airbnb, Uber, and Task Rabbit, just to name a few. (attribution: Copyright Rice University, OpenStax, under CC BY 4.0 license)

Online and digital business models allow almost anyone to start a business from scratch in what some call the democratization of free enterprise. An economy so open to new players is a significant step toward increased buyer access to goods and services at all levels, even as it raises legitimate questions about how to ensure trust between the transacting parties.

One issue facing the access economy is regulation. For example, should private individuals who rent out rooms be regulated like a Marriott hotel or perhaps a bed-and-breakfast operator, or simply be considered consumers allowing a guest to stay in their house? They are not only subject to income taxes on the money they earn but they are increasingly likely to be charged hotel or occupancy taxes. Some cities have passed ordinances to limit real estate rentals to minimum stays of a week or a month; shorter stays will be considered hotel rentals subject to regulations such as health and safety code rules. In the ride-sharing segment, some cities have said drivers must undergo the same scrutiny as taxi or limousine drivers, such as fingerprinting, commercial licensing, training, and background checks.

The access economy presents an ethical and regulatory challenge for all levels of government—balancing the need to have at least some rules to protect consumers with the desire to allow competition from new business models. Big businesses are lobbying legislative bodies to apply the same regulation to the access economy as to the traditional economy in an effort to reduce or eliminate the threat of competition. This, in turn, raises an ethical question for society as a whole. Traditional means of raising capital, whether through initial public offerings (IPOs) or venture capital, are often dominated by big players. Should access to capital remain limited to those who have influence, or should the government pursue policies aimed at facilitating access to capital by small businesses? In one sign of increasing acceptance of the access economy, traditional businesses are starting to invest in smaller, more nimble, platforms, as the following feature on Oasis Collections demonstrates.

CASES FROM THE REAL WORLD

Oasis Collections

Oasis Collections is a real estate rental marketplace or platform similar to Airbnb, with a few key differences. Founded in 2009, the company fills a market niche by matching house and condo owners with travelers who want something more personal than a hotel but more upscale than a room in someone's house.

Oasis sought venture capital funding but was turned down multiple times. An IPO was not feasible because the company was too small. This financing quandary demonstrates the limited access to capital that often forms a barrier for entrepreneurial startups to overcome. Oasis' founders turned to sources often used by entrepreneurs, including a mix of seed funding from founders, friends, and family, and angel funding from a private investor. The company operated on a relatively tight budget for several years.

In 2017, Hyatt Hotels decided to invest $20 million in Oasis, after it had proven it had a niche in the access economy. Steve Haggerty, Hyatt's global head of capital strategy, said the investment "reflects Hyatt's established strategy to super serve the high-end traveler by offering new experiences beyond traditional hotel stays. Travelers who book Oasis Collections homes are . . . leisure and often business travelers who seek more space for a longer time, but also want the peace of mind, personalized service and amenities they expect when staying with Hyatt."[62] Hyatt apparently now sees the access economic model as a force it cannot afford to ignore and has chosen to embrace and fund it. Oasis has the capital to expand its footprint, so CEO Parker Stanberry spends most of his time traveling to sign up new properties and new customers. "We definitely have our work cut out for us," he says. "We've got to hustle hard every day."[63]

Critical Thinking

- Can a sixty-year-old traditional hospitality corporation and a new access-economy startup thrive side by side? Or will the experiment crash and burn?
- How likely is it that a big business in a similar type of industry would buy up the related access-economy business or use their market power to crush them instead of integrating the new model as

Hyatt did? Defend your answer.

As the Oasis case shows, getting access to funding is often a challenge for entrepreneurs. An IPO is essentially a method of funding a startup by selling its stock to the public at large, a process heavily regulated by the government. The Securities and Exchange Commission (SEC) oversees the applicable federal laws, which require the filing of a registration statement and a full disclosure of financial information, along with months of effort by accountants, attorneys, underwriters, and company executives. The cost and complexity of this process usually outweighs the benefit for entrepreneurs who want to raise a modest amount of capital ($10 million or less).

However, as a matter of business ethics, businesses of all sizes should be able to participate fully in the U.S. economy and not be shut out by the "gatekeepers of capital"—the investment banking community. Thus, in 2012, Congress enacted new legislation called the JOBS (Jumpstart Our Business Startups) Act, which amended U.S. securities laws to enable small businesses to use a variation on a technique known as crowdfunding. Crowdfunding is already in use as a way to give or lend money to consumers and businesses through web portals such as GoFundMe. But those sites do not offer SEC-compliant sales of securities in a business, as the JOBS Act now permits emerging growth companies (EGCs) seeking capital to do. This new type of funding should help level the playing field for EGCs; many view it as a way of democratizing access to capital.[64] One entrepreneurial startup that used this new method successfully is Betabrand, a San Francisco–based retail clothing company that doubles as a crowdfunding platform. The company lets users of its platform crowdsource clothing concepts and develop prototypes into actual products.

LINK TO LEARNING

This website connects to one of several active business-oriented crowdfunding websites (https://openstax.org/l/53crowdfunding) to offer emerging growth companies or small business several avenues of funding, including equity, convertible notes, and debt. The primary advantage is the opportunity to raise equity capital without big fees and red tape.

The Gig Economy

Opportunities for limited-term employment, sometimes referred to as "gigs," have existed for decades in the music and entertainment industry; they have even been likened to the widespread small-scale self-employment typical of the pre-union and pre-Industrial eras.[65] What is new about gig work today is that it is often made possible by technology, which frees workers from the need to travel to the employer's workplace and allows them to work multiple jobs at once. This offers workers, and perhaps even managers, a new set of advantages and disadvantages in the employment equation.

The **gig economy** is an environment in which individuals and businesses contract with independent workers for short-term assignments, engagements, or projects, offering few or no benefits beyond compensation. A freelancer or contractor is a self-employed worker who may work with more than one client but who usually has a contract that covers the details of the job, including compensation. The terms freelancer and contractor are generally used interchangeably. However, if there is a distinction, it is that a freelancer is almost always self-employed and works for multiple companies, whereas a contractor may or may not be self-employed and may work for only one company at a time (Figure 10.8). Some may be happily committed to their independent status; others are involuntarily self-employed while they search for more permanent or full-time positions. Gigs might be full- or part-time; they might be limited to a specific task or a specific time; and they may serve as the worker's sole employment or as a "moonlighting" job. Regardless of the terminology, the trend toward a gig economy has begun.

Employment Relationships	
Employees	**Non-employees** **(Contractors, Freelancers, Gig workers)**
• Full-time • Single employer • Benefits • Employment taxes are split between employee and employer	• Part-time • Multiple employers (clients) • No benefits • Employment taxes must be paid entirely by employee

Figure 10.8   Different models of work include widely varying terms and conditions, but the two most basic divisions are listed. Of course, someone might also be an employee who works part-time and may or may not receive benefits, or a contractor might have a standing contract with a client that provides some benefits, although the contractor is not considered an employee. (attribution: Copyright Rice University, OpenStax, under CC BY 4.0 license)

A recent study by Intuit predicted that by 2020, a surprisingly large 40 percent of U.S. workers would be independent contractors, and according to the Freelancers Union, more than 55 million adults in the United States (that is, 35 percent of the U.S. workforce) already work as independent contractors and/or moonlighters.[66] The nature of freelance work leaves some workers searching for the qualities of traditional full-time work, and the Freelancers Union has attempted to provide them by giving its more than 375,000 members a voice through policy advocacy and access to some group benefits.[67]

Many people value the flexibility of freelance work hours. They work off premises (frequently at home), make their own schedules, and juggle assignments as needed. However, benefits such as health care and retirement plans are usually unavailable (unless an employment agency sponsors them for those it places in temporary work). Freelancers most often must establish their own retirement accounts and obtain their own health insurance through an employed spouse or partner or in a health care insurance exchange. Robert B. Reich, the former Secretary of Labor and professor at the University of California, Berkeley, says, "This on-demand economy means a work life that is unpredictable, doesn't pay very well, and is terribly insecure."[68]

Unlike employees on the payroll, gig workers must also pay both the employee's and the employer's halves of the federal payroll tax (referred to as FICA [Federal Contributions Insurance Act], which funds Social Security and Medicare). This combined tax currently totals 15.3 percent of a freelancer's earnings. Payroll taxes overall bring in about 24 percent of combined federal, state, and local government revenue, [69] making them the second-largest source of government revenue in the United States after individual federal income taxes. Here is one of the ethical issues employers face: Are they dodging their fair share of taxes and failing to offer benefits by forcing people who could be their employees into contract work instead?

CASES FROM THE REAL WORLD

Gig Work

Have you ever been a gig worker? A recent study found that 37 percent of U.S. workers participate in the gig economy, and government and other estimates say 40 percent will be working outside traditional full-time jobs by 2020. Clearly the gig economy is not a fad. The issue is often whether it benefits only the company or also the worker. Do people actually like being gig workers, or has the economy forced them into it, sometimes by taking second and third jobs?

A national survey by the Freelancers Union found that two in three of the 55 million U.S. workers who freelanced in 2016 did so because they wanted to, not because they were forced to; the other one-third did it out of necessity.[70] Although motivations for gig work may vary, it is clear that employers are benefitting. Of course, part-time contract workers are not new. What is new is the way gig work has spread to many white-collar professions. Here are two examples.

Joseph creates websites for a marketing company and a digital content studio. He also creates and edits motion graphics. "It's been a fun ride, tiring but fun," he says. "Finding time is always the struggle. I'm working on a freelance project every weekend." Joseph thinks gig work has helped him improve his graphic skills faster than he might have done in a traditional job. "I get to move around to different companies, and if one thing falls out, I still have other things I can fall back on—and it keeps me sharp."

Nicole, a mother of three, is a full-time clerk at a law firm, but she decided she needed extra money and signed up with a work-at-home call center. Her husband has joined too. Nicole says her gig job is one she could continue when she retires, and she likes that possibility. [71]

"This is the future of work," says Diane Mulcahy, a private equities investor whose clients often benefit financially from the use of gig workers. "The full-time employee is getting to be the worker of last resort."[72]

Critical Thinking

- Aside from the lack of benefits, what are the potentially negative effects for society of the gig economy?
- What happens to the concept of loyalty between worker and employer if we move to a mostly gig economy? Will that result be negative or positive? For whom, and why?

Microsoft was one of the first companies to save huge amounts of money by hiring contract workers, avoiding paying benefits and payroll taxes and escaping a wide variety of employment and labor laws. However, the company found itself the object of legal action by both the Internal Revenue Service (IRS) and its contract workers on the grounds that a large portion of its contract workforce should have been classified as employees instead.

Microsoft ended up conceding the IRS position that the workers were de facto employees. It issued W-2s (earnings statements) for the workers' past two years and paid its share of payroll taxes. It hired some of the workers as well, but others sued for fringe benefits they had been denied as freelancers. After lengthy litigation and appeals, in 2000, Microsoft agreed to pay thousands of plaintiffs a total of $97 million, the value of stock options they would have received if it had employed them. It was the largest settlement ever received by a group of temporary employees. Today, Microsoft has more 110,000 employees, and about 75 percent are temporary or contract workers. However, Microsoft says it now requires staffing companies to give temporary and gig workers it hires fringe benefits.[73]

A particularly hazy work relationship exists between employers and interns. Many business or other professional-track students seek—indeed, are encouraged to find—internships while still in school. Sometimes these positions are paid, sometimes not; some carry academic credit and some do not. The tasks interns perform, and therefore the quality of the professional experiences they gain, can vary widely. However, many interns clearly function as a source of unpaid labor. Ethical boundaries are often crossed, even if students are willing to undertake these positions. Although state labor laws governing internships vary, responsible companies will insist that their interns are paid for their services or receive academic credit, or both.

10.4 | Robotics, Artificial Intelligence, and the Workplace of the Future

Learning Objectives

By the end of this section, you will be able to:

- Discuss the application of robotics and the workplace changes it will bring
- Identify artificial intelligence applications in the workplace
- Explain the ethical challenges presented by the use of artificial intelligence

As we have seen earlier in this chapter, general advances in computer technology have already enabled significant changes in the workplace. In this module, we will look at how future workforce demographics may be affected by existing and emerging technologies. The combination of automation and robotics has already changed not only the workplace but everyday life as well. It also comes with a host of ethical and legal issues, not least being where humans will fit in the workplace of tomorrow. Managers of the future may ask, "Does my company or society benefit from having a human do a job rather than a robot, or is it all about efficiency and cost?"

Robotics and Automation in the Workplace

Advances in the field of **robotics**—a combination of computer science, mechanical and electronics engineering, and science—have meant that machines or related forms of automation now do the work of humans in a wide variety of settings, such as medicine, where robots perform surgeries previously done by the surgeon's hand. Robots have made it easier and cheaper for employers to get work done. The downside, however, is that some reasonably well-paying jobs that provided middle-class employment for humans have become the province of machines.

A McKinsey Global Institute study of eight hundred occupations in nearly fifty countries showed that more than 800 million jobs, or 20 percent of the global workforce, could be lost to robotics by the year 2030.[74] The effects could be even more pronounced in wealthy industrialized nations, such as the United States and Germany, where researchers expect that up to one-third of the workforce will be affected. By 2030, the report estimates that 39 million to 73 million jobs may be eliminated in the United States. Given that the level of employment in the United States in mid-2018 is approaching 150 million workers, this potential loss of jobs represents roughly one-quarter to one-half of total current employment (but a smaller share of employment in 2030 because of future population and employment growth).

The big question, then, is what will happen to all these displaced workers. The McKinsey report estimates that about twenty million of them will be able to transfer easily to other industries for employment. But this still leaves between twenty million and more than fifty million displaced workers who will need new employment. Occupational retraining is likely to be a path taken by some, but older workers, as well as geographically immobile workers, are unlikely to opt for such training and may endure job loss for protracted periods.

In developing countries, the report predicts that the number of jobs requiring less education will shrink. Furthermore, robotics will have less impact in poorer countries because these nations' workers are already paid so little that employers will save less on labor costs by automating. According to the report, for example, by the same date of 2030, India is expected to lose only about 9 percent of its jobs to emerging technology.

Which occupations will be most heavily affected? Not surprisingly, the McKinsey report concludes that machine operators, factory workers, and food workers will be hit hardest, because robots can do their jobs more precisely and efficiently. "It's cheaper to buy a $35,000 robotic arm than it is to hire an employee who's inefficiently making $15 an hour bagging French fries," said a former McDonald's CEO in another article about the consequences of robots in the labor market.[75] He estimated that automation has already cut the number of people working in a McDonald's by half since the 1960s and that this trend will continue. Other hard-hit jobs will include mortgage brokers, paralegals, accountants, some office staff, cashiers, toll booth operators, and car and truck drivers. The Bureau of Labor Statistics (BLS) estimates that eighty thousand fast-food jobs will disappear by 2024. As growing numbers of retail stores like Walmart, CVS, and McDonald's provide automated self-checkout options, it has been estimated that 7.5 million retail jobs are at risk over the course of the next decade. Furthermore, it has been estimated that as self-driving cars and trucks replace automobile and truck drivers, five million jobs will be lost in the early 2020s.

Jobs requiring human interaction are typically at low risk for being replaced by automation. These include nurses and most physicians, lawyers, teachers, and bartenders, as well as social workers (estimated by the BLS to grow by 19 percent by 2024), hairstylists and cosmetologists, youth sports coaches, and songwriters. McKinsey also anticipates that specialized lower-wage jobs like gardening, plumbing, and care work will be less affected by automation.

The challenge to the economy, then, will be how to address the prospect of substantial job loss; about twenty million to fifty million people will not be able to easily find new jobs. The McKinsey report notes that new technology, as in the past, will generate new types of jobs. But this is unlikely to help more than a small fraction of those confronting unemployment. So the United States will likely face some combination of rapidly rising unemployment, an urgent need to retrain twenty million or more workers, and recourse to policies whereby the government serves as an employer of last resort.

ETHICS ACROSS TIME AND CULTURES

Advances in Robotics in Japan

Japan has long maintained its position as the world's top exporter of robots, selling nearly 50 percent of the global market share in terms of both units and dollar value. At first, Japan's robots were found mainly in factories making automobiles and electronic equipment, performing simple jobs such as assembling parts. Now Japan is poised to take the lead by putting robots in diverse areas including aeronautics, medicine, disaster mitigation, and search and rescue, performing jobs that human either cannot or, for safety reasons (such as defusing a bomb), should not do. Leading universities such as the University of Tokyo offer advanced programs to teach students not only how to create robots but also how to understand the way robot technology is transforming Japanese society. Universities, research institutions, corporations, and government entities are collaborating to implement the country's next generation of advanced artificial intelligence robot technology, because Japan truly sees the rise of robotics as the "Fourth Industrial Revolution."

New uses of robots include hazardous cleanup in the wake of the 2011 earthquake and tsunami disaster that destroyed the Fukushima Daiichi nuclear power plant. After those events, Japan accelerated its development and application of disaster-response robots to go into radioactive areas and handle remediation.

In the laboratory at the University of Tokyo School of Engineering, advances are also being made in technology that mimics the capabilities of the human eye. One application allows scientists a clear field of vision in extreme weather conditions that are otherwise difficult or impossible for humans to study.

Japanese researchers are also developing a surgical robotic system with a three-dimensional endoscope to conduct high-risk surgery in remote mountainous regions with no specialized doctors. This system is in use in operating rooms in the United States as well, but Japan is taking it a step further by using it in *teletherapy,* where the patient is hundreds of miles away from the doctor actually performing the surgery. In Japan's manufacturing culture, robots are viewed not as threats but as solutions to many of the nation's most critical problems. Indeed, with Japan's below-replacement fertility since the mid-1970s, Japan's work force has been aging quite rapidly; in fact, beginning in the period from 2010 to 2015, the Japanese population started shrinking. Clearly, robots are potentially quite important as a means to offset prospective adverse consequences of a diminishing labor force.

Critical Thinking

- Does using robots cause a loss of jobs, a shifting of jobs, or both? How should society respond?
- How might the use of robots add to the increasing inequality in the U.S. economy?
- Do companies have an ethical responsibility to their workers to training or other support to workers displaced by automation?

Artificial Intelligence

Although some robots are remotely controlled by a human operator or a computer program written by a human, robots can also learn to work without human intervention, and often faster, more efficiently, and more cheaply than humans can. The branch of science that uses computer algorithms to replicate human intelligent behavior by machines with minimal human intervention is called **artificial intelligence (AI)**. Related professions in which the implementation of AI might have particular impact are banking, financial advising, and the sales of securities and managing of stock portfolios.

According to global consulting giant Accenture, AI is "a collection of advanced technologies that allows machines to sense, comprehend, act and learn." Accenture contends that AI will be the next great advance in the workplace: "It is set to transform business in ways we have not seen since the Industrial Revolution; fundamentally reinventing how businesses run, compete and thrive. When implemented holistically, these technologies help improve productivity and lower costs, unlocking more creative jobs and creating new growth opportunities."[76] Accenture looked at twelve of the world's most developed countries, which account for more than half of world economic output, to assess the impact of AI in sixteen specific industries. According to its report, AI has the potential to significantly increase corporate profitability, double rates of economic growth by 2035, increase labor productivity by as much as 40 percent, and boost gross value added by $14 trillion by 2035, based on an almost 40 percent increase in rates of return.[77] Even news articles have begun to be written by robots.[78]

A report by KPMG, another global consulting and accounting firm, indicates that almost 50 percent of the activities people perform in the workplace today could be automated, most often by using AI and automation technology that already exist. The ethical question facing the business community, and all of us on a broader level, is about the type of society in which we all want to live and the role automation will play in it. The answer is not simply about efficiency; a company should consider many variables as it moves toward increased automation (Figure 10.9).

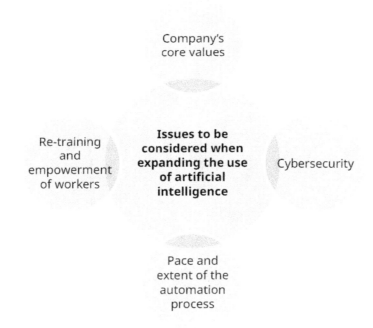

Figure 10.9 Managers should balance multiple variables as the workplace moves toward increased use of artificial intelligence, automation, and robotics. (attribution: Copyright Rice University, OpenStax, under CC BY 4.0 license)

For example, as AI programs become better able to interact with humans, especially online, should a company be required to inform its customers if and when they are dealing with any form of AI and not a person? If people cannot tell when they are communicating with an AI program and not a human being, has an AI-controlled computer or robot reached a form personhood? Why or why not? Although traditional business ethics can provide us with a starting place to answer such questions, we will also need a philosophical approach, because we also need to decide whether it is necessary to have consciousness to be considered a person. This issue is further muddied when a human employee largely is tapping AI i to serve customers or clients. Should this combination of human and AI assistance be made patently clear?

Another issue in AI and all forms of automation is liability. According to Reuters News, "lawmakers in Europe have agreed on the need for [European Union]-wide legislation that would regulate robots and their use, including an ethical framework for their development and deployment, as well as the establishment of liability for the actions of robots, including self-driving cars."[79] The legal and ethical questions in assigning liability for decisions made by robots and AI are not only fascinating to debate but also an important legal matter society must resolve. The answers will one day directly affect the day-to-day lives of billions of people.

 Key Terms

access economy a nontraditional business model in which consumers participate on both sides of a transaction, sometimes facilitated by a third party

artificial intelligence (AI) the branch of science that uses computer algorithms to replicate human intelligent behavior by machines with minimal human intervention

flextime a work schedule in which employees can select their own start and finish time

gig economy an environment in which individuals and businesses contract with independent workers for the completion of short-term assignments, engagements, or projects, offering few or no benefits beyond compensation

job sharing the use of two or more employees to perform the work of one full-time position

robotics a field of research that includes computer science, mechanical and electronics engineering, and science process with the objective to produce robots, or related forms of automation, to replicate human tasks

telecommuting working from a remote location (home or other space) by means of electronic connections

Summary

10.1 More Telecommuting or Less?

Remote workers save themselves the time and cost of a commute and are better able to balance work and home life. Companies often benefit from the higher productivity and lower turnover of telecommuting employees, and they can also provide a social benefit by permitting employees to avoid commuting, reducing traffic congestion and pollution. Some challenges of telecommuting for the manager are maintaining the privacy of the firm's data, transmitting corporate culture, defining performance objectives, and encouraging collaboration. Employees have the challenge of remaining focused on work when they are working elsewhere. Ethical companies support their remote workers by developing and encouraging trust and guarding against abuse. They also set clear and equitable expectations and rewards to ensure fairness and keep open the lines of communication.

10.2 Workplace Campuses

Traditional office buildings with separate workspaces for each worker are giving way to multifunctional worksites where employees are encouraged to actively collaborate. Some companies have expanded the workplace to include restaurants, recreation facilities, and convenient amenities to attract and retain employees. Other companies are building villages around their campuses to assist employees seeking to balance work and home life. These all-encompassing work environments have some potential downsides for employees, however, including a risk of tethering them to their workplaces. Their effects on local communities are being questioned as well.

10.3 Alternatives to Traditional Patterns of Work

When undertaken with equity and fairness, job sharing and flextime can create flexibility for workers who need or want to limit their hours. These practices allow employers to recruit more diverse employees, help them meet employees' need for work-life balance, and, in the case of job sharing, bring more than one person's perspective to problem solving. However, employers must clearly spell out expectations and procedures for each employee to ensure success.

Given flexible hours and job-sharing arrangements, the traditional employment-based U.S. economy appears to be in transition toward new business models that offer many opportunities but also serious challenges. Ethical issues in the access economy include the responsibilities of each of the parties in a sharing transaction and the character of any regulation, including taxes, that may be passed. In the gig economy, they include workers' insecure positions and lack of benefits, employers' responsibility for paying their fair share of social insurance (payroll) taxes, and the fair treatment of interns.

10.4 Robotics, Artificial Intelligence, and the Workplace of the Future

Initially, robots and AI inspire both intrigue and fear in most of us. Fear of losing jobs is a reality, but so too is intrigue about what the future holds. A key for companies is to help workers retrain to become part of that future.

Assessment Questions

1. Which of the following is not a prospective benefit to the firm of implementing a telecommuting program?
   A. higher productivity of telecommuting workers
   B. greater connectivity and collaboration among employees
   C. lower operating costs
   D. more satisfied workers

2. A successful telecommuting program would include which of the following?
   A. a written policy that spells out expectations
   B. an oral policy the manager can change at will
   C. subjective criteria for each individual worker
   D. preference for some people to telecommute over others

3. True or false? Telecommuting presents some difficulties for on-site technology departments providing security and technical assistance.

4. True or false? Some telecommuters may be penalized by a perception that they are lazy.

5. How can an employer develop trust in a telecommuting employee?

6. In what ways does telecommuting help companies recruit and retain employees?

7. When considering the issue of work-life balance, which of the following points does not apply?
   A. Each employee probably assesses this differently.
   B. Managers and workers as cohorts often have different perspectives on it.
   C. Workers with families at home should be entitled to a "better" balance.
   D. All employees have a right to pursue this.

8. Which of the following is not a potential downside of a corporate campus?
   A. Impaired productivity
   B. Reduced ability of labor markets to adjust to changing conditions
   C. Adverse impact on local businesses
   D. Increased fiscal burden on local government

9. True or false? The design of corporate campuses is meant to enhance opportunities for employees to collaborate.

10. Why do some companies provide free or inexpensive meals for their employees? Are they behaving ethically by doing so?

11. If you were designing an office building for a mid-size advertising firm, what ideas could you incorporate from this section to enhance collaboration?

12. Some employers allow workers a compressed work week as long as _____.
   A.   the work can be put off until the next week
   B.   the workplace is a store
   C.   it is a week in which a holiday falls on Monday
   D.   the employee can completely finish the work in a shorter time

13. The primary reason small-business entrepreneurs might want to hire mostly contract labor is that _____.
   A.   the cost of fringe benefits is reduced
   B.   only contract workers can be part-time but employees must be full-time
   C.   only employees can file workers compensation claims
   D.   it improves the company's stock price

14. True or false? One drawback to job sharing is that employees may become competitive with one another, which could cause communication difficulties.

15. True or false? The terms "sharing economy" and "access economy" both refer to a marketplace that differs from the traditional, more capital-intensive, shareholder-owned corporations.

16. How could offering a shared job help an employer recruit more employees?

17. Participating in the gig economy often means working for a company as a part-time worker with no guarantee the job will last. Why would someone do it?

18. What advantages does a company gain from hiring gig workers?

19. Robots have usually been operated by a human at the controls but now are becoming more independent. How?

20. Artificial intelligence and robotics in the United States are thus far largely unregulated. Do you see more regulations coming? Why or why not?

21. The use of robots at work _____.
   A.   can reduce the exposure of humans to dangerous working conditions
   B.   costs more than human labor
   C.   must first be approved by the Occupational Safety and Health Administration
   D.   is unlikely to affect the number of people in the overall workforce

22. True or false? Worker displacement is a problem that companies have a legal duty to address when implementing the use of robots.

23. Worker retraining programs for employees who lose their jobs to robots _____.
   A.   are a "Band-Aid" solution most of the time
   B.   will be needed only for a small minority of the workers who lose their jobs
   C.   are offered and funded by the employers only if a sufficient number of workers are displaced
   D.   are an obligation taken on by ethical companies

Endnotes

1. Global Work Analytics, FlexJobs, *2017 State of Telecommuting in the U.S. Employee Workforce*, June 2017. https://cdn.thepennyhoarder.com/wp-content/uploads/2017/06/30140000/State_Of_Telecommuting_U.S._Employee_Workforce.pdf (accessed March 2018); Patricia Reaney, "About One in Five Workers Worldwide Telecommute: Poll," *Reuters*, January 24, 2012. https://www.reuters.com/article/us-telecommuting/about-one-in-five-workers-worldwide-telecommute-poll-idUSTRE80N1IL20120124.
2. Ken Hess, "Death of the Office and Rise of the Telecommuter," *ZDNet*, June 2, 2014. http://www.zdnet.com/article/death-of-the-office-and-rise-of-the-telecommuter/.
3. "3 Reasons Why Telecommuting Is a Must Have for Working Parents," FlexJobs, April 24, 2013. https://www.flexjobs.com/blog/post/3-reasons-why-telecommuting-is-a-must-have-for-working-parents/; Karla L. Miller, "Work Advice: Working with Parents Who Work from Home," *The Washington Post*, January 14, 2013. https://live.washingtonpost.com/work-advice-101413.html.
4. Barbara Otto, "Survey: Telecommuting Is More Than a Perk for Workers with Disabilities," *Huffpost*, May 8, 2013. https://www.huffingtonpost.com/barbara-otto/telecommuting-is-more-than-a-perk_b_3239553.html.
5. Mike Maciag, "How Will the Growing Popularity of Telecommuting Impact Public Transit?" *Future Structure*, November 1, 2017. http://www.govtech.com/fs/transportation/How-Will-the-Growing-Popularity-of-Telecommuting-Impact-Public-Transit.html.
6. Sara Sutton Fell, "9 Ways Working from Home Saves You Money," *SFGate*, April 21, 2013. https://www.sfgate.com/jobs/salary/article/9-Ways-Working-from-Home-Saves-You-Money-4456584.php.
7. Nicholas Bloom, "To Raise Productivity, Let More Employees Work from Home," *Harvard Business Review*, January–February 2014. https://hbr.org/2014/01/to-raise-productivity-let-more-employees-work-from-home.
8. Amanda Gonzales, "Telecommuting Increases Employee Engagement, Productivity and Overall Happiness!" Colorado Department of Transportation, April 4, 2016. https://www.codot.gov/business/process-improvement/local-lean/telecommuting-increases-employee-engagement-productivity-and-overall-happiness.
9. Greg Kratz, "5 Benefits of Telecommuting for Employers and Employees," 1 Million for Work Flexibility, June 13, 2017. https://www.workflexibility.org/5-benefits-of-telecommuting-for-employers-and-employees/.
10. Carolyn Kylstra, "10 Things Your Commute Does to Your Body," *Time*, February 26, 2014. http://time.com/9912/10-things-your-commute-does-to-your-body/.
11. Andrea Loubier, "Benefits of Telecommuting for the Future of Work," *Forbes*, July 20, 2017. https://www.forbes.com/sites/andrealoubier/2017/07/20/benefits-of-telecommuting-for-the-future-of-work/#a4f6c9f16c65.
12. "Costs and Benefits: Advantages of Agile Work Strategies for Companies," http://globalworkplaceanalytics.com/resources/costs-benefits (accessed May 2018).
13. Syracuse Staff, "4 Benefits of Adopting Remote Employees," Martin J. Whitman School of Management, Syracuse University, September 11, 2015. https://onlinebusiness.syr.edu/4-benefits-of-remote-employees/.
14. Jessica Howington, "The Positive Environmental Impact of Remote Work," FlexJobs, August 9, 2016. https://www.flexjobs.com/blog/post/the-positive-environmental-impact-of-remote-work/.
15. Christopher Tkaczyk, "Marissa Mayer Breaks Her Silence on Yahoo's Telecommuting Policy," *Fortune*, April 19, 2013. http://fortune.com/2013/04/19/marissa-mayer-breaks-her-silence-on-yahoos-telecommuting-policy/.
16. Nicole Spector, "Why Are Big Companies Calling Their Remote Workers Back to the Office?" *ABC News*, July 27, 2017. https://www.nbcnews.com/business/business-news/why-are-big-companies-calling-their-remote-workers-back-office-n787101.
17. Emily Peck, "Proof That Working from Home Is Here to Stay: Even Yahoo Still Does It," *Huffpost*, December 6, 2017. https://www.huffingtonpost.com/2015/03/18/the-future-is-happening-now-ok_n_6887998.html.
18. "Pixar Headquarters and the Legacy of Steve Jobs," *Office Snapshots*, July 16, 2012. https://officesnapshots.com/2012/07/16/pixar-headquarters-and-the-legacy-of-steve-jobs/.
19. Rachael Go, "7 Deadly Disadvantages of Working from Home and How to Counter Them," *Hubstaff Blog*, January 9, 2018. https://blog.hubstaff.com/disadvantages-of-working-from-home/.
20. Trish Barnes, "Pros and Cons of Employing Telecommuters," *RMI*, June 23, 2016. http://rmi-solutions.com/blog/pros-and-cons-of-employing-telecommuters/.
21. Rachael Go, "7 Deadly Disadvantages of Working from Home and How to Counter Them," *Hubstaff Blog*, January 9, 2018. https://blog.hubstaff.com/disadvantages-of-working-from-home/.
22. Trish Barnes, "Pros and Cons of Employing Telecommuters," *RMI*, June 23, 2016. http://rmi-solutions.com/blog/pros-and-cons-of-employing-telecommuters/.
23. Parker Beauchamp, "Telecommuting: the Pros, Cons and Risks of Working from Home," INGUARD, July 24, 2015. http://www.inguard.com/blog/telecommuting-pros-cons-risks-working-from-home.
24. Parker Beauchamp, "Telecommuting: the Pros, Cons and Risks of Working from Home," INGUARD, July 24, 2015. http://www.inguard.com/blog/telecommuting-pros-cons-risks-working-from-home.
25. Larry Alton, "Are Remote Workers More Productive Than In-Office Workers?" *Forbes*, March 7, 2017. https://www.forbes.com/sites/larryalton/2017/03/07/are-remote-workers-more-productive-than-in-office-workers/#5e15316931f6.
26. Melanie Pinola, "Best Jobs for Telecommuting;" *Lifewire*, March 7, 2018. https://www.lifewire.com/best-jobs-for-telecommuting-2377295.
27. Sara Sutton, "Why Are Companies Still Avoiding Telecommuting?" *Entrepreneur*, November 28, 2014. https://www.entrepreneur.com/article/240189.
28. Nicole Fallon, "5 Issues Your Company's Telecommuting Policy Should Address," *Business News Daily*, March 31, 2017. https://www.businessnewsdaily.com/7749-create-telecommuting-policy.html.
29. Susanna Kim, "Best Buy Follows Yahoo's Lead, Takes a Look at Employees Working from Home," *ABC News*, March 6, 2013. https://abcnews.go.com/Business/best-buy-yahoo-questions-telecommuting/story?id=18666891.
30. "Workplace Flexibility's Win-Win Streak," MIT Management Executive Education, September 4, 2016. https://executive.mit.edu/blog/workplace-flexibilitys-win-win-streak#.WnOuzq6nEdU.
31. George Piskurich, *An Organizational Guide to Telecommuting: Setting Up and Running a Successful Telecommuter Program* (Alexandria, VA: American Society for Training and Development, 1998), 95.
32. Michael Boyer O'Leary, "Telecommuting Can Boost Productivity and Job Performance," *U.S. News & World Report*, March 15, 2013. https://www.usnews.com/opinion/articles/2013/03/15/telecommuting-can-boost-productivity-and-job-performance.
33. Samantha McDuffee, "Out of Sight, Out of Mind? 5 Virtual Team Building Activities That Work," Teambonding, February 9, 2017. https://www.teambonding.com/5-team-bondingtips-for-remote-employees/.
34. Mari Silipo, "Flexible Workspaces: What They Are and Why You Need Them," *TurningArt*, http://blog.turningart.com/flexible-workspaces-what-they-are-and-why-you-need-them (accessed May 1, 2018).
35. "Top Trends Shaping Design," *Gensler*, 2015. https://www.gensler.com/design-forecast-2015-the-future-of-workplace (accessed July 31,

2018).

36. David Streitfield, "Welcome to Zucktown. Where Everything Is Just Zucky," *New York Times*, March 21, 2018. https://www.nytimes.com/2018/03/21/technology/facebook-zucktown-willow-village.html.

37. Knoll Inc., *The Workplace Network*, 2015. https://www.knoll.com/media/286/198/Knoll-The-Workplace-NetWork.pdf.

38. David Streitfield, "Welcome to Zucktown. Where Everything Is Just Zucky," *New York Times*, March 21, 2018. https://www.nytimes.com/2018/03/21/technology/facebook-zucktown-willow-village.html.

39. Leanna Garfield, "Facebook and Amazon Are So Big They're Creating Their Own Company Towns – Here's the 200-Year Evolution," *Business Insider*, March 26, 2018. http://www.businessinsider.com/company-town-history-facebook-2017-9.

40. Matt Novak, "Blood on the Tracks in Pullman: Chicagoland's Failed Capitalist Utopia," *Paleofuture*, November 13, 2014. https://paleofuture.gizmodo.com/blood-on-the-tracks-in-pullman-chicagolands-failed-cap-1574508996.

41. Dirk Mateer and Lee Coppock, *Principles of Economics*, 2nd ed. (New York: W.W. Norton and Company, 2018), 451.

42. "Work Life Balance," Mental Health America. http://www.mentalhealthamerica.net/work-life-balance (accessed July 31, 2018).

43. Ryan Jenkins, "5 Ways Millennials Are Redefining Work-Life Balance," *Inc.*, February 5, 2018. https://www.inc.com/ryan-jenkins/this-is-how-millennials-view-work-life-balance.html.

44. Adam Rogers, "If You Care about Cities, Apple's New Campus Sucks," *Wired*, June 8, 2017. https://www.wired.com/story/apple-campus/.

45. Adam Rogers, "If You Care about Cities, Apple's New Campus Sucks," *Wired*, June 8, 2017. https://www.wired.com/story/apple-campus/.

46. Amy Moore, "Complete Guide to Apple Park," *Macworld*, February 20, 2018. https://www.macworld.co.uk/feature/apple/complete-guide-apple-park-3489704/.

47. Nathan Heller, "Is the Gig Economy Working?" *The New Yorker*, May 15, 2017. https://www.newyorker.com/magazine/2017/05/15/is-the-gig-economy-working.

48. Guy Standing, *The Precariat: The New Dangerous Class* (New York: Bloomsbury, 2011).

49. Greg Kratz, "How a Shorter Work Week Can Benefit Companies," 1 Million for Work Flexibility, June 6, 2017. https://www.workflexibility.org/shorter-week-can-benefit-companies-workers/.

50. John Duggleby and Brenda Russell, "Job Sharing: Twice the Benefits or Double the Problems?" Edward Lowe Foundation. http://edwardlowe.org/job-sharing-twice-the-benefits-or-double-the-problems-2/ (accessed May 1, 2018).

51. Beth Lewis, "Job Sharing for Teachers," ThoughtCo, July 9, 2017. https://www.thoughtco.com/job-sharing-pros-and-cons-2081950.

52. Amy Gallo, "How to Make a Job Sharing Situation Work," *Harvard Business Review*, September 23, 2013. https://hbr.org/2013/09/how-to-make-a-job-sharing-situation-work.

53. "Databases, Tables and Calculators by Subject," Bureau of Labor Statistics. https://www.bls.gov/data/ (accessed June 18, 2018).

54. Molly Thompson, "The Disadvantages of Job Sharing," *The Nest*. https://woman.thenest.com/disadvantages-job-sharing-5638.html (accessed June 20, 2018).

55. Andrew Saunders and Kate Bassett, "How to Make Job Sharing Work," *Management Today*, February 17, 2017. https://www.managementtoday.co.uk/job-sharing-work/your-career/article/1424603.

56. John Duggleby and Brenda Russell, "Job Sharing: Twice the Benefits or Double the Problems?" Edward Lowe Foundation. http://edwardlowe.org/job-sharing-twice-the-benefits-or-double-the-problems-2/ (accessed May 1, 2018).

57. David Burkus, "Everyone Likes Flex Time, but We Punish Women Who Use It," *Harvard Business Review*, February 20, 2017. https://hbr.org/2017/02/everyone-likes-flex-time-but-we-punish-women-who-use-it.

58. Jeanne Sahadi, "The 4-Day Workweek Is Real . . . for Employees at These Companies," *CNN Money*, April 27, 2015. http://money.cnn.com/2015/04/27/pf/4-day-work-week/index.html.

59. Susan M. Heathfield, "Advantages and Disadvantage of Flexible Work Schedules," The Balance Careers, March 19, 2018. https://www.thebalance.com/advantages-and-disadvantages-of-flexible-work-schedules-1917964.

60. "Managing Flexible Work Arrangements," *SHRM*, June 14, 2016. https://www.shrm.org/resourcesandtools/tools-and-samples/toolkits/pages/managingflexibleworkarrangements.aspx.

61. Eric Jaffe, "How Flexible Hours Can Harm Employees As Much As It Helps Them," *Fast Company*, June 25, 2014. https://www.fastcompany.com/3032310/how-flexible-hours-can-harm-employees-as-much-as-it-helps-them.

62. "Paychecks, Paydays, and the Online Platform Economy. Big Data on Income Volatility," JP Morgan, February 2016. https://www.jpmorganchase.com/corporate/institute/report-paychecks-paydays-and-the-online-platform-economy.htm.

63. Melissa Locker, "Oasis Is the Home-Sharing Company That Doesn't Consider Airbnb a Rival," *Fast Company*, December 21, 2017. https://www.fastcompany.com/40505734/oasis-is-the-home-sharing-company-that-doesnt-consider-airbnb-a-rival.

64. Kurt Stanberry, "Regulatory Relief for Small Businesses," *The Journal of International Management Studies* 12, no. 1 (2017): 83–87.

65. Liat Clark, "The Gig Economy Threatens to Take Us Back to Pre-Industrial Revolution Times," *Wired*, June 23, 2017. http://www.wired.co.uk/article/gig-economy-bank-of-england-worker-rights.

66. Brian Rashid, "The Rise of the Freelancer Economy," *Forbes*, January 26, 2016. https://www.forbes.com/sites/brianrashid/2016/01/26/the-rise-of-the-freelancer-economy/#2f40228f3bdf.

67. Freelancers Union. https://www.freelancersunion.org/about/ (accessed July 10, 2018).

68. Farhad Majoo, "Uber's Business Model Could Change Your Work," *New York Times*, January 28, 2015. https://www.nytimes.com/2015/01/29/technology/personaltech/uber-a-rising-business-model.html.

69. Amir El-Sibaie, "Sources of Government Revenue in the OECD, 2017," Tax Foundation, September 6, 2017. https://taxfoundation.org/sources-of-government-revenue-oecd-2017/.

70. Nancy Dahlberg, "The Gig Economy Is Big and Here to Stay: How Workers Survive and Thrive," *Miami Herald*, September 6, 2017. http://www.chicagotribune.com/business/ct-gig-economy-workers-20170906-story.html.

71. Nancy Dahlberg, "The Gig Economy Is Big and Here to Stay: How Workers Survive and Thrive," *Miami Herald*, September 6, 2017. http://www.chicagotribune.com/business/ct-gig-economy-workers-20170906-story.html.

72. Nancy Dahlberg, "The Gig Economy Is Big and Here to Stay: How Workers Survive and Thrive," *Miami Herald*, September 6, 2017. http://www.chicagotribune.com/business/ct-gig-economy-workers-20170906-story.html.

73. Steven Greenhouse, "Temp Workers at Microsoft Win Lawsuit," *New York Times*, December 13, 2000. https://www.nytimes.com/2000/12/13/business/technology-temp-workers-at-microsoft-win-lawsuit.html.

74. "Robot Automation Will Take 800 Million Jobs by 2030," *BBC*, November 29, 2017. http://www.bbc.com/news/world-us-canada-42170100.

75. Matt McFarland, "Robots: Is Your Job at Risk?" *CNN Money*, September 15, 2017. http://money.cnn.com/2017/09/15/technology/jobs-robots/index.html.

76. "What Is Artificial Intelligence (AI)?" Accenture. https://www.accenture.com/bg-en/artificial-intelligence-index (accessed January 15, 2018).

77. "What Is Artificial Intelligence (AI)?" Accenture. https://www.accenture.com/bg-en/artificial-intelligence-index (accessed January 15, 2018).

78. Chris Baraniuk, "Would You Care if This Feature Had Been Written by a Robot?" *BBC News*, January 30, 2018. https://www.bbc.com/news/business-42858174.

79. Ben Taylor, "Who's Liable for Decisions AI and Robotics Make?" *BetaNews*, March 21, 2017. https://betanews.com/2017/03/21/artificial-intelligence-robotics-liability/.

Figure 11.1 Business ethics starts right where you are and leads you down the road of life with a set of standards and rules to follow. (credit: modification of "We're on the Road to Nowhere" by Marc Dalmulder/Flickr, CC BY 2.0)

Chapter Outline

11.1 Business Ethics in an Evolving Environment

11.2 Committing to an Ethical View

11.3 Becoming an Ethical Professional

11.4 Making a Difference in the Business World

Introduction

Even though they are business decisions, the choices we make at work can be personal in that they begin with our use of conscience. Just as the human body requires nourishment and care, so the conscience needs attention. Developmental psychologists have long understood that the formation of conscience, and the emergence of an individual in whom being and doing are comfortably aligned, take place over time. There are no shortcuts. Imperfection, self-doubt, and mistakes are part of the process. But what counts in life—including our choice of profession as well as the way we live our personal lives—is the manner in which we apply wisdom, education, and experience in forming the decisions we make and in becoming the person we wish to be.

Facing the right direction may be difficult at first, but with each decision toward wholeness, the path becomes a little easier to tread. The reverse is also true. When we neglect or ignore our conscience, it becomes more difficult for us to turn around. This final chapter explores the process of becoming a professional with an unshakeable ethical stance in a changing world. Where do you stand on your own path in life, and more important, which direction are you facing (Figure 11.1)? In which direction will your choices regarding your work and career take you?

11.1 Business Ethics in an Evolving Environment

Not only does the world seem to have shrunk, but the twenty-first century pace of change seems to have sped up time itself. As the world becomes smaller and faster and companies adapt their practices to fit new conditions, the core of business ethics that guides corporate behavior remains the same, directed, as always, by shared values and morals as well as legal restraints. What happens when these are ignored? An example follows:

Rajat Gupta grew up in India, earned an MBA from Harvard, and prospered for years as managing director of McKinsey & Company, a preeminent management consulting firm. A respected business leader and cofounder of the Indian School of Business and the American Indian Foundation, Gupta served on many corporate and philanthropic boards. "Gupta was commended by people who knew him as a person who helped others. He was very active in providing medical and humanitarian relief to the developing countries. Born to humble circumstances, he became a pillar of the consulting community and a trusted advisor to the world's leading companies and organizations."[1] According to the Securities Exchange Commission, however, in 2009, Gupta provided hedge-fund manager and longtime friend Raj Rajaratnam with insider information about investor Warren Buffet's agreement to purchase shares in Goldman Sachs, an investment bank for which Gupta served as a corporate director. Gupta was convicted of felony securities fraud relating to insider trading (three counts) and conspiracy (one count) and sentenced to two years in jail plus $5 million in fines.[2] He had chosen to violate both business ethics and the law, as well as breaching his fiduciary duty as a corporate director.

When corporate managers follow codes of conduct in a virtuous fashion, the outcome is positive but tends not to make the news. That is not a bad thing. We should value ethical behavior for its own sake, not because it will draw media attention. Unethical behavior, on the other hand, is often considered newsworthy, as were the crimes of Rajat Gupta. In discussing his case, the Seven Pillars Institute for Global Finance and Ethics (an independent, nonprofit think tank based in Kansas City, Missouri, that helps raise public awareness about financial ethics) said, "As a true professional, the good manager strives to achieve a moral excellence that includes honesty, fairness, prudence, and courage."[3] These are some of the virtues ethical players in the corporate world display.

Respected businesses and managers adhere to a well-thought-out vision of what is ethical and fair. The primary purpose of business ethics is to guide organizations and their employees in this effort by outlining a mode of behavior that proactively identifies and implements the right actions to take, ones that avoid lapses in judgment and deed. For instance, as we saw in Defining and Prioritizing Stakeholders, identifying the needs and rights of all stakeholders, not just of shareholders, is a useful first step in fair and ethical decision-making for any business organization. The box that follows describes what happened when General Motors forgot this.

CASES FROM THE REAL WORLD

General Motors' Failure to Consider Stakeholders

General Motors (GM) has struggled with its brands and its image. Over the years, it has jettisoned some of its once-popular brands, including Oldsmobile and Pontiac, sold many others, and climbed back from a 2009 bankruptcy and reorganization. The automaker was hiding an even bigger problem, however: The ignition switch in many of its cars was prone to malfunction, causing injury and even death. The faulty switches caused 124 deaths and 273 injuries, and GM was finally brought to federal court. In 2014, the company reached a settlement for $900 million and recalled 2.6 million cars.

The case exemplifies the tension between the concept that "the only goal of business is to profit, so the only obligation that the business person has is to maximize profit for the owner or the stockholders" on one hand, and the ethical obligations a company owes to its other stakeholders on the other.[4] GM's failure to consider its stakeholders and consumers when choosing not to report the potential for malfunction of the ignition switches led to an ethical breakdown in its operations and cost the company and its customers dearly. In addition, by treating customers as only a means toward an end, the company turned its back on a generation of loyal buyers.

Critical Thinking

- What virtues and values shared by its long-time customers did General Motors betray by failing to disclose an inherent danger built into its cars?
- How do you think that betrayal affected the company's brand and the way car buyers felt about the firm? How might it have affected its shareholders' views of GM?

At first glance, you might not see many parallels between the purchase of a flask of wine in an ancient Greek marketplace and your online purchase of a week's worth of groceries with a single click. In both cases, however, and throughout all the generations in between, buyers and sellers would agree that customers are entitled to be treated with honesty and accorded fair value for their money. Business leaders should approach ethical issues with the same sense of the permanence of ethical values. Technological innovation has changed the business environment and our lives, but it does not change the basis on which we make ethical business decisions. It does however, cause us to *expand* the application of our ethical standards to new situations.

For example, ethical principles are now being applied to online business. One reason is so that managers can navigate the privacy issues raised by the wholesale collection and sharing (intentional and otherwise) of customer data.

> "The big ethical dilemmas of the twenty-first century have mostly centered on cybercrimes and privacy issues. Crimes such as identity theft, almost unheard of twenty years ago, remain a huge threat to anyone doing business online—a majority of the population. As a result, businesses face social and legal pressure to take every measure possible to protect customers' sensitive information. The rise in popularity of data mining and target marketing have forced businesses to walk a fine line between respecting customers' privacy and using their online activities to glean valuable marketing data."[5]

Which values are at play on the two sides of this dilemma? Which stakeholders are priorities at companies like Facebook and Equifax?

Another ethical dilemma arises for managers when government policy collides with a multinational corporation's global ethical standards. Although this clash can occur in many industries, the information industry offers a useful example. Google's stated mission is to "Organize the world's information and make it universally accessible and useful." From its founding, says the company's website, "our goal has been to develop services that significantly improve the lives of as many people as possible. Not just for some. For everyone."[6] This may not hold true in all Google's markets, however.

> "In 2006, [Google] launched a Chinese-language website in China and, contrary to its global ethical standards opposing censorship, agreed to Chinese government demands to eliminate links which the authorities found objectionable. For example, when a Web-surfer searched 'Tiananmen Square' on Google's Chinese-language website in Los Angeles, reports of the 1989 demonstrations popped up. Not so if the same surfer entered the same words on Google's Chinese-language site in Beijing (at various times either nothing or innocuous history came up)."[7]

In 2010, Google withdrew from China for a time, but it still wants to crack the huge market that country represents. It currently makes two applications available to Chinese users, but Gmail, YouTube, Google maps, and its search engine remain largely banned by the government.[8] Does Google have an obligation to follow its own internal value of providing information to its users, or to respect China's policy of censorship? Is its current strategy in China coherent, or does it open the door for ethical lapses?[9]

Consider one more of the many general ethical challenges managers of global businesses now face. The Cheesecake Factory, the California-based restaurant chain that prides itself on large portions and sumptuous desserts, opened a restaurant in Hong Kong in May 2017. Since then, the restaurant has been overwhelmed by customers intent on having not just a slice of cheesecake but an "American" experience. The restaurant's menu is the same in all of its two hundred stores around the world. Whether you are eating in Los Angeles, Hong Kong, or Dubai, you can order dishes with mozzarella, fontina, parmesan, cheddar, feta, or Swiss cheese, along with plenty of bacon, sour cream, and potatoes (Figure 11.2). The interior decor is also the same wherever you go, guaranteeing a uniform experience.[10]

Figure 11.2   Does the Cheesecake Factory in Dubai or anywhere else in the world have an obligation to give customers what they want, or what they need? Would compromise betray its mission? Would it disappoint customers? (credit: "cheesecake factory Dubai mall three" by Krista/Flickr, CC BY 2.0)

Does it raise any ethical issues for the Cheesecake Factory not to tailor its offerings to local tastes and norms, as competing chains have done? People in Hong Kong, for example, normally eat a diet with fewer calories and dairy products and that is much lower in fat and sugar than is typical in the United States. As one young customer at the Hong Kong outlet exclaimed, "Chinese people just cannot handle this much cheese."[11]

Yet the company is offering a product the great majority of the public wants. Does it owe them anything in addition? That is, does the Cheesecake Factory have an obligation to give customers what they *need*, rather than what they *want*? In many parts of the world, there is pronounced desire for many things American, in particular, and Western, in general. Do Western companies have a primary mandate simply to meet this want, or do they have an obligation to deliver what is better for others? This is a core ethical consideration that has implications for companies far beyond simple marketing strategies and tactics. To impose certain products and services on other cultures because Western nations believe these would be best for them certainly would be a form of imperialism. However, for corporations to satisfy expressed wants could be applauded as an honorable response to customers identifying their own preferences. To preemptively decide what ought to be consumed by others—because it is for their own good—might be a form of paternalism. Ultimately, do customers or do companies have the right to make these decisions?

You might answer that it would depend on the company and its products or services, and you would be right to see it in this light. What is unmistakable, however, is that these truly are decisions fraught with ethical dimensions. Business leaders must become accustomed to considering them in this way.

11.2 | Committing to an Ethical View

Professional values and ethical reasoning are traits valued by all good employers. In fact, we have seen throughout this book that employees' sound ethical decisions lead to higher profits in the long run. How do we develop the ability to make such decisions? We will see in the coming paragraphs that it takes discipline, commitment, and practice. Strong work and personal relationship matters, too.

Relationships Matter

Workplace research indicates that employees are more likely to be unethical when they are dissatisfied with their jobs or see their superiors acting unethically.[12] How do relationships influence this equation? A good example set at the top and the freedom to determine a comfortable work-life balance for oneself—all influenced by the organization's positive relationship with its employees—lead to a more ethical workplace. Consider Walmart's relationships with its many employees.

CASES FROM THE REAL WORLD

Walmart: "Save Money. Live Better."

With annual revenues of almost half a trillion dollars (2017), 2.3 million employees, and nearly twelve thousand stores worldwide, Walmart is the largest private employer on the planet (Figure 11.3).[13] In fact, it is bigger than many national economies, including some in the developed world. In 2007, it replaced its longstanding slogan, "Always Low Prices," with "Save Money. Live Better."[14]

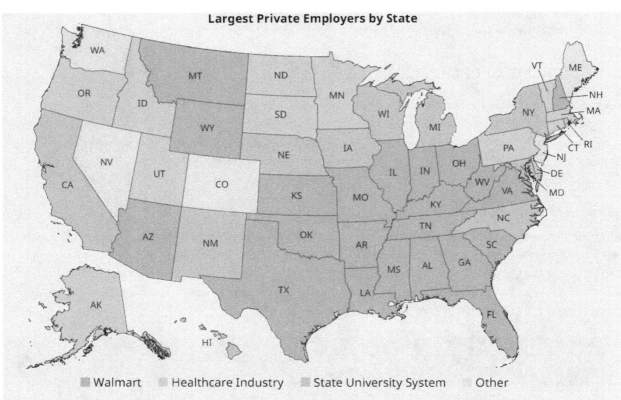

Figure 11.3   According to Walmart, ninety percent of people in the United States live within ten miles of one of its stores.[15] What does this say about the nature of for-profit business in the United States? What might such a map have looked like one hundred years ago? (attribution: Copyright Rice University, OpenStax, under CC BY 4.0 license)

Walmart attempts to demonstrate virtuousness by holding itself out as a responsible corporation, concerned especially for the lower-income families that make up the majority of its customers.[16] But the company has experienced problems over the years, including lawsuits over illegal firing of employees, withholding of overtime pay and benefits, violations of foreign workers' rights, wage violations, violations of child labor laws, and failure to provide health coverage where and when applicable.[17]

Thousands of Walmart's U.S. employees are also reported to be receiving public assistance to make ends meet.[18] Meanwhile, the Walton family, operators of the retailer that purports to help people "live better," recently made $12.7 billion in a single day.[19]

Critical Thinking

- If you were an upper-level manager at Walmart, what kinds of decisions would you expect to make regarding the company's challenges?
- As a Walmart manager, how would you view the company's relationships with its stakeholders, including its employees? How would that view guide your decision-making?
- As a company executive, would you try to increase employee benefits? Why or why not?

Where does a case like Walmart's leave us? If a corporation with 2.3 million employees globally has reason to be concerned that at least some are dissatisfied with the job and may have witnessed some degree of unethical management behavior, the firm might also need to assume that some of those employees could choose to act unethically in the course of any business day. Of course, no job is perfect, and most of us experience some Monday mornings when we do not necessarily want to go into the office or exert the energy to be productive. And a company that provides high-quality goods to consumers at relatively low prices should get at least some credit for treating consumers fairly and ethically. It remains true, however, that any firm that wishes its employees to act ethically in the workplace must develop managers who model such behavior consistently toward all the company's stakeholders. No other single act on the part of business leaders is as important as this in fostering ethical behavior on the part of employees.

Using Values to Make Hard Choices

According to the logic of the market, each of us is a commodity with specific assets, such as education, training, and job experience. But we are more than commodities, and what moves us are values. Can you identify your core values and imagine how you might live them in the workplace (Figure 11.4)? We'll return to this question at the end of the chapter.

Figure 11.4 Which values are important to you? Which will you choose to act on in your career? (credit: modification of "doors choices choose open decision" by qimono/Pixabay, CC0)

To make the difficult decisions that come with career, personal life, and the balance between both, we must identify our personal values. Values provide us with the *why* for doing what we do. As an entrepreneur, for instance, you may find yourself working nonstop, dealing with emergency phone calls at 3:00 a.m., and doing a great deal of soul-searching about the direction and culture of your new venture. These tasks collectively might serve as impediments to happiness unless they truly reflect your underlying values.

The Role of Loyalty

Customers often remain loyal to a brand because of its appearance, functionality, or price. Companies want loyal customers like these and will go to great lengths to keep them. These relationships are external relationships between the company as an organization and its customers as a group.

Internal relationships exist among people, including among managers, employees, suppliers, and distributors. The loyalty that forms good internal relationships and enables us to rely on one another to do our work is a matter of trust and develops over time. Although it may be tested by rivalry, resentment, misunderstanding, and personality or other conflicts, without such trust, a company cannot function properly.

However, as we have seen, loyalty between employee and employer is a two-way street. The organization takes the first step by hiring a candidate in whom it will invest time, training, and money, and whose success it will reward with recognition, raises, and bonuses. No employer wants to spend time and money nurturing new talent only to see people leave for another firm. Therefore, it falls to the new professional, in turn, to decide whether his or her values align with those of the organization, and if so, to demonstrate a commitment to grow with the company over time. Achieving such clarity about your career goals, the type of company you would be proud to work for, and your vision of your future self requires some self-scrutiny. In the process, you will further clarify your personal and ethical values and start to become an ethical professional.

11.3 | Becoming an Ethical Professional

"'Professionalism' is the conduct, aims or qualities that characterize or mark a profession or professional person. It implies there is a quality of workmanship or service. But in reality, it's more about ethical behavior in the workplace. Every organization knows that a professional and ethical reputation is the difference between success and failure, and they seek to keep those staff who are the most professional."[20]

Ethical professionals work for companies whose values align with their own. How do you evaluate a company to see whether it is a good occupational fit and one that will allow you to live your ethical values every day?

Finding the "Right Fit"

Ethics has become a major consideration for young people in their selection of work and career. The following observation about young British workers applies to their counterparts in the United States, as well: "There's a quiet revolution happening. . . but it's not about pay, hours or contracts. It's a coup d'état led by the nation's young, politically engaged jobseekers who demand employers enshrine values and ethics in their business model, not just profit."[21]

Many job seekers want to feel that what they are doing is not just making money but making a difference, that is, contributing to the company in unique ways that reflect their core values, conscience, and personality. They believe an individual has worth beyond his or her immediate work or position. Many modern companies thus try to give greater weight to the human cost of decisions and employee happiness. They know that, according to studies, employees in "companies that work to build and maintain ethical workplace cultures are more financially successful and have more motivated, productive employees."[22] The decision whether to transfer someone from Boston to Salt Lake City, for instance, would now likely include the employee from the beginning and consider the impact on family members and the employee's future, in addition to the needs of the company.

This was not always the case, and there are several reasons for the change. The first is that satisfied employees are more productive and feel greater commitment to the organization.[23] Second, there are more options for job seekers, which gives them more freedom to choose a company for which to work.

"When we graduate from school, or whenever we are thinking about changing jobs, we are matching three things in deciding on our "vocation"—the job market (Are there jobs and opportunities?), our skills (Do I have the right skills to succeed in a particular job?) and our passions or beliefs (What do I want to do?) [with the concept that] worthwhile work can be found in working in a corporate culture that respects its workers and their personal lives. You may work where management is supportive and workers thrive and advance, but you can also find yourself working in a toxic environment where human dignity is torn down every day and responding to one's family commitments is regarded as weaknesses."[24]

Many business journals report annually on how highly employees rate their work places (Figure 11.5). For example, you can consult *Fortune's* annual list of "100 Best Companies to Work For," which you can search by such factors as diversity, compensation, and paid time off. You can also consult specialized lists such as *Forbes'* "100 Best Workplaces for Women" and *Black Enterprise's* "50 Best Companies for Diversity."

Best U.S. Employers as Ranked by Employees

Employer	Rating
Costco	9.58
Google	9.57
REI	9.53
Memorial Hermann Health System	9.45
United Services Automobile Association	9.42
MD Anderson Cancer Center	9.40
Penn Medicine	9.34
Mayo Clinic	9.32
City of Austin	9.31
Wegmans Food Markets	9.30

Sources: McCarthy, Niall. "America's Best Large Employers." Statista. May 10, 2017. Kalogeropoulos, Demitrios. "Why Costco Doesn't Worry about Paying Workers $13 an Hour." The Motley Fool. Apr 29, 2015.

Figure 11.5 With insurance coverage for part-time workers, higher-than-industry-average pay, and an overall employee satisfaction rating of 9.58 of a possible 10, Costco is often rated the best large employer to work for by *Forbes* and Statista. It is not just a generous employer; it is efficient, too, operating on a profit margin that meets the norm in the retail grocery business. (attribution: Copyright Rice University, OpenStax, under CC BY 4.0 license)

A third reason more companies are considering what truly makes employees happy is that even more than loyalty, employees appear to value the freedom and responsibility to act as moral agents in their own lives. A *moral agent* is someone capable of distinguishing right from wrong and willing to be held accountable for his or her choices.

The exercise of moral agency includes making a judgment about the alignment of personal and corporate conscience. Rather than jumping at the first job offer, moral agents assess whether the values expressed by the organization conform with their own, while recognizing that there is no perfect job. Even the most ethical organizations make mistakes, and even the most corrupt have managers and workers of integrity (Figure 11.6). This is why the "right fit" is more likely to be a job in which you can grow or that itself will change in a way that allows you to find greater meaning in it.

Figure 11.6   Abuse of power may not come as a surprise, but it should not be "business as usual." A firm should balance profitability with responsibility to society in a way that lifts the communities and neighborhoods of which we are part. (credit: modification of "Los Angeles Women's March (Unsplash)" by Samantha Sophia/Wikimedia Commons, Public Domain)

It's Not About the Money—Is It?

You may follow a professional vocation that offers low pay or low status but yields nontangible rewards, such as nonprofit work, nursing, or teaching. Or you may find a position that pays a great deal and offers job security but leaves you feeling unhappy or unfulfilled. For some professionals, these might include law, accounting, dentistry, or anything else. The point is that occupations with high compensation and a certain stature do not always infuse their holders with the greatest psychological and emotional rewards, and it is different for each of us. In the best of all worlds, you might embark on a well-paying career that helps others or contributes a much-needed good or service to society. Finding such work is easier said than done, of course, because the aim of most jobs is not to help people find meaning or happiness. Where these do occur, they are often ancillary effects of work, whose real purpose is the profitability without which there would not be any jobs at all.

Also consider the gap between the purpose of the business and the purpose of the individuals in it. Except in a few startups, these purposes are not identical. Even artists, musicians, and independent practitioners who derive great meaning from their work are not immune to the frustrations over money or career that affect everyone else.

It has been estimated, however, that the amount of money needed to be happy is not actually that much, at least by Western standards, although it is well above the poverty line.[25] Most people find themselves somewhere in the middle in terms of satisfaction and pay. Finding the proper balance between the two for *you* is taking a step on the way to your growth as a professional. You will make that assessment not once but throughout your career as you move in and out of jobs. Even if it turns out to be the best decision of your life, the choice to work for a company because of its mission, leadership, or cultural values should be intentional and based on sufficient knowledge of the company and yourself. To be appreciated for your contributions in the workplace, to work with congenial colleagues, or to provide a product or service of which you are proud might rival money as your most intrinsic motivator at work. Studies attest to this and, as professionals of integrity, we must each decide for ourselves how strong a benefit salary alone is in the jobs we select.

LINK TO LEARNING

Watch the TEDx presentation "Money Can Buy Happiness" about money and its relationship to happiness (https://openstax.org/l/53MoneyHappy) **to learn more.**

The Role of Ethical Top Leadership

As you consider your future path, perhaps leading toward a leadership role, keep in mind that perhaps the most effective way ethical behavior is learned in a company is through the modeling of that behavior by senior executives and others in leadership positions. This modeling sets what is known as "tone at the top." Employees may already have a personal moral code when they join an organization, but when they see key figures in the workplace actually living out the ethical values of the company, they are more likely to follow suit and take ethics seriously. Leaders' ethical behavior is especially important in emerging fields like artificial intelligence, where questions of safety, bias, misuse of technology, and privacy are raised daily.[26] It is not enough to offer codes of conduct, training, reporting, and review programs, no matter how thorough or sophisticated, if management does not adhere to or promote them. These are tools rather than solutions. The solutions come from leaders using the tools and showing others how to do the same. This takes practice, reinforcement, and collaboration at all levels of an organization. The result will be a culture of ethics that permeates the company from top to bottom.

Even leaders can falter, as the following box demonstrates. Also read the stories of ten ethical leaders in the appendix Profiles in Business Ethics: Contemporary Thought Leaders.

CASES FROM THE REAL WORLD

Swanson's Rule #1: Don't Plagiarize

Bill Swanson, former CEO of the defense contractor Raytheon, became well known for publishing a booklet entitled *Swanson's Unwritten Rules of Management*, which included thirty-three brief maxims for achieving success in business and cultivating a virtuous life in the corporate world.[27] The list included items like the famous "Waiter Rule," which held that you can judge a person's character by the way he or she treats those in subservient positions.

Swanson was hailed as a sage of modern business whose rules had saved companies like Czar Entertainment and Panera Bread from making bad hiring decisions.[28] Then it was discovered that he had plagiarized the list from several sources.[29] The booklet was discontinued and Swanson's compensation and retirement package was modified downward.[30] As in similar cases of ethical lapse, however, the greatest damage was to his reputation, despite an otherwise distinguished 42-year career.[31]

Critical Thinking

- Does this case surprise you? Why or why not?
- What do you think is the effect on a company's employees of unethical behavior at the top?

Ethics matter not merely because acting unethically will end in a compliance problem or public relations nightmare but because ethics is a way of life, not a hurdle to overcome. Moreover, the benefit of ethical behavior can grow over time so that a company begins to attract other ethical professionals and develops a reputation for honesty, integrity, and dependability. In a globally competitive world, these are not inconsequential factors. In an ethical workplace, employee satisfaction creates more loyalty to the company and morale improves because employees and managers feel they are part of an effort they can be proud of. Business performance picks up in ways ranging from higher earnings per share to increased customer retention to more satisfied employees.

Consider the net income of two corporations that, as of 2018, have appeared on eleven consecutive annual lists of the world's most ethical companies as determined by the Ethisphere Institute (https://ethisphere.com). The first is United Parcel Service (UPS), founded in 1907, which earned net income of $4.91 billion in 2017.[32] The second is Xerox, founded in 1906, which earned net income of $195 million in 2017.[33] Notice the staying power of these two companies, as well. Each is more than a century old and has a global presence. To test the consumer confidence these corporations evoke, consider your own opinion of how reputable they are. Ask your friends and family, too.

Again, employee loyalty, a positive work environment, and strong financial performance are not accidents; they are the result of intentional efforts on the part of leadership and board members who provide ethical vision and a plan for execution to all stakeholders. Ethical business need not be a zero-sum game with winners and losers; it can create situations in which everyone wins. Is there a more attractive environment for those just starting out in their careers? To be part of something profitable, responsible, and individually uplifting justifies all the work required to get there.

11.4 | Making a Difference in the Business World

On what will you base your professional identity? Do you believe an employer's enlightened self-interest is enough to ensure the ethical behavior of employers and employees? Or do you embrace "the critical importance of individual ethical choice in making our organizations, our professions and our culture serve all of humanity"?[34]

As attractive as high salary and comfortable lifestyle are to many, the life of a true professional is guided less by the desire to amass material goods than by a willingness to adhere to a code of ethical behavior and make the sometimes selfless decisions that protect the public and the corporation from misdeeds. In ideal form, that code of behavior is an expression of everything we have covered in this text regarding virtue, character, commitment, resilience, and the use of professional skills and training for the benefit of others. As first-century BCE Jewish religious leader Rabbi Hillel is said to have put it, "If I am not for myself, then who will be? And if I am only for myself, then what am I? And if not now, when?"

Today, it is often said that what counts at the end of a career is not how much money we made or how high up the corporate ladder we climbed. Rather, the real test is the difference we made—whether we have helped others or succumbed to motives such as greed and hubris (excess pride). Hubris creates the delusion that we are above the law and will never get caught. It has been used to justify many ruthless decisions whose sole criterion, in the end, is the potential for personal gain. This book has provided many examples on which to reflect about whether taking this short-term view actually benefits the company. In fact, hubris has ruined many lives and taken down a number of companies. Some, like Enron and Theranos, were once touted as icons of efficiency and ethical leadership.

Identifying Your Values and Mission

The values we choose to honor are the essence of ourselves, and we carry them with us wherever we live, work, and play. As we noted, the career you choose should reflect your values, whether you work at a for-profit or nonprofit organization, at Wells Fargo Bank or Doctors Without Borders (a medical rescue organization). It also is possible that you might work for a for-profit company and volunteer extensively on your own or on behalf of your firm in the nonprofit sector. Whatever path your career takes, it remains important not to let your well-considered values be diminished by others who do not prize loyalty or industriousness, for instance. Your career is not a contest in which the person who finishes with the biggest portfolio or fastest jet skis wins anything other than an empty prize. It is far better to treat others with integrity and respect and be surrounded by the true emblems of a successful career—family, friends, and colleagues who will attest to the dignity with which you have worked. In the final analysis, if you achieve a life of honor, then you have won.

How do you keep personal values like integrity, fairness, and respect close at hand? The best way is by writing them down, prioritizing them, and fashioning them into a personal mission statement. Most companies have mission statements, and people can have them, too. Yours will guide you on your path, clear away distractions on the road, and help you correct any missteps. It should be flexible, too, to account for changes in yourself and your goals. Your mission statement is not a global positioning system so much as a compass that guides you toward discovering who you are and what drives you (Figure 11.7).

Figure 11.7   Professionals need to develop a personal mission statement to avoid straying from the path they have set for themselves. A personal mission statement can serve as an ethical compass, guiding an individual through his or her professional and personal life. (credit: modification of "adventure compass hand macro" by Unknown/Pixabay, CC0)

Let us write your mission statement. Because it will reflect your values, start by identifying a handful of values that matter most to you. You can do this by answering the questions in Table 11.1; you may also find it beneficial to keep a journal and update your answers to these questions regularly.

Identifying Your Values

1. Of all the values that matter to you (e.g., honesty, integrity, loyalty, fairness, honor, hope), list the five most important.

2. Next, write down where you believe you learned each value (e.g., family, school, sports team, belief community, work).

3. Write a real or potential challenge you may face in living each value. Be as specific as possible.

4. Commit to an action in support of each value. Again, be specific.

Table 11.1

Now you can incorporate these values into your mission statement, which can take the form of a narrative or action. There are many formats you can follow (see the Link to Learning box), but the basic idea is to unite your values with the goals you have set for your life and career. You can, for instance, link the benefit you want to create, the market or audience for which you want to create it, and the outcome you hope to achieve.[35] Keep your statement brief. Richard Branson, founder of the Virgin Group, wants "to have fun in [my] journey through life and learn from [my] mistakes." Denise Morrison, CEO of Campbell Soup, aims "to serve as a leader, live a balanced life, and apply ethical principles to make a significant difference."[36] Your own statement can be as simple as, for instance, "To listen to and inspire others," or "To have a positive influence on everyone I meet."

LINK TO LEARNING

Read this blog, "The Ultimate Guide to Writing Your Own Mission Statement," by Andy Andrews (https://openstax.org/l/53Mission) for more information about creating a personal mission statement.

Watch the TEDx talk "How to Know Your Life Purpose in Five Minutes" about the self and identifying values (https://openstax.org/l/53LifePurpose) to learn more.

Putting Your Values and Mission Statement to the Test

There may be no better place to put personal values and mission to the test than in an entrepreneurial role. Startups cannot be run on concepts alone. More than almost any other kind of venture, they demand practical solutions and efficient methods. Entrepreneurs usually begin by identifying a product or service that is hard to come by in a particular market or that might be abundantly available but is overpriced or unreliable. The overall guiding force that inspires the startup then is the execution of the company's mission, which dictates much of the primary direction for the firm, including the identification of underserved customers, the geographic site for a headquarters, and the partners, suppliers, employees, and financing that help the company get off the ground and then expand. In a brand-new organization, though, where does that mission come from?

The founder or founders of a firm develop the company's mission directly from their own personal beliefs, values, and experience; this is particularly true for nonprofits. Sometimes the inspiration is as simple as the recognition of an unmet need, such as the rising global demand for food. Bertha Jimenez, an immigrant from Ecuador who was studying engineering at New York University, could not help but be concerned that while craft breweries were riding a wave of popularity in her adopted city, they were also throwing away a lot of barley grain that still had nutritional value but that no one could figure out how to reuse. After a few attempts, Jimenez and two friends, also immigrants, finally hit on the idea of making flour out of this barley grain, and thus was born the Queens, New York–based startup Rise Products, whose website proclaims that "Upcycling is the future of food."

Rise Products does not only supplies local bakers and pasta makers with its protein- and fiber-packed "super" barley flour for use in products from pizza dough to brownies. It has also sent product samples on request to Kellogg, Whole Foods, and Nestlé, as well as to a top chef in Italy. Jimenez and her fellow cofounders say, "In the long term, we can bring this to countries like ours. We want to look at technologies that won't be prohibitive for other people to have."[37]

If we were to diagram the relationship between founders' values and the entrepreneurial mission, it would look something like this:

personal values → personal mission statement → entrepreneurial mission statement

Just as a personal mission statement can change over time, so can the company mission be adapted to fit changing circumstances, industry developments, and client needs. TOMS Shoes is another entrepreneurial firm founded to fill a need: For every pair sold, the company donates a pair of shoes to a child without any. Over time, TOMS Shoes has expanded its mission to also offer eyeglasses and improved access to clean water to people in developing countries. It calls itself the "One for One" company, promoting founder Blake Mycoskie's promise that "With every product you purchase, TOMS will help a person in need."[38]

The point is, if you have clarified your personal values and mission statement, there is almost no limit to the number of ways you can apply them to your business goals and decisions to "do good and do well" in your career. The purpose of business is relationships, and the quality of relationships depends on our acceptance of self and concern for others. These are developed through the virtues of humility on the one hand and courage on the other. The demanding but essential task of life is to practice both. In that way—perhaps *only* in that way—can we be truly human and successful business professionals.

Endnotes

1. Pratik Patel, "Applying Virtue Ethics: The Rajat Gupta Case," The Seven Pillars Institute for Global Finance and Ethics, February 11, 2013. https://sevenpillarsinstitute.org/applying-virtue-ethics-the-rajat-gupta-case/.
2. Anita Raghaven, "For Rajat Gupta, Returning Is a Hard Road," *New York Times*, August 15, 2017. https://www.nytimes.com/2017/08/15/business/dealbook/rajat-gupta.html; Patricia Hurtado, "Ex-Goldman Director Rajat Gupta Back Home after Prison Stay," Bloomberg, January 19, 2016. https://www.bloomberg.com/news/articles/2016-01-19/ex-goldman-director-rajat-gupta-back-home-after-prison-stay.
3. Samuel Clowes Huneke, "Raj Rajaratnam and Insider Trading," The Seven Pillars Institute for Global Finance and Ethics. https://sevenpillarsinstitute.org/case-studies/raj-rajaratnam-and-insider-trading-2/ (accessed June 30, 2018).
4. Chelsea Bateman, "General Motors: A Recall Nightmare (2014)," Business Ethics Case Analyses, November 23, 2015. http://businessethicscases.blogspot.com/2015/11/general-motors-recall-nightmare-2014_23.html.
5. Greg DePersio, "How Have Businesses Evolved over Time?" *Investopedia*. https://www.investopedia.com/ask/answers/022615/how-have-business-ethics-evolved-over-time.asp#ixzz5IJV5DK2U (accessed June 13, 2018).
6. Google. https://www.google.com/about/our-company/ (accessed June 29, 2018).
7. Ben W. Heinemen, Jr., "The Google Case: When Law and Ethics Collide," *The Atlantic*, January 13, 2010. https://www.theatlantic.com/politics/archive/2010/01/the-google-case-when-law-and-ethics-collide/33438/.
8. Sherisse Pham, "Google Now Has Two Apps in China, but Search Remains Off Limits," *CNN Tech*, May 31, 2018. http://money.cnn.com/2018/05/31/technology/google-in-china-files-app/index.html.
9. Ben W. Heinemen, Jr., "The Google Case: When Law and Ethics Collide," *The Atlantic*, January 13, 2010. https://www.theatlantic.com/politics/archive/2010/01/the-google-case-when-law-and-ethics-collide/33438/.
10. Julia Steinberg and Natasha Khan, "It Takes Careful Planning to Scale a Mountain of Cheese," *Wall Street Journal*, December 10, 2017. https://www.wsj.com/articles/it-takes-careful-planning-to-scale-a-mountain-of-cheese-1512930205.
11. Julia Steinberg and Natasha Khan, "It Takes Careful Planning to Scale a Mountain of Cheese," *Wall Street Journal*, December 10, 2017.

https://www.wsj.com/articles/it-takes-careful-planning-to-scale-a-mountain-of-cheese-1512930205.

12. Ellen Wulfhorst, "Work-life Balance Boosts Workplace Ethics: Survey," Reuters, April 16, 2007. https://www.reuters.com/article/us-work/work-life-balance-boosts-workplace-ethics-survey-idUSN1631548120070416 (accessed June 20, 2018).

13. Walmart, 2017 Annual Report. http://s2.q4cdn.com/056532643/files/doc_financials/2017/Annual/WMT_2017_AR-(1).pdf (accessed February 7, 2018).

14. Ylan Q. Mui and Michael S. Rosenwald, "Wal-Mart's New Tack: Show 'Em the Payoff," *Washington Post*, September 12, 2007. http://www.washingtonpost.com/wp-dyn/content/article/2007/09/12/AR2007091202513.html?hpid=moreheadlines.

15. Maria Halkias, "Wal-Mart CEO Thinks No One Should Pay $99 for Free Shipping," *Dallas Morning News*, June 2, 2017. https://www.dallasnews.com/business/retail/2017/06/02/wal-marts-a-giant-orange-machine-is-part-of-wal-marts-online-strategy.

16. Hayley Peterson, "Meet the Average Wal-Mart Shopper," *Business Insider*, September 18, 2014. http://www.businessinsider.com/meet-the-average-wal-mart-shopper-2014-9.

17. Timothy Jordan, "The Good, The Bad, and Wal-Mart," Workplace Fairness. https://www.workplacefairness.org/reports/good-bad-wal-mart/wal-mart.php (accessed February 8, 2018).

18. Krissy Clark, "Save Money. Live Better," *Slate*, April 2, 2014. http://www.slate.com/articles/business/moneybox/2014/04/walmart_employees_on_food_stamps_their_wages_aren_t_enough_to_get_by.html.

19. Rob Wile, "The Walmart Heirs Just Made $12.7 Billion in One Day," *Time*, November 17, 2017. http://time.com/money/5029034/walmart-fortune-heirs-12-7-billion-in-one-day/.

20. Darrell Brown, "Ethics and Professionalism in the Workplace," *Indianapolis Recorder*, September 15, 2016. http://www.indianapolisrecorder.com/business/article_36d05298-7b96-11e6-8226-033c365dab07.html.

21. Mathew Jenkin, "Millennials Want to Work for Employers Committed to Values and Ethics," *The Guardian*, May 5, 2015. https://www.theguardian.com/sustainable-business/2015/may/05/millennials-employment-employers-values-ethics-jobs.

22. "Employee Job Satisfaction and Engagement: Revitalizing a Changing Workforce," The Society for Human Resource Management. https://www.shrm.org/hr-today/trends-and-forecasting/research-and-surveys/Documents/2016-Employee-Job-Satisfaction-and-Engagement-Report.pdf (accessed February 10, 2018).

23. "Employee Job Satisfaction and Engagement: Revitalizing a Changing Workforce," The Society for Human Resource Management. https://www.shrm.org/hr-today/trends-and-forecasting/research-and-surveys/Documents/2016-Employee-Job-Satisfaction-and-Engagement-Report.pdf (accessed February 10, 2018).

24. Kirk O. Hanson, *The Six Ethical Dilemmas Every Professional Faces*. (Waltham, MA: Bentley University, Center for Business Ethics, February 3, 2014). https://www.bentley.edu/sites/www.bentley.edu.centers/files/2014/10/22/Hanson%20VERIZON%20Monograph_2014-10%20Final%20%281%29.pdf (accessed June 21, 2018).

25. Jill Suttie, "How Does Valuing Money Affect Your Happiness?" *Greater Good Magazine*, October 30, 2017. https://greatergood.berkeley.edu/article/item/how_does_valuing_money_affect_your_happiness.

26. Richard Nieva and Sean Hollister, "Read Google's AI Ethics Memo: 'We Are Not Developing AI for Use in Weapons,'" Cnet.com, June 7, 2018. https://www.cnet.com/news/read-googles-ai-ethics-memo-we-are-not-developing-ai-for-use-in-weapons/.

27. William H. Swanson, *Swanson's Unwritten Rules of Management* (Waltham, MA: Raytheon, 2005).

28. Del Jones, "CEOs Say How You Treat a Waiter Can Predict a Lot about Character," *USA Today*, April 14, 2006. http://www.ign.com/boards/threads/ceos-say-how-you-treat-a-waiter-can-predict-a-lot-about-character.115174051/ (accessed February 15, 2018).

29. Tom Ehrenfeld, "The Rewritten Rules of Management," 2–3. https://changethis.com/manifesto/23.RewrittenRules/pdf/23.RewrittenRules.pdf (accessed February 15, 2018).

30. Tom Ehrenfeld, "The Rewritten Rules of Management," 3. https://changethis.com/manifesto/23.RewrittenRules/pdf/23.RewrittenRules.pdf (accessed February 15, 2018).

31. "Bill Swanson: Biography," Raytheon. https://www.raytheon.com/rtnwcm/groups/public/documents/profile/bio_swanson.pdf (accessed February 16, 2018).

32. "UPS Growth Accelerates in 2017," February 1, 2018. https://globenewswire.com/news-release/2018/02/01/1329929/0/en/UPS-Growth-Accelerates-In-2017.html.

33. "Xerox Corporation Form 10-K," SEC filing. https://www.sec.gov/Archives/edgar/data/108772/000010877218000012/xrx-123117x10xk.htm.

34. Kirk O. Hanson, *The Six Ethical Dilemmas Every Professional Faces*, Bentley University: Center for Business Ethics, February 3, 2014. https://www.bentley.edu/sites/www.bentley.edu.centers/files/2014/10/22/Hanson%20VERIZON%20Monograph_2014-10%20Final%20%281%29.pdf (accessed June 21, 2018).

35. Jessica Stillman, "Here Are the Personal Mission Statements of Musk, Branson, and Oprah (Plus 7 Questions to Write Your Own)," *Inc.*, May 29, 2018. https://www.inc.com/jessica-stillman/how-to-write-your-own-personal-mission-statement-7-questions.html.

36. Drew Hendricks, "Personal Mission Statement of 13 CEOs and Lessons You Need to Learn," *Forbes*, November 10, 2014. https://www.forbes.com/sites/drewhendricks/2014/11/10/personal-mission-statement-of-14-ceos-and-lessons-you-need-to-learn/#1e7644621e5e.

37. Larissa Zimberoff, "From Brewery to Bakery: A Flour That Fights Waste," *New York Times*, June 25, 2018. https://www.nytimes.com/2018/06/25/dining/brewery-grain-flour-recycling.html. Rise Products. http://www.riseproducts.co/ (accessed July 1, 2018).

38. TOMS. https://www.toms.com/ (accessed July 1, 2018).

A The Lives of Ethical Philosophers

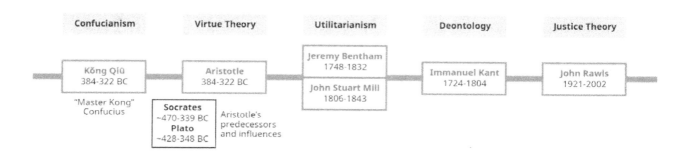

Figure A.1 Over time and in different parts of the world, philosophical ethics has occupied the thoughts of many significant thinkers. Here are the names and lifespans of some of those figures. (attribution: Copyright Rice University, OpenStax, under CC BY 4.0 license)

The Ethics of Aristotle: Virtue Theory

Aristotle, 384 BCE–322 BCE

Aristotle (384 BCE–322 BCE) was a student of Plato, who was himself a student of Socrates, one of the founders of Western philosophy. Aristotle spent about twenty years at Plato's Academy in Athens, first as a student and then as an associate. Later he tutored the young Alexander of Macedonia, who would become Alexander the Great.[i]

Aristotle eventually returned to Athens where he opened his own school, the Lyceum, and where he studied and taught extensively in philosophy, government, and the natural and social sciences. He, along with most of the classical Greek thinkers, believed that all academic disciplines were linked. They were far less inclined than we are to rigidly separate academic subjects.

Aristotle's principle work on ethics, *The Nicomachean Ethics*, was dedicated either to his father or son, both of whom were named Nicomachus, a popular name within his family. In *Ethics*, where Aristotle laid out the essence of virtue theory, he stated that if we truly desire people to be ethical, then we must have them practice ethics from an early age. Just as Plato claimed that unethical individuals are simply uneducated in ethics, so Aristotle held that constant practice is the best means by which to create ethical humans. He contended that men—for Aristotle, unlike Plato, education was restricted to males—who are taught to be ethical in minor matters as boys will automatically act ethically in all matters as they mature. Of course, a legitimate question regarding both philosophers is whether we believe they are correct on these points.

In *Ethics*, Aristotle introduced the concept of what is usually referred to as the golden mean of moderation. He believed that every virtue resides somewhere between the vices of defect and excess. That is, one can display either too little or too much of a good thing, or a virtue. The trick, as for Goldilocks, is to have just the right amount of it. Adding to the complexity of this, however, is the fact that striking the right balance between too

---

i Aristotle's family originated from a region in northern Greece that was adjacent to classical Macedonia, and his father, Nicomachus, had similarly tutored Alexander's father, Philip II of Macedonia.

much and too little does not necessarily put one midway between the two. The mean of moderation is more of a sliding value, fluctuating between defect and excess, but not automatically splitting the difference between them. Depending on the virtue in question, the mean may lie closer to a deficit or to a surplus. For example, take the virtue of courage (Figure A.2). For Aristotle, the mean laid closer to foolhardiness or brashness. It's not that foolhardiness is less a vice than cowardice; it's just that courage verges closer to the one than to the other.

Cowardice   Courage   Foolhardiness

Figure A.2   (attribution: Copyright Rice University, OpenStax, under CC BY 4.0 license)

What constitutes a virtue in the first place, according to Aristotle? Besides courage, the virtues include wisdom, kindness, love, beauty, honesty, and justice. These approximate the same virtues proclaimed by Plato.

Aristotle also speaks of *eudaemonia*, a perfect balance of happiness and goodness interpreted classically. Humans experience *eudaemonia* both in themselves and in the world when they act virtuously and live a life of rational thought and contemplation. As Aristotle argued, rational thought is the activity of the divine, so it is appropriate for men to emulate this practice, as well.

The Ethics of Bentham and Mill: Utilitarianism

Jeremy Bentham, 1748–1832

John Stuart Mill, 1806–1873

Jeremy Bentham, an attorney, became what we would today call a consultant to the British Parliament in the late-eighteenth century. He was given the task of devising a method by which members could evaluate the worth of proposed legislation. He took a Latin term—*util*, or utility, usefulness, or happiness—and calculated the number of utils in proposed bills. Essentially this quantified the scoring of upcoming legislation—those pieces with the greatest number of utils were given a higher ranking than those with the least.

Utilitarianism as an ethical system today, though it has application to many areas beyond that simply of lawmaking, holds to this same principle. When making moral decisions, we are advised to select that action which produces the greatest amount of good for the greatest number of people. If the balance of good or happiness or usefulness outweighs that of evil, harm, or unhappiness, then the choice is a moral one. On the other hand, if the balance of evil outweighs that of good, then the choice is immoral. Due to this emphasis on the outcome of ethical decisions, utilitarianism is classified as a consequentialist theory.

Bentham lays much of his theory out in *An Introduction to the Principles of Morals and Legislation* (1789). There, he proposes the hedonic calculus—from the Greek *hedone*, or pleasure—as a mechanism by which one can determine the amount of pleasure versus pain in moral choices.

Bentham found a ready supporter and lieutenant in James Mill (1773–1836), a Scottish lawyer who came to assist Bentham in championing utilitarianism as a political philosophy. And when Mill's son, John Stuart, was born, Bentham, having no children of his own, became his godfather. Together, Bentham and the elder Mill established a curriculum through which the younger Mill was schooled at home, an arrangement that was not uncommon in the early nineteenth century. John Stuart was evidently a prodigy and at an early age was taking on Greek, Latin, economic theory, and higher mathematics.

An odd twist accompanies the arrangements that Bentham made for his body after his death. Because donated cadavers were rare in teaching hospitals and this had led to a rash of grave-robbing, he stipulated that his body be dissected by surgeons for the education of their students, while in the presence of his friends. He further requested that, afterward, his body be re-stitched together, dressed in his own clothes, and perpetually displayed at what was then a new school that he had endowed, University College in London. To this day, Bentham's corpse, with a wax head to replace the original, mummified one, is posed in a glass case at meetings of the trustees of University College, all by provision of his will.

John Stuart Mill, as he reached adulthood, became a leader of the second generation of utilitarians. He broke with his mentor, though, in one significant way: by distinguishing between different levels of pleasure—higher and lower ones—and offering a means by which to determine where any given pleasure falls. While Bentham insisted that ranking pleasures were subjective and that no one could truly say that some pleasures were objectively more worthy than others, the younger Mill claimed that we could indeed specifically determine which pleasures were the higher ones by polling educated people. Those pleasures which were ranked highest by this select cohort were indeed the greatest ones, and those which were ranked least were the inferior ones.

Mill also refined the political applications of utilitarianism and, in so doing, laid the foundation for the political movement of libertarianism. Though he himself never used this term and probably would take issue with being labeled a libertarian were he alive today, he did introduce many of the principles that are esteemed by libertarians. In his most important work on political freedoms, *On Liberty* (1859), he introduced the no-harm rule. By this, Mill proposed that no individual be deprived of his or her right to act in any fashion, even a self-destructive one, provided that his or her action does not impinge *physically* on others.[ii]

For example, according to Mill, we may try to persuade an alcoholic to give up drinking. We may marshal our best arguments in an attempt to convince him or her that this is wrong and harmful—"remonstrate" is the verb that he employed. Still, if the alcoholic persists in drinking excessively despite our best efforts to encourage him or her otherwise, then no power of the state ought to be brought to bear to prevent him or her from drinking, unless and until the drinking causes physical harm to others. One can see the application of this to, say, motorcycle-helmet laws today. Mill would hold that even though the injury-preventing capacity of helmets clearly can be demonstrated, bikers still ought to be permitted to refrain from wearing them if they so choose.

The significance of utilitarianism in our era lies in the fact that many of us implement utilitarian thought processes when we have to make many ethical choices, even if we don't necessarily consider ourselves to be utilitarians. In addition, utilitarianism continues to influence new generations of philosophers and ethical thinkers, such as the Australian Peter Singer, an inspiration for the contemporary animal rights movement who is currently on the faculty at Princeton University.

A telling critique of utilitarianism, however, is the objection that it assays no good or evil in acts themselves, but only in the good or evil that these acts produce. If a proposed municipal, state, or federal law could be demonstrated to serve the defined interests of a majority at the expense of the interests only of a minority, then utilitarianism would suggest that such a law is good and moral. Little recognition appears within utilitarianism of the possibility of tyranny of the majority. Many critics of utilitarianism have scored this weakness of the ethical system. A persuasive instance of this is the short story "Those Who Walk Away from Omelas" by the American writer Ursula K. Le Guin (1929–2018).

The Ethics of Kant: Deontology

Immanuel Kant, 1724–1804

---

ii   A limitation within Mill's no-harm principle was its focus solely on physical harm without acknowledgement of the reality of psychological damage. He made no allowance for what the law today denotes as pain and suffering. In his defense, this concept is a twentieth-century one and has little credibility among Mill's contemporaries.

The sage of Königsberg in Prussia (now Kaliningrad in Russia), Kant taught philosophy at the University of Königsberg for several years. In fact, throughout a very long lifetime, especially by the standards of the eighteenth century, he never traveled far from the city where he had been born.

Kant's parents were members of a strict sect of Lutheranism called pietism, and he remained a practicing Christian throughout his life. Though he only occasionally noted religion in his writing, his advocacy of deontology cannot be understood apart from an appreciation of his religious faith. Religion and ethics went hand in hand for Kant, and God always remained the ground or matrix upon which his concept of morality was raised.

Though he never married, Kant was by contemporary accounts no dour loner. He apparently was highly popular among his colleagues and students and often spent evenings eating and drinking in their company. He frequently hosted gatherings at his own lodging and served as a faculty master at the university. He was also a creature of habit, taking such regular walks through the neighborhood surrounding campus that residents could tell the time of day by the moment when he would pass their doorway or window.

The term deontology stems from the Greek *deon*—duty, obligation, or command. As an ethical system, it is the radical opposite of utilitarianism in that it holds that the consequences of a moral decision are of no matter whatsoever. What *is* important are the motives as to why one has acted in the way that one has. So an action may have beneficial results, but still be unethical *if* it has been performed for the wrong reasons. Similarly, an action may have catastrophic consequences, but still be deemed moral if it has been done on the basis of the right will.

Not only is deontology non-consequentialist, it is also non-situationalist. That is, an act is either right or wrong always and everywhere. The context surrounding it is unimportant. The best example of this is Kant's famous allusion to an axe-murderer who, in seeking his victim, must always be told the truth as to his would-be victim's whereabouts. By Kant's reasoning, one cannot lie even in this dire circumstance in order to save the life of an innocent person. Kant was not diminishing the significance of human life in holding that the truth must always be told. Instead, he was insisting that truth-telling is one of the inviolable principles that frames our lives. To lie—even in defense of life—is to cheapen and weaken an essential pillar that sustains us. Kant knew that this example would draw critics, but he deliberately chose it anyway in order to demonstrate his conviction about the rightness of certain acts.

Perhaps the most well-known element of Kant's ethics is his explanation of the categorical imperative, laid out in his *Fundamental Principles of the Metaphysics of Ethics*, 1785. This intimidating phrase is just a fancy way of saying that some actions must always be taken and certain standards always upheld, such as truth-telling. The categorical imperative has two expressions, each of which Kant regarded as stating the same thing. In its first expression, the categorical imperative holds that a moral agent (i.e., a human being imbued with reason and a God-given soul) is free to act only in ways that he or she would permit any other moral agent to act. That is, none of us is able to claim that we are special and so entitled to privileges to which others are not also entitled. And in its second expression, the categorical imperative stipulates that we must treat others as ends in themselves and not just as means to our own ends. So we can never simply use people as stepping stones to our own goals and objectives unless we are also willing to be so treated by them.

Despite the enduring popularity of utilitarianism as an ethical system, deontology is probably even more pronounced within our moral sensitivity. Perhaps the best indicator of this is that most of us believe that a person's motives for acting ought to be taken into account when judging whether those actions are ethical or unethical. To witness a famous literary example of this, Victor Hugo made clear in *Les Misérables* that his protagonist, Jean Valjean, became a hunted man simply because he stole bread to feed his starving family. By Hugo's standards—and our own—Valjean truly committed no crime, and the tragedy of his life is that he must spend a significant part of it on the run from the dogged Inspector Javert.

Deontology, like all ethical systems, has its critics, and they zero in on its inflexibility regarding acts which may never be permitted, such as telling a lie, even if it is to save a life. Still, the system continues to inspire a devoted following of philosophers to this day. In the twentieth century, this was notably represented by the British ethicist W. D. Ross (1877–1971) and the American political philosopher John Rawls (1921–2002). Those who embrace deontology are typically attracted to its deep-seated sense of honor and commitment to objective values in addition to its insistence that all humans be treated with dignity and respect.

The Ethics of John Rawls: Justice Theory

John Rawls, 1921–2002

Though Rawls considered himself to be a utilitarian, he also acknowledged that his moral philosophy owed much to the social contract tradition represented over the past few centuries by John Locke and David Hume, among others. To complicate Rawls' philosophy even further, there was a bit of deontology exhibited in it, too, through Rawls' sentiment was that political freedoms and material possessions be distributed as fully and widely as possible precisely because it is the right thing to do.

Rawls is a uniquely American political philosopher, and this can be seen from his emphasis on political liberty. But this statement also speaks to his commitment to the utilitarianism of John Stuart Mill, the second-generation leader of that movement. Hence Rawls's assertion that he actually was a utilitarian at heart.

Whatever the influences on his thought, Rawls was the most significant political philosopher ever to emerge from the United States, and probably one of the most influential ethicists in the West over the past several centuries. He labeled his ethics to be "justice as fairness," and he developed it over nearly a lifetime. It was laid out formally in 1971 with the publication of his *A Theory of Justice*, a treatise of more than 550 pages. Still, preliminary drafts of what became this book were circulating within philosophical circles beginning in the late 1950s.

To be fair, Rawls insisted, human justice must be centered on a firm foundation comprising a first and second principle. The first principle declared that "each person is to have an equal right to the most extensive basic liberty compatible with a similar liberty for others." These liberties included traditional ones such as freedom of thought and speech, the vote, a fair trial when accused of a crime, and the ownership of some personal property not subject to the state's seizure. Very few commentators have criticized this principle.

It is the second principle, however, which has incurred the loudest objections. It consisted of two sub-points: first, socio-economic inequality is permissible only to the degree that it brings the greatest benefit to the least-advantaged members of society. (Rawls labeled this the *difference principle*.) And, second, authority and offices are to be available to everyone competent to hold them. (Rawls called this *fair equality of opportunity*.) Additionally, the training to ensure that all may merit these offices absolutely must be available to all.

What Rawls actually advocated was an at-least minimal distribution of material goods and services to everyone, regardless of what inheritance he or she might come by or what work he or she might engage in. And this tenet has incurred a firestorm of controversy. Many have embraced what they term Rawls' egalitarian perspective on the ownership of property. Yet others have argued that he ignored the unlimited right to ownership of personal property specifically predicated on hard work and/or bequests from family. On the other hand, pure Marxists have dismissed this principle as not going far enough to ensure that sizable estates, as well as the means of production, be extracted from the clutches of plutocrats.

How might society move toward justice as fairness? Rawls proposed a thought exercise: If we all could imagine ourselves, before birth, to be in what he calls the Original Position, knowing only that we would be born but without knowledge of what sex, race, wealth, ethnicity, intelligence, health, or family structures we would be assigned, then we necessarily would ensure that these two principles would be observed. We would do so because we would have absolutely no way of predicting the real-life circumstances which we would inherit post-birth and wouldn't want to risk being born into an impoverished or tyrannical environment.

The reason why we would be blind as to the world that each of us would inhabit would be because we would be cloaked by a "veil of ignorance" that would screen us from pre-knowledge of our circumstances once we were born—in other words, viewed from the original position, we wouldn't take the chance of suffering from political oppression or material poverty. Self-interest, then, would motivate us to insist that these minimum levels of political and material largesse would be the birthright of all.

Of course, we can't return to our pre-birth stage and so negotiate this sort of arrangement beforehand. Hence, the only way of creating this sort of world now would be to imagine that we were in the original position and deliberately build such a fair environment for all.

Given human nature and its inherent selfishness, is it reasonable to expect human beings to make a concerted effort to create the structures needed for justice as fairness? Perhaps not, but realize that Rawls was only following in the footsteps of Plato in his proposal to craft a perfect *polis*, or city-state, in *The Republic*. Therein Plato took all of the beauty and wisdom of the Athens of his day and imagined it without any of its limitations. Plato knew that this was an ideal, but he also realized that even an attempt to build such a city-state would produce what he regarded as much incalculable good.

B Profiles in Business Ethics: Contemporary Thought Leaders

Dan Bane, chairman and chief executive officer of Trader Joe's

With roots in Pasadena, California, the Trader Joe's brand is no stranger to ethical and sustainable business practices. At its origin, when it was a mere convenience store and still called Pronto Markets, founder Joe Coulombe opted to pay his employees at the median California family income rate. He did not want to exploit his employees the way he felt other large convenience chains did at the time.[i] After reading about the looming threats to the environment in 1970, Joe transformed his stores to become more health and environmentally conscious. Indeed, as far back as 1977, the growing chain of grocery stores began selling reusable "Save-A-Tree" canvas bags to its customers to encourage more environmentally friendly shopping practices.[ii]

These ethical principles, like the plastic lobsters it decorates its stores with and the Hawaiian shirts its employees wear, have become an integral and recognizable part of the Trader Joe's brand. With more than four hundred stores nationwide, this chain of grocery stores specializing in reasonably priced, high-end cheeses, wines, and organic foods is a beacon of ethical business practices in the grocery industry.

Joe Coulombe, the original Trader Joe, has long since given up his Hawaiian shirts and his role as leader of the company. Since 2001, Trader Joe's chief executive officer (CEO) has been Dan Bane. Bane has held firm on the ethical values established decades before. As part of his leadership approach, he often works in his stores so he can interact with customers and employees. He imagines the organizational principle at work at Trader Joe's as an inverted pyramid, where he as CEO sits at the bottom of the pyramid and the many employees and customers are at the top. He thinks of himself more like a conductor of an orchestra than a dictator shouting orders at his underlings.[iii]

Bane's Trader Joe's has seven core values: demonstrating integrity, being product-driven, producing customer "wow" experiences, challenging bureaucracy, seeking continuous improvement, treating the store as the brand, and being a national and neighborhood company.[iv] These core values are a roadmap for Bane and the company. As he sees it, it is his job to "make sure we stay on those [values] and preach those all the time."[v]

As an extension of its values, Trader Joe's tries to keep a close watch on its supply chain. In 2010, it was taken to task by environmental groups for selling seafood that had been harvested in environmentally unfriendly ways. Bane took this criticism to heart and pledged to do better. The company now sends its purchasers out to the very locations where they produce the product they sell. Bane wants to be certain that the suppliers are using practices that are consistent with Trader Joe's focus on environmental sustainability and even labor practices.[vi] As an added precaution, he also works with Greenpeace to keep the store shelves as green-friendly as possible.[vii]

i   Beth Kowitt, "Meet the Original Joe," *Fortune*, August 23, 2010, http://fortune.com/2010/08/23/meet-the-original-joe/.

ii   "Our Story: Timeline," Trader Joe's, https://www.traderjoes.com/our-story/timeline (accessed July 6, 2018).

iii   "The Gathering (Oct. 2013) with Dan Bane," Claremont Lincoln University, https://www.youtube.com/watch?v=CxUjovZDMbc (accessed July 6, 2018).

iv   Anthony Molaro, "The Trader Joe's Way for Libraries (a Manifesto Part III)," November 27, 2013, https://informationactivist.com/2013/11/27/the-trader-joes-way-for-libraries-a-manifesto-part-iii/

v   "The Gathering (Oct. 2013) with Dan Bane," Claremont Lincoln University, https://www.youtube.com/watch?v=CxUjovZDMbc (accessed July 6, 2018).

vi   "The Gathering (Oct. 2013) with Dan Bane," Claremont Lincoln University, https://www.youtube.com/watch?v=CxUjovZDMbc (accessed July 6, 2018).

vii   Jim Lichtman, "2016 – Over Already?," It's Ethics, Stupid!, December 31, 2016, https://ethicsstupid.com/accountability/2016-over-already/ (accessed July 6, 2018).

- Watch this video of Dan Bane discussing his position on ethics as CEO of Trader Joe's (https://openstax.org/l/53DanBane) to learn more.

Mary T. Barra, chairman and CEO of General Motors

Mary T. Barra was born into a General Motors (GM) family in Michigan. Her father worked for the GM brand Pontiac for nearly four decades and one of her first jobs was working at a GM plant herself checking the fender panels and hoods of cars rolling off the line when she was only eighteen years old.

After earning a degree in electrical engineering from the General Motors Institute (now called Kettering University) in Flint, Michigan, she returned to the company to work as an engineer for Pontiac's new sporty two-seater, the Fiero. After a few years working as an engineer, GM then sent her to Stanford University on a fellowship to earn a master of business administration. From there, she climbed the executive ladder, working in a variety of positions until, in 2014, she was named CEO of General Motors Company, becoming the first woman ever to hold that position at a major international automaker.[viii]

When Barra took the reins of the company, the once-dominant automobile manufacturer had undergone a considerable decline in influence and prestige. The Great Recession hit the already struggling company very hard. As a result, it was compelled to seek bankruptcy and government support. It also went through some painful downsizing, even going so far as to discontinue the very Pontiac division Barra once worked for as a young engineer.

Just a few years later, GM appears to have turned those lemons into lemonade. It is now a healthy company with billions in cash on its books and billions in earnings. How it got to this healthy position is due in large part to Barra's efforts to transform GM's famously large and clumsy bureaucracy, as well as her push to encourage diversity of thought, innovative ways of dealing with problems, and working more closely with GM's many stakeholders.[ix]

But, this success aside, there were huge ethical bumps in the road that appeared right at the time Barra took control. In the spring of 2014, a string of news stories emerged regarding possible defects in the Chevy Cobalt, a GM compact car that started coming off the line in 2004. These stories eventually uncovered the fact that GM insiders had known of the defect and covered it up for a decade, even when they knew the defect was causing needless injuries and deaths.

The press attention was a mounting disaster for GM, and Barra's action was crucial. As the country condemned GM, Barra announced that "whatever mistakes were made in the past, we will not shirk from our responsibilities now and in the future. Today's GM will do the right thing."[x] Barra jettisoned the "cost culture" that had precipitated the defect and cover-up, and replaced it with a "customer culture." She also reformulated GM's code of ethics and published a booklet on the code called *Winning with Integrity*. Although some have pointed to some weaknesses in the code, it remains an important step for GM in encouraging personal integrity and empowering GM employees to speak up.[xi] These days, GM and Barra hope the tragic lapse in ethics the company is now safely in the rearview mirror.

- Watch this video of Mary Barra discussing GM's response to the ignition switch recall (https://openstax.org/l/53MaryBarra) to learn more.

viii   Max Nisen, "How Mary Barra Went from Inspecting Fender Panels to GM's First Female CEO," *Business Insider*, December 10, 2013, http://www.businessinsider.com/mary-barra-gm-ceo-career-bio-2013-12.

ix   Rick Tetzeli, "Mary Barra Is Remaking GM's Culture—and the Company Itself," *Fast Company*, October 17, 2016, https://www.fastcompany.com/3064064/mary-barra-is-remaking-gms-culture-and-the-company-itself.

x   Phil LeBeau and Jeff Pohlman, "The Corporate Culture: Behind the Scenes at General Motors," CNBC, May 16, 2014, https://www.cnbc.com/2014/05/16/the-corporate-culture-behind-the-scenes-at-general-motors.html.

xi   Marianne Jennings and Lawrence Trautman, "Ethical Culture and Legal Liability: The GM Switch Crisis and Lessons in Governance," https://www.bu.edu/jostl/files/2016/08/JENNINGS_ARTICLE_MACROD-PDF.pdf (accessed July 6, 2018).

Marc Benioff, chairman, CEO, and founder of Salesforce

Marc Benioff took to computer entrepreneurism at an early age. At only 15 years old, he had already started his own software company. The profits from that company were enough to put him through college. When he graduated, he jumped right into a position at the software company Oracle, quickly climbing the corporate ladder and becoming the youngest vice president in the company's history within a few years.[xii]

Benioff eventually left Oracle to start his own software company, Salesforce. At its inception, Salesforce was a revolutionary approach to software, in that it delivers centrally hosted applications over the Internet to its clients. The bold move of charting a cloud approach to computing proved successful and, as of 2017, Salesforce was pulling in $8.39 billion in revenue.

Rather than take his success for granted, however, Benioff has tried to use his wealth and position of power to support ethical causes, such as promoting sustainable growth and diversity. He is a big supporter of stakeholder capitalism as well.[xiii] This is an approach to business that attempts to consider the interests of all major stakeholders rather than catering merely or disproportionately to the investors.

And Benioff has tried to put his money where his mouth is. Since 1999, he has maintained what he calls his "1-1-1 model." This is a company program that donates 1% of equity, 1% of employee time, and 1% of products to nonprofit organizations operating in locations where his companies do business. According to Benioff, this is just one way for him to demonstrate that "the business of business is improving the state of the world."[xiv] Another way is by ensuring that there is pay equity between men and women working in the same positions in his company. When Benioff realized a few years ago that men and women were not being paid at a comparable rate, he took action to change this.[xv]

Beyond philanthropy and striving for equity in his company, Benioff recognizes that technology innovators like himself need to take initiative in ensuring that business is done ethically. He knows that the volume of innovation coming out of the industry makes it difficult to manage, and he does not trust individual CEOs and companies to always do the ethical thing. "We're moving rapidly into a new world where we know the government is going to have to be involved in these next-generation technologies—like AI [artificial intelligence], biotech, etc.—which are all so new, and could have unintended consequences," he said in 2018. To manage the disruption that comes with these changes, he suggested it might be necessary to create a regulatory government body not unlike the Food and Drug Administration, except for technology.[xvi]

Recently, his ethical approach to business has led him to speak out on the autocratic style of many other leaders in Silicon Valley. Speaking in Davos, Switzerland, in 2018, Benioff challenged leaders in technology to step back from the all-too-common position he summarized as, "I'm the entrepreneur and I am in charge no matter what happens." Citing the infamous aggressive leadership style of Uber's founder and former CEO, Travis Kalanick, he warned against adopting this approach. Instead, he proposed they embrace the concept of trust.[xvii] "It's a culture issue. What is the most important thing in your company—is it trust or is it growth? If anything trumps trust, we are in trouble."[xviii]

xii   Matt Weinberger, "The Rise of Marc Benioff, the Flashy Billionaire Founder of Salesforce," *Business Insider*, March 17, 2016. http://www.businessinsider.com/the-rise-of-salesforce-ceo-marc-benioff-2016-3.

xiii   Rana Foroohar, "Marc Benioff: Taking on Silicon Valley's Noxious Culture," *Financial Times*, January 21, 2018, https://www.ft.com/content/117c23d2-fb6a-11e7-9b32-d7d59aace167.

xiv   "Pledge 1%," Salesforce.org, http://www.salesforce.org/pledge-1/ (accessed July 3, 2018).

xv   Lesley Stahl, "Leading by Example to Close the Gender Pay Gap," *60 Minutes*, April 15, 2018, https://www.cbsnews.com/news/salesforce-ceo-marc-benioff-leading-by-example-to-close-the-gender-pay-gap/.

xvi   Rana Foroohar, "Marc Benioff: Taking on Silicon Valley's Noxious Culture," *Financial Times*, January 21, 2018, https://www.ft.com/content/117c23d2-fb6a-11e7-9b32-d7d59aace167.

xvii   David Reid and Andrew Ross Sorkin, "Marc Benioff Launches Tirade against the Leadership Style of Silicon Valley," CNBC, January 23, 2018, https://www.cnbc.com/2018/01/23/davos-2018-marc-benioff-launches-tirade-against-the-leadership-style-of-silicon-valley.html.

- Watch this video of Marc Benioff discussing the crisis of trust in Silicon Valley (https://openstax.org/l/53MarcBenioff) to learn more.

John C. (Jack) Bogle, founder of The Vanguard Group

Born months before the infamous Black Thursday stock market crash of 1929, Jack Bogle knows from experience the social and economic cost of unethical and unregulated stock market speculation. In the depression that followed the crash, his family lost much of its wealth, and his father sunk into a destructive alcoholism that tore the family apart. He and his twin brother were compelled to enter the workforce at early ages, holding menial jobs like delivering papers and waiting on tables.[xix] The experience was formative for Bogle, who admits he feels sorry for those who do not grow up in circumstances where they have to work for what they need. Despite earning a comfortable fortune in managing mutual funds, Bogle remains reluctant to spend money on himself, believing that extravagance is a weakness that exposes him to unnecessary risk.[xx]

After graduating with a degree in economics from Princeton University in 1951, Bogle went directly into the banking and investment industries. He quickly demonstrated an aptitude for making wise investments and rose up the ranks at Wellington Fund, eventually becoming the chairman in 1970. In 1975, he founded The Vanguard Group, an investment firm based on the principle that fund shareholders own the funds and, therefore, own Vanguard. There are no outside owners seeking profits at Vanguard.[xxi]

This simple but revolutionary founding ethical standard has earned Bogle accolades from thought leaders around the world. Economist and former vice chair of the Federal Reserve, Alan S. Blinder, for example, has celebrated Bogle's "relentless voice, sharp pen, and indefatigable energy . . . prodding the mutual fund industry in particular, and the financial industry more generally, to embrace higher business, fiduciary, and ethical standards."[xxii]

Beyond establishing his client-centered approach to money management, Bogle has become an important voice advocating for ethical business practices. Too often, Bogle complains, CEOs in the investment business are compelled to make bets in the expectations market rather than to do what they are supposed to and build real corporate value. The result of this type of thinking and practice has been to distort the financial system. Instead, Bogle proposes following simple ethical guidelines such as seeking higher profits for investors rather than managers, treating the client as an owner rather than a customer, and limiting risk. These guidelines have worked for him and have made a lot of money for his clients. It turns out, he contends, that "good ethics is good business."[xxiii]

- Watch this video of John Bogle discussing the importance of ethics in leadership (https://openstax.org/l/53JohnBogle) to learn more.

---

xviii   "Marc Benioff: Trust Has to Be the Highest Value in Your Company," Salesforce.com, https://www.salesforce.com/company/news-press/stories/2018/012318/ (accessed July 3, 2018).

xix   Jonathan Berr, "Vanguard Founder John Bogle Sees No Good Alternatives to Indexing," Aol.com, February 13, 2010, https://www.aol.com/2010/02/13/vanguard-founder-john-bogle-sees-no-good-alternatives-to-indexin/ (accessed July 5, 2018).

xx   Chris Taylor, "Me and My Money: Jack Bogle," Reuters, September 11, 2012, https://www.reuters.com/article/us-column-taylor-bogle/me-and-my-money-jack-bogle-idUSBRE88A0LI20120911.

xxi   "A Remarkable History: Our Heritage," Vanguard, https://about.vanguard.com/who-we-are/a-remarkable-history/ (accessed July 5, 2018).

xxii   Taylor Larimore, "What Experts Say about Jack Bogle," Bogleheads.org, April 17, 2015, https://www.bogleheads.org/forum/viewtopic.php?t=163903.

xxiii   John C. Bogle, "Ethical Principles and Ethical Principals," a speech delivered at The Johnson School at Cornell University, November 11, 2010, http://johncbogle.com/wordpress/wp-content/uploads/2006/02/Cornell-11-11-10.pdf (accessed July 5, 2018).

Yvon Chouinard, founder, and Rose Marcario, CEO and president of Patagonia Works

Yvon Chouinard was introduced to rock climbing almost by accident. After taking an interest in falconry, an adult decided to teach the young Chouinard to rappel down a cliff to reach the cliff-side falcon nests. But it was not long before Chouinard was teaching himself how to climb up in the same way. Thus began a life-long love affair with climbing around the world. To support his climbing lifestyle, he learned to make and sell steel climbing pitons, the small metal spikes with an eyelet that climbers drive into the rock to guide their rope.

The piton business proved successful and eventually became Chouinard Equipment, the largest supplier of climbing hardware in the United States. But with this success, Chouinard was suddenly faced with his first ethical dilemma. As climbing became more popular, more pitons were driven into the rock, sometimes causing great damage. This was something Chouinard's internal sense of environmentalism could not tolerate, so he made the ethical move to phase out the pitons and sell more environmentally friendly aluminum chocks instead. Around this same time, Chouinard began experimenting in the active sportswear business. Soon the clothing line outpaced the gear line. The Patagonia clothing line was born.

Despite Chouinard's growing success, his interest in environmentalism never flagged. Indeed, if anything, it increased. The 1970s, 1980s, and 1990s were decades of increasing public awareness about the dangers of environmental neglect and the growing threat of climate change. It was at this time that terms like "acid rain," "the ozone layer," "global warming," and "deforestation" became common rallying cries for environmentalists around the world. Chouinard wanted to make Patagonia part of the movement for change. Beginning in 1986, Patagonia committed to donating 10% of its annual profits to environmental nongovernmental organizations (NGOs). Two years later, Patagonia led its own effort to save Yosemite Valley from overdevelopment.

This concern with environmentalism has continued with the coming on board of Rose Marcario as CEO in 2012. She shares Chouinard's goal of applying more ethical and environmentally friendly protection methods. Using solar energy and radiant heating in their plants and retail stores, Patagonia has been able to reduce its carbon footprint. It also strives to use recycled content in its clothing and to exclude dyes that require toxic ingredients. Patagonia also switched to using only organic cotton for its cotton products to reduce its reliance on chemical pesticides. Recently, Marcario has taken up environmental activism. Alongside Chouinard, Marcario decided to protest attempts to rescind the national monument designation of Bears Ears in southeastern Utah, first by withdrawing Patagonia from the annual Outdoor Retailer trade show in Salt Lake City in February 2017, and then by suing the Trump administration for its decision to reduce the monument's size.[xxiv] Like Chouinard, Marcario believes strongly in maintaining public lands free of private development. Many decades after it was founded as an outdoor clothing line, Patagonia's policies remain consistent with the environmental ethics of its founder.

- Watch this video of Yvon Chouinard discussing his position on environmentalism in business (https://openstax.org/l/53YvonChouinard) to learn more.

Tony Hsieh, CEO of Zappos

Born to Taiwanese immigrants in Illinois and raised largely in San Francisco's Bay Area, Tony Hsieh excelled at school as a child. He developed an interest in computers, which helped get him accepted to Harvard University, from which he graduated in 1995 with a degree in computer science. Upon graduation, he jumped right into the corporate world by taking a position at Oracle, a large database and software company.

---

xxiv   David Gelles, "Patagonia v. Trump," *New York Times*, May 5, 2018. https://www.nytimes.com/2018/05/05/business/patagonia-trump-bears-ears.html.

At the time, Hsieh felt he had made it. His hard work had paid off and he was now perched firmly on the ladder to corporate and business success. Five months later, however, Hsieh abruptly quit. "I did not want to carry on with my job just because it paid me a handsome salary. The job lacked creativity and the corporate environment wasn't my style."[xxv]

Within a few months, Hsieh and another former Oracle employee, Sanjay Madan, launched their own business from the stuffy confines of their apartment. The company was called LinkExchange, an innovative advertising cooperative that used the power of the emerging Internet to amplify advertising. The company proved to be a huge success. Within two years, it had acquired nearly half a million members and displayed ten million advertisements per day. Microsoft bought it in 1998 for $265 million.

After his success with LinkExchange, Hsieh was encouraged to become CEO of the newly created Zappos.com, an Internet shoe retailer. As CEO, Hsieh has embraced ethical behavior through what has been termed "radical transparency," where he openly shares his schedule and even his personal and company priorities. Hsieh believes strongly that this transparency helps build trust with his employees and other stakeholders.[xxvi]

Beyond transparency, Hsieh's ethical approach has created a strong office culture that encourages team unity, camaraderie, and employee empowerment. The organizational atmosphere at Zappos rejects hierarchy and management, and encourages creativity, even wackiness. And Zappos has extended this ethical approach to community involvement as well. Hsieh dumped his heart, soul, and $350 million of his own money into an urban revitalization project of the small part of Las Vegas surrounding the company. He has transformed it into vibrant and hip neighborhood of vinyl record shops, independent bookstores, trendy restaurants, and free live music. The company and its surrounding neighborhood are now almost seamless. As a result, periods of work and periods of play in the company also intermingle.[xxvii] In this way, the company is now a manifestation of Hsieh's bold rejection of the stiff corporate culture he rejected at Oracle. And it may very well transform corporate culture entirely.

- Watch this video of Tony Hsieh discussing the problem with some corporate culture (https://openstax.org/l/53TonyHsieh) to learn more.

Kim Jordan, CEO of New Belgium Brewing Company

In 1988, while working in Europe as an electrical engineer, Jeff Lebesch took a beer-tasting trip through Belgium riding atop a fat-tire bicycle. A couple years later he met Kim Jordan and they soon married. Both being beer aficionados, they could smell a great business opportunity bubbling up from Jeff's experience. Sensing that the famously bold flavors of Belgian beer were exactly what the American beer market lacked and needed, Jeff and Kim got to work testing methods and recipes in their Fort Collins, Colorado, basement. By 1991, New Belgium Brewing was born.[xxviii]

The brewery emerged at just the right time: Young Americans were just beginning to expand their general appreciation for craft brews. Over the next nine years, the company grew steadily. Then, in 2000, Jordan decided to grow the company in a new and radically different way. Inspired by her Quaker background, she

xxv   Udhaw Kumar, "Serial Entrepreneur Tony Hsieh: Quitting My Dream Job at Oracle Was the Best Decision," BrainPrick, June 21, 2012, http://brainprick.com/serial-entrepreneur-tony-hsieh-quitting-my-dream-job-at-oracle-was-the-best-decision/.
xxvi   David Henderson, "Tony Hsieh, a Leader Grounded in Ethics and Collaboration," davidhenderson.com, https://www.davidhenderson.com/2014/03/21/tony-hsieh-a-leader-grounded-in-ethics-and-collaboration/ (accessed June 28, /2018); David Rodic, "What I Learned from Studying Zappos CEO Tony Hsieh's Schedule for a Year," Business Insider, January 9, 2016, http://www.businessinsider.com/what-i-learned-from-studying-zappos-ceo-tony-hsiehs-schedule-2016-1.
xxvii   Roger D. Hodge, "First, Let's Get Rid of All the Bosses: A Radical Experiment at Zappos to End the Office Workplace as We Know It," The New Republic, October 4, 2015, https://newrepublic.com/article/122965/can-billion-dollar-corporation-zappos-be-self-organized
xxviii Tanza Loudenback, "Why the Maker of Fat Tire Bucked the Trend and Became 100% Owned by Its Workers," Business Insider, June 13, 2016, http://www.businessinsider.com/new-belgium-brewing-kim-jordan-2016-6.

started New Belgium's employee stock ownership program (ESOP). She had to battle the many advisers and accountants that came out against the move, but Jordan thought it was an important ethical move to give the employees a stake in the business.[xxix]

By 2012, Jordan had sold her last piece of ownership in the company to the ESOP. She knows that had she held onto this piece, she would have made even more money. But it was not necessarily money she was after. She wanted her employees to feel they were a part of the company and had a say in its operations. She felt this was the ethical and neighborly thing to do. According to Jordan, "We spend a lot of time at this thing called work, and if it can't feel warm and like everyone you see every day has your back, then I think that's a real tragedy." To Jordan's great credit, the ESOP has proven to be a great business success. In 2015, the company became the fourth largest craft brewer, selling nearly a million barrels in that year and pulling in $225 million in sales.[xxx]

And Jordan's ethical principles have been a driving force in the business even beyond transforming her employees into joint owners. New Belgium is particularly interested in demonstrating that it is environmentally safe and sustainable. For example, in 1998, it became the first U.S. brewer to power its entire operation with wind-produced electricity. In 2002, it completed a biological wastewater facility that would clean the water left over by the brewing process before releasing it back into the environment. It also uses natural draft cooling and swamp-cooling systems rather than the less environmentally friendly glycol-cooled systems for its cold storage.[xxxi]

Nor is Jordan content with only her environmental achievements. New Belgium Brewing is also a leader in philanthropy. It donates $1 to charities in its distribution territory for every barrel of beer it sells. Over the years, this has translated into millions of dollars in donations, and in 2018, the company projects that it will donate more than $900,000 to projects across the country.[xxxii] It also manages a volunteer corps it calls the Beer Scouts, which finds and helps supply volunteers for causes aligned with New Belgium's values.[xxxiii] Finally, it collaborates with a number of organizations supporting business ethics and nature conservation, such as Conservation Colorado, the Natural Resources Defense Council, and the American Sustainable Business Council.[xxxiv]

- Watch this video of Kim Jordan discussing New Belgium's position on sustainability (https://openstax.org/l/53KimJordan) to learn more.

Indra Nooyi, chairman and CEO of PepsiCo

What might a company like PepsiCo, known for selling sugar-filled sodas and junk food, teach us about ethical business practices? It might actually teach us quite a lot if CEO Indra Nooyi has anything to say about it.

Born in India and having immigrated to the United States at a relatively young age, Nooyi excelled at school and moved right into the business world after graduating from Yale University. In 1994, Nooyi came to PepsiCo

xxix   Chloe Sorvino, "New Belgium's Kim Jordan Talks about What It Takes to Be America's Richest Female Brewer," *Forbes*, July 16, 2016, https://www.forbes.com/sites/chloesorvino/2016/07/16/new-belgiums-kim-jordan-talks-what-it-takes-to-be-americas-richest-female-brewer/#76bc9c48b6d3; Dinah Eng, "New Belgium's Kim Jordan Is Tasting Success in Craft Brewing," *Fortune*, June 12, 2014, http://fortune.com/2014/06/12/new-belgium-kim-jordan/.
xxx   Chloe Sorvino, "New Belgium's Kim Jordan Talks about What It Takes to Be America's Richest Female Brewer," *Forbes*, July 16, 2016, https://www.forbes.com/sites/chloesorvino/2016/07/16/new-belgiums-kim-jordan-talks-what-it-takes-to-be-americas-richest-female-brewer/#76bc9c48b6d3.
xxxi   "New Belgium Brewing Wins Ethics Award," *Denver Business Journal*, January 2, 2003, https://www.bizjournals.com/denver/stories/2002/12/30/daily21.html.
xxxii   "Grants Program," New Belgium, https://www.newbelgium.com/sustainability/community/grants (accessed July 6, 2018).
xxxiii   "New Belgium's Beer Scouts," New Belgium, https://www.newbelgium.com/sustainability/community/beerscouts (accessed July 6, 2018).
xxxiv   "Policy and the Craft Beer Industry," New Belgium, https://www.newbelgium.com/sustainability/community/policyandindustry (accessed July 6, 2018).

as senior vice president for strategic planning. In 2006, she was promoted to president and CEO, and assumed the role of chairman in 2007. In August 2018, Nooyi announced she would be stepping down as CEO in October 2018 and leaving the position of chairman in early 2019. As CEO, she has tried to push PepsiCo in new and more ethical directions.

Nooyi devised a sustainable-growth agenda for the company based on three pillars. The first pillar has to do with health and well-being. Through acquisitions, mergers, and other internal changes, Nooyi has tried to transform the Pepsi brand into more of an agent for change and healthy living. She does not want the company to be known merely as the junk food and sugary soda company. She believes in providing options to consumers and in making sure that PepsiCo's traditional products are not unnecessarily unhealthy.

The second pillar is a focus on the environment. Nooyi has driven PepsiCo to take notice of its reliance on exhaustible resources like water and she has led efforts to encourage greater energy conservation and recycling efforts. These are issues that are very personal to Nooyi, who grew up in a water-distressed city in India. She wants to use PepsiCo's great resources not only to find ways to produce beverages that conserve water better but also to pass on this technology to local farmers so they can contribute to this process.

The third pillar is about empowering people who typically lack power. She has promoted outreach to women and minorities so they feel comfortable and supported in the company. To do this, she has created daycare centers in the bottling plants, added maternity and paternity leave as company benefits, and even made religious accommodations. As she sees it, she wants to make PepsiCo a place "where every employee can bring their whole self to work and not just make a living but also have a life."

Nooyi is a champion of what she calls "Performance with Purpose." By this she means recognizing that a company's performance in the marketplace is intimately connected to seeking ethical and sustainable approaches. Being a steward of the environment and encouraging tolerance and inclusion are not secondary functions for Nooyi; they are inherent in the company's approach to business. "If we don't focus on the environment, our cost will be too high. . . . and if we don't have the best and brightest people, we won't be able to deliver performance."

Performance with purpose is different from mere corporate social responsibility. As she explains, "Corporate social responsibility is about spending the money you make. You make money and then you give it to a couple of charitable causes in some distant lands and feel good. This is not a feel-good program. This is who we are. You talk about ethics. The ethics of our company is performative purpose. The ethics of our company is the deep-seated belief that large companies can actually make a difference to societies in which we operate."

- Watch this video of Indra Nooyi delivering the keynote address at the World's Most Ethical Companies Gala in 2018 (https://openstax.org/l/53IndraNooyi) to learn more.

Jostein Solheim, CEO of Ben & Jerry's

Cherry Garcia, Wavy Gravy, and Chubby Hubby are just a few of the wacky flavors churned out by the four-decades-old ice cream company, Ben & Jerry's. These quirky names are a reflection of the company's unique business style, something Jostein Solheim signed on to when he agreed to become CEO of the company in 2010.

Ice cream was nothing new to Solheim. Before becoming CEO, he had worked for Unilever's many ice cream brands like Breyers, Klondike, Popsicle, and Good Humor. Indeed, the Norway native calls himself "an ice cream guy." And he is wildly enthusiastic about maintaining Ben & Jerry's iconic weirdness, even celebrating Unilever's acquisition of the company by eating a full pint of Chunky Monkey.[xxxv]

---

xxxv   "Division President: Jostein Solheim, Ben & Jerry's Homemade," *Food Processing*, January 26, 2011, https://www.foodprocessing.com/ceo/jostein-solheim/ (accessed July 6, 2018).

But as Solheim knows, Ben & Jerry's is more than just an ice cream chain; it is also an organization dedicated to making a social impact. The founders of the Vermont-based company, Jerry Greenfield and Ben Cohen, transformed their ice cream–making success into a values-led social mission by supporting a host of ethical positions on such issues as responsible manufacturing, fair trade, and non–genetically modified organisms labeling.[xxxvi] And Solheim has embraced this important component too. He has led the company to establish public positions on racial justice in the United States, environmental activism, and even private prisons. "What inspires me," Solheim said, "is what social impact can we create with this business."[xxxvii]

The activism Solheim supports through Ben & Jerry's springs from his understanding of the stakeholders in his company. For example, he refers to the consumers as "fans." "They're more than just customers," he explains. "They are bigger stakeholders in our company and we have a responsibility to them beyond a basic transactional exchange of product." And the same goes for the suppliers, farmers, and NGO partners. "They all connect in a model we called 'linked prosperity,' which is circular and reinforcing."[xxxviii]

It is Solheim's vision to see Ben & Jerry's as a leader in ethical change. Making a values-led company that embraces the concept of linked prosperity also highly profitable is major step in transforming the standard business model. He believes it is inevitable that other businesses will catch on and recognize they, too, have ethical obligations to uphold community values and recognize how their work affects the larger global community.[xxxix]

- Watch this video of Jostein Solheim discussing his interpretation of conscious capitalism (https://openstax.org/l/53JSolheim) to learn more.

---

xxxvi   "Jostein Solheim," Conscious Capitalism, https://www.consciouscapitalism.org/people/jostein-solheim (accessed July 5, 2018).
xxxvii   Bill Snyder, "Jostein Solheim: Do Things You Passionately Believe In," Stanford Business, April 4, 2017, https://www.gsb.stanford.edu/insights/jostein-solheim-do-things-you-passionately-believe.
xxxviii   "Jostein Solheim of Ben & Jerry's: Empathy Is Not Simply the 'Flavor of the Month'," Medium, https://medium.com/change-maker/jostein-solheim-of-ben-jerry-s-empathy-is-not-simply-the-flavor-of-the-month-fc8c44242831 (accessed July 6, 2018).
xxxix   "Jostein Solheim of Ben & Jerry's: Empathy Is Not Simply the 'Flavor of the Month'," Medium, https://medium.com/change-maker/jostein-solheim-of-ben-jerry-s-empathy-is-not-simply-the-flavor-of-the-month-fc8c44242831 (accessed July 6, 2018).

c   A Succinct Theory of Business Ethics

The Nature of Business Ethics

Business ethics should be grounded in *deontology* more than in *utilitarianism*. That is, the ends should not typically be considered sufficient justification for the means when it comes to framing a business strategy. Rather, it is the means that ennoble the ends. Utilitarianism, as a consequentialist theory and when applied to business, emphasizes the greatest good (or profit) for the greatest number of shareholders. However, this may be inappropriate criterion for determining what is truly ethical in the conduct of business because business morality should not to be centered only on calculations of profit or loss. Deontology, on the other hand, focuses on the motives and reasons why entrepreneurs engage in business and the methods that they implement in doing so. Ultimately, both theories have a place in business practice, but a preference should be shown to deontology.

The honor or shame that accrues to business as a profession is directly attributable to the ethical practices of its leaders. So, if business as a whole has an unsavory reputation, it is a likely consequence of the practices in which management engages. And while this reputation is not easily changed, it can be improved through a diligent commitment by management to do so.

To pit *ethics* against *profits* and insist that a business leader must choose between the two is a false dichotomy. In truth, successful business can be practiced in ethical fashion. Further, ethical conduct by a business will naturally draw the loyalty of many consumers and clients. Not only that, but employees and other stakeholders of that business will also approve, and their relationship to the company might become even closer as a result.

Similarly, it diminishes ethics to insist that it is useful only for keeping business leaders out of jail and avoiding opprobrium, such as through social media. Ethical behavior *can* keep executives safe from indictment, but it also accomplishes much more. Ethical business practices honor the profession and endow it with integrity and credibility.

When it comes to hiring for and promoting within the workplace, merit and commitment should be assigned the highest value. At the same time, *merit* should not to be seen as a code word for discrimination; nor should it be disparaged. Business ethics applies to all people equitably in the sense that race, ethnicity, creed, sex, sexual orientation, age, and disability all are irrelevant to the abilities that they bring to the workplace.

The Nature of the Ethical Business Leader

An ethical business leader appreciates the existence of multiple stakeholders and accepts responsibility for all of them. These include employees, shareholders, customers/clients, vendors, suppliers, wholesalers, retailers, and the community as a whole within which a corporation resides. While not all stakeholders are *equal* in significance, they nonetheless *all are significant*.

Ethical entrepreneurs are good stewards of the social and physical environments where they do business. They safeguard the earth at the same time that they protect human capital.

In addition, the ethical executive engages in both private and corporate philanthropy. Thus, he or she is willing to commit a portion of the funds of his or her organization, as well as that of his or her personal wealth, to worthy charitable community organizations.

Corporate professionals earn respect through the manner in which they lead and conduct business. There is no positive correlation between the trappings of their success—the homes they own, the cars they drive, the clothes they wear—and their character as human beings. The limousines and jets that they commandeer and the vacation resorts that they frequent are externalities completely unconnected with what Martin Luther King, Jr., called "the content of their character." If anything, excessive material possessions blind business leaders to their most important managerial tasks.

In truth, leaders who are in business only for the salary and attending perquisites have found the wrong profession, for they will constantly endure frustration in bearing the responsibilities that come with the privileges.

And while successful executives are compensated more than their subordinates, it should not to be many multiples more. The less disparity that exists between the highest- and least-paid members of a company, the greater the level of teamwork and commitment that will prevail among all. In short, people will work harder and make a deeper commitment to a company that has a leadership team with which they can identify.

Additionally, an MBA is not a license for arrogance on the part of its holder. Ethical leaders are justifiably proud of their business acumen, but to lord it over others risks sacrificing their effectiveness as managers. Sometimes the least educated member of a firm may know the most about sustaining the dignity and self-worth of everyone on the team and, therefore, may be the most essential employee for the company to have for that purpose.

An accomplished executive is not insulated from his or her employees and should not be a "sir" or "ma'am" to subordinates, but rather a partner or colleague or coworker, and so, a concerned boss.

In this same way, ethical leaders are welcomed and admired instead of feared and resented. Respect from colleagues, employees, and competitors ultimately cannot be compelled. Instead, it flows naturally from the just and fair ways in which leaders manage and compete.

Worthy managers sustain the dignity and self-respect of all who surround them. This at once acknowledges the basic humanity of those with whom they work and simultaneously inspires them to contribute their best effort.

Similarly, the best business leaders take pride in the accomplishments of the business and its employees. This success may never be accorded directly to managers themselves, but employees assuredly recognize those bosses who help them accomplish their best. Further, it is precisely this kind of leader for whom most employees will be motivated to go above and beyond merely what is required of them on the job.

In short, ethical business executives become the enablers of professional success among their colleagues. This is not in the sense of being a slave to the business and its employees, but rather placing the interests of the firm and one's coworkers above those of oneself. When this occurs, the enterprise succeeds in a way in which all associated with it may take pride. This is actually the essence of the best business leadership.

A goal of a more egalitarian workplace—one in which managers and employees respect one another—is a renewed sense of loyalty among all who are there. Too often today we witness distrust along the management/labor divide. Each side accuses the other of harboring no commitment except to itself. Unfortunately, the accusation frequently is true. One way to dispel it is for business leaders to take the first steps in restoring the broken sense of obligation that owners and employees owe each other. This may be the most important task of business leadership now and going forward.

Answer Key

Chapter 1

1. A
2. True
3. Behaving ethically requires that we meet the mandatory standards of the law and then go above and beyond them to recognize that an action may be legal but we personally may consider it unacceptable. Ethical reasoning often is more topical than law and reflects the changes in consciousness that individuals and society undergo. Often, ethical thought precedes and sets the stage for changes in the law.
4. Normative ethical theories are philosophical theories based on reason that tell individuals how they ought to behave. Descriptive ethical theories are based on scientific evidence describing how people tend to behave in a particular context. The theories discussed in this book are normative.
5. B
6. False. In Friedman's view, a company's social responsibility consists of enhancing stockholder value.
7. CSR is the practice of viewing a business within a broader context, as a member of society with certain implicit social obligations, rather than considering the maximization of shareholder wealth as a company's sole purpose and objective.
8. In three columns, list stakeholders in order of perceived priority, their perceived interests, and the likely impact of the business decision on them. This will aid comprehension of the decision's impacts as well as provide justification for the course of conduct ultimately chosen.
9. The ethical behavior of managers has a positive influence on the value of a variety of components affecting the company's overall goodwill, including its brand, its workforce, and its customer relationships. Positive goodwill generated by ethical business practices, in turn, generates long-term business success.
10. True
11. D
12. Having a single ethical standard maximizes ethical behavior no matter who the other party is and supports an internally consistent rule of behavior toward all family, friends, customers, clients, and others with whom we interact.

Chapter 2

1. A
2. B
3. True
4. True
5. Because virtue ethics emphasizes individual character and conscience, it can have a tremendous influence on organizational culture by encouraging individuals to stand up for sound, ethical, and responsible business practices.
6. C
7. D
8. True
9. False. Confucius's hope for reform was the five great relationships that support Chinese society: parent/child, husband/wife, elder/junior sibling, master/apprentice, and ruler/subject.
10. Wholeheartedness and sincerity require not just competence but compassion when dealing with stakeholders and making executive decisions. Reflecting the overall Confucian concern for balance, they temper initiative and boldness with self-regulation.
11. A
12. B
13. True
14. False. In Confucian ethics, the locus of ethics and moral decision making was the family rather than the individual. The most important value was the development of humanity and putting an end to anarchy, and this was done best in the context of the family.
15. D
16. A
17. True
18. Utilitarianism is pervasive in contemporary business practice, management theory, and decision-making through cost-benefit analysis. Decisions are often made based on the "bottom line" of profit, numbers of stakeholders affected, or overall utility to the organization. Utilitarianism is reflected in this abiding emphasis on efficiency, often to the neglect of other factors.
19. Certainly there exists a need today to engage in political debate that includes all sides of an issue in

respectful ways. Mill's teaching on the role of free speech in society can be a starting point and a reminder of the importance of civil debate and freedom.

20. C

21. True

22. True

23. Utilitarianism is a consequentialist philosophy dependent solely on outcomes. Although focused on rights, Mill's utilitarianism also depends on results. Deontology is concerned with motive, duty, and one's obligation to act regardless of circumstances or outcomes.

24. Because Kantian ethics is about treating people not as means but as ends, this philosophy can influence nearly every aspect of business, from research and development to production, manufacturing, marketing, and consumption. It may be difficult to implement, however, because many businesses are focused on efficiency and production to the near-exclusion of other factors.

25. C

26. B

27. True

28. True

29. Rawls's theory has been called radical because it redistributes goods and services without regard for extenuating circumstances or historical context. It also has been accused of stifling enterprise, innovation, and investment.

Chapter 3

1. D

2. False. Amenities are additional resources made available to employees above and beyond wages, salary, or other standard benefits or obligations.

3. Regardless of the company or brand selected, responses should include some of the following: customers, clients, employees, shareholders, communities, government, media, and possibly the environment and other abstract concepts that represent resources or concerns of many people.

4. A

5. C

6. The normative approach is the fundamental basis of stakeholder theory and argues that stakeholders are ends unto themselves rather than means to an end. Thus, they have inherent value and cannot be looked at merely as instruments or as functional parts in an economic engine intended solely to generate profit for stockowners. That said, the instrumental and descriptive approaches also have their role in helping us to understand stakeholders and are mutually supportive of the normative approach.

7. The high-power, high-interest quadrant is most important because it represents stakeholders who both are highly interested in their relationship with the firm and have a high level of power or influence in the relationship.

8. C

9. True

10. The three components are people, profit, and planet.

11. The California Act requires businesses that operate in California to describe for consumers all components and activities of their supply chains.

12. True

13. C

Chapter 4

1. False. Social responsibility does not mean lower profitability, as the returns on social index funds have shown.

2. False. Milton Friedman argued that shareholders should be able decide for themselves what social initiatives to donate to or to take part in, rather than having a business executive or government decide for them.

3. A

4. D

5. One benefit is that consumers may prefer to purchase products from a socially responsible company. A second benefit is that CSR may attract more investors, or shareholders, who are interested in investing in the company.

6. Earth jurisprudence is an interpretation of law and governance based on the belief that society will be sustainable only if we recognize the legal rights of Earth as if it were a person.

7. B

8. D

9. True

10. C

11. False. Legal restrictions exist to limit the revolving door effect, but most relate only to direct government contracting and/or lobbying.

12. True

13. C

14. C

15. B

16. The First Amendment and free speech: The case was a challenge to the federal elections law limiting the amount of money a person or business can spend in support of a political candidate.

Chapter 5

1. A

2. Enculturation is the process by which humans learn the characteristics, values, and rules to participate in a society more generally, whereas acculturation is the introduction of the values, worldview, philosophy, or practice of one culture into another.

3. As an extreme preoccupation with buying and owning, consumerism runs counter to the new sensitivity to ethics and human flourishing in business, because it defines people not by their humanity but by their purchasing power.

4. False. Cultures often adapt to business rather than the other way around. As an example, U.S.-style jeans and baseball caps can now be found globally.

5. A

6. False. Certain core ethics exist throughout cultures and time, although they may manifest in different ways.

7. False. The UN Global Compact is a voluntary set of standards; it is not legally binding on countries or corporations.

8. *Shlensky v. Wrigley* gave boards of directors and management more latitude in determining how to balance the interests of stakeholders. This was in contrast to *Dodge v. Ford Motor Company*, which validated the rule of shareholder primacy.

9. C

10. True

11. Localization is the process of adapting a product for use or sale in other nations and cultures. This might include language translation, adapting content to the tastes and consumption habits of the local market, and converting measurements.

12. This can be a matter of managing expectations. Managers must do the work required for any business deal but deliver it in a way that is culturally sensitive, even if that means negotiating details like project deadlines and the conduct of meetings and agreeing to have different expectations of those in a different cultural context.

13. A

14. D

15. Conscience is the locus of ethical behavior in business because individuals acting in free association make up the business or organization. They are motivated by their inner voice to act responsibly toward each other and their stakeholders—or not.

16. Although many agree on the importance of goals like acting with honesty and fairness and treating people as ends rather than means, their implementation is extremely complex, because people have different understandings of what is honest, fair, or an end in itself. The result may be a series of diverse rules rather than one set.

17. A humanistic business model focuses on leadership development and the data of social science about how to motivate people. Humanities in ethics looks to case methods, novels, short stories, and plays to gain insight into human behavior.

Chapter 6

1. C

2. False. Sexual harassment is both unethical and illegal.

3. Surveys show that women value benefits related to childcare and health care more highly than do men, although the benefit mix any employee values most is an individual one.

4. Managers can model ethical behavior by example, and the company can offer training and communicate and strictly enforce a written policy.

5. B

6. False. Minimum wage can be set by city (municipal), state, or federal governments.

7. False. Minimum wages have not kept up with inflation; in fact, they have fallen far behind.

8. Cost of living variations and concern about a shrinking middle class are possible motives for a state to enact its own above-federal minimum wage.

9. Among the factors are discrimination, historical wage rates, and artificially manipulated job titles.

10. D
11. True
12. False. Right-to-work laws are state laws.
13. Union membership is low due to two primary reasons: the United States has switched from a manufacturing economy to a service economy, and the law now affords workers many of the protections they once got only through a collective bargaining agreement.
14. Most studies indicate that U.S. executives are paid much more highly than executives in other countries, including those that are very competitive with the United States. The pay ratio is approximately three hundred in the United States as compared with twenty-two in the United Kingdom and twelve in Germany.
15. False. If an employer is monitoring any device owned by the company, such as a telephone or computer, no advance notice is required.
16. False. No state completely bans drug testing. Some regulate it to make sure it is fair and accurate.
17. There are at least two reasons a company might want to monitor Internet use at work: productivity and electronic security. Managers do not want employees wasting time or exposing the company to breaches of data security, identity theft, or the legal ramifications of inappropriate or offensive behavior.
18. The two exceptions to the ECPA that weaken its protection are the business purpose exception, which allows monitoring if an employer can demonstrate a legitimate business purpose for doing so, and the consent exception, which allows employers to monitor employee communications provided employees have given their consent.
19. The answer is yes, as long as a company is responsible for what its employees do. Then businesses need to check for drugs due to reasons such as workplace safety and protection of property.

Chapter 7

1. C
2. B
3. True
4. Conflict of interest: The employee must not act in a way that would result in a conflict of interest with the employer.
5. Duty of confidentiality: Employers are well within their rights to expect employees to honor their duty of confidentiality and maintain the secrecy of such proprietary material as trade secrets, intellectual property, and customer data.
6. A. Employers can encourage positive behavior toward customers by empowering employees to use their best judgment when working with them.
7. B
8. True
9. Customers' perceptions are formed by the employees with whom they have contact, and these perceptions affect not only the company but all the employees who depend on its success for their livelihood.
10. D. Violence by a customer occurs when the violent person has a legitimate relationship with the business, perhaps as a customer or patient.
11. A
12. True
13. Employees owe each other courtesy and respect.
14. NIOSH indicates that violence at work usually fits into one of four categories: traditional criminal intent, violence by one worker against another, violence stemming from a personal relationship, and violence by a customer.
15. A
16. B
17. False. Despite legal and cultural differences that may allow bribes in other countries, U.S. firms and their employees are prohibited from paying them.
18. In addition to individuals, bribery injures competitors, the government, and the free-market system as a whole.
19. Factors that help establish the ethics and legality of gift giving include the value of the gift, its purpose, the circumstances under which it is given, the position of the person receiving it, company policy, and the law.
20. B
21. False. Generally speaking, labor law gives workers the right to discuss among themselves the specifics of their individual employment agreements, including matters of salary.
22. True
23. Employees can post information online about wages, hours, and working conditions, and that speech is protected by federal statute.
24. Employees should not seek revenge on a boss with whom they are angry. Of course, even if an employee has a personal revenge motive, if the company is actively breaking the law, it is still important that the

wrongdoing be reported.

25. The employee should usually try internal reporting channels first, to disclose the problem to management before going public.

Chapter 8

1. B

2. C

3. True

4. Studies indicate that the financial performance of companies with a diverse workforce is above average for their industries. The McKinsey and Company study noted in the chapter found that companies featuring great diversity in their workforces typically enjoyed earnings between 15 and 35 percent greater than their respective US industry medians.

5. The percentage of women in leadership positions remains much lower than for men, generally less than 20 percent of positions. The benefits of greater gender diversity in the workforce include improved internal relationships and employee morale and more effective internal and external communication. Studies have also shown that companies in the top 25 percent for executive and/or board diversity had returns on equity more than 50 percent higher than those companies that ranked in the lowest 25 percent.

6. C

7. A

8. False. In both cases, employers must be willing to make a reasonable accommodation for the employee.

9. The ADA's main requirement is that employers make reasonable accommodations for applicants and workers with disabilities to allow them to perform the essential functions of the job.

10. One example of religious apparel that is protected under Title VII is Muslim women's head scarves, which, in most situations, they may wear.

11. C

12. False. Title VII of the Civil Rights Act does not address sexual orientation and federal law does not prohibit discrimination based on this characteristic.

13. Yes. Approximately half of U.S. states have local laws that provide protection even though federal law does not; however, some of those states prohibit sexual orientation discrimination only in public workplaces, not private ones.

14. Yes. The law does not mandate or prohibit extending benefits to LGBTQ partners; it is up to the company.

15. A

16. C

17. True

18. Independent contractors are not covered by workers' compensation or unemployment insurance or health insurance coverage.

19. Yes. A state can set its own minimum wage higher than the federal level. Currently, twenty-nine states do so.

20. B

21. C

22. True.

23. False. Alternatives include the use of patient-drug databases, virtual drug trials, computer models and simulations, noninvasive imaging techniques, and microdosing.

24. U.S. companies lose sales abroad because they cannot sell products that were tested on animals in the European Union markets.

Chapter 9

1. C

2. False. Entrepreneurs are usually motivated by the hope of profit.

3. B

4. A

5. False. Caveat emptor means the buyer is principally responsible for purchase decisions, not the seller.

6. False. Research studies indicate that children are the least-discerning audience for much advertising content.

7. A

8. True

9. Arguably, yes. Residences and businesses in these catastrophe-prone areas certainly would benefit from coverage. The difficulty comes in paying for it; it can be very expensive given the potential for cataclysmic loss. So an apparatus that would combine payment on the part of the insured but supplemented with tax subsidies might be most fair.

10. Very. Though it is essentially illegal everywhere, traces of it remain.

11. Statistically, this makes sense, but it often plays out unfairly for those insured individuals who absolutely do not contribute to the higher incidence of claims in certain areas. For example, suppose you are a very safe driver in a neighborhood of dangerous drivers. Your premiums for auto insurance will reflect not so much your own safety record as the overall rate of claims in your community.

12. False. British merchant shippers began insuring themselves against loss of their cargos in the seventeenth century.

13. True

14. False. Employer-sponsored wellness programs carry some risk of invasion of worker privacy.

15. False. Most European countries have single-payer health care systems.

16. A

17. D

18. Yes, such a case could be made, particularly if the company is providing health coverage for its employees, because the cost of this coverage to the employer is driven by the number of health claims made against it by workers. Furthermore, absenteeism reflects the health of employees, and their actions off the job help determine this. Conversely, permitting employers to stipulate worker behavior when not on the clock places great oversight in the hands of management and reduces individual autonomy significantly.

Chapter 10

1. B

2. A

3. True

4. True

5. An employer can communicate clear expectations and then regularly check the employee's successful completion of tasks according to specifications.

6. Companies can use telecommuting to recruit and retain employees who wish to facilitate work-life balance, or employees from locations that are not within daily travel distance to the facility.

7. C

8. A

9. True

10. Making free or inexpensive food available in the workplace is a recruiting and retention tool. The employer may also hope that if food is available on the premises, employees will spend less time getting meals and more time working. It might be considered unethical to try to control employees' time and limit social interactions away from work.

11. Any new office building could incorporate shared and flexible work space to allow for greater collaboration among employees. Less space would be dedicated to individual offices. A manager would also want to include collaborative technology that allows employees to easily contact customers, vendors, and other suppliers.

12. D

13. A

14. True

15. True

16. Applicants who are interested in working fewer hours will be encouraged to apply for a job they would have to pass up if it were full-time.

17. Gig work allows flexible scheduling, the ability to work for more than one company at a time, and the ability to work more or fewer hours each week, as desired.

18. Advantages include reduced payroll taxes, reduced cost of benefits, and the ability to use and, hence, pay for workers only when they are needed.

19. The development of artificial intelligence allows robots to act on their own much more often, meaning humans do not always control them.

20. Likely yes, for example in the area of self-driving cars, where we have already (in 2018) experienced a pedestrian's death caused by a self-driving car.

21. A

22. False. Companies have no such duty.

23. D

Index

A

access economy, 309, 319
acculturation, 132, 155
advertising, 271, 290
Affordable Care Act (ACA), 286, 290
agribusiness, 253
amenities, 71, 89
Americans with Disabilities Act, 239
animal rights, 119, 253, 259
Aquinas, 33
Aristotle, 13, 28, 33, 40, 341
artificial intelligence, 317
artificial intelligence (AI), 316, 319
Athens, 28
automation, 315, 317
awareness, 42

B

Bane, 347
Barra, 348
Ben & Jerry's, 354
benefits, 166
Benioff, 349
Bentham, 44, 342
bias, 153
Bogle, 350
brand, 203, 226
branding, 203, 226
bribe, 214, 226
Buffet, 15
Burwell v. Hobby Lobby, 98
business, 133
business ethics, 9, 23, 326
business judgment rule, 97, 125
business purpose exception, 185, 190

C

cap and trade, 112, 125
carbon footprint, 107, 125
carbon tax, 115, 125
categorical imperative, 51, 59
Chouinard, 351
Citizens United, 123, 125
Citizens United v. Federal Election Commission, 104
Civil Rights Act, 233

claim, 276, 290
Clean Air Act, 117
closed shop, 179, 190
code of conduct, 210
Codetermination, 180
codetermination, 190
collective bargaining, 177, 190
Commerce Clause, 121, 125
comparable worth, 174, 190
compliance, 10, 23
confidentiality, 200
Confucius, 35, 40
consent exception, 185, 190
consequentialism, 46, 59
consumerism, 137, 155
control, 41
copayment, 284, 290
corporate culture, 18, 23
Corporate Equality Index, 246
corporate personhood, 104, 125
corporate social responsibility, 83, 95, 99
corporate social responsibility (CSR), 19, 23
corporate status, 95
cosmetic testing, 256
CSR, 83
culture, 133
cybersecurity, 211

D

deductible, 284, 290
Deepwater Horizon, 104, 122
defined-contribution retirement plans, 198
DeGeorge, 153
deontology, 11, 23, 52
descriptive approach, 73, 89
diffused stakeholder, 75, 89
diversity dividend, 236, 259
Dodge v. Ford Motor Company, 96
drug testing, 188
duty of confidentiality, 200, 226
duty of loyalty, 196, 197, 226

E

eBay Domestic Holdings Inc. v. Newmark, 100
EEOC, 163, 190
Electronic Communications Privacy Act of 1986, 185
employment at will, 188, 190

enabling stakeholder, 75, 89
enculturation, 132, 136, 155
entrepreneur, 266, 290
entrepreneurial culture, 269, 290
environment, 103, 106
Equal Employment Opportunity Commission, 163, 235
Equal Pay Act, 174
ethical maximum, 70, 89
ethical minimum, 70, 89
ethical relativism, 20, 23
ethics, 8, 23
eudaimonia, 29, 59
exigency, 79, 89

F

fair wage, 170
fiduciary duty, 100, 125
flextime, 308, 319
Ford, 96
Ford Motor Company, 96
Foreign Corrupt Practices Act, 215, 226
Friedman, 14, 99
functional stakeholder, 75, 89

G

gender diversity, 234
gender wage gap, 252
general index funds, 102
General Motors, 348
gig economy, 311, 319
Global 100, 107
globalization, 134, 137, 139
golden mean, 30, 59
goodwill, 17, 23
greenwashing, 86, 89

H

harassment, 211
harm principle, 48, 59
Hippocratic Oath, 10
honor, 33
Hsieh, 351
humanistic business model, 152, 155
Hume, 51

I

inclusion, 233, 259
income inequality, 247, 259
insider trading, 212, 226
instrumental approach, 73, 89

insurance, 276
integrity, 10, 23
intellectual property, 201, 226
internal marketing, 205, 226
internships, 314
ISO 14000, 109

J
job sharing, 306, 319
Jordan, 352
junzi, 36, 59
justice as fairness, 54, 59
justice theory, 54, 59

K
Kant, 11, 50, 344
Keystone XL pipeline, 118

L
labor union, 177
LEED certification, 110
li, 35, 59
limited liability, 94, 125
limited liability companies, 94
localization, 144, 155
long-term perspective, 14, 23
loyalty, 196

M
managerial ethics, 41, 59
Manhattan, 132
medical research, 255
mercantilism, 141, 155
middle class, 248
Mill, 47, 343
minimum wage, 171, 250
mission, 135
monitoring, 184, 186
moral agency, 153, 155
moral minimum, 99, 125
motive, 42
multipayer health care system, 281, 290

N
New Belgium Brewing, 352
non-compete agreement, 201, 226
nondisclosure agreement, 200, 226
nonsolicitation clause, 202, 226
Nooyi, 353
normative approach, 73, 89
normative ethical theories, 11, 23

normative stakeholder, 89
Normative stakeholders, 75

O
Obamacare, 286
Occupational Safety and Health Act, 162
organizational culture, 152
original position, 55, 59
OSHA, 162, 190

P
Patagonia, 351
pay ratio, 182, 190
pay secrecy, 218, 226
PepsiCo, 353
Phronesis, 13
phrónēsis, 29, 59
premiums, 276, 290
productivity, 181
Project Shakti, 101
psychological appeal, 273, 290
public health, 119
purpose, 135

Q
quan, 38, 59
qui tam provision, 221, 226
quid pro quo, 95, 125

R
Rawls, 54, 345
reasonable accommodation, 239, 259
redlining, 280, 290
religion, 146, 150
religious beliefs, 241
responsible employer, 160
right-to-work law, 190
Right-to-work laws, 178
robotics, 314, 317, 319
Rockefeller, 142, 147

S
Salesforce, 349
Sarbanes-Oxley, 124, 125
sexual harassment, 164, 190
sexual identification, 244
sexual orientation, 244
shareholder, 16, 23
shareholder primacy, 96, 125
Shlensky v. Wrigley, 97
short-term perspective, 13, 23

single-payer health care system, 281, 290
social contract, 14, 23
social contract theory, 55, 59
social index funds, 102
social media, 271
social responsibility of business, 71, 89
Solheim, 354
stakeholder, 68, 72, 75, 78
stakeholder claim, 72, 89
stakeholder management, 78, 89
stakeholder prioritization, 79, 89
stakeholders, 8, 23
states' rights, 121, 125
stockholder, 14, 23
subliminal advertising, 275, 290
sustainability, 107, 107, 112, 114, 117, 125

T
Tarbell, 142
telecommuting, 296, 319
telework, 296
The Vanguard Group, 350
trade secret, 200, 226
Trader Joe's, 347
tragedy of the commons, 105, 125
transparency, 160
triple bottom line (TBL), 85, 89

U
UN Universal Declaration of Human Rights, 149
unanimity of acceptance, 55, 59
undue hardship, 240, 259
Union of Concerned Scientists, 110
United Nations (UN) Global Compact, 143
universal health care system, 288, 290
universal values, 149, 155
utilitarianism, 11, 23, 44, 45, 47, 49
utility function, 46, 59

V
veil of ignorance, 55, 57, 59
virtue ethics, 28, 59
virtue theory, 12, 23

W
Weber, 268

wellness programs, 285, 290
whistleblowing, 220, 226
work style, 209, 226
work-life balance, 304
Worker Adjustment and
Retraining Notification (WARN)
Act, 161
workplace campus, 301
workplace discrimination, 164
workplace diversity, 232
workplace personalities, 209
workplace personality, 226
workplace violence, 210
Wrigley Company, 97

Z

Zappos, 352